John Pairman Brown
Israel and Hellas III

Beihefte zur Zeitschrift für die alttestamentliche Wissenschaft

Herausgegeben von
Otto Kaiser

Band 299

W
DE
G

Walter de Gruyter · Berlin · New York
2001

John Pairman Brown

Israel and Hellas

Volume III

The Legacy of Iranian Imperialism and the Individual

with Cumulative Indexes to Vols. I – III

W
DE
G

Walter de Gruyter · Berlin · New York
2001

♾ Printed on acid-free paper which falls within the guidelines of the ANSI
to ensure permanence and durability.

Library of Congress Cataloging-in-Publication Data

Brown, John Pairman.
    Israel and Hellas / John Pairman Brown.
       xxii 407 p.;   24 cm. – (Beihefte zur Zeitschrift für die alt-
testamentliche Wissenschaft ; 231)
    Includes bibliographical references and indexes.
    ISBN 3-11-016882-0
    1. Bible. O.T. – Extra-canonical parallels.   2. Bible. O.T. –
Comparative studies.   3. Greek literature – Relation to the Old
Testament.   4. Jews – Civilization – To 70 A.D.   5. Greece –
Civilization.   I. Title.   II. Series.
    BS410 .Z5 vol. 231
    [BS1171.2]
    221.6 s – dc20
    [880.9/42]   95-034023

Die Deutsche Bibliothek – CIP-Einheitsaufnahme

Brown, John Pairman:
Israel and Hellas / John Pairman Brown. – Berlin ; New York :
de Gruyter
   (Beihefte zur Zeitschrift für die alttestamentliche Wissenschaft ; ...)

Vol. 3. The legacy of Iranian imperialism and the individual with
cumulative indexes to vols. I – III. – 2001
   (Beihefte zur Zeitschrift für die alttestamentliche Wissenschaft ;
   Bd. 299)
   ISBN 3-11-016882-0

Printed in Germany
Disk conversion: Readymade, Berlin
Printing: Werner Hildebrand, Berlin
Binding: Lüderitz & Bauer-GmbH, Berlin

AUTHOR'S PREFACE

Kind reader!—you now have in your hands the final volume of this work on the two societies that underlie us all. Vol. I, some day to be subtitled "The Vocabulary of Social Enterprises," appeared in 1995 as BZAW 231. Here, more promptly than I dared hope, are just the materials promised in Vol. II, "Sacred Institutions with Roman Counterparts" (BZAW 276, 2000). The far-sightedness of Walter de Gruyter enables me to add here cumulative indexes forming a comprehensive atlas to the widely-scattered territories traversed in all three surveys.

As previously, the chapters appear in inductive rather than deductive format, with data before analysis; those who choose may adopt in their own work the policy of the Queen of Hearts, "Sentence first— verdict afterwards." Thus in Chapter 18 I record the switch in both Israel and Hellas from a (men's) culture of honor and shame to one of non-retaliation; and in Chapter 19 the growing urgency of a symbolic answer to the puzzle of death. What has happened? A revived imperialism (Chapter 20) has torn down the walls of the city-state, replacing the old family solidarity by a new individualism; and simultaneously transforming the old particularity, "We are different from the others," into a new universalism, "We are custodians of a treasure for the others." (In place of "universalism" I could have written more precisely "cosmopolitanism," but I hold to my original usage.) By the "legacy of Iranian imperialism" I mean the offices, modes of legitimation and sanctions developed by the Achaemenid Persian empire, in part on an Akkadian basis; by its heirs I mean Alexander and the Hellenistic kingdoms, Carthage, and Rome, as well as the Arsacid and Sasanid dynasties on old Iranian territory. As always, political disruption is symbolized by the fear of cosmic disruption; and I chronicle (Chapter 21) the increasingly supernatural character ascribed to the cosmos in miniature at its best, the Iranian vision of *paradise*.

Those first 21 chapters (excepting the introductory Chapter 1 and the linguistic Chapter 17) complete my gathering of data to document the comparison of classical Israel and Hellas. As the two societies approach confluence in the New Testament, their differences become more pronounced; and in Chapter 22 I reverse course and analyze their *complementarity*, which monopolized the attention of earlier authors (I.2-3). I document the confluence by a novel enterprise; a reconstruction (Chapter 23) of the foreign words in the Aramaic originals of Jesus' sayings—the stratum of the New Testament where we are most sure of an Aramaic base. And the surprising result is that his language contains vocabulary naming institutions of the four successive empires that occupied Palestine—Akkadian, Iranian, Greek and Latin—as their linguistic legacy. The final Chapter 24 puts the materials of all three volumes in logical and chronological order; Hebrew and Greek citations are no longer needed; and both the professional and the lay reader may now wish to begin there for an overall view of the whole. Its title could serve for the whole enterprise: the appearance of (non-identical!) twin free societies rejoicing in their *particularity*, which upon their overthrow by new empires gives way to a cosmopolitan *universalism*.

What is the relation of the 19 substantive chapters to each other and to the work as a whole? On the one hand, they have an *underlying unity*: each proceeds from one person's original vision of two new free societies in joint emergence—a vision hardly anticipated by previous authors known to him. On the other hand, each represents a *fresh beginning*: it proposes a realm of connection or parallelism, and explores that realm on its own terms; while it is further illustrated by other chapters, equally it offers something to them. With a couple of exceptions, the comparison is always between speakers of West-Semitic and Greek; only in the studies of the *templum* and *saeculum* (Chapter 15), and of the Ark and Janus (Chapter 16), is Hellas substantially replaced by Etruscanized Rome.

Thus, while those chapters are much more than a miscellany of "collected essays," they so far retain their original status as (actual or potential) journal articles that each can be read on its own terms without preconditions. Four (none previously published) in different ways lay out general themes: Chapter 1, on the new societies as revealed in their texts; Chapter 17, on historic and prehistoric levels of connection between Greek and Hebrew; Chapter 22, on the complementary differences between the two societies; Chapter 24, a summary of their evolution before and after imperial control. Throughout, the coming confluence of the two in the New Testament can be descried as a distant goal, explicitly treated in Chapter 23. The deepest penetration into the novelty of the two appears in Chapter 10 on the High God as guarantor of justice; the deepest into the New Testament in Chapter 18, on the new laws of human nature under Grace.

Readers, like some reviewers, may feel (correctly!) that this work fails to undertake three tasks: (1) an account of historical connections between the two societies; (2) a comparison of narrative themes between their stories; and (3) a theological analysis.

(1) I would have been glad to lay out deeper *historical connections* between Israel and Hellas if I had been able. The parallels in their social structures, often expressed in common vocabulary, leap to the eye (and ear); but I could form only general ideas of an explanation. Unlike some "Old Testament" scholars, I cannot break the Hebrew Bible down into strata, or date its materials to their proper century. My general suspicion is that many books grew by slow accretion, and contain both old and late materials; but mostly I cannot determine which are which. Connections between the two societies were at second or third hand, by sea and land, trade and war, dispersal of technology and social institutions, foreign women and male collectivities. Their shared features assume a common form because of the new emergence which they jointly represent: a critique of social and religious institutions expressed in alphabetic script. Perhaps a profounder analysis of the archaeological record will more closely document the dates and means of transmission.

(2) I have always had trouble keeping the plots of stories in my head, and I have minimized the *narrative parallels* between the two literatures here compared. Some of the most striking I owe to Martin West (II.280-286). There are supposed to be only so many plots available to world literature, and I lack fixed criteria to determine when narrative parallels prove historical connection, and when they simply flow from the general human condition. I suspect that there may exist a science of narrative structure which can distinguish between vague and precise parallels; if so, I have not found it.

(3) Above all, especially in this volume where it might be looked for, I emphasize that this is *not a work of theology*! Here throughout I do chronicle parallels between later Israel and Hellas in formulating the meaning of existence and giving answers to the unavoidable reality of death—that mystery (as Churchill is supposed to have said of the former Soviet Union) wrapped up in a riddle inside an enigma. At times my judgements are more positive, at times less so; but in general I find myself unable to affirm absolutely whether or not the ancient formulations are correct, inevitable, compelling.... My failure is compounded when I *can* translate the activities earlier ascribed to the High God into terms acceptable to environmentalism or sociology. Still I recognize that an evaluative treatment of what the ancients say about God or

death is a fully legitimate enterprise—very likely for somebody else, with different methods, in other books.

While this volume follows close on its predecessor, there are still new works to note. I have read the second edition of the Dictionary of Deities and Demons in the Bible (DDD²) with more care than the first; users will always discover something new, and I have lifted a number of citations with credit. I have consulted the materials, old and new, in the Textbook of Aramaic Documents from ancient Egypt (TAD) less than I should. I have learned quite a bit from the New Companion to Homer; but I miss in it articles on the role of the gods, characterization, the use of Homer by Vergil.... Margaret Williams' Diasporan Handbook has proved a very useful resource. German readers (I presume) will already have been looking up Ancient Near Eastern texts in the comprehensive TUAT, which shares its more-than-industrious editor with the BZAW; for English readers, perhaps the new enterprise Context of Scripture will one day supplement or replace ANET; but there is no substitute for the task I long ago gave up on—knowledge of the difficult original scripts.

This volume enters on new academic areas. Chapter 21 notes such materials for Iranian studies as have come my way; I am confident there is much more I have missed. But readers should note the value of the trilingual "Res Gestae Divi Saporis" for Iranian realities. The novel Chapter 23 makes much more extensive use of Rabbinic materials than the others; as of the Syriac and Latin versions of the Gospels, more for historical than for textual purposes.

In both preceding volumes, I unaccountably failed to credit Prof. Saul Levin for the elegant printouts of Arabic texts from his highly educated computer. Once again here he has taken time away from his own work to provide the reader with phrases from the Quran. In addition, readers owe to him the transcriptions of some vocalized Mishna texts from the Kaufmann codex in Appendix 4—to the best of my knowledge, not elsewhere available in print. Further, he read the chapters of this volume in MS at very short notice, and much improved them.

In December of 1999 I enjoyed the hospitality of the two institutions which have sponsored this enterprise: the Philipps-Universität at Marburg an der Lahn (founded 1527), which hosted a symposium for the 75th birthday of my editor Otto Kaiser; and Walter de Gruyter in Berlin (which I can now think of only as a city of snow...), beginning its *second* quarter-millennium, with special appreciation to Volker Gebhardt of the Division of Humanities, and Klaus Otterburig. Much thanks to my genial driver and companion Karl-Wilhelm Dahm. It was amazing for this American, after finding several doors closed in the States, to have others swing wide open in Germany! I know no easy way to express my indebtedness. And I suppose I should thank the inventors of WordPerfect for making possible a disk of the letter-text; much more then, de Gruyter's learned staff for transcribing the endless Greek and Hebrew font off my untidy hand, no better than it used to be.

Even text-editions of single authors may fall short of total correctness, and the reader should not expect the citations here from hundreds of authors in many languages to be absolutely error-free. (I know my unsystematic compromises between American and German typographical usage will satisfy no-one.) To have hired a very energetic and learned person to sit in a very large library checking everything on the proofs was out of the question, for expense and even more for time. More far-reaching are the author's defects of knowledge and interpretation, which only future research will amend. Many saving qualifications late in a paragraph are due to Levin's vigilant presence, "Do we really have the *Besserwissen* to correct two millennia later what the ancients affirmed about themselves?" With less pressure on me now to keep current in the literature, authors who wish assurance that I know about their works will receive warm thanks if they take the initiative to send me reprints or notices (at the address in the directories of APA or SBL).

I would be remiss not to thank Prof. Edward Lipiński here for the sumptuous gift of his "Dieux et déesses de l'univers phénicien et punique". This work would be longer and better if I entered at each relevant place what I should have learned from him; I will just say that wherever we treat the same topic, he knows more than I do. And special thanks to appreciative readers, who have made unique contributions which each will recognize: Louis Feldman, Margaret Miles, Bennett Simon, Zeph Stewart.

As always, Emily's silent example has reduced clutter, and would have done more if I had let it. Besides an immense relief now at seeing my manuscript in good hands and generating proofs, I feel also some sadness at writing FINIS to an investigation which began in Beirut already in 1960. My friend Cyrus Gordon had then just published "Homer and Bible"; and everybody (whether they admit it or not) owes the largest part of their formation to both Israel and Hellas. If I have succeeded to some degree in elucidating their connection, and setting up a cairn pointing future mountaineers further along the same trail, I shall be more than satisfied.

TABLE OF CONTENTS

ABBREVIATIONS AND BIBLIOGRAPHY (Cumulative)

Here are listed all works, both of general reference and specific studies, referred to in shortened form. This list as cumulative includes all titles appearing in the comparable sections of Volumes I and II, whether or not they are referred to in Vol. III, and updates their bibliographical data. Modern studies marked with an asterisk (*) are those I have found most useful.

ABD: D. N. Freedman (ed.), The Anchor Bible Dictionary; 6 vols.; New York: Doubleday, 1992.

ADPV: Abhandlungen des Deutschen Palästina-Vereins.

Ahiqar: Cowley pp. 212-220.

AJA: American Journal of Archaeology.

AJP: American Journal of Philology.

Aland, Synopsis: K. Aland, Synopsis Quattuor Evangeliorum; Stuttgart: Württembergische Bibelanstalt; 1964.

Amarna: J. A. Knudtzon, Die El-Amarna Tafeln; 2 vols.; repr. Aalen: Zeller, 1964. English translation and updates in W. L. Moran, The Amarna Letters; Baltimore: Johns Hopkins, 1992.

ANEP^2: James B. Pritchard (ed.), The Ancient Near East in Pictures Relating to the Old Testament; 2nd ed.; Princeton: University, 1969.

ANET^3: James B. Pritchard (ed.), Ancient Near Eastern Texts Relating to the Old Testament; 3rd ed.; Princeton: University, 1969.

ANRW: H. Temporini & W. Haase (eds.), Aufstieg und Niedergang der römischen Welt; Berlin: de Gruyter, 1972—.

Astour: Michael C. Astour, Hellenosemitica: An Ethnic and Cultural Study in West Semitic Impact on Mycenaean Greece; Leiden: Brill, 1965.

Bab. Talm.: Babylonian Talmud.

Back: Michael Back, Die sassanidischen Staatsinschriften...; Acta Iranica 18; 3 série, Textes et Mémoires vol. 8; Leiden: Brill, 1978.

BAGD: Bauer-Arndt-Gingrich-Danker, A Greek-English Lexicon of the New Testament; 2nd ed.; Chicago: University, 1979. 3rd ed. promised for 2000.

BAH: Bibliothèque Archéologique et Historique.

Bartholomae: Christian Bartholomae, Altiranisches Wörterbuch; Strassburg: Trübner, 1904.

BASOR: Bulletin of the American Schools of Oriental Research.

BCH: Bulletin de Correspondance Hellénique.

BDB: Brown, Driver & Briggs: Hebrew and English Lexicon.

BDF: Blass, Debrunner, Funk: A Greek Grammar of the New Testament.

Beentjes: Pancratius C. Beentjes, The Book of Ben Sira in Hebrew...; Supplements to Vetus Testamentum LXVIII; Leiden etc.: Brill, 1997.

Benz: Frank L. Benz, Personal Names in the Phoenician and Punic Inscriptions: A Catalog, Grammatical Study and Glossary of Elements; Studia Pohl 8; Rome: Biblical Institute, 1972.

Bernal: Martin Bernal, Black Athena: The Afroasiatic Roots of Classical Civilization. Vol. 1: The Fabrication of Ancient Greece 1785-1985; London: Free Association, 1987; Vol. 2: The Archaeological and Documentary Evidence; New Brunswick: Rutgers Univ. 1991.

BGU: Berliner Griechische Urkunden.

Bib. Arch.: Biblical Archaeologist.

BibZ: Biblische Zeitschrift.

Black: Matthew Black, An Aramaic Approach to the Gospels and Acts; 2nd ed.; Oxford: Clarendon, 1954.

Bogan: Zachary Bogan, Homerus Ἑβραΐζων sive comparatio Homeri cum scriptoribus sacris quoad normam loquendi: Oxford, 1658.

Bomhard & Kerns 1994: Allan R. Bomhard & John C. Kerns, The Nostratic Macrofamily: A Study in Distant Linguistic Relationship; Trends in Linguistics, Studies and Monographs 74; Berlin & New York: Mouton de Gruyter, 1994.

Bonfante, G. & L.: G. & L. Bonfante, The Etruscan Language: An Introduction; Manchester: University, 1983.

* Bonnet, Melqart: Corinne Bonnet, Melqart: Cultes et mythes de l'Héraclès tyrien en Méditerranée; Studia Phoenicia 8; Bib. de la fac. de phil. et lettres de Namur 69; Leuven: Peeters, 1988.

Borger: R. Borger, Die Inschriften Asarhaddons Königs von Assyrien; Archiv für Orientforschung Beiheft 9; 1956/1967.

Briant: Pierre Briant, Histoire de l'empire perse de Cyrus à Alexandre; 2 vols.; Achaemenid History X; Leiden: Ned. Inst. voor het nabije Oosten, 1996.

* Briquel-Chatonnet: F. Briquel-Chatonnet, Les relations entre les cités de la côte phénicienne et les royaumes d'Israël et de Juda; Orientalia Lovaniensia 46; Studia Phoenicia 12; Leuven: Peeters, 1992.

Brown, From Hesiod to Jesus: J. P. Brown, "From Hesiod to Jesus: Laws of Human Nature in the Ancient World," NovT 35 (1993) 313-343 [now revised here as Chapter 18].

Brown, Images: —, "Images and their Names in Classical Israel and Hellas," pp. 7-32 (with illustrations) of Asher Ovadiah (ed.), Hellenic and Jewish Arts: Interaction, Tradition and Renewal; the Howard Gilman International Conferences I; Tel Aviv: Ramoth, University; 1998.

Brown, Lebanon and Phoenicia: —, The Lebanon and Phoenicia: Ancient Texts illustrating their physical geography and native industries; Vol. I [all pub.] The physical setting and the forest; Beirut: American University, 1969.

Brown, LXX & Targum: —, "The Septuagint as a Source of the Greek Loan-Words in the Targums," Biblica 70 (1989) 194-216.

Brown-Levin, Ethnic Paradigm: J. P. Brown & S. Levin, "The Ethnic Paradigm as a pattern for nominal forms in Greek and Hebrew," General Linguistics 26 (1986) 71-105 [excerpted here in Vol. II, Chapter 17].

Bryce: Trevor Bryce, The Kingdom of the Hittites; Oxford: Clarendon, 1998.

* Burkert, Homo Necans: Walter Burkert, Homo Necans: The Anthropology of Ancient Greek Sacrificial Ritual and Myth; tr. P. Bing from the German ed. of 1972, and revised by the author; Berkeley: Univ. of California, 1983.

* Burkert, Or. Rev.: Walter Burkert, The Orientalizing Revolution: Near Eastern Influence on Greek Culture in the Early Archaic Age; Cambridge: Harvard, 1992: English tr. (with extensive revisions by the author) of Die orientalisierende Epoche in der griechischen Religion und Literatur (Sitzungsb. der Heid. Akad. der Wiss., Phil.-hist. Klasse, 1984).

Burkitt: F. Crawford Burkitt, Evangelion da-Mepharreshe...; 2 vols.; Cambridge: University, 1904.

BZAW: Beihefte zur Zeitschrift für die alttestamentliche Wissenschaft.

CAD: The Assyrian Dictionary of the University of Chicago.

CAH: Cambridge Ancient History.

* Cambridge Iliad: G. S. Kirk (general ed.), The Iliad: A Commentary; 6 vols.; Cambridge: University, 1985-1993.

* Casabona: Jean Casabona, Recherches sur le vocabulaire des sacrifices en grec des origines à la fin de l'époque classique; Pub. des Annales de la Faculté des Lettres Aix-en-Provence n.s. 56; Ophrys, 1966.

Casey: Maurice Casey, Aramaic Sources of Mark's Gospel; SNTSMS 102; Cambridge: University, 1998

* Casson, Periplus: Lionel Casson, The Periplus Maris Erythraei; Princeton: University, 1989.

CBQ: Catholic Biblical Quarterly.

CFHB: Corpus Fontium Historiae Byzantinae.

Chantraine: P. Chantraine, Dictionnaire étymologique de la langue grecque; histoire des mots; 4 vols.; Paris: Klincksieck, 1968-1980.

Charlesworth: J. Charlesworth (ed.), Old Testament Pseudepigrapha; 2 vols.; Garden City: Doubleday, 1983-1985.

CIJ: Corpus Inscriptionum Judaicarum, ed. J. B. Frey; New York: Ktav, 1975; Vol. II: Rome 1952.

CIL: Corpus Inscriptionum Latinarum.

CIS: Corpus Inscriptionum Semiticarum.

Claridge: Amanda Claridge, Rome: An Oxford Archaeological Guide; Oxford: University, 1998.

Context of Scripture: W. W. Hallo, ed.; in progress; Leiden: Brill, 1997—.

* Cook, Persian Empire: J. M. Cook, The Persian Empire; New York: Shocken, 1983.

Cook, Zeus: A. B. Cook, Zeus: A Study in Ancient Religion; 3 vols. in 5; Cambridge: University, 1914-1940.

Cooke: G. A. Cooke, A Text-Book of North-Semitic Inscriptions; Oxford: Clarendon, 1903.

* Cornell: T. J. Cornell, The Beginnings of Rome: Italy and Rome from the Bronze Age to the Punic Wars (c. 1000-264 BC); London: Routledge, 1995.

Corp. Christ.: Corpus Christianorum, series latina.

Cowley: A. Cowley, Aramaic Papyri of the Fifth Century B.C.; Oxford: Clarendon, 1923 [text numbers preserved in TAD].

CPG: E. Leutsch & F. G. Schneidewin, Corpus Paroemiographorum Graecorum; 2 vols.; Göttingen: Vandenhoek & Ruprecht, 1839-1851.

CPJ: V. A. Tcherikover & A. Fuchs, Corpus Papyrorum Judaicarum; 3 vols.; Cambridge: Harvard for Magnes Press, 1957-1964.

CR: Classical Review.

CRAI: Comptes Rendus de l'Académie des Inscriptions et Belles-Lettres.

CSCO: Corpus Scriptorum Christianorum Orientalium.

CSEL: Corpus Scriptorum Ecclesiasticorum Latinorum.

CSHB: Corpus Scriptorum Historiae Byzantinae.

Cuny: Albert Cuny, Invitation a l'étude comparative des langues indo-européennes et des langues chamito-sémitiques; Bordeaux: Bière, 1946.

Cur. Syr.: The Curetonian MS of the Old Syriac Gospels, ed. Burkitt.

Daremberg-Saglio: C. L. Daremberg & E. Saglio, Dictionnaire des antiquités grecques et romaines...; 5 vols. in 9; 1877-1919; repr. Graz: Akademische.

* DCPP: Edouard Lipiński (ed.), Dictionnaire de la civilisation phénicienne et punique; Brepols, 1992.

* DDD: K. van den Toorn et alii, Dictionary of Deities and Demons
in the Bible; Leiden: Brill, 1995; 2nd ed., 1999.

Debevoise: Neilson C. Debevoise, A Political History of Parthia; Chicago: University, 1938.

Delumeau: Jean Delumeau, History of Paradise: The Garden of Eden
in Myth and Tradition; tr. M. O'Connell; New York: Continuum,
1995; tr. of Une Histoire du Paradis: Le Jardin des délices; Paris:
Fayard, 1992.

de Ste. Croix: G. E. M. de Ste. Croix, The Class Struggle in the Ancient
Greek World from the Archaic Age to the Arab Conquests; Ithaca:
Cornell, 1981.

DHGE: Dictionnaire d'Histoire et de Géographie Ecclésiastiques.

Diocletian, Edict: see Maximum-Price Edict.

DISO: C.-F. Jean & J. Hoftijzer, Dictionnaire des Inscriptions Sémitiques de l'Ouest; Leiden: Brill, 1965 [now replaced by DNWSI]

DJD: Discoveries in the Judaean Desert.

DMG²: M. Ventris & John Chadwick, Documents in Mycenaean
Greek; 2nd ed.; Cambridge: University, 1973.

DNWSI: J. Hoftijzer & K. Jongeling, Dictionary of the North-West
Semitic Inscriptions; 2 vols.; Leiden: Brill, 1995 [replacing DISO].

* Drews, Bronze Age: Robert Drews, The End of the Bronze Age:
Changes in Warfare and the Catastrophe ca. 1200 B.C.; Princeton:
University, 1993.

Drews, Coming of the Greeks: —, The Coming of the Greeks: Indo-
European Conquests in the Aegean and the Near East; Princeton:
University, 1988.

Driver: G. R. Driver, Aramaic Documents of the Fifth Century B.C.
[the Arsames dossier]; 2nd ed. [with notes by W. B. Henning on
Iranian linguistics]; Oxford: Clarendon, 1957 [texts now revised in
TAD].

DSS/SE: F. G. Martínez & E. J. C. Tigchelaar, The Dead Sea Scrolls:
Study Edition; 2nd ed. (paper), 2 vols.; Leiden: Brill & Grand
Rapids: Eerdmans, 2000.

* Dubuisson: Michel Dubuisson, Le latin de Polybe: Les implications
historiques d'un cas de bilinguisme; Etudes et Commentaires 96;
Paris: Klincksieck, 1985.

Duchemin: Jacqueline Duchemin, Mythes grecs et sources orientales;
Paris: Les Belles Lettres, 1995 [reprints of articles with footnotes
abbreviated].

* Edwards, Kadmos: Ruth B. Edwards, Kadmos the Phoenician: A

XX   ABBREVIATIONS AND BIBLIOGRAPHY

Study in Greek Legends and the Mycenaean Age; Amsterdam: Hakkert, 1979.

* EFH: M. L. West, The East Face of Helicon: West Asiatic Elements in Greek Poetry and Myth; Oxford: Clarendon, 1997.

Ehrenberg-Jones: V. Ehrenberg & A.H.M. Jones, Documents illustrating the reigns of Augustus & Tiberius; 2nd ed.; Oxford: Clarendon, 1955.

Ellenbogen: Maximilian Ellenbogen, Foreign Words in the Old Testament: Their Origin and Etymology; London: Luzac, 1962.

Ep. Arist.: Epistle of Aristeas, ed. M. Hadas, Aristeas to Philocrates; New York: Ktav, 1973.

EPROER: Etudes préliminaires aux religions orientales dans l'Empire romain.

Erman-Grapow: A. Erman & H. Grapow, Wörterbuch der aegyptischen Sprache, 6 + 5 vols.; Leipzig: Hinrichs, 1926-1953.

Ernout-Meillet: A. Ernout & A. Meillet, Dictionnaire étymologique de la langue latine; 4th ed.; Paris: Klincksieck, 1959.

* Faure: P. Faure, Parfums et Aromates de l'Antiquité; Fayard, 1987.

FGH: F. Jacoby, Die Fragmente der Griechischen Historiker; Leiden: Brill, 1957—.

FHG: C. Müller, Fragmenta Historicorum Graecorum; 5 vols.; Paris: Didot, 1841-1870.

Field: F. Field, Origenis Hexapla; Oxford, 1875.

Fitzmyer, Wandering Aramaean: J. A. Fitzmyer, A Wandering Aramaean: Collected Aramaic Essays; SBLMS 25; Chico: Scholars, 1979.

Fitzmyer-Harrington: J. A. Fitzmyer & D. J. Harrington, A Manual of Palestinian Aramaic Texts; Biblica et Orientalia 34; Rome; Bib. Inst. Press, 1978.

* Fournet: Jean-Luc Fournet, "Les emprunts du grec à l'égyptien," Bulletin de la Société de Linguistique de Paris 84 (1989) 55-80.

Friedrich: Johannes Friedrich, Hethitisches Wörterbuch; Heidelberg: Winter, 1952.

Frisk: H. Frisk, Griechisches etymologisches Wörterbuch; 3 vols.; Heidelberg: Winter, 1960-1972.

FRLANT: Forschungen zur Religion und Literatur des Alten und Neuen Testaments.

FVS[8]: H. Diels & W. Kranz, Die Fragmente der Vorsokratiker; 8th ed.; 3 vols.; Berlin: Weidmann, 1956.

Gabba: Emilio Gabba, Iscrizioni greche e latine per lo studio della Bibbia; Sintesi dell'oriente e della Bibbia, Monografie 3; Torino, 1958.

GCS: Die Griechischen Christlichen Schriftsteller.

Geiger: Abraham Geiger, Judaism and Islam; New York: Ktav, 1940; first pub. as Was hat Mohammed aus dem Judenthume aufgenommen?, 1835.

Geus: Klaus Geus, Prosopographie der literarisch bezeugten Karthager; Studia Phoenicia 13; Orientalia Lovaniensia Analecta 59; Leuven: Peeters, 1994.

GGM: C. Müller, Geographi Graeci Minores; 2 vols.; Paris: Didot, 1855-1861.

Gignoux: Philippe Gignoux, Glossaire des Inscriptions Pehlevies et Parthes; Corpus Inscriptionum Iranicarum, Supplementary Series, Vol. I; London: Lund Humphries, 1972.

Gilgamesh: A Reader: John Maier (ed.), Gilgamesh: a Reader: Wauconda: Bolchazy-Carducci, 1997.

Gordon [A.], IILE: Arthur E. Gordon, Illustrated Introduction to Latin Epigraphy; Berkeley: Univ. of California, 1983.

* Gordon [C.], Before the Bible: Cyrus H. Gordon, Before the Bible: The Common Background of Greek and Hebrew Civilisations; London: Collins, 1962; the New York ed. (Norton, 1965) is entitled The Common Background of Greek and Hebrew Civilizations.

* Gordon [C.], Homer & Bible: —, Homer and Bible: The Origin and Character of East Mediterranean Literature; Ventnor (N.J.): Ventnor Publishers, 1967; repr. from HUCA 26 (1955) 43-108.

Greeks and Barbarians: J. E. Coleman & C. A. Walz (eds.), Greeks and Barbarians: Essays on the Interactions between Greeks and Non-Greeks in Antiquity and the Consequences for Eurocentrism; Occ. Pubs. of the Dept. of N. E. Studies and the Prog. of Jewish Studies, Cornell Univ., no. 4; Bethesda: CDL, 1997.

Head: Barclay V. Head, Historia Numorum: a manual of Greek numismatics; 2nd ed.; Oxford: Clarendon, 1911.

Helck-Otto: H.-W. Helck & E. Otto, Lexikon der Ägyptologie; Wiesbaden: Harrassowitz, 1972—.

Hoehner: H. W. Hoehner, Herod Antipas; Cambridge: University, 1972.

HSCP: Harvard Studies in Classical Philology.

HTR: Harvard Theological Review.

HUCA: Hebrew Union College Annual.

* Hughes: J. Donald Hughes, Pan's Travail: Environmental Problems of the Ancient Greeks and Romans; Baltimore: Johns Hopkins, 1994.

Hymn of the Pearl: A. A. Bevan, The Hymn of the Soul; Texts and Studies V.3; Cambridge: University, 1897 [Syriac text]: Greek text in M. Bonnet, Acta Apostolorum Apocrypha, II.2, Hildesheim: Olms, 1959, pp. 219-225 (Acta Thomae 108-114).

IDB: Interpreter's Dictionary of the Bible, 4 vols.; New York: Abingdon, 1962; with Supplementary Volume, 1976.

IEG: M. L. West, Iambi et Elegi Graeci; 2 vols.; Oxford: Clarendon, 1971.

IEJ: Israel Exploration Journal.

IESL: Saul Levin, The Indo-European and Semitic Languages: An exploration of structural similarities related to accent, chiefly in Greek, Sanskrit and Hebrew; Albany: State Univ. of New York, 1971.

IG: Inscriptiones Graecae.

IGLS: Inscriptions Grecques et Latines de la Syrie, in the series BAH.

IGRR: R. Cagnat & G. Lafaye, Inscriptiones Graecae ad res romanas pertinentes; vols. 1, 3, 4 [all pub.]; Paris, 1906-1927.

ILS: H. Dessau, Inscriptiones Latinae Selectae; 3rd ed.; 5 vols.; Berlin: Weidmann, 1962.

Inscr. Cret.: M. Guarducci, Inscriptiones Creticae.

Inscriptions de Délos: see LSJ xxixa.

Insler: S. Insler, The Gāthās of Zarathustra; Acta Iranica 8; 3 série, Textes et Mémoires 1; Leiden: Brill etc., 1975.

Inventaire: Inventaire des inscriptions de Palmyre; see Concordance in PAT 446-7.

JAAR: Journal of the American Academy of Religion.

JAOS: Journal of the American Oriental Society.

Jastrow: Marcus Jastrow, A Dictionary of the Targumim, the Talmud Babli and Yerushalmi, and the Midrashic Literature; 2 vols.; London: Luzac, 1903.

JBL: Journal of Biblical Literature.

* Jeffery: Arthur Jeffery, The Foreign Vocabulary of the Quran; Baroda: Oriental Institute, 1938.

Jennings-Gantillon: W. Jennings & U. Gantillon, Lexicon to the Syriac New Testament; Oxford: Clarendon, 1926.

Jer. Talm.: Jerusalem Talmud.

JHS: Journal of Hellenic Studies.

JNES: Journal of Near Eastern Studies.

Joüon: Paul Joüon, Grammaire de l'hébreu biblique; 2nd ed.; Rome: Inst. Bib. Pont., 1947.

JQR: Jewish Quarterly Review.

JRS: Journal of Roman Studies.

JSNT: Journal for the Study of the New Testament.

JSOT: Journal for the Study of the Old Testament.

JSS: Journal of Semitic Studies.

JTS: Journal of Theological Studies.
* Just: Roger Just, Women in Athenian Law and Life; London: Routledge, 1989.
KAI: H. Donner & W. Röllig, Kanaanäische und aramäische Inschriften; 3 vols.; Wiesbaden: Harrassowitz, 1962-4.
KASD: J. Friedrich, Kleinasiatische Sprachdenkmäler; Kleine Texte 163; Berlin: de Gruyter, 1932.
* Kaufman: Stephen A. Kaufman, The Akkadian Influences on Aramaic; Assyriological Studies 19; Chicago: University, 1974.
Kaufmann Codex: Georg Beer, Faksimile-Ausgabe des Mishnacodex Kaufmann A50; 2 vols.; Jerusalem, [5]728 [= 1967/8].
KB³: L. Koehler & W. Baumgartner, Hebräisches und Aramäisches Lexicon zum alten Testament; 3rd ed., 5 vols.; Leiden: Brill, 1967-1995.
Kent: R. G. Kent, Old Persian: Grammar, Texts, Lexicon; 2nd ed.; American Oriental Series vol. 33; New Haven: Am. Oriental Society, 1953.
KJV: King James Version of the English Bible.
Kock: T. Kock, Comicorum Atticorum Fragmenta; 3 vols.; Leipizg: Teubner, 1880-1888 [being replaced by R. Kassel & C. Austin, Poetae Comici Graeci; in progress; Berlin: de Gruyter, 1983—; not referred to here].
Kraeling: Emil G. Kraeling, The Brooklyn Museum Aramaic Papyri; New Haven: Yale, 1953 [texts now revised in TAD].
Krauss: Samuel Krauss, Griechische und lateinische Lehnwörter im Talmud, Midrasch und Targum; mit Bemerkungen von Immanuel Löw; Teil II; Berlin 1899; repr. Hildesheim: Olms, 1964.
KTU: M. Dietrich et alii, The Cuneiform Alphabetic Texts from Ugarit, Ras Ibn Hani and Other Places (KTU: second, enlarged edition); Abhandlungen zur Literatur Alt-Syrien-Palästinas und Mesopotamiens Bd 8; Münster: Ugarit-Verlag, 1995; replaces iidem, Die Keilalphabetischen Texte aus Ugarit; Teil 1; Alter Orient und Altes Testament Bd 24; Neukirchen-Vluyn, 1976.
LACUS: Linguistic Association of Canada and the United States.
Lampe: G. W. H. Lampe, A Patristic Greek Lexicon; Oxford: Clarendon, 1961.
LCL: Loeb Classical Library.
Levin, Saul: See IESL, SIE.
Levy: Jacob Levy, Neuhebräisches und chaldäisches Wörterbuch über die Talmudim und Midraschim; 4 vols.; Leipzig: Brockhaus, 1876.
* Lewy: Heinrich Lewy, Die semitischen Fremdwörter im griechischen; Berlin: Gaertner, 1895.

* Lieberman, Greek: Saul Lieberman, Greek in Jewish Palestine...; 2nd ed.; New York: Feldheim, 1965.

* Lieberman, Hellenism: —, Hellenism in Jewish Palestine...; New York: Jewish Theological Seminary of America 5711 / 1950.

LIMC: Lexicon Iconographicum Mythologiae Classicae; 6 vols., each in 2 parts; Zurich: Artemis, 1981-1994.

* Lipiński, Dieux et Déesses: E. Lipiński, Dieux et Déesses de l'univers phénicien et punique; Orientalia Lovaniensia Analecta 64; Studia Phoenicia 14; Leuven: Peeters, 1995.

LSAG²: Lilian H. Jeffery, The Local Scripts of Archaic Greece, rev. ed. by A. W. Johnston; Oxford: Clarendon, 1990.

LSAM: Franciszek Sokolowski, Lois Sacrées de l'Asie Mineure; École française d'Athènes, Travaux et Mémoires...fasc. 9; Paris: Boccard, 1955.

LSCG: —, Lois Sacrées des Cités Grecques; ibid. fasc. 18, 1969; LSCGSup, Supplément [to the older work by Prott-Ziehen]; ibid. fasc. 11, 1962.

LSJ: Liddell-Scott-Jones, A Greek-English Lexicon; 9th ed.; Oxford: University, 1940; with Revised Supplement by P. G. W. Glare, 1996.

Luther: Die Bibel...nach der Übersetzung Martin Luthers; Stuttgart: Württembergische Bibelanstalt, 1972.

* Margalith: Othniel Margalith, The Sea Peoples in the Bible; Wiesbaden: Harrassowitz, 1994.

* Masson, Recherches: Emilia Masson, Recherches sur les plus anciens emprunts sémitiques en grec; Etudes et Commentaires 67; Paris: Klincksieck, 1967.

Maximum-Price Edict: Marta Giacchero, Edictum Diocletiani et Collegarum...; Pubblicaz. dell'Ist. di Storia antica...dell'Univ. di Genova 8; 2 vols.; 1974.

* Meiggs: Russell Meiggs, Trees and Timber in the Ancient Mediterranean World; Oxford: Clarendon, 1982.

Meiggs-Lewis: R. Meiggs & D. Lewis, A Selection of Greek Historical Inscriptions to the end of the Fifth Century B. C., rev. ed.; Oxford: Clarendon, 1975.

Merkelbach-West: R. Merkelbach & M. L. West, Fragmenta Hesiodea; Oxford: Clarendon, 1967.

* Millar: Fergus Millar, The Roman Near East 31 BC—AD 337; Cambridge: Harvard, 1993.

* Miller, Spice Trade: J. Innes Miller, The Spice Trade of the Roman Empire, 29 B.C. to A.D. 641; Oxford: Clarendon, 1969.

Möller: Hermann Möller, Vergleichendes indogermanisch-semitisches Wörterbuch; Göttingen: Vandenhoek & Ruprecht, 1911.

Monier-Williams: M. Monier-Williams, A Sanskrit-English Dictionary; Oxford: Clarendon, 1899.

Morris: Sarah Morris, "Homer and the Near East," New Companion 599-623.

MUSJ: Mélanges de l'Université saint-Joseph (Beirut).

Muss-Arnolt: W. Muss-Arnolt, "On Semitic Words in Greek and Latin," TAPA 23 (1892) 35-156.

Musurillo: H. Musurillo, The Acts of the Pagan Martyrs: Acta Alexandrinorum; Oxford: Clarendon, 1954.

MVAG: Mitteilungen der Vorderasiatischen Gesellschaft.

Mynors: R. A. B. Mynors, Virgil: Georgics; Oxford: Clarendon, 1990.

Nauck: A. Nauck, Tragicorum Graecorum Fragmenta; 2nd ed.; Leipzig: Teubner, 1889 [partly replaced by TrGF].

NEAE: New Encyclopaedia of Archaeological Excavations in the Holy Land; 4 vols.; New York: Simon & Schuster, 1993.

New Companion: Ian Morris & Barry Powell, eds., A New Companion to Homer; Mnemosyne Supp. 163; Leiden: Brill, 1997.

New Documents: New Documents Illustrating Early Christianity; in progress; Macquarie: University; in progress, 1976— [pub. 1981—].

NovT: Novum Testamentum.

NTS: New Testament Studies.

NYT: New York Times.

OBO 129: B. Janowski et alii (eds.), Religionsgeschichtliche Beziehungen zwischen Kleinasien, Nordsyrien und dem Alten Testament [Symposion Hamburg 1990]; Orbis Biblicus et Orientalis 129; Göttingen: Vandenhoek & Ruprecht, 1993.

* OCD³: Oxford Classical Dictionary, 3rd ed. by S. Hornblower & A. Spawforth; Oxford: University, 1996.

OCT: Oxford Classical Texts.

ODEP³: F. P. Wilson, Oxford Dictionary of English Proverbs, 3rd ed.; Oxford: Clarendon, 1970.

Odes of Solomon: ed. J. H. Charlesworth; Chico: Scholars, 1977.

ODQ²: Oxford Dictionary of Quotations; 2nd ed.; Oxford: University, 1955.

OED: Oxford English Dictionary.

* Ogilvie: R. M. Ogilvie, A Commentary on Livy Books 1-5; Oxford: Clarendon, 1965.

OGIS: W. Dittenberger, Orientis Graeci Inscriptiones Selectae; 2 vols.; Leipzig: Hirzel, 1903-5.

OLD: P. G. W. Glare (ed.), Oxford Latin Dictionary; Oxford: Clarendon, 1982.

Old Syr.: Old Syriac Gospels, ed. Burkitt (q.v.).

OLP: Orientalia Lovaniensia Periodica.

* Otto: A. Otto, Die Sprichwörter und sprichwörtlichen Redensarten der Römer; Leipzig: Teubner, 1890.

* Oxford Odyssey: A. Heubeck et alii, A Commentary on Homer's Odyssey; 3 vols.; Oxford: Clarendon, 1988-1992.

Palingenesia 36; C. W. Müller et alii (eds.), Zum Umgang mit fremden Sprachen in der griechisch-römischen Antike; Kolloquium Saarbrücken 1989; Palingenesia 36; Stuttgart: Steiner, 1992.

* Pallottino, Etruscans: Massimo Pallottino, The Etruscans, tr. J. Cremona; Bloomington: Indiana Univ., 1975; tr. from the 6th Italian edition of Etruscologia; Milano: Hoepli, 1968.

Pal. Syr.: Agnes Smith Lewis & Margaret Dunlop Gibson, The Palestinian Syriac Lectionary of the Gospels; London: Kegan Paul, 1899.

Palm. Tar.: Palmyrene Tariff, PAT 0259.

PAT: Delbert R. Hillers & Eleonora Cussini, Palmyrene Aramaic Texts; Baltimore: Johns Hopkins, 1996.

PEQ: Palestine Exploration Quarterly.

Pesh.: The New Testament in Syriac [Peshitto]; London: British & Foreign Bible Society, 1950.

PG: J.-P. Migne, Patrologia Graeca.

Pickthall: M. Pickthall, The Glorious Koran: A Bilingual Edition...; Albany: State Univ. of New York, 1976.

Pindar ed. Bowra: C. M. Bowra, Pindari Carmina cum fragmentis; 2nd ed.; Oxford: Clarendon, 1947.

PIR: Prosopographia Imperii Romani.

PL: J.-P. Migne, Patrologia Latina.

PLF: E. Lobel & D. L. Page, Poetarum Lesbiorum Fragmenta; 2nd ed.; Oxford: Clarendon, 1963.

PMG: D. L. Page, Poetae Melici Graeci; Oxford: Clarendon, 1962.

Poultney: J. W. Poultney, The Bronze Tables of Iguvium; Philological Monographs XVIII; American Philological Association, 1959.

* Powell: Barry B. Powell, Homer and the Origin of the Greek Alphabet; Cambridge: University, 1991.

Powell, Homer & Writing: —, "Homer and Writing," New Companion 3-32.

P. Oxy.: Oxyrhynchus Papyri.

PRU iv: Jean Nougayrol, Le Palais Royal d'Ugarit IV: Textes accadiens des archives sud (Archives internationales); Mission de Ras Shamra IX; Paris: Imprimerie Nationale, 1956.

PW: Paulys Real-encyclopädie der klassischen Altertumswissenschaft, ed. G. Wissowa, 1894—.

RB: Revue Biblique.

REA: Revue des Etudes Anciennes.
RES: Répertoire d'Epigraphie Sémitique.
RGRW: Religions in the Graeco-Roman World.
RHR: Revue de l'Histoire des Religions.
Richardson: L. Richardson Jr., A New Topographical Dictionary of Ancient Rome; Baltimore: Johns Hopkins, 1992.
RLA: Reallexikon der Assyriologie; Berlin: de Gruyter, 1932—.
* Rosén: H. B. Rosén, l'Hébreu et ses rapports avec le monde classique: Essai d'évaluation culturelle; Etudes chamito-sémitiques Sup. 7; Paris: Geuthner, 1979.
RSV: Revised Standard Version of the English Bible.
SANT: Studien zum Alten und Neuen Testament.
Sapor, Res Gestae: A. Maricq, "Res Gestae Divi Saporis," Syria 35 (1958) 295-360; see also Back.
SBL: Society of Biblical Literature.
Script. Hist. Aug.: Scriptores Historiae Augustae.
SEG: Supplementum Epigraphicum Graecum.
SGDI: Sammlung der griechischen Dialekt-Inschriften; Göttingen 1884-1915.
SGHI: see Meiggs-Lewis.
SHA: Scriptores Historiae Augustae.
Sherk: Robert K. Sherk, Roman Documents from the Greek East: Senatus Consulta and Epistulae to the Age of Augustus; Baltimore: Johns Hopkins, 1969.
* SIE: Saul Levin, Semitic and Indo-European: The Principal Etymologies; with observations on Afro-Asiatic; Amsterdam Studies in the Theory and History of Linguistic Science; Series IV; vol. 129; Amsterdam/Philadelphia: John Benjamins, 1995.
SIG³: W. Dittenberger, Sylloge Inscriptionum Graecarum; 3rd ed.; 4 vols.; Leipzig: Hirzel, 1915-1921.
Sin. Syr.: the Sinaitic MS of the Old Syriac Gospels, ed. Burkitt.
Smallwood, Nerva: E. Mary Smallwood, Documents Illustrating the Principates of Nerva, Trajan and Hadrian: Cambridge, University; 1966.
SNTSMS: Society for New Testament Studies Monograph Series.
Sokoloff: Michael Sokoloff, A Dictionary of Jewish Palestinian Aramaic of the Byzantine Period; Ramat-Gan: Bar-Ilan, 1990.
Sperber (A.): Alexander Sperber, The Bible in Aramaic; 4 vols. in 5; Leiden, 1959.
Sperber (D.), Legal Terms: Daniel Sperber, A Dictionary of Greek and Latin Legal Terms in Rabbinic Literature; Bar-Ilan: University, 1984.
Spicq: Ceslas Spicq, Notes de léxicographie néo-testamentaire; 3 vols.;

Orbis biblicus et orientalis 22; Fribourg: Editions universitaires etc.; 1978-1982.

* Stern: M. Stern, Greek and Latin Authors on Jews and Judaism, 3 vols.; Jerusalem: Israel Academy of Arts and Sciences, 1974-1984.

Strack-Billerbeck: H. L. Strack & P. Billerbeck, Kommentar zum NT aus Talmud und Midrasch; 6 vols.; Munich: 1922-1961.

SVA: Die Staatsverträge des Altertums: Vol. ii, H. Bengtson & R. Werner, Die Verträge der griechisch-römischen Welt von 700 bis 338 v. Chr.; München: Beck, 1962; Vol. iii, Hatto H. Schmidt, Die Verträge der griechisch-römischen Welt von 338 bis 200 v. Chr., 1969.

* SVMB: The History of the Jewish People in the Age of Jesus Christ (175 B.C.—A.D. 135) by Emil Schürer, rev. by Geza Vermes, Fergus Millar & Matthew Black; Edinburgh: T. & T. Clark; 3 vols. in 4; 1973-1987.

TAD: B. Porten & A. Yardeni, Textbook of Aramaic Documents from ancient Egypt; Jerusalem: Hebrew University; 4 vols.; 1986-1999.

TAPA: Transactions of the American Philological Association.

Targums: see A. Sperber.

TDNT: Theological Dictionary of the New Testament.

TDOT: Theological Dictionary of the Old Testament.

* Telegdi: S. Telegdi, "Essai sur la phonétique des emprunts iraniens en araméen talmudique: Glossaire," Journal Asiatique 226 (1935) 224-256.

TLE: Massimo Pallottino, Testimonia Linguae Etruscae; Biblioteca di Studi Superiori XXIV; 2nd ed.; Firenze: La Nuova Italia, 1968.

TLL: Thesaurus Linguae Latinae.

TLZ: Theologische Literaturzeitung.

TrGF: Tragicorum Graecorum Fragmenta; Göttingen: Vandenhoek & Ruprecht; in progress, 1971—.

TUAT: O. Kaiser, ed., Texte aus der Umwelt des alten Testaments; in progress; Gütersloh: Mohn, 1982—.

TWAT: Theologisches Wörterbuch zum Alten Testament.

TWNT: Theologisches Wörterbuch zum Neuen Testament.

UNP: S. B. Parker (ed.), Ugaritic Narrative Poetry; Writings from the Ancient World 9; Society of Biblical Literature; Scholars, 1997.

UT: C. H. Gordon, Ugaritic Textbook; 3 vols; Analecta Orientalia 38; Roma: Pont. Inst. Bib., 1965 [Texts replaced by KTU, cross-references to UT provided in Vol. I only].

Vattioni: F. Vattioni, Le Iscrizioni di Ḥatra; Sup. n. 28 agli Annali vol. 41 (1981) fasc. 3; Napoli: Istituto Orientale di Napoli, 1981.

Vermeule: Emily Vermeule, Aspects of Death in Early Greek Art and Poetry; Berkeley: Univ. of California, 1979.

Vet. Test.: Vetus Testamentum.
* Weinfeld, Cov. Term.: Moshe Weinfeld, "Covenant Terminology in the Ancient Near East and its Influence on the West," JAOS 93 (1973) 190-199.
* Weinfeld, Loyalty Oath: —, "The Loyalty Oath in the Ancient Near East," Ugarit-Forschungen 8 (1976) 379-414.
* Weinfeld, Promise of the Land: —, The Promise of the Land: The Inheritance of the Land of Canaan by the Israelites; Berkeley: Univ. of California, 1993.
* Weinfeld, Social Justice: —, Social Justice in Ancient Israel and in the Ancient Near East; Jerusalem: Magnes & Minneapolis: Fortress, 1995.
West, M. L.: see EFH.
* West, Theogony: M. L. West, Hesiod: Theogony; Oxford: Clarendon, 1966.
* West, Works and Days: M. L. West, Hesiod: Works and Days; Oxford: Clarendon, 1978.
* Williams, Sourcebook: Margaret Williams, The Jews among the Greeks and Romans: A Diasporan Sourcebook; Baltimore: Johns Hopkins, 1998.
WUNT: Wissenschaftliche Untersuchungen zum Neuen Testament.
WVDOG: Wissenschaftliche Veröffentlichungen der Deutschen Orient-Gesellschaft.
ZAW: Zeitschrift für die alttestamentliche Wissenschaft.
ZDMG: Zeitschrift der deutschen morgenländischen Gesellschaft.
ZNW: Zeitschrift für die neutestamentliche Wissenschaft.

ERRATA to Vols. I & II

*: Line counted from bottom. Errata in the Indexes are omitted in view of the Cumulative Indexes in Vol. III.

Vol., page, line	In place of:	Read:
I.XXII.8	Bengston	Bengtson
I.119.19	Carthage	Sardinian "Carthage."
1.225 note 8.1	T. R. Bryce	T. B. Bryce
I.244 note 69	Chambray	Chambry
I.245.12*	Solomon Reinach	Salomon Reinach
I.282.2	Senaccherib	Sennacherib
I.320 note 64	Chambray	Chambry
I.325 note 104	Chambray	Chambry
II.19.8	aureum	aurea
II.27.11	*aduenae*	*aduenae esse*
II.39.10	Κλείω	Κλειώ
II.66.13*	*Iouem*	*Iouem enim*
II.66.7*	quidem mittit	mittit quidem
II.66.6*	deos enim	enim deos
II.66.3*	quod	quos
II.77.2*	*reuertantur*	*reuertentur*
II.97.14	*progenies*	*proles*
II.98 fn 42	86	I.86
II.120.6*	בֶן...בֶן	בַר...בַר
II.144.5	II Chron	I Chron
II.150 note 53.1	J. D. Wiseman	D. J. Wiseman
II.175 note 57.1	Matthias Delcor	Mathias Delcor
II.210.14*	הַהֲלוֹן	הַהֲלוֹן
II.233.18	*ordo saeclorum*	*ordo seclorum*
II.293.10*	קַדְמוֹן	קַנְמוֹן
II.305 note 92.2	Paradign	Paradigm
II.317.15*	a men	a man
II.318.10	[Lucian	[Lucian]
II.325.12	(II.000)	(II.281)

II.329.2*	λίθοις	πλίνθοις
II.330.23	1825	1835
II.331.18*	(Arabic font) *tadbaḥu*	*taḏbaḥu* [as transcribed]
II.333.12	"stream."	"spring."
II.336.12	בעצמן בעצמך	בעצמך

Chapter 18: The Double Laws of Human Nature[1]

A few lines of Hesiod's *Works and Days* are inverted and transformed in the Sermon on the Plain in the version of Luke.[2] The two versions constitute a double set of laws of human nature, which we label (18.1) after Simone Weil as operative under the respective regimes of "gravity" and "grace." Most of the materials in the old "gravity" format were available to Jesus in the Hebrew Bible or Mishna, although an editor of his sayings (often seen as gathered in a "Q-document") surely had a tradition of Hesiod's grouping. In both versions the "laws" of human nature appear in twin forms, both descriptive (like the laws of physics) and prescriptive (like the laws of a political state). In both versions the persons involved are labelled under the categories of friends and enemies (18.2), while the treatment of enemies is inverted under Jesus' regime of grace. The old regime of gravity emphasizes a recompense of injuries; the new regime of grace a recompense of benefits (18.3).

18.1 Gravity and grace

Hesiod makes a far-reaching distinction between friend and enemy (A), "Invite your friend to a banquet but leave out your enemy" (*Opera* 342):

τὸν φιλέοντ' ἐπὶ δαῖτα καλεῖν, τὸν δ' ἐχθρὸν ἐᾶσαι.

He goes on to discuss the best principles for borrowing and repaying grain (B), "Get a full measure from your neighbor and repay him in full, with the same measure, and with a better one if you are able, so

---

1 Revision of "From Hesiod to Jesus: Laws of Human Nature in the Ancient World," Nov. Test. 35 (1993) 313-343.

2 The connection was observed in part by M. Bouttier, "Hésiode et le serment sur la montagne," NTS 25 (1978/9) 129-130; but he misses the nice agreement in "measure for measure."

that if you fall into need in the future you will find him reliable"
(*Opera* 349-351):

εὖ μὲν μετρεῖσθαι παρὰ γείτονος, εὖ δ᾽ ἀποδοῦναι,
αὐτῷ τῷ μέτρῳ καὶ λώιον, αἴ κε δύνηαι,
ὡς ἂν χρηίζων καὶ ἐς ὕστερον ἄρκιον εὕρῃς.

He then recapitulates the first half of (A) and states a principle of
giving (C) in rough-hewn grammar and meter, "Love the one that loves
you... Give to whoever gives and do not give to whoever does not give"
(*Opera* 353-4):

τὸν φιλέοντα φιλεῖν ...
καὶ δόμεν ὅς κεν δῷ, καὶ μὴ δόμεν ὅς κεν μὴ δῷ.

Finally he replaces the infinitives of (C) acting as imperatives by
gnomic aorists, "For one gives to a giver, and does not give to a non-
giver" (*Opera* 355):

δώτῃ μέν τις ἔδωκεν, ἀδώτῃ δ᾽ οὔ τις ἔδωκεν.

The Gospel parallels in both content and connection are clustered
in Luk 6,27-38. (A) "Love your enemies" (6,27), ἀγαπᾶτε τοὺς ἐχθροὺς
ὑμῶν with three more parallels. (C) "Give to everyone that asks you"
(6,30), παντὶ αἰτοῦντί σε δίδου. (A) "But if you love those who love
you, what thanks do you get?" (6,32) καὶ εἰ ἀγαπᾶτε τοὺς ἀγαπῶντας
ὑμᾶς ...; "But love your enemies" (6,35); (C) "and lend expecting
nothing back," δανίζετε μηδὲν ἀπελπίζοντες; "and your reward will be
great." (C) "Give and it will be given you" (6,38) δίδοτε καὶ δοθήσεται
ὑμῖν; (B) "Good measure, pressed down, heaped up, running over, will
they give in your lap"; "for with what measure you measure it will be
measured back to you" ᾧ γὰρ μέτρῳ μετρεῖτε ἀντιμετρηθήσεται ὑμῖν.

Other versions of Luke's materials are in places closer to Hesiod.
Hesiod's parallelism in (A) appears at "You have heard that it was
said, 'You shall love your neighbor' (Lev 19,18 LXX) and hate your
enemy," ἀγαπήσεις τὸν πλησίον σου καὶ μισήσεις τὸν ἐχθρόν σου (Matt
5,43). There might be a reference to pagan Greek usage in "And if you
embrace your brothers only, what extra do you do? Do not even the
Gentiles (οἱ ἐθνικοί) do the same?" (Matt 5,47). Hesiod's verb φιλέω
appears at *Didache* 1.3 "But as for you, love those who hate you and
you will have no enemy," φιλεῖτε τοὺς μισοῦντας ὑμᾶς καὶ οὐχ ἕξεις
ἐχθρόν.[3]

---

3   The prudential addition is perhaps Stoic; see Epictetus *Enchiridion* 1.3 ἐχθρὸν
     οὐχ ἕξεις "You will have no enemy" if you make correct judgements about
     good and evil.

Hesiod and Jesus further agree in a double form of what we may call these "laws" of human nature, both prescriptive and descriptive. It is hardly different for Hesiod to say "give to the giver" and "one regularly gives to the giver." At Luk 6,35 Jesus appears to be stating an imperative "love your enemies"; but when he goes on "and your reward will be great," the first clause is turned into a condition, "*if* you love your enemies...*then* your reward will be great." The same grammatical ambiguity appears in highly condensed form in "Give and it will be given you."

Should we conclude that not merely has the collector of Jesus' sayings followed the arrangement of Hesiod, but that Jesus himself knew and transformed Hesiod's doctrines? But in fact for most of the themes Jesus had parallels to Hesiod in his own tradition, though not in Hesiod's arrangement.

(A) *Love friends, hate enemies.* We saw that a fuller parallel to Hesiod than Luk 6,27 was Matt 5,43 "You have heard that it was said, 'You shall love your neighbor and hate your enemy'." The quotation of Lev 19,18 LXX is clear enough, ἀγαπήσεις τὸν πλησίον σου ὡς σεαυτόν "you shall love your neighbor as yourself."[4] Where did Jesus find "hate your enemy"? We see below that Hesiod's contrasted treatment of friends and enemies runs through Greek literature from beginning to end. But Jesus had both sides of the contrast closer at hand. When David was mourning for Absalom, Joab appeals to the strongest heroic emotion, the fear of being shamed: "Today you have shamed (LXX κατῄσχυνας)[5] the face of all your servants...by loving those who hate you and hating those who love you" (II Sam 19,6-7):

חֹבַשְׁתָּ הַיּוֹם אֶת־פְּנֵי כָל־עֲבָדֶיךָ...לְאַהֲבָה אֶת־שֹׂנְאֶיךָ וְלִשְׂנֹא אֶת־אֹהֲבֶיךָ

where the LXX has τοῦ ἀγαπᾶν τοὺς μισοῦντάς σε καὶ μισεῖν τοὺς ἀγαπῶντάς σε. If Joab had been asked to state formally in reverse the true principles of heroic conduct, he could have said nothing but the words of Archilochus (III.8) "I know how to love my friend and hate

---

4   Kierkegaard somewhere says that "love your neighbor as yourself" left no loopholes for excuses not to love the neighbor. But Aristotle realistically saw that "a friend is another self" (*Eth. Nic.* 9.5, 1166a31), ἔστι γὰρ ὁ φίλος ἄλλος αὐτός with an elegant bit of grammar. It is taken up late in Latin by Ausonius 1.2 in a dedication to Syagrius, *communemque habitas alter ego Ausonium* "and as another self you inhabit a shared Ausonius"; apparently from this source *alter ego* became standard English. See further III.300.

5   Below (III.20) we discuss the deep connection between the Hebrew root בּוֹשׁ "be ashamed" and Latin *pudet*; as well as the physical accompaniments of shame, namely stinking and blushing, attested by all three languages Hebrew, Greek and Latin.

my enemy." The harshest thing one Greek could say of another (Lysias 6.7) was: he is one "who has this knack, to do his enemies no harm, but as much as he can to his friends," ὃς τέχνην ταύτην ἔχει, τοὺς μὲν ἐχθροὺς μηδὲν ποιεῖν κακόν, τοὺς δὲ φίλους ὅτι ἂν δύνηται κακόν. So Pope says of "Atticus" (Addison):

> Alike reserved to blame or to commend,
> A tim'rous foe, and a suspicious friend.

(B) *Measure for measure.* Contracts for repayment of grain on papyrus from Egypt specify the original lender's measure, both in Greek (μέτρῳ ᾧ καὶ παρείληφεν) and demotic.[6] (No centralized authority in the ancient world to standardize measures.) The Mishna (*Sotah* I.7) states the formula for recompense of ill, "With the measure that a man measures, they will measure to him":

במדה שאדם מודד בה מודדין לו

Jesus understands it primarily of benefit, Luk 6,38 (Matt 7,2, Mark 4,24) ᾧ γὰρ μέτρῳ μετρεῖτε ἀντιμετρηθήσεται ὑμῖν, Vg *eadem quippe mensura qua mensi fueritis remetietur uobis.*[7]

Luke (6,38) gives the extension "Good measure, pressed down, shaken together, running over shall they give (δώσουσιν) into your lap." Several features mark this as Palestinian. Eric Bishop[8] describes the measurement of grain in a Palestinian market place, in which the pressing, shaking, and heaping up all figure; the grain is measured in a container, but then poured out into the lap of the buyer's garment to take home; "they shall give" is an Aramaic passive as in the Mishna.

(C) *Not giving to the non-giver.* Here I find no verbal parallel in the Hebrew Bible or Talmudic; but the general principle of recompense for ills appears at Lev 24,19 (III.27) "As he did, so shall it be done to him," and Jud 15,11, where Samson says "As they did to me, so have I done to them."

Jesus transforms each of these inherited sentiments along similar lines. (A) "Love your friend" (nearly paralleled in Leviticus) becomes "love your enemies." (B) The sayings on "measure" initially seem more

---

6 B. Couroyer, "'De la mesure dont vous mesurez il vous sera mesuré,'" Revue Biblique 77 (1970) 366-370. The phrase in the text is from a grain-contract of 113 BC between two women of Pathyris designated as Persian: Naomsesis loans Theesis ten artabae of wheat to be repaid later on in the year without interest; B. P. Grenfell & A. S. Hunt, The Amherst Papyri Part II; London: Oxford, 1901; no. xlvi p. 56.

7 As an English proverb "Measure for measure" the application becomes indeterminate again as in Shakespeare's title; see ODEP³ 520.

8 Eric Bishop, Jesus of Palestine; London: Lutterworth, 1955; p. 80 quoting C. T. Wilson.

alike: but in fact Hesiod insists on the full measure to ensure a grateful neighbor in hard times to come, while the full measure in return that Jesus envisages is plainly transcendent. Hesiod expects the neighbor to be "reliable in the future"; Jesus bids us lend "expecting nothing in return." (C) "Give to the giver" becomes "give to whoever asks."

In the bulk of this chapter we lay out parallels between Hellas and Israel in the old inherited descriptive laws of human nature, and discuss antecedents for the fundamental inversion that Jesus applies to them. Here by the example of Plutarch we illustrate the wide popularity of Hesiod, and the beginnings in Greek (doubtless antedating Plutarch) of a more altruistic interpretation, which might by some route have influenced Jesus.

Plutarch in his *Moralia* often quotes the *Works and Days*; he also wrote a commentary on the poem which was excerpted and paraphrased by Proclus and from him copied into the scholia.[9] Plutarch sometimes commends the verses of Hesiod in their sober realism, sometimes finds them unjust or immoral; his admiration of the poet forces him to deal with the second group by pronouncing them inauthentic. Thus on the one hand he approves of Hesiod's sentiment "Invite your friend to dinner, leave out your enemy" (*Opera* 342) on the grounds that if you should invite your enemy, he will invite you in turn, and you will lose your necessary mistrust (ἀπιστίαν) of him;[10] "we shall abandon ourselves to the mercy of persons ill-disposed towards us."[11] But Plutarch rejected *Opera* 353-4 ("Love the one who loves you..."), as inauthentic; he feels that it makes giving compulsory and eliminates the pleasure in giving which Hesiod affirms; also, people could never becomes friends "if each waited for the other to make the first move."[12] Likewise he rejected *Opera* 267-273 (cited II.35) on "the all-seeing eye of Zeus" as guardian of justice on the grounds that "justice is to be chosen and injustice avoided even if there is no Providence," τὸ δίκαιον αἱρετόν, κἂν μὴ ᾖ πρόνοια, καὶ φευκτὸν τὸ ἄδικον; the lines are "unworthy of Hesiod's opinion on justice and injustice," ἀναξίους τῆς Ἡσιόδου περὶ δικαίων καὶ ἀδίκων κρίσεως.[13]

---

9   The fragments of Plutarch's commentary on the *Works and Days* are edited with translation by F. H. Sandbach in the Loeb edition of the *Moralia*, vol. xv (1969), pp. 104-227.

10   Plutarch *On Compliancy* 4 (= *Mor.* 530E).

11   Plutarch on Hesiod *Opera* 342-3, frag. 48 Sandbach (Loeb ed. xv.138).

12   Scholia and Tzetzes on *Opera* 353-4 = Plutarch frag. 51 Sandbach (Loeb ed. xv.142).

13   Plutarch frag. 38 Sandbach (Loeb ed. xv.122).

In these comments, though mostly quoted at second or third hand, we still see the first stages of a critique which could have led to the sweeping reversals of Hesiod's formulas in Jesus. No other Greek text was the subject of a commentary by an author in his own right as early as Plutarch; and the fact that almost every line of the *Works and Days* is quoted by somebody shows that it was an essential part of any Greek education anywhere. (The Homeric epics were equally popular or more so, but too long for a concise commentary, and also less consistently quotable.) Thus in particular Luke, who turns out quite acceptable Hellenistic Greek when he chooses, can hardly have been totally ignorant of Hesiod.

Here we label the two viewpoints of Hesiod and Jesus by a distinction drawn from Simone Weil. When in 1947 Gustave Thibon edited her *pensées*, he put at their head two which also give her book its title:

> Tous les mouvements *naturels* de l'âme sont régis par des lois analogues à celles de la pesanteur matérielle. La grâce seule fait exception.
>
> Il faut toujours s'attendre à ce que les choses se passent conformément à la pesanteur, sauf intervention du surnaturel.[14]

Weil sees the laws of human nature in the old order, operating under the regime of "gravity", as illustrated above all in Homer. In her essay on the *Iliad* she writes:

> La force, c'est ce qui fait de quiconque lui est soumis une chose.... Telle est la nature de la force. Le pouvoir qu'elle possède de transformer les hommes en choses est double et s'exerce de deux côtés: elle pétrifie différemment, mais également, les âmes de ceux qui la subissent et de ceux qui la manient.[15]

A cruder version is the "realistic" tradition of social analysis, as in Hobbes (*Leviathan* I.13): "during the time men live without a common Power to keep them all in awe, they are in that condition which is called Warre; and such a warre, as is of every man, against every man." So Machiavelli; or von Clausewitz with his three "reciprocal actions" (*Wechselwirkungen*) which remind us, as intended, of Newton's three laws. These "laws" as we saw in Hesiod waver between imperative and indicative, between prescriptive and descriptive, between the "laws" of ethics and of physics: men are urged to follow the only line open to them—the invariable practice of other men. There is only necessity along this route, especially when it is not recognized.

---

14   Simone Weil, La pesanteur et la grâce; ed. Gustave Thibon; Paris: Plon, 1948.
15   Simone Weil, "L'*Iliade* ou le poème de la force," La source grecque (Gallimard, 1953) 11-42; pp. 11, 32.

Thucydides, like Homer, goes beyond this "realism" by recognizing the necessity. On the revolution at Corcyra he remarks (3.82) "War is a stern teacher (ὁ δὲ πόλεμος ... βίαιος διδάσκαλος); in depriving men of the power of easily satisfying their daily wants, it brings most men's minds down to the level of their actual circumstances."[16] Later, the Athenians demand the surrender of Melos, not on grounds of right, but only of superior strength. The historian sets out a dialogue between the two parties, no doubt representing his own analysis. The Athenian position is (5.105):[17]

> Our opinion of the gods and our knowledge of men lead us to conclude that *it is a general and necessary law of nature to rule whatever one can* (διὰ παντὸς ὑπὸ φύσεως ἀναγκαίας, οὗ ἂν κρατῇ, ἄρχειν). This is not a law that we made ourselves, nor were we the first to act upon it when it was made. We found it already in existence, and we shall leave it to exist for ever among those who come after us. We are merely acting in accordance with it, and we know that you or anybody else with the same power as ours would be acting in precisely the same way.

Thucydides comments by narrating the disaster of the Sicilian expedition right afterwards; he has internalized the lesson of tragedy that overreaching leads to destruction, and finds it worked out in actual history.

Freedom is possible, Simone Weil would say, only under the regime of Grace. Under that heading we may group Jesus' formulations in the Sermon, which likewise waver between command and statement. Most people feel that only under special circumstances are Jesus' "laws" true or viable; elsewhere they are hopelessly "idealistic." Luther saw them as operative only between one Christian and another, who (like intelligent societies in the universe) were "few and far between": *Aber die Christen wonen (wie man spricht) fern von eynander.*[18] Schweitzer regarded them as an *Interimsethik*, valid only in the brief period before the full advent of the Kingdom of God.

But most people can no more deal with the "realistic" laws. Whereas Simone Weil sees them as self-evident statements of the way things are, public opinion has made "Machiavellian" an adjective for cynical manipulation. Here I propose that *the "idealistic" laws of human nature under "Grace" are* historically motivated logical *extensions of*

---

16   Translation after Rex Warner; Harmondsworth: Penguin; rev. ed., 1972.
17   Also in the translation of Rex Warner; compare the version of Hobbes, III.193.
18   "Von weltlicher Obrigkeit," D. Martin Luthers Werke vol. xi (Weimar, 1900) p. 251.

the "realistic" laws under "Gravity". Unlike Newton's laws in the physical world, in the human world of antiquity we find *two* sets of dynamical laws, one built on the other.

In 18.2 on "Friend and enemy" I suggest that the old heroic ideal of avoiding shame by "loving friend and hating enemy" went shipwreck on the growing interchangeability of friend and enemy. For its basis in the promises of the vassal-treaty dissolved as the city-state crumbled. In section 18.3 on the law of recompense, gathering up the themes "measure for measure" and "give to the giver," I suggest that the old insight about recompense of harm—blood shed demands more blood to be shed—required completion by a new insight into recompense of good. In each section I propose actual historical and linguistic contacts among the ancient societies.

18.2 Friend and enemy

18.2.1 Helping friends, harming enemies

Hesiod's sharp distinction (*Opera* 342) between the treatment due friend and enemy is normative for the writers who follow. Mary Whitlock Blundell in a beautiful chapter[19] has shown how it runs through Greek thought from beginning to end. It is most formulaic in a papyrus fragment of Archilochus[20]

ἐπίσταμαί τοι τὸν φιλέοντα μὲν φιλεῖν
τὸν δ᾽ ἐχθρὸν ἐχθαίρειν ...

"I know how to love my friend and hate my enemy." It is plain in Homer, where Odysseus tells Nausicaa that a man and woman happily married bring "many pains to their ill-wishers, and joy to their well-wishers," πόλλ᾽ ἄλγεα δυσμενέεσσι, / χάρματα δ᾽ εὐμενέτῃσι (*Od.* 6.184-5). Theognis 869-872 combines the sentiment with an elaborate oath: "May the great broad bronze heaven[21] overhead fall on me (the fear of men of old time), if I do not requite those who love me, and am not a sorrow[22] and great woe to my enemies":

ἔν μοι ἔπειτα πέσοι μέγας οὐρανὸς εὐρὺς ὕπερθεν
χάλκεος, ἀνθρώπων δεῖμα παλαιγενέων,
εἰ μὴ ἐγὼ τοῖσιν μὲν ἐπαρκέσω οἵ με φιλεῦσιν,
τοῖς δ᾽ ἐχθροῖς ἀνίη καὶ μέγα πῆμ᾽ ἔσομαι.

---

19   Mary Whitlock Blundell, Helping Friends and Harming Enemies: A Study in Sophocles and Greek Ethics (Cambridge: University, 1989), pp. 26-59.
20   Archilochus frag. 23.14-15 IEG = *P. Oxy.* 2310.
21   For the shared theme of the bronze sky see I.106-110.

An orator (Lysias 9.20) considers (as Jesus says of the ancients) that to harm enemies and help friends is a *commandment* (ἡγούμενος τετάχθαι τοὺς μὲν ἐχθροὺς κακῶς ποιεῖν, τοὺς δὲ φίλους εὖ). Sophocles has Creon tell his son Haimon that fathers desire obedient sons "to requite their enemy with ills, and honor their friend" (*Antigone* 643-644):

ὡς καὶ τὸν ἐχθρὸν ἀνταμύνωνται κακοῖς
καὶ τὸν φίλον τιμῶσιν ...

Pindar (*Pythian* 2.83-85) "May I love my friend (φίλον εἴη φιλεῖν), and as an enemy like the wolf track down my enemy (ποτὶ δ' ἐχθρὸν ἅτ' ἐχθρὸς ἐὼν λύκοιο δίκην), following in his crooked paths[23] this way and that." Thucydides 3.13 shows the Spartans as responding favorably to the appeal of Mytilene to assist its revolt, so as to be "aiding those whom one should and at the same time harming enemies:"[24] ἵνα φαίνησθε ἀμύνοντές τε οἷς δεῖ καὶ ἐν τῷ αὐτῷ τοὺς πολεμίους βλάπτοντες. Xenophon (*Cyr.* 8.7.28) attributes the same sentiment to the foreigner Cyrus, whose dying words to his sons are "By helping your friends you will also be able to punish your enemies" (τοὺς φίλους εὐεργετοῦντες καὶ τοὺς ἐχθροὺς δυνήσεσθε κολάζειν). So Machiavelli (*il Principe* 21), "A prince is further esteemed when he is a true friend and a true enemy (*vero amico e vero inimico*)," while putting in his own meaning.

Blundell[25] summarizes the Greek view:

> ...Harm Enemies tends more towards the descriptive, and Help Friends to the prescriptive. That is, it is generally taken for granted that everyone desires revenge on enemies, and that most people pursue it, but its violation is condemned primarily in terms of personal honour, and may even be praised. Help Friends, on the other hand, is less descriptive, since incentives to violate it in pursuit of self-interest easily arise and may be very powerful. To counteract such temptations, it acquires a more powerful prescriptive force backed by strong social disapproval of its violation.

The first half only of the formula also appears at Xenophon *Mem.* 2.3.8 εὖ ποιεῖν τὸν εὖ ποιοῦντα and often. It is a self-standing proverb in Latin, *amico amicus* (Plautus *Mil. Glor.* 658 etc.), "friend(ly) to a

---

22 For a highly probable Hebrew counterpart to ἀνίη "sorrow" see III.29.

23 For crooked (and straight) paths see II.46.

24 Probably Thucydides at 2.41 means to ascribe the same sentiment to the Athenians in Pericles' funeral oration, which Warner translates "and everywhere we have left behind us everlasting memorials of good done to our friends or suffering inflicted on our enemies"; but the Greek austerely just has μνημεῖα κακῶν τε κἀγαθῶν "memorials of harms and benefits" with no mention of the parties harmed or benefitted.

25 Blundell Helping Friends p. 57.

friend."[26] We saw at I.263 that the Psalmist (Ps 139,21-22) promises only the *second* half of the formula, "Do I not hate those who hate you?"; and reciprocally Yahweh (Ex 23,22) "I will be an enemy to your enemies." (Did neither Yahweh nor Israel have friends?) But elsewhere Yahweh does undertake both sides of the agreement: "I will bless those who bless you, and him who curses you I will curse" (Gen 12,3, cf I Sam 2,30):

וַאֲבָרֲכָה מְבָרֲכֶיךָ   וּמְקַלֶּלְךָ אָאֹר

Isaac intended to say of Jacob (Gen 27,29) "Cursed be every one who curses you, and blessed be every one who blesses you":[27]

אֹרֲרֶיךָ אָרוּר   וּמְבָרֲכֶיךָ בָּרוּךְ

Balaam did say it (Num 24,9 in reversed order), and Balak (Num 22,6) credits Balaam with the same talent.

The self-image of the hero is that of the Ancient Near Eastern ruler in the vassal treaty, and so moved across linguistic and cultural frontiers. In particular it underlies the Israelite covenant with Yahweh. The key element in the "loyalty oath" is the agreement of the vassal to have *the same enemies and friends as the lord*. At I.263-264 we document this as the central provision of treaties between unequals from Suppiluliuma the Hittite to Caligula.

18.2.2 Polarization of the "stranger"[28]

The heroic image starts to break down with the realization that only a razor-blade can be gotten between friend and enemy. Wagner lays out the typical situation in *Die Walküre*. Siegmund takes shelter from pursuit at Hunding's hearth; Hunding recognizes the bond of hospitality, accepts the role of host (*Wirt*), and makes Siegmund his guest (*Gast*). But when he hears Siegmund's story he recognizes an enemy (*Feind*), and on the morrow they must fight. Conversely, Jacob and Laban are on the verge of becoming enemies, but decide to make a covenant (Gen 31).

ξένος (Homeric ξεῖνος) from the sense "stranger, wanderer" (in the plural with ἱκετάων "suppliants" *Odyssey* 9.270 and πτωχοί "poor men" 6.208) normally is "one bound by ties of hospitality," either as guest (8.543) or as host (*Iliad* 15.532). Latin *hostis* shows a fuller

---

26 Greek and Latin texts in Otto Sprichwörter 23.
27 Note the flexibility of Hebrew grammar, where the subjects (coming first) are plural and the predicates singular; as much as to say "Of all those who curse you, each is cursed."
28 This section takes up again the theme of the city walls marking outsiders and insiders previously treated at I.159-162.

grasp of the Wagnerian dilemma and a semantic parallel to the Hebrew. Varro (*de lingua latina* 5.3) notes:

multa uerba aliud nunc ostendunt, aliud ante significabant, ut
hostis: nam tum eo uerbo dicebant peregrinum qui suis legibus
uteretur, nunc dicunt eum quem tum dicebant *perduellem*.

"Many words now indicate one thing, but formerly meant something
else, like *hostis*, for before by this word they meant a 'foreigner' subject
to his own laws, but now they so name one whom then they called
perduellis 'enemy'."[29] Likewise Cicero, though unclear about the sequence of meanings.[30] For in fact *hostis* is identical with the north-
European word for "host" or "guest," Gothic *gasts*,[31] Church Slavonic
gosti, at first "stranger" as with *hostis*. (German *Gast* and English
guest show a different specialization.)[32]

Out of *hostis* in its original sense Latin developed a word *hospes*; for
its formation Levin suggests a parallel with δεσἰπότης "master of the
house," i.e. "landlord, master of hospitality." Like ξένος it meant both
"guest" and "host": English *host* comes from *hospite(m)* through Old
French *hoste*. Plautus (*Most.* 479) shows both senses, *hospes necauit
hospitem captum manu* "the host overpowered his guest and murdered
him." Ovid (*Met.* 1.144) says of the Iron Age, *non hospes ab hospite
tutus*, naturally translated "guest was not safe from host," although
for lack of an example the opposite is also possible. Hence Livy

---

29　*Hostis* classically replaced *perduellis* in the specific sense of "public enemy,"
while *inimicus* was "private enemy": thus Cicero *pro lege Manilia* 28 *qui
saepius cum hoste conflixit quam quisquam cum inimico concertauit* "[Pom-
pey,] who more often engaged in battle with the enemy of the State than
another quarrelled with a private enemy."
30　Cicero (*de off.* 1.37): qui proprio nomine *perduellis* esset, is *hostis* uoca-
retur...*hostis* enim apud maiores nostros is dicebatur, quem nunc *peregrinum*
dicimus. Indicant Duodecim Tabulae...ADVERSVS HOSTEM AETERNA
AVCTORITAS. "He who by his proper name is a *perduellis*, 'enemy,' is called
hostis; ...for with our ancestors that one was named *hostis* whom we now call
peregrinus, 'foreigner.' The XII Tables [III.7, Loeb ed. p. 440]) show this
usage: ...'Title of ownership is permanent in dealings with a foreigner (*hostis*)'."
31　In the Gothic New Testament *gasts* invariably translates ξένος, e.g. at Matt
25,43.
32　On hospitality in the ancient world see Philippe Gauthier, "Notes sur l'étranger
et l'hospitalité en Grèce et à Rome," Ancient Society 4 (1973) 1-21; Otto
Hiltbrunner, "Gastfreundschaft und Gasthaus in der Antike," pp. 1-20 of H.
C. Peyer (ed.), Gastfreundschaft, Taverne und Gasthaus im Mittelalter; Schriften
des Historischen Kollegs, Kolloquien 3; München & Wien: Oldenbourg, 1983.
Hiltbrunner also has an extensive philological and historical discussion in
"Hostis und ξένος," pp. i.424-446 of Studien zur Religion und Kultur
Kleinasiens (FS F. K. Dörner); 2 vols. (= EPROER vol. 66); Leiden: Brill, 1978.

contrasts *hospes* "guest" with *hostis* "enemy," recognizing both the similarity in sound and the original connection. Hannibal said that "he had come to Gaul as a guest, not an enemy," *Hospitem enim se Galliae non hostem aduenisse* (Livy 21.24.4).[33]

The polarization of words meaning "foreigner, stranger" into "friend" and "enemy" depends on a division of mankind into insiders and outsiders. That very language brings to mind city-walls and the legal systems they inclose. Ovid (*Met.* 1.97) imagines a time when
> nondum praecipites cingebant oppida fossae

"not yet did steep moats surround cities." Vergil (*Georg.* 2.155-157) more realistically takes pride in the walls of Italian hill-towns:
> Adde tot egregias urbes operumque laborem,
> tot congesta manu praeruptis oppida saxis,
> fluminaque antiquos subterlabentia muros.

"Add so many famous cities and the results of labor, so many towns raised up by hand on sheer rocks, and rivers flowing below ancient walls." For (as Hesiod said, *Opera* 189) in the present iron age "one will sack another's city," ἕτερος δ' ἑτέρου πόλιν ἐξαλαπάξει. We noted (I.160, II.329) parallel understandings of the city-wall: Heraclitus said that "the people must fight for its law as for its wall"; so, when God "determined to lay in ruins the *wall* of the daughter of Zion...the *law* is no more" (Thr 2,8-9). When a stranger appeared at the gate, the question was whether he should be brought inside the walls under the protection of guest-friendship (ξενία, *hospitium*) or regarded as an outsider and therefore enemy. In Rome, all rights were inseparably bound up with citizenship, so that a foreigner without protection was truly an "out-law," who could be robbed or enslaved with impunity. Lévy-Bruhl[34] maintained that in early Rome "1° tout esclave est un étranger; 2° tout étranger est un esclave," "every slave is a foreigner and every foreigner is a slave."

18.2.3 The incognito of gods and men

The vicissitudes of war and trade ensured it that men in the ancient world constantly met strangers, who had a special claim on them: for

---

33 Xenophanes of Macedon, sent to negotiate a treaty with Hannibal, lied to Laevinus that he was seeking a Roman alliance, and Laevinus, believing it, *hostes pro hospitibus comiter accepit* (Livy 23.33.7) "graciously received enemies as guests."

34 Henri Lévy-Bruhl, "Théorie de l'esclavage," in his Quelques problèmes du très ancien droit romain (Paris: Domat-Montchrestien, 1934), 15-33; reprinted in M. I. Finley (ed.), Slavery in Classical Antiquity: Views and Controversies; 2nd ed.; Cambridge: Heffer, 1968, pp. 151-170.

it was generally agreed that to fear God is to love the stranger. This is clearly implied at Deut 10,18-20: "[Yahweh] loves the sojourner (אֹהֵב גֵּר) ...And you shall love the sojourner, for you were sojourners in the land of Egypt. You shall fear Yahweh your God..." Whenever Odysseus meets a strange people, he wonders within himself, "Are they violent, savage, unjust; or do they love strangers, and have a spirit that fears the divinity?":

ἦ ῥ᾽ οἵ γ᾽ ὑβρισταί τε καὶ ἄγριοι οὐδὲ δίκαιοι,
ἦε φιλόξεινοι, καί σφιν νόος ἐστὶ θεουδής.

So of the Cyclopes (*Odyssey* 9.175-6); of the Phaeacians (6.120-121); and even of transformed Ithaca (13.201-202). Also Alcinous (8.575-576) presumes that Odysseus will have been asking the same question.

Why is loving the stranger identical with fearing the god? For one thing, the god watches over strangers. Ps 146,9 "Yahweh watches over strangers," יהוה שֹׁמֵר אֶת־גֵּרִים. *Odyssey* 6.207-208 Nausicaa tells her girls that "All strangers and poor are under the protection of Zeus," πρὸς γὰρ Διός εἰσιν ἅπαντες / ξεῖνοί τε πτωχοί τε. Even more important, the gods disguise themselves as strangers to test the hospitality shown by mortals. At Gen 18,1-2 Yahweh appears to Abraham in the form of three men and receives proper hospitality; not so at Sodom.[35] When Antinous hits disguised Odysseus, even one of the arrogant suitors warns him that this may be a "heavenly god" (*Odyssey* 17.484-487), τις ἐπουράνιος θεός; "For the gods take on the likeness of strangers from all manner of lands, appearing in many forms, and wander through cities, inspecting both the arrogance and lawfulness of men":

καί τε θεοὶ ξείνοισιν ἐοικότες ἀλλοδαποῖσι,
παντοῖοι τελέθοντες, ἐπιστρωφῶσι πόληας
ἀνθρώπων ὕβριν τε καὶ εὐνομίην ἐφορῶντες.

When the Son of Man says "I was a stranger and you welcomed me" (ξένος ἤμην καὶ συνηγάγετέ με) Matt 25,35, it seems that he appears in *every* stranger. So Wotan in the *Ring* and its sources.[36] Ovid (*Met.* 8.626ff) tells how Jupiter and Mercury appear in disguise to Philemon and Baucis. Luke may have a Hellenistic original of Ovid's story in mind when he has the Lycaonians identify Barnabas and Paul respectively as Zeus and Hermes (Act 14,12, where of course the Vulgate has

---

35 Heb 13,2 probably has this in mind when it recommends hospitality (φιλοξενία) on the grounds that "some have entertained angels unawares," ἔλαθόν τινες ξενίσαντες ἀγγέλους.

36 Cristiano Grottanelli ("Ospitare gli dei: sacrificio e diluvio," Studi Storici 4 [1984] 847-857) compares the story of Abraham with that of Philemon and Baucis.

Jupiter and Mercury). It is scandalous to keep a stranger waiting (*Odyssey* 1.119), who must be served before his name is asked (1.124, 8.550). —Even though he may turn out to be either friend or enemy.[37]

Besides turning out to be a god in disguise, the stranger may prove to be a close relation of the unsuspecting party who meets him. The disguised one is nearly always a man, women did not get around in the world the same way. In all the tales, the stranger is curiously reluctant to reveal his true identity; it seems as if he has fallen in love with his incognito, recognizes the advantage it gives him, and wishes to keep it as long as possible. The disguise frees you from the limitations of your individuality. Odysseus delays as long as possible revealing himself to each ally at Ithaca. Joseph puts off declaring himself to his brothers through a long series of incidents. Jesus gives the two disciples at Emmaus many hints before they recognize him (Luk 24,31 ἐπέγνωσαν) in the breaking of bread. Aristotle (*Poetics* 11.4; 16) regards ἀνα-γνώρισις "discovery" as an essential part of tragedy, which may be of the true situation as in the *Oedipus Rex* rather than of a disguised person. The dramatists come to emphasize the revealing clue. Each tragedian has a scene in which Electra recognizes her brother Orestes: Aeschylus (*Choephoroi* 200) by his hair and footprints; Sophocles (*Electra* 1223) by his father's seal; Euripides (*Electra* 573) by a scar (as Odysseus to his nurse). Plautus took from Greek New Comedy the theme of the σύμβολον by which a long-lost party is recognized: originally the matching half of a broken potsherd; at *Pseud.* 55-57 both halves of the *symbolon* are the owner's "own likeness stamped on wax from his ring," *expressam in cera ex anulo suam imaginem.* For both Hebrews and Greeks, the dramatic situation *par excellence* is that in which a man appears in a different place or time or role from his original one, with all the consequences of his recognition as such.

18.2.4 Reciprocal borrowing of words for "sojourner"

The special status of the Hebrew and Greek words for "foreign sojourner" is indicated by the fact that each is marginally taken up into the other language. At II.291 we discussed how גִּיורָא, the Aramaic equivalent of Hebrew גֵּר, appears in the LXX with Jewish and Patristic Greek as γιώρας. At Matt 23,15 in the Peshitto προσήλυτον "proselyte" becomes גִּיורָא. Further: at Josephus *BJ* 2.521 ὁ τοῦ Γιώρα Σίμων is "Simon son of the proselyte"; hence Tacitus *Hist.* 5.12.3 *Bargioram* accus. with some confusion about his identity. Also at Dio Cassius

---

37   West (EFH 122-124, 183-185) discusses further examples of "theoxeny" where the stranger is revealed as a god.

65.7.1 Reimarus restored Βαργιώρας for MS Βαρπώρας. Jastrow 236c cites persons named בר גיורא. I wonder if Rabbinic גיורא "adulterer" is not the same word, a foreigner being automatically attributed sexual improprieties, as with Hebrew נָכְרִיָּה "foreign woman, i.e., prostitute."

Conversely ξένος entered Aramaic as אכסניא (apparently the abstract ξενία was heard as concrete). Thus at Matt 25,44 Peshitto "When did we see you...a stranger (ξένον)?" comes out אכסניא. A Palmyrene bilingual (PAT 0305, II.116) honors one who on the visit in AD 130/131 of Divus Hadrianus (θεοῦ Ἁδρ[ι]ανοῦ = א[נ]הדרין אלהא) provided oil to various parties:

ξένοις τε καὶ πολίταις

לבני מד[י]נתא ול[א]סטר[טומא?] ולאכסניא די אתא עמה

Greek "to foreigners and citizens"; Palmyrene "to the sons of the city and the army (στράτευμα ?) and the strangers (i.e. ξένοι) who came up with him." *Odes of Solomon* 17.6 has Christ say, "And I seemed to them like a stranger,"

ואיך אכסניא אסתברת להון

אכסניא is regular in Rabbinic. In particular, Hillel (*Lev. Rabbah* 34.3) told his disciples that he was going to bestow a kindness on a guest in his house, which turned out to be himself:

והדין נפשא עלובתא לאו אכסניא היא בגו גופא

"Is not the poor soul a guest in the body?" See the verses of the same Hadrian (SHA *Hadrian* 25)

animula uagula blandula
hospes comesque corporis...

"Little soul, wanderer, charming one, the guest and companion of the body..." *Hospes* is the natural version of ξένος. Behind the words of both Hillel and Hadrian I conjecture a Stoic formula *ἡ ψυχὴ ξένος ἐν τῷ σώματι "the soul is a stranger in the body," though I do not find it attested.[38]

18.2.5 Barbarians and Goyim

While the "stranger" (ξένος, גֵּר, hospes) may be either friend or enemy, Hebrew and Greek have unambiguous terms to denote the outsider

---

38 Nahum H. Glatzer, Hillel the Elder: The Emergence of Classical Judaism; New York: Shocken, 1956, p. 32: "Seneca, in part a contemporary of Hillel, spoke of the God who dwells as a guest in the human body; the Stoics often compared the soul to a guest in the body." But I have not easily found such passages. The closest is Dio Cassius 78.6a where Cornificia, commanded to kill herself, says "O miserable little soul, imprisoned in a foul body, go out, be freed," ὦ δυστυχὲς ψυχίδιον ἐν πονηρῷ σώματι καθειργμένον, ἔξελθε, ἐλευθερώθητι.

rejected as such: "barbarian" (βάρβαρος) and "Goy" (גּוֹי). But there is little overlap in their usage: here is a realm where Israel and Hellas show maximum variation (III.171). The barbarian is one who does not speak Greek; the Goy is one who worships some other god than the God of Israel. However, Demosthenes 21.150 speaks of his adversary Meidias "his true, natural barbarism and hatred of the gods" τὸ τῆς φύσεως βάρβαρον καὶ θεοῖς ἐχθρόν; compare Ex 23,22 (III.17) "I shall hate those who hate you." A melic poet in unknown context (PMG 929c) appears to have "Zeus thundered with his thunder against all that is barbarian," Ζεὺς μὲν ἐπέβρεμε βάρβαρα βροντᾷ;[39] compare I Sam 2,10 & 7,10 where Yahweh thunders against adversaries and Philistines.

Where the two societies come closest is the formula of rejection. Thales (Diogenes Laertius 1.33) thanks Fortune (Tyche) for three things: "I was born a human being and not a beast, a man and not a woman, a Hellene and not a barbarian," ἄνθρωπος ἐγενόμην, καὶ οὐ θηρίον...ἀνὴρ καὶ οὐ γυνή...Ἕλλην καὶ οὐ βάρβαρος. The Synagogue service begins:[40] "Blessed art thou, Lord our God, king of the universe, who hast not made me a foreigner (גוי)[41]...a slave (עבד)...a woman (אשה)." In even more exact parallels to the Synagogue triad, Aristotle in inferior status (Pol. 1.1.5 = 1252b5) groups barbarians, females and slaves; and Paul (Gal 3,28) on the contrary has "In [Christ] there is neither Jew nor Hellene, slave or free, male or female"—texts at I.234-235.[42]

Both Israelites and Hellenes were conscious of a difference from the peoples surrounding them, and at first emphasized that difference by downgrading their neighbors. But as their consciousness of their superiority grew more pronounced, and with loss of their civic autonomy to resurgent empires, both peoples also came to feel a mission to define the commonality of all human beings. Segal[43] in particular cites the

---

39 Add this to the passages (II.319) where the elements are a cognate accusative of the verb expressing their action, "rain rain, flash lightning" etc.
40 Already in David Hedegård, Seder R. Amram Gaon, Part I; Lund: Lindstedt, 1951, pp. 9-10 & daleth.
41 But in modern prayer books נכרי.
42 But the sentiment is universal, Isaac Watts Divine Songs for Children vi:
       Lord, I ascribe it to thy grace,
            And not to chance, as others do,
       That I was born of Christian race,
            And not a heathen or a Jew.
    Still elsewhere Watts remains the prince of English hymn-writers.
43 Charles Segal, "Classics, Ecumenicism, and Greek Tragedy," TAPA 125 (1995) 1-26, p. 14.

sophist Antiphon[44] "In this we have all been made barbarians to one another (βεβαρβαρώμεθα), since by nature we are all disposed alike in all respects, both barbarians and Hellenes...For we all breathe into the air with our mouths and nostrils." Eratosthenes (Strabo 1.4.9) rejected the opinion of those who advised Alexander "to treat Hellenes as friends and barbarians as enemies"; rather, such judgements should be made on the basis of "virtue and vice," ἀρετῇ καὶ κακίᾳ. "For (he said) many of the Hellenes are bad (κακούς) and many of the barbarians civilized (ἀστείους), in particular Indians and Arians; and likewise Romans and Carthaginians, governed so excellently." Jeremias[45] sees as underlying Jesus' work the prophetical vision of the "pilgrimage of the nations": thus at Isa 2,2 where the "mountain of the house of Yahweh" is established as the highest of mountains, "and all the Goyim shall flow to it," וְנָהֲרוּ אֵלָיו כָּל־הַגּוֹיִם. As the sense of a world-community became more profound, the original rationale for the existence of the city-wall and the particularistic city it enclosed faded away; see the discussion at I.161-162.

18.2.6 Love and hate

As only a fine line separates friend and enemy, so with love and hate. So of Amnon after his rape of Tamar, "the hatred with which he hated her was greater than the love with which he had loved her" (II Sam 13,15):

גְּדוֹלָה הַשִּׂנְאָה אֲשֶׁר שְׂנֵאָהּ מֵאַהֲבָה אֲשֶׁר אֲהֵבָהּ

here the nouns in the LXX become μῖσος and ἀγάπη (etymologically, as it seems); Vg *odium* and *amor*. So Catullus 85 *odi et amo* although he cannot explain it. In Hebrew the closeness of love and hatred is mirrored in the closeness of the roots אהב and איב (SIE 458); for the shift of /h/ to /y/ is no more than from the perfect הָלַךְ "he went" to the imperfect יֵלֵךְ and the hiphil הוֹלִיךְ, both as if from a root *ילך. They have taken up different slots in the language. איב appears as a verb only at Exod 23,22 "I will be an enemy to your enemies and an adversary to your adversaries"

וְאָיַבְתִּי אֶת־אֹיְבֶיךָ   וְצַרְתִּי אֶת־צֹרְרֶיךָ

Everywhere else it appears (as here) as a participle אֹיֵב. אהב appears only occasionally as the corresponding participle אֹהֵב. But they stand in the conclusion to the Song of Deborah (Jud 5,31) in modified parallelism, אוֹיְבֶיךָ...וְאֹהֲבָיו "your enemies...his friends" (LXX οἱ ἐχθροί

---

44   Diels-Kranz FVS[8] 87 B44, frag. B, col. 2.7-33.
45   Joachim Jeremias, New Testament Theology: The Proclamation of Jesus; tr. J. Bowden; New York: Scribner's, 1971; p. 247.

... οἱ ἀγαπῶντες) both times referring to Yahweh. Perhaps the participles are opposite specializations of an original meaning "foreigner,
stranger," depending on the determination of the stranger's status.

The relationship between אהב "to love" (with אַהֲבָה, both its infinitive and a noun) and Greek ἀγαπάω, ἀγάπη is perplexing. The Greek
verb is Homeric; until recently the noun was unknown before its use
in the LXX to translate אַהֲבָה, but now it has appeared as a woman's
name ΑΓΑΠΑ in a Thessalian gravestone of the 6th century BC.[46] The
LXX as often picked it to translate a Hebrew of similar sound, but that
does not settle the etymological relations one way or the other. The
relation is too close to be accidental, but it is unclear in what social
context such a noun should be borrowed. Levin (SIE 224-225) also
compares אהב with the root עגב "have intercourse(?)," restricted to
Ezek 23 and Jer 4,30; he regards the two Hebrew roots as representing
alternative hearings of some foreign verb, and the Greek as a loanword either from the Hebrew or from its source. The connection here
observed between אהב and איב further complicates the matter.

18.2.7 Shame and its physical manifestations

The definition of heroic conduct implies that *honor* is the typical virtue
of the hero, and *shame* the failing that he must at all costs avoid.
Hebrew and Greek everywhere presume the contrast, and occasionally
define it: Ps 4,3 עַד־מֶה כְבוֹדִי לִכְלִמָּה "How long shall my honor suffer
shame?"; Thucydides 1.5.1 says of piracy that once this trade had no
shame (αἰσχύνην), but rather brought some honor (τι καὶ δόξης).[47]

We are so far from the heroic age that "shame" seems to us to have
two diametrically opposed senses, depending on whether we are
ashamed at what we have done, or are ashamed even to think of an
immoral action that we have *not* done. At II.322 (III.3) we noted: at
II Sam 19,6 Joab tells David that by mourning for Absalom "You have
covered with shame (הִבַשְׁתָּ, LXX κατήσχυνας) the faces of all your
servants" who have themselves acted blamelessly; Hos 2,7 "For their
mother has played the harlot, she who bore them has acted shamefully
(הוֹבִישָׁה, LXX κατήσχυνεν)". So in Greek. Plato *Phaedrus* 257D,
Phaedrus says that statesmen "feel shame to write speeches" lest they

---

46   SEG 19 (1963) 422; see Oda Wischmeyer, "Vorkommen und Bedeutung von
     Agape in der ausserchristlichen Antike," ZNW 69 (1978) 212-238.

47   Honor and shame are felt to characterize Mediterranean society even today:
     David D. Gilmore (ed.), Honor and Shame and the Unity of the Mediterra-
     nean; special pub. of the American Anthropological Association 22, Washing-
     ton 1987.

be called Sophists (αἰσχύνονται λόγους τε γράφειν).[48] At *Gorgias* 494E
Callicles asks "Are you not ashamed, Socrates, of dragging our discussion into such [unseemly] topics [as the life of sexual perverts]?," οὐκ
αἰσχύνῃ εἰς τοιαῦτα ἄγων, ὦ Σώκρατες, τοὺς λόγους;—which in fact
Socrates has just done.[49] So with *pudor*: Cicero *pro Plancio* 27
adulescentis modestissimi pudor "the shyness of a most modest youth";
but Calpurnius *Decl.* 49 the adulterer *pudore torquetur* "is tormented
with shame." In an heroic shame-culture, whatever sets you aside from
your fellows is felt the ultimate disgrace, whether (from a later ethical
point of view) it is your fault or you are entirely blameless. In our
culture, shame at the thought of an immoral action we have *not* done
arises from our temptation to do it; Jesus in his sternest mood says
(Matt 5,28) "Whoever *looks* at a woman with an eye towards desiring
her..."

With II Sam 19,6 cited above we may compare the definition of
virtue at *Iliad* 6.209 μηδὲ γένος πατέρων αἰσχυνέμεν "not to shame the
race of one's fathers." Elsewhere in *Samuel* "to be brought to shame
in the presence of" is expressed by a root similar to בּוֹשׁ, namely בָּאַשׁ
"to stink," mostly passive, in the sense "be in bad odor with." Israel
stinks with the Philistines (I Sam 13,4):

וְנִם־נִבְאַשׁ יִשְׂרָאֵל בַּפְּלִשְׁתִּים

Achish thinks "David stinks with his people" (I Sam 27,12); the
Ammonites stink with David (II Sam 10:6); Absalom is to stink with
David (II Sam 16,21). The LXX (which translates literal uses of בָּאַשׁ
literally), in all four passages translates with a form of αἰσχύνη as it did
for בּוֹשׁ at II Sam 19,6. Perhaps the LXX thought these verbs were
forms of בּוֹשׁ "be ashamed."

Perhaps in some sense they were. Shame goes with nakedness and
sexuality. Gen 2,25 expects us to be surprised that Adam and Eve were
"naked and not (mutually) ashamed" (עֲרוּמִּים ... יִתְבּ׳שָׁשׁוּ). We saw that
a woman bearing the children of harlotry is ashamed (Hos 2,7 הוֹבִישָׁה,
κατήσχυνεν). When Jonathan makes excuses for David, Saul says that
he has made David his friend "to your shame and the shame of your
mother's nakedness" (I Sam 20,30):

לְבָשְׁתְּךָ וּלְב׳שֶׁת עֶרְוַת אִמֶּךָ

---

48 Socrates goes on to claim that in the laws they pass, statesmen *are* in effect
writing; but that does not affect Phaedrus' meaning. LSJ 43b end observes that
when αἰσχύνομαι middle takes an infinitive it denotes shame at the mere
thought of something shameful one has *not* done, while with the participle it
denotes shame at having in fact done something shameful.
49 The near-synonym αἰδώς mostly like Latin *pudor* means "sense of honor, self-
respect"; occasionally as an exclamation it suggests "Shame!" (*Iliad* 17.336).

(LXX αἰσχύνην *bis*). The sexual parts are מְבֻשָׁיו (Deut 25,11); and so αἰδοῖα, Latin *pudenda*. These are all matters which literally stink, so it would seem possible that בּוֹשׁ "be ashamed" is an abstract specialization of בָּאַשׁ stink." The latter's contexts run parallel. When David's servants had their clothes and beards half cut off, they were dishonored (different verb, נִכְלָמִים) and the Ammonites stank with David (II Sam 10,5-6). The hero much more even than we ourselves is demeaned by an invasion of his privacy. What was to make Absalom stink with David (נִבְאַשְׁתָּ) was taking his father's concubines (II Sam 16,21-22).

Levin[50] doubly compared Latin *te pudet* "you are ashamed" with Heb. תֵּבוֹשׁ* "you will be ashamed" (only the feminine תֵּבֹ֫שִׁי attested at Jer 22,22 etc): namely, in the personal prefixes and in the roots. The comparison is strengthened when we see that Latin *pudet* also is similar in sound to (unrelated) verbs meaning "stink": *foetet* (Plautus *As.* 894) and *putet* (Horace, *Serm.* 2.2.42). The latter is related to Greek πύθεται "rot" (*Iliad* 11.395). And so yet a fourth stem, perhaps also unrelated, *foedus* adjectival "offensive, repugnant": often with forms of *pudet*, thus Cicero *Phil.* 2.15 *foeditatem...impudentiam*; Tacitus *Hist.* 1.72 *foeda pueritia, impudica senecta* "his youth was unchaste, his old age corrupt." In a mixed metaphor the Israelites complain to Moses and Aaron (Exod 5,21) "you have made our breath stink in the eyes[!] of Pharaoh,"

הִבְאַשְׁתֶּם אֶת־רֵיחֵנוּ בְּעֵינֵי פַרְעֹה

where the Vulgate *quoniam* fetere[51] *fecistis odorem nostram coram Pharaoh*. Frisk[52] thinks the Indo-European words onomatopoetic, citing German *pfui* (so English *phew*): the nose is wrinkled up to keep the smell out, the lips are pursed and minimally opened to expel the stinking air without taking any more in. The Greeks exclaimed φῦ φῦ of smoke (Aristophanes *Lys.* 294). With Greek φῦσα "breath" compare Heb. יָפוּחַ Cant 2,17 "it breathes."

Later, in all three languages, the physical manifestation of shame is softened from stinking to *blushing*. At Plato *Protagoras* 312A Hippocrates blushes (ἐρυθριάσας) when forced to admit that he is in training to be a sophist, and can only agree when Socrates asks "Wouldn't you be ashamed for offering yourself to Hellenes as a sophist?" οὐκ ἂν αἰσχύνοιο εἰς τοὺς Ἕλληνας σαυτὸν σοφιστὴν παρέχων; where the participle shows that (by supposition) he *is* doing the shameful act. Pliny the Younger *Paneg.* 31.6: Egypt was ashamed of her sterility (the Nile

---

50   IESL 525; SIE 250-259; II.321.
51   Later spelling of *foetere*.
52   Frisk ii.622.

didn't rise), *pudebat* and blushed at it, *erubescebat*. What then does it mean to be "clothed with shame"?[53] See *Iliad* 9.372 (cf. 1.149) ἀναιδείην ἐπιειμένος, Job 8,22 יִלְבָּשׁוּ־בֹשֶׁת. Further, Ps 109,29 "May [my accusers] be wrapped in their shame as a garment":

וְיַעֲטוּ כַמְעִיל בָּשְׁתָּם

This is a natural description of blushing. Jer 8,12 (cf. 6,15) "Were they ashamed when they committed abomination? No, they were not at all ashamed; they did not know how to show contrition":

הֹבִשׁוּ כִּי תוֹעֵבָה עָשׂוּ גַּם־בּוֹשׁ לֹא־יֵבֹשׁוּ וְהִכָּלֵם לֹא יָדָעוּ

But here the Vulgate (followed by RSV) has *erubescere nescierunt* and perhaps that is a further connotation of the root כלם. Above all, II Sam 19,6 "covered their faces with shame" (cited above) can only refer to blushing. Likewise the later idiom בֹשֶׁת פָּנִים (cf. English *shamefaced*) at II Chron 32,21 etc.; Ps 44,16 "And shame has covered my face,"

וּבֹשֶׁת פָּנַי כִּסָּתְנִי

18.2.8 Loving the enemy

Plutarch partly refashions the ideas of friend and enemy. He begins his essay "How to profit by one's enemies" by admitting that "our friend-ships themselves involve us in enmities" (ταῖς ἔχθραις αἱ φιλίαι ἐμπλέκουσιν ἡμᾶς *Mor.* 86C). Having an enemy, he says, puts you on your guard, provides you additional incentive to morality, and gives you a greater chance than with a friend of showing magnanimity. Above all, it is from our enemies that we hear the truth about our-selves, ἀκουστέον ἐστὶ παρὰ τῶν ἐχθρῶν τὴν ἀλήθειαν (89C). Plutarch approaches the insight of Jung: in wartime, "in the judgment we pronounce upon [our enemy] we unwittingly reveal our own defects; we simply accuse our enemy of our own unadmitted faults."[54] The enemy whom we choose or who is chosen for us is the mirror of the shadow side of ourselves. So Athens had not long defeated the Persians

---

53 West (EFH 238-239) and I independently noted this striking parallel.
54 C. G. Jung, "General Aspects of Dream Psychology," The Structure and Dynamics of the Psyche (Bollingen Series XX, The Collected Works of C. G. Jung, vol 8); tr. by R. F. C. Hull; New York: Pantheon, 1953-1979; p. 270 sect. 516. From "Allgemeine Gesichtspunkte zur Psychologie des Traumes," Die Dynamik des Unbewussten; Gesammelte Werke Band 8 (Zurich & Stuttgart: Rascher Verlag, 1967) p. 307: "Unsere Mentalität ist dadurch charakterisiert— wie die Ereignisse in der Kriegszeit [Erster Weltkrieg] deutlich demonstriert haben—, dass wir mit einer schamlosen Naivität über den Gegner urteilen und im Urteil, das wir über ihn aussprechen, unsere eigenen Defekte verraten; ja, man wirft dem Gegner einfach die eigenen, nicht eingestandenen Fehler vor."

when she took a leaf out of their book and exacted tribute in Persian style from her subject states. Against that fatal tendency stands the saying ascribed to Pittacus of uncertain date, "not to speak ill of a friend or even an enemy," φίλον μὴ λέγειν κακῶς, ἀλλὰ μηδὲ ἐχθρόν (Diogenes Laertius 1.78). Epictetus goes farther, "when beaten to love those who beat you as a brother would," δερόμενον φιλεῖν αὐτοὺς τοὺς δέροντας ... ὡς ἀδελφόν (Arrian *Epic.* 3.22.54).[55]

It remained for Jesus absolutely to reverse the old formula, "love (Syriac אחבו)[56] your enemies," ἀγαπᾶτε τοὺς ἐχθροὺς ὑμῶν (Matt 5,44 = Luk 6,27), Vg *diligite inimicos uestros*. This is precisely the principle for which David was reproached by Joab; here Jesus is in a special way a "son of David." At Luk 6,35 the new formulation is repeated, and in that context as we saw it has an extended structure: "But love your enemies...and your reward will be great." The English *will* like the Greek future ἔσται is too precise. For the underlying Aramaic appears in the Syriac ונהוא as an imperfect of the verb: that is, it represents an action *in process of* happening; for Semitic hardly has a true way of speaking about the future even in the (later!) Indo-European sense (III.42 below). With this qualification, the saying has the pattern "Do A and B will happen" which I discuss in 18.3.

Did Jesus hold Jung's position, that by taking an enemy you become the thing that you hate, and that only by loving the enemy can this be avoided? At least he motivates his new way by the hope of becoming "sons of your Father in heaven" (Matt 5,45). He has not with the Stoics wholly abandoned his local citizenship for one of the world, because his reaction to the likely destruction of the Temple is one of sorrow. But Paul comes close to that point, I.162, "our commonwealth is in heaven" (Phil 3,20). So at Heb 13,12-14, Jesus "suffered outside the gate...for here we have no abiding city, but we look for that which is to come."

18.3 Recompense of injuries and benefits.

Here we begin with classical formulations of recompense, both human and divine, and make a circuit back to "measure for measure" and "give to the giver." Bismarck in 1886 said of the policy of the King of

---

55   Further passages on love of enemy in BAGD s.v. ἐχθρός p. 331b.

56   This Syriac form is usually thought Aphel of חב "was kindled, on fire." The translator, unaware of Hebrew אהב, found a verb sounding like the Greek with a different guttural.

Prussia, *sie macht sich nur durch Blut und Eisen,* "it can only be carried out through blood and iron."[57] See the harsh realism of von Clausewitz (*vom Krieg* 4.11):

> Let us not hear of Generals who conquer without bloodshed (*Menschenblut*). If a bloody slaughter is a horrible sight, then that is a ground for paying more respect to War, but not for making the swords we wear blunter and blunter by degrees from feelings of humanity, until one steps in with one that is sharp and lops off the arm from our body.

Blood and iron naturally go together. Quintilian (*decl.* 350) *caedes uidetur significare sanguinem et ferrum* "slaughter seems to mean blood and iron."[58] See the parallel passages with "sword" and "blood" cited at II.143: Isa 34,6; Lucan 7.317. Blood and iron may label two sets of parallel sayings dealing with recompense (both natural and human) for *injuries*; along with other proverbial expressions they by contrast underlie Jesus' teaching about recompense for *benefits*.

18.3.1 Blood for blood

Here there is a beautiful Hebrew-Greek parallel previously noted (I.5, II.279). Gen 9,6 has a lapidary construction (lost in the Versions) with assonance of "blood" and "man" and structure ABC:CBA

שֹׁפֵךְ דַּם הָאָדָם   בָּאָדָם דָּמוֹ יִשָּׁפֵךְ

"Whoever sheds the blood of man, by man will his blood be shed." Luther[59] rejected the view that this could be seen as a "plague or punishment of God on murderers" (*als von eyner plage und straff von Gott uber die moerder*) on the grounds that many murderers die of natural causes; he sees it rather as a law ordained by God (*recht von Gott befolhen*) mandating the death penalty ("...by man *shall* his blood be shed"), which is clear at Lev 24,21 "He who kills a man shall be put to death." But originally it recognizes an inescapable sequence of events, neither exactly "natural" nor "divine" in our sense, but rooted in the special character of blood, Gen 4,10 "The voice of your brother's blood is crying to me from the ground." For as Mephisto says (*Faust* I.1740), *Blut ist ein ganz besondrer Saft,* "Blood is a very special kind of sap."

The Greeks had that sense of blood very strongly: Euripides in *Electra* 857-858 has the Messenger say of Aegisthus' death at the hands of Orestes:

---

57 ODQ² p. 72.
58 Seneca *Epist.* 77.9 *non fuit illi opus ferro, non sanguine* "he needed neither iron nor blood" to commit suicide.
59 *Von weltlicher Obrigkeit,* Werke xi.248.

... αἷμα δ' αἵματος

πικρὸς δανεισμὸς ἦλθε τῷ θανόντι νῦν.

"Blood the bitter repayment of blood has come upon him who now lies dead." The Chorus in Aeschylus' *Choephoroi* 309-314 states the general principle: "For a hostile tongue may a hostile tongue be requited; Justice as she exacts the debt cries aloud; for a murderous blow let one repay a murderous blow. The doer shall suffer (δράσαντι παθεῖν)..."[60] And at 400-402, "There is a law (*nomos*) that bloody drops shed on the ground call for more blood." West (EFH 236, 575) adds the theme of the earth drinking the blood of the slain: Aeschylus *Eum.* 980 (cf. *Septem* 736, *Choeph.* 66) "the dust drinking the black blood of citizens":

πιοῦσα κόνις μέλαν αἷμα πολιτᾶν

Gen 4,11 of the ground "which has opened its mouth to receive your brother's blood from your hand."

Aeschylus in the *Eumenides* mythologizes the causative factor as the Erinyes, sniffing out spilled blood. One stained by involuntary homicide must seek asylum both in Israel (Num 35,9-15 etc.) and Hellas.[61] At Athens the Basileus conducted trials of animals and objects that caused death (Aristotle *Ath. Pol.* 57.4); the animal is to be killed and "cast outside the borders," ἔξω τῶν ὅρων τῆς γῆς...διορίσαι (Plato *Leg.* 873E) and even the tool is to be exiled. So in Israel the ox is stoned and its flesh may not be eaten (Exod 21,28). Exiles—murderers, avengers, involuntary slayers—may have carried the blood-formula from land to land. Either from Genesis 9 or independently it appears in an English phrase, first quoted from *Mirror for Magistrates* (1559)[62]:

Blood axeth blood as guerdone dewe.

Shakespeare gives it to Macbeth (*Macb.* III.iv.122):

It will haue blood they say: Blood will haue Blood.

A special stroke of his genius is the "It" without antecedent, Duncan's

---

60 Same phrase at Pindar *Nem.* 4.32 ῥέζοντά τι καὶ παθεῖν ἔοικεν "it is proper that one who has done something should also suffer it"; similarly Sophocles frag. 962 Radt (& Pearson) εἰ δείν' ἔδρασας, δεινὰ καὶ παθεῖν σε δεῖ "if you have done ill things, you must suffer ill things"; and see further Hesiod frag. 286 M-W cited in full at I.5.

61 Moshe Greenberg, "The Biblical Conception of Asylum," JBL 78 (1959) 125-132 with comparison of Greek legislation. See in particular Demosthenes 23.72 "The man convicted of involuntary homicide (ἐπ' ἀκουσίῳ φόνῳ) shall, on certain appointed days, leave the country by a prescribed route, and remain in exile until he wins reconciliation from a relative of the deceased." See Weinfeld Promise of the Land 29.

62 ODEP³ 69.

murder or the like: we break into the middle of Macbeth's stream of consciousness.

18.3.2 Iron for iron

Matthew (26,52) records the saying with its "chiastic" (ABBA) order "for all those who take the sword, by the sword shall perish":

πάντες γὰρ οἱ λαβόντες μάχαιραν ἐν μαχαίρῃ ἀπολοῦνται

This belongs to the old order; but when Jesus says "Put the sword[63] back in its sheath" he restores the freedom it denies. Even without the preface it goes beyond Machiavelli or Clausewitz: for it sees an inevitable chain of cause and effect (whether symbolized as natural or divine) by which the sword once taken up turns against the taker. The closest parallel to the seeming proverb "All those who take the sword..." is Latin, "to be killed with one's own sword," Terence *Adelph.* 958 *suo sibi gladio hunc iugulo* "I cut his throat with his very own sword"; Cicero *ad Caec.* 83 *aut tuo, quemadmodum dicitur, gladio aut nostro defensio tua conficiatur necesse est,* "Your case will necessarily fall either (as the saying goes) by your sword or by mine."[64] Luther in the same place[65] treated Gen 9,6 "Whoever sheds man's blood, by man shall his blood be shed" not as descriptive of divine judgement ("for many murderers die without the sword," *Denn viel mörder...on schwerd sterben*) but prescriptive, "one should justly kill him with the sword," *man yhn mitt recht durchs schwerd tödten solle.* He goes on to say that Matt 26,52 is to be understood in the same way, that is, as a commandment, *wilchs auch gleich wie das Gen. 9 zü verstehen ist.*

See further Prov 26,27 "He who rolls a stone, to him it returns." Two Hebrew texts approach the same thought.

(a) Prov 27,17 בַּרְזֶל בְּבַרְזֶל יָחַד "iron sharpens iron" where the form of the verb is uncertain but the general meaning is clear: LXX σίδηρος σίδηρον ὀξύνει, Vg *ferrum ferro acuitur.*[66] Latin *ferrum* could be derived from some such Near Eastern form (II.227). As the text continues "and a man sharpens the countenance of his neighbor" it is usually interpreted "insight or wit is contagious." In that understanding it is close to the current use of English *diamond cut diamond,* where a contest of wit is understood. But the old uses, going back to

---

63 The Peshitto here has the Persian imperial name of the sword ספסרא discussed at III.99.

64 See Otto 20 for further instances.

65 *Von weltlicher Obrigkeit,* Werke xi.248.

66 English "One knife whets another" since 1576 (ODEP³ 432).

1593[67], on the contrary imply a fatality by which a man's own talents are turned against him. So Webster (*Duchess of Malfi* V.v.91):

> Whether we fall by ambition, blood, or lust,
> Like Diamonds, we are cut with our owne dust.

If "iron sharpens iron" had an independent existence it could then have been a true predecessor of Jesus' saying. Bab. Talm. *Sanh.* 104a "weapon eating weapon," זין אוכל זין reflects the same thought.

(b) Jer 15,2 = 43,11 "Whoever is for the sword, to the sword" (with three other agents of death) אֲשֶׁר לַחֶרֶב לַחֶרֶב. This means something different, "whoever is destined for the sword shall go to the sword." The prophet does not specify what destines certain ones to the sword; the emphasis is on the apparently inscrutable divine decree.[68] But behind Jeremiah's saying may have lain the proverb in the sense that Matthew gives it.[69]

The military rhetoric of Latin poetry sets sword against sword. Thus in Dido's invocation of Hannibal (Vergil, *Aen.* 4.628-9):

> Litora litoribus contraria, fluctibus undas
> imprecor, *arma armis...*

"I call on shores [of Carthage and Italy] to be opposed to shores, waves to seas, *arms to arms.*" Silius, *Punica* 9.322-325, works out the details:

> ...galea horrida flictu
> aduersae ardescit galeae, clipeusque fatiscit
> impulsu clipei, *atque ensis contunditur ense*;
> pes pede, uirque uiro teritur...

"Helmet, vibrating at the clash with an opposing helmet, flashes fire; shield collapses under the impact of shield; and *sword is broken by sword*; foot is pressed against foot, man against man..."[70] The fatality of sword set against sword in battle implies a foregoing recompense by which the drawing of a sword elicits its counterpart.

---

67 ODEP³ 185.

68 In the adaptation at Rev 13,10 the sense of Jeremiah must have been intended, "Whoever is to be killed by the sword, by the sword will he be killed"; but some MSS assimilate it to Matthew, εἴ τις ἐν μαχαίρῃ ἀποκτείνει "whoever kills by the sword..."

69 I pass by the difficult verse Isa 27,7 "Has he smitten them as he smote those who smote them? Or have they been slain as their slayers were slain?" (RSV); it evidently envisages recompense of ill, but the parties involved are obscure.

70 See Baebius, *Ilias latina* 955 (ed. F. Vollmer, Poetae latini minores vol. II fasc. 3; Leipzig: Teubner, 1913) *ensem terit horridus ensis* "bristling sword wears down sword."

18.3.3 An eye for an eye

"Eye for eye." The causative factor in recompense of blood and iron was independent, although men might take upon themselves the role of its human agent. A third formula of recompense involves solely human retribution. At Matt 5,38 Jesus quotes and overrules "an eye for an eye and a tooth for a tooth" (Exod 21,23-24, Lev 24,19-20, Deut 19,21, with other applications). The Law may have a tradition of the Code of Hammurabi "If a man destroy the eye of another man, they shall destroy his eye."[71] Still the original motivation of the Hebrew law may have been humanitarian, to counteract vengeance of 7 times or 77 (Gen 4,24); Jesus is aware of that too, and rejects it in favor of forgiveness 7 times or 77 (Matt 18,21-22, cf Luk 17,4). The principle of Hammurabi and the Mosaic law is paralleled in Greece.[72] Demosthenes 24.140 says there was a law among the Locrians that "whoever gouges out an eye must let his own eye be gouged out," ἐάν τις ὀφθαλμὸν ἐκκόψῃ, ἀντεκκόψαι παρασχεῖν τὸν ἑαυτοῦ.[73] But already in the Mishna (*Baba Qamma* VIII) the retribution of "an eye for an eye" is replaced by a fine for "injury, pain, healing, loss of time and indignity." The continuity of Near Eastern law-codes is strongly marked by the appearance of the same formula expanded at Quran 5.46 "Eye for eye...tooth for tooth" (cited II.279).

18.3.4 The *lex talionis*

At Lev 24,19-20 the formula "eye for eye" is extended to an abstract principle in two forms. The first is "as he did, so shall it be done to him,"

$$\text{כַּאֲשֶׁר עָשָׂה כֵּן יֵעָשֶׂה לּוֹ}$$

LXX ὡς ἐποίησεν αὐτῷ, ὡσαύτως ἀντιποιηθήσεται αὐτῷ.
Here the Vulgate achieves extreme linguistic compression, *sicut fecit fiet ei.* In similar language applied to private justice, Samson says (Jud

---

71 Sect. 196, R. F. Harper, The Code of Hammurabi...; Chicago: University, 1904. The translation at ANET[3] 195 interprets it as of an aristocrat destroying the eye of a commoner, but still remaining liable to lose his own eye.

72 See Morton Smith, "East Mediterranean Law-Codes of the Early Iron Age," pp. 38*-43* of H. L. Ginsberg Volume (ed. Menahem Haran); Eretz-Israel vol. 14; Jerusalem: Israel Exploration Society etc., 1978. Smith does not cite this, but includes valuable materials on Egyptian law codes under Bocchoris (720-715 BC), Amasis (568-525) and Darius (522-485) from Diodorus and native Egyptian sources.

73 Diodorus 12.17.4 ascribes the same principle to Charondas at Thurii, and Diogenes Laertius 1.57 to Solon; all three texts casuistically discuss the penalty for destroying the only eye of a one-eyed man.

15,11) "As they did to me, so have I done to them"; and Luther, who several times cites the passage, justifies him as possessed by the Spirit, although Prov 24,29 forbids us to say, "As he did to me, so shall I do to him." See Aeschylus *Choeph.* 313 cited above (III.24) δράσαντι παθεῖν. A Latin parallel in the fictitious "acclamations" of the Senate after the death of Commodus (Script. Hist. Aug. *Commodus* 19): *carnifex unco trahatur...sic fecit, sic patiatur* "let the butcher be dragged with the hook...as he did, so let him suffer."

Lev 24,20 ends "as he does injury to a man, so shall it be done to him":

כַּאֲשֶׁר יִתֵּן מוּם בָּאָדָם כֵּן יִנָּתֶן בּוֹ

LXX καθότι ἂν δῷ μῶμον τῷ ἀνθρώπῳ, οὕτως δοθήσεται αὐτῷ. Here as elsewhere the LXX translates מוּם by a word of nearly identical sound, μῶμος, discussed at I.232. There we concluded that the word travelled in the negative as a description of perfection, "without flaw," more likely as applied to women (so in both Greek and Hebrew) rather than to sacrificial animals (not early so attested in Greek).[74] We found (II.279) that legal formulas travelled across the Mediterranean. In the first appearance of μῶμος in Greek, Antinous asks Telemachus (*Od.* 2.86) what he has said, "shaming us, and you would wish to attach blame to us," ἡμέας αἰσχύνων, ἐθέλοις δέ κε μῶμον ἀνάψαι. In the context of the heroic shame-culture, this usage is not far from the men's high-handed world envisaged by Leviticus.

All three of these formulas of recompense (whether carried out by nature, God or man) have the same noun—blood, iron or sword, eye— repeated in different constructions. Greek has many such proverbial expressions. Thus *Odyssey* 17.217-218 "now plainly a rascal is conducting a rascal (κακὸς κακὸν ἡγηλάζει) just as the god always leads like to like (τὸν ὁμοῖον...ὡς τὸν ὁμοῖον)." So Menander[75] "man saves man, and city city":

ἀνὴρ γὰρ ἄνδρα καὶ πόλις σῴζει πόλιν

Again,[76] "hand washes hand and fingers fingers"

χεὶρ χεῖρα νίπτει, δάκτυλοι δὲ δακτύλους

Aristotle[77] cites a line which ideally illustrates nominative and accusative in two declensions, "A thief knows a thief, and a wolf a wolf":

---

74   Brief discussion at Levin SIE 170 with no conclusion about the realm of transmission.

75   Menander, *Sent.* 31, ed. S. Jaekel, Menandri Sententiae; Leipzig: Teubner, 1954.

76   Menander, *Sent.* 832 Jaekel; see Petronius 45.13 etc. *manus manum lauat.*

77   Aristotle *Eudemian Ethics* 7.1.7 (1235a7), supplemented by *Nic. Eth.* 8.1.6 (1155a34), *Mag. Mor.* 2.11.2 (1208b10), *Rhet.* 1.11.25 (1371b10); along

ἔγνω δὲ φώρ τε φῶρα καὶ λύκος λύκον

It has gone into English as "set a thief to catch a thief" (since 1654).[78] In its folk-humor it still has something in common with the somber sayings on blood and the sword: in the end theft or rapine is recognized by those who share the same characteristics and is brought to justice, since the tradition varies whether or not "there is honour among thieves."[79] Further it suggests a mechanism by which the recompense of harm is carried out.

The correlative phrase with two nouns can paraphrase the second half of the heroic formula "and hate my enemies." Theognis (344) in his usual mood says "may I give hurts in return for hurts," δοίην δ' ἀντ' ἀνιῶν ἀνίας. Here the thought of "hate enemies" (18.2) is expressed in the language of recompense. Odyssey 15.394 ἀνίη "grief" is a phonetic parallel to אֲנִיָּה Isa 29,2 (here only and Thr 2,5) "mourning"; Hebrew -iyy- is parallel to a Greek long ī.[80] We saw above (III.8) that Theognis 872 wishes to be an ἀνίη to his enemies. The perfect phonetic agreement and substantial semantic closeness strongly suggests a linguistic connection, although the Hebrew does not indicate the exact social context.

The formula of recompense of ill (divine or natural) equally appears with a verb rather than noun as the parallel element. That Zen master Rabbi Hillel (Avoth II.7) saw a skull floating on the water and said, in a saying less opaque than many, "Because you drowned others, they drowned you; and in the end those who drowned you will be drowned":[81]

על דאטפת אטפוך   וסוף מטיפיך יטופון

This emphasizes the never-ending chain of recompense; Hillel hardly envisages the possibility that something might intervene to break it.[82] Or with correlative verbs: Prov 26,27 = Koh 10,8 "He that diggeth a

---

with Od. 17.218 he also cites "And jackdaw sits beside jackdaw," "Agemate pleases agemate."

78 ODEP[3] 810, which however misses Aristotle as the source. "The thefe knoweth the thefe, and the wolfe the wolfe" (1539) is older but obviously a translation from the Greek.

79 ODEP[3] 382.

80 In the Aeolic form ὀνίαισι (Sappho frag. 1.4) it has been compared with Latin onus "burden" and ὄνος "ass"; see II.51.

81 I am uncertain about both the spelling and vocalization of the four verb-forms of the root טוף.

82 Sap Sol 11,16 gives a rationalistic explanation, "through whatever things one sins, through them he is punished," δι' ὧν τις ἁμαρτάνει, διὰ τούτων καὶ κολάζεται.

pit shall fall therein" with parallels in both places. The self-imposed curses of the vassal treaty constitute an *ad hoc* creation of the same sequence; numerous examples at I.272-276 "As this animal is struck, so may I be struck" etc.

Latin has a noun for "exactness of retribution," *talio*. Thus in the Twelve Tables VIII.2 *si membrum rupsit, ni cum eo pacit, talio esto* "If a man maims another's limb, unless he makes agreement with him for it, let there be retaliation in kind."[83] Gellius 20.1.14 records the familiar phrase *lex talionis*. Quintilian (7.4.6) equates *talio* with *uim contra uim* "force against force"; Seneca (*Epistle* 81.7) imagines an opponent recalling Cicero's definition of justice (II.29): "it is of the nature of justice to give each his due: thanks for a benefit, recompense for an injury," *iustitiae conuenit suum cuique reddere, beneficio gratiam, iniuriae talionem.*

18.3.5 Recompense of benefits

Plato was the first to reject the idea of retaliation (*Crito* 49B): since "One must never do injustice" (οὐδαμῶς ἄρα δεῖ ἀδικεῖν), equally retaliation (ἀνταδικεῖν) or "doing injustice in return" is excluded. But what may seem the heartless mathematics of the *talio* in fact suggests a new way of looking at recompense, on the divine or natural rather than on the human side, by which it is exactly proportional to the original action, not merely in injury *but also in benefit*. Perhaps the processes of agriculture led to this insight. First in sowing. What would pass for a Neolithic saying is attested by Cicero as a proverb (*de orat.* 2.261) *ut sementem feceris ita metes* "as you have done your sowing, so shall you reap"; discussion at I.317-318.[84] In Hellas and Israel only the ill side is seen. Prov 22,8 (see Job 4,8; Hosea 8,7; 10.13) "he who sows injustice will reap calamity"; a fragment of Hesiod:[85]

εἰ κακά τις σπείραι, κακὰ κέρδεα κ'ἀμήσειεν

But Paul at Gal 6,7 impartially draws both sets of conclusions, "for whatsoever a man sows, that shall he reap."

Again, recompense of benefits is illustrated in measuring out the harvested grain (III.4). Jesus' saying on measure is largely positive (Luke 6,38, III.4) "With what measure you mete it will be measured to you in return." It is led up to by a sequence of four little clauses, two negative and two positive, preserved by Luke alone (6,37-38):

---

83   Cited from Festus 550,3 and other sources; Loeb ed. p. 476.
84   Parallels in Otto Sprichwörter 221.
85   Hesiod frag. 286 M-W, see I.5.

(a) Do not judge, and you will not be judged;
(b) Do not condemn, and you will not be condemned.
(c) Forgive, and you will be forgiven;
(d) Give, and it will be given you.

Matthew (7,1-2) reduces the sequence to (a), but with a different motivation *"so that you will not* be judged" and with an extension "for with what judgement you judge you will be judged." The formula can be extended: so I Clement 13.2[86] "be merciful, so that you may obtain mercy; ...as you do, so will it be done to you; ...as you do benefits, so will you receive benefit." The briefest form is (c), which Luke has in the form ἀπολύετε καὶ ἀπολυθήσεσθε; Polycarp *ad Phil.* 2.3 in different vocabulary ἀφίετε καὶ ἀφεθήσεται ὑμῖν.[87] The variant shows that cancellation of debts is the image; the Syriac of Luke is שרו ותשתרון, Vulgate *dimittite et dimittemini*.[88] Here the old law of recompense (divine or natural) of ill finds its briefest formulation as a new law of recompense of good. The grammar wavers between an imperative with result "Just try forgiving! You will be forgiven," and a statement of natural law, "If you forgive, you will be forgiven."

We all feel that language somehow corresponds to reality. The logic and brevity of δράσαντι παθεῖν, *sicut fecit fiet ei* dispose us to believe that things are really so; and the long view of history, in which no injustice survives forever, confirms it. Recompense may be delayed but is inevitable, "The mills of the gods grind slow, but they grind exceeding small,"[89]

ὀψὲ θεῶν ἀλέουσι μύλοι, ἀλέουσι δὲ λεπτά

But already Plutarch in his beautiful *de sera uindicta* "on the delay in divine punishment" (III.176) shows a convergence to Hebrew thought in ascribing the delay to God's *gentleness* (πραότητα, *Mor.* 551C). And *dimittite et dimittemini* is just as neat and persuasive. It induces us to look at history in a new way, where the fact of benefits done

---

86   Partly followed by Polycarp *ad Phil.* 2.3.

87   1 Clement 13.2 has ἀφίετε ἵνα ἀφεθῇ ὑμῖν.

88   The Lord's Prayer presumes the same law in form of a petition (Matt 6,12), ἄφες ἡμῖν...ὡς καὶ ἡμεῖς ἀφήκαμεν (I.250).

89   Hexameter in Sextus Empiricus *adv. math.* 1.287 with discussion at II.44. The familiar translation is due to Longfellow, "Though the mills of God grind slowly, yet they grind exceeding small; / Though with patience he stands waiting, with exactness grinds he all." He was working over the German of Friedrich von Logau, "Gottesmühlen mahlen langsam, mahlen aber trefflich klein; ...," but apparently did not realize that von Logau had it from the Greek; neither does the ODQ² 315, 317, from which I have this information.

claims by right a permanent place in the scheme of things. Jeremias[90] calls the passive in the conclusion of such sayings a "divine passive" or circumlocution for the name of God, and suggests such a translation as "Forgive, for there is one that forgives you." But that confines Jesus too strictly to the usages of his time; as they stand the passives simply define the way things are. What you send out into the world, he says, comes back to you from it, whether bad or good. The conclusion holds equally if Jesus used the Aramaic third-person plural "passive" as in the Mishna, "and they will forgive you."

As brief is the other positive formula, "give and it will be given you," δίδοτε καὶ δοθήσεται ὑμῖν, Syriac הבו ומתיהב לכון, Vulgate *date et dabitur uobis*. We may go back from grace to gravity and contrast heavy-footed Hesiod (*Opera* 354):

κaì δόμεν ὅς κεν δῷ, καì μὴ δόμεν ὅς κεν μὴ δῷ.

"Give to one that gives, and do not give to one that does not give," together with the prudential considerations that follow. Again in Hesiod the imperatives conceal a result "Give to one that gives, and when you are in need he will give to you in return." This runs parallel to what precedes it (*Opera* 353) τὸν φιλέοντα φιλεῖν "Love the one that loves you" with the same logic. That gave rise to 18.2, and now we see that the evolution of the law of recompense runs parallel to that of "friend and enemy." Hesiod, we might say, differs from Jesus in being *less* realistic; his realism is limited to the short run and a superficial consideration. In the long run, or a deeper consideration (Jesus says), the fact of giving, irrespective of the character of the receiver, of itself means that we are in turn a receiver.

Käsemann[91] defined NT formulas superficially like ours as "sentences of holy law," *Sätze heiligen Rechts*. Most are *negative* formulas of punishment: "If anyone destroys God's temple, God will destroy him" (I Kor 3,17); "If one does not recognize this, he is not recognized" (I Kor 14,38); "If any one adds to these words, God will add to him the plagues described in this book" (Rev 22,18); "Whoever is ashamed of me..., of him will the Son of man also be ashamed" (Mark 8,38). But they are a throwback: the old formula of negative recompense is applied to the new situation of the Church; the novelty of

---

90 Joachim Jeremias, New Testament Theology: The Proclamation of Jesus; translated by John Bowden; New York: Scribner's, 1971; p. 11. He finds about a hundred such uses of the "divine passive" in the sayings of Jesus.

91 Ernst Käsemann, New Testament Questions of Today; translated by W. J. Montague; Philadelphia: Fortress, 1969; chapter 3, "Sentences of Holy Law in the New Testament" (orig. published in German in NTS 1 [1954/5] 248-260).

Jesus—enlarging recompense of evil to recompense of good—hardly appears.

18.3.6 The grammar of recompense

The saying *"give* and it will be given you" has a polar counterpart in *"ask* and it will be given you" (Luk 11,9-10 = Matt 7,7-8) with its continuation "seek and you will find, knock and it will be opened to you." Rosén[92] boldly finds its antecedent in the motif of the New Comedy, illustrated in Menander's *Dyscolus*, where a lover or servant knocks on the door of the beloved, and draws conclusions about the availability of Greek comedy in Palestine. But the sayings have a more natural antecedent in the cryptic message which a beggar writes on a hospitable gate for his successors, "Knock and it will be opened to you, ask and it will be given you." And in that way the polarity with "Give and it will be given you" is naturally explained. Jesus sees the whole ladder of human society from bottom to top as enmeshed in a money-economy and a nexus of personal obligations (I.249). ʿAqiba in his great parable (*Avoth* III.17, cited I.75) says that "the net is cast over all living...the account-book (פנקס = πίναξ) is open." Everybody (except the single fortunate one at the top) is a debtor to somebody higher up; everybody (except the poor devil at the very bottom) is also a creditor of somebody lower. The fact that each of us plays both roles explains the logic of "Forgive us our debts as we forgive our debtors." In the same way Jesus assumes that each of us in our lives has an area of adequacy and an area of need. "Give and it will be given you" says that dealing with any excess in our adequacy benefits a (perhaps quite disparate) area of our need; "Ask and it will be given you" says that by publicizing our area of need our area of adequacy is enlarged.

At Luk 6,35 and 38 our two types of saying fall together in the pattern "Do A and B will follow": "Love your enemies...and your reward will be great"; "Give and it will be given you." The pattern δίδοτε καὶ δοθήσεται ὑμῖν where an imperative is followed by an indicative has been poorly treated by grammarians. Rosén cites Gen 42,18 זאת עשו וחיו "Do this and you shall live," LXX τοῦτο ποιήσατε καὶ ζήσεσθε (whence Luk 10,28). The standard Greek grammar[93] cites examples since *Iliad* 4.29:

ἔρδ'· ἀτὰρ οὔ τοι πάντες ἐπαινέομεν θεοὶ ἄλλοι

92 Haiim B. Rosén, "Motifs and ΤΟΠΟΙ from the New Comedy in the New Testament?," Ancient Society 3 (1972) 245-257.
93 E. Schwyzer & A. Debrunner, Griechische Grammatik, 2 Band; Handbuch der Altertumswissenschaft 2.1.2; Munich: Beck, 1966; p. 344.

"Do it; but not all we other gods will approve it"; and coming down to Joh 2,19 "Destroy this temple and in three days I will raise it up." But neither it nor the standard NT Greek grammars cite the much more obvious usage in the sayings of Jesus. We may say: Jesus' grammar records a forerunner (with, as we saw, its own special ambiguity) of a developed conditional sentence.

The meaning of the overall structure "If A, then B" or "Do A and B will follow" in Jesus' sayings has been defined by Robinson:[94]

> ...the message of Jesus consists basically in a pronouncement to the present in view of the imminent eschatological future. It is precisely this polarity...that can be detected as a structuring tendency in the individual logia...a structure in terms of two members, which can be related to the Jewish apocalyptic doctrine of two aeons as its *religionsgeschichtliche* background. The first member, the pronouncement to the present, is related primarily to the "present evil aeon"; the second member, the allusion to the near future, looks to the "aeon to come."

But the doctrine of "two ages" appears formally in the Gospels only in scattered sayings often thought late: "a hundredfold now in this time, ...and in the age to come eternal life" (Mark 10,30); "...will not be forgiven, either in this age or in that to come" (Matt 12,32); "the sons of this age marry...but those accounted worthy to attain to that age do not marry..." (Luk 20,34-35, cf 16,8). It puts the two halves of Jesus' sayings too much on a par. We should take the cue for our interpretation from the antecedents of the sayings in the realm of "gravity." Recompense of evil—the state of affairs in which those who hate the enemy are in turn hated, the shedder of blood has his blood shed, the drowner is drowned—is verified in an actual future, perhaps some distance off; but that future simply vindicates a reality which has already been created in the present by one hating the enemy and shedding blood. Recompense of good—the state of affairs in which those who love enemies are rewarded and the giver receives—is in Jesus' understanding as certain as recompense of evil *or more so*, and likewise vindicates a reality instantly created in the present by the doing of good. Still, in contrast, it is not invariably or primarily realized in a future in time; rather, in some state of affairs which is just as real as future time *or more so*, but which Jesus' silence and the Semitic verb-structure prevent us from placing at some definite point on the arrow of time.[95]

---

94 James M. Robinson, "The Formal Structure of Jesus' Message," pp. 91-110 of Current Issues in New Testament Interpretation [Otto A. Piper Festschrift], W. Klassen & G. F. Snyder, eds.; New York: Harper, 1962; see p. 97.
95 The status of these more-than-futures is discussed further at III.42.

Chapter 19: Blessedness in Better Lands

This chapter treats parallels between Israel and Hellas in their symbolic treatment of the rewards flowing from blessedness. The formulas of blessedness define a fortunate one as assured a transfer, in the future or something like the future, long lasting or permanent, into a happier realm, more literal or more metaphorical, conceived of in quasi-geographical terms. We begin (19.1) with an agreement in the literary form of the Beatitude: "Blessed are those who do A, for they shall receive B." We continue (19.2) with a general discussion of the future life, and (19.3) with the status of verbs indicating the future. We then (19.4-9) discuss six ideal settings in which blessedness is concretely realized. Next (19.10) we look at the criteria of blessedness as they develop at a later period, in particular involving the idea of the separated soul. Finally (19.11) we treat the vocabulary agreement in seeing the soul as a *pearl*. Wherever possible we anchor the comparisons to Greek-Semitic shared vocabulary, certain or plausible; some previously treated (like the *jasper* of the garden of jewels [19.7]), others new. Much of what we learned in Vols. I and II is here reviewed in a different light. Matters Egyptian appear more here than elsewhere, even though I continue to regret my inability to cite actual Egyptian texts.

19.1 The Beatitude as literary form

At the end of the period we consider, Jesus states the literary form of the Beatitude in its briefest possible form (Luk 6,20-21):

μακάριοι οἱ πτωχοί, ὅτι ὑμετέρα ἐστὶν ἡ βασιλεία τοῦ θεοῦ.
μακάριοι οἱ πεινῶντες νῦν, ὅτι χορτασθήσεσθε.
μακάριοι οἱ κλαίοντες νῦν, ὅτι γελάσετε.

Blessed are you poor, for yours is the kingdom of God.
Blessed are you who hunger now, for you shall be filled.
Blessed are you who weep now, for you shall laugh.

While this form seems primitive, in fact Jesus has condensed previous formulations, both in Hebrew and Greek, which were more diffuse; the paradoxical form of his statements stands in implicit contrast to the more natural logic of earlier texts. The first of the three Beatitudes refers no more to the present instant than do the last two; for throughout Jesus' thought, the "kingdom of God" is a state of affairs which is breaking in, imminent, but has not yet quite arrived. Matt 5,3-12 enlarges Luke's four beatitudes into eight (or nine), as it seems interpreting Luke's short versions and adding non-paradoxical sayings; the Apocalypse perhaps counted seven attributed to Jesus and adds seven more.

Hebrew sometimes omits the second clause "for he shall receive B" and substitutes additional definitions of the first, "Blessed is the man who does A." Also, like Greek, instead of the B clause or in addition to it, Hebrew may include the contrasted fate of one who is not blessed. (Jesus makes the contrast in a separate format of Woes [Luk 6,24-26, Matt 23,13-32].) And the "future" status of the B clause may only be implicit. A relatively simple example with both A and B doubled is Prov 3,13-14:

וְאָדָם יָפִיק תְּבוּנָה   אַשְׁרֵי אָדָם מָצָא חָכְמָה
וּמֵחָרוּץ תְּבוּאָתָהּ   כִּי טוֹב סַחְרָהּ מִסְּחַר־כָּסֶף

"Blessed (LXX μακάριος) is the man who finds wisdom, and the man who gets understanding; for its gain is better than the gain of silver, and better than gold its profit." The peculiar exclamatory form אַשְׁרֵי, "Oh the blessedness of...!," seemingly a masculine plural construct, is treated by Joüon[1] as a feminine singular construct. The word for "gold," חָרוּץ, is the Phoenician one which went over to Greek (I.303), for as we have seen proverbs are an international literature.

Prov 8,34-36 with typical expansions illustrates the finding of *life*: "*Blessed* is the man who listens to me [Wisdom, with two further clauses]; *for* he who finds me finds *life*, and obtains favor from Yahweh; but he who *misses* me does violence to himself; all who hate me love death."

אַשְׁרֵי אָדָם שֹׁמֵעַ לִי...
וַיָּפֶק רָצוֹן מֵיהוָה   כִּי מֹצְאִי מָצָאֵי חַיִּים
כָּל־מְשַׂנְאַי אָהֲבוּ מָוֶת   וְחֹטְאִי חֹמֵס נַפְשׁוֹ

In the contrasted clause note the use of the verb חטא, mostly "sin," in its original sense "miss the mark"; it is correctly translated by the LXX as ἁμαρτάνοντες, which had the same history (I.56).

---

1   Paul Joüon, Grammaire de l'hébreu biblique, Rome: Institut biblique pontifical; 1947; 215.

Psalm 1, a preface to the whole book, elaborates both the A and B clauses, as well as the contrast with the "wicked." It begins "Blessed is the man who does not walk in the counsel of the wicked"

אַשְׁרֵי הָאִישׁ אֲשֶׁר לֹא הָלַךְ בַּעֲצַת רְשָׁעִים

and continues with two more negative definitions of his standing and sitting. Then a positive one "But his delight is in the law of Yahweh":

כִּי אִם בְּתוֹרַת יהוה חֶפְצוֹ

followed by another positive one. The B clause becomes a simple future (or imperfect) without "for," "And he shall be like a tree planted by rivers of water":

וְהָיָה כְּעֵץ שָׁתוּל עַל־פַּלְגֵי מָיִם

with two metaphorical additions and one literal one. Then the contrast, "The wicked are not so, but are like the chaff which the wind drives away," followed by a negative future, "Therefore the wicked will not stand in the judgement":

עַל־כֵּן לֹא־יָקֻמוּ רְשָׁעִים בַּמִּשְׁפָּט

itself doubled. Finally both sections are summed up, "For Yahweh knows the way of the righteous, but the way of the wicked shall perish":

כִּי יוֹדֵעַ יהוה דֶּרֶךְ צַדִּיקִים וְדֶרֶךְ רְשָׁעִים תֹּאבֵד

The whole is the elaboration of an underlying simple structure which nowhere quite appears as such in the Hebrew Bible, "Blessed are those who do A, for they shall receive B." The genius of Jesus was to extract that kernel.

Classical Greek beatitudes appear above all in a formula of the Eleusinian mysteries. The most exact structure is in a fragment of Sophocles,[2] "*Triply blessed* are those of mortals who go to the house of Hades having seen these ceremonies; *for* to them alone is *living* granted there; to the others all things there are ill":

... ὡς τρισόλβιοι
κεῖνοι βροτῶν, οἳ ταῦτα δερχθέντες τέλη
μόλωσ᾽ ἐς Ἅιδου· τοῖσδε γὰρ μόνοις ἐκεῖ
ζῆν ἔστι, τοῖς δ᾽ ἄλλοισι πάντ᾽ ἐκεῖ κακά.

Here we note the emphasis on *life* of Prov 8,34-36, as well as the contrast with the "others." A fragment of Pindar[3] allows the "for" to be understood, "Blessed is he who goes under the earth having seen those things; he knows the end of life, and he knows its Zeus-given beginning":

---

2   Sophocles frag. 837 TrGF (iv.553) from Plutarch.
3   Pindar frag. 121 Bowra; from Clement Alex. *Strom.* 3.17.2, who refers it to "the mysteries in Eleusis," περὶ τῶν ἐν Ἐλευσῖνι μυστηρίων.

ὄλβιος ὅστις ἰδὼν κεῖν᾽ εἶσ᾽ ὑπὸ χθόν·
  οἶδε μὲν βίου τελευτάν,
οἶδεν δὲ διόσδοτον ἀρχάν.

Both are working over the formula in the *Homeric Hymn* to Demeter (2.480-2) containing a contrast but no B clause with "for," "Blessed is whoever of men on earth has seen these things; but whoever is uninitiated in the sacred things and has no share in them never has as his lot such things once he is dead, down in the mouldy darkness":

ὄλβιος ὃς τάδ᾽ ὄπωπεν ἐπιχθονίων ἀνθρώπων·
ὃς δ᾽ ἀτελὴς ἱερῶν, ὅς τ᾽ ἄμμορος, οὔ ποθ᾽ ὁμοίων
αἶσαν ἔχει φθίμενός περ ὑπὸ ζόφῳ εὐρώεντι.

Richardson[4] notes

> ὄλβιος usually has a strong material connotation...So here, the prosperity which the Mysteries bring comes in this life as well as after death...But the Greeks were always aware that ὄλβος and πλοῦτος were gifts of the gods. Hence these words acquired religious overtones.

Unlike the Hebrew, the Eleusinian beatitudes suggest no moral criterion; the important thing is simply to have *seen* what happened there.

A Greek beatitude on the theme of knowing rather than seeing is in Empedocles,[5] "Blessed is he who has acquired wealth of divine insights; wretched is he in whom dwells a darkened understanding about the gods":

ὄλβιος ὃς θείων πραπίδων ἐκτήσατο πλοῦτον,
δειλὸς δ᾽, ᾧ σκοτόεσσα θεῶν πέρι δόξα μέμηλεν.

Compare Prov 3,13 (III.36 above). He is echoed by Vergil *Georg.* 2.490 *Felix qui potuit rerum cognoscere causas*. Homer in place of ὄλβιος has μάκαρ, which in the form μακάριος became standard later and appears in the Greek of Jesus' Beatitudes. *Odyssey* 5.306 "Triply blessed and four times are the Danaans who perished then..."[6]

τρισμάκαρες Δαναοὶ καὶ τετράκις οἳ τότ᾽ ὄλοντο.

The climax "three and four" also appears at Prov 30,15-31 and in Amos 1. Greek μάκαρ vocative appears at *Iliad* 3.182. But originally, it seems, μάκαρες mostly refers to the gods: thus *Iliad* 1.406 μάκαρες θεοί; of the chthonic gods Aeschylus *Choeph.* 476 μάκαρες χθόνιοι. At Hesiod *Opera* 141 of the semi-divinised heroes of the silver age "They are called the blessed dead under the earth,"

---

4   N. J. Richardson, The Homeric Hymn to Demeter; Oxford: Clarendon, 1974, 314.
5   Empedocles frag. 132, FVS[8] i.365.
6   Vergil translates it at *Aen.* 1.94 *O terque quaterque beati*.

τοὶ μὲν ὑποχθόνιοι μάκαρες θνητοὶ καλέονται.

Thus presumably the "Isles of the Blessed" (III.49 below), ἐν μακάρων νήσοισι *Opera* 171 and elsewhere, originally referred to the gods, though later it is applied to fully human heroes. On the other hand, μακάριος can only refer to human beings; Levin explains this from its being a kind of patronymic, "having a god as a father or protector." Hebrew has comparable semantic fields: בָּרוּךְ may describe either God or a human being, but אַשְׁרֵי a human being only.

The etymology of μάκαρ is enigmatic (II.10). There is no other adjective in -αρ and no reason to derive it from an unattested neuter noun. In principle Vermeule[7] accepts an Egyptian etymology; but there is no consensus on the original. Two authors compare Egyptian *m3ᶜ ḥrw* "justified of voice," applied to the dead one as identified with Osiris.[8] Another compares Egyptian *mᶜr* "fortunate," applied to the holy dead.[9] Pierce rejects both etymologies.[10] Rendsburg[11] with regret rejects Bernal's etymology to *m3ᶜ ḥrw* in favor of a highly speculative etymology from Semitic *brk* "bless." McGready[12] mentions neither; nor does Fournet, our most reliable analyst. We need an Egyptologist to study the phonetics and to cite actual hieroglyphic texts.

The grammar of a Beatitude is a hidden statement of cause and effect. It affirms that anyone who does A will reach the desirable result B; thus the good fortune of such a one can be celebrated in advance. Most often the desirable result is the translation of the fortunate one into a pleasant and perhaps death-free environment, whether seen more literally or more symbolically. The organization of this chapter classifies texts according to the topography of the better land that the blessed one inherits.

---

7   Vermeule, Aspects of Death 72-73.
8   Alexandre H. Krappe, "Μάκαρ," Revue de Philologie 66 (1940) 245-6; Constantin Daniel, "Des emprunts égyptiens dans le grec ancien," Studia et acta orientalia (Budapest) 4 (1962) 13-23. For the Egyptian see Erman-Grapow ii.17-18.
9   Bertrand Hemmerdinger, "Noms communs grecs d'origine égyptienne," Glotta 46 (1968) 238-247; for the Egyptian see Erman-Grapow ii.48.
10 Richard H. Pierce, "Egyptian loan-words in ancient Greek?," Symbolae Osloenses 46 (1971) 96-107, p. 105.
11 Gary A. Rendsburg, "*Black Athena*: An Etymological Response," Arethusa Special Issue, Fall 1989, The Challenge of *Black Athena*, 67-82; p. 79.
12 A. G. McGready, "Egyptian Words in the Greek Vocabulary," Glotta 46 (1968) 247-254.

19.2 The future life and the Egyptians

It is natural to interpret the seemingly future expectations in literary beatitudes as the hope of life beyond death. We associate Israel with the resurrection of the dead, Hellas with the immortality of the soul. But compared with the peoples around them, each nation, above all in its classical period, is strikingly this-worldly. So Spronk, reviewing research into a "beatific afterlife in ancient Israel,"[13]

> As soon as the Old Testament was not regarded anymore as a collection of proof-texts to be used in support of the traditions of the church, it appeared to contain very few references to a happy afterlife and to speak rather negatively about the world of the dead.

Emily Vermeule will not let us read *Odyssey* 11 literally:[14] the actions of the heroes in the underworld "are not true reflections of popular beliefs about the dead, so much as stage directions for a theatrical mysterious scene." Behind the poetry, she states (p. 123) the true state of affairs (and compare another quotation from her at I.55):

> It is part of the Greek legacy to the West, and almost a definition of humanism, that the Greeks found grief, defect and mortality, when faced with gallantry of mind, to be better than unearthly states of blessed existence.

How did the notions of resurrection and immortality grow from those soils? Because (I suggest) Israel and Hellas broke through in parallel to a *new realism* about death; see the texts laid out at I.56-58, II.37. Precisely by that realism they were able to transcend death.

In the end Spronk (p. 344), with much difficulty, concludes that Israel did indeed have some concept of a "beatific afterlife." Why is it then so muted?

> This reluctance to speak about help of YHWH after death is neither due to a lack of confidence in this matter nor to the fact that the Israelites would have lacked the natural human interest in life after death, but primarily to the fear of becoming entangled in the Canaanite religious ideas about life and death.

Vermeule (p. 96) tentatively sets Greek rationalism against a presumed background of Mycenaean religious ideas, but warns us:

---

13   Klaas Spronk, Beatific Afterlife in Ancient Israel and in the Ancient Near East; Alter Orient und Altes Testament, Band 219; Neukirchen-Vluyn: Neukirchener Verlag, 1986; p. 66.

14   Vermeule (fn 7 above) 29.

The Mycenaeans are unfairly blamed for being old, dark, bloody and chthonic, bound to peculiar vegetation cults and ancient Aegean mother goddesses, an irrational and illiterate people too primitive for the ordered splendors of Olympian religion and the civilized restraints of classical thought.

Still, neither Canaanite nor Mycenaean religious ideas are easy to reconstruct in any detail. What we can say confidently about Israelites and Greeks is that each formed many ideas over against *Egypt*. Martin Bernal, who in *Black Athena* derives much of Greek culture from Egyptian, misses the novel humanism in which Greece transcends Egypt, and the fact that in it Greece is comparable to Israel rather than to Egypt.

Both peoples found Egyptians xenophobic: it was an abomination for Egyptians to eat bread with Hebrews (Gen 43,32); they would not kiss a Greek for fear of contamination nor eat food cut with a Greek knife (Herodotus 2.41.3). Both note Egyptian funerary practice as an exotic curiosity. Of three grades of embalming (ταρίχευσις), each took 70 days (Herodotus 2.86-88). According to Gen 50,3 only 40 days are required for embalming, but the Egyptians mourned for Jacob 70 days, and perhaps there is some confusion. Phoenicians used myrrh for embalming (II.326). Herodotus 2.86.5-6 lists substances used in embalming: myrrh (σμύρνη), cassia (κασίη), frankincense (λιβανωτός) and nitre (λίτρον); all have equivalents in Biblical Hebrew. Nitre (I.241) is Egyptian *ntrj*,[15] cf. νίτρον Hippocrates (*Airs* 7.53), Jer 2,22 נֶתֶר. Also gum (κόμμι, Herodotus 2.86.6), Egyptian *ḳmj.t*,[16] appears in the Mishna (*Shabb.* XII.4) as קוֹמוֹס.[17]

We saw further (I.209) that the body to be embalmed (Herodotus 2.86.6) is wrapped with "a shroud of byssos," σινδόνος βυσσίνης, a beautiful international phrase appearing in Akkadian, Rabbinic, and Josephus. Since σινδών appears also in Egyptian as *šnḏwt* (II.295, original language uncertain), we should ask the Egyptologists whether a mortuary text exists with the three words "nitre, gum, *sindon*". The shroud especially made its way to other lands: Joseph of Arimathea "wrapped in a shroud" Jesus' body, ἐνείλησεν τῇ σινδόνι (Mark 15,46); "Rabbi was buried in a single shroud,"

בסדין אחד נקבר רבי

(Jer. Talm. *Kilaim* 32b4) so as not to encumber his resurrection body. The text goes on to explain "A garment that descends with a man to Sheol returns with him,"

כסות היורדת עם אדם לשאול היה באה עמו

---

15 Erman-Grapow ii.366.
16 Erman-Grapow v.39.
17 With an Aramaic translation קומא at Bab. Talm. *Gittin* 19a.

19.3 The grammatical status of the future

The beatitude in its final definitive form, that given it by Jesus (III.35 above), has its "for" or B clause expressed in Greek future verbs, χορτασθήσεσθε "you shall be filled," γελάσετε "you shall laugh." In Syriac (as in Psalm 1, III.37 above) they come out as Semitic imperfects, (Luk 6,21) תסבעון "you shall be full," תגחכון "you shall laugh." Classical Hebrew beatitudes, like those at Eleusis, leave it more open whether they refer to a present or a future fulfilment. Can we properly talk of future verbs at all?

An ambitious beginning linguist switched his major when the lecturer warned him, "There is no future in Indo-European"... Most Greek futures are slightly modified aorist subjunctives. Thus at Rev 14,13 "Blessed are the dead who henceforth die in the Lord...so that they may rest (ἵνα ἀναπαήσονται) from their labors," the MSS show variants ὅτι (P[47]) for ἵνα, and ἀναπαύσωνται (aor. subj.) and ἀναπαύσονται (future). At *Iliad* 7.29 "let us halt (παύσωμεν) war" the verb is aorist subjunctive, the form with long vowel standardized in Attic; but so is it at 21.314 "so that we may halt (παύσομεν) the savage man," the form with short vowel standardized in Attic as future. In the New Testament, when the difference in pronunciation between long and short was being lost and syntax was loosened, the two forms are close to optional variants. Since (as the Greeks knew well) we can never absolutely predict the future, any statement about the future will express volition or uncertainty.

Latin makes what we call its futures in two manners, depending on the conjugation and aspect of the verb, whether active or designating a state of being. Thus at Matt 5,6-7 "Blessed are they who hunger and thirst for righteousness, for they shall be filled (Vg *quoniam ipsi saturabuntur*). Blessed are the merciful, for they shall obtain mercy (*quia ipsi misericordiam consequentur*)." Verbs of the third and fourth conjugations make a future like *consequentur* from the present subjunctive *consequantur* (Latin having lost the aorist) with a change of vowel as in the Greek; verbs of the first and second conjugation make it by adding a form of the verb "to be," *satura-bu-ntur* like English "they *shall be* filled." The two formations, which grammars lump together as future, have slightly different meanings corresponding to the status of the verb. Third conjugation verbs, old consonantal stems having mostly active sense, modify a wish to form the future; first and second conjugation verbs, derived with a vowel suffix and often "stative" in sense, make a statement about the present, "they are *going to be* filled."

Any original Semitic that we can imagine had no unambiguous way of indicating the future by a verb alone, and Biblical Hebrew (unlike Greek and Latin) never clearly filled the gap. In the Syriac of Jesus' Beatitudes (as in the B clauses of Psalm 1) the B clauses are all in the "imperfect." The Semitic verb has two principal forms. In the perfect, denoting a completed action, the verb root as primary comes first, and is followed by a suffix indicating the person and number (and in some forms gender) of the subject. In the imperfect a prefix describing the subject (as primary, with some ambiguity) comes first, followed by the verb root (as liable to uncertainty) and perhaps a suffix denoting number. Semitic grammar does not presuppose a linear timeline of past, present and future; and even in Indo-European with its clear present ("primary") and past ("secondary") tenses, the aspect of the action is equally important, whether single and completed, or repeated and incomplete. In the moods, time is lost and aspect remains. In Semitic, the imperfect can represent (from our point of view) various types of actions in the present, continued actions in the past, and possible events in the future. But those distinctions are not made as such. Hence if there should prove to be states of affairs that cannot easily be placed on a timeline, Semitic has no problem about speaking of them in the imperfect—or even the perfect, if their certainty can be surely affirmed.

What then is the B or "for" clause of a Beatitude speaking about? It gives the reason for the affirmation (or exclamation) of the A clause, "Blessed is the one who does A" or "O the blessedness of the one who does A!" In Greek it appears to be placed in a linear future. But still two thousand years later we are waiting for the hungry to be fed and the mourners to be comforted. If Jesus truly expected the kingdom of God to irrupt fully into the time sequence chronicled by historians, and in the near future, he was in error. The alternative is that his Greek futures (which are surely just a translation of Aramaic imperfects) in fact like many Hebrew imperfects point to a state of affairs partially or wholly *out of history*. Literal-minded ages think of the general resurrection of the body as necessarily coming at a definite date in the temporal sequence—even though the sequence may wind up at that point and give way to eternity. But the Semitic languages are under no such necessity.

Most modern lovers of literature, whether religious-minded or secularist, admire both Hebrew and Greek texts for the realistic light that they throw on the complexities of human motivation: Thucydides' unsparing portrayal of the overweening pride that brought Athens down; the Court Chronicle (II Sam 9-20) for its objective depiction of the complex relations among David, Absalom, Joab and all the others. Those texts are also admired for their faithful delineation of human dignity in the face of certain downfall and death. It is only natural then that many readers should take with equal seriousness what the texts say, for example in beatitudes, about the coming and certain reward of virtue. Classicists tend to err by taking the depiction of the Islands of the Blessed or Plato's better world of jewels as merely metaphorical, pointing to something unknown in itself either to the old author or to us, perhaps only imaginary. Religious Jews and Christians tend to err by taking the depiction of the resurrection of the body or the New Jerusalem as merely literal, to be accepted or rejected in the same simple-minded way by us as (they presume) it was intended by the author. Here I try to discuss the representations of both Hellas and Israel as nearly as possible on the same level.

Since the present world is the only one we know, descriptions of a better world must inevitably take the form of the present one somehow transformed. In the six sections that follow (19.4-9) I take up themes of a mythical geography, pointing to the reward of the blessed, and to some degree shared by Israel and Hellas. The settings vary in the closeness of the parallels, in the degree to which they involve common vocabulary, and in the type of expectations they raise. They are interconnected, and our arrangement is to some degree arbitrary. In some, Egyptian themes appear which I cannot document to the same degree of exactness. In others, the Semitic equivalents are only partial. I propose that in their different ways they all point to the possibility of a fulfilment outside the temporal sequence rather than within it, but illustrated by various idealizations of the earth's geography. They are arranged roughly by the degree of idealization, from less to more.

19.4 The meadow of lilies

We do not know what the initiants saw at Eleusis to give them the certainty of future life: perhaps the resurrection of Persephone from the underworld? But the Homeric Hymn to Demeter, our principal source, begins with a scene which imprints itself firmly on our memory: Persephone with the Oceanids "in a soft meadow" (λειμῶν' ἄμ μαλακόν *Hom. Hymn* 2.7), no doubt stream-watered, picking flowers—roses, crocus, violets, iris, hyacinth; and above all the narcissus which Gaia pushed up as a snare (δόλον)[18] to her, and from whose roots Hades

---

18   Compare the "snares of Sheol" חֶבְלֵי שְׁאוֹל Ps 18,6.

sprang into the upper world. In the list which Persephone herself gives of the flowers (*Hom. Hymn* 2.427) she includes "lilies, a wonder to see," λείρια, θαῦμα ἰδέσθαι. There is a nice agreement with Hebrew in that the elements in a triple division of the universe (see I.267 & II.56) *rejoice*, and in the same order heaven-earth-sea. "And the whole broad heavens above and the whole earth laughed [at the beauty of the narcissus] and the salt swell of the sea" (*Hom. Hymn* 2.13-14):

... πᾶς δ᾽ οὐρανὸς εὐρὺς ὕπερθε
γαῖά τε πᾶσ᾽ ἐγέλασσε καὶ ἁλμυρὸν οἶδμα θαλάσσης

Ps 96,11 "Let the heavens rejoice and the earth be glad; let the sea roar, and all that is in it":

יִשְׂמְחוּ הַשָּׁמַיִם וְתָגֵל הָאָרֶץ   יִרְעַם הַיָּם וּמְלֹאוֹ

The scene of Persephone's abduction (on the border between a this-worldly and other-worldly landscape) is the ill-defined "Nysian plain," Νύσιον ἂμ πεδίον (*Hom. Hymn* 2.17). We saw (II.4) that Cicero (*Verr.* 2.4.106) locates the myth of Ceres and Proserpina at Enna of Sicily. The case of Persephone reminds us of mortal Europa. Herodotus begins his History (1.2, cf. 4.147) by rationalizing the abduction of the Phoenician king's daughter Europa. Hesiod told the story in its original mythical form in his lost *Catalogue of Women* and we have a summary:[19] "When Zeus saw Europa the daughter of Phoenix in a meadow with maidens picking flowers he fell in love with her." The setting and theme are identical to that of Persephone, only the god and his ruse are changed. The story is told most fully by the Hellenistic poet Moschus (ab. 150 BC) in his *Europa* (2.32), which tells how "she picked sweet-smelling lilies from the meadow,"

ἢ ὁπότ᾽ ἐκ λειμῶνος ἐΰπνοα λείρι᾽ ἀμέργοι

in addition to all the other flowers they picked (2.63-71). In general Moschus works over the Hymn to Demeter. The scene of Europa's story that captured the imagination of vase painters was Zeus as the bull carrying her off across the sea, full of marine life. Sidon in autonomous coinage under Rome shows Europa on the bull, bringing the Greek motif back to its supposed original home.[20]

In a fragment of Pindar[21] the heroic dead live in "meadows of purple roses," φοινικορόδοις δ᾽ ἐνὶ λειμώνεσσι shaded with *libanos*. A meadow

---

19   Scholiast on *Iliad* 12.292, Hesiod frag. 140 Merkelbach-West; see papyrus fragments of the actual verses, frag. 141.

20   G. F. Hill, Catalogue of the Greek Coins of Phoenicia; London: British Museum, 1910; Plate XXIII.

21   Pindar frag. 114 Bowra, from two quotations by Plutarch; see I.211-212 for text and III.52 below.

is regularly "soft," μαλακός as being stream-watered; *Odyssey* 6.292 of Scheria, in the grove of Athena "a spring flows, and about it is a meadow,"

...ἐν δὲ κρήνη ναίει, ἀμφὶ δὲ λειμών.

The blessed underworld of Vergil has its "green valley" (*conualle uirenti, Aen.* 6.679) and "fields renewed by brooks" (*prata recentia riuis* 6.674). Similar is an ideal landscape of the Psalms. We noted the "tree planted by rivers of water" of Ps 1,3 (III.37 above); so at the familiar Ps 23,2 "He makes me lie down in green pastures, he leads me beside still waters,"

בִּנְאוֹת דֶּשֶׁא יַרְבִּיצֵנִי   עַל־מֵי מְנֻחוֹת יְנַהֲלֵנִי

We expect to find the Shulamite in such a setting, Cant 2,1, "I am a crocus[22] of Sharon,[23] a lily of the valleys (Vg *lilium conuallium*)":

אֲנִי חֲבַצֶּלֶת הַשָּׁרוֹן   שׁוֹשַׁנַּת הָעֲמָקִים

Greek has three words for "lily" (cf. I.331). κρίνον (since Herodotus 2.92 κρίνεα pl.) has no etymology. σοῦσον, mostly known as lily ointment, σούσινον, is a loan from שׁוֹשַׁנָּה. The λείριον of Persephone and Europa is known to Homer, but only in peculiar metaphors, *Iliad* 3.152 ὄπα λειριόεσσαν "lily-like (?) voice" of the cicada.[24] The abnormal parallel λείριον / *līlium* marks the word as Mediterranean, as we would expect from the use of the lily in Minoan art. See then Hittite *alil, alel* "flower"[25] and Egyptian *ḥrr.t*.[26] The word continued in Coptic, and the Bohairic translator[27] of Matt 6,28 "lilies of the field" (τὰ κρίνα τοῦ ἀγροῦ) used the old word *hreri* ⲚⲚⲒⲤⲢⲎⲢⲒ Ⲛ̄ⲦⲈ ⲦⲔⲞⲒ just as the Vulgate did, *lilia agri*. Fayyumic *hlēli* shows the same variation r/l as between Greek and Latin.[28]

Jesus' Semitic verse about the ravens and the lilies (Luk 12,22-31, a little more concrete than Matt 6,25-33), is in a special way an ideal landscape. Readers may be disturbed that "providential" care for food

22 Cf. Akkadian *ḫabaṣillatu* "fresh shoot of reed" (CAD); assuming that the ṣ was once a ḍ, we might compare ἀσφόδελος "asphodel" as a Mediterranean noun.
23 At I.35 we tentatively compared "Sharon" with Greek Σάρων near Troizen and the Saronic gulf.
24 Janko on *Iliad* 13.830 χρόα λειριόεντα ("lily-fragrant skin"?) in the Cambridge Iliad thinks λείριον in all senses from an adjective λείριος "bright," and λείριον "lily" a derivative of this. But that does not explain Latin *līlium* or the other seeming cognates. See II.300.
25 Johannes Friedrich, Hethitisches Wörterbuch...; Heidelberg: Winter, 1952; 19.
26 Erman-Grapow iii.149.
27 The Coptic Version of the New Testament in the Northern Dialect; Oxford: Clarendon, 1898; 4 vols.; i.42.
28 W. E. Crum, A Coptic Dictionary; Oxford: Clarendon, 1939; 704.

and clothing is presupposed: "Of how much more value are you than the birds!...How much more will he clothe you?" Are there then no hungry, no naked in the world? I cannot easily find a commentator who says so, but the passage can be taken seriously only if it is about the new life of the resurrection: it is in the coming kingdom that all are made to lie down at table and clothed more splendidly than Solomon, as Paul expects to be "clothed upon" (II Kor 5,4, see I.58, III.143). So the Galilaean field in which the ravens are fed and the lilies clothed becomes transparent to a realm in which no human beings are in want.

19.5 A mountain in the north

Three Hebrew texts describe a mountain in the north where death is overcome; they bring in also two other themes which below we treat separately, the realm without tears (in 19.6 below) and the jewelled realm (19.7). Isa 25,6-8, seemingly a fragment, speaks of "this mountain" but does not further define it: "And Yahweh of hosts will make for all peoples on this mountain a feast of fat things...":

וְעָשָׂה יהוה צְבָאוֹת לְכָל־הָעַמִּים בָּהָר הַזֶּה מִשְׁתֵּה שְׁמָנִים

And it goes on, "He has swallowed up death forever,[29] and Lord Yahweh will wipe away the tear from all faces,"

בִּלַּע הַמָּוֶת לָנֶצַח וּמָחָה אֲדֹנָי יהוה דִּמְעָה מֵעַל כָּל־פָּנִים

Here only, in a phrase naturally much echoed in the New Testament, does the Hebrew Bible with full clarity define a victory over death. Ugaritic Mot is also put to death, but the story is different:[30]

> tiḥd bn ilm mt, bḥrb tbqᶜnn, bḫtr tdrynn, bišt tšrpnn, brḥm tṭḥnn, bšd tdrᶜnn
>
> [ᶜAnat] seizes the son of the gods Mot, with a sword she cleaves him, with a fan winnows him, with fire burns him, with a mill grinds him, in the field sows him.

Here mysteriously Mot after being cleaved gets the full treatment applied to grain—apparently with the expectation of his rising again. Milton (*Par. Lost* 3.250-253) in his highest vowel-harmony has Christ exploit the paradox:

---

29   The reading at I Kor 15,54, κατεπόθη ὁ θάνατος εἰς νῖκος "Death has been swallowed up in victory," not derived from the LXX, shows that the first verb was read as passive.

30   KTU 1.6.II.30-35; tr. ANET³ 140b; UNP 136.

> But I shall rise Victorious, and subdue
> My Vanquisher, spoild of his vanted spoile;
> Death his deaths wound shall then receive, & stoop
> Inglorious, of his mortall sting disarm'd.

Ez 28,11-19 is a lament over the fallen "king of Tyre" (perhaps the god Melqarth) which gives a Phoenician version of the myth of "Eden the garden of God": this garden has no trees but is instead a garden of jewels (19.7 below) and gold with which the king was "covered," and seems identical with the "holy mountain of God." Here is another mountain related to Tyre and surely north of Israel which through its jewels partakes of eternity.

Isa 14,12-20 is another lament, this time more ironical, over fallen "Day Star son of Dawn" who said in his heart "I will go up to heaven, above the stars of El; I will set my throne on high; and I will sit on the mountain of assembly, on the flanks of Saphon

$$\text{וְאֵשֵׁב בְּהַר־מוֹעֵד בְּיַרְכְּתֵי צָפוֹן}$$

I will go up over the heights of the clouds, I will be like ʿElyon." Hebrew צָפוֹן came to mean "north," but originally named Kasios the mountain of Ugarit (I.98-105); it is surely a mountain-name in this phrase, compare Isa 37,24 יַרְכְּתֵי לְבָנוֹן "on the flanks of Lebanon." Hebrew knows a divine assembly over which Yahweh presides:[31] Ps 82,1 "Elohim has taken his place in the council of El (LXX ἐν συναγωγῇ θεῶν); in the midst of the gods he holds judgment,"[32]

$$\text{אֱלֹהִים נִצָּב בַּעֲדַת־אֵל} \qquad \text{בְּקֶרֶב אֱלֹהִים יִשְׁפֹּט}$$

Perhaps Kasios was the site where the gods assembled. To the extent that we can identify these three texts, Hebrews knew, likely through their neighbors, of a divine mountain in the north where the gods assembled and death was overcome.

Likewise Greeks knew Olympos as a mountain to the north where the gods assembled. Its immutability is emphasized in the unique text *Odyssey* 6.42-46

> Οὔλυμπόνδ', ὅθι φασὶ θεῶν ἕδος ἀσφαλὲς αἰεὶ
> ἔμμεναι· οὔτ' ἀνέμοισι τινάσσεται οὔτε ποτ' ὄμβρῳ
> δεύεται οὔτε χιὼν ἐπιπίλναται, ἀλλὰ μαλ' αἴθρη
> πέπταται ἀνέφελος, λευκὴ δ' ἐπιδέδρομεν αἴγλη·
> τῷ ἔνι τέρπονται μάκαρες θεοὶ ἤματα πάντα.

"...to Olympos, where they say the seat of the gods is forever safe; it is not shaken by winds or ever wet by rain, nor does snow approach it; but a cloudless aether is spread out, and a bright gleam runs over

---

31   See II.54, 66, 98, 105.
32   In Ps 82 as rarely elsewhere the expected *Yhwh* is replaced by *Elohim*.

it; in it the *blessed* gods rejoice all their days." The Greek was widely imitated. Lucretius 3.18-22 describes "quiet seats" untouched by wind, cloud or snow. Vergil builds phrases from Lucretius into his description of "Elysium" with a beautifully disparate pair of predicates (*Aen.* 6.639-640) *Largior hic campos aether et lumine uestit / purpureo*, "Here the aether that envelops the fields is broader and with a purple light." Tennyson applies it to "the island-valley of Avilion" in the *Morte d'Arthur* "Where falls not hail, or rain, or any snow"; and to the abode of the gods in *Lucretius*, "Where never creeps a cloud, or moves a wind /...Nor sound of human sorrow mounts to mar / Their sacred everlasting calm!" Elsewhere Olympus is more realistically described as snowy, νιφόεντος Ὀλύμπου (Hesiod *Theog.* 794, cf. *Iliad* 1.420 etc.). The Olympus of *Odyssey* 6 can only be free of snow because it pierces *above* the realm of clouds (see Isa 14,14 above) into the immutable realm of aether.

19.6 *The ends of the earth*

"Ends of the earth" in Greek names, among other sites, the Islands of the Blessed, which first appear in Hesiod *Opera* 166-173[33] in his account of the fourth race of heroes, "demigods" (ἡμίθεοι 160), including those who fought at Thebes "for the flocks of Oedipus" and at Troy over Helen.

ἔνθ', ἦ τοι τοὺς μὲν θανάτου τέλος ἀμφεκάλυψεν,
τοὺς δὲ δίχ' ἀνθρώπων βίοτον καὶ ἤθε' ὀπάσσας,
Ζεὺς Κρονίδης κατένασσε πατὴρ ἐν πείρασι γαίης,
καὶ τοὶ μὲν ναίουσιν ἀκηδέα θυμὸν ἔχοντες
ἐν μακάρων νήσοισι παρ' Ὠκεανὸν βαθυδίνην·
ὄλβιοι ἥρωες, τοῖσιν μελιηδέα καρπὸν
τρὶς ἔτεος θάλλοντα φέρει ζείδωρος ἄρουρα.

There [at Thebes and Troy] the end of death covered some of them; but to others father Zeus son of Kronos gave a living and abodes apart from men, and established them at the *ends of the earth*. And they dwell there with a mind free from care in the Islands of the Blessed by Ocean with its deep currents, fortunate heroes, for whom the grain-giving earth bears honey-sweet crop, ripening three times a year.

---

33 Omitting the five verses ("173a-e" in West's numbering) following 173 in some papyri, of which the first ("173a") was formerly added from late sources as vs 169, here omitted.

Their admission comes, it would seem, from their social status both in war and peace. We noted above (III.39) that the "Islands of the Blessed" probably once referred to a home of the gods; West however observes "But by Hesiod's time μακάρων may have come to be understood of the fortunate pensioners." The "ends of the earth," πείρατα γαίης, is a more widely used description. It appears at the peculiar myth of *Iliad* 14.200-207 (= nearly 14.301-306); Hera goes there to reconcile Oceanus the "origin of the gods" (θεῶν γένεσιν) and mother Tethys. (Here, in contradiction to Hesiod, Ocean and Earth are the origin of the gods.)[34]

The Islands of the Blessed appear again in a long development in Pindar's second Olympian ode, vss 56-80, now strongly moralized. The arrogant who die up here are immediately punished under earth (56-60). Others are rewarded in two phases. In the first, with equal nights and days, in sunshine, the good (ἐσλοί) get a living without labor, neither farming nor seafaring, but "with those honored by the gods, all who rejoiced in keeping their word[35] live a *life without tears*, while the others have pain not to be dwelt on" (61-67)

> ...ἀλλὰ παρὰ μὲν τιμίοις
> θεῶν οἵτινες ἔχαιρον εὐορκίαις
> ἄδακρυν νέμονται
> αἰῶνα, τοὶ δ' ἀπροσόρατον ὀκχέοντι πόνον.

This stage is temporary and still subject to temptation. But those who have kept their soul (ψυχάν) free from injustice for three times in both realms (ἐστρὶς ἑκατέρωθε, i.e. here and below) go the way of Zeus[36] (Διὸς ὁδόν) to the tower of Kronos [unknown]; "there ocean breezes blow around the Island of the Blessed" (μακάρων νᾶσον); on land and sea trees bear gold for chaplets (68-74). There Rhadamanthys sits [as judge] beside the husband of Rhea [Kronos] along with Peleus, [Phoenician!] Kadmos and Achilles (75-80).

Here in the Island of the Blessed (now singular), along with the heroes also sit the Titan Kronos and demigod Rhadamanthys—perhaps the original "blessed" inhabitants. Already in the first stage the heroes "live a tearless existence" (ἄδακρυν νέμονται αἰῶνα) as in Isa 25,8. The Hebrew theme recurs at Ps 116,8-9 (cf. 56,14) "For you

---

34   At *Odyssey* 9.284 the formula ἐπὶ πείρασι γαίης is used in a local sense, "at the boundaries of your land" (Scheria). For the formula in *Odyssey* 4.563 (the Elysian fields) and in the *Hymn* to Aphrodite (5.227) see III.51 below.

35   Covenant keeping, like oath keeping, also brings permanent life. Ps 103,17-18 "But the steadfast love of Yahweh is from everlasting to everlasting...to those who keep his covenant."

36   Cf Jer 5,4 "the way of Yahweh," דֶּרֶךְ יהוה, LXX ὁδὸν κυρίου.

have delivered my soul from death, *my eye from tears*, my foot from stumbling; I shall walk before Yahweh in the lands of the living":

כִּי חִלַּצְתָּ נַפְשִׁי מִמָּוֶת אֶת־עֵינִי מִן־דִּמְעָה אֶת רַגְלִי מִדֶּחִי
אֶתְהַלֵּךְ לִפְנֵי יהוה בְּאַרְצוֹת הַחַיִּים

The "land (or lands) of the living" (cf. Ps 27,13 and III.61) suggests at least an embryonic concept of a better realm where death is absent. Isa 25,8 is quoted (again not from the LXX) with reference to Jerusalem at Rev 7,17 (cf. 21,4) "And God will wipe away every tear from their eyes," καὶ ἐξαλείψει ὁ θεὸς πᾶν δάκρυον ἐκ τῶν ὀφθαλμῶν αὐτῶν. Rev 21,4 adds a further reminiscence of Isa 25,8 "And death shall be no more"; Rev 7,17 adds "and he will lead them to fountains of waters of life," καὶ ὁδηγήσει αὐτοὺς ἐπὶ ζωῆς πηγὰς ὑδάτων which suggests an echo of Isa 49,10 "and by springs of water he will guide them," and more distantly of Ps 23.

Both Hesiod and Pindar on the "Islands of the Blessed" are working over what Menelaus is told (*Odyssey* 4.563-8) by truthful Egyptian Proteus, the Old Man of the Sea. Menelaus will not die back in Argos:

ἀλλά σ᾽ ἐς Ἠλύσιον πεδίον καὶ πείρατα γαίης
ἀθάνατοι πέμψουσιν, ὅθι ξανθὸς Ῥαδάμανθυς,
τῇ περ ῥηΐστη βιοτὴ πέλει ἀνθρώποισιν·
οὐ νιφετός, οὔτ᾽ ἄρ χειμὼν πολὺς οὔτε ποτ᾽ ὄμβρος,
ἀλλ᾽ αἰεὶ Ζεφύροιο λιγὺ πνείοντος ἀήτας
Ὠκεανὸς ἀνίησιν ἀναψύχειν ἀνθρώπους.

But the Immortals will bring you to the Elysian Field and the *ends of the earth*, where is blond Rhadamanthys, where life is easiest for men; there is no snow, nor much winter, nor ever rain; but always Ocean sends up breezes of fresh-blowing Zephyrus to refresh men.

Here only the Elysian Field (the name unexplained) appears originally in Greek; what is said about it accords almost completely with the Islands of the Blessed. At *Odyssey* 4 only Menelaus is said worthy to go there (on the grounds of his being husband of Helen and so son-in-law of Zeus, vs 569); but Hesiod and Pindar add other heroes, generally or by name.

In a reversal of the rape of Proserpina and Europa, Tithonus was carried off by Eos the Dawn; "he lived by the streams of Ocean at the *ends of the earth*" (*Hom. Hymn* to Aphrodite 5.227):

ναῖε παρ᾽ Ὠκεανοῖο ῥοῆς ἐπὶ πείρασι γαίης.

At I.111-112 we noted that Eos carrying off Tithonus appears in Attic vases as *winged*; and with Vermeule compared Ps 139,9 "Let me take the wings of the dawn, and dwell in the uttermost parts of the Sea":

אֶשָּׂא כַנְפֵי־שָׁחַר   אֶשְׁכְּנָה בְּאַחֲרִית יָם

LXX εἰς τὰ ἔσχατα τῆς θαλάσσης. It seems that Eos also has her dwelling, perhaps at the end of her day's course, near the Islands of the Blessed, for it is by Ocean at the ends of the earth. In contrast with the heroes of the Islands, those carried off find it bittersweet: for Tithonus has no choice in the matter, and eventually withers away; the Psalmist is trying to evade Yahweh but does not succeed. Still for better or worse we have a Hebrew parallel to the far-off abode by Ocean.

In Hebrew the girl of Canticles is herself identified with the whole gamut of fragrances (Cant 4,13-14; I.91-97). In Greek all the sites are scented with Phoenician spices. *Iliad* 8.1, "Eos with her saffron garment went out over all the earth,"

Ἠὼς μὲν κροκόπεπλος ἐκίδνατο πᾶσαν ἐπ' αἶαν

Her peplos is either dyed or scented with saffron, as her *croceum...cubile* (Vergil, *Georg.* 1.447, I.71); and the abode of the Blessed is shady with libanos. Pindar in a fragment of a *Dirge*[37] (cited I.212, III.45) describes the surroundings and life of the heroic dead without here naming it. Their happiness (ὄλβος) is complete, their dwelling is in "meadows of purple roses, shaded with libanos, hung with golden fruits"; and the whole place is fragrant from the incense of continual sacrifices. And in a nice agreement with Egyptian texts and monuments he defines the occupations of heroes in that better world.

Pindar goes on to say that of the dead below, "some delight in horses and games, some in checkers (πεσσοῖς), some in lyres." They are following the example of Penelope's suitors (shortly themselves to go below the earth) who "gladdened their hearts with checkers outside the gates" (*Odyssey* 1.107):

πεσσοῖσι προπάροιθε θυράων θυμὸν ἔτερπον

Vermeule[38] shows an Attic black-figured amphora with Aias and Achilles at a gaming-board, and another such board with winged daimons holding magic staffs. This is an Egyptian theme; on p. 77 she shows a painting from Thebes of the 19th Dynasty of one playing a board-game with "the Invisible Opponent." Plato says (*Phaedrus* 274C) that the Egyptian god Thoth "invented games of checkers and dice," Θεύθ...εὑρεῖν πεττείας καὶ κυβείας. A possible Near Eastern etymology for πεσσός, originally just "pebble," appears at Mark 15,24 Peshitto "and they threw lots for them," ווארמיו עליהין פסא (namely, the soldiers for Jesus' garments), for βάλλοντες κλῆρον. Mark cites the LXX of Ps 22,19 יַפִּילוּ גוֹרָל where גּוֹרָל was originally "pebble" (II.22). So ψῆφος "coun-

---

37   Pindar frag. 114 Bowra.
38   Vermeule pp. 80-81.

ter, vote" was once "pebble."[39] ἀστράγαλοι meant both "knuckle-bones" and "dice."

So perhaps did κύβος although attested is only "cubical die."[40] Dice in various metaphors are constant in classical Greek poetry; see particularly Sophocles[41] "the dice of Zeus always fall favorably" (no doubt for Zeus...):

ἀεὶ γὰρ εὖ πίπτουσιν οἱ Διὸς κύβοι

Do the gods play games with us?[42] (Einstein explicitly said that "God does not play dice with the universe.") The dice are attested as Egyptian by Herodotus 2.122, who says of his mythical king Rhampsinitus that "he went down living to the place that the Hellenes believe to be Hades, and there played dice with Demeter; sometimes he defeated her, sometimes he was defeated by her":

ζωὸν καταβῆναι κάτω ἐς τὸν οἱ Ἕλληνες Ἀίδην νομίζουσι εἶναι, κἀκεῖθι συγκυβεύειν τῇ Δήμητρι, καὶ τὰ μὲν νικᾶν αὐτήν, τὰ δὲ ἐσσοῦσθαι ὑπ' αὐτῆς.

Demeter here is surely Egyptian Isis.[43] Likewise Plutarch[44] has Hermes playing checkers with the Moon, Ἑρμῆν...παίξαντα πεττία πρὸς τὴν Σελήνην. M. Masson[45] compares Arabic كَعْب *ka*ᶜ*b(un)* which can mean both "knucklebone" and (with different plural) "die"; اَلْكَعْبَة *al-ka*ᶜ*batu* is "the Kaaba, the *cubical* building" (*Quran* 5.95, 97).[46]

39　From ψῆφος comes very common Rabbinic פסיפס "stone, checker, mosaic cube."

40　Caesar's "let the die be cast" is ἀνερρίφθω κύβος (Plutarch *Caesar* 32) using a familiar phrase appearing also at Menander frag. 59 Körte from the *Arrephoros*; see Suetonius *Julius* 32 *alea iacta est*.

41　Sophocles frag. 895 TrGF iv.574.

42　So Fitzgerald (*Rubaiyat* 49, 1st ed.), whether giving a Persian or British sentiment: "'Tis all a Chequer-board of Nights and Days / Where Destiny with Men for Pieces plays, / Hither and thither moves, and mates, and slays, / And one by one back in the Closet lays."

43　There is a full commentary by Alan B. Lloyd, Herodotus Book II vol. iii (=EPROER 43); Leiden: Brill, 1988 pp. 56-57. In an Egyptian story the prince Setne Khmamwas wins a magic book of immortality written by Thoth through playing checkers with the spirit of the dead Naneferkaptah; Miriam Lichtheim, Ancient Egyptian Literature: A Book of Readings; Vol. III: The Late Period; Berkeley: Univ. of California, 1980; pp. 132-3.

44　Plutarch *de Iside et Osiride* 12 = *Mor.* 355D.

45　Michel Masson, "KUBOS: un mot grec d'origine sémitique?," La linguistique 22 (1986) 143-148.

46　The word moved back from Greek into Rabbinic: κυβεία "dice-playing" (or metaphorically "trickery," Eph 4,14) appears at Mishna *Sanh.* III.3 המשחק בקוביא "one who plays at dice."

Pindar in *Olympians* 2 (not so in Frag. 114 as we have it) strongly ethicizes the version of the Islands in Hesiod and of the Elysian Field in the *Odyssey*. So even more fully Plato (*Gorgias* 523B) says that there was a law of Kronos, still existent among the gods:

Whatever man passes his life in a just and holy manner (δικαίως...καὶ ὁσίως), when he dies he goes to the Isles of the Blessed and lives in all happiness (εὐδαιμονίᾳ), free of ills; but the one who has lived unjustly and godlessly (ἀδίκως καὶ ἀθέως) goes to the prison of punishment and justice which they call Tartarus.

Finally there is a possible agreement between Hebrew and Greek in a word defining the "islands" or "coastlands" of the Mediterranean. Isa 41,5 shows that they are equivalent to the "ends of the earth":

רָאוּ אִיִּים וְיִירָאוּ   קְצוֹת הָאָרֶץ יֶחֱרָדוּ

"The coastlands have seen and are afraid, the ends of the earth (LXX τὰ ἄκρα τῆς γῆς) tremble." They are the "coastlands of the sea," Isa 24,15 בְּאִיֵּי הַיָּם, LXX "islands" ἐν ταῖς νήσοις...τῆς θαλάσσης. We saw above (*Iliad* 8.1, III.52) that Eos with her saffron garment went out "over all the earth," πᾶσαν ἐπ' αἶαν. It is the "life-bearing[47] earth" (φυσίζοος αἶα *Iliad* 3.243 = *Odyssey* 11.301) that holds the bodies of the dead. Like γαῖα and γῆ, αἶα means "the whole earth" and never comes in the plural; if it did, *αἶαι would be a very close parallel to the construct plural אִיֵּי *'iyyey*. As the actual words exist, a connection between them is speculative but enticing.

19.7 The jewelled world

Among the Hebrew versions of the mountain of the north, we discussed (III.48 above) Ez 28,12-19, the lament over the "king of Tyre" who was in "Eden, the garden of God" (vs 13), or as it seems alternatively "on the holy mountain of God." Its distinctive feature is the nine precious stones with which the king is "covered," perhaps identified. Two of the stones, jasper and sapphire (I.87-90, 332), have certain equivalents in Greek, and a third, בָּרֶקֶת, a highly probable one in emerald (I.18, 122, 332; II.293). It is characteristic of Hebrew thought that its equivalent is demythologized and attached to the priesthood. The whole list also appears in the High Priest's breastplate (Ex 28,17-20) plus three new items in row three. Gilgamesh in Tablet IX of his epic appears to have entered a garden of jewels.[48] We saw in our

---

47   For the ambiguity of φυσίζοος see II.38.
48   ANET³ 89b.

discussion (I.87-90) that two of the jewels, jasper and emerald, also appear as the geologic formation of Plato's true Earth (*Phaedo* 110D), of which our jewels down here below are only rubble. Also precisely the three stones of the Phaedo, jasper and sard and emerald, appear in the throne at Rev 4,3.

Here we need only summarize that the importation of the jewels to Greece, with their Oriental names, also brought the idea of the better world of which the precious stones are the infrastructure. In Ezekiel 28 that world is on a mountain and is called "Eden," the garden of God; here we have a unique Phoenician parallel to Hebrew myth. The relation of the "king of Tyre" to that garden and mountain is mysterious but deep. The myth of the *Phaedo* has further contacts with Hebrew thought. Plato says that humanity lives around the Sea "like ants or frogs around a marsh" (*Phaedo* 110C); Isa 40,22 that God "sits on the circle of the earth, and its inhabitants are as grasshoppers" (I.88, 110). Plato (109E) imagines that one "might become winged and fly" (πτηνὸς γενόμενος ἀνάπτοιτο) above our earth like the Psalmist taking the "wings of Dawn" (III.51 above). And he insists again and again on the pleasure of viewing that earth, it is "a delight for the blessed viewers" (θέαμα εὐδαιμόνων θεατῶν 111A) like the garden of Eden (עֵדֶן) or delight (Ez 28,13, Vg *in deliciis paradisi Dei*).

19.8 The garden with four rivers

Calypso's island Ogygia (νῆσον ἐς Ὠγυγίην *Odyssey* 1.85) is "far-off" (τηλόθ᾽ ἐοῦσαν 5.55) from Olympus, therefore somewhere in the West along with the Islands of the Blessed. While she, unlike Eos, is sedentary, Odysseus' situation is much like that of Tithonus. In its symmetry her garden has a Near Eastern pattern (briefly discussed at I.140-141). Beside her cave surrounded with trees "four springs nearby flowed with shining water, next to each other, but each one turned in a different direction" (*Odyssey* 5.70-71):

κρῆναι δ᾽ ἑξείης πίσυρες ῥέον ὕδατι λευκῷ,
πλησίαι ἀλλήλων τετραμμέναι ἄλλυδις ἄλλη.

Calypso has no need to bother with gardening, for the streams water a wild vine with grape clusters right by her cave (5.68). For Mediterranean peoples, who on the whole preferred fruit to vegetables, "gardens" were closer to what we would call orchards. In the big orchard of Alcinous in Scheria (ὄρχατος *Odyssey* 7.112, unrelated to English *orchard*) were "pear-trees and pomegranates and apple trees with fine fruit and sweet figtrees and flourishing olives" (*Odyssey* 7.115-116,

II.11). Beside these were vineyards. (But the πρασίαι of 7.127 are surely vegetables.) Although the Phaeacians in most respects are quite human, apart from not being given to war, the trees are half magical, for (7.117) "their fruit is never spoiled or lacking" winter or summer.

Calypso's garden island is nicely paralleled by the Garden of Eden with *its* four rivers and fruit trees. From Roman sources we saw evidence (I.158) that Eden was envisaged as a mountain, and that it too was surrounded with a vine, just as Milton imagined it. Odysseus has to admit that mortal Penelope, while circumspect (περίφρων 5.216-8), is inferior to the immortal and unaging Calypso. Still he is homesick, and finally the goddess, urged on by Hermes, helps him go away. But only the domesticity he has known makes him dissatisfied. Even less does Adam (one should think) have any cause for discontent, with a lovely consort at his side:

Adam the goodliest man of men since born

His Sons, the fairest of her daughters *Eve*. (*Par. Lost* 4.323-4) Still as events turn out he also must leave, in his case along with Eve, now a mere mortal Penelope.

Further, Calypso's Ὠγυγίη has a distant linguistic connection with Eden, which was planted מִקֶּדֶם (Gen 2:8), more likely "in the east" (κατὰ ἀνατολάς LXX), though some connotation of "in ancient times" (Vg *in principio*) cannot be ruled out (III.126). The two words have complex associations through Thebes.[49] Ancient and modern commentators on the Odyssey are uncertain whether Ὠγυγίη is a name or an adjective, and if the latter, what it means. In either case it must bear some relationship to the ancient figure Ὤγυγος, known to Pausanias 9.5.1 as autochthonous founder of Boeotian Thebes. But elsewhere the founder of Thebes is Kadmos (Κάδμος) the Tyrian who came to Greece in search of his sister Europa (Herodotus 2.49.3, 4.147.4) and founded Thebes; and he is surely connected with the בְּנֵי קֶדֶם "sons of the east" of Gen 29,1 etc. (discussion at I.37). The *Iliad* calls the Thebans Καδμείωνας (4.385 etc.); compare the people הַקַּדְמֹנִי Gen 15,19. Herodotus 5.58-59 relates that the Phoenicians who came with Kadmos also brought the alphabet, γράμματα...Φοινικήϊα or Καδμήϊα. Sophocles (*OR* 1, I.37) suggests that "Kadmos" *meant* "ancient." If "Kadmos" were once known as a descriptive adjective, "Easterner" or "ancient one" or both, the true name of the founder of Thebes in legend might have been Ogygos, so that Pausanias would be reconciled with the rest

---

49   For bibliography on Ogygos and allied words see II.188.

of Greek tradition.[50] And Agag (אֲגַג), perhaps one of the בְּנֵי קֶדֶם (I.37 note 149), might carry the same name, with its initial vowel reduced as in Phoenician.

19.9 The starry robe of the cosmos

In a final symbol of eternity, garments take on the starry attributes of the cosmos, immutable (or nearly so); and the cosmos conversely is seen as a garment. Aaron's tunic (Ex 28,4 etc. כְּתֹנֶת, LXX χιτών) is barely described in the Pentateuch; Josephus (AJ 3.161, I.208) calls it one-piece; in Alexandrian Judaism it has become a robe depicting the universe. Philo[51] says that to Aaron "it has been granted to wear a *tunic* that is a replica of the entire heavens," χιτῶνα ἐνδύεσθαι τοῦ παντὸς ἀντίμιμον τοῦ οὐρανοῦ. So Sap Sol 18,24 "on his long garment was the whole cosmos," ἐπὶ γὰρ ποδήρους ἦν ὅλος ὁ κόσμος.[52] Such a robe is attested for rulers. Demetrius Poliorcetes (Plutarch *Dem.* 41.4) had a cloak (χλανίς), "the likeness of the world and the heavenly bodies," εἴκασμα τοῦ κόσμου καὶ τῶν κατ' οὐρανὸν φαινομένων. Nero, to celebrate his Olympic victories, rode in Augustus' chariot (Suetonius *Nero* 25.1) *in ueste purpurea distinctaque stellis aureis chlamyde* "in a purple garment and a cloak picked out with golden stars." A relief of Mithras from Rome[53] shows the deity wearing a cloak with seven stars, no doubt for the sun, moon and planets; another such was found in the Mithraeum of Phoenician Sidon, now in the Louvre.[54] Robert Eisler[55] shows how the starry robes of Holy Roman Emperors, still extant, come down from classical Rome.

The shield on which Hephaistos beats out the whole universe (*Iliad* 18) once *was* the universe, as the God of Genesis beats out the "firmament" (רָקִיעַ) as a metal dome; both reflect the then current state of

---

50 Egyptian Thebes was also called "Ogygian" as if also founded by Ogygos (Aeschylus *Persae* 37). The connection between the two cities Thebes remains mysterious.
51 Philo *de somn.* 1.215 (LCL v.412) and similarly elsewhere.
52 See the commentary in David Winston, The Wisdom of Solomon; The Anchor Bible; Garden City: Doubleday, 1979; 321-322.
53 LIMC vi.2.338, Mithras no. 132.
54 Illustrated in the excellent work of my student Nina Jidejian, Sidon through the Ages; Beirut: Dar el-Machreq, 1971; no. 208.
55 Robert Eisler, Weltenmantel und Himmelszelt: Religionsgeschichtliche Untersuchungen zur Urgeschichte des antiken Weltbildes; 2 vols.; München: Beck, 1910.

bronze technology (I.109). We saw how the allegorist Heraclitus sees the poet (or god) as "hammering out in bronze Achilles' shield as an image of the cosmic totality." So heaven and earth are naturally seen as woven, even though as other clothes "they will all wear out like a garment" (Ps 102,27):

וְכֻלָּם כַּבֶּגֶד יִבְלוּ

For it is Yahweh (Isa 40,22; cf Ps 104,2) "who stretches out the heavens like a curtain, and spreads them like a tent to dwell in":

הַנּוֹטֶה כַדֹּק שָׁמַיִם   וַיִּמְתָּחֵם כָּאֹהֶל לָשָׁבֶת

There is a beautiful parallel in a fragment of Pherecydes, the early Greek mythographer.[56] Zas (Zeus) marries Chthonie (Earth) and on the third day of the wedding "Zas fashions a robe both big and beautiful, and on it he embroiders Earth and Ogenos (Ocean)..." Ζᾶς ποιεῖ φᾶρος μέγα τε καὶ καλόν, καὶ ἐν αὐτῷ ποικίλλει Γῆν καὶ Ὠγηνόν. Clement of Alexandria,[57] who quotes Pherecydes to illustrate Greek plagiarism, compares *Iliad* 18.483 "And on the shield (Hephaistos) made earth, sky and sea"

Ἐν μὲν γαῖαν ἔτευξ᾽, ἐν δ᾽ οὐρανόν, ἐν δὲ θάλασσαν.

Goethe's Erdgeist describes its activity (*Faust* I.508-509): "So I work at the roaring loom of time and create the living garment of the divinity,"

So schaff' ich am sausenden Webstuhl der Zeit
Und wirke der Gottheit lebendiges Kleid.

In an autobiographical painting, the Spanish symbolist Remedios Varo shows a roomful of identical blond girls in a tower weaving the landscape of the spherical earth, *Bordando el manto terrestre* (1961).[58]

The veil of the second Temple at Jerusalem has Greek parallels both in its making and its unmaking. Josephus (*BJ* 5.212-214) describes the colors of the veil (καταπέτασμα) and says that it depicted everything in the sky except the Zodiac. Mishna *Sheqalim* VIII.5 in one reading says that it was woven by 82 young girls. Lieberman[59] cites other Rabbinic texts to the same effect and compares the girls who wove the Peplos of Athena, between 7 and 11 years old.[60] He regards the parallel

---

56 FVS[8] i.48; see the new edition of the fragments with copious commentary, Hermann S. Schibli, Pherekydes of Syros; Oxford: Clarendon, 1990; esp. frag. 68 (pp. 165-7) and the text, pp. 51-61.
57 *Stromateis* 6.2.94, ii.429 ed. Stählin-Früchtel[3] (GCS 52[15]).
58 Edouard Jaguer, Remedios Varo, tr. [from French to Spanish] by José Emilio Pacheco; Mexico City: Editiones Era, 1980; pp. 32-33.
59 Saul Lieberman, Hellenism in Jewish Palestine 167-9.
60 *Etymologium Magnum* 149.19; he cites further Frazer on Pausanias 2.574 & 3.592.

as arising, not from historical connection, but from the need to have the weaving done by girls under the age of puberty so that the work would not be defiled by their menstruation.

The veil of the Temple long before the catastrophe of AD 70 had a checkered history. Matthew (27,51) affirms that at the death of Jesus the veil (καταπέτασμα) was rent from top to botton. In 169 BC an earlier veil (also καταπέτασμα), perhaps already with the constellations on it, was confiscated by Antiochus IV (I Makk 1,22) of Syria. But now Pausanias 5.12.4 says that "Antiochus" dedicated for the temple of Zeus at Olympia "a woollen veil, ornamented with Assyrian embroideries and with a dye of purple of the Phoenicians," παραπέτασμα ἐρεοῦν κεκοσμημένον ὑφάσμασιν Ἀσσυρίοις καὶ βαφῇ πορφύρας τῆς Φοινίκων. It is enticing to think that the Jerusalem veil ended up at Olympia. Pelletier[61] regards the Antiochus of Pausanias as Antiochus III; and observes that, even if Pausanias meant Antiochus IV Epiphanes, he plundered other temples, so that the veil of Olympia cannot be proved the Jerusalem one. But in fact no other such veil is attested.

19.10 Conditions for entrance

Who may enter the better world? Among the Greeks, as time went on, the criterion shifted, as we saw, from military heroes to the morally just. In Israel, the question of Ps 15,1 (cf. Isa 33,14-16) "Yahweh, who shall sojourn in your tent? Who shall dwell on your holy hill?," never has a ritual answer, but from the beginning an ethical one, "He who walks blamelessly, and does what is right..." We may think of the question as introducing a little moral catechism or "entrance liturgy" (II.263, 280). The Psalms further hint that such a one will escape death. Ps 16,10-11 "For thou dost not give up my life to Sheol, or let thy pious one see the Pit. Thou dost show me the path of life; in thy presence is fullness of joy; in thy right hand are pleasures for evermore." Ps 49,14-16 "Death shall be the shepherd" (מָוֶת יִרְעֵם) of the foolish; "But God will ransom my life from the hand of Sheol; he will surely rescue me."

Weinfeld[62] compares these texts from the Psalms specifying who may enter the Temple to Demotic texts on the doorposts and lintels of

---

61   André Pelletier s.j., "Le 'voile' du temple de Jérusalem est-il devenu la 'portière' du temple d'Olympie?," Syria 32 (1955) 289-307.

62   Moshe Weinfeld, "Instructions for Temple Visitors in the Bible and in Ancient Egypt," Scripta Hierosolymitana 28, Egyptological Studies; Jerusalem: Magnes, 1982; 224-250.

Egyptian temples in the Hellenistic period. He points further to nice Greek parallels. A stone from Delos of the Roman period[63] records that some party has reengraved from a broken stele

> the notice regarding entrance into the temple of Zeus Kynthios and Athena Kynthia, [namely] with pure hands and soul, wearing white clothing, barefoot, having sacrally abstained from a woman and meat; and not to carry in...nor a key, nor an iron ring, nor a belt, nor a purse, nor military weapons...

[ἀν]έργαψεν τὴν προγ[ραφὴν] ἰέναι εἰς τὸ ἱερ[ὸν τοῦ] Διὸς τοῦ Κυνθίου [καὶ τῆς] Ἀθηνᾶς Κυνθί[ας χε]ρσὶν καὶ ψυχῇ καθα[ρᾷ, ἔ]χοντας ἐσθῆτα λευ[κήν, ἀνυ]ποδέτους ἀγνεύοντας [ἀπὸ γυν]αικὸς καὶ κρέως [καὶ μηθὲ]ν εἰσ[φ]έρειν...[μη]δὲ κλειδίον, μηδὲ δακτύλιον σιδηροῦν, μηδὲ ζώνην, μηδὲ βαλλάντιον, μηδὲ ὅπλα πολέμια...

There is a superficial parallel where Jesus tells his followers "not to carry purse or bag or shoes" (Luk 10,4) μὴ βαστάζετε βαλλάντιον, μὴ πήραν, μὴ ὑποδήματα; Mark 6,8 permits a ζώνην but no copper in it (they and Matthew differ in other respects as well). Here the motive is not purity for a temple but voluntary poverty for the road. But there is a deep substantive parallel in Ps 24,3-4:

מִי־יַעֲלֶה בְהַר־יהוה   וּמִי־יָקוּם בִּמְקוֹם קָדְשׁוֹ
נְקִי כַפַּיִם וּבַר־לֵבָב

"Who shall ascend the hill of Yahweh? and who shall stand in his holy place? One clean of hands and pure of heart..." With the LXX ἀθῷος χερσὶν καὶ καθαρὸς τῇ καρδίᾳ we may compare in the Delos text [χε]ρσὶν καὶ ψυχῇ καθα[ρᾷ]. Does this represent influence of Hellenistic Judaism on the Greek world?

Mitchell Dahood in his bold reworking of the Psalms[64] sees "resurrection and immortality" affirmed in many more passages.[65] He further claims what he calls the "mythological motif of the Elysian Fields" in several others, though without any discussion of Greek texts. He translates Ps 5,9 נְחֵנִי בְצִדְקָתֶךָ "lead me into your meadow" by arbitrarily giving צְדָקָה a second meaning.[66] More plausible is his new Hebrew

---

63 Sokolowski, LSCG Sup 59 = Inscriptions de Délos 2529. See further other inscriptions there cited.

64 Mitchell Dahood, S.J., Psalms; Anchor Bible; 3 vols.; Garden City: Doubleday, 1966-1970.

65 Dahood vol. I. p. xxxvi, citing further Pss 5,9; 11,7; 17,15; 21,7; 27,13; 36,9-10; 37,37-38; 41,13; 61,14; 73,23-24.

66 Two pieces of evidence, both shaky. (a) Dahood translates Ps 23,3 יַנְחֵנִי בְמַעְגְּלֵי־צֶדֶק "he will lead me into luxuriant pastures" by assuming it parallel to vs 2, though remote, בִּנְאוֹת דֶּשֶׁא יַרְבִּיצֵנִי. He notes that at Ps 65,12-

word אוּר "meadow" (interpreted, as he sees it, in the MT as אוֹר "light") on the basis of three pieces of evidence.[67] (a) In view of Ps 116,9 (III.51 above) which he translates "I shall walk before Yahweh in the Fields of Life":

אֶתְהַלֵּךְ לִפְנֵי יהוה בְּאַרְצוֹת הַחַיִּים

he reads Ps 56,14 "That I might walk before God in the field of life":

לְהִתְהַלֵּךְ לִפְנֵי אֱלֹהִים בְּאוֹר הַחַיִּים

where some MSS of the LXX for בְּאוֹר have ἐν χώρᾳ. (b) By repointing the obscure Ps 97,11 MT אוֹר זָרֻעַ he translates "A sown field." (c) At Gen 11,28 etc. בְּאוּר כַּשְׂדִּים "in Ur of the Chaldaeans" in the LXX is ἐν τῇ χώρᾳ. Hence he translates Ps 36,10 בְּאוֹרְךָ נִרְאֶה־אוֹר "in your field we shall see the light," assuming word-play.

Without such reconstruction a comparable meaning (we saw) can be obatined from a smaller number of Psalms, even though on a minimal reading Sheol or death can mostly be made a metaphor of the ills of this life. The natural interpretation however is a dawning conviction, cautiously phrased, that the care of God for the just extends also beyond death. So Plato admits (*Gorgias* 523A) that his thought may be felt as a myth (μῦθον), although he regards it as a true account (λόγον).

19.11 The separable soul and its image, the pearl

Greeks, who agreed with Hebrews that something, however unsatisfactory, survived the death of the body, called it the *soul*, ψυχή. The *psychai* of the dead in art are tiny winged men; they can be weighed against each other as in Egypt.[68] At *Iliad* 22.209 Zeus weighs the fates of Achilles and Hector. See further evidence from Greek and Hebrew for the international spread of just weights (II.46). It would be tempting to discuss here Bernal's proposal[69] to derive Κήρ "personification of Death" from Egyptian *k3* "a particular aspect of the soul"; but I am incompetent to deal with either the phonetic or the semantic side of the Egyptian. The original sense of the Greek is not obvious; Homeric κήρ can be just "death"; Achilles accuses Agamemnon of cowardice (*Iliad*

---

13 מַעְגָּלֶיךָ is parallel to נְאוֹת. (b) In his comment on Ps 5,9 (vol. i.34) he rearranges Ps 143,10-11 to run parallel "With your good spirit lead me into the level land (בְּאֶרֶץ מִישׁוֹר); for your name's sake, O Yahweh, grant me life in your meadow (בְּצִדְקָתֶךָ)." But when he comes to Ps 143 (vol. iii.322) he tacitly abandons this proposal.

67   Dahood I.222-223.
68   Vermeule pp. 9, 76, 161-2.
69   Communication of January 1996.

1.228) "for all that [fighting] seems to you to be death," τὸ δέ τοι κῆρ εἴδεται εἶναι.

Plato makes the soul the more valuable part of us, locked up in the body as in a prison (*Phaedrus* 250C, *Phaedo* 81E, 82E); to have entered this world at all, something in us must have died, and "the body is our grave" τὸ μὲν σῶμά ἐστιν ἡμῖν σῆμα (*Gorgias* 493A). Greek texts cited at I.207 make the body the *tunic* (χιτών) of the soul; at III.15 we saw that Hillel and Hadrian make the soul a *guest* in the body.

There is a metaphorical name for the "soul" in the later period with an unquestionable correspondence between Greek and Semitic: the name of the "pearl," μαργαρίτης, known since Theophrastus *de lap.* 36, appears to be a loan from some unknown Oriental language, perhaps of the Indian subcontinent. Frisk ii.174 thinks it may have come through Iranian, citing Middle Persian *marvarit*. Quran 55.58 *alyāqūtu walmarjānu* ٱلۡيَاقُوتُ وَٱلۡمَرۡجَانُ is probably "jacinth (ὑάκινθος Rev 21,20) and pearl." It is borrowed in Latin as fem. *margarita* (Cicero *Verr.* 4.1), also as neuter, Tacitus *Agric.* 12.6 *gignit et Oceanus margarita* "also the Atlantic generates pearls." Augustus called Maecenas his *Tiberinum margaritum* "pearl from the Tiber" (Macrobius *Sat.* 2.4.12, cited I.89). In Rabbinic, Mishna *Kelim* XI.8 מרגליות plural. At Rev 21,21 each gate of New Jerusalem is a single pearl.

Roman trade usages of the pearl went directly into Rabbinic. Scaevola (*Digest* 35.2.26) speaks of a *lineam margaritorum triginta quinque* "a string of 35 pearls." *Cant. Rabbah* on 1.10 "The 70 members of the Sanhedrin were strung after [Moses and Aaron] like a string of pearls," בלוניא של מרגליות. Perhaps 35 pearls was standard so that the Sanhedrin was seen as a double strand.

The ancients of course knew that the pearl was an animal product, so that it is particularly appropriate for something living. Thus Jer. Talm. *Kilaim* 32c47, one dying outside Israel says "I am about to lose my pearl [evidently 'my life'] in the midst of an unclean land":

אנא מובד מרגליתי גו ארצא מסאבתא

A trader at *Ex. Rabbah* 30.24, hearing of bandits (לסטים = λῃσταί) ahead, exchanges his wares (פרקמטיא = πραγματεία) for jewels and pearls (מרגליות). He tells the bandits they are worthless and is let go, but later in the city he opens his cases (גלוסקמאות = γλωσσόκομον Joh 12,6[70]) and they find him selling the pearls for gold.

Above all the pearl appears in Matthew's tiny parable (13,45-46) of the trader who finds one precious pearl (μαργαρίτην, Syriac מרגניתא,

---

70 Here the Peshitto transliterates גלוסקמא.

Palestinian Syriac (מרגלי) and "went and sold all that he had and bought it":

ἀπελθὼν πέπρακεν πάντα ὅσα εἶχεν καὶ ἠγόρασεν αὐτήν

Peshitto Syriac: אזל זבן כל מא דאית לה וזבנה

The parable has extensive afterlife in unexpected places. A Rabbinic story (Bab. Talm. *Shabb.* 119a) seems like a parody, with the pearl buyer coming to a bad end:

Joseph who kept the Sabbath has a rich Gentile neighbor. Chaldaeans (כלדאי) tell the neighbor that Joseph will consume his property. "He went and sold all his property and bought a pearl with it":

אזל זבנינהו לכולהו ניכסי זבן בהו מרגניתא

He hides it in his turban, but the wind over a bridge blows it off, a fish swallows it, and Joseph buys the fish on the eve of Sabbath. For the Aramaic here is almost identical with the Syriac of Matt 13,46 above. Note the folk-motif (I.304) of the valuable object found in the fish: the stater which Peter is to find in the fish's mouth (Matt 17,27); Polycrates' ring (Herodotus 3.41) which it is impossible for the owner to get rid of, like any ineluctable destiny. In the Rabbinic story it is impossible for the owner to *keep* it.

The Syriac church Father Ephrem (III.141 below) has five enigmatic hymns *On the Pearl*.[71] The significance of all these pearls is spelled out in the beautiful *Hymn of the Pearl* from the Acts of Thomas, the crown of Syriac literature.[72] The speaker was brought up "in my kingdom, in my Father's house" in the East in luxury. But he is stripped of his "purple toga" (לטוגי ד זחוריתא vs 10) and told to go to Egypt and bring back "the one pearl (מרגניתא) which is in the midst of the sea, near the loud-breathing serpent." He goes to Egypt but forgets his mission until a living letter in the form of an eagle arrives from his Father, the King of Kings, reminding him of his duty. He charms the serpent by the names of his Father and Mother, takes the pearl, strips off his unclean dress, and returns to the East, where his living toga, a double of himself, comes to meet him.

The hero's "purple toga" is either a supplement or a Semitic parallel to his jewelled robe; compare Livy 34.7.2 *praetextis purpura togis* "togas bordered with purple." One or both is quasi-animate and acts

---

71 Nos. 81-85 of his *Hymns de Fide* (against the Arians), ed. Edmund Beck, CSCO 154-5 (= Scriptores Syri 73-74) Louvain 1955.

72 Syriac text edited by A. A. Bevan, The Hymn of the Soul, Texts and Studies V.3; Cambridge: University, 1897. The Greek text appears in a single MS of the Acts, ed. Maximilianus Bonnet, Acta Apostolorum Apocrypha, Vol. II.2; repr. Hildesheim: Olms, 1959; *Acta Thomae* 108-113, pp. 219-224.

as a double of himself, a Zoroastrian motif. Dion. Hal. 3.61.1 says that
Romans call embroidered purple robes like those of the kings of Lydia
and Persia τόγας; Strabo 3.2.15 refers to τογᾶτοι "those wearing the
toga" in Spain. A Byzantine chronicler of AD 419 describes an assas-
sination by sword in which the victim's "cloak and toga were
pierced,"[73] ὥστε τὸ πενόλιον αὐτοῦ καὶ τὴν τόγαν τρηθῆναι. The
Rabbis disapproved of going out in a toga (טגא) since such was worn
by idolaters (Sifre Deut. 81, cf. 234).[74] The descriptions of the robe
echo what Ammianus Marcellinus 23.6.84 (see I.59) says of Sasanid
dress, indumentis... lumine colorum fulgentibus vario "clothes shining
with variegated light of colors" and ornamented with pearls. The
Hymn's use of toga makes a Roman comparison; for the special
garment is a token of a rightful place in the Kingdom of the Father, as
the toga was the badge of Roman citizenship and emblem of peace:
cedant arma togae said Cicero in his poem on his consulate (de off.
1.77), "let arms yield to the toga" (I.58).

The theme of the merchant in Matthew appears here in that the hero
(vs 18) passes the borders of Mesene (מישן), "the meeting-place of the
merchants of the East," צובא דתגרי מדנחא. For the caravan terminus
Mesene see Excursus H. There is surely a Gnostic element in that his
unclean dress must be his human body; but no other Gnostic text has
the poetry of this one. The figure of the hero himself wavers between
representing Christ coming to earth and Everyman, forgetful of his
divine upbringing and mission until he is reminded by revelation. In
either case the pearl is the soul, either of all humanity or of the
individual.

Heinz Kruse[75] compares the Syriac Hymn of the Pearl (which he
prints in full in transcription) both with Matthew's tiny parable of the
Pearl and with Luke's favorite parable of the Prodigal Son. He proposes that the Hymn is an intermediate stage between the Gospel
parables and the verse parable in the fourth chapter of the Buddhist
Sanskrit Lotus Sutra (Saddharma-puṇḍarīka-sūtra), which he also prints
in transcription with translation. It has strongly influenced Japanese
Buddhism, which entitles it myōhō-renge-kyō (II.166). Here is an
instance where it is plausible to maintain that Christianity has influenced the living development of Buddhism.

---

73   Chronicon Paschale 310, PG 92.792A.
74   Translated by H. Bietenhard, Sifre Deuteronium; Judaica et Christiana Bd 8;
      Bern etc.: Lang, 1984, pp. 258, 553.
75   Heinz Kruse, "The Return of the Prodigal: Fortunes of a Parable on its Way
      to the Far East," Orientalia 47 (1978) 163-214; reprint kindly sent me by the
      author.

Excursus H: Mesene and the caravan trade

The hero of the *Hymn of the Pearl* (III.63, vs 18)[1] says "I passed the borders of Mayshan, the meeting place of the merchants of the East":

עברת תחומי מישן צובא דתגרי מדנחא

παρελθὼν δὲ καὶ τὰ τῶν Μοσάνων μεθόρια, ἔνθα ἐστὶν τὸ καταγώγιον τῶν ἀνατολικῶν ἐμπόρων.

The true Greek (not known to the translator) is Mesene, Μεσήνη (Dio 68.28.4, who calls it an island), properly a district rather than a city, the terminus of the caravan route from Palmyra on the Persian Gulf. Numerous bilingual Greco-Palmyrene honorific inscriptions from the agora of Palmyra describe the caravan trade and its entrepreneurs. Several items of its vocabulary fall under the lingua franca of the Roman period. They are here set within what we know about the history of Mesene. In particular I reprint a remarkable Greek-Parthian bilingual (the Parthian mostly in Aramaic ideograms) from Seleucia of Tigris on a bronze statue of a divinity, Heracles-Verethragna.

A Palmyrene bilingual of AD 135 (PAT 1397) honored "Julius Maximus, centurion of Legion —"[2]

יוליס מכסמס קטרינא די לגיונא

It was set up by Marcus Ulpius Abgar and the "sons of the caravan" (בני שירתא): Palmyrene, "which came up with him from Charax of Mayshan":

די סלקת עמה מן כרך מישן

Greek, "those from Spasinou Charax," οἱ ἀπὸ Σπασίνου Χάρακος. Nowhere in the Greek side of the Palmyrene bilinguals does Μεσήνη appear. In an inscription of AD 140 to an unknown honoree (PAT 1412)[3] the

---

1   Greek version 109.
2   Legionary number omitted by the Palmyrene; the Greek of this line is lacking.
3   Other Palmyrene texts treating Vologaisa are PAT 0197, 0262, 0279; and a long new bilingual edited by H. J. W. Drivers, "Greek and Aramaic in Palmyrene Inscriptions," pp. 31-42 of M. J. Geller et alii (eds.), Studia Aramaica: New Sources and New Approaches; Journal of Semitic Studies Supplement 4; Oxford Univ. Press, 1995.

caravan has come up (Palmyrene) "from Charax of Mayshan to Vologaisia and Tadmor"; (Greek) "from Charax to Palmyra <and> Vologaisia":

מן כרכ[א] די מישן לאלגשיא ולתדמר

παραγενομένη ἀ[πὸ τ]οῦ Χάρακος εἰς Πάλμυρα <καὶ> Ὀλογασίαν
συνοδία.

Vologaisia (*Vologesocerta* Pliny 6.122) was the foundation of Vologases
I of Parthia (ab. AD 51-79)[4] near ancient Babylon; the Palmyrene has
the logical order, since the caravan stopped off at Vologaisia en route
to Palmyra. Already we have several items of the caravan vocabulary,
and I briefly treat them before going on with the history of Mesene /
Charax Spasinou.

"*Merchants.*" From the *Hymn of the Pearl* 18 (above) we saw that
Syriac תגרי corresponds to ἔμποροι "merchants." Likewise Matt 13,45
the "trader (ἐμπόρῳ) seeking goodly pearls" comes out in the Syriac
תגרא. The place of trade, Matt 22,5 ἐμπορίαν or Joh 2,16 ἐμπορίου
went into Latin as *emporium* and Rabbinic as אמפורין.[5] The Aramaic
is a loan from Akkadian *tamkaru* "merchant." Also in Rabbinic תגרא;
thus Bab. Talm. *BM* 40b

זבון וזבין תגרא איקרי

"If one buys and sells [at the same price], can you call such a one a
trader?" The Targum Pseudo-Jonathan to Gen 25,3 gives both words
as simple equivalents, תגרין ואמפורין. Likewise in the Palmyrene
bilinguals the two words correspond. Thus an honorific inscription of
AD 161 for a *bouleutes* of Syrian Antioch (PAT 1373, see II.107) is set
up by "the merchants who came up from (Greek adds Spasinou)
Charax":

οἱ ἀναβάντες ἀπὸ Σπασίνου Χάρακος ἔμποροι.

תגריא די סלק מן כרכא

Thus in several Aramaic dialects (Rabbinic, Palmyrene, Syriac) the
word "merchant" תגרא (itself a loan from Akkadian) has a fixed Greek
equivalent ἔμπορος.[6]

"*Caravan.*" In the Palmyrene inscriptions the caravan is called
שירתא = συνοδία. Thus an honorary inscription of AD 159 to M. Ulpius
Yarhai (PAT 1409)[7] is set up by "the caravan which came up from
Spasinou Charax":

4   N. C. Debevoise, A Political History of Parthia; Chicago: University, 1938,
     p. 204.
5   The transliteration אמפוריא (e.g. Mishna *BM* II.1) was interpreted אין פה ראיה
     "there is no mark of ownership here" and transferred to mean "brand new."
6   From the nature of the Nabataean texts it does not appear in them.
7   Here only and at PAT 0274 does אספסנא appear in Palmyrene Aramaic.

[ἡ] ἀναβᾶσα ἀπὸ Σπασίνου Χάρακος συνοδία

שירתא די סלקת מן כרך אספסנא

(I find no obvious West-Semitic etymology for שירתא.) The "chief of a caravan" רש שירתא (or רש שירא PAT 1373) becomes in Greek (PAT 0294)[8] συνοδιάρχης and also elsewhere ἀρχέμπορος (PAT 0282). Now we can see that at Luk 2,44 Jesus' parents thought he was "in the caravan," ἐν τῇ συνοδίᾳ (where Vg in comitatu does not quite capture the Near Eastern flavor).[9] (At Gen 37,25 "caravan" is אֹרְחַת.) At Arrian Epict. 4.1.91 a cautious traveler on a road infested with bandits (λῃσταί) waits for the "caravan of a legate or...proconsul," συνοδίαν ἢ πρεσβευτοῦ...ἢ ἀνθυπάτου. An enigmatic inscription from Rome (CIL I².2519)[10] speaks of a magister... synhodi societatis cantorum Graecorum "master of the synod of the society of Greek singers"; the "synod" is a gathering of a religious or social organization. σύνοδος has its ecclesiastical sense at least since Dionysius of Alexandria (mid-3rd century), ἐν ταῖς μεγίσταις τῶν ἐπισκόπων συνόδοις (cited by Eusebius HE 7.5.5) "in the largest synods of bishops." The Greek went once into Rabbinic in a text[11] quoted by lexica, "I and my angels were thy escort":

אני ומלאכי נעשינו סינודיא שלך

The "palisade." The city Charax was originally, before silting from the two great rivers stranded it inland, on the coast of the Persian Gulf NE of what is now Kuwait. Pliny 6.139 on Charax describes how its first independent ruler Spaosines (in his spelling), king ab. 140-120 BC, protected it against the flooding Tigris and Euphrates with a palisade, oppositis molibus; hence Σπασίνου Χάρακος (Josephus AJ 20.22). χάραξ, originally "sharpened stake," is classical for "palisade, fortified camp." This must be the origin of Aramaic כרך "fortified city," whose attestation is all comparatively late (cf. SIE 246); so Joh 11,54 Pesh כרכא for πόλιν; Nabataean of Petra (CIS 2.350)[12] כרכא "wall" of a tomb; and Targumic and Rabbinic. In Hebrew at Mishna Meg. I.1

---

8   Greek broken, but word intact in PAT 0262.
9   Syriac לויתהון "their company."
10 In a text with earlier spelling from the same stone the synod comes out SVNHODO.
11 Yelammedenu on Num III.40 as quoted by Krauss 390 and Jastrow from the lexicon Aruch; but in the text printed by H. Bietenhard, Midrasch Tanhuma B: R. Tanhuma über die Tora, genannt Midrasch Jelammedenu; Judaica et Christiana Bd 6; Bern etc.: Lange, 1984, p. 214, it comes out "I and the angels were thy advocate (סינוגריה)," i.e. συνηγορία.
12 This etymology would be excluded if the word really appeared in the Aramaic of Elephantine; but in fact כרכיא at Cowley 26.3 etc. must rather be "Carians" (I.31).

כרכין המוקפין חומה

"cities encircled by a wall." It is familiar in Arabo-French from the great Syrian Crusader fortress *Krak des Chevaliers*.

The city and its district had a romantic history for five centuries. Some continuity is provided by the coins, as analyzed by Nodelman[13] and his successors, but their witness remains problematic; a recent discovery has thrown much new light on it. It was founded by Alexander as one more Alexandria (Pliny 6.138). Hyspaosines, originally satrap of Antiochus IV,[14] became its king and struck his own tetradrachms; he is known from late Babylonian cuneiform texts.[15] His name appears at Delos: in 179 BC there was a lion's head "the gift of Hyspasines the Bactrian, son of Mithroaxes"[16] Ὑσπασίνου Μιθροάξου Βακτριανοῦ ἀνάθεμα as well as a relief of an Hyrcanian dog.[17] Pliny calls the king *Spaosines Sagdonaci filius* with considerable textual variation; if this were misunderstanding of a Greek original "Spasines the Sogdian," the Delian dedications could be the king's very own and Mithroaxes his father.[18] Bellinger[19] by a series of conjectures thinks that he was through his mother the grandson of Euthydemus king of Bactria.

At Charax Spasinou, Izates of Adiabene, welcomed by king Abennerigos (Ἀβεννήριγος, Josephus *AJ* 20.22-34), surely ᶜAbd-nergal (I) "slave of Nergal" (reigning ab. AD 10-13, 22-36 according to Nodelman 121), was converted to Judaism by a travelling merchant. There was an ongoing Jewish community there. The Talmud (Bab. Talm. *Qidd.* 72b) felt that the priests of מישן were "not scrupulous about divorced women."[20] The grave of a Jewish woman from Mayshan,

13   Sheldon Arthur Nodelman, "A Preliminary History of Characene," Berytus 13 (1960) 83-121.
14   Pliny 6.138 *Antiochus quintus* counting differently.
15   T. G. Pinches & Terrien de Lacouperie, "A Babylonian Tablet...," The Babylonian and Oriental Record 4 (1889/1890) 131-144. Pinches also knew a further Akkadian text of Hyspaosines still unpublished; see his The Old Testament in the Light of the Historical Records and Legends of Assyria and Babylonia; London: SPCK, 1903, p. 483.
16   Inscriptions de Délos 442.B.109; same information at 443.Bb.33 the next year.
17   *Ibid.* 1432.Aa.II.27, prob. 153/2 BC.
18   For Hyspaosines died at the age of 85 ([Lucian] *Makrobioi* 16), and if with Nodelman we place his death at 120 BC, he was born in 205 and would have been an ambitious young man of 26 in 179.
19   A. R. Bellinger, "Hyspaosines of Charax," Yale Classical Studies 8 (1942) 53-67.
20   Elsewhere those of Mesene are impudent (*Qidd.* 49b, *Yeb.* 17a), and Babylonian traders traveled there regularly (*Baba Qamma* 97b).

"Sarah known as Maxima," was found at Beth-Shearim in Palestine (CIJ ii.1124), Μισηνη Σαρα ἡ Μάξιμα. An inscription from Hatra of the 1st/2nd century CE (KAI 247) may refer to trade with Mayshan, במשן. The *Periplus Maris Erythraei* 35 mentions its port "Apologos" (Hellenizing of a local name);[21] Isidoros the historian of Parthia was a native of Charax. In AD 116 Trajan, after taking Ctesiphon, traveled to the Gulf, was welcomed by Athambelos (V) (Ἀθάμβηλος) of Spasinou Charax, and standing by the sea with Alexander in mind, said that he would also have crossed over to India if he had been young (Dio 68.29). Mani the prophet as a young man about AD 235 lived with the sect of "Washers" according to an Arab chronicler at "Dastu-maisān" (دستميسان), "the city of Maysan" in Persian form.[22]

A flood of light on Mesopotamian history and Mesene in the second century CE comes from a bilingual Greco-Parthian inscription of AD 151; it is on the two thighs of a statue of Heracles, 85 cm high, found in clandestine excavations at Seleucia on the Tigris, the capital of Parthia.[23] Parthian script developed insensibly from Aramaic texts with a few Iranian loanwords to Iranian texts with a few Aramaic ideograms; the Parthian text here is at the mid-point of evolution, where most of the text is in Aramaic ideograms but the Iranian substructure is plain. I print it in square Aramaic characters. One item that betrays the underlying text as Iranian is the order of "king of kings," against Semitic idiom but following Iranian.

Ἔτους τοῦ καθ᾽ Ἕλληνας βξύ βασιλεὺς βασιλέων Ἀρσάκης Ὀλόγασος, υἱὸς Μιραδάτου βασιλέως, ἐπεστρατεύσατο Μεσσήνηι κατὰ Μιραδάτου βασιλέως υἱοῦ Πακόρου τοῦ προβασιλεύσαντος καί, τὸν Μιραδάτην

---

21 Ed. Lionel Casson; Princeton: University, 1989; see his discussion pp. 179-180.
22 Gustav Flügel, Mani, seine Lehre und seine Schriften...Aus dem Fihrist des Abû'lfaradsch Muḥammad ben Isḥaḳ al-Warrâḳ, bekannt unter dem Namen Ibn Abî Jaʿḳûb an-Nadîm...; Leipzig: Brockhaus, 1862; p. 83.
23 First published by Wathiq Ismail al Salihi, "Mesenes' [sic] Bronze Statue of 'Weary Hercules'," *Sumer* 43 (1984)219-234; texts edited by Fabrizio A. Pennachietti, "L'Iscrizione bilingue greco-partica dell' Eracle di Seleucia," *Mesopotamia* 22 (1987) 169-185; I have not seen the long study by Paul Bernard, "Vicissitudes au gré de l'histoire d'une statue en bronze d'Héraclès entre Séleucie du Tigre et la Mésène," Journal des Savants 1990 3-68. Discussion by D. T. Potts, "Arabia and the Kingdom of Characene," pp. 136-167 of *idem* (ed.), Araby the Blest: Studies in Arabian Archaeology; Copenhagen: Univ. of Copenhagen; 1988; G. W. Bowersock, "La Mésène antonine," pp. 159-168 of T. Fahid (ed.), L'Arabie préislamique et son environnement historique et culturel; Univ. des Sciences humaines de Strasbourg, Travaux du centre de recherche sur le Proche-orient et la Grèce antique 10; 1989.

βασιλέα ἐγδιώξας τῆς Μεσήνης, ἐγένετο ἐνκρατὴς ὅλης τῆς Μεσήνης καὶ
εἰκόνα ταύτην χαλκῆν Ἡρακλέους θεοῦ, τὴν μετενεχθεῖσαν ὑπ' αὐτοῦ
ἀπὸ τῆς Μεσήνης, ἀνέθηκεν ἐν ἱερῷ τῷδε θεοῦ Ἀπόλλωνος τοῦ χαλκῆς
πύλης προκαθημένου.

...א[רש]ך ולגשי מלכין מלכא ברי מתרדת מל[ך] כת[ש]ו על מישן ברא
מתרדת מלכא ברי פכור מלכין מלכא מתרדת מלכא מן תמה מרדפו.
חמך מישן אחדו. זנה פתכר ורתרגן אלחא מה מן מישן חיתה ניכנדן
בתירי 17 חקאימו

Greek: "In the year of the Greeks 462 the king of kings Arsaces Ologasos,
son of king Miradates, took the field at Messene against king Miradates son
of that Pacorus who ruled before him; he drove king Miradates out of
Mesene and gained control of all Mesene; and set up this bronze statue of
the God Heracles, which was brought by him from Mesene, in this temple
of the god Apollo who watches over its bronze gate."

Parthian: "...A[rsa]ces Vologases king of kings, son of king Mithridates, [fought] in Mayshan against king Mithradates, son of Pacorus
king of kings. And he drove king Mithridates out of there. He conquered
all Mayshan. He inscribed and set up this statue of the god Verethragna,
which was taken from Mayshan, on the 17th of [the month] Tyr."

In the Parthian, כת[ש]ו "fought" is probable, cf. Joh 18,36 Pesh
מתכתשין for ἠγονίζοντο. In the logograms ḥeth is three times written
"incorrectly" for he, as in אלחא "god" (normally אלהא). ḥmk "all" and
nykndn "inscribed" are genuine Iranian (Pennachietti 176). פתכר "image" line 8 is Iranian already naturalized in Aramaic, so that its status
whether as Iranian or logogram is ambiguous. See III.96 for its history.

In neither language of the inscription does "Charax" appear, and
district or city are just "Mesene." The date of AD 150/151 for the
bilingual is given by the Greek dating to year 462 (of the Seleucid era
of 312/11 BC). This Vologases king of Parthia ruled from AD 148-192,
called Vologases III by Debevoise 270 and Vologases IV by Potts 150;
he is known from Greek and Latin literary witnesses to the history. His
father is now identified as a Mithradates, probably "Mithradates IV"
of Parthia, known previously only from his coins (ab. AD 128-147).
Mithradates son of Pacorus (where the Parthian adds "king of kings")
is the Meredat king of Mesene of Nodelman previously also known
only from coins (reigning according to Nodelman AD 131-143, but
now known to have reigned at least until 150). He is now further
attested by the Greek of the Palmyrene inscription PAT 1374 (Palmyrene fragmentary) of AD 131 where the merchants (ἔμποροι) in Spasinou
Charax honor Yarhai son of Nebozabad "citizen of Hadriana Palmyra,
satrap of Thilouana under Meeredates king of Spasinou Charax":

Ἁδριανὸν Παλμυρηνόν, σατρά[π]ην Θιλουανων Μεερεδάτου βασιλέως
Σπασίνου Χάρακος.

(Palmyra called itself "Hadriana" from some benefit bestowed by the
Emperor; Red Sea captains of Hadriana Palmyra ['Αδριανῶν Παλμυ-
ρηνῶν ναυκλήρων 'Ερυθραϊκῶν] are attested in an inscription from
Coptos.)[24] Thilouana may be Tylos (Bahrein), Strabo 16.3.4 etc. This
Mithradates of Mesene felt himself so much a king that he appointed
a Palmyrene as "satrap" under him.

Pacorus can be nobody but the long-reigning Parthian king Pacorus
II (AD 78-115, known from Pliny the Younger *Epist.* 10.74 to Trajan);
the text implies that Pacorus controlled Mesene and set up his son
Mithradates in his place; and that Mithradates at some point made
himself independent until he was expelled by another Parthian king
Vologases. This is the first genuinely historical Parthian text; it is
exceptional in that the monarch's actual name Vologases is given in
addition to the dynastic name Arsaces (which alone appears in the
Greek letter of Artabanus III at Susa, AD 21).[25] It is remarkable to
have the Iranian equivalent Verethragna of Heracles; it is a title of
Indra as "slayer of the demon Vṛtra," Vedic *Vṛtrahan* and Avestan
Verethragna. We now learn that the Heracles on the coins of Mesene
was in part understood as Verethragna. Early Sasanian kings, beginning with "Vahram I" (ab. AD 273-276) called themselves Vahram
(Οὐαραράνης) after the god; so Agathias 4.24.5-8[26] in his survey of the
Sasanids, who adds that one called his son σεγανσαά "king of kings".[27]

---

24 L'année épigraphique 1912.171.
25 C. B. Welles, Royal Correspondence in the Hellenistic Period: A Study in
    Greek Epigraphy; New Haven: Yale, 1934; no. 75.
26 CSHB 6.260; ed. R. Keydell, CFHB 2.154 (Berlin: de Gruyter, 1967).
27 For the changes of the Iranian title "king of kings" see III.83.

Chapter 20: Iranian Imperialism and the Rebel Victim[1]

I use "imperialism" without any rigorous definition simply to mean the control of a military power over other peoples, as originally illustrated in the Near East by the Hittites, the Egyptians and the Assyrians (the last followed by the Chaldaean rulers of Babylon). But neither Israel nor Hellas had more than dim memories of the Hittite empire; the historic Greeks did not know Egypt until the end of its imperial days when Necho took Cadytis (Gaza) ab. 609 BC (Herodotus 2.159) and fought at Megiddo 605 BC (II Reg 23,29; Jer 46,2). Greek records of Akkadian rule are scanty. If Herodotus did indeed visit Babylon, it had already been a city ruled by the Persian empire for sixty years before his birth about 480 BC. Since our overall subject is the parallel history of Israel and Hellas, here in their relations to Near Eastern powers, for us "imperialism" begins with the form it took under the Old Persian or Achaemenid Empire,[2] from the capture of Babylon by Cyrus in 539 BC to the victory of Alexander over Darius III at Arbela in 331 BC. Relations with Persia dominate all Greek history before Alexander. In Israel they underlie the last historical books, Ezra and Nehemiah (perhaps somewhat out of chronological order); as likewise the first Aramaic archives, the papyri of Elephantine in Egypt (495 to about 400 BC) and the Arsames dossier (about 410 BC).

Our initial theme is the continuity of Persian imperial power and of its symbols (20.1) in its successor states. Among these are two native

---

1   Extensive revision of my "Prometheus, the Servant of Yahweh, Jesus: Legitimation and Repression in the Heritage of Persian Imperialism," pp. 109-125, 317-325 of David Jobling et alii (eds.), The Bible and the Politics of Exegesis [Norman K. Gottwald Festschrift]; Cleveland: Pilgrim, 1991.

2   The most accessible and reliable history is J. M. Cook, The Persian Empire; New York: Shocken, 1983. That by A. T. Olmstead, History of the Persian Empire; Chicago: University, 1948, is often conjectural, especially in its account of Zoroaster in respect to the Achaemenids. The exhaustive and extremely dense treatment by Pierre Briant, Histoire de l'empire perse de Cyrus à Alexandre; 2 vols.; Achaemenid History X; Paris: Fayard, 1996, is bound to win the day, but at present is still the property of specialists alone.

Iranian dynasties. Eighty years after Arbela a new Iranian empire, the Parthian, appears in the shadowy figure of Arsaces, about 250 BC, whose name was officially adopted by all his successors until AD 227.[3] The Parthian empire was ended by a new Iranian dynasty, the Sasanids, under their first king Ardashir about AD 227. The Sasanid Sapor (Σαπώρης, Parthian *Šhypwḥr*, AD 240-272) left a great trilingual inscription at Naqš-i-Rustam in Greek, Parthian and Sasanid Middle Persian (or Pehlevi), called by moderns the *Res Gestae Divi Saporis*.[4] But Persian symbolism was earlier adopted by Alexander and his successors in Syria, Egypt, and Asia Minor; and some of its techniques were passed on to Carthage through Persian control of the Phoenician seaboard. Thus as Rome successively took over the Punic and Hellenistic empires, and faced Parthia across the Syrian desert, it triply fell heir to Persian techniques of legitimation and repression. A notable theme here is the imperial boast of world control "from sunrise to sunset."

Central to Greek, Israelite and Christian history are rebels, humiliated but (in their different ways) defiant: the Prometheus of Aeschylus, the Servant of Yahweh in Deutero-Isaiah, and Jesus called the Christ. In a section (20.2) on the rebel victim, I propose that both Prometheus and the Servant of Yahweh are envisaged by their poet-creators as crucified resisters to the Persian system. Nobody doubts that Jesus was crucified by the Roman imperial power: his assimilation to the Suffering Servant in the New Testament, and to Prometheus in much modern thought, does not then rest on arbitrary connection but on a solid historical basis, since Rome, above all in the Near East, falls heir to Persian imperial techniques. To the extent that the victims are rebels, Persian and Roman imperial titles are ascribed to them.

At 20.3 I summarize some sources for symbolic attributes of the Iranian monarch and then lay out testimony to the offices of Persian imperialism and their successors: the "king of kings," the satrap, the ambassador or legate, the Magi, and military ranks. In each case

---

3   The basic study remains that of N. C. Debevoise, A Political History of Parthia; Chicago: University, 1938. Early references to the "Parthians" (e.g. Herodotus 7.66.1) are to an Iranian group invaded by the Scythians some time before 250 BC (Strabo 11.9.2); the Arsacid "Parthians" appear to represent a fusion of the two peoples.

4   Greek and partial transcription of the Iranian versions by A. Maricq, "Res Gestae Divi Saporis," Syria 35 (1958) 259-360; full Iranian texts in M. Back, Die sassanidischen Staatsinschriften; Acta Iranica 18; 3rd ser.; Leiden: Brill, 1978; glossary in Gignoux. Why was there a Greek version? See Zeeb Rubin, "The Roman Empire in the *Res Gestae Divi Saporis*," Electrum (Kraków) 2 (1998) 177-185.

Iranian words and phrases continue through the ancient world. A Hellenistic offshoot is the title *kosmokratōr*, "world-ruler." The great perquisite and legitimation of both Great King and satraps is their control of the hunting-parks or "paradises," artificial and natural, studied in our Chapter 21.

The *modes of legitimation* of the Persian ruler are concentrated in his investiture (20.4) with diadem, signet and sword, and the obeisance of prostration due him; they were known at Rome, but mostly as exotic, so that native functional equivalents were developed. The *modes of sanction* available to him (20.5) are control over the bodies of his subjects through taxation, conscription (already treated at II.52-53), flogging and tattooing, and ultimately crucifixion—the fate of all three rebel victims. The sanctions were continued by Rome essentially unchanged. But history reverses the verdict on the rebel victims (20.6), and canonizes them as in the end victorious.

20.1 The continuity of Iranian imperialism

An excerpt from the otherwise unknown Roman historian Aemilius Sura is preserved in the text of Velleius 1.6.6:

> Assyrii principes omnium gentium rerum potiti sunt, deinde Medi, postea Persae, deinde Macedones; exinde duobus regibus Philippo et Antiocho, qui a Macedonibus oriundi erant, haud multo post Carthaginem subactam deuictis summa imperii ad populum Romanum peruenit.

> The Assyrians were the first of all peoples to hold universal power, then the Medes, after them the Persians, then the Macedonians; then through the defeat of the two kings Philip (V of Macedon) and Antiochus (III of Syria), of Macedonian origin, not long after the overthrow of Carthage (201 BC), supreme power passed to the Roman people.

The text picks up an old historico-mythical scheme of four or five successive realms, but still corresponds more or less to reality.[5] At Dan 2,35-45 it is combined with the motif of four successive ages of metal, which in Hesiod appears apart from world empire (I.302). Appian (quoting a lost book of Polybius at *Punica* [8] 132) says that Scipio at the final destruction of Carthage in 146 BC thought of the fall of Troy, Assyria, the Medes, Persia, Macedon, and in some future of Rome

---

5   See the discussion at I.302 and by West, EFH 312-319.

itself.[6] Dionysius of Halicarnassus (1.3.3) lists previous empires—the Assyrian, Median, Persian, Macedonian, and the Successors—and adds, "But Rome is the first and only one recorded from the beginning of time to have made the rising and setting of the sun the boundaries of its dominion":

πρώτη καὶ μόνη τῶν ἐκ τοῦ παντὸς αἰῶνος μνημονευομένων ἀνατολὰς καὶ δύσεις ὅρους ποιησαμένη τῆς δυναστείας.

Actually, Dionysius is applying an old Oriental theme to Rome. Esarhaddon defines his realm as "from rising of the sun to the setting of the sun."[7] So Mal 1,11 (cf. Ps 50,1; 113,3), probably in the Persian period, proclaims "From the rising of the sun to its setting my name is great among the nations":

כִּי מִמִּזְרַח־שֶׁמֶשׁ וְעַד־מְבוֹאוֹ גָּדוֹל שְׁמִי בַּגּוֹיִם

LXX διότι ἀπ' ἀνατολῶν ἡλίου ἕως δυσμῶν τὸ ὄνομά μου δεδόξασται ἐν τοῖς ἔθνεσιν, Vg *ab ortu enim solis usque ad occasum magnum est nomen meum in gentibus.* Aeschines 3.132 says that Xerxes wrote in letters to Greece (in a Greek version?) that he was "despot of all men from sunrise to sunset," δεσπότης ἐστὶν πάντων ἀνθρώπων ἀφ' ἡλίου ἀνίοντος μέχρι δυομένου. The Romans relished the idea: Sallust (*Cat.* 36.4) speaks of the *imperium populi Romani* "at a time when all peoples from sunrise to sunset, overcome by its arms, obeyed it," *cui cum ad occasum ab ortu solis omnia domita armis parerent.*[8] This is the imperial background to Jesus' claim, "Many will come from east and west (ἀπὸ ἀνατολῶν καὶ δυσμῶν) and recline with Abraham, Isaac and Jacob in the kingdom of heaven" (Matt 8,11).[9] When Muhammad made the same boast, "Say: To Allah belong the East and the West," قُل لِّلّٰهِ ٱلْمَشْرِقُ وَٱلْمَغْرِبُ (Quran 2.142) it was shortly to acquire imperial reality also. In a parodistic passage, Joyce says of Queen Victoria, "For they knew and loved her from the rising of the sun to the going down thereof, the pale, the dark, the ruddy and the ethiop."[10]

---

6   Polybius, who was present at the scene and is our ultimate source, in his extant work at 1.2.7 makes Persia, Sparta and Macedon the precursors of Rome in its drive "to make the whole world subject to them," πᾶσαν … τὴν οἰκουμένην ὑπήκοον αὐτοῖς.

7   D. J. Wiseman, The Vassal-Treaties of Esarhaddon; London: British School of Archaeology in Iraq, 1958; i.8 (= *Iraq* 20); translation at ANET³ 534.

8   Further classical usages of the theme "empire from sunrise to sunset" are gathered by E. Fraenkel, Horace; Oxford: Clarendon, 1957; 451, on *Carm.* 4.15.14-16 *et imperi / porrecta maiestas ad ortus / solis ab Hesperio cubili.*

9   J. Jeremias, New Testament Theology; New York: Scribner's, 1971; 245-7 makes Matt 8,11 Jesus' appropriation of the prophetic theme "the pilgrimage of the nations"; see III.17.

10   Joyce, Ulysses chap. 12.

The exact nature of Achaemenid rule is much debated, as likewise whether "imperialism" was consciously intended as a Roman foreign policy.[11] Here, rather than attempting to plumb the motives of rulers, I lay out the more accessible techniques of control, both positive (legitimation) and negative (sanctions). Ideal elements of the Iranian heritage will be those embedded in Persian loanwords,[12] or calques, however transformed, on the very scene of the former empire. The Eastern empires regularized their techniques of control in the face of resistance by less autocratic states. The triumph of those techniques lay in their adoption by the West through the transformation of states once democratic (Athens, a great exactor of tribute) or oligarchic (Carthage and Rome) into capitals of empire.

The ongoing vitality of imperial techniques in their Roman form is surprisingly attested by Edward N. Luttwak, both a Roman military historian and an American strategic analyst, in his comparison of the two situations, written during the Cold War:

> We [Americans], like the Romans, face the prospect not of decisive con-
> flict, but of a permanent state of war, albeit limited. We, like the Romans,
> must actively protect an advanced society against a variety of threats rather
> than concentrating on destroying the forces of our enemies in battle. Above
> all, the nature of modern weapons requires that we avoid their use while
> striving to exploit their full diplomatic potential.[13]

Again, on the dilemma of tying down troops to police remote frontier regions (Judaea then, South Korea now), Luttwak adds:

---

11   P. Veyne ("Y a-t-il eu un impérialisme romain?," Mélanges de l'Ecole française
      de Rome: Antiquité 87 [1975] 793-855) says that Rome had no fixed policy
      of imperial expansion; W. V. Harris (War and Imperialism in Republican
      Rome, 327-70 B.C.; Oxford: University, 1979) says that it did; M. I. Finley
      ("Empire in the Greek and Roman World," Greece and Rome 2nd ser. 25
      [1978] 1-15) with nuances shifts the discussion onto the benefits of empire. See
      the articles in two collective volumes: M. T. Larsen (ed.), Power and Propa-
      ganda: A Symposium on Ancient Empires: Mesopotamia; Copenhagen Studies
      in Assyriology 7; Copenhagen; Akademisk Forlag, 1979; P. D. A. Garnsey &
      C. R. Whitaker (eds.), Imperialism in the Ancient World; Cambridge: Univer-
      sity, 1978.
12   On the Greek side, see B. Hemmerdinger, "158 noms communs grecs d'origine
      iranienne, d'Eschyle au grec moderne," Byzantinoslavica 30 (1969) 18ff; on
      the Rabbinic, S. Telegdi, "Essai sur la phonétique des emprunts iraniens en
      araméen talmudique: Glossaire," Journal Asiatique 226 (1935) 224-256.
13   E. N. Luttwak, The Grand Strategy of the Roman Empire from the First
      Century A.D. to the Third; Baltimore: Johns Hopkins, 1976; p. xii.
14   Ibid. 81.

It is for this reason [the need of quick response] that American troops must be stationed in the theater itself, with the resultant diseconomy of force, regardless of the obvious political functions that these deployments also serve.[14]

In the late Roman republic and early Empire, contemporaries saw Rome and Parthia as equals and rivals. Thus Pliny 5.88 describes Palmyra:

...ac uelut terris exempta a rerum natura, priuata sorte inter duo imperia summa Romanorum et Parthorum, et prima in discordia semper utrimque cura.

...as it were separated by nature from other lands, with a unique destiny between the two supreme empires of Romans and Parthians, and at any beginning of controversy a matter of concern to both sides.

(But the Palmyrene Aramaic inscriptions, while very often with Greek versions, contain few loanwords from Iranian.) Strabo 11.9.2[15] considers that by "the size of their empire" the Parthians have become "rivals to the Romans," ἀντίπαλοι τοῖς Ῥωμαίοις κατὰ μέγεθος τῆς ἀρχῆς. (But at 16.2.20 Strabo speaks of Roman soldiers deployed in Syria as a defence only against *bandits*.) Justin 41.1.1, referring to the time of Trogus, *Parthi, penes quos, uelut diuisione orbis cum Romanis facta, nunc Orientis imperium est* "The Parthians, by whom, as if a division of the world with the Romans had been made, now is held the empire of the Orient." Herodian 4.10.2[16] calls them the two "greatest powers," ἀρχάς...μεγίστας. And so Bab. Talm. *Yoma* 10a "The destroyers of the Second Temple shall fall by the hand of Persia [i.e. Parthia]":

עתידים מחריבי בית שני לפול ביד פרס

20.2 *The rebel victim*

In the Hellenistic world, hidden currents of sympathy flowed among resistance movements. Vogt[17] thinks that the slave revolt of Eunous in Sicily (136-132 BC) had relations to the Seleucid kingdom and was likely "influenced by the Maccabean war of liberation." Eunous was a follower of the "Syrian goddess," that is, Atargatis; he called himself

---

15 And similarly Dio Cassius 40.14.3.
16 See further the texts cited in George Rawlinson, The Sixth Great Oriental Monarchy, or the Geography, History and Antiquities of Parthia; London: Longmans, 1873; p. vi: in particular Velleius 2.101.2, Tacitus *Ann.* 15.13.
17 Joseph Vogt, "The Structure of Ancient Slave Wars," Ancient Slavery and the Ideal of Man; Cambridge: Harvard, 1975, 39-92, esp. 52, 67.

"Antiochus" and the rebels "Syrians."[18] Toynbee[19] compares the Gospels to Plutarch's biographies of Hellenistic and Roman popular leaders. With Matt 8,20 (cf. Luk 9,58) "Foxes have holes (φωλεούς), and birds of the air have nests; but the Son of Man has nowhere to lay his head," he compares the saying of Tiberius Gracchus: "The wild beasts that roam over Italy have a hole (φωλεόν), to each is its lair or nest; but the men who fight and die for Italy have no share in anything but air and sunshine" (Plutarch *Gracchi* 9.4).

Here I suggest that in an earlier period, symbolic figures of victimization and rebellion under Persian imperial rule—likewise joined by hidden currents of sympathy—appear in Aeschylus' Prometheus and the Suffering Servant of Second Isaiah. Podlecki[20] sees the *Prometheus Bound* as a critique of tyranny in the Greek city-states. But its Zeus, the "new tyrant among the gods" (νέος...τύραννος ἐν θεοῖς, *PV* 310) is a more universal figure; the scene is Scythia, the play includes two surveys of what is in effect the Persian empire (*PV* 408ff, 705ff). Io's tormentor Argos, with his "crafty eye" (*PV* 569 δόλιον ὄμμα), is reminiscent of the "King's Eye," or intelligence service (Herodotus 1.114.2 ὀφθαλμὸν βασιλέος).[21]

The more we meditate on Zeus' attributes in the play, the more parallels we find to the Great King. Above all, the running critique of tyranny in the play agrees with the critique of tyranny that Herodotus puts in the mouth of the Persian Otanes in a famous debate. Aeschylus' Oceanus says that in Zeus "a harsh monarch, in no way *accountable*, is ruling" (*PV* 324):

τραχὺς μόναρχος οὐδ᾽ ὑπεύθυνος κρατεῖ

The Persian Otanes says that, in contrast with the monarch, when the majority is in charge it exercises "accountable rule" (ὑπεύθυνον...ἀρχήν), Herodotus 3.80.6. (The annual εὔθυνα, "public examination of the

---

18   Diodorus 34/35.2.7, 24. Vogt (p. 70) is more speculative when he suggests that Aristonikos of Pergamum the rebel leader (133-129 BC), in calling his following of poor man and slaves "Heliopolitai" (Strabo 14.1.38), that is, "citizens of Sun City," had in mind Heliopolis-Baalbek of Syria.

19   A. J. Toynbee, A Study of History; 12 vols.; London: Oxford, 1934-1961; vi.414.

20   A. J. Podlecki, The Political Background of Aeschylean Tragedy; Ann Arbor: Univ. of Michigan, 1966; 101-122.

21   Another internal intelligence agency, the "King's Ears" (τὰ βασιλέως ὦτα Xenophon *Cyr.* 8.2.10, cf. Aristotle *Pol.* 3.11.9 = 1287b30) is attested in Egyptian Aramaic (Cowley 27.9): "The judges, officers and 'ears' who are over the province":

דיניא תיפתיא נושכיא זי ממנין במדינתא

For "ear" in Old Persian is *gauša* (Kent 182).

conduct of officials," was an essential feature of Athenian democracy.)
Prometheus refuses to flatter (θώπτειν) Zeus (*PV* 937); Otanes says
that the tyrant will reject a flatterer (θωπί, Herodotus 3.80.5).
Prometheus says, "So the arrogant are accustomed to show their
arrogance":
οὕτως ὑβρίζειν τοὺς ὑβρίζοντας χρεών
(*PV* 970); Otanes recalls the ὕβριν of Cambyses (Herodotus 3.80.2).

A recent touring Vatican art exhibit included a black-figured
Laconian vase of about 555 BC attributed to the Arkesilas painter.[22]
Prometheus is tied to a column at right while the eagle attacks his chest;
at the left, Atlas holds up a starry sky. The two antagonists of Zeus are
punished together as in Hesiod (*Theog.* 517-525) and Aeschylus (*PV*
348). The Catholic context irresistibly defined the scene as a crucifixion, complete with the carrion bird that in the old curse (I.280-282)
preys on the defenseless body. A full-size sculptural grouping from
Aphrodisias shows Prometheus being unchained by Heracles.[23] Aeschylus uses what was then the technical term for "crucify." Hephaistos
says, "I will peg you (προσπασσαλεύσω) to this inhospitable rock" (*PV*
20); Herodotus 9.120.4 ends his history with a description of how, in
reprisal for numerous crucifixions by the Persians, the Greeks took
Artayctes to a hill overlooking Xerxes' pontoon bridge, where they
"pegged him (προσπασσαλεύσαντες) to a plank and hung him up."

The nineteenth century read Aeschylus' play as an attack on *all*
authorities, political and religious. Shelley, in the Preface to his
Prometheus Unbound, refused the theme of "reconciling the Cham-
pion with the Oppressor of mankind"; in the play (III.iv.471) he
plainly identifies omnipotent Jupiter, responsible for "thrones, altars,
judgment-seats, and prisons" with the Christian God.[24] Marx, in the
Preface to his doctoral thesis,[25] calls Prometheus "the most eminent
saint and martyr in the philosophical calendar." A cartoon of 1843 on

---

22 Black-figured kylix from the Museo Gregoriano Etrusco. See Metropolitan
    Museum of Art, The Vatican Collections: The Papacy and Art; New York:
    Abrams, 1983 p. 185 no. 101; C. M. Stibbe, Lakonische Vasenmaler des
    sechsten Jahrhunderts v. Chr.; 2 vols.; Studies in Ancient Civilization 1;
    Amsterdam: North-Holland, 1972; no. 196 pl. 63. See further I.125.
23 Kenan T. Erim, Aphrodisias: City of Venus Aphrodite; Muller, Blond &
    White, 1986; 118 etc.
24 Shelley's work along with many others is discussed by Jacqueline Duchemin,
    Prométhée: Histoire du Mythe, de ses Origines orientales à ses Incarnations
    modernes; Paris: Belles Lettres, 1974.
25 K. Marx & F. Engels, Collected Works; London: Lawrence & Wishart, 1975-;
    i.31.

the censoring of the *Rheinische Zeitung* shows Marx as Prometheus, chained to a printing press.[26] Posted to the press is a canceled page of the journal; the chain leads up to the leg of a heavenly throne. Marx's heroic figure is surrounded by lamenting Oceanids, done in the style of the odalisques of Ingres. His liver is being attacked by the crowned Prussian eagle, also tethered to the throne; a long line of carrion birds in the sky await their turn.

One theological reaction to the revival of Prometheus was to reject whatever atheists accepted, at the cost of having to swallow Aeschylus' Zeus as a portrait of God. Thus Karl Barth writes enigmatically on Rom 7,7:

> Under the scrutiny of law men become sinners...; for in the end human passion derives its living energy from that passionate desire, *Eritis sicut Deus!* ...Can there be any affirmation of passion that outstrips the passion with which Prometheus robs Zeus of his fire and uses it for his own advantage?[27]

(But Kratos [Aeschylus *PV* 8] says that Prometheus benefitted mortals, not himself.) Hans Küng spells out the underlying thought when he rejects the rebellion of "rising up defiantly against the power of the gods, like emancipated, autonomous Prometheus."[28] Environmentalists do better justice to the genuine ambivalence of the tragedy when they accuse Prometheus of the crime of bringing the primordial technology of fire to earth.

The New Testament suggests an ambiguous parallel between Christ and Prometheus. The risen Jesus tells Paul, "It hurts you to kick against the goads" (πρὸς κέντρα λακτίζειν Act 26,14). So a classical proverb: Pindar *Pythian* 2.94-96 ποτὶ κέντρον...λακτιζέμεν; Aeschylus *Agam.* 1624; Euripides *Bacchae* 795. Less closely, Oceanus advises Prometheus not to "offer your limbs to the goads" (Aeschylus *PV* 323 πρὸς κέντρα κῶλον ἐκτενεῖς). But in our times the Christian-Marxist dialogue, over against Barth and his followers, almost fully engrafted Prometheus onto Christ.[29] Thus in the enormous work of the reluctant atheist Ernst Bloch:

> Prometheus, through his poet Aeschylus, became as it were the founder of his own religion, one which did not of course blossom out. It had to remain unblossomed in the spirit of its rebellion, firstly because a social mandate

---

26   *Ibid.*, vol. i, plate facing p. 374.
27   Karl Barth, The Epistle to the Romans; London: Oxford, 1933; 236.
28   Hans Küng, On Being a Christian; New York: Doubleday, 1978; 431.
29   James Bentley, "Prometheus Versus Christ in the Christian-Marxist Dialogue," JTS 29 (1978) 483-494.

such as that of Moses against the Pharaoh, of Jesus against Caesar, was wanting.[30]

The Czech theologian Jan Milič Lochman—in words now applicable to the former Soviet tyranny—demands a place for Prometheus in theology, in three areas: (1) challenging the idea of God as "an inhuman superstructure imposed on humanity from above"; (2) revealing that inertia in face of God's promise of liberation is as great a sin as *hybris*; (3) pointing to grace as that which "mobilizes human creativity," a driving force for "Promethean existence."[31]

Toynbee sees the "creative power of suffering" as equally illustrated by Prometheus, the Suffering Servant, and Christ, but misses the imperial settings.[32] Jesus was crucified by order of the Roman prefect of Judaea. But the New Testament writers, for whom it was dangerous to underline that fact, explained it by Hebrew antecedents—above all, by Isaiah 53 (with the other Servant poems) and Psalm 22. Luk 22,37 cites Isa 53,12 from the LXX. The Ethiopian eunuch (Acts 8,22-23) cites Isa 53,7-8. I Peter 2,22-25 extensively uses Isa 53,5-12. Isaiah 53 is also quoted explicitly at Joh 12,38; Rom 10,16; 15,21. Isa 50,6 LXX "and my cheeks to blows" (τὰς δὲ σιαγόνας μου εἰς ῥαπίσματα) underlies Matt 5,39 "whoever gives you a blow on the right cheek" (ῥαπίζει εἰς τὴν δεξιὰν σιαγόνα) and is cited at Justin *Apol.* 1.32.2. Mark 15,34 places the opening of Psalm 22 on Jesus' lips, and adds echoes of the psalm that are formalized by the other Evangelists: Mark 15,24 "and they divided his garments" echoes Ps 21,19 LXX which is formally cited by Joh 19,24; Mark 15,29 "wagging their heads" probably echoes Ps 21,8 LXX, and Matt 27,43 "He trusted in God, let him deliver him" makes the connection explicit; Mark 15,36 surely echoes Ps 68,22 "they gave me vinegar to drink."

C. H. Dodd sees certain Hebrew texts as a substructure of New Testament theology, with Isaiah 53 and Psalm 22 at the heart of one of four groups, in each of which the writers remain "true to the main intention" of the Hebrew text.[33] We may add that Psalm 22 has vocabulary links to Second Isaiah: the human figure is a "worm" (תּוֹלַעַת, Ps 22,7; Isa 41,14); "all the ends of the earth" (כָּל־אַפְסֵי־אָרֶץ, Ps 22,8; Isa 45,22) will return to God.

30 Ernst Bloch, The Principle of Hope; 3 vols.; Cambridge: MIT Press, 1986; iii.1213.
31 J. M. Lochman, Christ and Prometheus? A Quest for Theological Identity; Geneva: World Council of Churches, 1988; 28-33.
32 Toynbee, A Study of History, xii.617.
33 C. H. Dodd, According to the Scriptures: The Sub-Structure of New Testament Theology; London: Nisbet, 1952; 108-110.

And as soon as we ask what the Hebrew poems are *about*, the imperial setting returns. It is arbitrary to interpret them in terms of sickness or leprosy and then make the adversaries metaphorical. The Greek translators long before Jesus found a crucifixion in them: thus Ps 22,17.c LXX "they have pierced my hands and feet," ὤρυξαν χεῖράς μου καὶ πόδας. The "dogs" of Ps 22,17.a are naturally interpreted as carrion feeders around their helpless prey. The New Testament citations make the best sense if their authors *correctly* interpreted the Hebrew poems as arising from a situation of imperial oppression like their own—and in fact (we shall see) its ancestor. Isaiah 53 is certainly of the Persian period, and Psalm 22 will fit there. A century of scholarship summed up by North[34] asked only who the servant was, not what happened to him or who did it. If we do ask, we will most naturally conclude that the Servant poems are images, self-censored but recognizable, of the *crucifixion under the Persians of an ideal figure representing Israel*. Thus Toynbee, in comparing the Servant with Prometheus and both with Christ, was a better historian than he realized.

20.3 Iranian imperial offices

A variety of sources combine to give an overall picture of the Iranian court from Darius to the Parthians.

(a) *Obeisance.* A Treasury relief from Persepolis shows an unidentified king receiving obeisance (being "blown a kiss").[35]

(b) *Darius at Susa.* Darius the Great, in a newly found statue from Susa, has his name and title "King of kings" in four languages on his robe and thigh.[36]

(c) *Investiture.* At Josephus *AJ* 20.32, Monobazus is made king of Adiabene (ab AD 45) in Iranian fashion with the diadem (διάδημα), his father's signet (σημαντῆρα), and the ceremonial sword (σαμψηράν, III.99). (The monarch is attested as *Monobazus* at Tacitus *Ann.* 15.1, and as מונבז at Mishna *Yoma* III.10.)

---

34   C. R. North, The Suffering Servant in Deutero-Isaiah: An Historical and Critical Study; London: Oxford, 1948.

35   Cook Plate 9. I have heard a rumor, which I cannot easily substantiate, that this scene is copied in a Persian shield of the "Alexander sarcophagus" from Sidon—which would therefore represent a more Persian conception than previously thought.

36   Headless statue of Darius at Susa with an honorific inscription in Akkadian, Elamite, Old Persian and Egyptian on the folds of his robe: Cook plate 35; M. Kervran et alii, "Une statue de Darius découverte à Suse," Journal Asiatique 260 (1972) 235-266.

(d) *Christ as Parthian monarch.* At Rev 19,11-16 (cf. 17,14; I Tim 6,15) the Christ as the "Word of God" appears with (1') many diadems (διαδήματα); (2') a sword (ῥομφαία) coming from his mouth; (3') on his robe and on his thigh (μηρόν) a name written, "King of kings and Lord of lords":

Βασιλεὺς βασιλέων καὶ κύριος κυρίων.

Also at Rev 19,4 (4') the elders prostrate themselves (προσεκύνησαν) before God.

(e) *The king's Gate.* The *Hymn of the Pearl*[37] represents a redeemer-messenger coming down from a court based on the Parthian monarchy. He returns to "the gate of the King of kings," vs 104:

לתרעא...דמלך מלכא

Here (20.3-5) we survey modes in which the Old Persian empire and its successor Iranian states defined, legitimated and defended their own status. By their subjects, these symbols were seen in a double light: as illegitimate claims to be rejected, but also as the basis of counter-claims in rebellion. Further, some were taken over by the Hellenistic states or Carthage, and from them adopted by Rome in a similar pattern. We begin with offices and their titles.

20.3.1 "King of kings"[38]

This title appears first occasionally in the usage of Egyptian and Assyrian kings,[39] where however "king of kings" was never formulaic. Ezek 26,7 (cf Dan 2,37) applies the title to Nebuchadrezzar, but it seems not to be attested in Akkadian texts; did the Chaldaean take over a Median title? It first became so under the Achaemenids, where Darius in the first line of the Behistun inscription calls himself *xšāyaθiya xšāyaθiyānām* (Kent 116). Artabanus III the Parthian, in a Greek inscription of AD 21, calls himself "Arsaces king of kings,"[40] βασιλεὺς βασιλέων Ἀρσάκης. The title has a Hebrew counterpart at Deut 10,17 (cf Ps 136,2-3, Dan 2,47) where Yahweh is "God of gods and Lord of lords,"

---

37 For editions of this text see III.63.
38 "King of kings" was briefly treated at II.297.
39 J. G. Griffiths, "βασιλεὺς βασιλέων: Remarks on the History of a Title," *Classical Philology* 48 (1953) 145-154; G. Schäfer, "König der Könige"— "Lied der Lieder": Studien zum paronomastischen Intensitätsgenitiv; Abhandlungen der Heidelberger Akademie der Wissenschaften, Phil.-hist. Klasse, 1973, 2; Heidelberg: Winter, 1974.
40 C. B. Welles, Royal Correspondence in the Hellenistic Period: A Study in Greek Epigraphy; New Haven: Yale, 1934; p. 299 no. 75 line 1. The ascription to Artabanus III comes from the date.

אֱלֹהֵי הָאֱלֹהִים וַאֲדֹנֵי הָאֲדֹנִים

LXX θεὸς τῶν θεῶν καὶ κύριος τῶν κυρίων, Vg *deus deorum et dominus dominantium*. It seems probable that Deuteronomy was late enough to reflect Medo-Persian usages. We saw (above) that in the Apocalypse of John the Christ appears as the Word of God with his name written "on his robe and on his *thigh*"; the form of the title is derived from Deuteronomy, but the iconography mirrors the statue of Darius at Susa, where the "name" (now quadrilingual) appears on the robe covering the king's thigh. In a statue of a warrior or god, the thigh is the place where his identification belongs: so in the archaic Greek Mantiklos statuette from Thebes (I.45), and the Parthian statue of Heracles/Verethragna from Seleucia (III.69). For the thigh is where his creative energy resides.

The usage is reflected in Aramaic at Ezra 7,12 מֶלֶךְ מַלְכַיָּא of some Artaxerxes, and at Memphis (482 BC) of Xerxes (חשיארש, KAI 267). (Xerxes appears as אֲחַשְׁוֵרוֹשׁ at Ezra 4,6.) It appears in Greek in a Roman re-engraving of an apparently genuine letter of Darius.[41] Pompey refused that title to the Parthian (Plutarch *Pomp.* 38.2); but Suetonius *Calig.* 5 says that the *regum...regem* joined in mourning Caligula's death. In Sapor's inscriptions the Iranian is masked by Aramaic ideograms. But it is transcribed by Ammianus 19.2.11, who in a beautiful text records the battle cries on Roman and Sasanid sides in a siege of AD 359 where he himself was present and barely escaped:

> Nostris uirtutes Constanti Caesaris extollentibus ut domini rerum et mundi, Persis Saporem *saansaan* appellantibus et *pirosen*, quod "rex regibus imperans" et "bellorum uictor" interpretatur.

> Our men were extolling the virtues of Constantius Caesar as 'Lord of all things and of the world,' while the Persians were calling Sapor *saansaan* and *pirosen* [this form not elsewhere attested], which mean 'king ruling over kings' and 'victor in battle'.

Saansaan, a phonetically simplified descendant of the Old Persian, has the genitive plural first as in Byzantine σεγανσαα (Agathias 4.24)[42] and modern Persian *šāhan-šāh*. The imperial titles of the two realms are brought into absolute confrontation.

What does the title mean? Schäfer[43] suggests that it has the same force as "Song of songs," שִׁיר הַשִּׁירִים, which can hardly have been

---

41   Meiggs & Lewis, SGHI no. 12.
42   CSHB 6.261.5; Agathias gives a false etymology but transmits the title correctly.
43   Footnote 39 above.

intended as "a large composition composed of collected songs" (though in fact it is just that!), but must mean "song *par excellence.*" However some of the usages of "king of kings" demand the meaning "king ruling over other kings," and all are consistent with it.[44] So understood, the title paradoxically betrays political weakness: the overlord cannot supplant tributary kings and must leave them in place. Aeschylus (*Pers.* 24) calls Xerxes' generals "kings subordinate to the Great King,"

βασιλῆς βασιλέως ὕποχοι μεγάλου

Antony called his sons by Cleopatra "kings of kings" and gave them lands he did not control—thus Armenia, Media and Parthia to his son Alexander (Plutarch, *Ant.* 54.4). The romantic Diodorus (1.47.4) puts "king of kings" on the monument of his "Osymandyas" (Ὀσυμανδύας), really the Ramesseum of Thebes—the basis of Shelley's sonnet

I met a traveler from an antique land.

Two inscriptions from the last days of Palmyrene power further illustrate the title "king of kings" and show another Roman office going into Semitic. (I) A posthumous inscription of king Septimius Odainath of Palmyra, killed in AD 267, describes his statue (PAT 0292, AD 271)

צלם ספטמיוס אדי[נת] מלך מלכא ומתקננא די מדנחא כלה

"Statue of Septimius Odainath, king of kings and corrector of the whole Orient". (II) In the "milestone of Zenobia" (PAT 0317, bilingual, the Greek fragmentary) the queen mother appears under her native name בתזבי[45] as "mother of the king of kings,"

אמה די מלך מלכא

namely her son Septimius Wahballath Athenodoros, who is also "illustrious king of kings and corrector of the whole Orient,"

[נהי]רא מלך מלכא ואפנרתטא די מדנחא כלה

Here "corrector," which in the inscription of Odainathus appears in a

---

44 The same meaning is required by the Silver Latin usage of *dux ducum* to describe ancient heroes and in particular Agamemnon: Ovid *Her.* 8.46 *dux erat ille ducum.* At Cicero *Att.* 14.17a.2 Agamemnon is *regum regi.* Cf. Seneca *Agam.* 39 *rex ille regum, ductor Agamemnon ducum.* Hence Jerome at I Chron 7,40 (with no antecedent in the Hebrew or LXX) *duces ducum.* The phrase went back into Rabbinic—from Latin verse!. *Num. Rabbah* 7.3:

מלך בשר ודם יש לו דכסין אף האלהים יש לו דכסין ונשיא נשיאי הלוי
אמר ר׳ יהושע בן לוי דוך דוכנים היה

"A king of flesh and blood has *duces,* and God also has *duces;* '[Eleazar was] prince of the princes of the Levites' [Num 3,32]; Rabbi Joshua son of Levi says that he was *dux ducum.*"

45 As also at PAT 0293; in both places the Greek has familiar Ζηνοβία.

Palmyrene translation, is simply transcribed from Greek ἐπανορθω-τής.[46]

In all our languages "king of kings" or its equivalent becomes a divine title. Thus in archaic Latin the *Carmen Saliare* of the Salian priests had *diuum deo supplicate* "supplicate the god of gods" (Varro *de ling. lat.* 7.27). In Aeschylus *Sup.* 524 the Chorus addresses Zeus ἄναξ ἀνάκτων, μακάρων μακάρτατε "lord of lords, most blessed of the blessed," which (in spite of the Egyptian setting) must have conveyed a Persian flavor to the audience. In later Stoic usage (Dio Chrysostom 2.75) Zeus becomes "great king of kings," μέγας βασιλεὺς βασιλέων.[47] It is Hellenistic that II Makk 13,4 (see Enoch 9.4) calls the God of Israel βασιλεὺς τῶν βασιλέων. Rabbi ᶜAqabya (II.297) went one step further (*Avoth* III.1): "Know before whom you are to give account: before the King of the kings of kings":

לפני מלך מלכי המלכים

where the sense "king ruling over kings who rule over kings" is required. Speratus the Scillitan martyr of AD 180[48] rejects the Emperor as if in fact the Emperor had the Iranian title, and in his place confesses God as *domnum meum, imperatorem regum et omnium gentium*, "my Lord, Emperor of kings and of all peoples." But when the Anglican liturgy addresses God in modified court terms, "thy divine majesty," it is comparison and not contrast. Audiences must stand for Händel's *Hallelujah Chorus* on "king of kings and lord of lords," as at a Court occasion.

20.3.2 The satrap[49]

Darius' administrative innovation was to put each province (Herodotus 3.89) under a "kingdom-protector" or satrap, *xšaçapāvā* (*Beh.* 3.14, 56). Xenophon *Oec.* 4.11 σατράπης records the governor of a Persian province or "satrapy" (σατραπηΐας Herodotus 3.89.1 accus. pl.). Vari-

---

46   The office of Odainath is paraphrased but verified in the SHA *Vita Gall.* 10, *Odenatus rex Palmyrenorum optinuit totius Orientis imperium*, "Odenatus king of the Palmyrenes received rule over the whole Orient." From the time of Trajan, *corrector* is used technically of Imperial commissioners sent out to restore order. So SHA *XXX Tyr.* 24.5 *correctorem totius Italiae*; ILS 9467 (AD 250) τῆς Ἀσίας ἐπανορθωτήν of Annius Sabinus, also prefect of Egypt. An alternative Greek translation appears in the διορθωτὴν τῶν ἐλευθέρων πόλεων "corrector of the free cities" of Asia—a personage who lays out the prerogatives of his office to Epictetus (Arrian *Epict.* 3.7).

47   Elsewhere (II.88) Zeus and Yahweh are both "great king of the gods."

48   Herbert Musurillo, The Acts of the Christian Martyrs; Oxford: Clarendon, 1972; p. 82 no. 6.

49   Briefly treated at II.296.

ously spelled: Στρούσης ἐξαιτράπης ἐὼν Ἰωνίης in a treaty inscription of Miletus, ab. 390 BC[50] "Strouses satrap of Ionia"; participle Μαυσσώλλου ἐξαιθραπεύοντος (Caria, 367-354 BC)[51] "when Mausollus was satrap"; Theopompus has ἐξατράπης.[52] These forms closer to the Iranian, with folk-etymology to ἐξ. Lycian *kssadrapa*;[53] in the Xanthos trilingual the Greek and Aramaic have nouns ξαδράπης = חשתרפנא, the Lycian a verb *χssaθrapazate* "he was satrap."[54] The Aramaic here represents nearly the same transcription as the Aram. of Dan 3,3 אֲחַשְׁדַּרְפְּנַיָּא; cf the Hebrew, Esther 8,9 (cf Ezra 8,36) הָאֲחַשְׁדַּרְפְּנִים.[55] In Arsacid usage (OGIS 431, Bisitun) the title is applied back to the king: Γωτάρζης σατράπης τῶν σατράπων "Gotarzes (king AD 38-51) satrap of satraps." Latin *satrapa* is mostly literal, but see Terence *Heaut.* 452-3 *satrapa si siet / amator* "though her lover is rich as a satrap."

The word in Aramaic form went into Egyptian, *ḫšdrpn*.[56] All these transcriptions agree in the stem with the Sasanid form, Sapor *Res Gestae* 62 σατράπου, Parthian *ḫštrp*, Pehlevi *štrp*. In Old Persian *xšaçapāvā* "kingdom-protector" the stem *pavan* in -*n* is attested in the Aramaic and hieroglyphic forms. The first term of the compound in all other languages is not Old Persian but Median, as shown by the agreement of Avestan *xšaθrəm* "kingdom" (*Yasna* 30.8) with the name *Xšaθrita* assumed by the Median rebel Fravartish / Phraortes (Darius *Beh.* II.15, IV.19). For proto-Iranian *θr* is preserved in Avestan and Median but becomes ç in Old Persian (Kent 31). Old Persian had a limited royal and ceremonial status. The working language of the empire was Median, as was its personnel, for the Greeks knew the Iranian invaders as Medes: Thucydides 1.18.1 "the battle at Marathon of Medes against Athenians," ἡ ἐν Μαραθῶνι μάχη Μήδων πρὸς Ἀθηναίους. A bronze helmet at Olympia was dedicated by the Athenians from the Persian wars, "To Zeus, the Athenians, capturing it from the Medes,"[57] ΔΙΙ ΑΘΕΝΑΙΟΙ ΜΕΔΟΝ ΛΑΒΟΝΤΕΣ.

---

50 M. N. Tod, a Selection of Greek Historical Inscriptions; Vol. II, From 403 to 323 B.C.; Oxford: Clarendon, 1948; II.113.41-43 (p. 37).
51 Tod II.138.2 (p. 112).
52 Jacoby FGH 115 F 103.
53 Friedrich, KASD 62 no. 40d.
54 Henri Metzger et alii, Fouilles de Xanthos Tome VI, La stèle trilingue du Létôon; Paris: Klincksieck, 1979.
55 The LXX Ms "A" of Jud 16,8 interprets the Philistine סַרְנֵי as satraps, σατράπαι, and so Vg *satrapae*.
56 Erman-Grapow iii.339.
57 Margaret C. Miller, Athens and Persia in the fifth century BC: A study in cultural receptivity; Cambridge: University, 1997; 42, with references.

The highest perquisite of both the Great King and the satraps was the forested hunting-park or *paradise*, planted or natural; we discuss it in the following chapter, and in particular its role in the satrapies.

20.3.3 The *cosmocrator*

The Persian example of a world-ruler both inspired Alexander and gave him a title *cosmocrator*, both in Greek and Rabbinic. Otherwise the extensive Hellenistic influence on West Semitic mostly involves cultural terms brought by Greeks to Palestine. In the Alexander romance[58] Nectanebo tells Olympias at the prince's birth "shortly you will give birth to a world-ruler," ἄρτι τέξεις κοσμοκράτορα. Two successive paragraphs of the Jerusalem Talmud (*Aboda Zara* 42c.53-71) speak of Alexander and a world-ruler. "Alexander the Macedonian" (אלכסנדרוס מקדנון) is shown with a ball in his hand[59] "but [unlike God] does not rule over the sea"; a "king of flesh and blood" (מלך בשר ודם) may be called a world-ruler (קוזמוקרטור) but does not rule over the sea; plainly the two are identified. In Greek the word was perhaps originally cultic: *Orphic Hymn* 4.1-3 Οὐρανέ ... κοσμοκράτορ "O Sky World-Ruler." At Eph 6,12 demonic powers are called "the world-rulers (κοσμοκράτορας) of this darkness," in *contrast* to rulers of "blood and flesh" (πρὸς αἷμα καὶ σάρκα).

In the second century CE the title is applied to the Emperor. In a Greco-Nabataean dedication[60] from Rawwafah (N. Hejaz) to Marcus Aurelius and Lucius Verus (AD 166-169) the Greek calls the two rulers κοσμοκρατόρων and the Nabataean perhaps

מתתמ[כי]ן ל[כ]ל [ע]ל[מ]א]

from the root תמך (also in Biblical Hebrew) "grasp." A dedication at Rome (IG 14.926) of the Gazaeans (Γαζαίων) to Gordianus III calls him κοσμοκράτορα. The Gazaeans say that they are setting up this honorary inscription by the command "of their ancestral god," τοῦ πατρίου θεοῦ whom we know (II.71,117) to be Marnas god of the

---

58 Pseudo-Callisthenes, *Historia Alexandri Magni* 1.12, ed. C. Müller post Arrianum; Paris: Didot, 1877.

59 Roman coins of several emperors show the emperor with an orb in his hand; e.g. an aureus of Constantine: Harold Mattingly, *Roman Coins from the earliest times to the fall of the Western Empire*; 2nd ed.; London: Methuen, 1960; LIV.5.

60 J. T. Milik, "Inscriptions grecques et nabatéennes de Rawwafah," *Bulletin of the Institute of Archaeology* (London) 10 (1971) 54-57; see M. G. A. Bertinelli "I Semiti e Roma: Appunti da una lettura di fonti semitiche"; pp. 145-181 of *Serta historica antiqua*; Roma: Bretschneider, 1986; p. 169.

rains. Eusebius (*Vita Const.* 3.46.1 = PL 20.1105C) has Helena refer to her only son Constantine as βασιλεῖ μονάρχῳ κοσμοκράτορι "king, monarch, world-ruler." The closest Latin equivalent would be *terrarum rectorem* (ILS 112A).

Midrash further inflates the imperial imagery: thus (*Exod. Rabbah* 5.14) "That day was the day of Pharaoh's ambassadors (פרוזבוטי i.e. πρεσβευταί cf III.90), and all the kings came to honor him, and they brought gifts (דוראות, i.e. δωρεάς) of crowns and crowned him, for that was the day of the world-ruler (קוזמוקרטור)." Again (*Esther Rabbah* 1.12) "No king who is not a world-ruler of the universe can sit on [Solomon's throne],"

כל מלך שאין קוזמוקרטור בעולם אינו יושב עליו

where the redundant בעולם shows that the force of κοσμο- was lost. (Although Alexander appears to be a *cosmocrator*, Midrashic legend does not make him sit on Solomon's throne.) Also the "angel of death" (מלאך המות) is a *cosmocrator* (*Lev. Rabbah* 18.3).[61]

20.3.4 The ambassador

Any empire needs ambassadors to its subordinate states and neighbors. Artabanus III, in his Greek inscription of AD 21 to Susa,[62] is confirming the election of a city treasurer. In praise of the treasurer, whose election had been irregular, the king notes that at his own expense he has devoted himself on the city's behalf to "two embassies" (line 6), ἀμφοτέρας τὰς πρεσβείας; probably earlier reference had been made to an "ambassador," πρ[εσβευτοῦ]. How was the office named in Iranian? Plutarch *Alexander* 18.5[63] says of Darius that "he became king instead of courier," ἐξ ἀστάνδου βασιλεὺς γενόμενος. Here the importance of the office is minimized but a surely genuine Iranian loan-word appears. Hesychius records what must be the same word as ἀσκανδής "messenger"; the *t* in Plutarch is either phonetic simplification, or a copying error in uncials for *ἀσγανδης. Recently Iranian testimony to what again must be the same word has appeared in Buddhist Sogdian, zyʾnt, ʾstʾnk.[64] But it is frequently attested in Targumic Aramaic and

---

61 For the later history of the idea, see François de Polignac, "Cosmocrator: l'Islam et la légende antique du souverain universel," pp. 149-164 of M. Bridges & J. Ch. Bürgel (eds.), The Problematics of Power: Eastern and Western Representations of Alexander the Great; Schweizer Asiatische Studien; Mon. Band 22; Bern etc.: Lang, 1996.

62 See note 40 above.

63 Similarly Plutarch *Mor.* 326E, 340C.

64 H. Happ in Glotta 40 (1962) 198-201; W. P. Schmid, *ibid.* 321.

Peshitto Syriac as איזגדא "messenger," evidently as a loan-word from Iranian.

Thus Targum Onqelos at Gen 32,3 has אזגדין for Hebrew מַלְאָכִים. The abstract πρεσβεία "legation, embassy" occurs in the sayings of Jesus. Luk 14,32, in the parable of the two kings with unequal forces: "While the other is still far off, [the weaker] sends an embassy (πρεσβείαν) and asks terms of peace." At Luk 19,12-14 a nobleman has gone off to a far land to acquire a kingdom; "but his citizens hated him, and sent an embassy (πρεσβείαν) after him, saying 'We do not want this one to rule over us'." Both times the Vulgate has correctly *legationem*; the Pesh makes it concrete, "ambassadors," איזגדא.

The two usages in Luke suggest not merely typical but specific Near Eastern situations. Just after Jesus' death, about AD 35, the army of Herod Antipas of Galilee was defeated by Aretas of Nabataea when some of Antipas' allies went over to the other side (Josephus *AJ* 18.114); Antipas the tetrarch was called a king[65] and Aretas really was one, though neither campaigned in person. This could have colored the earliest versions of Luk 14,32, which originally might have rested on recollections of earlier battles among the vassal kinglets of the Near East. The situation in Luk 19,14 (it is often observed) reflects the situation in 4 BC after the death of Herod the Great, when his son Archelaus went to Rome to lobby with Augustus for the title 'king,' and is opposed by a "legation of Jews" (πρεσβεία Ἰουδαίων, Josephus *AJ* 17.300), fifty in number, individually designated as πρέσβεις. The incident fits poorly into the parable of the minas, but evidently some strong motivation put it in there. The situation is partially reversed at *Exod. Rabbah* 42.3:

> Parable of a province that sent a legate (i.e. πρεσβευτής) to crown a king:

משל למדינה ששלך פרוזבוטיס לעטר למלך

While he was absent the sons of that province rose up, overthrew the images and stoned the likenesses (האיכונים, i.e. εἰκόνια).

In Paul's usage the 'legate' becomes a messenger from God to human beings. At II Kor 5,20 Paul speaking editorially says "We act as ambassadors on behalf of Christ," ὑπὲρ Χριστοῦ οὖν πρεσβεύομεν, where Pesh has the plural noun in place of the verb, חנן איזגדא, Vg *legationem fungimur*. Eph 6,19-20 "to make known the mystery [of

---

65   Mark 6,22 etc., see Harold W. Hoehner, Herod Antipas; Cambridge: University, 1972; 149-151.

the Gospel],[66] for which I am an ambassador in bonds,"
γνωρίσαι τὸ μυστήριον [τοῦ εὐαγγελίου] ὑπὲρ οὖ πρεσβεύω ἐν ἁλύσει;[67]
Peshitto:

אכרז ארזא דסברתא הו דאנא איזגדה בשעלתא

At Philemon 9 where Paul calls himself a πρεσβύτης "old man," many
follow Bentley in emending to πρεσβευτής "ambassador" (unless
πρεσβύτης itself can mean that [Levin]).

Two Aramaic texts suggest that behind Paul lies a doctrine (Zoroastrian? Gnostic?) of a Messenger come down from a higher world to
enlighten those below, where (in Paul's terminology) it would have
been the Christ rather than the Apostle who is the "messenger." The
hero of the *Hymn of the Pearl* is in effect a legate from the King of
Kings to mankind, though not called such. He has with him two
messengers (vs 16), פרוקין, Greek ἡγεμόνων; and his home is in effect
the Parthian court, for when he falls asleep (37-8) "a *proclamation* was
made in our kingdom that all should speed to our gate, / kings and
princes of *Parthia* and all the nobles of the East":

דכלנש לתרען נשתנז   ואתכרז במלכותן

וכל רורבני מדנחא   מלכי ורשי פרתי

The actual Iranian word appears in a Mandaean text[68] "My good
messenger of light (אשגאנדי טאבא דנהירא) who travelleth to the house
of its friends."

20.3.5 The Magi[69]

In Herodotus 1.101 the Μάγοι are a Persian tribe, who play an increasingly great role in internal politics (Herodotus 3.63.2). The history of
the Magian pretender there is in a general way confirmed by Darius at
Beh. I.36 (Kent 117) *I martiya maguš āha Gaumāta nāma* "There was
one man, a Magian, Gaumata by name"; here the Akkadian is
ma-gu-šu.[70] At Elephantine (Kraeling 4.24) a document is witnessed by

---

66   Omitted by Codex B.

67   Here the Peshitto has two or even three Iranian words: further, ארזא "mystery"
    and אכרז "proclaim," if this is not just a borrowing from Greek κηρύσσω but
    a conflation with a native Iranian word.

68   E. S. Drower, The Canonical Prayerbook of the Mandaeans; Leiden: Brill,
    1959, p. 107 sect. 107 (with copy of original MS at p. 144); transcription in
    E. S. Drower & R. Macuch, A Mandaic Dictionary; Oxford: Clarendon, 1963,
    p. 40 s.v. *ašganda*.

69   The Magi have appeared previously at I.95, 212, 342; II.39, 296.

70   L. W. King & R. C. Thompson, The Sculptures and Inscription of Darius the
    Great...; London: British Museum, 1907; p. 165.

two "magi," each designated מגשיא, one with a name from Mithras, מתרסרה. A Greco-Aramaic bilingual from Cappadocia (*KAI* 265) has denominative verbs ἐμάγευσε = מגיש[71] "conducted Magian ceremonies" for Mithra.

Mostly in the West the magus, however influential, is distrusted: so in Heraclitus[72]; likewise in Sophocles *OT* 387, where Oedipus condemns Teiresias as "such a trickster magus," μάγον τοιόνδε μηχανορ-ράφον. (But a plausible reading of the newly-found Derveni papyrus[73] at vi.2-3 regards them as powerful, "the incantation of the *magoi* is able to change the *daimones* when they get in the way," ἐπ[ωιδὴ δ]ὲ μάγων δύν[α]ται δαίμονας ἐμ[ποδὼν] γι[νομένου]ς μεθιστάναι.) Act 13,8 shows us one such as an apparent historical figure, Ἐλύμας ὁ μάγος; and so 8,9 Σίμων ... μαγεύων "Simon Magus." The μάγοι from the East (Matt 2,1), Syriac מגישי, are given uniquely honorific treatment in the ancient world. At Rome the fall from favor of M. Scribonius Libo Drusus was due to his being led into "the prophecies of the Chaldaeans and the rites of the Magi," Tacitus *Ann.* 2.27 *Chaldaeorum promissa, magorum sacra.* Nero thought that such rites could raise the spirits of his murdered mother, Suetonius *Nero* 34.4 *facto per magos sacro euocare Manes.* Sapor in his *Res Gestae* names one *Krtyr ʾḥrpty* (Parthian 28), Greek 66 Καρτειρ μάγου. This Kartir the Magian has left his own Middle-Persian inscription where he calls himself (line 1) in its usual defective spelling *Kltyl mgwpt* "Kartir chief magus."[74]

20.3.6 The chiliarch and the centurion

At least in theory ancient armies had, besides other ranks, rulers of thousands and hundreds (II.236). Thus Ex 18,21 (cf. I Sam 22,7)

שָׂרֵי אֲלָפִים שָׂרֵי מֵאוֹת

(besides rulers of fifties and tens) where LXX χιλιάρχους καὶ ἑκατοντ-άρχους, Vg in Roman fashion *tribunos et centuriones.* Herodotus 7.81 says that the Persian army under Xerxes had rulers of ten thousands (μυριάρχας), of thousands (χιλιάρχας), of hundreds (ἑκατοντάρχας) and of tens. Of these the rulers of thousands are the best attested otherwise. The Iranian original appears in Sapor's *Res Gestae* 23 as *ḥzrwpt* (transcribed in Greek as αζαροπτ etc.), where the first part of the compound corresponds to Sanskrit *sahásram* "thousand." A more

---

71   Here the *y* in *mgyš* seems to denote the *i* vowel of the intensive ("piel").
72   Heraclitus frag. 14, Diels-Kranz FVS[8] i.154.
73   A. Laks & G. W. Most (eds.), Studies on the Derveni Papyrus; Oxford: Clarendon, 1997; pp. 11 & 95.
74   Text in Back (footnote 4 above).

classical transcription in Hesychius ἀζαραπατεῖς.[75] It appears further in Rabbinic, נזירפמי Bab. Talm. *Shabb.* 139a along with "Magi," אמגושי. One such *par excellence* seems to have commanded the Persian king's bodyguard of a thousand (Aeschylus *Persae* 304); Alexander took over the office, and Antipater installed his own son Cassander as chiliarch (Diodorus 18.48). Hence χιλίαρχος went into standard Hellenistic usage. Judas Maccabaeus (I Makk 3,55, 165 BC) in his army appointed leaders of thousands (χιλιάρχους), hundreds (ἑκατοντάρχους), fifties and tens; the same structure is presumed in the Qumran *War Scroll* (1QM IV.1-5).

The Roman legion of 6,000 was normally made up of 10 *cohortes* of 600 men each, each containing 6 *centuriae* of 100. The legion had 6 military tribunes (*tribuni militum*) instead of the 10 we would expect to command the cohorts, but we regularly find a military tribune commanding a single cohort; the exact structure is unclear to me. (Or did the effective infantry amount to just 6 cohorts?) Latin writers so refer to the officers of foreign armies: Justin 14.1.7 speaks of *centuriones* in the Macedonian army of Eumenes; at 22.1.10 Agathocles in the army of Syracuse is first *centurio* and then *tribunus militum*. Polybius 1.23.1 etc. seems to exaggerate the tribune's command from 600 to 1,000 by giving him the Hellenistic title χιλίαρχος; the Latin occasionally went over into Greek τριβούνους (Dionysius Hal. 2.7.3). Polybius once (6.24.5) transcribes Latin *centurio* as κεντυρίωνας; but the Latinism becomes frequent in Greek inscriptions and papyri. Josephus (*BJ* 2.577-578, AD 66) says that he himself "organized his army along Roman lines" (ῥωμαϊκώτερον ἔτεμνεν τὴν στρατιάν), and appointed rulers of ten ("decurions," δεκαδάρχαις), rulers of a hundred (ἑκατοντάρχαις), of a thousand (χιλιάρχοις), and over these commanders of larger bodies; but he may exaggerate the extent or Roman character of the reorganization, since the structure follows the Maccabean.[76]

Near Eastern armies and militias then show the same pattern, naming their officers in Greek or Latin; it is probably meaningless to ask whether they follow Hellenistic, Roman or even Persian prototypes, since a uniform structure had imposed itself. A Nabataean inscription of AD 8 at el-Hejra in Saudi Arabia[77] marks the tomb of "Ḥaninu

75 Hesychius A.1441 (i.52 Latte), defined inaccurately as εἰσαγγελεῖς "messengers"; with transposition, Ctesias FGH 688 frag. 15.46 ἀζαβαρίτης.

76 See Israel Shatzman, The Armies of the Hasmonaeans and Herod: From Hellenistic to Roman Frameworks; Texte und Studien zum antiken Judentum 25; Tübingen: Mohr, 1991; p. 158.

77 Cooke no. 82 = CIS 2.201; it is dated by the 17th year of Aretas (IV), 9 BC— AD 40; he appears at II Kor 11,32 (cf. II.117).

Hephaistion chiliarch":[78] חנינו הפסתיון כלירכא. Another from the same site (CIS 2.217), also under Aretas and under the protection of the god Dusares (דושרא, Greek Δουσάρης [I.333]), is of the "centurion Shaʿdallahi son of Zabda":

שעדאלהי קנטרינא בר זבדא

The centurion (ἑκατοντάρχης) in charge at Leukē Kōmē the port of Petra (*Periplous Maris Rubri* 9) is surely also a Nabataean. Both chiliarch and centurion appear in Rabbinic, but out of historical context, in vague tables of precedence: thus כלירכין *Qoh. Rabbah* XII.7; קיטרין *Sifre Deut.* 309. The dedications at Palmyra to a קטרינא (PAT 1397 etc.) are to centurions in numbered Roman legions. Still all these officers, Roman or indigenous, are stepping into the boots of their Hellenistic and Iranian predecessors.

The primacy of the Roman military structure in our minds deceives us into transforming indigenous officers of the New Testament into Romans, both in Galilee and Judaea. In *Galilee* it is plain that when Herod Antipas invites to his birthday (Mark 6,21) his χιλιάρχοις, Peshitto כילירכא, Vg *tribunis*, these are not Romans, since he enjoyed a nominal independence free of military occupation; they are officers in his local militia which made such a poor showing against Aretas (Josephus *AJ* 18.114, III.90). It is his soldiers whom John Baptist (Luk 3,14) told to "be content with your wages," ὀψωνίοις, Pesh אפסוניתכון, Vg *stipendiis* (II.110).

At Capernaum Jesus meets a "ruler of a hundred", Matt 8,5 ἑκατόνταρχος, Luk 7,2 ἑκατοντάρχης, Pesh קנטר, Vg *centurio*. He is described as a non-Jew—perhaps an Idumean like his master Antipas. The "centurion" is one of the "first men of Galilee" (Mark 6,21) like the *epitropos* Chuza (Luk 8,3) and Antipas' boyhood comrade Μαναήν (Act 13,1).[79] Joh 4,46-53 seems to have the same event in mind, and calls the personage a "king's man," βασιλικός. With his soldiers he is

---

78 J. M. C. Bowsher ("The Nabataean Army," pp. 19-30 of D. H. French & C. S. Lightfoot, eds., The Eastern Frontier of the Roman Empire...; part 1; British Institute of Archaeology at Ankara, Monograph 11; 1989; p. 21) thinks that Haninu "may have emulated the specific rank as well as the name of Alexander's famous companion [Hephaistion]"; see Arrian *Anab.* 7.14.10.

79 Perhaps this Manaen is the grandson of that Menahem the Essene (Josephus *AJ* 15.373) who predicted the accession of Herod the Great; less likely the same man as the Menahem of Mishna *Hag.* II.2. Theodore Zahn with exceptional ingenuity proposed that the "centurion" of Capernaum *was* Manaen of Acts, on the grounds that the officer is the person of highest rank converted in the Gospels, and Manaen the highest-ranking convert in Acts.

presumably guarding the customs house (τελώνιον Mark 2,14) on the main N-S road. Sherwin-White writes:

> This centurion cannot be a Roman soldier, though the story implies that he is not a Jew. Capernaum was in the heart of the tetrarchy of Herod. Galilee was never part of a Roman province until the death of Agrippa I in A.D. 44. The centurion must be a soldier of Herod [Antipas], who certainly affected Roman terminology.[80]

In *Judaea* at the mocking of Jesus the σπεῖραν (Vg *cohortem*) of Mark 15,16 is beyond doubt a Roman body, and its (undesignated) commander would have been a military tribune or χιλίαρχος as at Act 21,31. Likewise the centurion (Mark 15,39 κεντυρίων) at the Cross is a Roman soldier.[81] But at Joh 18,12, who are the "cohort and the chiliarch and the assistants of the Judaeans" (ἡ οὖν σπεῖρα καὶ ὁ χιλίαρχος καὶ οἱ ὑπηρέται τῶν Ἰουδαίων)? Excursus I proposes that they are a *detachment of the Temple police*.

20.4 Symbolic attributes of the Iranian monarch

The poet of the Persian period called "Deutero-Isaiah" represents Cyrus as being called to his historic mission by the God of Israel (Isa 45,1-7). Morton Smith[82] points out that much of the material here also appears in the Akkadian decree of Cyrus,[83] and the conclusion follows that the poet is repeating what was being said about Cyrus in his milieu. (Smith increases the parallels by assuming that the "Servant poem" of Isa 42,1-4 "Behold my servant whom I have chosen" also refers to Cyrus, rather than [as usually] to an ideal representative of Israel.) Smith goes on to the sensational conclusion that the concept in the Hebrew Bible of the world's creation by God originated with II Isaiah rather than with the Priestly writer of Genesis 1 or elsewhere; and that the poet-prophet took it or augmented it from the Zoroastri-

---

80   A. N. Sherwin-White, Roman Society and Roman Law in the New Testament; Oxford: Clarendon, 1963; p. 124. Another example of Antipas' Roman terminology is the σπεκουλάτορα (Mark 6,27) who beheaded John Baptist, Pesh אספוקלטרא, Vg *speculatore*. The word is frequent in Rabbinic, with nice parallels to Latin and Greek usage: thus *Num. Rabbah* 19.26 "no man praises his executioner," אין אדם מקלס לאיספקלטור שלו.

81   The revisers of Mark found this unliterary, whence Matt 27,54 ἑκατόνταρχος, Luk 23,47 ἑκατοντάρχης.

82   Morton Smith, "II Isaiah and the Persians," JAOS 83 (1963) 415-421.

83   ANET³ 315-316.

anism of Cyrus. At II.58 we summarize the agreement of the Avestan *Yasna* 44 with II Isaiah and other sources in an "Indo-European catechism" of the creator God: "Who created light and darkness?"

The political and cosmic role of the Iranian Great King, "King of kings," is as we saw reinforced by a series of attributes which reflect that role. Here we consider a series of such: his sacred *image*; his *diadem*; obeisance or *prostration* in his presence; his *gate*; and end with an attribute as much belonging to the sanctions exercised by him as to his legitimation—his *sword*.

20.4.1 The image of the Great King

Above (III.83) we saw that the vision of the "Word of God" at Rev 19,11-16 contains Hebrew elements (like the "rod of iron," Ps 2,9) grafted onto a pictorial representation of the Parthian king, including two of the three elements in his investiture (Josephus *AJ* 20.32), the diadem and the sword. In Old Persian such a representation is called *patikara*; Darius (*Beh.* IV.71) so refers to the sculptures surrounding his text at Behistun. In trilingual inscriptions of the Sasanids Artaxaros and Sapor a 'relief' is named by Parthian *ptkr* = πρόσωπον.[84] The word continued to be written in the same manner in Parthian as when it originally entered imperial Aramaic as a loanword eight centuries earlier. In a text of the 5th century BC from Tarsus (KAI 258), פתכר זנה "this statue" refers to a lost relief or sculpture. The bronze Heracles/Verethragna from Seleuceia on the Tigris (III.70) calls itself a פתכר = εἰκόνα. At Elephantine פתכר likewise is "sculpture" and the unique compound פתכרכר "sculptor."[85]

At Isa 8,21 Targum Jonathan has פתכריה for וּבֵאלֹהָיו "and by his gods"; similarly at Amos 5,26, Zeph 1,5. In a beautiful agreement, MS "93" of the LXX at Isa 8,21 has πάταχρα; at Isa 37,38 MS "B" has πάταρχον with metathesis (πάτεχρον correctly in copies known to Theodoretus[86]). Theodoretus in his commentary on Isa 8,21[87] records that πάταχρα stood in some of his MSS there and adds τὸ γὰρ παταχρῆ Σύρων μέν ἐστιν ὄνομα, σημαίνει δὲ τῇ Ἑλλάδι φωνῇ τὰ εἴδωλα "For *patachrē* is a word of the Syrians, and in the Greek

---

84   E. Herzfeld, Paikuli: Monument and Inscription of the Early History of the Sasanian Empire, 2 vols; Forschungen zur islamischen Kunst III; Berlin 1924, p. 84; the Greek texts alone are printed at OGIS 432, 434.
85   Driver 9.1-2.
86   Theodoretus ad Isa 37,38, *in Isaiam* 11.392 ed. Guinot iii.374, Sources chrétiennes 276.
87   *Ibid.* 3.716, Guinot i.316.

language it means 'idols'." Since the word appears nowhere else in Greek or Rabbinic, it must have entered the LXX and the oral Targumic tradition at the same place and time.[88] By "Syrians" Theodoretus may mean the usage of the Syriac churches: at I Kor 8,4 εἴδωλον the Peshitto has פתכרא; the later Syriac of Rev 9,20 has two Iranian words ולפתכרא (i.e. *daiva!*) לדיוא for τὰ δαιμόνια καὶ τὰ εἴδωλα.

20.4.2 The Great King's diadem

The primary emblem of the Persian king's authority was the διάδημα, a cloth headband. Darius on the Behistun relief apparently wears the diadem over the tiara.[89] The diadem was adopted by Alexander (Arrian *Anab.* 7.22) and Seleucus, and continued by the Parthian kings, where the Surena invested the new king with it (Tacitus *Ann.* 6.43). Iranian for "diadem" seems unknown; curiously the Greek went into Pehlevi as *dydymy*.[90] The "kingly crown" that Shakespeare has Antony offer Caesar was really a *diadema* (II.111). The proposal that Caesar be styled *rex* rested on a convenient Sibylline prophecy that "the Parthians could only be conquered by a king" (*Parthos nisi a rege non posse uinci*, Suetonius *Julius* 79.2-3). That would have made Rome one more monarchy on the Parthian-Seleucid model—the only one available. The emperors were so far above wearing the diadem themselves that they bestowed it on Armenians and such: Tiberius early in his career on Tigranes III, Nero on Tiridates.[91]

20.4.3 Obeisance and prostration

The recognition of royal authority in one wearing the diadem was the act of προσκύνησις, whose meaning changed over the years. In 66 BC Tigranes I of Armenia came to Pompey on horseback with the diadem over his tiara; Pompey made him dismount, and he then threw off his

---

88 In my "The Septuagint as a Source of the Greek Loan-Words in the Targums," *Biblica* 70 (1989) 194-216, p. 203, on general considerations I presume that the Targum has it from the LXX, as is surely the case with Greek loan-words in the Targum. But if the two texts were being formed simultaneously (although the Targum took centuries longer to achieve written form than the Greek), perhaps the Greek has it from the Aramaic, where it was well established.

89 Photo in Cook *Persian Empire* plate 8; Xenophon *Cyr.* 8.3.13 says that Achaemenids wear the diadem over the tiara.

90 Gignoux 22.

91 Suetonius *Tib.* 9.1, *Nero* 13. These dynasts with their Iranian names were surely of different culture from any subjects speaking what we know as "Armenian."

diadem and did obeisance (προσκυνοῦντα) to the Roman (Dio Cassius 36.52.3). When Cinnamus the pretender in AD 37 recognized Arta-banus III as king, he first did obeisance (προσκυνήσας) and then transferred the diadem from his own head to the other's (Josephus *AJ* 20.65). The shift of meaning in προσκυνέω, in spite of other theories,[92] is best explained by the development of Persian ceremonial. The Greek literally means "blow a kiss," and just that is done by an inferior to the king in a relief from Persepolis.[93] As social differences widened, the act became prostration and carried the meaning of the Greek verb with it.[94] At first Greeks rejected *proskynēsis*, but in spite of resistance Alexander took it over from Persian court ceremonial.[95] It is Hellen-istic usage that προσκυνέω is the regular LXX translation for the anomalous verb השתחוה; it is unclear what precise act it denotes in the earlier strata of the Hebrew Bible. Persian style so imposed itself that the verb, no doubt with the sense "fall prostrate," is standard in Matthew's Gospel for respect shown to Jesus.[96] It was appropriate that Satan, perhaps with Ahriman somewhere in his background, should ask Jesus to "fall down and worship him" (πεσὼν προσκυνήσῃς Matt 4,9). It was even more appropriate that Magi, looking for a king of the Jews, "fell down and worshipped him" (Matt 2,11), for a council of "wise men and Magi" also played a role in the designation of the *Parthian* king (Strabo 11.9.3).

20.4.4 The Great King's gate

One more tableau of the Parthian court appears in the *Hymn of the Pearl* 104. The court is defined as the "gate of the king of kings":

לתרעא...דמלך מלכא = τὰς τοῦ βασιλέως θύρας

---

92   H. Greeven (TDNT 6.759) thinks that προσκυνέω originally implied respect to a *chthonic* deity, on the grounds that kissing one such would require prostra-tion!

93   Relief from the Persepolis treasury (Cook, Persian Empire, plate 9; see III.82); the king has not been surely identified. The gesture of "blowing a kiss" is described by Apuleius *Met.* 4.28.

94   R. N. Frye, "Gestures of Deference to Royalty in Ancient Iran," Iranica Antiqua 9 (1972) 102-107, analyzes a variety of gestures shown on the monuments. Herodotus 1.134.1 shows how the rank of one being saluted determines the gesture.

95   Herodotus 7.136; Xenophon *Anab.* 3.2.13; Arrian *Anab.* 4.10-12; Plutarch *Alex.* 74.

96   In Mark προσκυνέω appears only in Roman context: by the one who has the "Legion" (Mark 5,6) and in mockery by the Roman soldiers (15,19). In Luke it may belong only to the Temptation narrative (Luk 4,7-8), for Western witnesses omit it at Luk 24,52.

as the Ottoman court was the *Sublime Porte*. Xenophon *Anab.* 1.9.3 knows that noble Persian youth were educated "at the gates of the king," ἐπὶ ταῖς βασιλέως θύραις. The same idiom appears at Esther 2,19, "the king's gate":[97] שַׁעַר הַמֶּלֶךְ.

20.4.5 The Great King's sword

At III.82 we saw that Monobazus was invested in Iranian fashion with a sword, σαμψηράν (Josephus *AJ* 20.32). The word is plainly Iranian; Sapor *Res Gestae* 64 had one "Papak the sword-bearer," Parthian *P'pk spsyrdr*, Greek Παπάκου τοῦ σπαθοφόρου.[98] The loanword in Greek further in a fragment, perhaps from Arrian's *Parthica*[99] δῶρα φέρει Τραϊανῷ ὑφάσματα σηρικὰ καὶ σαμψῆρας "N. brings gifts to Trajan of silk garments and swords." A papyrus[100] has σαμσειρὰ Ἰταλική "an Italian sword"; the editors in an addendum (I.iii.86) explain Persian *šamšer* as a compound, *šam* 'claw' + *šer* 'lion,' but I cannot verify this.

Above all the word appears in Aramaic. Thus in Rabbinic, Bab. Talm. *Baba Bathra* 21b "he drew his sword," שקל ספסרא. Similarly in Syriac, *Odes of Solomon* 28.5 "And the dagger shall not divide me from him, nor the sword"

וחרבא לא תפלגני מנה אפלא ספסרא

And frequently in the Peshitto New Testament, although its distribution beside other Aramaic words for "sword" is peculiar. Thus at Act 16,27 the jailer, proposing suicide, "drew his sword," σπασάμενος τὴν μάχαιραν, Pesh נסב ספסרא. At Matt 26,55 (cf. Mark 14,48, Luk 22,52) Jesus addresses his adversaries, "Have you come as against a bandit (λῃστήν) with swords (μαχαιρῶν) and staves to take me?" Here the Pesh has בספסרא; the Palestinian Syriac (and the Pesh of Luk 22,52) correctly translate λῃστήν with לסטיא.

There is a remarkable variation between Matt 26,52a and b. In the first half-verse, "Put your sword back in its place," ἀπόστρεψον τὴν μά-

---

97 The book of Esther is not a mere historical romance, for it has access to good tradition. Thus in Hegay (הֵגַי Esther 2,8), eunuch over Xerxes' harem, it records one Hegias, the sole historical Greek person named in the Hebrew Bible; he must be the "Hegias of Ephesus," named in Xerxes' court by Ctesias, FGH 688 frag. 13.27; see I.34.

98 He takes the place of Gaubaruva (Γωβρύης Herodotus 3.70) the spear-bearer (*arštibara*) of Darius and Aspacana (Ἀσπαθίνης, see II.6) his bow-bearer (*vacabara*); Kent 140.

99 *Suda* iv.319 Adler.

100 *Pap. Giessen* 47.11, ed. O. Eger et alii, Griechische Papyri im Museum des oberhessischen Geschichtsverein zu Giessen; Leipzig: Teubner 1910, I.ii.

χαιράν σου εἰς τὸν τόπον αὐτῆς the Pesh has Iranian אהפך ספסרא לדוכתה.
And so at Joh 18,11 with θήκη "sheath," βάλε τὴν μάχαιραν εἰς τὴν θήκην,
the Pesh likewise has סים ספסרא בחלתה.[101] But in the proverb Matt
26,52b "for all those who take the sword shall perish by the sword,"
πάντες γὰρ οἱ λαβόντες μάχαιραν ἐν μαχαίρῃ ἀπολοῦνται all the Syriac
versions have Aramaic סיפא, thus Pesh:

כלהון גר הנון דנסבו סיפא בסיפא נמותון

It is hard to discern the dialectal register of the two translations in the
Pesh of Matt 26,52. The seeming proverb "All those who take the
sword..." with Rabbinic סיפא might either be colloquial, or quotation
of an archaic saying. The command "Put the sword back in its place/
sheath" with Iranian ספסרא might be either correct literary eastern
Aramaic or a colloquial reminiscence. What seems clear is that the
original usages of ספסרא in Aramaic must have carried the connotation
of Parthian political power. Then it applies also to the sword of minor
Near Eastern powers like the police force of the high priests, "Have
you come out to take me as against a bandit with *swords* and staves?"
Perhaps also in Iranian it had a metaphorical force "that which divides
one person from another" as in "not peace but a sword" (Matt 10,34)
and the *Odes of Solomon*.

20.5 Imperial sanctions

During the Old Persian or Achaemenid empire, Jews were in intimate
touch, both in Babylonia and the Palestinian satrapy, with the new
rulers of the Near East. Since 597 BC there had been a Jewish exile
community in Babylon. Soon after the accession of Darius I in 522 BC
he controlled what Herodotus 3.91 calls his fifth province, including
"Phoenicia, Palestinian Syria and Cyprus"; it is the seventh in Darius'
own list (*Beh.* I.12-17), "those who are beside the sea." (Already in
546 BC Cyrus controlled Sardes, and from that time on Greeks somewhere were ruled by Iranian-speaking officials.) Deutero-Isaiah has
God call Cyrus his 'Anointed' (Isa 45,1 מְשִׁיחוֹ, LXX τῷ χριστῷ). Ezra
and Nehemiah record, along with Aramaic documents from Egypt and
the Arsames dossier, many facets of Persian imperial rule in Palestine.
    After the formation of the new Arsacid or Parthian dynasty,
Babylonia and the Jewish community there were under Iranian rule by

---

101 Circe with different vocabulary expresses the exact same command to Odysseus,
    Od. 10.333 ἀλλ' ἄγε δὴ κολεῷ μὲν ἄορ θέο.

the death of Mithradates I in 138/7 BC.[102] In 40 BC Pacorus I, son of king Orodes II of Parthia, seems to have been co-regent in his own right. With the satrap (of an uncertain area, Josephus *AJ* 14.330) Barzaphranes and the Roman renegade Q. Labienus,[103] Pacorus took advantage of the absence of M. Antonius and invaded Syria and Palestine (Dio 48.24-26); in Jerusalem they installed the Hasmonean claimant Antigonus as king (Josephus *BJ* 1.269), which office he held as Mattathias[104] until the Romans reclaimed control. Antonius executed him in 37 BC (Dio 49.22.6) and installed as king Herod the Great.[105] During the career of Jesus, Judaea was ruled by Tiberius (AD 14-37) far to the west, brooding on the Palatine or at Capri. Much nearer at hand was the Parthian king Artabanus III (AD 12-ca. 38, with gaps?), whose winter palace was at Seleuceia near Babylon (Strabo 16.1.16); for a while his rival Vonones was interned by the Romans in Syria as a check on the incumbent (Josephus *AJ* 18.52; Tacitus *Ann.* 2.58). In AD 35, Artabanus wrote to Tiberius demanding Vonones' treasure and impertinently offering to annex the former empires of Cyrus and Alexander (Tacitus *Ann.* 6.31).

From the beginning of the new Iranian dynasty of the Sasanids under king Ardashir (ab. AD 227), Edessa, the home of Syriac Aramaic, was close to the sphere of influence of his son and successor Sapor I (reigned AD 240-272). Sapor in his *Res Gestae* 19 states that in AD 260 when he captured the Roman emperor Valerian he besieged Carrhae and Edessa/Urha (Greek Κάρρας καὶ Ἔδεσσα, Parthian *H'rn W'wrḥ'y*), although it is doubtful[106] that Edessa was actually taken. Thus during the formative period of the Syriac Gospels their language went on being influenced by Iranian.

The Old Persian empire took over many of the administrative sanctions of the Assyrians and neo-Babylonians, whose exactions were vividly recalled in Israel, dimly in Hellas also. Plato (*Laws* 685C, see I.329) imagines that at the time of the Trojan war "those [hostile to Trojan power], relying on the power of the Assyrians sited at Ninos [Nineveh], boldly raised the war against Troy"; and adds "as now we

---

102 Discussion in Debevoise 27; Jacob Neusner, A History of the Jews in Babylonia; I. The Parthian Period; Leiden: Brill, 1965, 21.
103 Labienus on a famous coin with a Parthian horse on the reverse calls himself Q. LABIENVS PARTHICVS IMP (erator); Mattingly (note 59 above) p. 80 & Plate XIX.20. In Roman tradition that should have meant "Commander in a victory over the Parthians"; it is unclear what Labienus meant by it.
104 So on his bilingual coins, SVMB i.281.
105 See further for these events Debevoise 110-120.
106 Millar 167.

fear the Great King, so those of old feared the then established authority." Rumors of Assyrian power surely are reflected in Homer. The
whole spectrum of humiliations inflicted on the bodies of the captured,
living or dead, by the Assyrians—impaling, flaying, hanging up[107]—is
echoed in the last books of the Iliad. Somehow the word got around.
But with Homer, what in the Assyrian reprisals is "national propaganda, to intimidate potential enemies of the king, is turned to the
expression of the final horror of the death of noble warriors, and to the
last extremity of passionate heroic hatred."[108]

Here we record some of the sanctions either developed by the Old
Persian empire or taken over by it from the Assyrians, beginning with the
mildest (taxation, bureaucracy). The deprivation of freedom through
requisitioning and conscription (*angareia*) has been treated above at
II.52-53. (Homeric ἄγγελος "messenger," unexplained from IE, may be
an earlier loan of the unknown [Akkadian or Iranian?] original of
ἄγγαρος "courier.") We end with the forms of corporal punishment:
tattooing and flogging, and the ultimate sanction, crucifixion.

20.5.1 Taxation

Aramaic Ezra three times (4,13; 4,20; 7,24) has the phrase "tribute,
custom or toll" with slight variations; Ezra 7,24

$$\text{מִנְדָּה בְלוֹ וַהֲלָךְ}$$

Vulgate *uectigal et tributum et annonas*; at 4,20 *tributum et uectigal
et reditus.* מנדה also appears in the Arsames dossier (Driver 8.5); הלכא
frequently there and elsewhere.[109] Kaufman recognizes these as from
Akkadian *maddattu, biltu, ilku*; and thinks (p. 44) that they represent
"a threefold list of Persian taxes represented in L(ate) B(abylonian) by
the forms *ilku, baru,* and *nadi/anatu.*" The words thereafter drop out
of Aramaic almost completely.

In contrast מֶכֶס "tax" appears in the Hebrew Bible at Num 31,28ff
(and there only) where LXX τέλος; the corresponding noun of agent
"publican" is Rabbinic מוכס, Palmyrene מכסיא, Peshitto מכסא representing τελώνης in the Gospels. Kaufman 72 derives מֶכֶס from *miksu*
'tax,' and the nouns of agent probably from Akkadian *mākisu*. Either
this is a late addition to Numbers or an early influence of Akkadian

---

107 ANET³ 276, 288, 295.
108 Jasper Griffin, Homer on Life and Death; Oxford: University, 1980; p. 46.
109 מנדה or מדה also at Ezra 6,8 (Aram.), Neh 5,4, Kraeling 5.7.
110 H. W. F. Saggs, "The Nimrud Letters, 1952—Part II," Iraq 17 (1955) 126-
       160; Letter XII.10-20 (p. 128) speaks of "tax-collectors (who were) over the
       wharves [?] of Mount Lebanon" taxing timber, and "a tax-collector (*ma-ki-su*)
       who (had been) in the warehouses of Sidon."

bureaucracy on Hebrew. An Akkadian letter from 740-705 BC[110] records tax-collectors taxing timber on Lebanon. Mishna *BQ* X.1 תיבת המוכסין "the chest of the tax-collectors." τελώνιον "customs house" (Mark 2,14), Pesh בית מכסא, Vg *teloneum*.[111] The same equivalence τελώνης = מכסא also at Palmyra, where the Tariff (I.7) records "disputes between the traders (III.66) and the publicans:

ζητήσεις...[με]ταξὺ τῶν ἐνπόρων πρὸς τοὺς τελῶνας

סרבנין...ביני תגרא לביני מכסיא

The N.T. Vulgate *publicanus* traps us into thinking of the Gospel τελῶναι as in some sense Romans. Eventually some of the proceeds did get back to Rome from both Galilee and Judaea through tribute. But through all changes of regime the reliable tax-collectors were locals who knew the scene. The tax-collector of Capernaum was a local, Levi son of Alphaeus (Mark 2,13; see II.120) or Matthew the Evangelist (Matt 9,9; 10,3); even in Roman Judaea the "chief tax-collector" of Luk 19,2 (ἀρχιτελώνης, Pesh רב מכסא, Vg *princeps publicanorum*) is a local, Zacchaeus. Tax-collection like banditry is hereditary: Bab. Talm. *Shebu.* 39a "You will find no family with a tax-collector, where they are not all tax-collectors; or with a bandit (λῃστής) where they are not all bandits":

אין לך משפחת שיש בה מוכס שאין כלה מוכסין ושיש בה ליסטין שאין כלה לסטין

20.5.2 The bureaucracy

פֶּחָה is used of an Assyrian captain (it seems correctly) at II Reg 18,24, where LXX τοπάρχου and Vulgate *satrapam* (anticipating its later Persian use). At Jer 51,23 of Babylonian officials, פַּחוֹת וּסְגָנִים (for the latter see below). At Esther 3,12 of Persian governors. At I Reg 10,15 retroactively applied to the time of Solomon, פַּחוֹת הָאָרֶץ; there is no other evidence that it was adopted this early in the monarchy. (But Levin thinks this text a precious witness to early usage.) In Biblical Aramaic at Ezra 5,14, again in Persian context. At Elephantine it designates Persian provincial governors or satraps: Bigway of Judah בגוהי פחת יהוד (Cowley 30.1), Sanballat of Samaria סנאבלט פחת שמרין (30.29).[112] It seems abbreviated from Akkadian *bēl paḥāti* "lord of a district."

The subordinate to a פחת is סגן, applied to both Assyrian and Babylonian officials, nearly always with פַּחוֹת: Ezek 23,6 etc.; Jer 51,23

---

111 Also on stone the Greek enters Latin as a loanword: in North Africa a *teloneum* is repaired (CIL 8.12314); in Ephesus is one Quintus a *teloniarius* (CIL 3.13677).

112 This Sanballat is likely the same man as סַנְבַּלַּט of Neh 2,10 etc.; and Bigwai the Bagoses of Josephus *AJ* 11.297-301.

etc.; of Medes Jer 51,28. It is taken up as a title of Judaean officials at Neh 2,16 etc. Biblical Aramaic סְגְנַיָּא וּפַחֲוָתָא Dan 3,2 etc. סגן is constant at Elephantine for the Persian governor but also of civilians, Cowley 26.9 סגן נגריא "head of the carpenters." Kaufman 97 takes it from Akkadian *šaknu*.

> In all periods, *šaknu* could refer to officials on two distinct levels of the administrative hierarchy: provincial governors (appointed by the king), and officials subordinate to provincial governors and other high officials... Note also that a *šaknu* in charge of a garrison...could also be called "governor" (*bēl pāḫiti*).[113]

There is an unique Mishnaic description (see I.198) of a Hellenistic ceremony where a bull (השור) with gilt horns (וקרניו מצופות זהב) is brought to Jerusalem (*Bikkurim* III.3). When they got near "the governors, the prefects and the treasurers went out to meet them":

הפחות והסגנים והגזברים יוצאין לקראתם

These are evidently officials of the Temple. *Avoth* III.2 quotes Rabbi Ḥanina (חנינא) deputy of the priests (סגן הכהנים) "Pray for the peace of the government." In the LXX of Nehemiah (2,16 etc.) the סְגָנִים are translated στρατηγοί "commanders" and are surely heads of the Temple police (III.115, where Hanina is identified with Ananos the στρατηγός of the Temple [Josephus *AJ* 20.131]). Thus *Bikkurim* testifies to two groups of Temple officials with Assyrian titles, פחות and סגנים, and a third, the treasurers, with a Persian one (גזברים, Ezra 1,8). For this Iranian word see III.240.

The same Akkadian term appears much earlier in a different transliteration, *skn* at Ugarit, which knows a "mayor of the city" (*skn qrt* KTU 4.609.10) and a "superintendent of the house" (*skn bt* KTU 7.63.5). The Ahiram inscription of Byblos speaks of "a governor among governors," סכן בסכנים (KAI 1.1); the "New City" or Carthage of Cyprus has a mayor, סכן קרתחדשת (KAI 31.1). At Isa 22,15 Shebna is סֹכֵן. Thus the same Akkadian title is taken up in West Semitic at widely separate periods with slightly different phonetics for (so far as we can determine) nearly the same office.

20.5.3 Tattooing and flogging

C. P. Jones, in a notable article,[114] proposed that Greek (and Latin) *stigma* normally means "tattoo," not "brand"; certainly the verb στίζω

---

113 CAD 17.1.191.
114 C. P. Jones, "*STIGMA*: Tattooing and Branding in Graeco-Roman Antiquity," JRS 77 (1987) 139-155. But in the American Civil War, Union deserters were

means "prick," so that on a previous view its use for "brand" could be only metaphorical.[115] Penal tattooing was a Persian innovation in Greece: Xerxes tattooed the Thebans taken at Thermopylae with the "royal stigmata," ἔστιξαν στίγματα βασιλήϊα—as earlier he had symbolically done to the Hellespont (Herodotus 7.233.2, 7.35.1)! The Athenians, quick studies, tattooed Samian captives with their owl, and the Samians in turn tattooed Athenians with their trireme.[116] The Syracusans tattooed Athenians with their horse (Plutarch *Nic.* 29). A στιγματίας was a runaway slave caught and tattooed.[117] In Latin such a tattoo was normally of three letters, for example *FVR* "thief."[118] The Romans saw it as an act of "writing."[119] The mark of the Beast (Rev 13,16) on forehead or right hand is then primarily a mark of ownership; here also it is of three letters, interpreted as numbers. At Jewish Elephantine the owner's name was marked on the right hand of a slave.[120] A soldier was in a status close to slavery, and a captured deserter also was tattooed (Aeschines *Emb.* 79). During the Roman proscriptions, masters (who feared a recurrence of slave revolts) treasured the memory of "a tattooed slave who saved the master that had tattooed him" (Dio Cassius 47.10.4), στιγματίας...τὸν στίξαντα... ἔσωσεν.

The meaning of *stigma* is extended to the permanent scars from flogging, as in "one tattooed (στιζόμενος) by the rod" (Aristophanes *Wasps* 1296). When Paul says "I carry the marks (στίγματα) of Jesus on my body" (Gal 6,17), he surely means that he had been flogged by Jews and Gentiles (II Kor 11,24-25; Act 16,23) just as Jesus had been— hardly that he had been made a slave to Christ by religious tattooing.

---

branded D with a hot iron on the cheek. One Army physician, Dr William Minor, carried out the punishment under orders (Simon Winchester, The Professor and the Madman; New York: HarperCollins, 1999). His obsessive memory of the act helped push him over the brink to violent and delusionary madness. Most of his latter years were spent at the Broadmoor Criminal Lunatic Asylum in England, where he became the most valued single contributor to the Oxford English Dictionary.

115 Still the scars of flogging are called a *stigma*, so a brand could also have been so named.

116 Photius, *Samiōn ho dēmos* as printed by G. F. Hill, Sources for Greek History...; 2nd ed.; Oxford: University, 167; Plutarch *Per.* 25 through misunderstanding reverses the situation. Actually, it is easier to imagine Xerxes taking a hot iron to the sea; and on second thought this raises doubts about Jones' doctrine in general.

117 Athenaeus 13.612C; Cicero *de off.* 2.25; a female runaway tattooed, Aristophanes *Lys.* 331.

118 Plautus *Aul.* 325, speaking of a "three-letter man," *trium litterarum homo.*

119 Quintilian 7.4.14, *si quis fugitiuo stigmata scripserit.*

120 Kraeling no. 5.7.

The Franciscan understanding of the *stigmata* has lost the imperial reference. Jewish Aramaic reveals its underclass status by having *two* foreign words for "flogging," one from each of two empires. Ezra 7,26 has a descending scale of penalties "death, *flogging*, confiscation of goods, imprisonment":

לְמוֹת...לִשְׁרֹשׁוּ...לַעֲנָשׁ נִכְסִין וְלֶאֱסוּרִין

that the LXX παιδείαν is correct is shown by Egyptian Aramaic, where סרושיתא is a punishment for slaves.[121] The word is Iranian; it appears in the Avestan hymn to Mithra in the phrase *yo ništayeiti kǝrǝtǝe sraošyąm* "who orders the execution of punishment."[122]

Roman practice was found different and abhorrent enough that *flagellum* was taken into Greek as φραγέλλιον (Joh 2,15, Pesh פרגלא, Vg *flagellum*) and thence into Palestinian Aramaic פרגל.[123] Cicero (*Rab. Perd.* 12) regards *flagella* as worse than *uirgae* "rods"; Horace *Serm.* 1.3.119 speaks of the *horribili flagello*. There is a striking parallel to the Passion in near-identical form in several Rabbinic texts, here taken from *Mekilta* on Exod 20,3-6,[124] a dialogue between an unidentified onlooker and a Jewish martyr.

על שמלתי את בני ישראל	מה לך יוצא ליהרג
על שקראתי בתורה	מה לך יוצא לישרף
על שאכלתי את המצה	מה לך יוצא ליצלב
על שנטלתי את הלולב	מה לך לוקח מאה פרגל

"—Why are you being led out to be killed? —Because I circumcised my son to be an Israelite. —Why are you being led out to be burned? —Because I read in the Torah. —Why are you being led out to be *crucified*? —Because I ate the unleavened bread. —Why are you getting a hundred *lashes*? —Because I did the ceremony of the Lulab." In this text "crucified" is the West Aramaic verb. Here the Jewish community reacts to its persecution, probably under Hadrian, as the Christian sect to *its* persecution.

20.5.4 Crucifixion

Assyria has justifiably had a bad name for "frightfulness," Hitler's *Schrecklichkeit*. Persia and Rome are sometimes given credit for mitigating it. But, as with the Allied victors in World War II, their route

---

121 Driver no. 3.6; note the accurate distinction between the two Avestan sibilants.
122 I. Gershevitch, The Avestan Hymn to Mithra; Cambridge: University, 1959; para. 109.
123 At Mark 15,15 Codex Bezae has the more correct φλαγελλώσας with vulgar ρ written over the first λ in the corrector's hand.
124 *Mekilta* ed. Lauterbach ii.247. Nearly the same text at *Lev. Rabbah* 32.1 and *Midrash on Psalms* 12.5. Further discussion at Sperber Legal Terms 153-4.

to take over its sway lay through mass killings. When Darius took Babylon, he crucified three thousand citizens (Herodotus 3.151.1). Cyrus the younger was praised (Xenophon *Anab.* 1.9.13) for making highways safe for Hellene and barbarian by lopping off hands and feet and gouging out eyes of criminals. At home, when M. Licinius Crassus defeated Spartacus in 71 BC, six thousand captives were strung up all along the road from Capua to Rome (Appian *Civil Wars* 1.120). (Readers may recall that Crassus was defeated and killed by the Parthian Surena at Carrhae, 53 BC, and his head used in a performance of Euripides' *Bacchae* at the Hellenized Parthian court [Plutarch *Crassus* 33].) When Rome in the same year (146 BC) took Carthage and Corinth, it thus found sanctions for imperial control ready at hand: conscription, tattooing and flogging, crucifixion. In the opposite sense to what the poet intended, *Graecia capta ferum uictorem cepit*, "Captured Greece took her fierce victor captive" (Horace *Epist.* 1.1.156).

For crucifixion was standard procedure in the Hellenistic empires, particularly the Seleucid.[125] The Maccabees saw themselves as Hellenistic monarchs, and Alexander Jannaeus crucified eight hundred captives while drinking and reclining with his concubines (Josephus *BJ* 1.97). Carthage made a specialty of crucifying its own defeated generals as well as captured enemy ones (Polybius 1.11.5, 1.24.6; Diodorus 25.10.2). The Carthaginians were then imitated by mutineers (Polybius 1.79.4). One Mago in 296 BC enticed the suffetes of Gades into his hands and then scourged and crucified them (Livy 28.37.2). One Hannibal crucified the runaway Campanian slave Spendius, but was himself captured by Spendius' allies, who took their friend down and put Hannibal up in his place (Polybius 1.86.4-6). Hannibal the great crucified a false guide in Italy *ad reliquorum terrorem* (Livy 22.13.9), *pour encourager les autres*. Goya's *Los Desastres de la Guerra* (ab. 1815, pub. 1863), still so upsetting to us, are pale reflections of the ancient realities.

Thereby Carthage continued Assyrian and Persian practice, evidently mediated by the Phoenician cities, which owed their independence and prosperity to their inland neighbors. Phoenicia alone could supply various luxury goods as well as "the enormous quantities of iron required by the Assyrian 'war machine'."[126] The Assyrians, while striving to control the coastal cities, granted them quasi-autonomous status to engage in the sea-trade at which they felt themselves incom-

125 Hengel 73-76 (note 128 below).
126 Susan Frankenstein, "The Phoenicians in the Far West: A Function of Neo-Assyrian Imperialism," Power and Propaganda (ed. Larsen, see note 11 above) 263-294, esp. 272, referring to A. L. Oppenheim.

petent (I.302). Thus the example of Carthage was closest at hand for Rome. Rome herself had an archaic version of the penalty in the old formula of execution *arbori infelici suspendito* "hang him from a barren tree" (II.247,321).[127] This may be Etruscan and itself Oriental in view of Deut 21,22 "hang him on a tree." But the Roman ruling class had more solidarity than the Carthaginian, and as a result the punishment was transformed from one of nobles to one of slaves.

Crucifixion was then the sanction *par excellence* from Akkadian Babylon to the new Babylon Rome (Rev 14,8 !). Hengel[128] has covered most of the Greco-Roman materials. At Rome, crucifixion was "the slaves' punishment," *seruile supplicium*.[129] It would seem already a paradox then that Jesus should have been so executed as "king of the Jews." But with the Old Persian kings, crucifixion was the punishment of pretenders to the diadem.

Darius says of Fravartish (Φραόρτης Herodotus 2.96) that he "fixed him on a stake (*uzma*)", *uzmayapatiy akunavam* (*Beh*. II.76).[130] In the Babylonian version this becomes "Then upon a stake (*za-qi-pi*) did I affix him."[131] This is the language of the Assyrian kings and of the (eastern) Peshitto Syriac version of the Gospels (III.110). Crucifixion was exercised by the Persian empire especially on those of high rank: Herodotus records the crucifixion of Magi (1.128), others of rank (4.43), rebellious Greeks (3.125, 6.30). Lampon proposes that Pausanias avenge his uncle's impaling by crucifying the corpse of Mardonius (Herodotus 9.78), and we saw (III.79) how Herodotus (9.120) ends his tale by Greeks taking over the punishment. Glaucon presumes that the just man will be "scourged, racked, bound, have his eyes burned out and in the end be impaled (ἀνασχινδυλευθήσεται)" (Plato *Rep*. 361E). Clement of Alexandria applies Plato's text to Jesus.[132]

On the cross, Jesus says (Luk 23,43) "Today thou shalt be with me in Paradise." The *paradise* or hunting-park remained the prerogative of the Parthian king and his satraps. Thus in Iranian context the Passion narrative assumes a different shape; although Jesus is executed as a pretender to some diadem, he is in fact its legitimate wearer.

---

127 Livy 1.26.4 etc.
128 Martin Hengel, Crucifixion in the ancient world and the folly of the message of the cross; tr. John Bowden; Philadelphia: Fortress, 1977.
129 Valerius Maximus 2.7.12, and numerous other sources gathered by Hengel, 51-52.
130 Cf. *Beh*. III.52.
131 Section 60 of the Akkadian version as transcribed by King & Thompson (note 70 above), p. 182.
132 Clement Alex. *Stromateis* 5.108.2 (GCS 52 [15] 308).

The essence of the punishment is deterrence through public humiliation. Prometheus must be "*taught* to accept the tyranny of Zeus," ὡς ἂν διδαχθῆ τὴν Διὸς τυραννίδα /στέργειν (Aeschylus *PV* 10-11); the psalmist says "all who see me mock at me," כָּל־רֹאַי יַלְעִגוּ לִי (Ps 22,8); opponents say, "If we let him go on thus, every one will believe in him" (Joh 11,48). *Esther Rabbah* I.12[133] reads "Where the bandit (λῃστής) steals, there is he crucified":

הין דליסטאה מקבח תמן מצטלב

with the Western verb "to crucify." (λῃστής is the regular equivalent of Latin *latro*.) This runs parallel to Roman practice and may reflect it (*Digest* 48.19.28.15):

Famosos latrones in his locis, ubi grassati sunt, furca figendos compluribus placuit, ut et conspectu deterreantur alii ab isdem facinoribus et solacio sit cognatis et adfinibus interemptorum eodem loco poena reddita, in quo latrones homicidia fecissent.

Most authorities have determined that notorious brigands should be crucified at the site of their activities, so that on the one hand others may be deterred from such crimes by the spectacle, and on the other that it may be a solace to the relatives and kin of those killed that the punishment was carried out in the same place where the bandits committed murders.

Deterrence and solace!—exactly the themes of contemporary advocates for the death penalty.... Polybius, according to Pliny (8.47), saw lions (!) by the same logic crucified in Africa "because the others would be deterred from [harming human beings] by fear of a similar punishment," *cruci fixos...quia ceteri metu poenae similis absterrerentur eadem noxa.*

Jesus' saying on "bearing one's cross" appears six times: Matt 10,38, 16,24; Mark 8,34 (and 10,21 as var. lect.); Luk 9,23, 14,27. The Syriac versions show a dialectal distinction for "cross" between eastern זקיפא and western צליבא. The Sinaitic Syriac has זקיפא where attested (all except Matt 16,24, Luke 14,27); the Curetonian (wholly lost for Mark) has צליבא in three passages, זקיפא at Matt 16,24. The Peshitto has זקיפא everywhere except צליבא Luke 14,27. The Palestinian Syriac has צלבא in the two texts where it is extant (Matt 10,38; Mark 8,34).

In Rabbinic the root צלב underlying צליבא has only the concrete meaning "hang, impale." In Semitic generally the root זקף has a neutral meaning "raise up," which becomes "crucify" only as a euphemism.[134]

---

133 Cited by Sperber Legal Terms 108.
134 In Biblical Hebrew only at Ps 145,14; 146,8, which already show Aramaic influence.

Akkadian *zaqīpu* appears (as in the Babylonian version of Darius' Behistun inscription) in the texts of several Assyrian kings, *ana* GIŠ *zi-qi-pi uzaqqip* "I impaled on stakes."[135] The semantic shift is illustrated at Ezra 6,11 where if anyone alters Darius' edict, "a beam shall be pulled out of his house, and he shall be *lifted up* and impaled upon it":

יִתְנְסַח אָע מִן־בַּיְתֵהּ וּזְקִיף יִתְמְחֵא עֲלֹהִי

Hence a subtle dialectal distinction at Joh 19,6 Peshitto where the chief priests cry out "Crucify him, crucify him!," Pesh צלוביהי; and Pilatus answers "Take him yourselves and crucify him" (וזוקפוהי)."[136] The chief priests are represented as speaking in Palestinian vernacular, Pilatus in the dignified euphemism of eastern Syriac, "lift him up." (If the scene is fully historic, the chief priests in their excitement would use Aramaic and require an interpreter, and Pilatus would respond in Greek.) In the six versions of Jesus' saying, the Curetonian and Palestinian reflect the western vernacular, the Sinaitic and Peshitto literary eastern usage.

It has often been observed[137] that a special usage of the Fourth Gospel must rest on Aramaic: namely, that whereby ὑψωθῆναι "to be lifted up" refers both to the Crucifixion and Ascension (or some equivalent in the author's mind); thus at John 3,14; 8,28; 12,32-34. We can now specify that John's contact is surprisingly with what we have called *eastern* Aramaic where זקף "lift up" becomes a euphemism for "crucify." (The Syriac versions of John's Gospel all miss this effect, translating throughout with forms of רום.) This is one piece of evidence that זקיפא "cross" was in fact current in the West. But most likely the Aramaic of Jesus' saying used the unambiguous western vernacular צליבא "cross," while the Syriac versions progressively introduce the euphemistic Akkadian eastern usage.

20.6 *The rebel victim as victor*

Prometheus is fed on by an eagle; the psalmist is encircled by dogs (Ps 22,17). Each has fallen victim to the old curse, "Your dead body shall be food for all the birds of the air, and for the beasts of the earth" (Deut 28,26 etc., see I.280-282). But the exposed corpse may have a

---

135 CAD xxi.58a.

136 The Old Syriac is lacking here, the Palestinian Syriac in both places has forms of צלב.

137 See references in Matthew Black, An Aramaic Approach to the Gospels and Acts; 2nd ed.; Oxford: Clarendon, 1954, p. 106; Kaufman 112.

female companion who keeps off the carrion eaters "day and night": Rizpah for the bodies of her sons (II Sam 21,10); Aphrodite for Hector's body (*Iliad* 23.185-186). She runs much risk, for the imperial power that crucifies the man also prostitutes the woman (I.247-249), as with Jannaeus (III.107): "Women are ravished in Zion...princes are hung up by their hands" (Thr 5,11-12, under the Babylonian Chaldaeans). Pheretima, queen of Cyrene, even more barbarously crucified the men of Barca and nailed their wives' breasts to the city wall (Herodotus 4.202). Each of the rebel victims has a prostituted female companion. Prometheus has Io, the concubine of Zeus; the Servant of Yahweh has the "captive daughter of Zion" (Isa 52,2), who has been sold into slavery, that is, prostitution (Isa 50,1); Jesus has the Magdalen from whom seven demons had gone out (Luk 8,2), often (though incorrectly) identified with the prostitute of Luk 7,36-50. At Joh 19,25 the Magdalen is replaced by Jesus' mother, another Rizpah; early representations of the Crucifixion show John and the Virgin on the left, the other three women at the right.

The demand of Socialist theology for a Promethean Christ was realized pictorially by the Mexican muralist José Clemente Orozco in three exemplars of manhood.[138] In the Prometheus of Pomona (1930) the Titan, cramped under a Gothic arch, brings down fire from heaven; in a side panel, Zeus, Hera and Io. The Christ of Dartmouth (1932-34) is shown frontally as Vitruvian man, his left hand raised before a rubbish heap of weapons, a broken Ionic column, and a Buddha. In his right hand he holds an axe with which he has just chopped down his cross behind him. His feet are still skeletal; his resurrection body in lurid reds and blues is emerging from his split thighs. Nearby, ferocious vultures are on another rubbish heap of Western culture. As a ten-year-old I saw the artist at work, and it is alleged that I appear as one of the blond schoolchildren in the New England panel. The Man of Fire of Guadalajara (1938-39) stands overhead in the cupola of the Hospicio Cabañas as if seen from below, beside three prostrate blue figures. He is naked; his arms, legs and head are burning.

The unity of suffering and exaltation in all three figures is very marked, as in John's double theme of Christ being "lifted up" both on the cross and in the Ascension. At II.268 we discussed the symbolism of Yahweh with his axe: destroying presumptuous empires (Isa 10,15) as they previously had taken an axe against the forest of Lebanon;

---

138 All these works are illustrated in D. Elliott (ed.), ¡ Orozco! 1883-1949; Oxford: Museum of Modern Art, 1980.

turning the Roman *fasces* against collaborators (Matt 3,10 // Luk 3,9). Today, in decades that must undo the damage done by the axe and fire to the planet's rain forests, the axe has become as ambivalent a symbol as fire, the supposed monopoly of the Mazdaean Achaemenids, brought down by Prometheus. Orozco thus transfers the real complexity of Aeschylus' Prometheus to the axe-bearing Christ. Evidently the Man of Fire of Guadalajara has also brought down fire from heaven—we may hope, not in vengeance (Luk 9,54), nor as insupportable nuclear power, but as the "refiner's fire" of Mal 3,2. "I came to cast fire upon the earth, and would that it were already kindled!" (Luk 12,49).

Excursus I: The Temple police at Jerusalem

In 165 BC (III.93) Judas Maccabaeus (I Makk 3,55) appointed commanders of thousands and hundreds in his army; and in AD 66 Josephus by his own account (*BJ* 2.577-578) "organized his army along Roman lines," including the same two ranks. Was that a novelty or a continuation? Just after the death of Herod the Great in 4 BC, when his army still existed, his son Archelaus (Josephus *AJ* 17.215, cf. *BJ* 2.11) sent "a cohort of heavy infantry with their chiliarch," σπεῖράν τε ὁπλιτῶν χιλίαρχόν τε to suppress disorders. Whenever a military force is recorded in Jerusalem, it has the same structure. What happened to the force commanded by Herod the Great and Archelaus? The Fourth Gospel, which unawares has preserved a number of valuable historical notes, may suggest a clue. According to Joh 18,3, at the arrest of Jesus, Judas brought the "cohort" and assistants from the chief priests and Pharisees; they are summarized at 18,12, "The cohort and the chiliarch and the assistants of the *Ioudaioi*": ἡ οὖν σπεῖρα καὶ ὁ χιλίαρχος καὶ οἱ ὑπηρέται τῶν Ἰουδαίων, Vg: *Cohors ergo et tribunus et ministri Iudaeorum*. Pesh:

הידין אספיר וכילירכא ודחשא דיהודיא

Further, in the Palestinian Syriac ὑπηρέται comes out as הפריטיא.

If τῶν Ἰουδαίων goes not merely with the ὑπηρέται, but also with the σπεῖρα and χιλίαρχος, the "cohort and chiliarch" are already defined as Jewish. This may be John's intent. But perhaps, however he understood them, he is defining two groups. The *speira* and the chiliarch obviously go together; over against them are set the assistants of the *Ioudaioi*. Who are these two groups? We begin with the second.

In John's Gospel, οἱ Ἰουδαῖοι like a number of other ambiguous terms fluctuates between two poles (II.257). In the writer's thinking about his own time it designates "Jews" as over against "Christians" (or however he named the community to which he belonged). In his sources, or in his thinking about the time of Jesus, it can simply mean "Judaeans." Joh 7,1 contrasts them with Galilaeans: "And after this Jesus walked about in Galilee; for he did not want to walk about in

Judaea (ἐν τῇ Ἰουδαίᾳ), because the Judaeans (!, οἱ Ἰουδαῖοι) sought to kill him." At Joh 3,1 Nicodemus is naturally identified as "a magistrate of the Judaeans," ἄρχων τῶν Ἰουδαίων. Here at Joh 18,3 ὑπηρέται τῶν Ἰουδαίων has both colorations: in his own time it means "assistants of the Jewish people [responsible for Jesus' death]"; in Jesus' time it means "assistants of the Judaean temple."

The ὑπηρέται appear in a police role in the subsequent narrative (Joh 18,22; 19,6) with "Jewish" authorities; at 7,32.45-46 with chief priests and Pharisees; and at Mark 14,54-5 (// Matt 26,58), 65 with the chief priest and the Sanhedrin (ὅλον τὸ συνέδριον Mark 14,55). At Act 5,21-26 they appear with the chief priest, the Sanhedrin, and "all the gerousia"; and in particular with the "commander of the temple" (Act 4,1; 5,24-26), ὁ στρατηγοὺς τοῦ ἱεροῦ, Vg magistratus templi, Pesh ארכונא דהיכלא the "archon." At Luk 22,52 (cf 22,4) there are several "commandants of the temple," στρατηγοὺς τοῦ ἱεροῦ. (Here the Old Syriac has "soldiers," אסטרטיוטא, but this may just be an error for אסטרטיגא.) These parties have available a prison (Act 5,22-23), φυλακή or δεσμωτήριον with guards (φύλακες). These materials in all four Evangelists and Acts make it perfectly plain that there was a Temple police organized in military fashion. Herod the Great (Josephus BJ 1.656) "handed over to the assistants to execute" (παρέδωκεν τοῖς ὑπηρέταις ἀνελεῖν) those who had taken down the golden eagle. Josephus (BJ 6.294) confirms that when the Temple gate opened of itself "the guards of the temple reported it to the commander," οἱ τοῦ ἱεροῦ φύλακες ἤγγειλαν τῷ στρατηγῷ (Tacitus Hist. 5.13 reports the same prodigy, apertae repente delubri fores, II.243.)

The στρατηγοί appear in the LXX as translating סְגָנִים: Neh 13,11 Nehemiah complains to the סְגָנִים (LXX στρατηγοῖς, Vg magistratus) that the Levites are not being taken care of. Thus the סְגָנִים are the heads of the Temple police. Mishna Bikkurim III.3 (III.104) notes them together with the פחות and the treasurers (גזברים). Furthermore there was a single סגן par excellence who stood beside the High Priest in certain ceremonies.[1] Often though not invariably the principle of Jer. Talm. Yoma 41a5 was followed, "One was not appointed high priest before he had served as sagan":

לא היה כהן גדול מתמנה להיות כהן גדול עד שהו נעשה סגן

Here we can make a remarkable combination between Josephus and the Mishna. About AD 50 (C. Ummidius Durmius) Quadratus, governor of Syria, sent to Rome Jewish leaders whom he held responsible for

---

1   Mishna Yoma III.9; VII.1; see J. Jeremias, Jerusalem in the Time of Jesus, Philadelphia: Fortress, 1967; pp. 160-162; SVMB ii.277-278.

a slaughter of Samaritans. Among them were Ananias the high-priest
AD 47-59 (SVMB ii.231; Acts 23,2; 24,1) and his son Ananos (Josephus
BJ 2.243); at *AJ* 20.131 Josephus omits the family connection, but
adds that Ananos was στρατηγός, i.e. commander of the Temple.
Mishna *Avoth* III.2 speaks of a R. Ḥanina the "commander of the
priests" (סגן הכהנים) and gives him the the uniquely pro-Roman sentiment: "Pray for the peace of the Government; for without the fear of
it, we would have swallowed each other up alive":

הוי מתפלל בשלומה של מלכות שאלמלא מוראה איש את רעה חיים
בלענו

R. Ḥanina is supposed to have survived the destruction of the Temple;
this saying must come before AD 70. It is difficult not to identify him
with the Ananos of Josephus. No doubt if the high priesthood had
continued Ananos/Ḥanina would have had aspirations for it. At Mishna
Zeb. IX.3 R. Ḥanina quotes his father (unnamed) as having rejected
blemished beasts from the altar.

This police must have operated under regulations. One was surely
the warning notice of which we have two copies (*OGIS* 598, often
reprinted):[2]

Μηθένα ἀλλογενῆ εἰσπορεύεσθαι ἐντὸς τοῦ περὶ τὸ ἱερὸν τρυφάκτου
καὶ περιβόλου. ὃς δ' ἂν ληφθῇ ἑαυτῷ αἴτιος ἔσται διὰ τὸ ἐξακολουθεῖν
θάνατον.

"No alien may enter inside the balustrade around the Temple and the
enclosure; whoever is caught will have himself to blame for the imme-
diate consequence of his death." Josephus (*BJ* 5.193-4, cf *AJ* 15.417)
describes the δρύφακτος and the στῆλαι "some in Greek, others in
Latin letters, that no foreigner should enter the holy place," αἱ μὲν
Ἑλληνικοῖς αἱ δὲ Ῥωμαϊκοῖς γράμμασιν, μηδένα ἀλλόφυλον ἐντὸς τοῦ
ἁγίου παριέναι. Again, (*BJ* 6.124-6) he has Titus ask John of Gischala
if it was not the Jews themselves who set the balustrade around the
sanctuary, and put up stelae in Greek and Latin (γράμμασιν Ἑλληνικοῖς
καὶ ἡμετέροις) warning that no one should violate it; and if it was not
the Romans who permitted the Jews to execute violators. While we
have found no Latin version, all else fits the inscription. Who could
have set it up? It is the descendant of an earlier regulation in a letter

---

2   See Elias Bickerman, "The Warning Inscriptions of Herod's Temple," pp. 210-
     224 of Studies in Jewish and Christian History vol. II; Arbeiten zur Geschichte
     des antiken Judentums und des Urchristentums 9; Leiden: Brill, 1980.

of Antiochus III (223-187 BC) preserved in Josephus *AJ* 12.145-6 which begins with almost the same words.[3] Herod the Great must have renewed it on his own authority; the vague threat of death suggests a public lynching tacitly approved by the authorities. A Roman version would certainly have mentioned a Roman authority. It was on the basis of this regulation and presumption that the crowd tries to kill Paul (Act 21,30).

Who are the *speira* and its chiliarch? Polybius 11.23.1 uses σπεῖρα for maniples of 200 and says that three make up the κοόρτις. σπεῖρα is a Hellenistic use of a word for "bundle" to mean "tactical military unit." At II Makk 8,23 τῆς πρώτης σπείρας "the first division" is one of 4 divisions of 1,500 men each of Judas Maccabeus' army of 6,000. Here the total corresponds to a legion, but a true Roman legion had no division into four parts. Later σπεῖρα is used for a cohort only. In the Greco-Latin bilingual IGRR i.896 (from the Bosporus) there is a formal equivalence *miles coh(o)r(tis)* = στρατιώτης σπίρης. Josephus at *BJ* 3.67 attests Roman σπειρῶν operating independently of legions, composed of 1000 men or 600 plus cavalry—plainly true (single or double) cohorts. At Act 21,31 (cf 10,1; 27,1) over a Roman σπείρης (Vg *cohortis*, Pesh. אספיר) there is correctly a "chiliarch." Bab. Talm. *Berakh.* 32b appears to say of the "legions" of stars "and for each legion I created for it 30 cohorts,"

וְעַל כָּל לִגְיוֹן בָּרָאתִי לוֹ שְׁלֹשִׁים קַרְטוֹן

which would make the קַרְטוֹן a maniple; but the Talmud has only a vague idea of Roman military organization. σπεῖρα also went into Rabbinic as אספיר (Midrash Ps 15,6) or צפירה (*Mekhilta* on Exod 15,2).[4]

Most commentators like Winter[5] take it for granted that the *speira* of Joh 18,12 is the Roman cohort stationed in Jerusalem with its commander. The Roman cohort appears at Mark 15,16 and parallels as mocking Jesus; the Roman cohort and its chiliarch appear at Act 21,31, for the officer turns out to be the Roman citizen Claudius Lysias (Act 23,26). But John's narrative makes poor sense if his *speira* and chiliarch are Romans: obviously they are in charge of "the assistants of the Judaeans," and a Roman detachment would take the prisoner to their own praetorium, not deliver him to the deposed high-priest

---

3   See the discussion by Bickerman "Une proclamation Séleucide relative au temple de Jérusalem," pp. 86-104 of the same work as in the prev. note.
4   *Mekilta* ed. Lauterbach ii.24.
5   Paul Winter, On the Trial of Jesus; Studia Judaica Band 1; Berlin: Gruyter, 1961; p. 45.

Annas. Also, Pilatus would have to have given orders for the Roman cohort to carry out the arrest; but by John's own showing at 18,29 he knows nothing about the case, and the supposed Romans have disappeared, since none of the detachment enter the praetorium so as not to be defiled. Thus as in the Synoptics it must be a detachment from the Temple authorities, here seen more formally than as a disorderly ὄχλος (Mark 14,43) "from the chief priests and scribes and elders."

Thus if John's terminology has any kind of historical basis, and is not invented from thin air, we learn that the Temple police were organized in Roman fashion with the normal Greek equivalents of "tribune" and "cohort." This is the conclusion at which our most careful student of the history, Josef Blinzler, arrives;[6] and I do not see how it can be avoided. Even after the death of Herod the Great, at least one *speira* with its chiliarch remained intact (Josephus *AJ* 17.215). In line with the conservative nature of the military at all times, we find the same structure attested at Joh 18,12, with the former army now fallen back on the core of the Jewish state, the Temple. The chiliarch of Joh 18,12 is either a subordinate of the *strategos* of the Temple (Act 4,1; *AJ* 20.131), who is the then *sagan* of the priests (*Avoth* III.2); or else (if the police consisted of only one cohort) the very man himself. Joh 18,13 alone says that the detachment first led Jesus to Annas before taking him to Caiaphas (Matt 26,57; Joh 18,24). Perhaps Annas' son Ananos was already in the ranks at the time of Jesus' arrest, and moving up to replace his father twenty years later.

Jeremias (p. 180) presumes that the "guard" at the tomb of Matt 27,65 must, if historical, be Jewish, for Roman soldiers could never admit to falling asleep on duty (Matt 28,13); then ἔχετε κουστωδίαν is not imperative but indicative, "you have a guard"; Vg *habetis custodiam*, Sin.Syr. אית לכון קסטודי. κουστωδία in the sense "guard" follows the regular pattern by which Latinisms like *custodia* taken over into Greek prefer a concrete to an abstract sense. The usage is not just Matthew's, for the word had already gone into Rabbinic: Jer. Talm. *Ned.* 41b45:

לקסטודייא שהיתה עוברת

"like a prison guard which was passing by." Here again then we find that the Temple police are following Roman military practice and terminology—this time not Greek but Latin.

Thus the "cohort" (σπεῖρα) and its "tribune" (χιλίαρχος) of Joh 18,12 like all their context have nothing to do with the Roman occu-

---

6   Josef Blinzler, Der Prozess Jesu; 4th ed.; Regensburg: Pustet, 1969; pp. 94-101.

pying forces. The cohort is unrelated to the Roman cohort of Mark 15,16 // Matt 27,27; the tribune is unrelated to the Roman tribune of Act 21,31 along with *his* cohort. Rather the cohort and tribune of Joh 18,12, along with the "assistants" (ὑπηρέται), form part or all of a Jewish militarized police force of the Temple under the high priest. As with the Nabataean army and that of Herod Antipas in Galilee, they are set up on the Roman pattern, as an inheritance from the army of Herod the Great, and before him from the Maccabean army; and take their names from the normal Greek translation of Latin terminology. Jerusalem then at the time of Jesus (whenever the governor was in residence, III.267) held two military structures exactly parallel, Roman and Jewish, in uneasy coexistence.

Chapter 21: Paradise and the Forest of Lebanon

21.1 Columbus and the Earthly Paradise

On October 18, 1498 [Old Style of course] Columbus wrote to Ferdinand and Isabel(la) from Hispaniola an account of his third voyage, expressing his conviction that he had found the Earthly Paradise, *el parayso terrenal*. We do not have his MS, but a hand copy by Bartolomé de Las Casas with the heading:

La ystoria del viaje qu'el almirante don Christóval Colón hizo la tercera vez que vino á las Yndias, quando descubrió la Tierra Firme, como lo enbió á los reyes desde la isla Española.

> Account of the voyage which the Admiral Don Christóval Colón made the third time that he came to the Indies, when he discovered mainland [the South American continent], as he sent it to the Sovereigns from the island Española.[1]

This is the document in which he expresses his conviction that the Western hemisphere, unlike the Eastern, was not truly spherical:

Mas este [hemisperio] digo que es como sería la mitad de la pera bien redonda, la qual toviese el peçon alto, como yo dixe, ò como una teta de muger en una pelota redonda.

> But I say that this [hemisphere] is as it were the half of a very round pear which has a raised stalk, as I have said [above, same page], or like a woman's nipple on a round ball.[2]

---

1   Edited and translated by Cecil Jane, Select Documents illustrating the four voyages of Columbus...; vol. II; Hakluyt Society second series No. LXX, 1933; repr. Millwood: Kraus, 1967; p. 3. The Admiral appears to have been born in Genoa as Christoforo Colombo, but all his letters are in Castilian like this one, and his name in Spanish Christóval (as here) or Christóbal. I do not know on what authority the date of the letter rests. These passages are discussed by Kirkpatrick Sale (The Conquest of Paradise: Christopher Columbus and the Columbian Legacy; New York: Knopf; 1990, 174-177)—a work very harsh on Columbus and the whole enterprise of European colonization.

2   Jane, *ibid.*, p. 31.

The Admiral reached this surprising result partly by observations misunderstood (he felt that he was sailing uphill), partly by theory (the Earthly Paradise would have had to be on a raised mountain to survive the Flood). His further indications that he was in the vicinity of the Paradise were the mildness of the climate, *la suavíssima temperancia*, and the outflow of fresh water (the mouths of the Orinoco river in the bay of Paria), *tanta cantidad de agua dulçe* (p. 39); for Paradise, he knew, was the source of four great rivers. He realizes that the summit on which the paradise lies, and from which the water comes, could not be reached, *y creo que nadie no podría llegar al colmo*; but, he says, "I am firmly convinced in my own mind that the Earthly Paradise is there, where I have said" (p. 43):

> Mas yo muy assentado tengo en el ánima que allí, adonde dixe, es el parayso terrenal.

Amerigo Vespucci and his successors in Brazil make the same judgement.[3] Likewise in North America:

> George Alsop advertised Maryland as the only "Terrestrial Paradice." Its very trees, plants, fruits, flowers and roots spoke in "Hieroglyphicks of our Adamitical or Primitive situation," and their general effects and properties still bore "the Effigies of Innocency according to their original Grafts."[4]

All these travelers are drawing from a long tradition of speculation around the Biblical data of "paradise." The word is Iranian, entering Greek and Hebrew at the same time to designate the same thing—the hunting parks and timber preserves of the Old Persian satraps. How did it come to have all the resonances which Dante, Shakespeare, Milton, Goethe and so many others have exploited? Here is a word and concept that has infiltrated from Iran through classical Greek and Hebrew into the Septuagint, the New Testament, Jewish apocrypha, the Quran, and the Church Fathers—Greek, Syriac and Latin—and so on to the Renaissance and Reformation. It gathers up what Greeks said about the Islands of the Blessed and the Elysian Fields; and both the Hebrew and Phoenician versions of the Garden of Eden. No other

---

3   Jean Delumeau, History of Paradise: The Garden of Eden in Myth and Tradition; tr. Matthew O'Connell; New York: Continuum, 1995 (tr. of Une Histoire du Paradis: Le Jardin des délices; Paris: Fayard, 1992); pp. 109-115.
4   C. L. Sanford, The Quest for Paradise; Urbana: Univ. of Illinois, 1961; 84, citing George Alsop, A Character of the Province of Maryland, 1666; reprinted in Publications of the Maryland Historical Society no. 15; Baltimore, 1880; p. 37 [not seen by me].

single word creates anything like such unity among all these seemingly disparate cultures. What can we learn from its history?

We begin with the point at which "paradise" enters Greek and Hebrew history, the enclosures of the Persian king and satraps (21.2). The usage is verified by two original Iranian texts (21.3). The status of the Lebanese forest as timber-preserve was anticipated long before by the expeditions of Sumerian and Akkadian kings and the myth of Gilgamesh (21.4). Before extensive naval warfare the original forests of the Mediterranean were most impressive (21.5); logging on the Lebanon was controlled by bureaucratic officials (21.6). After the word "paradise" entered Greek and Hebrew it was diminished to denote any garden (21.7). But in later Judaism and the New Testament it is supernaturalized to denote the restoration of Eden (21.8). Ephrem of Nisibis in the Syriac church retains a lively sense of the symbolism (21.9). This religious usage went side by side with the deforestation of the actual Lebanese "paradise" and other Mediterranean woodlands (21.10). I end with a few excerpts from the enormous Patristic, medieval and later literature (21.11).

And we start with the Greek Xenophon, like Columbus an explorer of new realms, but on land, and initially as attached to a ragtag army, of which he later became the general.

21.2 The satrapal hunting parks

In 401 BC Cyrus, younger son of Darius II of Persia, led an army of Greek mercenaries from Sardes to overthrow, if possible, his elder brother Artaxerxes II who had just succeeded to the throne. After seven days' march they reached Kelainai, a large and prosperous city of Phrygia (Xenophon *Anab.* 1.2.7-9):

> There Cyrus had a palace (βασίλεια) and a large *paradeisos* full of wild beasts (παράδεισος μέγας ἀγρίων θηρίων πλήρης), which he used to hunt from horseback whenever he wanted to give himself and his horses exercise. The river Maeander flows through the middle of the *paradeisos*, and its springs are from the palace.... The Great King also has has a fortified palace (βασίλεια ... ἐρυμνά) in Kelainai at the springs of the Marsyas river, at the foot of the acropolis. ...Here Xerxes, when he retreated from Hellas after his defeat, is said to have built the [royal] palace and the acropolis of Kelainai.

When they reached Syria they encamped at the river Dardas (1.4.10):

Here was the palace of Belesus governor (ἄρξαντος)[5] of Syria, and a very large and beautiful *paradeisos*, with all the fruits that the seasons produce (παράδεισος πάνυ μέγας καὶ καλός, ἔχων πάντα ὅσα ὧραι φύουσι); but Cyrus cut it down and burned the palace. After Cyrus' death in battle the Hellenes encamped at Sittake on the Tigris (2.4.14) "near a large beautiful *paradeisos* thick with all kinds of trees," ἐγγὺς παραδείσου μεγάλου καὶ καλοῦ καὶ δάσεος παντοίων δένδρων.

The *paradeisoi* that Xenophon saw were at once hunting-parks for the king and his satraps; timber-reserves; and sites for fortified "palaces" or glorified hunting-lodges built over self-contained water supplies. The orchard on the Dardas is probable but not certain. Meiggs[6] sees them more as parks strictly speaking, "trees for pleasure," with their function as "hunting reserves" secondary. Briant[7] emphasizes their symbolic role in investing the satrap with derivative attributes of the king; along with their ancillary villages he sees them as ideal agricultural models of land-development, *vitrines idéologiques*; he proposes further[8] that each satrapy in principle had one or more, and draws up a list of those known. Fauth[9] focuses on the cultic and propagandistic role of the king and satraps in planting the park, and stocking[10] and then hunting the animals.

In the twentieth year of some Artaxerxes, Nehemiah the Jew, the king's cupbearer, asked for permission to rebuild the walls of Jerusalem. The books of Ezra and Nehemiah are in some confusion: if the monarch was Artaxerxes I, the date would be 445/4 BC; if Artaxerxes II, 385/4 BC. In either case, the events are within a generation of Xenophon one way or the other. Nehemiah asks (Neh 2,8) for "a letter to Asaph, keeper of the king's *pardes*, that he should give me timber":

---

5   But at *Anab.* 1.1.2 and frequently Xenophon uses the proper term "satrap," σατράπης, for the Persian governors (III.86).

6   Russell Meiggs, Trees and Timber in the Ancient Mediterranean World; Oxford: Clarendon, 1982; 270-2.

7   Pierre Briant, Rois, Tributs et Paysans: Etudes sur les formations tributaires du Moyen-Orient ancien; Annales littéraires de l'Univ. de Besançon, 269; Paris: Belles-Lettres, 1982; 451-456. This is the best account of the Persian "paradises" known to me.

8   *Ibid.* p. 451 note 109.

9   Wolfgang Fauth, "Der königliche Gärtner und Jäger im Paradeisos: Beobachtungen zur Rolle des Herrschers in der vorderasiatischen Hortikultur," Persica 8 (1979) 1-53; reprint kindly sent me by the author.

10   The stocking of animals is plausible in itself, but not (that I can see) attested in any ancient text.

וְאִגֶּרֶת אֶל־אָסָף שֹׁמֵר הַפַּרְדֵּס אֲשֶׁר לַמֶּלֶךְ אֲשֶׁר יִתֶּן־לִי עֵצִים

LXX ("II Esdras 12,8") καὶ ἐπιστολὴν ἐπὶ Ἀσαφ φύλακα τοῦ παραδείσου, ὅς ἐστιν τῷ βασιλεῖ, ὥστε δοῦναί μοι ξύλα; Vg *et epistulam ad Asaph custodem saltus regis ut det mihi ligna*. On the parallel of the rebuilding done by Ezra under Cyrus (Ezra 3,7) the "king's *pardes*" can only be the forest of Lebanon. Here alone do we have testimony to the Persian bureaucracy (18.6 below), in which an official (with a West-Semitic name) must grant permission for all logging in the *pardes*. In another place[11] from my seven years in Beirut I have chronicled the exploitation of the Lebanese cedar forest from earliest contacts with Egypt to the time of Justinian, AD 527.

Two mutually contradictory themes run through the descriptions of the forest *paradeisoi*. On the one hand, their great age and the size of the trees is emphasized. A century after Xenophon, Theophrastus (*Hist. Plant.* 5.8.1) had apparently been on the Lebanon:

> In Syria in the mountains the cedar-trees reach an exceptional height and thickness; some are so large that three men cannot join hands around them; and in the *paradeisoi* they are even larger and finer.

> ἐν Συρίᾳ γὰρ ἔν τε τοῖς ὄρεσι διαφέροντα γίγνεται τὰ δένδρεα τῆς κέδρου καὶ τῷ ὕψει καὶ τῷ πάχει· τηλικαῦτα γάρ ἐστιν ὥστ' ἔνια μὲν μὴ δύνασθαι τρεῖς ἄνδρας περιλαμβάνειν· ἔν τε τοῖς παραδείσοις ἔτι μείζω καὶ καλλίω.

Quintus Curtius 8.1.12 affirms that a forest in "Bazaira" (somewhere in Bactriana) had been "intact from cutting for four consecutive generations," *quattuor continuis aetatibus intactum saltum fuisse*. In the poem of Ez 31,3-9 the cedar of Lebanon has become the world-tree: its head is in the clouds, its roots go down to the subterranean Deep (תְּהוֹם vs 4), all birds nest in its branches, all animals give birth underneath it, all nations live under its branches; the place where it grows is in the "garden of Elohim" (בְּגַן אֱלֹהִים), and since all the "trees of Eden" envy it, it appears that the Lebanon is an alternative placement in Phoenician myth (as at Ez 28,13, III.48) of the garden of Eden. The forest *paradeisoi* could not possibly have been created by the Persians *de novo*. Rather the Great King annexed the principal existing forest lands, some like the Lebanon still holding the climax vegetation from after the last glacial period or before (for the Lebanon it seems was

---

11 My The Lebanon and Phoenicia, Chapter V, pp. 175-212. The materials have been worked over again by Meiggs op. cit. (note 6 above), Chapter 3, "The Cedars of Lebanon," pp. 49-87, with generous acknowledgements to myself.

never glaciated). Many no doubt were already held as the property of native kings, perhaps principally as timber preserves. The king and his satraps threw some kind of boundary around them, further stocked them with game, built hunting-lodges or "palaces" for king or satrap (or both as at Kelainai), provided them with supervisors (perhaps disposing troops), and gave them a uniform legal status.

But the hoary antiquity of the forest was tempered by the doctrine that the king or satrap himself must have planted it. Xenophon (*Oecon.* 4.20-24)[12] has Cyrus the younger, at that time satrap of Lydia, show Lysander the Spartan his "paradise at Sardes," τὸν ἐν Σάρδεσι παράδεισον, and pride himself that some of the trees "I even planted myself," ἃ καὶ ἐφύτευσα αὐτός. Berossos describes the "hanging *paradeisos*" of Babylon built by Nebuchadrezzar (Ναβουχοδονόσορος nominative),[13] in fact a whole novel creation. In a new palace he built high stone terraces imitating mountain scenery,

> he planted them with trees of every sort, and so worked up and completed the so-called "hanging *paradeisos*," because his wife, who had been brought up in Media, had a longing for mountain scenery.[14]

> καταφυτεύσας δένδρεσι παντοδαποῖς, ἐξειργάσατο καὶ κατεσκεύασε τὸν καλούμενον κρεμαστὸν παράδεισον, διὰ τὸ τὴν γυναῖκα αὐτοῦ ἐπιθυμεῖν τῆς ὀρείας διαθέσεως τεθραμμένην ἐν τοῖς κατὰ Μηδίαν τόποις.

Only the king who in theory planted the trees may cut them; Artaxerxes II (Plutarch *Art.* 25.2) must set an example to his own soldiers of cutting down a tree for firewood by "taking an axe," λαβὼν πέλεκυν. It was an act of war when Cyrus cut down the paradise of Dardas (Xenophon *Anab.* 1.4.10 above); or when Agesilaus in 396 BC

---

12   This text was the occasion for Sir Thomas Browne's work on the number 5, *The Garden of Cyrus*: "All stories do look upon *Cyrus* as the splendid and regular planter."

13   Josephus, *con. Ap.* 1.141 = Berossos FGH 680 F8.141. Cf Diodorus 2.10.2.

14   The "hanging garden" cannot long have outlived the Chaldaean kings of Babylon. But it was quickly invested by the Greeks with a dreamlike Orientalism and appears throughout the Middle Ages in the lists of the "seven wonders," beginning with the first, *Anth. Pal.* 9.58 by an Antipater, perhaps of Sidon. Antipater's list also included Pheidias' statue of Zeus at Olympia; the Colossus of the Sun at Rhodes; the Pyramids of Egypt; the Mausoleum of Halicarnassus; the temple of Artemis at Ephesus; and the walls of Babylon. Gradually the Pharos of Alexandria (which remained standing until the 15th century) displaced the walls of Babylon. The Seven Wonders are mentioned by Strabo 17.1.33 (ἐν τοῖς ἑπτὰ θεάμασι) and Pliny 36.30 (*septem miracula*) but not listed by either author. See now the OCD³ 1397.

(Diodorus 14.80.2) "destroyed the *paradeisos* of Tissaphernes" at Sardes, ἔφθειρε…τὸν παράδεισον τοῦ Τισσαφέρνους. In 350 BC (Diodorus 16.41.5) when the Sidonians at Tripolis of Phoenicia "destroyed the royal *paradeisos*, in which the Persian kings had been accustomed to take their recreation, by cutting down the trees" (τὸν μὲν βασιλικὸν παράδεισον … δενδροτομήσαντες διέφθειραν), it was plainly a declaration of war which served the further purpose of getting timber for their new fleet of triremes.

The logic behind this apparently contradictory belief is to assimilate the king to the divinity who (with more antecedent time at his disposal) was credited with having planted the forest in the beginning. The principal documentation is Hebrew.[15] The vine from Egypt overshadowed even the "cedars of El" (Ps 80,11) אַרְזֵי־אֵל (but RSV "mighty cedars"). We may compare the "oak" (φηγός) of Zeus (*Iliad* 5.693, 7.60). Ps 104,16 "The trees of Yahweh[16] are watered abundantly, the cedars of Lebanon which he planted":

יִשְׂבְּעוּ עֲצֵי יהוה   אַרְזֵי לְבָנוֹן אֲשֶׁר נָטָע

LXX χορτασθήσεται τὰ ξύλα τοῦ πεδίου, αἱ κέδροι τοῦ Λιβάνου, ἃς ἐφύτευσεν.

The God of Israel as planter is of course primarily recorded at Gen 2,8 "And Yahweh the God planted a garden in Eden, in the East (?—*miqqedem*)":

וַיִּטַּע יהוה אֱלֹהִים גַּן־בְּעֵדֶן מִקֶּדֶם

It will be worthwhile to survey the Versions to see the changes that the verse undergoes. It is essentially unchanged in Targum Onqelos:

ונצב יוי אלהים גנתא בעדן מלקדמין

The Septuagint makes the momentous innovation of replacing the "garden" by a "paradise": καὶ ἐφύτευσεν κύριος ὁ θεὸς παράδεισον ἐν Ἐδεμ κατὰ ἀνατολάς; it also renders מִקֶּדֶם unambiguous "in the East." The Peshitto Syriac follows either the Hebrew or Targum in reading מן קדים but knows the LXX also, from which it draws "paradise":

ונצב מריא אלהא פרדיסא בעדן מן קדים

The Old Latin follows the Septuagint, *et plantauit Deus paradisum in Eden contra orientem*.[17] Only at this date (to our knowledge) does

---

15 See further the extensive documentation of Fauth, note 9 above.

16 But the fact that most MSS of the LXX have τοῦ πεδίου suggests that its Hebrew was שדי read as "field," but intended as שַׁדַּי "Shadday." And this is preferable, for how could Yahweh have an old cult on the Lebanon? (Ps 29 must be the transposition of a Phoenician hymn.)

17 Attested in this wording in the Latin of Irenaeus *con. Haer.* 5.5.1, ed. A. Rousseau et alii, Livre V, Sources chrétiennes 153; Paris: Cerf, 1969, p. 64.

paradisus enter Latin; Gellius 2.20.4 cites it as Greek. The Vulgate, where we must see Jerome's own hand, treats "Eden" as a common noun "pleasure," and reinterprets מִקֶּדֶם as "in the beginning," *plantauerat autem Dominus Deus paradisum uoluptatis a principio*. The first of these changes follows the LXX of Gen 3,23 where for "And Yahweh the God sent him out of the garden of Eden":

וַיְשַׁלְּחֵהוּ יהוה אֱלֹהִים מִגַּן־עֵדֶן

the LXX has ἐκ τοῦ παραδείσου τῆς τρυφῆς "from the garden of delight."

But the word "paradise" was extended to rather different kinds of enclosures with different functions. We have seen that some contained "palaces," perhaps grander than hunting-lodges, in some cases fortified. Greek βασίλεια may represent Old Persian *apadāna* in the inscriptions of Artaxerxes II: thus (Kent 155) *[imām] apadānam stūnāya aθagainam* "[this] palace of stone in its columns." The Iranian went into Hebrew at Dan 11,45 וְיִטַּע אָהֳלֵי אַפַּדְנוֹ "And he shall pitch the tents of his palace" (Vg *Apedno* as if a proper noun), thought to refer to Antiochus IV Epiphanes. Hence in more secular usage to Rabbinic אפדנו "country place" (e.g. Bab. Talm. *Keth.* 62a). The tomb of Cyrus the elder was at Pasargadae "in the royal enclosure," ἐν τῷ παραδείσῳ τῷ βασιλικῷ (Arrian *Anab.* 6.29.4). East of Syrian Apamea stood the "fortified town Caphrena," *oppidum Caphrena munitum* (Pliny 6.119); it was "called Palace of the Satraps where tribute was brought," *Satraparum Regia appellatum quo tributa conferebantur*. Here only do we read of a centralized site for the satraps generally, though no paradise is there mentioned. But not far off was the site near the springs of the Orontes seemingly called "Paradise" as a proper noun (Strabo 16.2.19, Pliny 5.82); it may be identical with the "Triple Paradise" (τριπαράδεισος) of Diodorus 18.39.1, and perhaps is still marked by the pyramid of Hermel with its reliefs of hunting scenes.[18]

Perhaps the original function of the paradises was as hunting parks; this is attested by Xenophon for Media in his fictional biography of Cyrus the elder.[19] The paradises which were simply maintained in the wild state must have served above all as timber-preserves; this is the case without doubt for the paradise of Mount Lebanon, where further it is hard to imagine wild game having been released, or extensive hunting from horseback on the steep slopes. Alexander built part of his

---

18   D. Krencker & W. Zschietzschmann, Römische Tempel in Syrien; Arch. Inst. des Deutschen Reiches, Denkmäler antikes Architektur; Band 5; 2 vols.; Berlin: 1938; p. 161.

19   Xenophon, *Cyr.* 1.3.14; 1.4.5; 8.1.38; 8.6.12.

Red Sea fleet in Babylon from "the cypresses in the groves and paradises (ἐν τοῖς ἄλσεσι καὶ τοῖς παραδείσοις)" (Strabo 16.1.11).[20] Others like the paradise of Cyrus the younger and that of Tissaphernes at Sardes may have in fact been like modern parks with only moderate-sized trees and created from the ground up by the satrap. The language which Xenophon (*Anab.* 1.4.10, III.122) uses of the paradise of the satrap Belesus on the Dardas river suggests that it contained fruiting trees and perhaps was primarily an orchard. The text on which Briant relies for his idea of the paradise as a center of agricultural development is Xenophon, *Hell.* 4.1.15. In 395 BC Agesilaus goes to Dascyleium of Lesser Phrygia:

> where lay the palace (βασίλεια) of Pharnabazus, and around it many large villages (κῶμαι) with abundant provisions, and fine areas for hunting (θῆραι), some in enclosed parks, others in open spaces (αἱ μὲν καὶ ἐν περιειργμένοις παραδείσοις, αἱ δὲ καὶ ἀναπεπταμένοις τόποις). Beside it flowed a river full of all kinds of fish; and there were abundant birds for skilled fowlers.

So *paradeisos* covered a wide variety of environments from wild mountainous forests to artificial parklike gardens to whole village complexes.

21.3 Original Iranian texts

One feature common to all these types of "paradise" must have been the fact of their enclosure, as we just saw at Dascyleium. Forests, whether natural or artificial, which served mainly as the home of wild animals to be hunted must have been walled around, both to keep the animals (just indigenous or also imported?) in and poachers out. We shall see (III.135) how Hadrian surrounded the remnants of the Lebanese cedar forest with hundreds of inscriptions to forbid unauthorized logging; no signs of walls are reported by Breton, but there may have been some fencing in antiquity. The more artificial paradises were not intended as leisure playgrounds for citizens of nearby towns (if any) or inhabitants of villages, but for the Great King, the satrap and their entourages; for this there must at least have been a fence clearly marking its boundary. Quintus Curtius 8.1.11-13 describes the eastern district which he calls Bazaira:

---

20 Other ships were built in segments in Cyprus and Phoenicia and dragged overland to Thapsacus!

Barbarae opulentiae in illis locis haud ulla sunt maiora indicia quam magnis nemoribus saltibusque nobilium ferarum greges clusi. Spatiosas ad hoc eligunt siluas crebris perennium aquarum fontibus amoenas; muris nemora cinguntur turresque habent uenantium receptacula. Quattuor continuis aetatibus intactum saltum fuisse constabat cum Alexander cum toto exercitu ingressus agitari undique feras iussit.

There is no greater sign of barbarian opulence in those parts than the herds of noble wild beasts, penned in great woods and parks.[21] To this end they select extensive forests made pleasant by numerous perennial springs; the woods are surrounded with walls and have towers as blinds for the hunters. It is known that the forest had been untouched for four successive generations when Alexander entered with his whole army and ordered the beasts to be beaten up on every side.

The parallel usage of Nehemiah and Xenophon (with his successors) shows that the word is Iranian. There can be no doubt that in Old Persian and Median it named the satrapal hunting parks and gardens. The constant statement or implication that the paradise must be an enclosure in fact springs from the word's etymology. It appears once (only) in Avestan at *Videvdat* 3.18[22] where its form and etymology are believed clear. It is used of the "enclosure" to be built around a man who has perpetually defiled himself by carrying a corpse single-handed: *pairi.daēzą̄n pairi.daēzayą̄n* (with cognate accusative masculine plural of the noun preceding the verb), "they shall heap up a surrounding wall."[23] The noun (Frisk s.v.) would be exactly cognate with Greek masc. *περίτοιχος, nearly attested in the neuter in different grade περίτειχος LXX II Reg 25,1 for דָּיֵק "siege-wall."[24]

It is remarkable that in this unique Avestan usage the word is used in a highly pejorative context. It may also appear in nearly the honorific sense of the Greek and Hebrew in an Old Persian text of Artaxerxes II at Susa in four copies (Kent 154-5), where the key words are of uncertain meaning:

vašnā A(ura)M(azda)hā imām hadiš tya ji-va-di-ya pa-ra-da-ya-da-a-ma adam akunavām.

---

21   Greek παράδεισος never went into Latin *paradisus* until the Old Latin versions of the Bible, so Curtius uses what vocabulary he has.

22   C. Bartholomae, Altiranisches Wörterbuch; Strasbourg: Trübner, 1904; 865; translation of this text in Fritz Wolff, Avesta, die heiligen Bücher der Parsen...; Strasbourg: Trübner, 1910; p. 328.

23   The *i* in Avestan *pai-* is a regular phonetic phenomenon by which the *i* following the *r* is anticipated.

24   See II.296 for a likely connection of the Iranian and Hebrew.

Kent prefers "By the favor of Ahuramazda this is the palace (*hadiš* = ἕδος) which I built in my lifetime as a pleasant retreat," but notes (p. 195) the version of Emil Benveniste "paradis de vie." The Old Persian word can be identified with the Avestan form under plausible assumptions.[25] And since παράδεισοι are attested at Susa (Aelian *Hist. Anim.* 7.1 in fantastic context), likely "paradise" is intended in the Susa Old Persian texts also.

21.4 Gilgamesh and the forest of Lebanon

What became the "paradise" of the Lebanon was from the beginning of history an object of aggression from the East. Rowton,[26] going as far as possible behind the historical cuneiform sources, concludes:

> Now the Gilgamesh epic probably originated, at least in oral form, ...not much later than the middle of the third millennium B.C. And if we go back that far in time there is no difficulty in believing that this valley [between Mt. Hermon and the Lebanon] was a scene of surpassing sylvan beauty, with the two great mountains, deep in forest, soaring on either side.

Moderns, relying on modern translations of the Gilgamesh epic, see its hero as the first representative of Western humanism—perhaps the only such in Mesopotamian literature. What is he about? He is assigned or undertakes the task of overcoming Huwawa (Old Babylonian version) or Humbaba (Assyrian) the guardian[27] of the Cedar Forest:

> At whose name the lands are ever in terror
> I will conquer him in the Cedar Forest!
> ...My hand I will poise and will fell the cedars,
> A name that endures I will make for me!
> ...Huwawa—his roaring is the storm-flood,
> His mouth is fire, his breath is death![28]

---

25 The second *d* of the Old Persian corresponds to Median and Avestan *r* (Kent 33b); Levin conjectures that in this later Old Persian the distinction between the prefixes *para* and *pariy* may have become blurred.

26 M. B. Rowton, "The Woodlands of Ancient Western Asia," JNES 26 (1967) 261-277; p. 267. In general see Horst Klengel, "Der Libanon and seine Zedern in der Geschichte des Alten Vorderen Orients, " Das Altertum (Berlin) 13 (1967) Heft 2, 68-76.

27 In the translations available I do not find that Huwawa is anywhere given this exact description, but his role seems clear enough.

28 Old Babylonian Version III.v.2-3; ANET[3] 80a.

Originally the Cedar Forest was surely in the West, not very closely located in real geography; perhaps on the Amanus or the Lebanon. Humbaba is a formidable adversary, though not clearly defined. In a new fragment of the Old Babylonian the scene becomes precise:

> E[nkidu] killed [the *watchman*] of the forest,
> At whose word Saria[29] and Lebanon [*trembled*].[30]

There is no extended account of felling the cedars; in the Hittite version[31] it appears that Gilgamesh has cut down a single cedar (standing for the whole forest? or a world-tree?) before he and Enkidu dispatch Humbaba.[32]

We are obviously meant to identify sympathetically with Gilgamesh in his contest with the fearsome Humbaba, and in his failure (Tablet XI end) to grasp the plant of rejuvenation. The serpent which eats the plant of youth in his place and sheds its slough made its way as far as Greece (I.16). But how does he look in the light of history? The epic suggests no motivation for felling the cedar except that it is there. Historic rulers cut cedar for the practical purpose of building temples: thus first the Sumerian Gudea (ab. 2000 BC).[33] Ashur-Nasir-Pal (883-859 BC) cut cedar on the Amanus; Tiglath-Pileser III (744-727) built his palace at Calah with Lebanese cedar; Sennacherib (705-681) cut very large cedar logs in Sirara (Hermon) and used them to build his palace; similarly Esarhaddon (680-669) and Ashurbanipal (668-633).[34] There is a beautiful agreement with the Akkadian texts in the words which Isa 37,24 (= II Reg 19,23) puts in Sennacherib's mouth:

אֲנִי עָלִיתִי מְרוֹם הָרִים   יַרְכְּתֵי לְבָנוֹן
וְאֶכְרֹת קוֹמַת אֲרָזָיו   מִבְחַר בְּרֹשָׁיו
וְאָבוֹא מְרוֹם קִצּוֹ   יַעַר כַּרְמִלּוֹ

"I went up to the height of the mountains, the slopes of Lebanon; again and again I cut[35] the highest of its cedars, the most choice of its

---

29   Mt Hermon, Bib. Hebr. שִׂרְיֹן Deut 3,9; Ps 29,6.
30   New fragment, ANET³ 504b.
31   ANET³ 82a.
32   I here omit consideration of the difficult and fragmentary Sumerian version (ANET³ 47-50) "Gilgamesh and the Land of the Living." See Aaron Shaffer, "Gilgamesh, the Cedar Forest and Mesopotamian History," JAOS 103 (1983) 307-313.
33   ANET³ 268-9; The Lebanon and Phoenicia 176-7.
34   Texts and references in my The Lebanon and Phoenicia 179-195.
35   So I translate the imperfects of the Hebrew in both books, which bolder editors would like to convert to preterites, וָאֶכְרֹת etc.

junipers,[36] and ascended to its farthest height, the forest of its planta-
tion." It would almost seem that the prophet had some idea of
Sennacherib's actual words (on the "Bull Inscription") "Asshur and
Ishtar...showed me how to bring out the mighty cedar (GIŠ *eri-ni*), logs
which had grown large in the days gone by, and had become enor-
mously tall as they stood concealed in the mountains of Sirara."

In the texts of the (Sumerian and) Akkadian rulers, the obstacle to
timber-cutting are the kings whose territory they had to pass through;
Humbaba has disappeared. While the use of the cedar-logs to build
palaces is emphasized, the exploit is not merely practical; perhaps even
the reverse, the palaces are proof of the king's symbolic prowess as
shown in entering the forest. Solomon's palace "the House of the
Forest of Lebanon" (I Reg 7,2), בֵּית יַעַר הַלְּבָנוֹן, unlike the Akkadian
ones, had not merely cedar beams but cedar pillars, it reproduces the
forest. The motive of the Akkadian rulers is then similar to that of
Gilgamesh: an heroic accomplishment. Is the obstacle that Gilgamesh
had to meet merely mythological? If Humbaba corresponds to a reality, it would have to be a forest predator; since the lion was familiar
to Mesopotamian heroes, the predator would have to be the *bear*. To
a symbolic mind, the bear would be the agent or representative of the
guardian deity of the forest. We have seen (II.180-184) that both
Yahweh of Israel and Melkarth of Tyre have ursine characteristics.
Perhaps once the god of the cedar forest was Shadday (III.125) although in Psalm 29 it is Yahweh: it seems he has replaced a Phoenician
deity.[37] As the Mesopotamian kings made claim to the coastland and
its tutelary deities, to cut its timber is their right and their boast; they
carry out in reality what the epic projects in myth.

Likewise the Phoenician monarchs considered the forest was theirs
by right; Hiram of Tyre sends wood and carpenters to David (II Sam
5,11); Hiram sends Solomon timber for his palace and temple, but
Solomon must provide the labor, and in addition cede cities (I Reg
5,15-32; 9,10-14). Josephus (*con. Ap.* 1.106-120) cites the Hellenistic
writers Menander of Ephesus and Dios to the same effect.[38] Still the
Israelite kings not merely regard the Assyrian kings as invaders but as

---

36 From בְּרוֹשׁ (in its Aramaic equivalent, e.g. Rabbinic ברתא [Jastrow i.198])
    comes βόρατον Diodorus 2.49.4; βράθυ Dioscorides 1.76, τὸ Βράθυ Philo
    Byblius (FGH 790 fr. 2.9) as name of a mountain.
37 See Fritz Stolz, "Die Bäume des Gottesgartens auf dem Libanon," ZAW 84
    (1972) 141-156.
38 FGH 783, 785.

usurpers of the forest claimed for their own God. Isaiah goes on to say
(37,26-29) that it had been Yahweh's purpose all along that Sennacherib
should rage against him, and therefore that "I will put my hook in your
nose and my bit in your mouth." Thus what seems humanistic to us in
Gilgamesh seems both imperialist and blasphemous to the Hebrew
prophet in Sennacherib. The ironical lament of Isa 14 over the "king
of Babylon," where the junipers and cedar say "since you were laid
low, no hewer has come up against us" (14,8) may be a later addition
to the book, looking at Nebuchadrezzar's logging on the eastern Lebanon.[39] Thus we possess recorded contrasting views of the same trans-
action as they appeared to the two opposing parties.

21.5 Original forests of the Mediterranean[40]

At the end of the last glacial age a remarkable climax vegetation grew
up around the Mediterranean in spite of its moderate and erratic
rainfall. Although many mountains, including the Lebanon, were not
glaciated, the rising sea-level created a new regime of temperature and
rainfall. Theophrastus, in a passage which we quoted in part above
(III.123; *Hist. Plant.* 5.8.1,3), further observes:

> any tree, if it is let alone and not cut, left in its natural position, becomes
> remarkable in height and thickness. In Cyprus the kings did not cut the trees,
> both because they took good care of them and husbanded them, and also
> because it was difficult to get the timber out. The timber cut for the eleven-
> oar ship of Demetrius [Poliorcetes] was 13 spans long [about 25 m.], and
> besides being of marvellous length was without knots and smooth. But they
> say that the trees of Corsica are much the largest of all; for while both the
> fir (ἐλάτη) and pine (πεύκη) in Latium are very handsome, being bigger and
> finer than those of [southern] Italy, they are puny compared with the trees
> of Corsica.... The country of the Latins is well-watered. The coastal plain
> bears laurel (δάφνην), myrtle, and wonderful beech (ὀξύην); of the last they
> cut timbers big enough to run the whole length of the keel of an Etruscan
> ship. The hill-country bears pine and fir.

---

39   The Lebanon and Phoenicia 195-199.
40   Generally for this section see Meiggs Trees and Timber (note 6 above) *passim*;
     Olli Makkonen, Ancient Forestry: An Historical Study; 2 parts; Acta Forestalia
     Fennica 82 (1967) & 95 (1969); Helsinki; Ellen Churchill Semple, "Climatic
     and Geographic Influences on ancient Mediterranean Forests and the Lumber
     Trade," Annals of the Association of American Geographers 9 (1919) 13-37
     (= pp. 261-296 of her The Geography of the Mediterranean Region: Its
     Relation to Ancient History; New York: Holt, 1931).

Theophrastus, born in barren Lesbos and settling in barren Athens, must have travelled to some extent in order to have discovered the wealth of an actual forest; evidently not to Corsica (where he quotes others) but perhaps to Italy and the Lebanon. Plato in the unfinished myth of the *Critias* (see II.68) imagines that once the sea-level of Attica had been lower before the present mere skeleton of the land was left— 9,000 years before his time [just right for the last glaciation!]:

> It had much timber in the mountains, of which clear evidence still remains. For there are mountains today which can only produce nourishment for bees [from the scrub-flora of the maquis]; but it is not long since that trees for roofing the largest buildings were cut from them, and the roofs are still intact. There were also other tall cultivated trees which provided a great deal of pasturage for flocks. Likewise the country turned to good use the yearly rain from Zeus, not as now wasting what flows from the bare ground to the sea; but since it had deep earth and received the rain into it, it stored up the water from the heights behind impervious clay such as potters use.[41]

Thucydides 1.2.5 says that "Attica because of its mostly thin soil did not attract invaders" (τὴν γοῦν Ἀττικὴν ἐκ τοῦ ἐπὶ πλεῖστον διὰ τὸ λεπτόγεων ἀστασίαστον οὖσαν) like other parts of Greece; but this may reflect conditions after deforestation rather than before.

Theophrastus' testimony about the old forests in Cyprus is brought forward by Strabo 14.6.5:

> Eratosthenes says that in ancient times the plains [of Cyprus] had gone to wood, so that they were covered with thickets (δρυμοί) and were not farmed. He goes on to say that the mines helped somewhat in this situation, since men cut down the trees for the smelting of copper and silver; the building of fleets was of further assistance, since the sea was now sailed without fear [of pirates] and [was patrolled] by naval forces. Even so they were not able to stem [the growth of timber], and so they permitted those able and willing to cut it out and hold the cleared land as their own property, free from taxes.

Rostovtzeff[42] thinks that the period of protection attested by Theophrastus was by the autonomous city-kings of the fourth century BC; the period of exploitation by the fleets of Antigonus and Demetrius; and adds a probable period of management of the forests by the Ptolemies. Thirgood, who had been a forester in Cyprus, chronicles its ongoing deforestation, climaxed by Turkish "aerial incendiary bomb-

41 *Critias* 111C-D.
42 M. Rostovtzeff, Social and Economic History of the Hellenistic World; Oxford: Clarendon, 1953; 3 vols.; iii.1612 note 113.

ing" of the forests in July 1974.[43] By the Roman period the greatest
natural resource of the Mediterranean was regarded as a nuisance and
obstacle to agriculture; and its wasteful utilization in metallurgy, naval
building and indiscriminate clearing was seen as the greatest of benefits
to the state.[44]

In ancient Lebanon, which I know best, on one hand the perennial
springs were fuller and more constant throughout the year from reten-
tion of water by the soil. The most conspicuous example of many is the
river which bursts out from an underground limestone cavern (flowing
over impenetrable clay) at Afqa (I.245); Ps 104,10 "You who make
springs break out in the valleys; they run between the hills":

הַמְשַׁלֵּחַ מַעְיָנִים בַּנְּחָלִים   בֵּין הָרִים יְהַלֵּכוּן

And further, the water received on the land was actually greater, from
the dripping of fog off needles onto the ground, and from greater
rainfall than now through the transpiration of water vapor from the
forests. The coastal redwood forests of California show the same
pattern. Vaumas[45] believes (like Rowton) that the entire Lebanon and
Antilebanon were originally forested, with hardwoods and pine on the
western slope of Lebanon up to about 1300 meters; cedar (*Cedrus
Libani*) and Cilician fir (*Abies cilicica*) up to 2000 meters; and juniper
(*Juniperus excelsa*) on both slopes of both mountains above 2000
meters. The ARBORVM GENERA IV of Hadrian (III.000) can mostly
be identified. Mouterde[46] is certain that they included the cedar, the
Cilician fir, and the *Juniperus excelsa*; for the fourth, ancient species
identifications need not have exactly corresponded with ours. In the
north there are small remnant forests of cedar today on the eastern
slopes of Lebanon, and Nebuchadrezzar (we saw) logged them about
587 BC. The Cilician fir, better preserved today in Turkey, must have
produced on the Lebanon long trunks suitable for masts, but was cut
back early and scarcely shows in the Akkadian records. The *Juniperus
excelsa*, today very much degraded, once also was a great forest tree.
Even the picturesque cedars of Bsharre, preserved in the sacred enclo-

43 J. V. Thirgood, Man and the Mediterranean Forest: A history of resource
    depletion; London etc.: Academic, 1981; 148.
44 See Julia E. Burnet, "Sowing the Four Winds: Targeting the Cypriote Forest
    Resource in Antiquity," pp. 59-69 of S. Swiny et alii (eds.), Res Maritimae:
    Cyprus and the Eastern Mediterranean from Prehistory to Late Antiquity;
    Atlanta: Scholars, 1997.
45 Etienne de Vaumas, Le Liban: Etude de géographie physique; 3 vols.; Paris:
    Firmin-Didot, 1954; I.286.
46 Paul Mouterde, "Note sur les essences forestières du Liban," Mélanges de
    l'Univ. saint Joseph 25.3 (1942/3) 48-49.

sure of a Maronite monastery, show a low branched habit from dys-
genic selection by centuries of grazing goats; the ancient cedar was a
tall forest tree (see Theophrastus, III.123).

Not long before Hadrian, Tacitus in his famous phrase (*Hist* 5.6) is
struck above all with the shade of the forest in its semi-tropical environment: "among such heats, Lebanon is dark with shade and constant
with snows (*tantos inter ardores opacum fidumque niuibus*); it generates and fills the Jordan river." The sacred wild place of the Hebrew
Bible is the slope of Lebanon—very likely adapting Phoenician literary
motifs now lost. Here from Psalm 104, besides the streams breaking
out in the ravines between the hills with the sea broad beneath, are the
ibex and coney, the wild asses and lions, the stork building her nest in
the junipers above the cedar-line. What is most impressive in the
California forests of the coastal redwood (*Sequoia sempervirens*) is not
even the height and shade of the trees, but their enormous vegetative
power in springing up from the roots of the cut or fallen, and the
energy in the twisted buttresses that they throw out on whatever side
their stability is threatened.

21.6 Bureaucratic control of logging

After the liquidation of the Persian empire by Alexander, in some
places the former paradises were kept up, but not under that name.
Thus the forest of Lebanon was controlled or exploited by successor
monarchs: by Antigonus in 315 BC (Diodorus 19.58.1-5); by Antiochus
III of Syria after 200 BC (Josephus *AJ* 12.141); by Agrippa II of Judaea
in AD 50-68 (Josephus *BJ* 5.36-38).[47] But the old name "paradise"
does not reappear. The Hellenistic monarchs who controlled the forest
of Lebanon must have done so through a bureaucracy more or less
patterned on the Persian as recorded in Neh 2,8; for it reappears in the
Roman period under Hadrian.

Aristotle (*Pol.* 6.5.4 = 1321b31, 7.11.4 = 1331b15) records ὑλωροί
"forest-keepers," but does not specify the area or their duties. When
Pharnabazus promises the Spartans timber for ships ἐν τῇ βασιλέως
(Xenophon *Hell.* 1.124-5) at Mt Ida in Phrygia (410 BC), the forest,
though in his satrapy, was at least nominally held by the Great King.
Latin inscriptions in the Roman world have been thoroughly enough
investigated so that we can say with some confidence: Only on the
Lebanon did Romans record systematic forest management. Hadrian

---

47   See my Lebanon and Phoenicia 206-210.

put up boundary markers on the living rock at what must have been
the perimeter of the Lebanese forest in his own day; the extent of
deforestation is indicated when we discover that today without exception they stand in the midst of treeless rocky shale. They were restudied
under dangerous political conditions by Jean-François Breton,[48] who
was unable to enter the northern Lebanon at all. Still he saw or
republished a total of 187 inscriptions.

The key to their abbreviations is his IGLS 5001, now on the campus
of the American University of Beirut:

    IMP(eratoris) HAD(riani) AVG(usti) DEFINITIO SILVARVM
"Boundary of the forests of the Emperor Hadrian Augustus." Many of
them further read, mostly in abbreviations (IGLS 5124)

    ARBORVM GENERA IV CETERA PRIVATA
"Four species of trees [are forbidden]; others are private." Above we
discuss likely identifications of the four species. Two inscriptions show
procurators of Augustus who have inherited the task of Asaph. IGLS
5096:

    IMP(eratoris) HAD(riani) AVG(usti) VIG(ilis?) C(aius) VMBRIVS
   PROC(urator) AVG(usti) IMP(eratoris) I(terum) S(alutati) P(osuit)
"Of the Emperor Hadrian Augustus. Gaius Umbrius, guard(?), procu-
rator of Augustus when saluted for the second time as Emperor, placed
it." And finally (IGLS 5186, cf. 5185) on the eastern slope of the
Lebanon, where Nebuchadrezzar cut timber:

    IMP(eratoris) H[AD](riani) AVG(usti) D(e)F(initio) S(iluarum) XII
   P(er) PR(ocuratorem) Q(uintum) VET(ium) RUF[u]M
"Boundary [marker] no. 12 of the forests of the Emperor Hadrian
Augustus, by the procurator Quintus Vetius Rufus."

21.7 The garden as private paradise

In the Hellenistic period Xenophon's word *paradeisos* is privatized to
mean "garden" simply. Hebrew offers a transitional usage at Koh 2,5,
where the supposed Solomon says "I made myself gardens and
paradises, and planted in them trees bearing every kind of fruit":

עָשִׂיתִי לִי גַּנּוֹת וּפַרְדֵּסִים   וְנָטַעְתִּי בָהֶם עֵץ כָּל־פֶּרִי

LXX ... κήπους καὶ παραδείσους, Vg *hortos et pomaria*. The date of

---

48   Jean-François Breton, Les Inscriptions forestières d'Hadrien dans le mont
    Liban, IGLS VIII,3; BAH 104; Paris: Geuthner, 1980. In the forthcoming
    Barrington Atlas of the Greek and Roman World (Princeton) I sketch the forest
    as it existed under Hadrian on the basis of Breton's maps.

Qoheleth must be late Persian or early Hellenistic; the ostensible author is given the style of an ancient Near Eastern monarch or divinity, setting out trees in a grand enclosure; but the reality is of a rich man planting a garden. The usage is clear in Rabbinic, Mishna *Arakh.* III.2 בפרדסות סבסתי "in the gardens of Sebaste." An inscription from Sardes of about 305 BC,[49] where the *paradeisos* of Tissaphernes was perhaps still remembered, uses παράδεισοι as "gardens" only. In Egypt, Nicias gives Zeno's agent Apollonius fruit trees from his παραδείσους and so reports on January 19, 257 BC.[50] The citizens of Itanos on Crete about 246 BC dedicate "the garden (παράδισον) by the gate" as a sacred precinct (ἱερὸν τέμενος) to Ptolemy III Euergetes and queen Berenice.[51] Antiochus IV Epiphanes set out vast parks (παραδείσοις...παμμήκεσι, Josephus *AJ* 12.233) on his country estates. In the Greek of the "Rosetta stone" (OGIS 90.15, 196 BC) the παράδεισοι (the Demotic version otherwise) are plantations of palms and other fruiting trees taxable for the benefit of the "gods," Ptolemy V and his sister-wife. An Egyptian Jew fancifully imagines himself as an irrigation-canal leading from the Nile (Sirach 24,30) "And I was like a canal from a river, like a watercourse I entered a garden":

κἀγὼ ὡς διῶρυξ ἀπὸ ποταμοῦ, καὶ ὡς ὑδραγωγὸς ἐξῆλθον εἰς παράδεισον.

Josephus like Theophrastus *Hist. Plant.* 9.6.1 (I.96) names as "paradises" the plantations of Jericho (*BJ* 4.467) and Judaea (6.6); when he describes the "paradises" of Solomon (*AJ* 8.186, cf. 7.347) he may have Jerusalem gardens in mind.

The usage of the Septuagint partly (and perhaps always in original intent) follows the same pattern, translating גַּן by παράδεισος. Thus at Num 24,6 for כְּגַנֹּת עֲלֵי נָהָר it has ὡσεὶ παράδεισοι ἐπὶ ποταμῶν; at Jer 29,5, where the prophet addresses the exiles in Babylon, he says "Plant gardens and eat their produce":

וְנִטְעוּ גַנּוֹת וְאִכְלוּ אֶת־פִּרְיֶן

LXX ("36.5") φυτεύσατε παραδείσους .... The "garden" of *Susanna* is a παράδεισος throughout. But where the LXX likewise makes the garden of Eden a "paradise" (perhaps anticipated by the usage of Cant 4,13) it creates a new concept.

---

49   W. H. Buckler & D. M. Robinson, Greek Inscriptions from Sardes I, AJA 16 (1912) 1-82; no. I col. 1 line 15.

50   C. C. Edgar, Zenon Papyri Vol. I, Catalogue général des antiquités égyptiennes du Musée du Caire 79.1; Le Caire 1925, no. 59033, p. 54. The Zeno papyri contain at least 17 references to a *paradeisos*: P. W. Pestman (ed.), A Guide to the Zenon Archive (P. L. Bat. 21); 2 vols.; Leiden: Brill, 1981, ii.696.

51   SIG³ 463.

21.8 The restoration of Eden

We saw (III.125) that the LXX of Gen 2,8 and 3,23 translates the "garden" as "Paradise." Likewise in most of the prophetic passages referring to Eden (Isa 51,3; Ez 28,13; 31,8-9; Joel 2,3) for גַּן the LXX has παράδεισος with variations. At Ez 31,3-9 the cedar of Lebanon is envied by the cedars in the "garden of God" and the "trees of Eden"; this strongly suggests that in the Phoenician myth of Ez 28,13 Eden is on Lebanon. In the erotic symbolism of Canticles the body of the beloved is assimilated to the landscape of Lebanon. In her virginity she is like the satrapal forest (Cant 4,12-13) "a garden locked...a fountain sealed":

גַּן נָעוּל...מַעְיָן חָתוּם

LXX κῆπος κεκλεισμένος, πηγὴ ἐσφραγισμένη, Vg *hortus conclusus, fons signatus*. Thus she herself becomes a "paradise of pomegranates," פַּרְדֵּס רִמּוֹנִים, παράδεισος ῥοῶν, Vg *paradisus malorum punicorum*. To that extent Canticles anticipates the LXX in seeing Eden as the satrapal paradise.

Rabbinic is hesitant about making the connection; in its thought Paradise becomes a place of danger. Tosefta *Hagigah* 2.3:[52]

> Four men entered Paradise: Ben ʿAzzai, Ben Zoma, the Other (Elisha b. Abuyah, אלישע), and R. ʿAqiba. [In the same sequence] One gazed and perished; one gazed and was smitten; one gazed and 'cut down sprouts' [apostatized];[53] one went up whole and came down whole.

ארבעה נכנסין לפרדס בן עזיי ובן זומא אחר ור׳ עקיבא אחד הציץ
ומת אחד הציץ ונפגע אחד הציץ וקיצץ בנטיעות ואחד עלה בשלום
וירד בשלום

The verbs associated with ʿAqiba indicate that this Paradise is *above* the earth. The Targums do not recognize this special usage; Aramaic פרדיסא appears in the Targ. Jon. of Jud 4,5 as "garden"; in Targ. Ps.-Jon. of Gen 14,3 etc. for "valley"; but never for "Eden." Thus the Talmudic text rests on the LXX naming of the garden of Eden as "paradise," while shifting the site.

---

52 Ed. Saul Lieberman; Jewish Theol. Sem. of America, 5722/1962; p. 381. A different version of this passage at Bab. Talm. *Hag.* 14b.

53 Jastrow 1407 explains this idiom (which is said to continue into modern Hebrew also) as "corrupting the youth," i.e. the "new shoots" in the garden of society.

54 J. T. Milik & M. Black, The Books of Enoch: Aramaic Fragments of Qumran Cave 4; Oxford: Clarendon, 1976; 232. Translation in Charlesworth I.28. How did the Aramaic come to be lost? The Vulgate explains! Enoch "was translated" (Heb 11,5 *translatus est*)—evidently into Ethiopic...—and thereafter the original "was no more to be found" (*non inueniebatur*).

Non-canonical Judaism continues more boldly along the same line. The Aramaic original of *I Enoch* 32 from Qumran[54] has "And I passed on to the Paradise of Righteousness":

ואחלפת ליד פרדס קשט[א]

Sibylline Oracles 1.24-25 with an Homeric reminiscence "in ambrosial Paradise," ἐν παραδείσῳ / ἀμβροσίῳ. The *Testament of Levi* 18.10,[55] perhaps here with a Christian overlay, says that "one will open the gates of Paradise," ἀνοίξει τὰς θύρας τοῦ παραδείσου. The concept is that Eden, long ago debarred from humanity by cherubim and the fiery sword, has again become accessible. Latin *IV Esdras* 8.52 has God say to Ezra "because it is for you that paradise is opened, that the tree of life is planted," *Vobis enim apertus est paradisus, plantata est arbor uitae.*

A possible pagan echo of the LXX usage appears in Aristides *To Rome* 99: among the benefits brought by Rome καὶ ἡ γῆ πᾶσα οἷον παράδεισος ἐγκεκόσμηται "And the whole earth has been beautified like a *paradeisos.*" If this reflects solely Hellenistic usage, the rhetorician is comparing the earth to a garden. But the scope of the comparison, anticipating medieval thought, suggests that some resonance of Eden has come to his ears. Thus Aristides can be added to the authors who may have had knowledge of the Greek Bible: Ovid (I.55), Vergil (I.173), Horace (II.78), Lucan (II.143), Athenaeus (I.122), Diodorus (III.321), "Longinus" 9.9, and Plutarch and Lucian (II.168).

The Apocalypse of John reverses the expulsion of mankind from Eden but otherwise does not conceptually go beyond the Septuagint. Rev 2,7 "To him that conquers I shall grant to eat of the tree of life which is in the paradise of God." At Gen 3,22 this is precisely the outcome feared by God, as a result of which mankind must leave the Garden; John says that the judgement has now been reversed. The expression could not possibly be derived from working over the language of the Hebrew Bible or the Targum; like much in this book it presupposes the LXX.

At II Kor 12,2-4 Paul speaks of a man in Christ fourteen years ago, whom most commentators consider to be Paul himself. Paul says two things about him, that "such a one was seized to the third heaven," ἁρπαγέντα τὸν τοιοῦτον ἕως τρίτου οὐρανοῦ; and "that he was seized to paradise and heard unspeakable words," ὅτι ἡρπάγη εἰς τὸν παράδεισον καὶ ἤκουσεν ἄρρητα ῥήματα. Commentators ancient[56] and modern differ about the relation between the "third heaven" and

---

55   Ed. M. de Jonge; Leiden: Brill, 1978. Translation in Charlesworth I.795. See Psalms of Solomon 14.3.

56   Lampe s.v. *paradeisos* p. 1011 col. 2, B2 quotes Fathers who take various positions about the relation of the "third heaven" and "paradise."

"paradise," and whether the third heaven was the highest to which one could attain or an intermediate state. The parallelism of the two clauses suggests that the two were more or less identified; but we need not assume that in Paul's thought the topography of either was precisely located. Since here if anywhere we have the exact language of the historical Paul, we must conclude that he has taken a step beyond the usage of the Septuagint; for there is nothing in the passage to suggest that "paradise" is the garden of Eden. Rather it is a special realm or place of revelation, which it is more natural to locate in the heavens than anywhere else. Paul here as elsewhere anticipates the experience and language of ʿAqiba;[57] both locate Paradise above rather than on the earth, both visit it unscathed.

The dialogue which Luke (23,42-43) gives to the good bandit and Jesus suggests a different equivalence: "Jesus, remember me when you come into your kingdom," Ἰησοῦ μνήσθητί μου ὅταν ἔλθῃς εἰς τὴν βασιλείαν σου; "Verily I say to you, today you will be with me in paradise," ἀμήν σοι λέγω, σήμερον μετ᾽ ἐμοῦ ἔσῃ ἐν τῷ παραδείσῳ. The historical Jesus normally speaks of "the kingdom of God" or equivalently "of heaven"; "your kingdom" reminds us of Luk 22,28 "so that you may eat and drink at my table in my kingdom (ἐν τῇ βασιλείᾳ μου)." We cannot be certain then at 23,42-43 of piercing behind Luke's language to anything earlier. The Fathers are divided[58] whether "paradise" here is identified with "heaven" or distinct from it. But the dialogue suggests that "Jesus' kingdom" and "paradise" are treated as alternative symbols. It is more natural here than in Paul to take "paradise" as the restored garden of Eden, which the Apocalypse presumes has been reopened by the work of Christ. Luke (intentionally or by good luck) has here contrasted two Persian themes (III.108). For crucifixion was the preferred punishment meted out by the Great King to rebels or pretenders. Thus Jesus, while being put to death as a pretender, is represented as making an audacious claim to future presence in the satrapal or regal *paradeisos*. And that means that correspondingly he is making the claim for himself as its rightful regal or divine proprietor.

21.9 The vision of Ephrem Syrus

The novel concept of Paradise in the New Testament as the place forbidden to Adam and reopened by Christ is variously interpreted by

---

57   See their common use of *arrabo* "pledge" (I.75, 77).
58   Lampe p. 1012 col. 1 (*paradeisos* C4).

the Fathers, especially the Greek, working hard to fit it in to the categories of their thought. But in the Semitic world it is understood in a more comprehensive manner in the fifteen *Hymns of Paradise* (מדרשא דפרדיסא) by Ephrem of Nisibis (AD 306 [?] to 373).[59] These Syriac hymns are all written in six-line syllabic stanzas with the syllables arranged in the pattern: 5+5, 5+5, 5+5, 5+2, 5+5, 5+5. There is much rhyming and assonance. It is unclear whether Ephrem may have known some Greek. But, except for loan words from Greek, most or all of which can be attested from elsewhere in Syriac, neither his syllabic metric, nor verse-forms, nor thought can plausibly be derived from any Greek original. But there are remarkable continuations of Rabbinic thought.

For Ephrem, "paradise" is not one state of affairs contrasted with "heaven" or the "kingdom," but the unique scene, both of creation, where Adam and Eve were placed and then expelled, and of the consummation when it was reopened by Christ. (It was precisely when Jesus' side was pierced by the lance [Joh 19,34] that the fiery sword was removed.[60]) Paradise is envisaged as a mountain, for otherwise it would have been destroyed by the Flood (*Hymn* 1.4.1-3):

חזיתה לפרדיסא	בעינא דרעינא
סימין תחית רומה	ורומא דכל טורין
רשא דממולא	לעקבוהי מטא בלחוד

With the eye of my mind	I gazed upon Paradise;
the summit of all mountains	is lower than its summit,
the Crest of the Flood	reached only its foothills.

This mountain encircles the whole earth, beyond the sea in every direction (*Hymn* 2.6.4-5):

---

59 The Syriac is edited with German translation by Edmund Beck, Des Heiligen Ephraem des Syrers Hymnen de Paradiso und Contra Julianum; CSCO vols. 174-5 (Scriptores Syri tom. 78-79); Louvain; 1957. His edition, following the British Museum MS add. 14571, dated AD 519, has no vowel-markers and only a few conventional points to distinguish grammatical forms with identical consonants. Consequently a deep understanding of both grammar and MS usage (which I do not possess) is required to translate these compressed and allusive texts. There is a beautiful French translation by the Lebanese Jesuit René Lavenant: F. Graffin (ed.), Ephrem de Nisibe, Hymns sur le Paradis; Sources Chrétiennes 137; Paris: Cerf, 1968. I have followed with some modifications the translation in the excellent edition of Sebastian Brock, Saint Ephrem: Hymns on Paradise; Crestwood (N.Y.): St Vladimir's Seminary Press, 1990. Ephrem on Paradise is anticipated by the Syriac Odes of Solomon 11.18.

60 *Hymn* 2.1 refrain with Graffin's note.

הויו אסר חצוהי   דעלמא

לימא חזיק רבא   שבבא הו דעליא

[Paradise] girds the loins of the world; encircling the great sea, neighbor
to the beings on high.

As we know, God planted it in the beginning (*Hymn* 6.10.1-2):

חילא דלא עמל   דרעא דלא לאא

שתלה לפרדיסא   צבתה דלא עמלא

The effortless power, the arm which never tires,
planted the Paradise, adorned it without effort.

After Adam's departure it had a "fence" put around it—namely, a סינא,
the word which the Rabbis used for the "fence around the Torah"
(*Avoth* I.1, see I.161), סיג לתורה (*Hymn* 4.1.6):

כרובא ושנן חרבא   סינה דפרדיסא

The cherub and the sharp sword were the fence of Paradise.

At Mark 12,1 when one puts a fence (φραγμόν) around his vineyard,
Pesh has סינא.

To accommodate different categories of people, both in the beginning and the end, Paradise has several regions. Simple-minded people,
הדיוטא (i.e. ἰδιῶται)[61] who sinned out of ignorance, after expiation are
established by the Good One at the "border of Paradise" בריכא דפרדיסא
(*Hymn* 1.16). In the center of the Garden was the Tree of Knowledge
(3.3). At the summit is the Tree of Life, "the sun of Paradise"
שמשא דפרדיסא (3.2.2). The levels are summarized at 2.11.5-6:

ארעה לתיבא   מצעתא לזדיקא

רומה לנציחא   ולשכינתא רשה

Its ground level for the penitent,   its middle for the just,
its top for the victorious,   its summit for the *Shekinah*.

In the Syriac realm the Rabbinic concept of the שכינה or tabernacling
presence of God (I.180) is continued in the Christian church. And it
reappears further at Quran 9.26 (II.330) "Then Allah sent down his
Sakinah on his Messenger": ثُمَّ أَنْزَلَ ٱللّٰهُ سَكِينَتَهُ عَلَىٰ رَسُولِهِ.

The reopening of Paradise was due to Christ, seen under many
images, in particular as the "athlete," אתליטא = ἀθλητής (12.6.1).[62] But
we have our own part to play (2.2.1):

---

61   Thus at I Kor 14,16 ἰδιώτου the Syriac has הדיוטא and the Vg *idiotai*; compare
     Mishna *Qidd.* I.6 ההדיוט.

62   The true Christian is seen as an athlete, ὡς τέλειος ἀθλητής at Ignatius *Polycarp*
     1.3; see Rabbinic אתליטיס *Gen. Rabbah* 77.3. ἀθληταί were introduced into
     Jerusalem by Herod the Great (Josephus *AJ* 15.269) and brought their name
     into the language. Similar metaphorical use in Latin, Varro *Res Rust.* 3.5.18
     nos athletae comitiorum "we old hands at politics."

מכא חשול סב לך   קלידה דפרדיסא

Forge here and take with you   the key of Paradise.

That would be in identical Greek *τὴν κλεῖδα τοῦ παραδείσου "the key of Paradise."[63] For (15.6.1-3) our intelligence (בוינא) is like a treasurer (גזברא)[64] who can fit a key to each locked door (תרע דאחיד). Paradise would be defiled by the presence of chalcedony (קרכדנא) or beryl (ברולא), 7.4—this text goes beyond Plato *Phaedo* 110D and Ez 28,13 (cited I.87), in both of which texts our jewels are good enough to belong to the better land (III.55).[65]

In the restored Paradise human beings are marked above all by the "robe of glory," אסטל שובחא[66] which they were given and lost at the beginning, but now get back in even finer fashion, the "robe of the house of Adam" (6.9.3) לאסטלא דבית אדם with the Greek loanword στολή.[67] Here several themes come together. The "tunics of skin" of Gen 3,21 (כָּתְנוֹת עוֹר) it appears were reinterpreted as "garments of light" (אוֹר for עוֹר)—perhaps an original more ethereal bodily substance (cf. I.207). But they also are parallel (in whichever direction the influence ran) to the supernatural garment or toga which the Zoroastrian awaits after death, in some sense his alter ego in heaven, and which we saw coming to meet the hero in the Syriac *Hymn of the Pearl* (III.63). And Paul says (II Kor 5,4, cf. I.58) "we do not wish to be unclothed but to be clothed upon," οὐ θέλομεν ἐκδύσασθαι ἀλλ' ἐπενδύσασθαι. The early Church, much as it strives to overcome Gnostic or neo-Platonic dualism, remains uneasy about sexuality and cannot abide nakedness. Especially in the Syriac realm, profoundly influenced by Iran, its ideal humanity is clothed from head to foot in iridescent garments like Sasanid nobles (I. 59).

---

63 The Latin equivalent actually appears in Tertullian *de anima* 55.5 addressing Christ, *tota paradisi clauis tuus sanguis est* "your blood is the whole key of paradise." See also de Quincey, *Confessions of an English Opium Eater* ii "Thou hast the keys of Paradise, oh just, subtle and mighty opium!" (cited from ODQ² 172.19). For "key" see II.169.

64 For the "treasurer" see III.240.

65 Biblical Heb. כַּדְכֹּד Ez 27,16 "some jewel" cannot be brought into original relation with the jewel χαλκηδών Rev 21,19 (with folk-etymology to the city Chalcedon?); Rabbinic has an alternative spelling כרכד, which could be the common scribal confusion of daleth and resh, but more likely represents partial assimilation as here to the Greek word.

66 Ephrem *Hymnen de ieiunio* 3.2.6, ed. E. Beck CSCO 246-7 = Scriptores Syri 106-7 (Louvain 1964); discussion Brock pp. 66-72.

67 For στολή in Rabbinic see III.245.

21.10 Deforestation in the Lebanon and the Mediterranean[68]

The forests described by the ancient sources are today reduced to scattered groves, degraded stands, or nothing. A survey of deforestation begins thus:

> There is a close interconnection between ruined cities and ruined land. The fact that the broken statues and scattered column drums of the centers of ancient civilization have deforested and eroded landscapes as their settings does not seem to be an accident. The general impression of synchronicity, the contemporaneous ruin of ancient societies and ancient environments, has been inescapable.[69]

The authors quote the intuitive judgement of Thoreau:

> The civilized nations—Greece, Rome, England—have been sustained by the primitive forests which anciently rotted where they stand. They survive as long as the soil is not exhausted. Alas for human culture! Little is to be expected of a nation, when the vegetable mould is exhausted, and it is compelled to make manure of the bones of its fathers.

The authors feel that 90% of the wood used in the ancient world (in the natural form or as charcoal) was as fuel. Strabo 5.2.6 (II.224) found Populonia nearly deserted (ἔρημον) apart from some reworking of the ore from Elba (Aithaleia), while Diodorus 5.13 (following Poseidonius about 90 BC) describes the furnaces of Aithaleia itself as in full operation. The decline was probably less due to depletion of the ore than to exhaustion of the mainland forests by which it was smelted. On the Lebanon, the damage done in the ancient and medieval world was much extended by the wood-burning Turkish railroad engines in World War I, which Hitti[70] estimates took 60% of the remaining

---

68   See E. W. Beals, "The Remnant Cedar Forests of Lebanon," The Journal of Ecology 53 (1965) 679-694; Marvin W. Mikesell, "The Deforestation of Mount Lebanon," The Geographical Review 59 (1969) 1-28. More generally: John D. Currid, "The Deforestation of the Foothills of Palestine," Palestine Exploration Quarterly 116 (1984) 1-11; William C. Brice, "The Desiccation of Anatolia, " pp. 141-147 of idem (ed.), The Environmental History of the Near and Middle East Since the Last Ice Age; London etc.: Academic, 1978; Marvin W. Mikesell, "Deforestation in Northern Morocco," Science, Aug. 19 (1960), Vol. 132, No. 3425, 441-448.

69   J. Donald Hughes & J. V. Thirgood, "Deforestation, Erosion and Forest Management in Ancient Greece and Rome," Journal of Forest History, April 1982 (vol. 26) 60-75. This thought is expanded in Hughes' chapter "Deforestation, Overgrazing, and Erosion" (Pan's Travail 73-90).

70   Philip K. Hitti, Lebanon in History from the earliest times to the present; London: Macmillan, 1957; 34.

forest. When the forests had been reduced to stumps, new shoots and scrub, the omnipresent goat finishes off the damage by constantly grazing off the sprouts before they can grow beyond its height. Eupolis the comic poet (Macrobius 7.5.9 = Kock i.269 frag. 14, cf Hughes 78) has a chorus of goats in five elegant lines list the plants they graze— a catalogue of the *maquis* flora. On the Lebanon, where our documentation is best and which I tried to study exhaustively, the documented timber use in the ancient world was for two main purposes: building of temples and of naval fleets. Of the two, shipbuilding appears to have been by far the more destructive.

The ancient world saw two great periods of naval shipbuilding: the naval arms race of 315-250 BC and the civil wars of the generals of the Roman republic. Our best figures for Lebanon are from 315 BC (Diodorus 19.58) when Antigonus had 8,000 men logging and sawing and 1,000 yoke of oxen dragging the timber down—perhaps for one full summer season. A temple took something like the same labor as one of these fleets: Solomon had labor-conscription of 30,000 men to cut the Lebanese timber for his temple, but used only 10,000 at a time on the mountain (I Reg 5,27). However, temples lasted for hundreds of years; Solomon's timbers presumably endured with some replacements until Nechuchadrezzar burned the temple to the ground in 586 BC (II Reg 25,9). The longest-lived Athenian trireme was in use 26 years; at the outbreak of the Second Punic War in 218 BC, Rome had 200 quinqueremes which were almost certainly those built or captured from Carthage in 242 BC.[71] In periods of action their life-expectancy was much shorter; many no doubt were sunk or scrapped in the month they were commissioned. Thus beside the fifteen or so temples in the ancient world known or conjectured to have been roofed with Lebanese cedar, the maintenance of the fleets controlling (among other things) the Phoenician cities was a far greater burden. The systematic Romans, locking the barn door after the horse had been stolen, put men who were probably procurators of the treasury, C. Umbrius and Q. Vettius Rufus, over the remains of the forest.

In the same way, the destruction of the great pine trees of New England was due to the insatiable demand of the British navy for masts. Malone[72] shows how the New England forests were a key element in colonial relations, and discusses two English policies:

---

71 Lionel Casson, Ships and Seamanship in the Ancient World; Princeton: University, 1971; 90, 120.
72 Joseph J. Malone, Pine Trees and Politics: The Naval Stores and Forest Policy in Colonial New England, 1691-1775; New York: Longmans 1964, ix.

The first visualized New England as a more useful unit of the colonial system through realizing its potential as a producer of naval stores [pitch and tar]. The second sought to safeguard the supply of masts for the Royal Navy, the most important sources of masts being the stands of tall *Pinus strobus*, or white pine, in New England. Both of these policies were expressions of the mercantilistic viewpoint.

We saw (II.268) that the death of a hero on the battlefield is compared by the *Iliad* (13.389-391 = 16.483-485) to the cutting of a great tree by woodworkers on the mountains with their sharp axes for ship timber. When Vergil (*Aen.* 2.624-631) adapts the old simile to describe the fall of *Neptunia Troia*, in principle he has the understanding of modern historical ecologists: when the forest that was the wealth of a city falls, the city falls. So far as the Germanic motif of a world-tree has entered here, it testifies to the same insight, that the life of civilization as a whole is dependent on the forest under which it grew and which nurtured it. Solomon's palace, we saw, with its cedar beams was a literal reconstruction of the forest; the temple on every Greek acropolis replants the forest in stone, though it might be roofed with timber. The makers attest to the interconnection of the forest and the temple, but are insufficiently aware that the temple can in no manner serve as substitute.

21.11 Later history of Paradise

In a few places Christian commentators, looking back to the Greek world, see it as a distorted version of the Biblical witness. So Tertullian (*Apol.* 11-13) rebuts critiques of Christian doctrine by pointing out that Greek paganism had comparable doctrines—which could only be inaccurate echoes of Biblical truth:

> Omnia aduersus ueritatem de ipsa ueritate constructa sunt.... Et si paradisum[73] nominemus, locum diuinae amoenitatis recipiendis sanctorum spiritibus destinatum, maceria quadam igneae illius zonae a notitia orbis communis segregatum, Elysii campi fidem occupauerunt. Unde haec, oro uos, philosophis aut poetis tam consimilia? Nonnisi de nostris sacramentis.

> All things against the truth were fabricated from the truth itself.... And if we speak of paradise, a place of divine pleasantness destined to receive the spirits of the saints, separated from the knowledge of the world at large by a wall composed of a certain fiery zone—the Elysian fields previously

---

73   Here Tertullian uses *paradisus* in his own language—to designate the temporary abode of saints until the general Resurrection?

captured belief [for a comparable tale]. From what source, I inquire, did philosophers and poets acquire notions so similar [to ours]? It could only have been from our mysteries.

Again, an apparently Christian scholiast on Hesiod *Opera* 171 "in the islands of the blessed" (ἐν μακάρων νήσοισι III.49):

μακάρων νήσους νῦν παράδεισον αἰνίττεται, ὅ ἐστι τὸ παρ᾽ αὐτοῖς Ἠλύσιον πεδίον λεγόμενον, παρὰ τὸ ἄλυτα τηρεῖν τὰ σώματα τὰ ἀθάνατα, ἢ παρὰ τὴν λύσιν τῶν κακῶν.

"By 'islands of the blessed' [Hesiod] hints at Paradise, which is what they called the Elysian field—either because it keeps bodies free of decay (*alyta*) and immortal, or from the dispersal (*lysis*) of ills"; the text then goes on to cite *Odyssey* 4.563-4 (III.51).[74]

From some Jewish-Christian or Jewish source, the name and concept went into Islam.[75] Twice only *firdaws(un)* appears in the Quran. At 18.107 "Lo, those who believe and do good works, theirs are the *gardens of Paradise*

لَهُمْ جَنَّتُ ٱلْفِرْدَوْس

for welcome." At 23.10-11 "Those are the heirs who *will inherit Paradise*"

ٱلَّذِينَ يَرِثُونَ ٱلْفِرْدَوْسَ.

In this manner Islam was preformed at its very beginning for its fateful acceptance in Iran. The national poet of Persia, author of the *Shahnameh*, took the pen-name Firdawsi (AD 941-1020), an Iranian word, but in its Arabic form. In the Moslem world it entered folklore.

The Venetian Marco Polo, after decades of travels, by all appearances real, was imprisoned at Genoa in 1298/9; he told his experiences to his fellow-prisoner Rustichello of Pisa, who wrote them down in (Old) French.[76] Chapters 41-43 describe what Marco learned about the Old Man of the Mountain (*le Viel de la montagne*) and his Assassins (*asciscins*). A few lines from the start of the tale will give something of its flavor:

---

74 A. Pertusi, Scholia Vetera in Hesiodi Opera et Dies; Pubb. dell' Univ. catt. del S. Cuore n.s. vol. 53; Milano: "Vita e Pensiero"; 1955; pp. 66-7.

75 An attempt has been made to derive the description of the doe-eyed houris of the Moslem Firdaws from Ephrem *Hymns on Paradise* 7.18; it is refuted by Graffin *ad loc.* (p. 103).

76 Luigi Foscolo Benedetto, Marco Polo: Il Milione; Comitato geographico nazionale italiano Pubb. N. 3; Firenze: Leo S. Olschki, 1928. Levin tells me that *Il Milione* was in origin a nickname of Marco's, *(E)milio*, later misunderstood as a title of his book. The Tuscan and Venetian versions must all be secondary or tertiary translations from the French. It is said that no two manuscripts have the same contents, and it seems that a big task of textual criticism remains, both of the French and of its relation to the other versions.

> Le Viel estoit appellé en lor lengajes Alaodin. Il avoit fait fer entre deus montagnes, en une valé, le plus grant jardin et les plus biaus que jamés fust veu.... Et encore hi avoit fait faire conduit, que por tel coroit vin, et por tel lait, et por tel mel, et por tel eive. Il hi avoit dame et dameseles, les plus bielles dou monde, les quelz sevent soner de tuit enstrumenti et chantent et calorent miaus que autres femes. Et fasoit le Vielz entendre a sez homes que cel jardin etoit *parais*.

The English Mandeville,[77] drawing (it appears) mostly from Marco, tells the story of Gatholonabes the proprietor of the castle with its wondrous garden and "welles faire and noble and alle envyround with ston of iaspre, of cristalle, dyapred with gold and sett with precious stones and grete orient perles." To his hired murderers he makes this promise:

> For after hire deth he wolde putten hem into another paradys that was an c. fold fairere than ony of the tothere, and there scholde thei dwellen with the most fairest damyselles that myghte be and pley with hem eueremore.

The Latin and especially the Greek Fathers of the church did their best to organize what the two Greek Testaments say about Paradise into a consistent topography and history. But since the texts reflect floating symbolic concepts, their best efforts could only result in irreconcilable contradictions.[78] Was the paradise of Eden the same as the "paradise of God" (Ez 28,13 LXX)? Was the "third heaven" into which Paul was caught up the same, or higher, or even lower, than the paradise of which he says the same (II Kor 12,2-3)? Was paradise an intermediate state, where the souls of the just await the general resurrection?[79] A text cited by Lampe[80] asks "where do you think Paradise is?" and answers "Some say it is heavenly and perceptible by the intellect; some earthly and perceptible by the senses":

> οἱ μὲν γὰρ αὐτὸν λέγουσιν ὑπάρχειν ἐπουράνιον νοητόν, οἱ δὲ ἐπίγειον αἰσθητόν.

The language of Columbus and his contemporaries about "the earthly Paradise" (*el parayso terrenal*) would suggest that it was contrasted with a distinct heavenly Paradise; but in fact I do not find that any Patristic or medieval author clearly affirms the existence of two concurrent paradises.

---

77   Ed. M. C. Seymour; Oxford: Clarendon, 1967; chap. 30 p. 202.
78   The Patristic discussions are conveniently summarized in the extensive citations of Lampe 1010-1013 and Delumeau's History of Paradise (note 3 above).
79   Texts for this Lampe 1011b C.2, especially Irenaeus *Haer.* 5.5.1 (PG 7.1135AB). Ephrem includes this as one of the zones of a stratified Paradise (III.142).
80   Ps. Caesarius of Nazianzen, *Dial.* 141 (PG 38.1089).

In Dante, *Paradiso* becomes the preferred name of the true heavens, and the earthly paradise appears at the summit of Mount Purgatory, but not under that name, nor even under the name of Eden. But further, in what C. S. Lewis calls the invention of romantic love, Paradise is internalized: Dante first knew it in Beatrice, and she needs to tell him (*Paradiso* 18.21) "Paradise is not in my eyes alone,"

Che non pur ne' miei occhi è Paradiso.

This leads naturally to the usage of Shakespeare, where *paradise* is mostly a stock concept with sexual overtones; most intensely at *Romeo and Juliet* III.ii.82 where Juliet marvels that Romeo can have so murderous an impulse

In mortall paradise of such sweet flesh.

The process becomes complete in Milton, where ostensibly Paradise at first is the name of the earthly paradise alone.[81] At the end of the sequel (*Paradise Regain'd* 4.612-613) the Angelic Quires celebrate Christ's victory over temptation:

For though that seat of earthly bliss be fail'd
A fairer Paradise is founded now.

Here almost uniquely we have the concept of two consecutive realms of paradise, on earth and in heaven. But in *Paradise Lost* the commentators Michael and Satan, in different ways speaking for the poet, explicitly subordinate the garden of Eden to internal spiritual states. Where the Angel recommends to Adam the cultivation of the virtues, they become a "happier" substitute for the garden (*Par. Lost* 12.583-587):

...add Love,
By name to come call'd Charitie, the soul
Of all the rest: then wilt thou not be loath
To leave this Paradise, but shalt possess
A paradise within thee, happier farr.

When the fallen angel voyeur sees the conjugal delights of the first human beings, he says (*Par. Lost* 4.505-508):

Sight hateful, sight tormenting! thus these two
Imparadis't in one anothers arms
The happier *Eden*, shall enjoy their fill
Of bliss on bliss, while I to Hell am thrust

Here Satan professes what Milton cannot, that sexual love has taken precedence over any other realm of fulfilment, it is "the happier *Eden*."

---

81 The centuries of speculation which lie behind Milton have been excellently studied by Joseph E. Duncan, Milton's Earthly Paradise: A Historical Study of Eden; Minneapolis: Univ. of Minnesota, 1972—the most helpful work on the topic I have found.

And since the authors of Genesis and Canticles were poets, Ephrem and Milton (and Dante also, in spite of his greater reworking of the tradition) grasp their thought better than all the theologians who came in between.

Philologists too have their own thoughts, and perhaps some final paragraphs on the understanding of paradise will be permissible. That Median princess, homesick for her native hills and forests, had the "hanging paradise" of Babylon built for her. Whenever the Persian Great King, coming from barren, dry and treeless Iran (Herodotus 9.122 has it called "rough" and "miserable," τρηχέαν...λυπρήν), in his conquest of the West found running streams and forests, he enclosed them and claimed them as his own *paradeisos*. Near Eastern rulers, though they had in mind building temples and fleets, perhaps obscurely realized that their "enclosures" represented the world at its best, and that it stood or fell with them.

One secret current of Patristic or medieval thought affirmed that the whole earth was intended as Paradise.[82] Thus Hugh of St Victor[83]:

> Unde et quidam affirmant totam terram futuram paradisum, si homo non pecasset, totam autem factam exsilium per peccatum.

"So some affirm that the whole earth was to become paradise, if man had not sinned, and that the whole earth became exile through sin." So Luther tentatively in his *Table Talk* in the winter of 1542/1543:[84]

> *Genesis* ist ein hoch buch; es liset sich niemer mer aus. Die ersten 5 capitel vorstehet man grundlich nicht. *Totus mundus* ist *paradisus* gewesen, oder ist jhe sehr weit umbfangen gewesen, umb Jerusalem her; denn die vier flus umbher gehörn all hinein. Abr die sindflut hatt es darnach gar zurissen.

> *Genesis* is a lofty book; it is never read all the way through. The first five chapters are fundamentally not understood. *Totus mundus* became *paradisus*, or [it] came to be very broadly encompassed, round about Jerusalem; for the four rivers all belong around there. But the Deluge quite destroyed it afterward.[85]

Similarly Sir Thomas Browne, *The Garden of Cyrus*, dedication: "But the Earth is the Garden of Nature, and each fruitful Country a Paradise."

---

82   Delumeau 150-151 documents it from several authors seemingly not reprinted since the 16th century.

83   Hugo de S. Victore, *in S. Scripturam* on Gen 2,10 (PL 175.39D).

84   D. Martin Luthers Werke: Kritische Gesamtausgabe; Tischreden 5. Band; Weimar: Böhlaus, 1919; pp. 199-200 no. 5505. But I understand that else-where he rejects this opinion.

85   I thank Levin for this translation.

The Old Persian kings then (we may say) had a true sense of what the earth was meant to be. The environmental catastrophe of the ancient Mediterranean world has become a prototype and warning of the current environmental crisis of the whole planet. Robert Pogue Harrison sees that crisis running parallel to a psychic crisis:[86]

> Because we exist first and foremost *outside of ourselves*, forests become something like an ancient and enduring correlate of our transcendence. And because our imagination is a measure of our ecstasis, the history of forests in the Western imagination turns into the story of our self-dispossession.

And further: part of our mind knows that the earth, even under the best ecological management, can survive for many millions of years yet but not forever. If that prospect is inacceptable to us (perhaps it is inacceptable to all), and if still we do not give up hope, we are driven like the ancients to affirm an eternal paradise—every minute and acre of the planet taken up constantly into eternity. But that eternity, like the corresponding resurrection of the body, can contain forever only what once existed on earth. Our cue then when we pass from scholarship to activism is to recreate the paradise wherever we are. The whole planet is to become Lebanon. And of course, as Ephrem and Milton remind us, that presupposes wholly new levels of justice and charity throughout the global society.

So we may strongly affirm the horticulturists who ship seedlings of Lebanese cedar (or of California redwoods, or the *Metasequoia* of China) to gardens and forests around the globe. The tomb of George and Martha Washington at Mount Vernon, not built until thirty years after his death in 1799, is today shaded by a fine Lebanese cedar with its resinous fruiting cones like striated green apples. The custodians like Xenophon solemnly affirm to tourists that it was planted by none other than the President himself. It is a handsome tree surely over a century old, I am unclear whether seedlings had gotten to England or France in his time. Still the guides are correct in principle when they insist that none but the proprietor may plant paradise. When not just every botanical garden in the world, but every street and back yard, holds (along with native plants) green and growing trees of Lebanese cedar, we may affirm that Paradise has begun to reconquer the planet.[87]

---

86   Robert Pogue Harrison, Forests: The Shadow of Civilization: Chicago: University, 1992; 201.

87   When the text was already in page proof I saw the collective volume edited by G. P. Luttikhuizen, Paradise Interpreted: Representations of Biblical Paradise in Judaism and Christianity; Themes in Biblical Narrative 2; Leiden: Brill, 1999. These essays and my chapter supplement each other extensively.

Chapter 22: Complementarity of Israel and Hellas

That ideal diligent reader for whom we all write deserves, after a thousand pages on the likenesses of Israel and Hellas, a chapter on their differences. It is not easy to keep in mind simultaneously a pair of correlative truths: (I) Two things contrasted must be comparable; (II) Two things compared can always be contrasted. For (I) things can be contrasted only with respect to some attribute, which constitutes a ground of comparison between them. And (II) when things are compared in their possession of some attribute, they must possess it in different and contrasted ways, otherwise they would be identical. The authors who contrast Israel and Hellas (I.3-4)—Arnold, Boman, Havelock, Auerbach—lose sight of truth I, following Tertullian (*de praescript. haer.* 7.9, I.161, II.85). For when he asked, "What do Athens and Jerusalem have to do with each other?," *Quid ergo Athenis et Hierosolymis?*, he failed to answer his own question by noting that each city was the center of a free society generating a novel literature. It may have seemed that in previous chapters we in turn lost sight of truth II! Anyway here we begin to remedy that defect.

Children in a family create environmental niches, each claiming vacant territory: one is tidy, one messy; one loud, one quiet; one industrious, one lazy. The classical Hebrew and Greek worlds are a little more distant than that, cousins rather than siblings, in touch only at one or more removes, through trade by land and sea; wars of their allies; common subjection to imperialism; foreign princesses and mercenaries, colonists, artisans, exiles. But the principle of differentiation still holds. In their joint breakout from ancient Near Eastern absolutism, each develops its own version of newly emergent freedom. They fit neatly into each other, supplementing each other's strengths, remedying each other's defects, just as the bright masculine positive sun-principle or Yang fits into the dark feminine negative moon-principle or Yin.[1] Partially in the

---

1   The Greek and Latin names of the luminaries follow the Chinese gender: ἥλιος with σελήνη, *sol* with *luna*. But both feminine moon-words are adjectives by etymology, not nouns. The genders of the various Semitic names are fluctuating.

Septuagint, and fully in the New Testament, the cousins are married and produce a novel offspring, in some ways more vigorous than either, while each maintaining its individuality. We may then describe the reciprocal relationship of Israel and Hellas as one of *complementarity*.

Every comparison we have made in the preceding chapters can be seen from the other side as a contrast. Here we lift out the most coherent from among all those contrasts. In some places we rework themes of our predecessors. At the end we revert to the conventional wisdom—not all that incorrect—which sees Israel as the fountainhead of religion, Hellas of science. Perhaps the novel framework we set around those timeworn materials will put them in a fresher light.

The initial obvious difference we find between the two societies is *style of dialogue* (22.1): in Israel between man (or an occasional woman) and God, in Hellas between man and man. It is explained by differences both in time and in space. In time (22.2): Israel as an *old* society, Hellas as a *young* one. And in space (22.3): Israel as a society *just inside* the Ancient Near East locked into land-trade, Hellas as one *just outside* enjoying a cosmopolitan sea-trade.

Each of those three contrasts has a further extension. The contrasted dialogues generate different imaging of the *divine* (22.4): in Israel concrete symbols are never fully adequate pointers to God; Hellas is content with them. As the two societies look behind them in time to varying distances (22.5), Israel goes back so deeply as to gain a vision of historical *survival*; Hellas can only see so far as to identify the situations which create *tragedy*. Looking out in space from their center, the two societies adopt different standards of *membership* (22.6): Israel sharply within its speech-community accepts only those reputed to have the same *lineage*; Hellas accepts as its own all those who speak the same *language*.

Where the two societies merge in the *New Testament* (22.7), the same three contrasts regarding divinity, time and space determine the nature of the confluence and the respective roles of the two parents in the merger. There follow two sections regarding the character of the *written texts* which the two societies (and now also the early Church) hand down to us. Partly due to intrinsic features of the two languages, partly to technical features of their scripts (arising from their respective insider and outsider status), their *literary canons* (22.8) markedly differ: small and fixed in both Testaments, large and open in Hellas. Closely related is their degree of *translatability* (22.9): high in Hebrew texts, due to their concrete character and relative lack of internal elegances; variable in Greek, where the New Testament in the end moves back toward the simplicity of Hebrew.

In the period of the Greek New Testament and Rabbinic exegesis, each society takes on *attributes of the other* (22.10). But the contemporary perception of Israel as the source of *religious faith*, Hellas of *reason and logic* has its own legitimacy (22.11). In the end we revert to the geographical contrast of the two societies. Modern nations in their claims on the individual approach the absolutist character of the Ancient Near Eastern empires as mediated to us via Rome. The places where the two traditions are transmitted to us—the congregation and the classroom—speak to us from the same place as their forerunners did: Hebrew-Christian religious faith offers guidance and critique of our world from the *inside*, Greek scientific reason as from the *outside*.

22.1 Complementarity in style of dialogue

We approached the common features of Israel and Hellas (I.1) through their architectural deposits in our cities: a university where Greek texts are widely read in translation, and, among a smaller circle, in the original; around it, churches where the Hebrew Bible (along with the Greek New Testament) is publicly read in translation, and a synagogue or seminary where it is studied in the original. Buildings where people read books!—often silently, but sometimes, in the old style, out loud. For what purposes? For the light that those books, the earliest records that lie behind us, studied somewhere in every generation, throw on our own institutions, which they more than anything else created. And therefore for help in forming our own thought and character within those institutions.

The Greek enterprise most directly formative for us is philosophy, which trains us to think clearly about our world and ourselves. We may take Plato's Dialogues as the books, and the classroom as the normal site, where Greek reason is most accessible. The Hebrew enterprise most directly formative for us is a proclamation about the source of justice, by which we are empowered to search out the places where justice is needed, and to strive for it. We may take prophetic works like Jeremiah as the books, and the place of worship as the normal site, where that proclamation is most accessible.

How do Plato's Socrates and Jeremiah most clearly differ? Socrates is constantly in dialogue with other human beings (always in fact men) of different viewpoints, from which ideally a resolution on a higher level is achieved; whereas Jeremiah is in dialogue only with God. (In this context, by "God" we mean the seemingly external source of novel thoughts that one finds in one's heart, challenging or confirming one's "own" thoughts.) Perhaps none of Plato's Dialogues records an actual conversation, but they may have been acted out in the Academy. Jeremiah 36 describes how the prophet spoke out or dictated his message for others to pass on (I.47). His first chapter records dialogue between himself and God, in which God puts words in the prophet's mouth. (The same experience is attested by Greek poets who find a message not their own put on their tongue.)

For any particular Israelite, there is only one pre-existing point of view on a topic. Any other is the prompting of God; we may if we wish attribute it to the unconscious side of the speaker, but for him it is the word of Another, with whom he enters into confrontation. Adam and Job hear unexpected responses from their God. For the Greek, things come in contrasted pairs, both of which are affirmed: the very structure of the language encourages sentences to come with μέν "on the one hand," δέ "on the other."[2] (Only the context tells us whether Hebrew *wa-* is better heard as "and" or "but.") A Greek's neighbor can be counted on to provide an opposite to his thought, there is no need to wait for a suggestion from the gods.

22.2 *Israel as an old society, Hellas as a young one*

How to explain the contrast: dialogue of man and man in Hellas, of man and God in Israel? Hellas is an experimental society with no fixed view how a city-state should be governed, about the nature of the gods, what duties a man has to his neighbor. Israelites at each epoch feel that such questions are settled by a known relationship between themselves and their God, although we looking back perceive big changes. We can understand the contrast in two ways: here by a contrast in *time*. All falls into place when we see Hellas, in spite of its seeming old legendary memory, as a *young society* where the historical period is disconnected from the heroic age; and Israel, in spite of its innovations over against the Near Eastern empires, as an *old society* with a long continuous memory (of course holding legendary elements) spanning many setbacks and recoveries. A couple of features show this contrast.

22.2.1 Literacy

Genesis is the history of a people without writing. But writing is there in the background, and the Hebrews show no interest in its origins;

---

2   Levin, "The Connective 'Particles' of Classical Greek Discourse," CUNY
     Forum 1979 nos. 5-6, pp. 52-58, proposes in fact that behind μέν is a word for
     "hand," cf Latin *manus*.

they were surely aware of both cuneiform and hieroglyphic before they began using the local alphabet. Pharaoh's signet ring (Ex 41,42) can have had no other function than to authenticate documents produced by Joseph. In Exodus, writing appears abruptly in the command to Moses (Ex 17,14) "Write this as a memorial in a book":

כְּתֹב זֹאת זִכָּרוֹן בַּסֵּפֶר

At Ex 24,4 Moses writes the words of Yahweh, and reads the book of the covenant to the people (Ex 24,7). We are to assume that the two tables of stone, "written with the finger of God" (Ex 31,18), had been written previously. The Rabbis further take it for granted that both Moses and his God wrote in Hebrew.

The Homeric poems presuppose writing only where Proetus gives Bellerophon a baneful message (*Iliad* 6.168-169, I.49); no language is suggested if indeed the "scratchings" are not pure ideograms. Herodotus (5.58-59), recognizing a novelty, has great interest in the introduction of "Phoenician" or "Cadmeian scratchings" (I.37, 44). Nowhere do classical Greeks betray any knowledge that an earlier form of their own language (and apparently others) was written in the Mycenaean palaces and in Minoan Crete.

22.2.2 Genealogy

Hebrew writers take it for granted that in principle the descent of every Israelite back to the beginning of humanity was known, even though parts of the tradition might be conflicting or unrecorded. The backbone of the historical books is genealogy. And so in the New Testament. Matthew records the descent of Jesus from Abraham in 3x14 = 42 generations; Luke records 56 (perhaps = 4x14) generations back to Abraham and 20 more back to Adam. Two Punic inscriptions of the third century BC, one from Sardinia (KAI 68) and one from Carthage (KAI 78), each gives a man 16 generations of ancestors, taking the ancestry back to the seventh century.

In classical Hellas, few genealogies go back before one's grandfather. Within the legendary heroic past a man could boast of knowing five generations back; (*Iliad* 6.145-211) Aeolus father of Sisyphus of Glaucus of Bellerophon of Hippolochus of another Glaucus. The seven generations of Tiresias can be counted (II.159). Thomas[3] documents the few claimed genealogies. An isolated stone of Chios[4] records the

---

3   Rosalind Thomas, *Oral Tradition and Written Record in Classical Athens*; Cambridge: University, 1985.
4   SGDI 5656.

ancestors of one Heropythos to 14 generations. When historic Greeks draw their genealogy back to the heroic age, the intervening generations are normally not listed. According to Pherecydes,[5] Hippocrates the physician traced his ancestry back (along different lines) to Heracles in 20 generations and to Asclepius in 19. Hecataeus told Egyptian priests that his family went back to a god in the 16th generation (Herodotus 2.143). The missing generations are unrecorded from Euagoras of Cyprus back to Teucer,[6] Andocides to Odysseus,[7] Alcibiades to Eurysaces (and therefore Zeus).[8] The exception is that of Miltiades to a son of Ajax, where the generations are in fact given;[9] but Thomas (161-3) finds even the historical part contradicted by external evidence. She sees these genealogies less as deposits of oral tradition than as artificial constructions by professionals. Only in Sparta was a genealogy of kings recorded: Leonidas (I) king 490-480 BC was the descendant of Heracles through 20 generations (Herodotus 7.204); Leotychidas likewise was the son of Heracles through 20 generations (the last few not kings, Herodotus 8.131). In the second passage Herodotus notes in contrast that the Athenian commander was just "Xanthippus son of Ariphron."

Thus, apart from the genealogies of Sparta, there is a break in Greek legendary memory between the fall of Troy and the earliest historical records of the mainland city-states. It was honorific to claim an heroic ancestor; superfluous to search out the generations in between. That selective memory corresponds to the break in literacy between the end of Linear B and the first alphabetic inscriptions. As Greeks contrasted their rainfall with Egyptian irrigation (I.22), and their alphabet with hieroglyphics (I.28), so their recent appearance: the Egyptian priest tells Solon (Plato *Tim.* 22 B) "you Hellenes are only children," Ἕλληνες ἀεὶ παῖδές ἐστε. The partly legendary Israelite record for the period of Joshua and the Judges is still a unique witness behind the scenes to the disruptive societies which ended the palace cultures of the eastern Mediterranean. As a result, the Hebrews felt that they had a continuous unbroken record extending indefinitely far back into prehistory.

---

5   FGH 3 frag. 59.
6   Isocrates *Euagoras* 12-19.
7   Plutarch *Alcib.* 21.1 = Hellanicus FGH 323a frag. 24.
8   Plato *Alcib. I* 121A.
9   Marcellinus *Vita Thuc.* 2-4 = Pherecydes FGH 3 frag. 2.

22.3 Insiders and outsiders of the ancient Near East

We suggested (I.22-28) four conditions necessary (but not sufficient) for the emergence of a new freedom over against the ancient Near East: (1') *geographical*—a defensible citadel surrounded by rain-watered fields; (2') *technological*—iron for weapons and tools, lime for water-proofing cisterns (II.324) in the dry summer; (3') *social*—elements of democracy; and (4') *scribal*—a phonetic alphabetic script. Here the geographical is key. For five thousand years autonomous local societies have never appeared in Egypt or Iraq, because of central bureaucratic control over the only source of water, the river. The Hittite empire, in rain-watered territory, did not generate free cities either: here other explanations come into play—the lack of a phonetic alphabet, the lack of access to the sea. For precisely the Hittite successor states closest to the Greek are on the sea like Lycia, which eventually borrowed a phonetic script from Greece.

Earlier I presupposed, but should have added, one more condition: (5') *proximity* to the Near Eastern empires which developed technology, city-life, commerce, central administration, standing armies, literacy (mostly non-phonetic), organized cult—even though all under absolutist regimes. Those conditions delimit both in time and space the places where (in Lincoln's words) a "new birth of freedom" was possible. Neither during the rise of the Near Eastern empires nor their decay: *early in the Iron Age* then. Neither at the heart of the ancient Near East, nor beyond the sphere of its trade and influence: therefore either *just inside* the ancient Near East, or *just outside*. As it turned out, the decisive evolution took place in *only one society* "just inside," namely Israel; and in *only one society* "just outside," namely Hellas. Greeks described irrigation in Egypt as outside visitors, Hebrews from a memory of having lived there (I.22); Herodotus describes brick-making in Babylon as of his own day, Hebrews as at its first building (I.83). It might seem that Latins and Etruscans were nearly as ready as Hellas to take the decisive step forward to a free society; but except by language they were in the Greek sphere of influence from the beginning, and it is speculative to ask how they might have developed without it. The position of Israel inside the Ancient Near East explains why it could not see itself otherwise than as an old society; the position of Hellas outside meant that it could only be a new society.

Their respective situations also gave Israelites and Greeks contrasted relationships to their neighbors. Israel was in effect a landlocked country, and her foreign trade was carried by caravans, which further did not normally take Hebrews far from home; it is an Ishmaelite spice caravan (Gen 37,25) that carries Joseph to Egypt. Greeks, living in a land of drowned mountain-ranges, naturally travelled and traded by sea; more extensively even than the Phoenicians they engaged in colonization. Only for the time of Solomon do Hebrews remember a time of sea-trade, perhaps inflated in memory.

What resources did young Israel and Hellas have? Originally the Hebrews had few cultural institutions not available to their neighbors— the maritime and colonizing Phoenicians, the even more landlocked Ammonites and Moabites. Their language was at most a distinct dialect of Canaanite, but fully comprehensible to their neighbors; the earliest Yahwism reconstructible hardly differs from the cult of Chemosh attested in the inscription of king Mesha of Moab; their sacrificial cult, mostly monopolized by a hereditary priesthood, in early texts shows no special originality.

The peoples of Canaan sat where armies of the great empires, Egyptian, Mesopotamian, and Hittite,[10] passed back and forth. It is unclear whether the memory of an Egyptian captivity is truly part of the earliest Israelite tradition; and, even if so, how it distinguished them from their neighbors—for the Philistines likewise remembered their arrival from "Caphtor" (Crete?) and the Aramaeans from un-known "Kir" (Amos 9,7). With the advantage of hindsight we can see the first shoots of independence in the unconquerable hill-villages of Israel. But they had little independent cultural heritage. Their original-ity then had to rest on the decision—which their defensible geographi-cal position made possible—to *accept or reject* inherited Near Eastern elements. But the historian cannot get so close as to say why the decision was made there rather than in Phoenicia, Moab or Damascus.

Hellenic culture in large part grew up in cities formerly of the Minoan-Mycenaean world with their palaces, scribal literacy, luxury goods, commerce reaching Cyprus, Phoenicia, Ugarit, Egypt. But its *remembered* beginnings are later and further away, on both sides of the upper Aegean, where the Homeric epics record an indigenous culture, with tenuous recollections of the Hittites (II.85). M. L. West has shown how Akkadian phrases made their way into the epic; we have seen how shared Mediterranean enterprises contributed vocabulary to both Hellas and Israel, as well (surely) as to lost literatures. Early on, Hellas is aware of the Near Eastern empires out there as representing a higher level of material culture; unlike Israel, it was not frightened off by them. Its inherited Indo-European language and institutions were so

---

10   Hittites at the battle of Kadesh on the Orontes, 1274 BC (Bryce 256-263).

strong, and its character so robust and curious, that it saw the empires rather as societies to be learned from. Hence in Hellas we find a series of borrowings from the Near East, some (by comparison with Israel) progressive, others retrograde.

Thus we may enlarge our former contrast to a geographical-cultural one:

Israel is an old inland society just inside the ancient Near East, the terminus of trade-routes by land, struggling to escape, which however it can do only in the most critical areas.

Hellas is a new seaboard society just outside the ancient Near East, to which the Mediterranean is open for trade and colonization, enjoying indigenous cultural resources, on which the Near East exercises an ongoing fascination.

Now Hellas, now Israel is the cultural innovator.

22.3.1 Hellas as the cultural innovator

Israel and Hellas share over against the Near East a *sacrificial cult* (I.186-187) with special vocabulary and practices. Although in the beginnings of Israel any man may be his own priest (Gideon at Ophrah, Jud 6,25), in the centralized kingdom sacrifice becomes the monopoly of an hereditary priesthood, down to the Maccabean priest-kings and the High Priests of the Herodian temple. From the time when "every man did what was right in his own eyes" (Jud 21,25), a steady retrograde movement leads back to the ancient Near Eastern pattern. While both cult and priests are criticized, there is no suggestion of carrying it out without them. By contrast, in Hellas from the beginning every man can sacrifice for himself.

Again in the realm of *kingship*. The emergence of Israel as a true state coincides with the taking-up of Near Eastern patterns of kingship. Israel hardly existed as such until the elders came to Samuel and said (I Sam 8,5) "Give us a king to judge over us like all the *Goyim*":

עַתָּה שִׂימָה־לָּנוּ מֶלֶךְ לְשָׁפְטֵנוּ כְּכָל־הַגּוֹיִם

When the state split into two at Solomon's death it is taken for granted that both parts will be under kingship; the independent state recreated by the Maccabees was under rulers who called themselves king or high priest. There is always some current of thought in Israel for which kingship contradicts its true nature—but none which has any substitute for it. The Minoan and Mycenaean palaces were surely the residence of kings. But from the time of Homer on (Vol. II, Chapter 12) Greek kingship everywhere except in Macedon (perhaps not Greek-speaking) undergoes a progressive reduction. Other patterns of Indo-

European social structure win out, take over the city of Rome, influence Carthage, and perhaps by reflex Phoenicia also. The invention of
the Polis in its Greek form weakened any residual Indo-European
kingship and blocked any takeover of the absolutist functions of Near
Eastern kingship, which Greeks (correctly) saw as an alien tyranny.

So with *literacy*. From somewhere in Canaan, Hebrews inherited a
phonetic consonantal alphabet, for we find one such four centuries
before them at Ugarit, though still in cuneiform script. Its inadequacy
is sufficiently marked that (I.49, II.325) every Hebrew written text
required an accompanying tradition of recitation. By inspired reinter-
pretation of the Phoenician alphabet (I.38-43) Greeks made it into a
nearly adequate record of their language, from which oral recitation
was possible. The results for the production and preservation of texts
were profound (III.185).

And finally in the realm of *science*. Through unclear modes of
contact, Greeks learned from Babylonians the art of astronomy (which
they partly disengaged from astrology), and, mostly as an independent
development, the logic of mathematics, in particular geometry. There
is no such takeover in Israel.

22.3.2 Israel as the cultural innovator

At the earliest point where we can see both societies, Israel is on its way
to a full *monotheism*, while Hellenes (in spite of Zeus' role as king of
the gods) have an extended *pantheon*[11] as in Babylon, Ugarit, Egypt,
Phoenicia. Far from feeling threatened by Near Eastern pantheons,
Greeks either adopted their members outright or identified them with
local divinities. Indo-European antiquity also had such a pantheon, but
of the divine names only Zeus the father is inherited by Hellas. For
some Greek divinities we can find a home here or there around the
Aegean; others remain mysterious; but the Near Eastern pantheons
were the pattern. The *Iliad* is prematurely rationalistic in that immortal
gods serve as comic relief against the all-too-mortal heroes; Aeschylus
and Pindar recover the gods' reality. The religious development in
Israel is a progressive deepening in the concept of the single God whom
in principle it professes from the beginning. The development in Hellas
is a philosophical movement towards affirmation of a single deity—at
the cost of losing such functions as the Hesiodic understanding of Zeus
to be the guarantor of justice.

---

11   See II.281 and West, EFH 107-113 for the pantheon.

With the monotheism of Israel goes rejection of *divination*. The Urim and Thummim no doubt represent a purified form of divination; but there are almost no relics of divination by the flight of birds, thunder, or the appearance of portents; the sacrificial regulations (I.185) to prevent divination by the form of the liver show that it was known and rejected. Joseph (Gen 44,5) has a silver cup with which he supposedly divines (נַחֵשׁ יְנַחֵשׁ בּוֹ, LXX οἰωνισμῷ οἰωνίζεται, Vg *augurari*);[12] but it plays no essential role as such in the tale. Hellenes, feeling that divided rule in the pantheon left much undecided, saw nothing to be lost by assessing the whims of Moira or Tyche through divination. In this respect Etruscans and Romans are more Greek than the Greeks; here as elsewhere they must have had a direct conduit to the Near East which bypassed the Greek mainland.

Above all, the *failure* of Israel to develop a slave-economy comparable to that of Athens is a progressive feature. The exceptional level of democracy in Athens is precisely correlated with its slave-economy, in which slaves were likely a third of the free population. Homer never brings on a male slave designate *doulos*, although he is aware of the "day of slavery" (δούλιον ἦμαρ, *Iliad* 6.463 etc.). While in Israel both foreigners and Hebrews could become slaves, a bad conscience about the institution led to provisions at least theoretical for their emancipation. The slaves (δοῦλοι) in Jesus' parables (translated "servants" in the RSV) represent a partial Hellenization of the social structure. But Exod 21,21 does say "for the slave is his silver"; so Aristotle calls a slave a "living tool" (ἔμψυχον ὄργανον, *Eth. Nic.* 8.13 = 1161b4); as in the Roman Empire with its vast expansion of slavery equivalently *instrumentum uocale* "a speaking tool" (Varro *de R. R.* 1.17.1).

The role of Yahweh as creator gives the *natural order* a numinous character lacking in Hellas. Psalm 104 affectionately surveys the Lebanese coastline from the high springs on the mountains down through the forest to the sea, along with the birds and beasts on each level as well as the human habitation. While Theophrastus admires the Lebanese forest, the Hebrews see it as an integral part of the divine order. Already the environments best known to the Greeks were much degraded, and none of the gods claimed the forest as a special province.

And, while we hear much about lawgivers and laws in the Greek tradition, and find much miscellaneous ethical advice in both prose and poetry, there is nothing like the Hebrew Ten Commandments

---

12   The Versions interpret the Hebrew by the role of "augury" through bird-flight in their own societies. But the supposed divination may be one more of Joseph's false clues.

representing a *fixed traditional moral code*. The body of Delphic sayings attributed also to the Seven Sages could be expanded or contracted at will.[13] Familiarity has dulled the novelty we ought to feel in the notion of a unique High God sufficiently in touch with his people to deliver in person an easily remembered set of principles for life in community.

22.4 Transcendence or immanence of the divine world

The most obvious difference between the two societies is Hebrew monotheism over against the Greek pantheon (III.161). "Monotheism" deserves two qualifications, which however do not seriously affect its difference from the Greek pattern. (1) *The divine names.* Strata of the Hebrew Bible employ different divine names, which have been interpreted as the usage of different tribal groupings: "Yahweh" (יהוה with unknown vowels) as revealed to Moses, though in the narrative used since Gen 2,4; "Shadday" (שַׁדַּי) as archaic usage by the Patriarchs and in the book of Job; "El" (אֵל) also archaic but less clearly located. *Adonay* (אדני) "Lord" from a title becomes the pronunciation of יהוה. (Perhaps "Elohim" [אֱלֹהִים] with its anomalous grammar was seen as a neutral term to cover all the others.) But it is precarious to ascribe different characters to the three or four names; and any differences that existed were (it appears) successfully bridged over. (2) *Gods of neighbors.* At one point Yahweh is seen (like Zeus!, II.88) as "a great king above all gods" (Ps 95,3); but (Ps 96,5) "all the

---

13   Plato (*Protagoras* 343A, *Charmides* 164D) attests that the familiar sayings, Laconic in their bevity, Γνῶθι σαυτόν "Know thyself" and Μηδὲν ἄγαν "Nothing in excess," were inscribed on the temple at Delphi (but they have not been found there). They appear on a stone at Thera (of a gymnasium?) of the fourth century BC (IG 12.3.1020). Stobaeus 3.1.172, printed in Diels-Kranz FVS[8] i.62-66, lists up to 20 for each of the Seven Sages. A stone from Miletus of the third century BC, perhaps at a gymnasium or school (SIG[3] 1268 with very full commentary by Diels), has a selection. Another list from Stobaeus 3.1.173 (summarized by Diels) begins
  Ἕπου θεῷ. Νόμῳ πείθου. Θεοὺς σέβου. Γονεῖς αἰδοῦ.
  "Follow God; obey the law; honor the gods; respect parents" with the same partial theism as in writers of the second century CE (III.176); and a little overlap with the Ten Commandments. The Miletus stone (I.15-16) echoes the familiar theme "Help friends, harm enemies" (III.3) Φίλους εὐνόει. ['Ε]χθροὺς ἀμύνου. Diels asserts that "this Delphic religion retained its force through all of antiquity until the capture of Constantinople, and was never fully displaced either by the Jewish Decalogue or Gospel precepts." It constitutes, we may say, a Greek open ethical canon in contrast to the Hebrew closed ethical canon.

gods of the peoples are idols." There is a tension, not fully resolved until late, between seeing foreign cults by analogy with Israelite as to a definable high being, and seeing them as merely empty; but that tension does not seriously undercut the Hebrews' understanding of their own cult.

Since for Hebrews the primary dialogue is between man and God, it is a key matter how that God is understood. Since there is ultimately no other true god in Israel from whom Yahweh its God needs to be distinguished, a visual representation of Yahweh is at the least superfluous; and in fact was absolutely rejected. Nowhere are the relations of the two societies to the ancient Near East more opposite than in the realm of the plastic arts. Archaic Greeks took the image of the standing youth or *kouros* (human or divine) from Egypt, while bringing it to life; composite animals, Gorgons and griffins, from the Hittite world. The language used about the God of Israel attributes to him, as to a mountain and to the Greek gods, the features of a man's body: arms and legs, hands and feet; a face, eyes and ears, nostrils (to express his anger). You would think him "anthropomorphic," as Strabo 17.1.28 noted that Egyptian temples had "no statue, or at least none of human form, but of one of the irrational beasts," ξόανον δ' οὐδέν, ἢ οὐκ ἀνθρωπόμορφον, ἀλλὰ τῶν ἀλόγων ζῴων τινός. But here Israel differs most strongly from its neighbors, where Melqarth, identified in an Aramaic inscription, appears in a stele of Aleppo carrying an axe.[14] Millar[15] discusses the theory of Bickerman[16] that the cult set up in the Temple of Jerusalem by Antiochus IV Epiphanes in 167 BC was not Hellenizing at all, but an adaptation of Syrian aniconic practice whereby the altar itself (I.202) became the cult-object. Still, the old Hebrew practice is a better testimony to aniconic worship. Here is a realm where the fascination exercised on the Greek imagination by the Near East outside Israel is patent and long-continuing, however much Greeks improved on their models; and where correspondingly the stubbornness of Israel in breaking with the Near East is stiffest. Both strategies, the ways of affirmation and of rejection of images, represent complementary aspects of how humanity views the divine. Neither warrants one of the labels "progressive" or "retrograde."

The *linguistic* "anthropomorphism" of both Hebrew and Greek occasionally results in parallel expressions. Thus Ex 13,9 "For with a

---

14   ANEP² 499; KAI 201.

15   Millar, Roman Near East, 12-13.

16   Elias Bickerman, The God of the Maccabees...; tr. H. R. Moehring; Studies in Judaism in Late Antiquity 32; Leiden: Brill, 1979 p. 70.

strong hand (LXX ἐν γὰρ χειρὶ κραταιᾷ) Yahweh has brought you out of Egypt":

כִּי בְּיָד חֲזָקָה הוֹצִיאֲךָ יהוה מִמִּצְרָיִם

Iliad 15.694-5 "and Zeus pushed[17] [Hector] forward with his most long hand," τὸν δὲ Ζεὺς ὦσεν ὄπισθε / χειρὶ μάλα μεγάλη. Similarly the eye of the high God is spoken of (I.272, II.34, III.5). But in poetic comparisons, a small but significant difference makes the Greek divine realm immanent, and the Hebrew one transcendent. In Hellas, natural objects are seen as an adequate symbol of the divine; in Israel, inadequate. The difference is especially noteworthy where the vocabulary as such is shared.

Gold and jewels. For Pindar (frag. 209, I.73) "gold is the child of Zeus," Διὸς παῖς ὁ χρυσός; again (*Olymp.* 1.1-2):

Ἄριστον μὲν ὕδωρ, ὁ δὲ χρυσὸς αἰθόμενον πῦρ
ἅτε διαπρέπει νυκτὶ μεγάνορος ἔξοχα πλούτου.

> Water is preeminent and gold, like a fire
> burning in the night, outshines
> all possessions that magnify men's pride.[18]

What could be better than gold? Hebrew finds something, Prov 8,10-11

קְחוּ־מוּסָרִי וְאַל־כָּסֶף   וְדַעַת מֵחָרוּץ נִבְחָר
כִּי־טוֹבָה חָכְמָה מִפְּנִינִים

(Wisdom speaking) "Take my instruction rather than silver, and knowledge rather than refined gold; for wisdom is better than jewels"; and similarly Prov 3,13-14; 8,19. Proverbs here as we have often noted is in the Phoenician orbit, using the foreign name of gold which went into Greek, rather than native זָהָב.[19]

Sand and stars. Again, in Israel, Hellas and Rome the sand on the seashore and the stars stand for what is uncountable (I.314-316), even though certain ones are given credit for having counted them: Archimedes and Archytas (Horace *Carm.* 1.28.1-2) the sand, Yahweh the stars (Ps 147,4). But once something is *more than* the sand, Ps 139,17-18 "How precious to me are thy thoughts, O El!...if I count them, they are *more* than the sand,"

אֶסְפְּרֵם מֵחוֹל יִרְבּוּן

Time and eternity. Time (χρόνος), says Plato (*Timaeus* 38B), and the heavens came into being together, so that, if necessary, they should be

---

17 Aristarchus and papyri for ὦρσεν.
18 Trans. F. J. Nisetich, Pindar's Victory Songs; Baltimore: Johns Hopkins, 1980. Rather than a tendentious version of my own, I follow this which I do believe conveys the implications of the original.
19 But where the actual names of jewels appear, jasper and emeralds, both Greek and Hebrew use them as adequate symbols of a better world (I.87).

dissolved together; but earlier (37D) when he calls time "a certain moving image of eternity" (εἰκώ...κινητὸν τοῦ αἰῶνος) he describes it as an "eternal image," αἰώνιον εἰκόνα (with a different form of the accusative for elegance). Heraclitus[20] says that "this cosmos, the same for all beings, was made by no gods or men, but always was and is and shall be ever-living fire, kindled by measure and extinguished by measure":

κόσμον τόνδε, τὸν αὐτὸν ἁπάντων, οὔτε τις θεῶν οὔτε ἀνθρώπων ἐποίησεν, ἀλλ᾽ ἦν ἀεὶ καὶ ἔστιν καὶ ἔσται πῦρ ἀείζωον, ἁπτόμενον μέτρα καὶ ἀποσβεννύμενον μέτρα.

Both authors in spite of subtleties appear to be saying that time and the universe partake of eternity; conversely then, eternity can be grasped through the objects of the universe. In clear contrast, Ps 102,27 (see the whole context) says of heavens and earth "They will perish, but you endure; they will all wear out like a garment":

הֵמָּה יֹאבֵדוּ וְאַתָּה תַעֲמֹד וְכֻלָּם כַּבֶּגֶד יִבְלוּ

22.5 Tragedy and survival

A further difference between the societies emerges from the centrality of the tragic vision in Hellas and its absence in Israel. Tragedy, says Aristotle (*Poetics* 13.5), is the story of one who falls into misfortune (δυστυχία) through some flaw (ἁμαρτία). The story of the *Iliad* is the anger or grudge (μῆνις) of Achilles responsible for the death of his best friend Patroclus. The story of Oedipus is the hot temper of one who in a crossroads encounter kills another old enough to be his father. The story told by Thucydides is the disaster of the Sicilian expedition arising from the Athenians' inflated estimate of their own abilities, documented in Pericles' Funeral Oration—much admired, not always for the right reasons. Perhaps it will be agreed that a pattern here runs through earlier Greek literature. Is it to be found in Hebrew?[21] David

---

20   Heraclitus frag. 30 FVS[8] from Plutarch.

21   Here I disagree with Flemming A. J. Nielsen, The Tragedy in History: Herodotus and the Deuteronomistic History; Journal for the Study of the Old Testament Supplement Series 251; 1997. Nielsen finds to his own satisfaction a tragic theme running through the Hebrew Bible. Like some others of an American-Danish school (III.328), he dates the final redaction of the Biblical history (including its "tragic" elements) so late that it could reflect Herodotus. His last sentence (p. 164): "Thus it becomes probable that [the Deuteronomistic History] was written at a time and in a milieu where the Hellenistic influence was important in the Israelite or more correctly, the Jewish tradition." But this bold claim is not buttressed by any proposed linguistic borrowing from Herodotus or Greek generally, such as we find in Qoheleth or Daniel.

suffers reverses seen as caused by his own failings, like the death of his first child by Bathsheba, but his life goes on as life does—the story seems more based on real life than Greek tragedy. The story from Genesis to Kings is the continuity of a people in spite of all setbacks. The Exile is seen as retribution for the faults of Judah, but only Lamentations makes it a total disaster. II Kings ends with Jehoiachin eating at the king's table. In spite of harsh words against Babylon, Jeremiah says in God's name to the actual exiles there (29,7) "But seek the peace of the city where I have sent you into exile":

וְדִרְשׁוּ אֶת־שְׁלוֹם הָעִיר אֲשֶׁר הִגְלֵיתִי אֶתְכֶם שָׁמָּה

Hebrews looking beyond their own traditions, to Egypt or Babylonia, were in touch with societies that traced their history hundreds and thousands of years into the remote past; and, even while struggling to escape, they learned from those empires to record and cherish their own distant history. For a supremely practical purpose. Levin on *Elohim* in the Hebrew Bible says:[22]

> The conviction of the Bible authors [about the nature of the Hebrew God] came (I think) from observing which patterns of human association are viable in the long run, and which ones end in failure. Their wisdom was a kind of pre-scientific sociology, far-sighted and practical at the same time; modern research is more methodical but not more acute or penetrating. They fastened upon the relation of father to son, as the basis of society and of all wholesome growth and development.

Thus the distinction between clean and unclean beasts is a traditional hygiene; the development of the (seemingly) instinctive abhorrence of incest is an observational eugenics; the Sabbatical rest of the land (II.25) is a heuristic agronomy. All such principles in the books of Moses required data over numerous generations in order to be verified. In contrast, the moral and social principles in Hesiod's *Works and Days*, while often persuasive and in agreement with Moses, rest mostly on one man's observations, even though (no doubt) drawing to some degree on traditional experience.

The Hellenes at no period had a long enough history behind them, legendary or historical, to say for certain which patterns of life in the human family (particular or universal) were sustainable in the long run. But they had a long enough history to say that certain patterns of life were self-destructive and doomed to failure even in a short run. The formative events of Israelite history made it the primary depository in

---

22 Saul Levin, Guide to the Bible; 5th ed.; laser-printed; State Univ. of New York at Binghamton, 1996; p. 12.

the ancient world of both levels of wisdom. Moderns with our individualism, like the Greeks, need to identify and ward off social patterns
which will implode upon ourselves in our own lifetimes. But with the
flux of technological innovation and changing family structures we are
giving up even the prospect of founding a dynasty; we expect in
advance that our grandchidren will strike out in diferent ways. The
uniqueness of the Kennedy clan is just the fact of its existence with a
seeming unchangeable Catholicism. For ourselves we can hardly imagine any proposal (in the nature of things never fully demonstrative)
that certain social patterns over an indefinite period of time actually
work.

22.6 *Criteria of membership: lineage vs. language*

Israelites, once they undertook to define themselves over against other
peoples, precisely because they differed so slightly in material culture
from other Canaanites, adopted a rigid definition of the difference
between themselves and their neighbors. Thus they answered the question, "What makes us different from other peoples?," much otherwise
than the Greeks. יִשְׂרָאֵל is masculine (except when seen as an army)
while Ἑλλάς is feminine.[23] At I.22 we brought the two names so far as
possible together.[24] Israel/Jacob is the father of *twelve* tribes. Hellen is
the father of three in Hesiod[25] "And from Hellen the war-loving king
came Doros, Xouthos and Aiolos the chariot-fighter"

Ἕλληνος δ' ἐγένοντο φιλοπτολέμου βασιλῆος
Δῶρός τε Ξοῦθός τε καὶ Αἴολος ἱππιοχάρμης

Xouthos was the father of Achaios (Ἀχαιός), and of Ion (Ἴων) the
ancestor of the Ionians (Apollodorus 1.7.3) with their *twelve* cities in
Achaea and in Ionia (Herodotus 1.145, II.205). But Hellenes came to
name themselves not after the man but the region Ἑλλάς, whose
original referent is variously reported, but which already Hesiod *Opera* 651-3 uses for the whole Achaean host: "...Aulis, where once the
Achaeans, after waiting out a storm, gathered a great host from sacred
Hellas (Ἑλλάδος ἐξ ἱερῆς) to Troy the land of fair women."

Herodotus also uses "Hellas" as a feminine adjective to denote the
Greek *language.* At 6.98.3 he explains the names of the Persian kings
"in Greek," κατὰ Ἑλλάδα γλῶσσαν; at 9.16.2 he represents a Persian

---

23 But we should resist the temptation to see the polar opposites Israel/Hellas as
     masculine/feminine, much less with the other attributes of Chinese Yang/Yin.
24 And see on "amphictyonies" of twelve peoples at II.203.
25 Hesiod frag. 9 Merkelbach-West.

as "speaking in Greek" to a Theban, τὸν Πέρσην...Ἑλλάδα γλῶσσαν
ἱέντα. Later Ἑλληνιστί is the only way of saying "in Greek." Plato
(*Tim.* 21E) says that the "founding divinity" (fem.!, θεὸς ἀρχηγός) of
Egyptian Sais "is named in Egyptian Neith, in Greek...Athena,"
Αἰγυπτιστὶ μὲν τοὔνομα Νηίθ, Ἑλληνιστὶ δέ...Ἀθηνᾶ. At Xenophon
Anab. 7.6.8 Seuthes the Thracian "had an interpreter, although he
himself understood most of what was said in Greek," ἔχων ἑρμηνέα,
ξυνίει δὲ καὶ αὐτὸς Ἑλληνιστὶ τὰ πλεῖστα. At Act 21,37 the tribune
Claudius Lysias (23,26), taking Paul for a different agitator, is surprised that he can understand Greek, Ἑλληνιστὶ γινώσκεις;, Syriac
יוֹנָאִית יָדַע אַתְּה "Ionian," Vulgate *Graece nosti?* Thus the primary connotation of "Hellas" comes to be *the land and society of all those who
speak Greek.*

When an earlier Alexander of Macedon urged the Athenians to
submit to Xerxes, and the Spartans urged them to stand fast, the
Athenians said No to Alexander, and to the Spartans defined the
features of their commonality which blocked any thought of becoming
traitors (Herodotus 8.144.2):

> τὸ Ἑλληνικόν, ἐὸν ὅμαιμόν τε καὶ ὁμόγλωσσον, καὶ θεῶν ἱδρύματά
> τε κοινὰ καὶ θυσίαι, ἤθεά τε ὁμότροπα...

> The Hellenic [nation], being of one blood and one language, along with
> the common shrines and sacrifices of the gods, as also the customs arising
> from a shared upbringing....

Here four things are seen as constituting the Hellenes: common descent, language, temples and customs. But Isocrates (*Panegyricus* 49-
50) sets a priority among them:

> But so far has our city [Athens] left behind other men in regards to
> thought and speech (τὸ φρονεῖν καὶ λέγειν), that her pupils have become
> teachers of the others, and have brought it about that the name of the
> Hellenes no longer is felt to refer to a race (τοῦ γένους) but a mental
> disposition (τῆς διανοίας), and that those are called Hellenes who share our
> education (τῆς παιδεύσεως τῆς ἡμετέρας) rather than a common descent (τῆς
> κοινῆς φύσεως).

Earlier Isocrates had said that the best sign of "our [Athenian] education" (τῆς παιδεύσεως ἡμῶν) was "things said" (τὰ λεγόμενα) by those
who "use speech well," τοὺς λόγῳ καλῶς χρωμένους. While like other
men he puts his own profession in first place, his claim that the use of
language is the surest sign of Hellenism is supported by Herodotus'
usage.

Israelites have no specific name for their language. Isa 19,18 "the lip
of Canaan" (שְׂפַת כְּנַעַן) defines the common language of Canaan (I.7),

including Hebrew, Phoenician, Moabite, Ammonite—and perhaps even Philistine, so far as its speakers had taken over Canaanite as with king Achish of Ekron (II.298). At II Reg 18,26 the contrast between "Judaean" (יְהוּדִית) and "Aramaic" (אֲרָמִית) refers to the peoples who spoke those tongues rather than to any clear concept of the languages themselves. In John's Gospel, Ἑβραϊστί is attached to proper names which can only be Aramaic, Βηθζαθά (5,2), Γαββαθά (19,13), Γολγοθά (19,17); it then likewise refers to the language spoken by people who called themselves "Hebrews," rather than to any clear distinction between what we know as Hebrew and Aramaic. In the Hellenistic period, most must have thought the Aramaic they spoke simply a vernacular form of the Hebrew they heard in the synagogue without full understanding; only an occasional Rabbi and Jerome understood the true situation (III.205).

The fact that all Hebrews speak the same language is taken for granted but not emphasized. Ezekiel (3,5) is told, "You are not sent to a people hard of lip and heavy of tongue, [but] to the house of Israel":

כִּי לֹא אֶל־עַם עִמְקֵי שָׂפָה וְכִבְדֵי לָשׁוֹן אַתָּה שָׁלוּחַ אֶל־בֵּית יִשְׂרָאֵל

even though his message will be more acceptable to foreigners than to Israel. One dialectal difference in the sibilants is noted, between Gileadite שִׁבֹּלֶת "ear of wheat" and Ephraimite סִבֹּלֶת (Jud 12,6); modern scholars find others. Moabite and Phoenician inscriptions prove that those languages, along with Hebrew, were closely related dialects of Canaanite and mutually comprehensible. We find little difference between the material cultures of Israel and Phoenicia (I.7), so that Phoenicians could transport to Hellas many objects, institutions and words today only attested from Israel. But the Israelites found a world of difference in cult and manners. (It is unknown how the much broader cults at Elephantine were regarded in Jerusalem....) Commonality of language hardly appears as a definition of what constitutes Israel. When Hebrew was replaced by Aramaic (which had previously supplanted Akkadian in Babylon) at the Exile, with Phoenician succumbing somewhat later, the self-image of the Israelites was if anything intensified. For many centuries *no* Jew grew up speaking either Hebrew or Aramaic as his mother tongue. But there never came a time when a speaker of Greek would call a non-speaker a Hellene.

Thus "Israel" refers to a markedly smaller group than those who spoke the same language: namely, those who in the categories of Herodotus had the same shrine (ἵδρυμα) of the same God, with the same sacrifices (θυσίαι) and customs (ἤθεα)—all codified in the books of the Law. The name "Israel" reflects the conviction that those commonalities were restricted to clans or families tracing their ancestry (physically or conventionally) to the twelve sons of Jacob/Israel.

Herodotus vaguely takes it for granted that the community of those who speak Greek is coterminous with those of common descent; Isocrates sharply defines it that language correctly used *rather than lineage* is what defines a Hellene.

The same contrast defines how the two peoples thought of *outsiders*. While Cretans (themselves mostly Greeks, but marginalized) are distrusted by other Greeks generally as liars, and Cilicians suspected as bloodthirsty (I.30-32, II.315), Carians are looked down on as speaking strangely, Καρῶν βαρβαροφώνων "Carians speaking barbarously" (*Iliad* 2.867), and therefore a suitable *corpus uile* for taking risks with (Cicero *pro Flacco* 65). Sanskrit *barbara* "non-Aryan" is conventionally taken as the source of βάρβαρος with the onomatopoetic connotation "stammering"; but Levin finds it poorly attested and proposes that in fact it is derived *from* the Greek.[26] Hellenes never hold it against "barbarians" that they worship the wrong gods. On the contrary, the gods of foreigners are just the gods of the Hellenes under different names: Babylonian Belos is Zeus (Herodotus 3.158.2), Egyptian Neith is Athena; Aphrodite has different names among Assyrians, Arabs and Persians (Herodotus 1.131.3). For Hebrews, the error of the Goyim is to worship the wrong god in the wrong way. David says to his God (II Sam 7,23) "And what one (LXX ἄλλο reading אחר "other") nation on earth is like your people, like Israel, whose God(s?) went[27] to redeem them to himself as a people?":

וּמִי כְעַמְּךָ כְּיִשְׂרָאֵל גּוֹי אֶחָד בָּאָרֶץ אֲשֶׁר הָלְכוּ־אֱלֹהִים לִפְדּוֹת־לוֹ
לְעָם

Initially Israel and Hellas, through their presumed superiority respectively in worship and in language, see themselves as set apart from other nations. (But precisely through that superiority they later come to see themselves as having a universal mission with something of infinite value to offer to all.)

Israel as defined by its lineage is much smaller than Hellas as defined by its language. The area of all peoples who spoke dialects of Canaanite

---

26 Older etymologists assumed that Akkadian *barbaru* must somehow reflect an Indo-European word also attested in Sanskrit; but in fact the Akkadian means simply "wolf"; and Frisk, who at i.220 suggests that the Indo-European is derived from Akkadian or its Sumerian counterpart BARBAR, at iii.49 recognizes the true state of affairs.

27 The plural הָלְכוּ suggests that the reference is to the gods of another nation: none such went out to create a people. I Chron 17,21 simplifies, reading הָלַךְ singular, "a people [Israel] whom God went out to redeem to himself as a people."

(including then Punic of Carthage) is larger than Israel, and more nearly comparable with the area of all who spoke Greek. But there was no common history or cult holding Canaanite speakers together: Egypt and Babylon put down attempted coalitions; there is no record that Carthage brought texts from the homeland. In the Near East, far from imposing their language on neighbors, Canaanites in the north and east kept losing adherents to speakers of Aramaic—which really *was* a missionary language, although likewise without common history or cult. At the earliest point where we can see the spread of Greek-speakers, they are held together by the Homeric poems—doubtless earlier by predecessors of those poems, heroic lays about the siege of Troy. And so with cult. Greeks fought with each other as often as neighbors anywhere in the ancient world; but they held the same pantheon of gods, and the festivals of those gods in peacetime were a bond of union. In Canaan, as elsewhere in the Near East (and more conventionally in Homer), the enmities of peoples were symbolized and reinforced by the presumed enmities of their gods.

To determine who their true associates were, Israelites looked back in time, to the genealogy theoretically known through tradition or writing; Greeks looked out in space, to see whom they could understand by virtue of their speaking the same language. Sea-trade further naturally gave Greeks a spacious outlook and a familiarity, at least superficial, with foreigners—Carians, Cilicians, Lydians, Libyans, Lycians, as well as Cretans, half foreigners; Israel knew those as mercenaries serving in their midst,[28] and their land-neighbors mostly as potential rivals in war. Through that trade the Anatolians learned Greek and after Alexander joined the Greek world. Through their relations with Mesopotamia and Egypt, Hebrews felt themselves surrounded by monuments of a distant antiquity, and in their tradition maintained connections (however adversarial) with those remote eras. When Greeks came to see those same monuments, they could only interpret them as *somebody else's* antiquity. The legendary migration of Danaus and his daughters (I.227) from Egypt, or of Cadmus from Phoenicia (I.37), is not thought of as bringing any knowledge of foreign social institutions.

---

28   Only the Lycians are unattested in the Hebrew Bible, though their own name of Τερμίλαι (Herodotus 1.173) appears in the Xanthos trilingual as *Trm̃mile*, תרמילא (I.29-31). But like the Hellenistic Lycians, the *Lukka* appear at Amarna 38.10 as pirates, and less certainly in Egyptian, Ugaritic and Hittite texts (RLA "Lukka" vii.161-163).

22.7 Confluence in the New Testament

The worlds of Israel and Hellas come into full contact with the conquest of the Near East by Alexander, when speakers of Aramaic (including now Jews) took on simplified Greek as a second language. Already before Alexander (I.34) Phoenician Tripolis had its Greek name, and Greek loanwords, γλύφω "carve" and στατήρ "stater" (II.299) had infiltrated the Aramaic of Egypt. The book of Jeremiah (42-44) shows that a substantial Jewish population had made its way into Egypt; along with other nationalities they came to the new city of Alexandria and prospered, and there the Hebrew Bible was translated into Greek, according to the legend of Aristeas by seventy (-two) scholars. A Greek-speaking school of Jewish philosophy grew up, attested by the *Wisdom* ascribed to Solomon, and later by Philo. Perhaps more from Alexandria than Jerusalem, Greek-speaking synagogues grew up around the Mediterranean, wherever Jewish traders or artisans took up residence.

The book of Acts (however schematic its history), along with the letters of Paul, shows that Christianity spread out from those Hellenistic synagogues before forming its own congregations. An Aramaic-speaking Jewish-Christian church in Palestine maintained a shadowy existence for many decades, but left little record. All the preserved literature of the earliest Church is in Greek. Only in Edessa of Syria did Aramaic-speaking Christians form their own church and translate the Greek New Testament into their dialect, Syriac. Not until after Constantine did Aramaic-speaking Christians in Palestine itself produce a translation in *their* dialect, the so-called "Palestinian Syriac," now extant except for fragments only in the Gospels. With both, at most some lingering traditions remained of the Aramaic originals of Jesus' sayings. (But the Syriac versions are precious reconstructions of the original [III.203], for they were made by men whose native language was Aramaic, living under conditions not all that different from Galilee.)

Hellenistic Judaism died out except so far as its Greek Bible was preserved in the new Christian Church; the Greek-speaking synagogues were the seed-bed of the Church, which however became so threatening that they reverted to Hebrew or eventually went out of business. Some texts will document the continuance of Hellenistic synagogues. An inscribed pillar in Greek from Aphrodisias of Asia Minor of the third century CE[29] lists a large number of men with Jewish names and a not

---

29   Joyce Reynolds & Robert Tannenbaum, Jews and God-Fearers at Aphrodisias: Greek Inscriptions with Commentary; Cambridge Philological Society Sup.

much smaller list of men with pagan names introduced by καὶ ὅσοι θεοσεβις. The first nine of the *theosebeis* are noted as βουλ(ευτής)—i.e. members of the city Senate or of a synagogue organization? We have here the same two categories as those attested at Antioch of Pisidia in varying formulas, Act 13,16 ἄνδρες Ἰσραηλῖται καὶ οἱ φοβούμενοι τὸν θεόν and 13,43 τῶν Ἰουδαίων καὶ τῶν σεβομένων προσηλύτων. So at Athens (17,17) Paul converses in the synagogue with τοῖς Ἰουδαίοις καὶ τοῖς σεβομένοις. Of individuals, σεβόμενος τὸν θεόν (Act 16,14; 18,7). Joh 9,31 θεοσεβής may reflect the Hellenistic category. Evidently at Aphrodisias a category of *theosebeis* (partial or full converts?) joined Jews in the synagogue, and surely the bulk of the service must have been in Greek with readings from the LXX.[30]

On February 8, AD 553 Justinian issued an edict at Constantinople[31] on languages in the synagogue worship and some other topics. The Greek text is the original, the ancient Latin translation is faulty. He has received petitions from one or both parties of those who wish to use Hebrew or Greek in the service. He permits both, and Latin too (τῆς Ἰταλικῆς); he prefers the Septuagint on the grounds that prophecies to the coming Christ appear more clearly in it, but grudgingly permits that of Aquila (Ἀκύλου) also. He absolutely forbids use of the δευτέρωσιν which must surely be the Mishna. Reading between the lines, we may conjecture that Hebrew liturgy along with the Mishna was winning the day, but that advocates of the Septuagint remained, whom the Emperor supports as far as he can.

We think of the New Testament as the Greek account of a Jewish spiritual movement. But that omits an important factor, by leaving the character of the Greek account undefined. Back to Alexander: how did the Macedonian conceive the idea of a campaign against the Near East? It was already united in the Persian empire: with a few exceptions like Phoenician Tyre, there would be no independent centers of resist-

---

Vol. 12; Cambridge: University, 1987. Discussion by Louis H. Feldman, Jew and Gentile in the Ancient World: Attitudes and Interactions from Alexander to Justinian; Princeton: University, 1993; pp. 362-369.

30 An inscription of uncertain Imperial date from the theatre at Miletus (Gabba 33) has ΤΟΠΟΣ ΕΙΟΥΔΕΩΝ ΤΩΝ ΚΑΙ ΘΕΟΣΕΒΙΟΝ "Place of the Jews known as *theosebeis*"—i.e. semi-converts?

31 Corpus Juris Civilis, III, Novellae [of Justinian], Berlin: Weidmann, 1895, ed. R. Schoell & W. Kroll, no. 146 pp. 714-718. Greek text, translation and discussion in Amnon Linder, The Jews in Roman Imperial Legislation, Detroit: Wayne State & Jerusalem: Israel Academy, 1987, pp. 402-411. See also James Parkes, The Conflict of the Church and the Synagogue: A study in the origins of antisemitism; Cleveland: Meridian & Philadelphia: Jewish Pub. Soc. of America, 1961; pp. 251-253.

ance. We said that Hellas (to which we may now add Macedon) was a society just outside the ancient Near East, with its own resources, but on which the Near Eastern empires exercised an ongoing fascination. One of the items in that fascination, it now turns out, was precisely the lure of empire! Athens for a time under Pericles maintained an empire with taxation—but over *poleis* which remained independent. Alexander has been called the last of the Achaemenids; from them he learned the very concept of a world-empire. After Alexander's victories and death, Palestine shifted between Ptolemaic and Seleucid control; then after a brief heady independence under the Maccabees, it fell under Rome, whether or not it was ruled by nominally autonomous client-kings, a Herod or Agrippa in Jerusalem, an Antipas in Galilee. And the Romans in turn had learned how to conduct an empire from their competitors, the Semitic Carthaginians and the Hellenistic kingdoms. Rome also was the student of ancient Near Eastern imperialism, at one more remove.

The courts of the Palestinian client-kings, in particular the Herods, intermarrying with other Near Eastern dynastic houses, must have been largely Greek-speaking. Roman administration in the East operated almost exclusively in Greek. Thus Greek was not merely the language of trade and of an upper-class culture in Palestine; above all, it was the language of *imperial control*. The three languages of the lingua franca are mirrored in the three facets of the New Testament: its narrative and spiritual theme is Israelite; its linguistic form and social institutions are Greek; but the political reality it faces is Roman. We may then redefine the confluence of Israel and Hellas in the New Testament. Its founding events exist just inside the ancient Near East, at the heart of old Israel; they are shaped and narrated by the language and spirit of Hellas—but a Hellas that had learned from its stance just outside the Near East what it meant to speak for an empire. In those special senses, its matter is Israelite and its form Hellenic.

We may now look at some features of Christianity in relation to its parents, in the same sequence as at 22.4—22.6 above.

22.7.1 Language about God in the New Testament

One thing that sets the New Testament apart from Greek literature—classical, contemporary to it or subsequent—is its unargued presupposition of a single God. How did the New Testament as a Greek book achieve that certainty? The obvious answer is, From the Greek Bible, the Septuagint. While we can detect several translators at work, each with some peculiarities, their differences do not at all coincide with the great variety of styles in the Hebrew Bible. Hebrew *Esther*, which nowhere mentions the God of Israel or his name, has additions in the Greek which abundantly make up for that defect. It is in the Septuagint that the conviction of a single God enters the stream of Greek literature.

A belated and partial record of the innovation brought by the Septuagint appears in philosophical writers of the second century CE. Epictetus (in Arrian 1.3.1-3) found no inconsistency in saying "*God* is the father of men and of *gods*," ὁ θεὸς πατήρ ἐστι τῶν τ᾿ ἀνθρώπων καὶ τῶν θεῶν, and then in going on to assume that one knows himself to be "the son of *Zeus*," τοῦ Διὸς υἱός. For Marcus Aurelius 12.5 it is the same thing to say "you are arguing with *God*," δικαιολογῇ πρὸς τὸν θεόν and "we were debating with the *gods*," διελεγόμεθα τοῖς θεοῖς. Plutarch in his beautiful essay "On those whose vengeance by *the divine* is delayed," Περὶ τῶν ὑπὸ τοῦ θείου βραδέως τιμωρουμένων (*Mor.* 548A) can speak (551C) of "the gentleness[32] and magnanimity that *God* displays," τὴν πραότητα καὶ τὴν μεγαλοψυχίαν[33] ἣν ὁ θεὸς ἐνδείκνυται. I suggest that the alternative of expressing their thought in the "theistic" mode is due to the subterranean influence of Hellenistic Judaism. Epictetus knows that Jews have specific dietary regulations (Arrian 1.11.12-13, 1.22.4); Marcus at least knows of the Jews and finds them unruly (Ammianus 22.5.5);[34] Plutarch (*Quaest. Conviv.* 6.1-2 = *Mor.* 671-2; see I.158) has a speaker to his own satisfaction prove that the god of the Jews is identical with Dionysos.

Thus the New Testament uses and much extends a language about God already implanted in Greek by the Septuagint, and being adopted by Greek writers of the second century CE. But it goes beyond both Hebrew austerity and Greek tentativeness in its language about God as Father, concerned for every sparrow and hair, ravens and lilies; it sees a specific new series of events as the work of God in history; in its universality it breaks down all remnants of both Hebrew and Greek ethnocentrism. One factor of its success in the Greco-Roman world was its reinforcement of the optional theism already current there.

22.7.2 Why is the New Testament not a tragedy?

Like the Hebrew Bible, and deriving from it, the New Testament looks back to the remotest origins of humanity. We said that the lack of

---

32   πραότης is used in the LXX only of human beings, e.g. Sirach 3,17.

33   MSS μεγαλοπάθειαν, a non-word.

34   See Stern ii.605 who cites the variant readings of the adjective by which Marcus describes the Jews, *inquietiores, inertiores, ineptiores.*

tragedy in the Israelite world was due to the conviction that the pattern of life chronicled in the Hebrew Bible, and deposited in the Law, was a guarantee for continuance of the family and people that led it. But not continuance of the individual. What would happen if external events blocked the continuance of family and people? Such immortality as the classical Hebrew man knows is derived from the conviction that his sons and their sons have a promised future existence. Any individual life after death was at best ambiguously hinted at in the Psalms (III.000). Ezekiel's vision of the valley of dry bones coming to life (37,1-14) is explicitly a symbol of the reviving of the exiled collective people, not of individuals. The conviction of a future continuance was not shaken by the Babylonian exile; it *was* shaken by the Maccabean martyrs, and at that time a doctrine of the "resurrection" of the dead explicitly appears (Dan 12,2; II Makk 12,43-45).

The narrative of the Gospels up until the end reads for all the world like a tragedy. The coming destruction of Jerusalem, which colors all the New Testament through prophetic expectation, perhaps in places through *vaticinia ex eventu*, even more than the Exile raised doubts about any future continuance of the Jewish people. All along, Greek heroes and ordinary people found only partial comfort in the continuance of their descendants after their own death. The Homeric heroes were more interested in perpetual fame (I.10-11). The prospect of going down to Hades monopolized Greek attention more strongly than Sheol for the Hebrews. And so (Chapter 19) the lively imagination of the Greeks more strongly than with the Hebrews constructed hopes of blessedness in better lands, first for military heroes, then for the morally virtuous. Perhaps the Hellenization of the Near East then assisted the Rabbis in constructing the doctrine of the תחית המתים (II.169) out of the ambiguous hints in the Psalms.

But no historical antecedent explains Paul's confident hope in the reality of Christ's resurrection as a pledge of his own; nor the multiform Gospel narratives of Jesus' resurrection appearances. That conviction was one of two or three features of the new faith which commended it to the masses of the Hellenistic-Roman world, oppressed by the fear of death. What is marginal in Judaism becomes absolutely central in Christianity, based on narratives with no correspondents in Israel.

The last of the thirteen principles of faith of Maimonides, inserted in our prayer books in Hebrew, is that "there will be a raising of the dead at the time when it shall please the Creator":

שתהיה תחית המתים בעת שיעלה רצון מאת הבורא

In the formation of American Reform Judaism it was explicitly dropped.

The "Pittsburgh Platform" of 1885, the basic statement of Reform from 1889 to 1937, says:[35]

> We reassert the doctrine of Judaism, that the soul of man is immortal, grounding this belief on the divine nature of the human spirit.... We reject as ideas not rooted in Judaism the beliefs both in bodily resurrection and in Gehenna and Eden (Hell and Paradise) as abodes for everlasting punishment or reward.

And that high-water mark of liberalism has not been fully reversed.

The Nazi Holocaust, the greatest trauma to Israel in all of history, was named Shoah after Zeph 1,15:

יוֹם עֶבְרָה הַיּוֹם הַהוּא...יוֹם שֹׁאָה וּמְשׁוֹאָה

Vg *dies irae dies illa...dies calamitatis* (שֹׁאָה) *et miseriae*. It drove occasional Jewish thinkers like Richard Rubenstein towards something like atheism:

> When I say we live in the time of the death of God, I mean that the thread uniting God and man, heaven and earth, has been broken. We stand in a cold, silent, unfeeling cosmos, unaided by any purposeful power beyond our own resources. After Auschwitz, what else can a Jew say about God?[36]

But Zephaniah (1,14) still called it "the great day *of Yahweh*":

קָרוֹב יוֹם-יהוה הַגָּדוֹל

Vg *iuxta est dies Domini magnus*. Rubenstein finds that inacceptable:

> Traditional Jewish theology...has interpreted every major catastrophe in Jewish history as God's punishment of a sinful Israel. I fail to see how this position can be maintained without regarding Hitler and the SS as instruments of God's will. ...The idea is simply too obscene for me to accept.

And still contemplation of the *Shoah*, which has created overwhelming political support for the state of Israel among Jews both in America and elsewhere, has not created an overwhelming agreed conviction of the resurrection among them. Perhaps this "Sadducean" tendency (Mark 12,18) comes from a feeling that Christianity has preempted the doctrine.

---

35 Encyclopaedia Judaica; Jerusalem: Macmillan, 1971, xiii.570-571. Neil Gilman (The Death of Death: Resurrection and Immortality in Jewish Thought; Woodstock [Vermont]: Jewish Lights, 1997) considers that Maimonides in fact found the doctrine of resurrection problematical, and (p. 154) "care[d] desperately that Jews understand the afterlife in terms of spiritual immortality." Gilman further chronicles the substantial replacement of resurrection by immortality in both the Reform and Conservative wings of American Judaism.

36 Richard L. Rubenstein, After Auschwitz: Radical Theology and Contemporary Judaism: Indianapolis etc.: Bobbs Merrill, 1966; pp. 152-153. This is the original edition; later ones somewhat soften the thought.

Thus, without intending it, modern Hebrew has found the name of what English calls the "Holocaust" (itself a word with endless overtones) in the text which above all for the Christian West evokes the death of the individual and of the creation. The sequence *Dies Irae* is anonymous; its popular attribution to Thomas of Celano rests on no specific evidence. It first appears in MSS of 1255, and was adopted in the Tridentine Missal for a Requiem mass. The haunting melody, uniquely for Gregorian, infiltrates modern compositions since the *Symphonie Fantastique* of Berlioz. The author appears to be using Augustine *de civ. Dei* 18.23 or some such source for the Sibylline verses:

> Dies irae dies illa
> Soluet saeclum in fauilla
> Teste Dauid cum Sibylla.

For the *tuba mirum spargens sonum* see the texts cited at II.234, 262; for the *liber scriptus*, see Rev 5,1 and ʿAqiba's ominous *pinax* (*Avoth* III.17, I.75 etc.).

22.7.3 Membership: why did Christianity win out?

Why did Christianity catch on so widely in the Roman world—and beyond—when the Greek language and the Jewish synagogue as such did not? (At 22.11 below we discuss how one component of Hellenism, reason and logic, has seemingly caught on universally, outdoing all competitors...) Its success can in large part be laid simply to the fact that it does not need to recognize the existence of any outsiders. In both Hellas and Israel, the old rejection of the foreigner, barbarians or *goyim*, was replaced by a new conviction that one's own culture contained a precious novelty which deserved to be made available to all peoples (III.309). But Hellas and Israel were never able to make that gift unconditional: the Greeks could not separate it from their language, the Hebrews from their ancestry. In the New Testament with its new universal appeal, both blockages were overcome.

The simplicity of New Testament Greek gave it a special translatability, so that the new community was not restricted to any *language*; the abandonment of circumcision removed the restriction to any *lineage*. Christianity can be seen as the creation of a new family, in principle universal: "Behold my mother and my brothers!" (Mark 3,34). A conscious decision to join (risky in the first centuries) must be made; but the act of entrance by baptism was non-threatening, the door was kept open for all. The pre-existing harmony between Hellenic and Hebraic cultures analyzed in these volumes explains in part why the new Church found footing throughout the Greco-Roman world—and to its Bible added superstructures of Greek philosophy and Roman law.

22.8 *Literary canons, closed and open*

Primarily we know the two peoples through their texts—Hellas secondarily through its art and architecture. During the long centuries
when the texts were preserved by Rabbinic and Byzantine scribes, their
status differed somewhat: among Jews the canon is seen as the charter
of an ongoing community; in the Greek world, the texts are studied for
their own sake, in tension with the new Christian books. In both
worlds, the texts become the subject of a large exegetical literature.
Earlier (I.10-14) we compared Hebrew and Greek texts in several
characteristics: their continuity of preservation, their phonetic script,
their origin from a whole people, their theism and humanism, their
exemplary character and originality. Those mark the common status of
the texts as recording, and constituting, a new emergent of self-knowl-
edge and freedom in sister societies. But the two bodies of texts have
obvious differences also.

Hebrew literature is a sharply defined canon of twenty-four books
(five of law, four each of Former and Latter Prophets, eleven of
writings). One can read it through in translation in a few weeks—
though not exhaust it in a lifetime. Greek literature is a much larger
body of verse and prose, which only the brazen-gutted (χαλκέντεροι)
can work through; Egyptian papyri (many literary) and inscriptions
put it beyond any individual's scope. What accounts for the difference?
In part (we saw) the small size of Israel over against Hellas, due to its
more rigid self-definition (III.168). In part technical features of Hebrew composition and deficiencies of its script; but these also can be
attributed to its being inside the ancient Near East, and to the restricted realms in which it was able to manage a clean breakout.

Scattered evidence suggests that Hebrew literature was once somewhat more extensive than now. The compilers of the history in a few
places quote from a collection of verse. From the "Book of the Up-
right" (סֵפֶר הַיָּשָׁר) comes David's lament over Saul and Jonathan (II
Sam 1,19-27); Joshua's couplet on the arrest of sun and moon (Jos
10,12-13, where however the LXX omits the attribution); and the
verse of Solomon on the completion of the Temple (I Reg 8,12-13,
attributed at 8,53a LXX to some book).[37] From "the Book of the Wars
of Yahweh" comes the geographical note at Num 21,14. Kings and
Chronicles (with Neh 12,23) often cite other chronicles variously

---

37   The LXX attributes it to "The Book of the Song" (ἐν βιβλίῳ τῆς ᾠδῆς), where
     perhaps the Hebrew read ספר השיר as a variant of ספר הישר.

entitled.[38] Still, the Rabbis who discussed the status of the 24 books found no competitors; rather, they raised doubts about some of the Writings. At most, the canonical books existed in variant forms, as witnessed by the changed order of materials in the LXX of II Kings, Jeremiah and Proverbs. (But the Qumran MS of Jeremiah 4Q72 seems to follow the Masoretic order.)

The classical passage is Mishna *Yadayim* III.5, "All the sacred Writings render the hands unclean":

כל כתבי הקדש מטמאין את הידים

The only doubts were whether the Song of Songs and Qoheleth were sacred writings. R. ʿAqiba summed up what became the ruling, "All the writings are holy, but the Song of Songs is the Holy of Holies":

כל הכתובים קדש ושיר השירים קדש קדשים

Rab Judah said in the name of Samuel, "[The scroll of] Esther does not render the hands unclean" (Bab. Talm. *Megillah* 7a):

אסתר אינה מטמאת את הידים

paraphrasing, the editor asks incredulously whether Samuel truly believed that Esther "was not spoken through the Holy Spirit":

לאו ברוח הקודש נאמרה

In the end all preserved books ended up on nearly the same level.

The manuscripts from Qumran provide fragments of Aramaic Tobit;[39] Aramaic Enoch (I.16, 151; II.332); Hebrew Jubilees;[40] and perhaps the Testaments of the Twelve Patriarchs. The Manual of Discipline, War Scroll and Psalms from Qumran are compositions of the sect itself. All these materials are in a wholly other—I will say *inferior*—realm beside the Hebrew Bible. The book of Sirach occupies a middle ground. The endless Rabbinic literature —even including its crown jewel, the tractate *Avoth* of the Mishna—purports to be commentary rather than supplement to the Hebrew Bible, although the careful reader finds important advances, as in the doctrine of the "raising of the dead."

The Greek books best attested in manuscripts either imposed themselves on the whole people, or were chosen out by γραμματικοί for preservation as models of their kind. These are more than what we

---

38 But the "Book of the Chronicles of the Kings of Media and Persia" at Esther 10,2 may be a mere invention. For after the Daiva inscription of Xerxes, the cuneiform record of later kings markedly deteriorates. We have no evidence that specifically Aramaic chronicles existed, and it is not easy to imagine how the author of Esther would have gotten hold of such.

39 DJD xix.1-79, 1995, ed. J. Fitzmyer; see I.309.

40 DJD xiii.1-185; 1994.

mean by "grammarians": they did declamations themselves (Polybius 32.2.5); they were previously called κριτικοί (Dio Chrysostom 53.1). Aristophanes ὁ γραμματικός arranged the dialogues of Plato in trilogies (Diogenes Laertius 3.61); Aristarchus the great Homeric critic is called ὁ γραμματικώτατος (Athenaeus 15.672A). Other books came through dark ages in a few manuscripts or a single one; fragments of many others are preserved in the sands of Egypt. While the Library at Alexandria contained far more works than we possess, popular taste and the grammarians certainly retained a selection well above the average. All evidence indicates that the lost epics stood on a far lower level than the *Iliad* and *Odyssey*. Already Solon, it was said (Diogenes L. 1.57) decreed that the Homeric poems should be recited in some fixed order, τά τε Ὁμήρου γέγραφε ῥαψῳδεῖσθαι.

The criterion for choosing the dramas to be preserved is uncertain: literary excellence? suitability for teaching beginners? grammatical interest? Probably not suitability for performance, the Hellenistic and Roman periods put on their own plays. The entire corpus of tragedy made its way safely to Alexandria. Lycurgus[41] sponsored a law that the tragedies of Aeschylus, Sophocles and Euripides "should be written out and preserved in a public place," ἐν κοινῷ γραψαμένους φυλάττειν and that the "city scribe" (τὸν τῆς πόλεως γραμματέα) should rehearse the actors from those copies. Ptolemy II Philadelphus of Egypt put down a deposit of fifteen talents of silver to borrow the originals from Athens for copying; but when he got them, he sent copies back to Athens and kept the originals, forfeiting the fifteen talents.[42] The time and place are unknown at which were made the selections from the corpus that have come down to us.

The grammarians had some historical interest, for they preserved a sequence of historians: Herodotus, Thucydides, Xenophon, Arrian, Polybius. In that respect they were like the makers of the Hebrew Bible, who forcibly shaped available materials into a single narrative from the beginning to the Exile—and then abbreviated it from a new point of view in Chronicles, with a later appendix in Ezra and Nehemiah. The Greek historians lent themselves to that treatment, in that Thucydides consciously sets himself up as a successor to Herodotus, and Xenophon to Thucydides. Either grammarians or philosophers determined that Plato and Aristotle needed to be read; we admire their choice, much as we would like to have more writings of the Presocratics and Stoics. But

---

41   *Lives of the Orators* preserved in the appendix to Plutarch's *Moralia*, 841E.
42   Surprisingly recorded by Galen in his commentary on the *Epidemics* of Hippocrates, Kühn xvii.1.607.

because several different criteria were operative, many minor works came through also.

The whole enterprise of classical studies would be different if the holdings of the Library of Alexandria had been preserved entire or in part.[43] It would be more like the study of medieval or modern literature, where nobody can read everything, and both casual readers and scholars must rely initially on other people's judgement. Perhaps Greek literature would be *less* influential than now, since even its best works would seem more optional. But that imaginary contrast mirrors the actual relation of our present "canon" of Greek literature to the Hebrew Bible. For Jews, Christians and ordinary readers alike, the limitations of the Hebrew Bible make each book precious in a special way, over against the chaotic spread of even the Greek literature we do possess. If instead of our thirty-two Greek tragedies we had just the *Oedipus Rex* and thirty-two Hebrew works like *Job* (if indeed such ever existed...), the *Oedipus* would take on an even more absolute character, and we would find limitations in *Job* now invisible. The Hebrew Bible (and after it the New Testament) is comparatively so short and imposing that, even outside the communities where it is heard in a special sense as Revelation, it is taken in utmost seriousness as an object with no obvious parallel.

But this does not yet explain why the Greek canon was so much bigger than the Hebrew one in the first place. In part it is because the community of those who spoke Greek—from Massilia to Cyprus, from the Black Sea to Libya—was much bigger than the twelve tribes of Israel, or even than all those (including Carthaginians) who spoke a dialect of Canaanite. But it also has to do with differences between the Greek and Hebrew languages, and between the alphabetic scripts in which they were respectively expressed.

22.8.1 Memorizability of languages

Greek verse is much more memorizable than Hebrew. At I.47-48 we insisted that equally in Israel and Hellas all "literary" compositions existed primarily as oral performances. But long Greek compositions were easier to get by heart. Ion the rhapsode had *Iliad* and *Odyssey* by heart (Plato *Ion* 530B); in a few months a bright American twelve-

---

43 It is unclear how long any particular collections of the Library were preserved. Already in Caesar's siege of Alexandria in 48 BC some of the Library at least was burned (Plutarch *Caesar* 49.3; Dio Cassius 42.38.2); under Aurelian, AD 272, the library of the Bruchion was in large part destroyed (Ammianus 22.16.13-15).

year-old learned to recite *Iliad* 1.1-52 with good conventional pro-
nunication and moderate understanding. The reason is that Greek is
fully syllabic, and in hexameter (as in iambic) it has a form of verse
where varying syllabic patterns are controlled by an overall fixed
structure. Unlike the Sapphic stanza, paralleled in Sanskrit, dactylic
hexameter has no Indo-European parallels. But the obscure words in
hexameter, besides metrical anomalies only explained by an older form
of the language, show that it had a long previous history in Greek and
in the Aegean.

In contrast, the Hebrew short indistinct vowel (*shewa*) prevents any
syllabic analysis. (Syriac verse, which had the same problem, is supposed to have a syllabic pattern [III.141]; but it is surely on a Greek
model.) Hebrew verse is thought accentual, with patterns such as 3:3,
2:2, and (in the קִינָה or lament) 3:2; but poetical books vary greatly in
the accuracy of the accentual count, with Psalms among the most
irregular. A rare syllabic approximation to the Greek pattern will point
up the differences. Gen 9,6[44] "He who sheds the blood of man, by man
shall his blood be shed":

שֹׁפֵךְ דַּם הָאָדָם   בָּאָדָם דָּמוֹ יִשָּׁפֵךְ

šopḗk dám hɔ'ɔdɔ́m ‖ bɔ'ɔdɔ́m dɔmṓw yiššɔpḗk

has an elegant ABC:CBA pattern with B and C rhyming, and (by
chance or intention?) all full vowels. Its 6:8 pattern of syllables is
occasionally found in hexameter: see Hesiod *Opera* 348 "Not even an
ox would die, if it were not for a bad neighbor"[45]

οὐδ' ἂν | βοῦς ἀπόλοιτ' ‖ εἰ | μὴ γεί|των κακὸς | εἴη

The Hebrew line is easily memorizable, but isolated. It has no distinction of long and short syllables; and no vowel harmony, for of its 14
vowels, 8 are identical, the *qɔmɛṣ*. The Greek line is not especially
musical, but of its 14 vowels, there are 7 different, and the commonest,
ᾰ and ει, only occur 3 times each. The metrical pattern is commoner
in Latin. Vergil *Georg.* 2.490

félīx | quí potu-lít ‖ rē-|rúm cog-|nóscere | caúsās

(III.38), where further each of the six vowels under the ictus is different
(I.12).

Hebrew texts, both prose and verse, were undoubtedly recited orally
each in its appropriate context. But in contrast to Greek, both prose
and verse are broken up into short sections, memorizable by diligence
rather than by internal cues. As we saw (I.47) in our study of Jeremiah

---

44 Often previously cited here in other contexts: I.5, II.279, III.23.
45 West explains, "Friendly neighbors would often be able to prevent the loss of
    the animal by their own intervention or by timely warning."

36, for a longer recitation, particularly with a mixture of prose and verse, a scroll was essential as *aide-mémoire*. Alma-Tadema's notorious *A Recitation from Homer*,[46] besides other anachronisms (square Roman columns, doubled roses, public affection to a young *lady*) has the reciter use a scroll, which would have mortified Ion.[47]

22.8.2 Superiority of Greek script

Likewise differences in alphabetic scripts blocked large-scale composition in Hebrew but encouraged it in Greek. The deciding element is the appearance of the vowels in Greek script (I.41-43), derived in part from the vocalic offglides in Semitic script (i.e. diphthongs in -y and -w) but entered with full consistency. Several features of the Hebrew language as the Masoretes heard it made any simple marking of its vowels impractical. Classical Arabic (and in part Ugaritic) marks only three vowels *aiu*, with a further notation in Arabic for long vowels.[48] The vowel system of Phoenician is unknown. But Hebrew has seven vowel qualities (further modified by offglides), of which three also come short, in addition to the vocalic *shewa*. In the inflection of nouns and verbs, the vowels shift in complex patterns; the numerous variants show that oral usage fluctuated. It might have happened that the original writing system included vowels by imposing an artificial unity. It did not. From Phoenician or some predecessor Canaanite dialect, Hebrew, like Aramaic, adopted the 22-letter alphabet of consonants only, which unlike the vowels were extremely stable.[49] The frication of single stops after a vowel, although surely an old feature of the Hebrew dialect, did not block recognition of the stop and the fricative as to be represented by the same letter. As we saw (III.160), in Israel pressure for innovation had to be selective. Where the society could get by with what it found around it, it kept things unchanged; as with kingship and the sacrificing priesthood, so with the alphabet.

As a result, only simple Hebrew texts could be read aloud from a previously unseen document (I.49-50).[50] Our Phoenician inscriptions,

---

46 1885, Philadelphia Museum of Art.
47 Alma-Tadema, I am sure without knowing it, comes closer to restoring an Homeric recitation in *Roman* Greece.
48 Emphatic consonants in Arabic color the vowels following, but the script has never marked this feature of the language, and the coloration is never phonemic.
49 Probably in fact Hebrew had more than 22 consonantal sounds (II.324), and the scribes improvised with the alphabet they were given.
50 See now the English version of S. Levin's fundamental article, "The 'Qeri' as the Primary Text of the Hebrew Bible," *General Linguistics* 35 (1997) 181-223, ed. J. P. Brown (Levin Festschrift).

which modern scholars believe we mostly understand, were perhaps intended as simple texts. But Ugaritic verse, comparable to Hebrew, must conceal many subtleties forever lost for its want of vowels. If the book of Job had been transmitted without vowels, nobody could understand it even so far as we do today, nor read it out aloud. As a result, as Levin has shown, each book of the Hebrew Bible required for its preservation—that is, for its ongoing oral recitation—a *double tradition*: the written text which reminded the reciter of the unpredictable materials coming next; and an oral tradition of the pronunciation, above all of the vowels.

Now Hebrew society was a small one, with limited specialization of function. Each division of our Hebrew Bible was the property of one group in society: the books of the Law, probably of the priests; the Former Prophets, perhaps of court historians; the three major prophets, each of a group of disciples like Jeremiah's Baruch; Proverbs (I have suggested) of a banker class; Psalms of some Temple functionaries. But most of the groups were not full-time scribes or grammarians. Each had the double task of safeguarding the written text of their book, and of teaching young men to pronounce it exactly according to the received tradition. The total of 24 books must then represent about the maximum that Israelite society could find custodians for. When a new composition like the Book of Job came on the scene, it must either be rejected or completely assimilated.

The contrast with Greek compositions is then clear. The very earliest Greek scrolls, it is true, were not all that easy to read from either. The lines may have been βουστροφηδόν "as an ox plows a field" (I.11), the first beginning at the right, the second at the left, and so on; there were no word divisions, the lines of verse were probably unmarked. West in his *Works and Days* p. 60 creates a sample of what its first text may have looked like.[51] But the indispensable phonetic feature of the vowels was present. A reciter, faced with such a scroll even of an unfamiliar text, had two sets of data previously internalized: the patterns of the hexameter, and the two or three possible accentuations of a word with known letters. After having heard the *Works and Days* or a book of Homer a few times, he would have the sounds recalled to his mind by the written text, since most of its phonetic features were represented there somehow. The most important function of the written text was as a corrective of creative or unintentional oral changes. The prose of Herodotus or Thucydides would seem a tougher nut to crack. But long prose texts, written later, must have been set out more

---

51   But Levin thinks the early poetic scrolls were already easier to read than this.

clearly; and their transmission by itself shows that their script was lucid enough for the reader—people read aloud even to themselves—to proceed through the text at normal speed, and provide it with the proper word-divisions and accents. The particles marked the pauses—they were put into the original oral text for precisely that purpose.

Thus the character of the Hebrew canon was the product of several factors all working in the same direction. Its mandatory character was in part the result of its small size. Its small size was due to (1) the small size of the community that preserved it; (2) the resistance of Hebrew texts to memorization; (3) the defects of the writing system, which required a separate dual tradition of each preserved work. Likewise in reverse for the Greek "canon." Its more nearly optional character was in part the result of its large size. Its large size was due to (1) the widespread geographical spread of its writers and custodians; (2) the memorizability of Greek verse; (3) the merit of the writing system, which did not require prior hearing to the comprehension of a written verse or prose text.

22.8.3 The canon of the New Testament

The New Testament, although written in Greek, looks more like a compact Hebrew compilation than an expansive Greek one. But soon enough, in the Greek, Latin and Syriac churches, a very copious literature sprang up, larger than the preserved body of pagan Greek and Latin literature, perhaps also than the Rabbinic. In the judgement of its own authors, as in the judgement of their contemporaries and of moderns, this work is commentary on an original which infinitely surpasses them. Augustine's *Confessions* stands by itself for many centuries as a book running parallel to the New Testament with a narrative of experience. Although the defects of the Hebrew writing system no longer blocked the production of the earliest Christian literature, the mere fact of the limited Hebrew canon seemingly operated to keep the New Testament down to size. Further, it came from a small community with not many natural writers in a very few generations.

The formation of the New Testament canon generated what today we *mean* by a "book": the codex. Perhaps at first each book of the New Testament was written on a scroll—smaller than the scrolls of the 24 books of the Hebrew Bible, as befitted a community on the road. But the first witnesses to the New Testament text, the papyri from Egypt, are written in a new format, the codex—the form of our printed books today—which then spread to all Greek and Latin books, and eventually most Jewish ones also.[52] From Christians or Moslems the Masoretes took the idea of a non-sacred codex to record their pronunciation of the text, while scrolls of the Torah went on containing just the sacred consonants. Levin explains the advantages of the codex in the new situation:[53]

> For many generations the leading Christians were chiefly adult converts from pagan worship.[54] That circumstance disposed them all the more to a book form that made the entire text quickly accessible.... In exegetical works above all, where they were commenting on a given holy book, they needed other relevant passages to prove or confirm their point.

Roberts & Skeat, while doubting this argument, provide additional support for it (p. 50):

> ...one thinks of Augustine in the famous 'Tolle, lege' episode [*Conf.* 8.(12).28], when he kept a finger in the codex of the Pauline Epistles to mark the place of the providential passage he had found.

And so Augustine (*Conf.* 4.[3.]5) *de paginis poetae cuiuspiam...cum forte quis consulit* "When by chance one consults the *pages* of a certain poet."[55] For any Church use—the Gospel locally received, Paul's letters—there was pressure to have a single codex.

In two respects then the New Testament *reflects* its Palestinian setting: in spite of all appearances it turns out to be a non-tragedy (22.7.2) like the Hebrew Bible; it likewise has a small closed canon. In two respects it *breaks* with both Israel and Hellas: in principle it has no need for a definition of insiders (22.7.3), and therefore ultimately no need for a definition of outsiders; its enlarged language about God (22.7.1) goes beyond both. Its use of the Greek language reflects a later development in Hellas: not just as the common tongue of the Greek city-states, but the new function of Greek as the instrument of imperialism, first of Macedon, then of Alexander's successors, then finally of Rome.

---

52 Colin H. Roberts & T. C. Skeat, The Birth of the Codex; London: British Academy, 1983; 38-41. They list eleven Christian Biblical papyrus manuscripts which they judge to be of the second century CE; all are in codex form.
53 Saul Levin, "From Scrolls to Codex: The Ancient and the Medieval Book," Mediaevalia 12 (1989 [for 1986]) 1-12, esp. p. 4.
54 [I would add that many converts had passed through an intermediate stage as "God-fearers" in the Hellenistic synaogue. JPB]
55 The SHA *Hadrian* 2.8 has Hadrian consult the *Vergilianas sortes* to discern Trajan's attitude towards him, and end up with a passage in Book 6. This presupposes a codex, for unrolling a scroll you would know just about what you were getting; but this authority is unreliable, and I wonder if the *Aeneid* existed in codex form in the early second century CE.

22.9 Translatability of Hebrew and Greek texts

What does it say about a text in one language that its key features are translatable into another—easily? with difficulty? hardly at all? I have heard that the Russian of Tolstoy and Dostoievsky is not so essential as to render the English versions seriously defective; certainly the story-line comes through with abundant clarity. It might seem that the elegant linguistic structure of Shakespeare renders him less translatable. But the German version of August Wilhelm von Schlegel and Ludwig Tieck (1796-1833) has so won the day that Germans tend to think of Shakespeare as a poet of their own language! For one thing, all agree in the supremacy and variety of his characterization, which no translation can spoil. But further this is also because "die Stammesverwandtschaft des deutschen und englischen Idioms mächtig zu Hilfe kam."[56] *Tempest* IV.i Folio:

> And like the baseless fabricke of this vision
> The Clowd-capt Towres, the gorgeous Pallaces,
> The solemne Temples, the great Globe it selfe,
> Yea, all which it inherit, shall dissolue,
> And like this insubstantiall Pageant faded
> Leaue not a rack behinde: we are such stuffe
> As dreames are made on; and our little life
> Is rounded with a sleepe...

Schlegel:

> Wie dieses Scheines lockrer Bau, so werden
> Die wolkenhohen Türme, die Paläste,
> Die hehren Tempel, selbst der grosse Ball,
> Ja, was daran nur teil hat, untergehn;
> Und, wie dies leere Schaugepräng' erblasst,
> Spurlos verschwinden. Wir sind solcher Zeug
> Wie der zu Träumen, und dies kleine Leben
> Umfasst ein Schlaf...

The two metrics run parallel, with an extra syllable at the end where the vocabulary warrants it. The most conspicuous loss is the Latinism *insubstantiall*, which German has no good parallel for. On the same grounds, both Greek prose and verse ought to have been quite translatable into Latin. And in fact, the meters of verse were taken over and

---

56 Wilhelm Dechelhäufer, W. Shakespeare's dramatische Werke; übersetzt von August Wilhelm von Schlegel und Ludwig Tieck; 13th ed.; Stuttgart etc.: Deutsche Verlags-Anstalt; ca. 1891; p. XI.

if anything improved; but Roman writers and poets set themselves other tasks than the translation of Greek.

For the Greek church of the East, the Bible is the Septuagint plus the Greek New Testament, in uneasy coexistence with the texts of pagan Hellas. For the Latin church of the West, the Bible is Jerome's Vulgate, in uneasy coexistence with the texts of pagan Rome. Jerome's Old Testament is a more adequate and nobler version than the Septuagint; his Gospels often unconsciously restore the lapidary brevity of the underlying Aramaic. In both Testaments his excellence springs from his guilty knowledge of the Latin classics.

Greek texts were never fully translated into Latin: the western Middle Ages knew Aristotle best. The key event was the capture of Constantinople by French and Venetian crusaders in AD 1204. It appears that from there Greek MSS were brought west as far as to England. The victors set up Latin principalities in Greece and appointed their own bishops there; and the land was opened to western scholars. The Britisher John Basingstoke took lessons in Athens from one Constantina, to whom remarkable psychic powers were attributed, daughter of an archbishop of Athens.[57] On his return he translated a Greek grammar into Latin ("*Donatus Graecorum*," not extant?); in 1235 he was Archdeacon of Leicester and a friend of Robert Grosseteste, bishop of Lincoln, who probably learned Greek from him.[58] From some such underground source the Fleming William of Moerboke also learned Greek, became the Pope's contact with the Eastern church, and at the end of his life (ab. 1278-1286) was the Latin archbishop of Corinth.[59]

The *Nicomachean Ethics* of Aristotle were first completely translated by Grosseteste about 1245; the *Politics* by Moerboke (who had previously translated most of Aristotle's works on logic) about 1260. There is a large MS tradition of these medieval translations. When Aquinas quotes rather than paraphrases Aristotle we can mostly pinpoint the version. Thus he quotes[60] the *Eth. Nic.* 1132a22 as *iudex est iustum animatum*; the Greek is ὁ γὰρ δικαστὴς βούλεται εἶναι οἷον δίκαιον ἔμψυχον "for the judge wishes to be as it were living justice,"

---

57 This archbishop must be one of the latter Greek archbishops of Athens, listed at DHGE v.22 s.v. "Athènes," either displaced by the Frankish bishop or maintaining a shadowy claim to legitimacy.

58 Dictionary of National Biography; Oxford: University, vol. i (1917), 1274-1275.

59 L. Minio-Paluello, art. "Moerbeke, William of" in Dictionary of Scientific Biography ix.434-440; New York: Scribners, 1974.

60 *Summa Theol.* Secunda Secundae, quaest. 58, art. 1 ad quintum.

where Grosseteste[61] *iudex enim vult esse velud iustum animatum.*
Elsewhere[62] he quotes *Pol.* 1252b28 as *perfecta enim communitas
civitas est*; the Greek is ἡ δ' ἐκ πλειόνων κωμῶν κοινωνία τέλειος πόλις
"the perfect partnership composed of several villages is the Polis,"
where already the *translatio imperfecta* attributed to Moerboke has[63]
ex pluribus vicis communitas perfecta civitas. When the Clerk of
Oxenford has

> Twenty bookes, clad in blak or reed,
> Of Aristotle and his philosophie

these are expensive bound Latin manuscripts of Moerboke's versions,
for the subject is *logyk.*

In the three hundred years after Grosseteste and Moerboke, Greek
achieved an overwhelming role in education. Roger Ascham was tutor
to princess Elizabeth (born 1533) as a teenager from 1550-1552; and
speaks of her later:[64]

> ...our most noble Queen Elizabeth, who never took yet Greek nor Latin
> grammar in her hand, after the first declining of a noun and a verb; but only
> by this double translating [to English and back again] of Demosthenes and
> Isocrates daily, without missing every forenoon, and likewise some part of
> Tully [Cicero] every afternoon, for the space of a year or two, hath attained
> to such a perfect understanding in both the tongues, and to such a ready
> utterance of the Latin, and that with such a judgment, as they be few in
> number in both the universities, or elsewhere in England, that be in both
> tongues comparable with her majesty.

(But Ascham might not have reported it if the Princess ever sulked, or
played hooky, or muffed a translation....) He runs through her praises
at the time in a letter to Sturm, April 4, 1550 (Old Style),[65] in which
he speaks of her *ingenium sine muliebri mollitia, labor cum virili
constantia*; and adds that the morning began with the New Testament
and included Sophocles.

---

61   *Aristoteles Latinus* xxvi.1—3.3 p. 234.
62   *Summa Theol.* Prima Secundae, quaest. 90, art. 2 ad finem.
63   *Aristoteles Latinus* xxix.1 p. 5. The full Latin translation of the *Politics*,
      unquestionably done by William of Moerboke, is critically edited from the
      MSS by F. Susemihl parallel to the Greek in his major edition *Aristotelis
      Politicorum Libri Octo cum uetusta translatione Guilelmi de Moerbeka*; Leip-
      zig: Teubner 1872. For the translation is so exact that the readings of the
      underlying Greek MS are mostly discernible—an excellent witness, several
      centuries older than our extant MSS.
64   In his *Schoolmaster*, ed. Giles, Whole Works: London, 1864 iii.180, repr. New
      York: AMS, 1965.
65   Giles i.191.

For an age when both Hebrew and Greek texts were translated into a vernacular we go to that same sixteenth century. In the later Middle Ages there was a thin stream of knowledge of Hebrew, mostly derived from Jewish converts; it was much augmented when the Jews were expelled from Spain, 1492. Northern Europe is the key; for there the Latin Vulgate is rejected in favor of new translations, which, above all in England and Germany, formed the basis of a renewed vernacular literature. The rediscovery of the Bible in the Protestant Reformation of northern Europe comes nearly at the same time as the Italian Renaissance of classical, and in particular Greek, learning.

Luther's German New Testament was published in 1522 and his complete Bible in 1534. Parts of William Tyndale's Old Testament (with some use at least of the Hebrew) were published in 1530 and 1537, parts copied by Myles Coverdale in 1535. Genesis 3 in Tyndale's version will show how it set the standard for all that followed:[66]

> But the serpent was sotyller than all the beastes of the felde which ẙ LORDE God had made / and sayd unto the woman, Ah syr [!] / that God hath sayd / ye shall not eate of all manner trees in the garden. And the woman sayd unto the serpent / of the frute of the trees in the garden we may eate / but of the frute of the tree ẙ is in the myddes of the garden (sayd God) se that ye eate not / and se that ye touch it not: lest ye dye.

The successive versions won the heart of English-speaking people, both as the newly provided text of the religion they had long professed, and as the standard of their own language.

The Gospels and the Revelation of John, as sharing the Semitic substructure of the Hebrew Bible, found equal resonance in English; Acts as a flowing narrative presented little difficulty either. Paul's letters and especially Romans, in spite of Luther's championing of them, are true Greek texts and difficult ones at that, and in many versions come out crabbed. A few classical Greek *prose* texts found adequate translations at nearly the same time as the English Bible and remained influential. North's Plutarch (1579, second hand from a French version) underlies Shakespeare's *Julius Caesar* and *Antony and Cleopatra*[67] and contributes much to their elegance. Sometimes the poet had nothing to do but an easy versification:

---

66 David Daniell (ed.), Tyndale's Old Testament...In a modern-spelling edition; New Haven: Yale, 1992; I restore Tyndale's spelling from Daniell's plate of the Pentateuch of 1530.

67 See especially North's version of Cleopatra in her barge, lightly adapted by Shakespeare and from him by Eliot in *The Waste Land*.

Furthermore, there was a certaine Soothsayer that had geven Caesar warning long time affore, to take heede of the day of the Ides of Marche, (which is the fifteenth of the moneth) for on that day he shoulde be in great daunger. That day being come, Caesar going unto the Senate house, and speaking merily to the Soothsayer, tolde him, The Ides of Marche be come: So be they, softly aunswered the Soothsayer, but yet are they not past.

Thomas Hobbes published his translation of Thucydides in 1629; he found much in the Greek (we may assume) that he already believed, and took more from it. A recent study[68] finds Thucydides deeper than his translator:

> Is it realistic [with Hobbes] to assume that all people act predictably, that they are always guided strictly by self-interest, that all other motivations are a sham—or, if genuine, so rare that to take them into account is useless? ...According to Thucydides, human beings are multifaceted, so that it becomes necessary, for example, to examine individual leaders and to listen seriously to their reasons for acting a certain way.

But Hobbes so resonated with the historian that his interpretations continue to hold the field. We may compare Hobbes' manly version of the Melian Dialogue (5.105.1) with Rex Warner's (III.7):

> For of the gods we think according to the common opinion; and of men, that for certain by necessity of nature they will every where reign over such as they are too strong for. Neither did we make this law, nor are we the first that use it made: but as we found it, and shall leave it to posterity for ever, so also we use it: knowing that you likewise, and others that should have the same power which we have, would do the same.

In English (I cannot speak for German) the translations of Greek *verse* accentuate the peculiarities and faults of each age. Chapman's *Iliad* (1616), which Keats found a "pure serene," for us is Elizabethan bombast with its seven-beat lines and rhyme:

Achilles' banefull wrath resound, O Goddesse, that imposd
Infinite sorrowes on the Greekes, and many brave soules losd
From breasts Heroique—sent them farre, to that invisible cave
That no light comforts; and their lims to dogs and vultures gave.

Here "resound" replaces ἄειδε "sing," "breasts" is padding, Ἄϊδι gets a popular (but uncertain) etymology, and "lims" replaces αὐτούς "themselves." Pope's version (1715) is hardly a translation, but a whole new

---

68   Laurie M. Johnson, Thucydides, Hobbes, and the Interpretation of Realism; De Kalb: Northern Illinois Univ. Press, 1993; 201-203.

construction of images, built distantly on the Greek narrative: "It is a pretty poem, Mr Pope, but you must not call it Homer":[69]

> Achilles' wrath, to Greece the direful spring
> Of woes unnumber'd, heav'nly Goddess, sing!
> That wrath which hurl'd to Pluto's gloomy reign
> The souls of mighty chiefs untimely slain:
> Whose limbs, unburied on the naked shore,
> Devouring dogs and hungry vultures tore...

"Limbs" and "vultures" show that Pope had Chapman before him. Homer is read in the twentieth century through translations which are at least accurate, line-by-line, and idiomatic, like Richmond Lattimore's (1951), but hardly memorizable:

> Sing, goddess, the anger of Peleus' son Achilleus
> and its devastation, which put pains thousandfold upon the
>   Achaians,
> hurled in their multitudes to the house of Hades strong souls
> of heroes, but gave their bodies to be the delicate feasting
> of dogs, of all birds...

But here *hurled* still reflects Pope.

English versions of tragedy in the late 18th and 19th centuries are even more precious and mannered than of epic; in the 20th century even less singable or memorizable.[70] Still, only in our century have educators felt obliged to make Greek books widely available to the cultivated reader, whereas in the 16th century there was a growing cry for Hebrew books (along with the Greek New Testament) to be accessible to men, women and children in the pews. And it is intrinsically harder to spoil Hebrew than Greek. To our ears the Septuagint did its best to spoil Hebrew, but the New Testament writers—all steeped in the Septuagint—turned it into a people's mode of expression. Modern versions of the English Bible have successively watered down the elevation of the Authorized Version, and the vogue of inclusiveness has rejected the goal of accuracy which originally motivated the new translations. Greek epic and tragedy until recently brought out the worst instincts of translators; today, only their incapacities. The structure of Hebrew narrative comes from the unavoidable sequence of events; Greek adds antitheses and (in epic) the verse-pattern. My own translations in these volumes follow the least objectionable patterns available, and strive for nothing more than a mediocre accuracy.

---

69   Richard Bentley, in Samuel Johnson's *Life* of Pope.
70   See Eliot's critique of translations in "Euripides and Professor Murray," Selected Essays 1917-1932; New York: Harcourt Brace, 1932; 46-50.

What does this tell us about Hebrew and Greek texts in the worlds of their origination? The only narratives in Ugaritic are mythical verse; Hebrews surely rejected any models they might have found in Akkadian literature. If we imagine Hebrew narrative coming out of hill-villages remote from Canaanite cultural influence, we can only conclude that isolation and a dawning sense of freedom brought into being a wholly new level of transcription for popular stories and sagas. The figures of Hebrew narrative are archetypes we instantly recognize: apart from a few abstract terms of psychology or ethics, the vocabulary is of concrete nouns and verbs whose translation into other languages is as near as possible automatic. The Greek of the New Testament narratives, in view of its Semitic background, has many of the same features. Only at the end of a long Greek prose development did Plutarch approach a comparable level of simplicity. The excellence of Hobbes' Thucydides is a shining exception.

Besides its built-in difficulty, Greek verse had complex antecedents. Behind the Homeric epics we can discern a background of shorter lays in somewhat different dialects, but in the same old metrical form, though not as such known elsewhere in Indo-European. The elaborate structure of Greek drama, both tragic and comic, with its variety of meters, dialects and styles, requires an extensive prior history. In Hebrew, lack of defined syllables, meter, vowel harmony as vehicle of expression means that *less is lost* in translation (for there is less to be lost). Likewise the New Testament is eminently translatable for the same reason as Plutarch. This does not mean that the Hebrew Bible is less deep or universal than Greek works, just that it has fewer secrets. (But I should add that there are many more Hebrew phrases we simply do not understand, for want of parallels.) Thus a paradox: the clannish and isolated Hebrews produced a more generally accessible work than the outgoing Greeks! Hebrew verse texts, though less memorizable than Greek, are more translatable.

But it is not the sole (though the final) task of literature to show what humanity may become; a necessary preliminary task is to define also what humanity is. While people in readiness to hear the Biblical texts hear them correctly, and pattern their lives according to them; people not so ready, or with distorted psyches, hear them incorrectly and do much damage. Indispensable to undoing the damage is the laborious work of scholarship, trained (normally) on other texts, classical or indigenous. So a further item in the complementarity is the relative accessibility (in translation) of the books of Israel (including the New Testament); and the greater precision of the texts of Hellas, necessary in training people how to read such books.

22.10 Reciprocal takeover of attributes

Although today in the West the heritage of Israel is seen as religious faith, and of Hellas as scientific reason, this was not so clear in the first centuries of our era. Directly after the formation of the New Testament, each society takes on features of the other. Thus the large fact of *Greek religion* has a sociological continuation in the Church. The cathedral of Syracuse incorporates the Doric columns of the temple of Athena Nike of the fifth century BC; the Romans built the columns into walls; the Christian basilica changed at least internal arrangements; under Islam a minaret was built;[71] the eighteenth century added a rococo façade. Each successive cult involved processions, singing, vestments, a contrast between leaders and people.

More generally, Greek civilization is built on the necessity of *myth*. In Chapter 19 we saw how much more strongly than Hebrews, Greeks needed to find a sequence of better lands, offering blessedness first to heroic figures, then to all. Plato ends his major dialogues with a myth concretely supporting the theoretical conclusions of the discussion. The myth of the *Phaedo* (I.87-88) agrees in two contrasting elements with Israel: human beings around the Mediterranean like ants or frogs around a marsh; over against them a better world of jasper and emerald. And wherever we could make a comparison like this, it was always Hellas that had fantastic elements, merging true and ideal geography, while Israel retains a dignified realism in descriptions of the earth, and a sober transcendence about its God.

As Greek ultimate affirmations rest on Mediterranean myth, parallel to Hebrew-Phoenician ones and in part derived from them, so Rabbinic exegesis rests on a basis parallel to Greek logic and Roman law, perhaps derived from them. To give the Greeks exclusive credit for an inheritance of Reason ignores the logical principles developed by the Rabbis to interpret the Torah.[72] Some themes they pick up are illustrated in Plato *Laws* 7.793AB (Daube 243). It begins with a distinction between ἄγραφα νόμιμα "unwritten customs" and τῶν

---

71   That is my recollection from a visit in summer 1960, but I cannot easily verify it.

72   Lee I. Levine, Judaism and Hellenism in Antiquity: Conflict or Confluence?; Seattle: Univ. of Washington Press, 1998; 113-116 briefly discusses two positions on the degree to which the Rabbis borrowed from Greco-Roman thought. He calls Saul Lieberman a "minimalist": Hellenism in Jewish Palestine; New York: Jewish Theol. Sem. of America, 5711/1950; "Rabbinic Interpretation of Scripture," 47-82. He calls David Daube a "maximalist": "Rabbinic Methods of Interpretation and Hellenistic Rhetoric," HUCA 22 (1949) 239-264.

[νόμων] ἐν γράμμασιν τεθέντων "written laws";[73] and goes on that "very old ancestral customs when properly founded and become habitual, acting as a shield hold subsequently written laws in full safety": πάτρια καὶ παντάπασιν ἀρχαῖα νόμιμα, ἃ καλῶς μὲν τεθέντα καὶ ἐθισθέντα πάσῃ σωτηρίᾳ περικαλύψαντα ἔχει τοὺς τότε γραφέντας νόμους. A heathen asked Shammai (Bab. Talm. *Shabb.* 31a) "How many Torahs (כמה תורות do you have?" and he answered "Two, written and oral":

שתים תורה שבכתב ותורה שבעל פה

ʿAqiba (*Avoth* III.14), defining more closely *Avoth* I.1 (our I.161) said "Tradition is a fence to the Law," מסורת סיג לתורה.

The seven exegetical principles of Hillel (Tosefta *Sanhedrin* 7:11; *Sifra* introd.) owe something to Hellenistic-Roman logic. —In particular the first, קל וחומר "Light and Heavy," i.e. *a minori ad maius*: "If P holds in the trivial case A, *how much more so* in the weighty case B." Again at Bab. Talm. *Shabb.* 31a Hillel brings a proselyte to reason קל וחומר on Num 1,51: a stranger (הַזָּר, where Hillel includes even king David) who approaches the tabernacle is put to death; and the proselyte concludes "how much more one like myself!" At about the same time the logic appears in pagan Greek: Diodorus 1.1.2, when fictitious mythology about Hades begets piety, "how much more (πόσῳ μᾶλλον) does history, the prophetess of truth (τὴν προφῆτιν τῆς ἀληθείας) and metropolis of all philosophy (τῆς ὅλης φιλοσοφίας οἱονεὶ μητρόπολιν)" build character![74] It is striking in the New Testament. Luk 12,28 (cf 11,13) "If God so clothes the grass of the field, how much more (πόσῳ μᾶλλον) you?" where Pesh כמא יתיר, Vg *quanto magis*. Rom 11,12 "If the fall [of the Jews] is the wealth of the world...how much more (πόσῳ μᾶλλον) their fulfilment?" The NT usage is often taken as reflection of the Rabbinic logic; but I suggest that both it and the Rabbinic ultimately are from Latin: Cicero *de Oratore* 3.213 *quanto ...magis admiraremini si audissetis ipsum* "How much more would you have marveled if you had heard [Demosthenes] in person?" Still, Rabbinic logic, whatever its source, was deeply internalized.[75] The Euro-

---

73 Aristotle (*Rhet.* 1.13.2 = 1373b5) divides law (νόμον) into ἄγραφον and γεγραμμένον. Rabbinic borrows the first word in a whole Greek sentence, unattested in Greek and perhaps parodied or misunderstood:

פרא בסיליאוס נומוס אגרפוס

(Jer. Talm. *Rosh hash.* 57a75 bottom), i.e. παρὰ βασιλέως νόμος ἄγραφος "For the King, the law might as well not have been written down, he need only observe it if he wishes to."

74 See Josephus *BJ* 2.365.

75 We saw (II.214, 278) that a parallel development of legal logic leads from the case-by-case style of the Roman XII Tables and the Covenant Code of Exodus

pean Jewish community, its intellect practiced by those centuries of exegesis, led the modern world in various enterprises: rational philosophy with Spinoza, economics and sociology with Marx, psychology with Freud, physics with Einstein.

22.11 Faith and reason

Today the polarity between Israel and Hellas is mostly seen as one between religion and science, faith and reason. An influential and in places helpful treatment of the theme "Faith and Reason" appears in an encyclical (September 15, 1998) of John Paul II.[76] The contrast is partly a simplification in view of the realms where each society trespasses on the presumed monopoly of the other. The two concepts nearly fall together in Hebrew, where "truth" (אֱמֶת) comes from the root אמן "be reliable," as is clear from the form Ps 91,4 אֲמִתּוֹ "[God's] reliability," LXX ἡ ἀλήθεια αὐτοῦ, Vg *ueritas eius*. Thus at I Reg 22,16 Ahab says to Micaiah, "How many times shall I adjure you that you should speak nothing to me but the truth in the name of Yahweh?"

אֲשֶׁר לֹא־תְדַבֵּר אֵלַי רַק־אֱמֶת

LXX ὅπως λαλήσῃς πρός με ἀλήθειαν, Vg *ut non loquaris mihi nisi quod uerum est*. Greek ἀληθής "true" does not have the modern connotation of something's being in conformity with the real world, but of its unavoidability, "that which cannot escape notice."

Still current perceptions are historical facts with their own legitimacy. Until recently in Europe and the United States, "faith" *meant* the profession of Judaism or Christianity; and still today communities here adhering to Islam, Buddhism, Hinduism are seen as to some degree alien. And even more so "reason" *means* the habits of thought derived from Greek philosophers—as filtered through Latin understanding. To discuss the truth or falsity of the insights in the ancient Near Eastern empires would be waste effort; we know too much about their restricted social systems. Does that mean that Hebrew or Greek insights likewise should be considered outmoded? It might seem that the question arises principally with Jewish-Christian faith; and that the process of reasoning, once grasped by the Greeks, is mandatory and unchanging. But our theme of complementarity suggests that the two should be more nearly parallel.

---

to the codifications, contemporary with each other, of the Roman lawyer Gaius and the Mishna.

76 Printed in Origins: CNS Documentary Service, Oct. 22 1998, vol. 28: no. 19. The English translation is due to the Vatican, and appears to have the same authenticity as the Latin original *Fides et Ratio*, which I have not looked up.

Today relations are the exact opposite of what they were in the later Middle Ages. *Then* society was based on a generally accepted system of belief, and secular Greek rationalism was only just making its way. *Today* Christian (and Jewish) belief is marginalized as a private choice, while Greek rational thought seems everywhere triumphant. In the United States, government must everywhere permit, but nowhere authorize, the places of worship where a transcendent source of justice is proclaimed. And even though the study of the classical languages has retreated, Greek literature in translation is the solidest part of the university canon (such as it is...), with the English Bible as a very optional extra.

If we take the present situation as a permanent state of affairs, the whole enterprise of these volumes is put under a cloud. For it would mean that the breakout of Israel from the ancient Near East, though admirable in many ways, was still darkened with the uncritical beliefs of its origins; and that only the Greeks were sufficiently distant to throw off their pantheon, god by god, and (with much backsliding into myth!) move towards a full reliance on reason. Here our historical study throws us back to look at ourselves. In *my* best understanding, does reason, carried through sufficiently far, demand to be completed by an affirmation of faith? or does it leave faith as an optional or arbitrary supplement to itself?—the position which faith occupies in all of American law, and in much American practice. (But Presidential candidates must belong to a Christian church; most weddings are performed by clergy; department stores, if they wish to end the year in the black, play Christmas carols in December.)

We may here settle for a minimum definition of faith: affirmation of a providential God watching over events. For early Israelites with an indefinite future ahead, it was enough to affirm that continuance of their family in ongoing time was thereby secured. In the formative period of Judaism and the New Testament, when the final destruction of the Temple and the dispersal of the Jewish people were in the cards, Providence required further a symbolism of the resurrection of the body. For us likewise, with the certainty that life on this planet, even if prolonged for millions of years, will eventually be wiped out by a dying sun, it may still require something more than even the continuance of history over that period. To affirm the values in a secularized Hellenism or Judaism, celebrating their human cultures but rejecting what they say about God or the gods, blessed lands or the restoration of the dead, is much less than they affirmed about themselves. If that is all our famous Greco-Roman or Jewish-Christian heritage amounts to, we are being given a much reduced inheritance by the probate court of history. We do not have a long enough view to know whether either tradition will continue to blossom if it is so far cut off from its roots; or whether humanity will be psychically able to continue its enterprise if all it can see ahead, near or far, is a blank wall.

We said (III.154) that the enterprises of those two old societies are continued among us in two places: classroom and congregation. They teach and pass on, respectively, the use of logic and the use of trust. In a kind of meta-logic and meta-trust, let us ask what functions they perform in our society. They are parallel and contrasted: each relies on books handed down from its mother society to train contemporaries in urgent tasks likewise inherited from it. They are equally inevitable structures of our society. In their graciousness they freely make those books available for private study, and many people do learn calculus and read the Bible on their own, or home-school their children. People in a society without classrooms or congregations would not have those options. The teaching may be poorly or well done; the congregation may be formed on too narrow or broad a basis. But if a community abandons traditional formats it must improvise, and its improvisations will not be better than what they replaced. —And classroom and congregation each has a style. While the style can be learned by self-study, it is the group which preserves and carries the style on. We have near-universal agreement that the style of the classroom is indeed indispensable for approaching the problems and tasks of our society with commitment and understanding. Is the style of the congregation equally a necessary prerequisite for something?

It used to be taken for granted that membership in the congregation was the necessary prerequisite for a sound family structure, training children (and parents too) in responsibility. Today families alienated from the old congregations, or unaware of them, are doing about as well as the meeting-goers. Perhaps everything would run downhill if the congregations simply disappeared—an unlikely event, as most sociologists would agree. It used to be taken for granted that the congregations were the organ of society from which aid went out to the poor, hungry, sick, suffering. Since then government first took on those tasks, then dropped a number of them, asking the congregations to fill in the gap. But the homeless, hungry, mentally disturbed walking the streets present a bigger task than congregational charity can easily take on.

Marx in the last of his eleven Theses on Feuerbach[77] says: "Die Philosophen haben die Welt nur verschieden *interpretiert*, es kömmt

---

77   Written in 1845, not published until 1888 (by Engels); often taken as a summary of Marx's essential insights.

drauf an, sie zu *verändern*." The world is changed in many ways by many agents—governments, corporations, wars, revolutions.... The changes that do the least damage, and have the brightest future, are those brought by people working out of faith communities by nonviolent direct action for new levels of justice. Susan B. Anthony (1820-1906) out of a Quaker heritage participated in the three great women's tasks of the nineteenth century: temperance to rescue their menfolks from drunkenness; abolition of slavery; their own suffrage. Gandhi from his Hindu background (with a little help from British thought) discovered a peaceful way for a people to recover its autonomy. The American revulsion against the war in Viet Nam elicited Buddhist allies who thought as we did. César Chavez carried the banner of the Lady of Guadalupe to campaign for the rights of farmworkers. Martin Luther King Jr out of the Black church, Dorothy Day and the Berrigan brothers out of Irish Catholicism, did what we know. As technology, law, physics, healing only arise from a place where reason is allowed free play; so the grassroots commitment to peace, justice and the integrity of creation (in the formula of the World Council of Churches) only arise from the heart of faith communities. That is less a theoretical doctrine than an observational fact. Direct action on a purely secular base tends to be grim, austere; faith adds an indispensable *joy*. People have the option of dispensing with the classroom and the faith communities in their own lives; society as a whole will either nurture both or do without their products.

With respect to the ancient Near Eastern empires, we saw, the two societies of Hellas and Israel grew up, respectively, just outside and just inside. Since nothing ever fully dies, modern states to some degree inherit the status of those empires: our law and the very concept of law is Roman; Rome historically continued the imperialist techniques invented by those regimes. Correspondingly then the two free traditions ever since maintain something of their original stance over against the inheritors of those original empires here. The Greek tradition of reason looks at our institutions in guidance and critique as from the *outside*; the Hebrew-Christian tradition of faith in guidance and critique as from the *inside*.

We have been so well trained by the classroom and our Hellenic tradition of logic generally that the first thing we ask, when we come to face the Hebraic tradition of faith in the congregation, is "Is it *true*?" That question is more in the style of the classroom than of the congregation. But also, the validity of scientific theories developed in the laboratory and classroom is judged by their results: does relativity or the proposed structure of DNA explain observed facts? Then it should be fair to say, The validity of an insight nurtured in the congregation of faith is judged by its results: the campaign for change that flows from it. If such campaigns for change are necessary for the continuance of our society in justice, and if (as seems to be the case) they emerge primarily from faith communities, the faith of such communities is a necessary structure of our society.

Chapter 23: The Foreign Vocabulary of Jesus' Aramaic[1]

The full confluence of Israel and Hellas comes in the New Testament, a Greek record of a Jewish movement. Its Semitic grounding is restored by its translation into dialects of Aramaic: the Syriac of Edessa, first in two unpointed MSS of the Gospels,[2] and then the complete New Testament, the Peshitto;[3] later a Palestinian dialect version of the Gospels in Syriac script.[4] Of all the New Testament strata, at least the sayings attributed to Jesus mostly rest on an Aramaic original. Here with caution I study the vocabulary of that original, as best it can be reconstructed. I guess that Mark's incidents rest on an oral Aramaic base, and that a Greek document behind Matthew and Luke rested on a written Aramaic one; but I hardly use those guesses. I am sure that some sayings were reworked or created in Greek; but I am not sure which. The sayings are the best record imaginable of one who, like Socrates, trusted his hearers to preserve whichever of his words they wished. I add a few sayings from other Galilaeans in the Gospels. It is doubtful that the Syriac translators had an oral tradition of Jesus' Aramaic; but, speaking as they did his mother tongue, and living in communities like his, they are still our best witness to it. Differences in dialect are partly correctible from Rabbinic.

We will find that the Aramaic noun-vocabulary underlying Jesus' sayings, far from being one more witness to primeval Semitic, *was heavily infiltrated by the languages of imperial rule in Palestine—*

---

1   A condensation has appeared as "The Noun-Vocabulary of Jesus' Aramaic," pp. 240-278 of C. E. Evans (ed.), The Interpretation of Scripture in Early Judaism and Christianity...; JSPSS 33, SSEJC 7; Sheffield: Academic, 2000.

2   The two MSS are the Curetonian (London and Berlin) and the Sinaitic palimpsest (St Catherine's, Sinai); edited by F. C. Burkitt, Evangelion da-Mepharreshe...; 2 vols; Cambridge: University, 1904. The translation may go back to the late second century CE.

3   The New Testament in Syriac; British and Foreign Bible Society: London, 1950.

4   A. S. Lewis & M. D. Gibson, The Palestinian Syriac lectionary of the Gospels...; London: Kegan Paul, 1899.

Akkadian, Iranian, Greek and Latin.[5] The foreign vocabulary is shown
as deeply rooted in Palestinian Aramaic by its appearance in Rabbinic
(where Aramaic and Hebrew are nearly interchangeable); and in the
Arabic of the Quran![6] Echoes of Gospel and Talmud in the mouth of
the Prophet show contact with Jewish or Jewish-Christian groups;
their anomalous form may be partly due to a sectarian source, partly
to his own speculations. Some of the Akkadian loans go back as far as
to Ugarit, documenting continuity of foreign themes in Semitic religious expression in the two millennia between 1400 BC and AD 600.

In (23.1) we note evidence for native Aramaic in the sayings of
Jesus. We then treat foreign words in the restored Aramaic of the
sayings from the successive imperial languages. In (23.2) we discuss
items borrowed from *Akkadian* of Babylon, including names of social
groups and features of urban design. In (23.3) we treat *Iranian*
loanwords in the sayings: abstractions, words of Medo-Persian administration and religion, some entering Greco-Latin like *gaza* "treasure."
In (23.4) paradoxically we treat *Greek* loan-words in the restored
Aramaic of the sayings, as evidenced by those very words in our Greek
New Testament! The sayings resemble Midrash and Targum in their
use of such. They name imported elements of Greek culture except
three for key features of Judaism (III.247)—Law, Covenant, Sanhedrin.
In (23.5) we treat *Latin* loanwords in the Aramaic sayings, all mediated through Greek: actual transcriptions, as of coins and measures;
and Greek equivalents for terms of administration from the Roman
chancery. Finally (23.6) we survey elements of a *lingua franca* in
Roman Palestine: a vocabulary shared by Aramaic, Greek, and Latin,
nearly all of Greek origin or of Latin mediated by Greek. Its primary
monument is the New Testament, which owes to it its high translatability.

---

5   The foreign vocabulary of Syriac is discussed by Sebastian P. Brock, "Greek
     Words in the Syriac Gospels (*Vet* and *Pe*)," Le Muséon 80 (1967) 389-426;
     John F. Healey, "Lexical Loans in Early Syriac: A Comparison with Nabataean
     Aramaic," pp. 73-84 of Studi Epigrafici e Linguistici sul Vicino Oriente antico
     12 (1995), a special issue on "The Lexicography of the Ancient Near Eastern
     Languages" with many valuable essays.

6   For the foreign vocabulary of the Quran see Jeffery. An especially nice item is
     Latin *castra* "camp." Frequent in Greek papyri of the Roman period; see IGRR
     3.237 κάστρα. Rabbinic קסטרא *Deut. Rabbah* 1.16 and Mishna קצרה, *Arach.*
     IX.6 קצרה הישנה של צפורים "the old camp of Sepphoris." Quran 22.44 Allah
     destroys many a *qaṣrin* قصر. So the Middle East is covered with sites bearing
     the name of "Camp," *Qaṣr*, just as Britain with sites called *Chester*: Bede 2.2
     *ad Ciuitatem Legionum, quae a gente Anglorum Legacaestir, a Brettonibus
     autem rectius Carlegion.*

23.1 The sayings of Jesus as Aramaic

In Palestine in the first century of our era, what languages were learned by children from their mothers and playmates?[7] Certainly Greek in some upper-class urban quarters; but it is unclear how far Greek percolated down to villages. We cannot pinpoint any groups where Hebrew was so learned. From the Jewish exile onwards, Aramaic steadily replaced Canaanite dialects including Hebrew. (But it is hard to document a shift from *Phoenician* Canaanite to Aramaic.) In written Palmyrene and Nabataean Aramaic (as with the Ituraeans, who left no Semitic texts) men's names are of Arabic formation. The Moslem conquest took over an area speaking dialects of both Arabic and Aramaic, which latter colors the colloquial Arabic of each land till this day.

Aramaic of Damascus spread to Babylon as the medium for trade and administration of the Old Persian empire rather than cuneiform, because it was simpler and written with pen and ink. When the leaders of Jerusalem ask the Rabshakeh to speak in "Aramaic" which they understood, and not in "Judaean" which the people understood (II Reg 18,26, see I.7), they had in mind the nationality of the speakers, not some perceived difference in the languages. The *Epistle of Aristeas* 10 (followed by Josephus *AJ* 12.15) makes an unclear distinction between the language of the Law and "Syrian." But Jerome and the Rabbis understood the difference. Where Laban and Jacob give the "heap of witness" (Gen 31,47, II.132) Aramaic and Hebrew names respectively, the Vulgate adds *uterque iuxta proprietatem linguae suae*, "each in the style of his own tongue." At Dan 2,4 Jerome notes the transition from *sermone... hebraeo*; the materials that follow *hebraicis quidem litteris sed lingua scribuntur chaldaica, quam hic syriacam uocat* "are written in Hebrew letters but the Chaldaean language, which [the text in his translation] calls 'Syrian'."[8] R. Samuel b. Nahman said (*Gen. Rabbah* 74.14): "Do not think lightly of the Aramaic language (לשון ארמי)! For the Holy One honors it in Torah, Prophets and Writings" citing Gen 31,47; Jer 10,11; and Dan 2,4.[9] R. Johanan advised against praying in Aramaic "for the Ministering Angels do not understand Aramaic" (Bab. Talm. *Shabb.* 12b, *Sotah* 33a):

שאין מלאכי השרת מכירין בלשון ארמי

---

7   See Joseph A. Fitzmyer, "The Languages of Palestine in the First Century A.D.," CBQ 32 (1970) 501-531, reprinted in his A Wandering Aramean: Collected Aramaic Essays; SBLMS 25; Chico: Scholars, 1979, 29-56.

8   Jerome *in Danielem* I; CC series latina 75A p. 785.

9   Aramaic is contrasted with the "holy tongue," i.e. Hebrew, at *Sotah* 49b.

Josephus first wrote the *Jewish War* in his "ancestral tongue" (τῇ πατρίῳ, *BJ* 1.3) for "upland barbarians" (τοῖς ἄνω βαρβάροις). Nabataeans? This must be Aramaic, for no non-Jews understood Hebrew. John's Gospel (III.170) designates Aramaic place-names as Ἑβραϊστί—i.e. the language spoken by Hebrews. Paul makes a speech τῇ Ἑβραΐδι διαλέκτῳ Act 21,40; but even if he could extemporize in Hebrew, his hearers would not understand it. What language did Josephus think he was writing? what language did Paul (or Jesus!) think they were speaking? What but a vernacular form of their difficult sacred Book! Only Rabbis knew that the Targum was in a different language from the original; others surely thought it the modernization of an archaic text, as Greeks today read Homer in a version with accentual hexameter.

Some late Jewish texts are in forms of Hebrew: the inner documents of the Qumran sect, the bulk of the Mishna. Others in Aramaic: papyri of the 5th century BC from Elephantine, apocryphal documents from Qumran, the Targums. Ezra and Daniel in both. Qumran Hebrew is archaizing,[10] Mishnaic Hebrew scholastic (but colored with Aramaic forms). Scattered inscriptions and papyri from the first century CE and later are in a confusing mix of Hebrew and Aramaic (with Greek too). Most of Hillel's sayings (from school context) are in Hebrew, but some (more popular) in Aramaic: thus the sequence beginning "Whoever makes his name great loses his name" (*Avoth* I.13):[11] נגיד שמא אבד שמה. The clearest proof that the native language of Jesus' Galilee was Aramaic lies in the Greek Gospels themselves.[12]

23.1.1 Some indications of Aramaic in the sayings

Inconclusive data. Some evidence excludes neither Hebrew nor Greek as the original language of the sayings.[13] Thus while Galilaean place-

---

10 W. M. Schniedewind, "Qumran Hebrew as an Antilanguage," *JBL* 118 (1999) 235-252, sees it as "created by conscious linguistic choices intended to set the speakers and their language apart from others."

11 Likewise the saying "Is not the poor soul a guest (אכסניא) in the body?" (*Lev. Rabbah* 34.3, III.15, with the Greek word ξένος also!).

12 Maurice Casey, Aramaic Sources of Mark's Gospel (SNTSMS 102; Cambridge: University, 1998) 1-72, surveys previous research into possible Semitic originals of N.T. strata, and finds the best treatment to be that of Matthew Black, An Aramaic Approach to the Gospels and Acts; 2nd ed.; Oxford: Clarendon, 1954.

13 Greek for Jewish concepts is inconclusive. Thus προσήλυτος Matt 23,15 "proselyte," Pesh גיורא (II.291, III.14); φυλακτήρια Matt 23,5 "prayer-boxes," Pesh תפיליהון; ἔθνη "Gentiles"; συναγωγή "synagogue," Pesh כנושתא; ἄγγελοι "angels."

names are Semitic (Βηθσαϊδά and Καφαρναούμ Matt 11,21-23), they might have been spoken as Greek just as in our text.[14] So for the Twelve (Mark 3,16-19).[15] *Calques* of Hebrew idiom were likely drawn from the LXX: Luk 21,24 στόματι μαχαίρης "by the mouth of the sword" is at Gen 34,26 LXX where Heb. לְפִי־חֶרֶב; Mark 13,20 πᾶσα σάρξ "all flesh" is frequent in the LXX, e.g. Gen 6,12 where Heb כָּל־בָּשָׂר; Matt 16,17 σὰρξ καὶ αἷμα "flesh and blood" (cf. Gal 1,16) echoes Sirach 17,31 (Heb. lost) with constant Rabbinic מלך בשר ודם "king of flesh and blood."

Data proving a Semitic original, but not which. Transcriptions: κορβᾶν Mark 7,11 "gift" is Hebrew קָרְבָּן, but κορβανᾶς Matt 27,6 "treasury" is Aramaic;[16] ῥαββί Matt 23,7-8 "my great one, Rabbi," here first in Greek, might as well be Hebrew רבי (post-Biblical). *"Son of X."* Thus "sons of the bridechamber" (Mark 2,19); "sons of the kingdom" straight or ironically (Matt 8,12; 13,38); "son of Gehenna" (Matt 23,15 with a double Semitism); "son of peace" (Luk 10,6); "sons of this age" (Luk 16,8) over against "sons of light" (Luk 20,34);[17] "sons of the resurrection" (Luk 20,36).[18] *Awkward translations.* Jesus' prayer surely had a clear adjective for "bread"; ἐπιούσιον (Matt 6,11 = Luk 11,3) shows that the translator found no natural Greek for it. The abstracts of Mark 2,21 show unfamiliarity with household terms: "Nobody sews a piece (ἐπίβλημα) of unshrunk cloth on an old garment; if one does, the patch (πλήρωμα) tears away from it." Luk 11,41 πλὴν τὰ ἐνόντα δὸς ἐλεημοσύνην is hardly Greek.[19]

Clear transcriptions of Aramaic. The vocative "Satan" Σατανᾶ (Mark 8,33) is surely Aramaic and corresponds to Pesh definite סטנא;[20] LXX in Hebrew form only at I Reg 11,14 σαταν; in Aramaic form Sirach

---

14 Sepphoris appears as Σαμφουρεῖν at Joh 11,54 in Codex D.

15 Thus most of the apostles carry Semitic names; but Ἀνδρέας and Φίλιππος are Greek, Θαδδαῖος probably represents an Aramaic version of Θεόδοτος, and Βαρθολομαῖος is probably Aramaic-Greek "son of Ptolemy."

16 So Josephus *AJ* 4.73; Josephus at *con Ap.* 1.167 cites Theophrastus (Stern i.12) to the effect that the Tyrians forbid κορβάν as a foreign oath.

17 The Qumran War Scroll (1 QM 1.1) defines itself as the war of the "sons of light" (בני אור) against the "sons of darkness" (בני חושך).

18 *The two ages.* The contrast between "this age" (העולם הזה) and "the age to come" (העולם הבא) runs through Rabbinic Judaism (e.g. *Avoth* IV.16, cited II.233). Three Gospel sayings echo it (III.34), but all may be editorial work.

19 But we may doubt Black's proposal (p. 2) of a mistranslation which Matt 23,26 has right, for there is little evidence that Matthew and Luke knew a sayings-collection in different translations from the Aramaic.

20 As applied here to Peter, "Satan" may just mean etymologically "tempter."

21,27 τὸν σατανᾶν. ῥακά Matt 5,22 "stupid" can only be Aramaic ריקא "good-for-nothing"[21] and is so interpreted by the Peshitto רקא. *Words of power*. To the deaf man (Mark 7,34) Jesus says ἔφφαθα; Pesh makes it intensive reflexive אתפתח 'ĕṯpattaḥ, and Jastrow (ii.1251) so reads *Lev. Rabbah* 22.4 (Aram.) "he who was blind was opened":[22]

דין דהוה סמי אתפתח

At Mark 5,41 the best MSS have ταλιθὰ κοῦμ "girl, get up": טליתא is Targumic; the Pesh writes a final *-i*, קומי, but the Greek attests an Aramaic feminine imperative the same as the masculine.[23] *The word from the Cross*. In the quotation from Ps 22,2 at Mark 15,34 = Matt 27,46 most MSS have σαβαχθανι for Aramaic שבקתני.[24] The name of God is ἐλωι (for Aramaic אלהי in most MSS of Mark), ἠλι (for Hebrew אלי) in a few; likewise ἐλωι in אB of Matthew.[25] The Hebrew is a learned correction. We have Targums to Psalms[26] with nearly the Gospel form; they were not written down so early, so Jesus' usage shows an oral Aramaic translation in synagogue school or worship. *Festivals*. πάσχα Matt 26,2 "Passover" is the LXX form for Targumic פסחא. σάββατον Mark 2,27 etc. is often plural (Mark 3,4); it is Targumic שבתא (Ex 16,28) interpreted as a Greek plural of a festival,

    Translations of Aramaic. Mistranslations. At Matt 7,6 "Give not the holy to dogs" the original must have been "a gold ring" with an Akkadian loanword in Rabbinic Aramaic (III.230).[27] *Alliteration*. Syriac verifies it at Matt 11,17 "We piped to you and you did not *dance*, we

---

21   Bab. Talm. *Taanith* 20b ריקה כמה מכוער "Wretch, how ugly you are!"

22   BAGD interpret it as simple peʿal reflexive, but equally Aramaic.

23   The unique perfect middle imperative πεφίμωσο Mark 4,39 addressed to the sea "be muzzled" suggests a Greek magical formula (papyri cited by Erwin Rohde, Psyche..., 2nd ed.; Freiburg: Mohr, 1898; ii.424). When Jesus walks on the sea and encourages the disciples (Mark 6,50 = Matt 14,27) θαρσεῖτε "be of good cheer," the Peshitto transliterates the root תרסו as a word of power (II.282).

24   Codex D both places has ζαφθανι for Hebrew עֲזַבְתָּנִי. Codex B in Mark strangely has the corrupt ζαβαφθανι.

25   Mark 15,25 "He is calling for Elijah" suggests rather the Hebrew form, but is outweighed by the evidence for the Aramaic verb.

26   Luis Diez Merino, Targum de Salmos, Bibliotheca Hispana Biblica 6; Biblica Poliglotta Complutense; Tradición sefardí de la Biblica Aramea IV,1; Madrid: Instituto "Francisco Suárez"; 1982. But I cannot elsewhere easily find a study discussing the origin or date of the Psalms Targum.

27   Black pp. 143-177 proposes many passages where he sees the Greek as misunderstanding an Aramaic original; but only a few rise to a high level of plausibility.

mourned to you and you did not *lament*," where the Peshitto has forms
of the same root:[28]

זמרן לכון ולא רקדתון   ואלין לכון ולא ארקדתון

Debt as sin. ὀφείλω often refers to literal debt;[29] but Luke 13,4 preserves a Semitism, "Do you think that [the eighteen] were 'debtors'
(ὀφειλέται) more than all the men in Jerusalem?" And so in the Lord's
Prayer (Matt 6,12, see I.250) the Peshitto preserves "debts" and "debtors":

ושבוק לן חובין איכנא דאף חנן שבקן לחיבין

Here the original meaning may well have been literal, but the Pesh
must understand "sinners." *"Lord."* Greek κύριος surely demands
Aramaic מר. Mark 13,35 "householder," κύριος τῆς οἰκίας, Pesh
מרה דביתא; Rabbinic[30] מארי ביתא. Matt 11,25 "Lord of heaven and
earth," κύριε τοῦ οὐρανοῦ καὶ τῆς γῆς, Pesh מרא דשמיא ודארעא; Dan
5,23 מָרֵי־שְׁמַיָּא, Cowley 30.15 ליהו מרא שמיא "to Yahu lord of heaven."

23.1.2 Sobriquets coined by Jesus

Jesus as second Adam renames the persons and agencies around him—
above all himself.[31] Many names are sardonic; he takes people ironically at their own evaluation or that of others. I call them by a French
term of uncertain origin, *sobriquets*. Any Rabbinic parallels are distant, for he radically transforms whatever he takes up. Some are
transcribed in our Greek Gospels, some translated. Most require an
Aramaic origin.

23.1.2.1 Sobriquets in transcribed Aramaic

Kephas. Mark 3,16 gives Simon's new name in Greek, Πέτρος; Matt
16,18 explains it, after all along calling him Peter. Joh 1,41 gives the
Aramaic Κηφᾶς with translation Πέτρος, which latter he thereafter
uses.[32] Paul mostly calls him Κηφᾶς (Gal 1,18 etc.); Πέτρος only at Gal

---

28   Black 118-142 has many back-translations of sayings with predominant con-
      sonantal sounds appropriate (as he deems) to the context; but his retroversion
      into Galilaean Aramaic would have admitted other possibilities.
29   The root חוב is common in Elephantine Aramaic to denote a legal liability, thus
      (Kraeling 4.14) "And if I start a suit against you with mention of that house,
      I shall be liable (אנה אחוב) and shall give you silver, 5 karsh..." חובא "sin"
      seems commoner in Rabbinic Aramaic than Hebrew.
30   Jastrow 834a citing *Gen. Rabbah* 58.
31   This and the next section expand a paragraph in my "The Son of Man: 'This
      Fellow'," Biblica 58 (1977) 361-387, pp. 370-371.
32   Here the renaming is reciprocal, for Simon's brother Andrew has just said "We
      have found the Messiah," where the narrator adds "which is translated
      'Christ'."

2,7-8. The Syriac has כאפא throughout. At Matt 16,13-23 Jesus calls Simon the Rock, and then right away Satan. "Rock" must be sardonic, either literally as "thick-headed" or ironically as "unstable." כיפא is Aramaic: Bab. Talm. *Moed Qatan* 25b כיפי דברדא "stones of hail."

"Sons of thunder." At Mark 3,17 James and John are called Βοανηργές. They rather than the Baptist or Jesus take on Elijah's role of bringing fire from heaven (Luk 9,54; II Reg 1,9-12). Cf. the (Aramaic?) place-name "Sons of Lightning," בְּנֵי־בָרָק Jos 19,45 (II.63). Mark's Greek is corrupt (the Βανηρεγες of MS 565 seems the correction of one knowing Syriac); Pesh has בני רגשי "sons of tumult" which it explains from the Greek as בני רעמא.

Beelzebul. For Βεεζεβούλ (better attested than correct Βεελζεβούλ) the Syriac has בעלזבוב and Vg *Beelzebub*,[33] identifying him with the god of Ekron, II Reg 1,2-16. That god is "Lord of the flies" (I.219-221): either deformation of some original; or honorific, "Averter of flies from the sacrifice." Mark 3,22 has Jerusalem scribes say "He has Beelzebul"; but with a final *l* it appears nowhere previously short of Ugaritic,[34] so this may be Mark's own deduction. Perhaps then it is Jesus' coinage: Matt 10,25 "If they have called the master of the house (οἰκοδεσπότην, Vg *patrem familias*, Pesh למרי דביתא) Beelzebul..." Demons are squatters in the house of a man's body (Matt 12,44 = Luk 11,25), so "master of the house" fits their chief. זְבֻל "divine residence" is Biblical Hebrew, e.g. בֵּית זְבֻל I Reg 8,13; then this designation uniquely is based on Hebrew.

Mammon. Luk 16,9 μαμωνᾶ τῆς ἀδικίας "unrighteous wealth" is doubly Semitic, (more normal Greek τῷ ἀδίκῳ μαμωνᾷ Luk 16,11). Pesh interprets as an Aramaic definite ממונא. Rabbinic "property": *Avoth* II.12 "Let the property of your associate be dear to you as your own":[35]

יהי ממון חברך חביב עליך כשלך

Personified in "You cannot serve God and Mammon" (Matt 6,24 = Luk 16,13).

Gehenna. γέεννα (cf. James 3,6) from Heb. גֵּי (בֶן) הִנֹּם "valley of (the son of) Hinnom," meaning uncertain. The Greek ending points to unattested Aramaic; Jos 18,16 LXX MS "B" Γαιεννα. First "garbage dump," then "place of perpetual fire." Matt 23,15 "son of Gehenna,"

---

33 The Old Latin in part has correctly *Beelzebul*.
34 KTU 1.6.IV.16 *zbl bʿl arṣ*, perhaps "Prince Baal of the earth"; discussion I.220.
35 Also in the Damascus Document (CDC 14.20), context broken; and frequent in Aramaic as "money" (Sokoloff 311).

υἱὸν γεέννης (Pesh ברה דגהנא); Bab. Talm. *Rosh hash.* 17b בני גהנם "sons of Gehenna."

Abba. Jesus calls God "Father," perhaps as an orphan, for Joseph early leaves the tale. Aramaic translated Mark 14,36 ἀββᾶ ὁ πατήρ; Peshitto אבא אבי as if already obscure. So Paul twice (Rom 8,15; Gal 4,6).[36] Does אבא reflect a child's language "Daddy" (II.317)? Colloquial at Mishna *Sanh.* III.2 נאמן עלי אבא "My father is acceptable to me [as judge or witness]." Bib. Heb. rarely calls God "Father" (II.57).[37]

23.1.2.2 Sobriquets preserved in Greek

The "whited sepulchres" of Matt 23,27, τάφοις κεκονιαμένοις, are a one-time sobriquet. Again, when Jesus calls Herod Antipas the tetrarch "that fox (jackal?)," τῇ ἀλώπεκι ταύτῃ Luk 13,32.[38]

"*Hypocrites.*" Classical ὑποκριτής is a stage "actor," as "responding" to the chorus. Surely in Jesus' lifetime Sepphoris had a theatre seating 4,500.[39] Nabataean תיטרא[40] is part of a tomb. Bab. Talm. *Megillah* 6a has "theatres and circuses of Edom," i.e. Philadelphia of Ammon:[41] תיאטריות וקרקיות שבאדום. ὑποκριταί can only be "actors" at Matt 6,2.5.16: they sound a trumpet, stand and pray, disfigure their faces, all "to be seen (or praised) by men." Matt 6,2 Pesh as often has נסבי באפא, which elsewhere means "showing partiality, respecting one [influential] person above another." At Luk 20,21 where adversaries

---

36 BAGD 1 call ἀββᾶ an Aramaic vocative incorrectly interpreted as a definite, whence Greek ὁ πατήρ nominative instead of πάτερ vocative; but what can they mean by a Semitic noun in the vocative?

37 It is a striking coincidence that "Father in heaven" (ὁ πατὴρ ὁ ἐξ οὐρανοῦ Luk 11,13) restores the old Indo-European title of the Sky Father, Ζεὺς πατήρ and *Iuppiter* (II.55).

38 The Greek is inappropriately feminine, so the Peshitto masculine תעלא must represent the original.

39 Zeev Weiss, "Sepphoris," NEAE iv.1324, who regards it as built "in the early first century CE, possibly in the reign of Antipas." An early date is confirmed by the familiarity of the Gospels with acting. It was the first part of the city you would arrive at, walking up from the SE. Already Herod the Great had built a theatre in Jerusalem (Josephus *AJ* 15.268), along with others in Sidon and Damascus (*BJ* 1.422).

40 CIS ii.163.2, Seia.

41 Classically theatre and circus overlap: Vergil *Aen.* 5.289 *theatri circus* "the circus of a theatre"; Plutarch *Aem. Paull.* 32.1 "in the equestrian theatres which [the Romans] call circuses," ἔν τε τοῖς ἱππικοῖς θεάτροις ἃ κίρκους καλοῦσι; and in Roman law (*Novell.* 98.359) *processiones...esse uolumus septem, omnes in circo et in arena et in theatro* "we wish there to be seven processions, all in the circus, the arena and the theatre."

say "you show no partiality," οὐ λαμβάνεις πρόσωπον, the Peshitto has
לא נסב אנת באפא.[42] Why did Aramaic apply "lifting up faces" to
actors? See Matt 7,5 = Luk 6,42 "Actor (ὑποκριτά), first take the beam
(δοκόν) out of your eye," Pesh:

נסב באפא אפק לוקדם קריתא מן עינך

Thw actor wore a *wooden mask* for characterization and acoustics.
One who objects to the splinter in his brother's eye is an actor; he has
on a whole wooden mask or "beam." The Greek is classical: Aristotle
Ars Rhet. 1413b28 ὁ τὴν δοκὸν φέρων "one whose face is immobile,
who wears a mask." Then נסב באפא was reinterpreted "one who wears
a mask"; Jesus sees the actor as presenting a false face of virtue.

"*This generation.*" Jeremias[43] noted Jesus' fourteen sayings about ἡ
γενεὰ αὕτη as "of extreme rebuke" to the unresponsive contemporary
world. It is the exact opposite of the kingdom of God, for they are
introduced identically by a double question: Luk 13,18 "What is the
kingdom of God like, and to what shall I compare it?" followed by a
double parable; Luk 7,31 "To what shall I compare the men of this
generation, and what are they like?" followed by their reactions to
John and Jesus.[44]

"*The kingdom of heaven (of God).*" Jesus' overarching concept is
assembled from scattered usages.[45] The obligation to recite the Shemaᶜ
is to take on "the yoke of the kingdom of heaven," עול מלכות שמים
(Mishna *Berakh.* II.2); Targum Jonathan on Sach 14,9 has "And the
kingdom of Y. shall be revealed upon all the inhabitants of earth in
that time":

ותתגלי מלכותא דיוי על כל יתבי ארעא בעידנא ההוא

Elsewhere[46] I arrange Jesus' sayings about the kingdom in four groups:
"the kingdom is at hand" as subject of verbs;[47] "to enter the king-

---

42   Similarly in the Targum: at Deut 10,17: God is no respecter of persons,
     לֹא־יִשָּׂא פָנִים, LXX οὐ θαυμάζει πρόσωπον, Onqelos לית קדמוהי מסב אפין.
     Sokoloff (p. 70b sect. 9) gathers texts for Palestinian Aramaic usage.

43   Joachim Jeremias, New Testament Theology: The Proclamation of Jesus; tr.
     John Bowden; New York: Scribner's, 1971; p. 135.

44   Behind Jesus' usage lies in part Deut 32,5 "a crooked and perverse genera-
     tion," where LXX γενεὰ σκολιὰ καὶ διεστραμμένη is quoted at Phil 2,15. An
     early editor of Mark 9,19 (P⁴⁵ et al.) added καὶ διεστραμμένη to ὦ γενεὰ
     ἄπιστος, for Matt 17,17 = Luk 9,41 so knew Mark.

45   Full inventory of Rabbinic texts by D. C. Duling in ABD iv.50-56. Jesus' usage
     was surely uniform, either "kingdom of heaven" or "kingdom of God," but
     now unrecoverable.

46   Article "Kingdom of God" in Encyclopedia of Religion (New York: Macmillan,
     1987) viii.304-312; xvi.682.

47   "Thy kingdom come" in context derives from the Aramaic Qaddish (II.29).

dom"; the kingdom as object of search and struggle; "in the kingdom" seen as a banquet at the end of time. Jesus' awareness of current expectations appears in the polemic against them: it is not enough to say "Lord, Lord" (Matt 7,21); it is nearly impossible for a rich man to enter the kingdom (Mark 10,23); it does not come with signs (Luk 17,20).[48] Once his irony flashes out: Semitic "sons of the kingdom," which at Matt 13,38 defines the good seed, marks false confidence at Matt 8,12 "the sons of the kingdom will be cast into outer darkness."

"The Son of Man." Late sayings about a "son of man" coming in glory (e.g. Mark 14,62) probably reflect a Church development resting on Dan 7,13. Still they follow the rule that "Son of Man" is only put in Jesus' mouth. In the earliest sources Jesus plainly so refers to himself. Twenty years ago[49] I proposed that this was the most ironic of his sobriquets, resting on what others called him, "this fellow." It rests on Aramaic בר נשא "a man." At Luk 7,34 = Matt 11,19 he represents opponents as saying, "Lo, a *fellow* (ἄνθρωπος) who is a glutton and winebibber"; this is their response to the fact as he describes it, "The *Son of Man* (ὁ υἱὸς τοῦ ἀνθρώπου) came eating and drinking." He adopts the persona of adversaries. At Mark 2,1-12 where the scribes say, "Why does *this one* (οὗτος) speak thus?...Who can forgive sins but God alone?," Jesus answers in a broken sentence, "But that you may know that the *Son of Man* has authority on earth to forgive sins..." His answer has most point if they asked him "Why does *this fellow* speak thus?" Thus "Son of Man" parallels his naming of the other actors on his stage.[50]

"Sinners," "publicans and harlots." Jesus uses "sinner" in the literal sense on occasion.[51] In contrast stands the far-reaching irony at

---

48   Matthew alone (3,2) represents John Baptist as proclaiming "Repent, for the kingdom of heaven is at hand"; it is unclear whether this is John's own usage or a retroversion of Jesus'. The episodes which represent others as somehow anticipating the kingdom—Joseph of Arimathea (Mark 15,43), Pharisees (Luk 17,20), disciples (Matt 18,1, Luk 14,15)—if historical, attest less a pre-existing expectation than a partial response to Jesus' own teaching.

49   "The Son of Man: 'This Fellow'," *Biblica* 58 (1977) 361-387. Delbert Burkett, *The Son of Man Debate: A History and Evaluation* (Cambridge: University, 1999; p. 34) rejects this proposal on the grounds that "the Gospels never represent Jesus' opponents as using the expression [Son of Man]." But in fact *anthropos* can represent nothing else in Aramaic.

50   Casey 112-117 surveys early Aramaic usage of "son of man." Sokoloff 100b referred me to Jer. Talm. *Yebamoth* 13a23 (tr. Neusner) "By your lives! I gave you a son of man who is as good as I am":

חייכון בר נש דכוותי יהבית לכון

51   Thus "this adulterous and sinful generation" (Mark 8,38); "the Son of Man is betrayed into the hands of sinners" (Mark 14,41 pars.). He does not dissent

Mark 2,17 "Those who are well do not need a doctor, but those who are sick; I did not come to call righteous but sinners." He adopts the usage of those who call themselves "well" and "righteous." Are they not the ones in most need of his treatment? But they can receive only the medicine of denunciation or parable. At Luk 15,7 he speaks as if beside one repentant sinner there are ninety-nine just persons needing no repentance.[52] In both places adversaries call his associates "(publicans and) sinners" (Mark 2,16; Luke 15,2); and the Evangelists naively assume that these are two actual categories of Galilaeans.

See again Matt 11,19 = Luk 7,34, "Behold a man who is a glutton and winebibber, the friend of publicans and sinners,"... τελωνῶν φίλος καὶ ἁμαρτωλῶν. Luk 7,29 puts publicans on the scene but no sinners. "Sinners" is genderless, contrary to Jesus' pairing of male and female examples.[53] The parallel is perfect at Matt 21,31 "the publicans and harlots (τελῶναι καὶ πόρναι) precede you into the kingom of God" (I.248-9; II.333). That is how adversaries designated his followers![54] Jesus accepts the designation, as Willie Stark (in Robert Penn Warren's *All the King's Men*) wins over the country folk by calling them "Friends, red-necks, suckers and fellow hicks."[55]

"Men" and other adversaries of God. Over against God, Jesus sees a front of mixed adversaries. "You cannot serve *God* and *Mammon*" (Matt 6,24); "If Satan casts out Satan, ...how shall *his kingdom stand*? ...But if I by the spirit (Luke *finger*) of God cast out demons, then the *kingdom of God* has come upon you" (Matt 12,26-28); "Give the things of *Caesar* to Caesar and the things of *God* to God" (Mark

---

when others call themselves a sinner: Peter (Luk 5,8); the publican (Luk 18,13). The editor, the Pharisee, and Jesus all agree that the woman of the city is a sinner (Luk 7,37-49). Most strongly he seems to accept the conventional designation at Luk 6,32-34 "Even sinners lend to sinners."

52 In the parable of the Pharisee and publican the latter is indeed a sinner—but much more so the righteous Pharisee (Luk 18,9-14). In the humanistic parable of the Prodigal Son (Luk 15,11-32) the younger brother is in effect a sinner and the elder righteous, and in a rare exception both are treated sympathetically.

53 A man losing a sheep, a woman a coin (Luk 15,2-10); a man with mustard seed, a woman with leaven (Matt 13,31-33 = Luk 13,18-19); one man and woman taken, one of each left (Matt 24,40-41 = Luk 17,34-35).

54 At Matt 5,46-47 they become "publicans...Gentiles" (τελῶναι...ἐθνικοί); at Justin *Apol.* I.15.9-10, with a better tradition than the Synoptic, "[male] prostitutes...publicans" (πόρνοι...τελῶναι).

55 Quakers take their name from their opponents, and perhaps Methodists. H. B. Mattingly ("The Origin of the Name *Christiani*," JTS n.s. 9 [1958] 26-37) thinks "Christians" were so named in Latin form at Antioch (Act 11,26) after the Neronian claque of *Augustiani* (Tacitus *Ann.* 14.13-15).

12,17).[56] "Men" also join the front, Mark 8,33 pars. "You do not think (οὐ φρονεῖς) the things of *God* but the things of *men*." "So that you may not appear fasting to *men* but to your *Father*" (Matt 6,18); "This is impossible with *men* but not with *God*" (Mark 10,27); "What is high among *men* is abomination before *God*" (Luk 16,15). Since in Aramaic "men" is "sons of man," it can also form puns or riddles with "Son of man": Luk 6,22 "Blessed are you when the sons of men (Peshitto בני נשא) hate you...on account of the Son of Man (i.e. 'this fellow,' Peshitto ברה דאנשא)."[57]

23.1.3 "Amen I say to you"

ἀμὴν λέγω ὑμῖν is a running formula of emphasis with variations.[58] It is often dropped by Luke (assuming he uses Mark) or Hellenized to ἀληθῶς. Matthew (19,23; 24,2) twice adds it to Mark; Matthew and Mark prefix it to materials in editorial style; simple λέγω (ὑμῖν) is frequent. But obviously it was there in the tradition from the beginning. What is its grammar? One verse has it followed by a strong Semitism: Mark 8,12 ἀμὴν λέγω ὑμῖν εἰ δοθήσεται τῇ γενεᾷ ταύτῃ σημεῖον "a sign will *not* be given to this generation." Is this simply imitating the LXX? Heb 3,11 quotes Ps 95,11 LXX "As I swore in my anger, They shall *not* enter my rest,"

ὡς ὤμοσα ἐν τῇ ὀργῇ μου, εἰ εἰσελεύσονται εἰς τὴν κατάπαυσίν μου.

אֲשֶׁר־נִשְׁבַּעְתִּי בְאַפִּי   אִם־יְבֹאוּן אֶל־מְנוּחָתִי

But the LXX text had its own authority. Here I boldly assume that Mark 8,12 (alone!) records the original Aramaic construction.

Hebrew negative oaths have a paradoxical grammar.[59] I Sam 19,6 Saul says to Jonathan of David, "As Yahweh lives, he shall *not* be put to death," חַי־יהוה אִם־יוּמָת, LXX Ζῇ κύριος, εἰ ἀποθανεῖται just like Mark 8,12. Joüon 503-505[60] explains the use of אִם as contamination

---

56 As with Mammon and Satan, *Caesar* is a pan-Aramaic name: Nabataean (Cooke no. 98, AD 47) שנת שבע לקלדיס קיסר "The seventh year of Claudius Caesar"; Bab. Talm. *Gitt.* 56a "Nero Caesar" נירון קיסר; Palm. Tar. 103 "Germanicus Caesar" גרמנקוס קיסר.

57 Mark 9,31 "The Son of Man is delivered into the hands of the sons of man"; and passages where "man" likewise stands in riddles with "Son of Man" (Mark 2,27-28; 8,37-38; 14,21). See Biblica 58 (1977) 372.

58 Sometimes in the singular ἀμὴν λέγω σοι; doubled in John, ἀμὴν ἀμὴν λέγω ὑμῖν.

59 Positive oaths too, here I simplify by considering only the negative ones.

60 Joüon prefers this to the explanation that a curse-formula is omitted in a negative oath; for an oath of God has the same grammar, Ez 20,3 "As I live, I will *not* be questioned by you," חַי־אָנִי אִם־אִדָּרֵשׁ לָכֶם, ζῶ ἐγὼ εἰ ἀποκριθήσομαι ὑμῖν.

with a curse, e.g. II Reg 6,30-31[61] "Thus may God do to me and more also, *if* the head of Elisha ben Shaphat remains on him today":

כֹּה־יַעֲשֶׂה־לִּי אֱלֹהִים וְכֹה יוֹסִף אִם יַעֲמֹד רֹאשׁ אֱלִישָׁע בֶּן־שָׁפָט עָלָיו הַיּוֹם

In effect Saul says "God do so to me and more also if David is put to death." Jesus says not to swear at all (Matt 5,33-37; 23,16-22); but rather (Matt 5,37) "Let your word be Yes Yes, No No," ἔστω δὲ ὁ λόγος ὑμῶν ναὶ ναί, οὒ οὔ. This may mistranslate an original better rendered at James 5,12 "Let your Yes *be* Yes, and your No, No," ἤτω δὲ ὑμῶν τὸ ναὶ ναὶ καὶ τὸ οὒ οὔ.[62] But Jesus needed to certify sayings by a formula, which as it seems inherited the oath-grammar. Rabbinic has the same grammar for an oath as Biblical Hebrew.[63] The woman suspected of adultery (Num 5,20) takes an oath with "Amen" and normal (non-paradoxical) grammar (Mishna *Sotah* II.5) "Amen that I have *not* gone astray...Amen that I have *not* become defiled":

אמן שלא שטיתי...אמן שלא נטמאתי

Then we can transform Jesus' negative statements introduced by "Amen": "As I speak to you truly, [may I be proved a false prophet]— if a sign is given this generation" (Mark 8,12); —if a prophet is honored in his own country" (Luk 4,24); —if a slave is greater than his master" (Joh 13,16); —if stone is left on stone" (Matt 24,2). I leave it open whether *all* the "Amen" sayings can be so explained.

23.1.4 Counter-indications of a Greek original?

We found no evidence for a Hebrew original of the sayings: in two words which echo Biblical Hebrew (זְבוּל "residence," III.210; מוֹרֶה "rebellious," III.250) Jesus may be making a learned pun. Are there counter-indications to suggest that the sayings were originally Greek?

(1') *The Greek tradition.* The "Synoptic problem" reveals a complex pre-history of the Gospel materials in Greek. Where Matthew and Luke agree with Mark, many conclude that both knew Mark in Greek; I would add, in an early editing with traces in the later MSS of Mark's text.[64] The common materials of Matthew and Luke, mostly sayings,

---

61 This passage is almost unique in that the content of "God do so to me and more also" is indicated by a preceding action, where the unnamed king tears his garments and so puts a conditional curse on himself to be torn; see I.272.

62 I wonder if Matthew's formulation lies behind the double ἀμὴν ἀμὴν of John's Gospel.

63 M. H. Segal, A Grammar of Mishnaic Hebrew; Oxford: Clarendon, 1927; 216.

64 My "An Early Revision of the Gospel of Mark," JBL 78 (1959) 215-227.

are often attributed to a Greek document ("Q"), better preserved by
Luke; I see Matthew as attesting a broad Greek revision of "Q",[65]
Mark as excerpting an earlier stage of the revision.[66] But far enough
back on any line we come to matter which demands an Aramaic
original, at least for the sayings. That Aramaic had a primarily oral
tradition; for the sayings are so novel as to be unintelligible in an
unpointed text.[67]

(2') *Greek grammar in the sayings.* Of all the sayings, the evangelists
or their sources write most freely in the parables. Luke in the Prodigal
Son has nine aorist participles introducing a main verb (15,17 ἐλθὼν
ἔφη) instead of Semitic parataxis, along with two genitive absolutes
(15,14.20). But (III.245) the parable also includes four Greek words
which went into Aramaic; Luke may have elegantly translated an
Aramaic source but retained Greek vocabulary which he found there
in transcription.

(3') *Use of LXX in the sayings?* Sometimes Jesus seems to presuppose the LXX just where it differs from the Hebrew. That could lead
to one of two unpalatable conclusions: (a) Jesus the boy knew Greek,
and the Nazareth rabbi explained the Hebrew Bible out of the LXX;
or (b) such passages were created by the Evangelists (or their Greek
sources) out of whole cloth. The first seems unlikely for a country
village; the second undercuts the evidence that Jesus was concerned to
interpret the Bible correctly. But we can modify the first: the rabbi
explained the Hebrew text out of a Targumic tradition more Hellenistic than that finally recorded in Onqelos and Jonathan.

The image of God. Jesus asks "Whose is this image (εἰκών)?" (Mark
12,16), and goes on (I.299) "Give God the things of God," i.e. one's
whole self.[68] The underlying connection is Gen 1,26 LXX where humanity is made κατ' εἰκόνα ἡμετέραν καὶ καθ' ὁμοίωσιν "after our image
and likeness" (בְּצַלְמֵנוּ כִּדְמוּתֵנוּ). Jesus would seem to be using the LXX.
But here Targum Pseudo-Jonathan[69] has בצילמנא כדייוקננא, where
דייוקננא is a distortion of איקוניא, since at Gen 5,3 the LXX for בְּצַלְמוֹ
has εἰκόνα and Pseudo-Jonathan correctly now איקוניא. As Onqelos and

65 My "The Form of 'Q' Known to Matthew," NTS 8 (1961/2) 27-42.
66 My "Mark as Witness to an Edited Form of Q," JBL 80 (1961) 29-44.
67 The unpointed MSS of the Old Syriac and Palestinian must then have been
    simply an *aide-mémoire* for readers already familiar with the matter.
68 Compare *Avoth* III.7 "Give him what is his, for you and yours are his,"
    תֶּן־לוֹ מִשֶּׁלּוֹ שָׁאַתָּה וְשֶׁלְּךָ שֶׁלּוֹ citing I Chron 29,14 "Of your own have we given
    you."
69 E. G. Clarke, Targum Pseudo-Jonathan of the Pentateuch [Brit Mus MS Add
    27031]; Hoboken: Ktav, 1984.

Jonathan frequently transliterate the LXX into Aramaic,[70] so Pseudo-Jonathan; it is the deposit of a tradition going back to rabbis who knew the LXX. Jesus might have asked "Pharisees and Herodians" (Mark 12,13) "Whose image is this?" either in Greek with εἰκών or in Aramaic with איקוניא. And Rabbis used איקונין of the "image" (εἰκόνιον) of the Emperor. *Exod. Rabbah* 30.16: "Parable of a man who insulted the *image* of the king and was brought before the *bema* (βῆμα). The king said, 'Have you not read in my *decree* (διάταγμα) that whoever touches my image is lost?'"

משל לאדם קנח איקונין של מלך ועלה לבימה אמר המלך לא קראת
בדיוטגמא שלי שכל מי שנוגע באיקונין שלי הוא אבד

A den of bandits. At Mark 11,17 Jesus quotes Jer 7,11 LXX for the Temple as a "den of bandits," σπήλαιον λῃστῶν. λῃστής is the fixed equivalent for Latin *latro* "bandit" and pejorative (III.260) for quasi-Messianic uprisings. He implies that the Temple authorities, rather than any resistance fighters in the hills, are the true *latrones* subverting law and order. This overtone is lost if Jesus cited the Hebrew מְעָרַת פָּרִצִים. But λῃστής went widely into Aramaic ליסטיס, and the Peshitto of Mark here has מערתא דלסטיא. A Jerusalem Targum of Jeremiah might have used ליסטיס here—or the Nazareth rabbi might so have interpreted.[71]

Fitzmyer[72] surveys evidence that Jesus spoke Greek, and occasions on which he might have spoken in Greek; but thinks it unlikely that he would ever "teach and preach in Greek." Selby[73] from Welsh usage holds:

> On the basis of the structure which Jeremias provides, it is evident that the Evangelists were aware that in some situations (home, discipleship groups, synagogue) Jesus spoke in Aramaic, whilst, in the world at large, he spoke Greek.

---

70 My "The Septuagint as a Source of the Greek Loan-Words in the Targums," Biblica 70 (1989) 194-216.

71 Cases treated elsewhere. —At the Last Supper (I Kor 11,25) Jesus calls the cup the "new covenant," διαθήκη (Jer 31,31 LXX); it has the overtone "last will and testament" like Rabbinic דייתיקי (III.248). —At Luk 23,43 "in Paradise" presupposes that Eden is renamed Paradise as in the LXX and apocryphal Judaism (III.140). —At Matt 5,35 Jesus calls earth the "footstool (ὑποπόδιοιν) of [God's] feet," quoting Isa 66,1 LXX; Beit Shammai (III.244)—equivalent to a Targum—has אפופודים.

72 Joseph A. Fitzmyer, "Did Jesus Speak Greek?," Biblical Archaeology Review, Sept./Oct. 1992, 58-63 (with footnotes 76-77).

73 G. R. Selby, Jesus, Aramaic and Greek; Doncaster: Brynmill, 1990; 104.

Most of the sayings are spoken to Galilaeans—men, women, and children; some no doubt understood Greek, all had Aramaic for mother tongue. The situation of Jesus in Galilee over against urban Greek culture is like that of César Chavez over against dominant Anglo culture. Chavez grew up in Yuma, Arizona in a Spanish enclave. He spoke Spanish at home but in school had to learn English. He told his biographer,[74] whenever he spoke Spanish "I remember the ruler whistling through the air as its edge came down sharply across my knuckles." Still, his work came to require contact with Anglo sympathizers, as in the liberal churches. Jesus was organizing (if we may so speak) much more in his own community, and went outside mostly in confrontation. But on occasion a group in front of him might all understand Greek, but not Aramaic. He might then formulate his thoughts in Greek. What kind of Greek?

I have often heard Chavez speaking English. It was clear and expressive. But I felt that what he said in English had been previously formulated in Spanish. My Palestinian students in Beirut had good English; but they said nothing they could not have said better in Arabic. A Semitic substructure underlay their English. A Lebanese professor discarding a document told the secretary "Tear it and throw it," missing the idiom "Tear it *up* and throw it *away*." So I conclude: even if Jesus sometimes did deliver his message in Greek, it was a message initially formulated in Aramaic.

23.1.5 Jesus as Semitic poet?

Bultmann is gratified when the sayings fall into Semitic poetical format, even while concluding that somebody other than Jesus spoke them. Thus at Matt 8,20 "The foxes have holes, and the birds of the sky nests; but the Son of Man has not where to lay his head," he notes the nested antithetic and synonymous parallelisms.[75] Burney,[76] writing after Bultmann's first edition but oblivious of it, used the Semitic structure of the sayings—including those of John's Gospel—as proof of their authenticity:

---

74   Jacques E. Levy, Cesar Chavez: Autobiography of La Causa; New York: Norton, 1975; 24.

75   Rudolf Bultmann, The History of the Synoptic Tradition, tr. John Marsh; 2nd ed.; Oxford: Blackwell, 1968; p. 81.

76   C. F. Burney, The Poetry of our Lord: An Examination of the Formal Elements of Hebrew Poetry in the Discourses of Jesus Christ: Oxford: Clarendon, 1925; p. 9.

> The Aramaic renderings of our Lord's sayings which form a marked feature in the book aim at conforming, so far as may be, with the Galilaean dialect, which was doubtless that spoken by our Lord and His disciples.

Black accepts Burney's proof "that the sayings of Jesus are cast in the form of Semitic poetry, with such characteristic features as parallelism of lines and clauses, rhythmic structure, and possibly even rhyme" (p. 105); and concludes (p. 142):

> Jesus did not commit anything to writing, but by His use of poetic form and language He ensured that His sayings would not be forgotten. The impression they make in [Black's reconstructed] Aramaic is of carefully premeditated style and studied deliverances; we have to do with prophetic utterances of the style and grandeur of Isaiah...

His phonetic observations would be more persuasive if the text were the Syriac, and not Galilaean Aramaic after his own reconstruction. Schwarz[77] draws similar conclusions from even more heavily restored verse. Fitzmyer[78] notes the lack of Aramaic poetry to compare with the sayings; but adds "I am not calling in question the existence of the rhythmic sayings attributed to Jesus in the Greek gospels or even their poetic character."

All that suggests that Jesus' Aramaic was an exemplary Semitic language, comparable in resources and power to the Hebrew of Job or Isaiah, used by Jesus with equal skill. That is not wholly misleading, but it leaves out the prehistory of Aramaic. Hebrew was the language of a clannish people, whose poets relied heavily on their predecessors back to Ugaritic. Aramaic all along was the working language of empires, and everywhere it picked up elements of local vocabulary. In the centuries after Jesus it did generate admirable poets in its Syriac dialect: the unknown authors of the *Odes of Solomon* and of the *Hymn of the Pearl*; the odes of Ephrem of Nisibis. Their verses are full of Greek loanwords. Ephrem was a cloistered monk. Much more did Jesus, a man of the streets and fields, use words in the air to describe the village culture of Galilee from which he drew his lessons. A few generalizations ("Ask and it will be given you") do use only the Semitic verb structure (III.33); elsewhere he calls the objects around him by the names in popular usage.

---

77 Günther Schwarz, "Und Jesus sprach": Untersuchungen zur aramäischen Urgestalt der Worte Jesu; BWANT 6.18 (118); Stuttgart: Kohlhammer, 1985; p. 121.

78 "The Study of the Aramaic Background of the New Testament," p. 17 of the work cited in note 7 above.

23.2 Akkadian in the Aramaic of the sayings

Already in the 7th century BC Aramaic the pen-and-ink business language of Babylon was displacing Akkadian as the vernacular also. The Jewish community deported to Babylon in 597 BC heard Akkadianized Aramaic all around it. (The Babel story nicely fits such a linguistic mixture.) It picked up that language and sent it back home. In the 5th century the Jewish military at Elephantine was entirely Aramaic-speaking. Neh 8,8 may mean that Ezra read the Law in Hebrew and interpreted it in Aramaic. Kaufman[79] distinguishes between Akkadian loanwords in Aramaic, and agreements where both simply record original Semitic stock. These loanwords, which hardly made their way into Greek, are distinct from the earlier Akkadian words which went into Ugaritic or Phoenician and thence to Greek (II.292). The Akkadian in Jesus' sayings reflects the Exile: (23.2.1) occupations and social groups; (23.2.2) urban design; (23.2.3) miscellaneous terms including business and trade. In the sayings of Jesus, as in Rabbinic and in real life, Babylonian Judaism is marvelously restored from the dead.

23.2.1 Akkadian names of occupations and social groups

Babylon of the exile was an old city with a stratified society where each social group was distinct and named. Both that rigid structure and its names were exported back to Palestine, and recorded in the Talmud and in the Aramaic behind Jesus' sayings.

(1) *"Student."* μαθητής is standard for Jesus' "disciples," Pesh. תַלְמִידָא: I Chron 25,8 מֵבִין עִם־תַּלְמִיד "teacher and student alike"; Hebrew of *Avoth*. From Akkadian *talmīdu* "apprentice, student"; only in Akkadian does the form in *ta-* designate occupations (Kaufman 107). In a double proverb, Matt 10,24 (Luk 6,40; Joh 13,16) "A student is not above his teacher, nor a slave above his master," οὐκ ἔστιν μαθητὴς ὑπὲρ τὸν διδάσκαλον, οὐδὲ δοῦλος ὑπὲρ τὸν κύριον αὐτοῦ where Pesh:

לית תלמידא דיתיר מן רבה ולא עבדא מן מרה

Aramaic[80] "the student disagrees with his teacher" תלמידא פליג על רבה.

---

79 Stephen A. Kaufman, The Akkadian Influences on Aramaic; Assyriological Studies 19; Chicago: University, 1974.
80 Cited by Sokoloff 583 as at Jer. Talm. *Qidd.* 64d13, but the citation seems erroneous.

Bab. Talm. *Berakhoth* 58b illogically conflates the two forms, "It is enough for a slave to be as his Rab":[81] דיו לעבד שיהא כרבה.

(2) *"Carpenter."* Galilaeans (Mark 6,3) call Jesus "the carpenter (τέκτων, Pesh נגרא), the son of Mary," marking him an orphan. Cowley 26.9 "head of the carpenters" סנן נגריא. From Akkadian *naggāru*, itself from Sumerian NAGAR;[82] hence Arabic surname *najjār* نَجَّار.[83] Matt 13,55 "the son of the carpenter" (Pesh ברה דנגרא) shows the trade hereditary; Bab. Talm. *Aboda Zara* 50b (Amos 7,14) "I am not a carpenter nor the son of a carpenter," לית נגרא ולא בר נגרא of a self-taught Rabbi. Akkadian "carpenters" are specifically woodworkers; Jesus perhaps commuted to rebuild Sepphoris, *burned* (ἐνέπρησεν Josephus *AJ* 17.289) by P. Quinctilius Varus in 4 BC. (Varus died with the loss of three legions in Germany, AD 9.)

(3) *"Physician."* In proverbs: Mark 2,17 "Those who are well do not need a physician (ἰατροῦ, Pesh אסיא)"; Luk 4,23 "Physician, heal yourself," ἰατρέ, θεράπευσον σεαυτόν, Pesh אסיא אסא נפשך.[84] From Akkadian *asû*, itself from Sumerian A.ZU;[85] old Israel records no physicians! They are presumed rapacious: Jer. Talm. *Taan.* 66d26 "Honor your physician (איקיר לאסייך) before you need him"; Bab. Talm. *B.Q.* 85a "A physician who heals for nothing is worth nothing," pure Akkadian (III.229): אסיא דמגן במגן.[86] The "proverb" (παραβολή, מתלא) at Luk 4,23 is international, perhaps Akkadian: *Gen. Rabbah* 23.4 "Physician, physician, cure your lameness!" אסיא אסיא אסי חוגרתך. At Aesop 69 (Chambry) the frog claims to be a physician, but the fox objects, πῶς σὺ ἄλλους σώσεις σαυτὸν χωλὸν ὄντα μὴ θεραπεύων "How will you save others when you can't cure your own lameness?"[87] It is

---

81   Rengstorf in TDNT iv.439 thinks that *talmīd* "came into Judaism from the educative process of the Greek and Hellenistic philosophical schools"; but the word and at least some of the context reflects Babylonian usage.

82   Kaufman 75, CAD xi.I.112.

83   Ugaritic *ngr* (KTU 1.16.IV.3 etc.) was translated "carpenter" by Gordon, but now Parker (UNP 36) makes it "herald," I do not know on what basis. In the sense "carpenter" it would seem a plausible early loan from Akkadian. Luk 23,31 "For if they do this in the green wood, what will happen in the dry?" surely betrays a carpenter's language: note also its (Roman?) logic *a minori ad maius*; the Aramaic passive "they do"; the hint of a final cosmic conflagration.

84   אסיא is attested in Palmyrene (PAT 0050, AD 213) and Nabataean (CIS 2.206, Hegra, AD 26).

85   Kaufman 37, CAD i.II.344.

86   In Homer healing like carpentry is hereditary: *Iliad* 11.512-518, Machaon the physician (ἰητρός) is "the son of Asclepius the faultless physician."

87   Similarly in verse, Babrius 120.7-8. More Greek versions in S. J. Noorda, "'Cure yourself, doctor' (Luke 4,23); Classical parallels to an alleged saying of Jesus,"

transformed at Mark 15,31, "Others he saved (ἔσωσεν, Pesh אחי),
himself he cannot save."[88]

(4) *"A poor man."* πτωχός common, Pesh. מסכנא. Koh 9,15 "A poor
wise man," אִישׁ מִסְכֵּן חָכָם.[89] Frequent in Rabbinic. From Akkadian
muškenu;[90] the poor *(muš-ke-nu)* address Šamaš daily. In the Quran in
lists of the needy, "kinsmen, orphans, travelers, the poor," e.g. 30.28
miskīnu مسكين. Thence to Spanish *mezquino*, attested AD 950;[91] surely
Moorish beggars pointed to themselves, *miskīn, miskīn!* For in 1884 in
Algeria is attested the phrase of *lingua franca* (III.265) *moi meskine, toi
donnar sordi* "I am poor, give me sous!" where *meskine* was correctly
perceived as shared between French and Arabic. Via Provençal to
Italian at Dante *Inferno* 27.115, one of the "black Cherubini" claims
Guido *tra' miei meschini* "among my servitors." Modern French
mesquin "meager, beggarly" continues the old sense; curiously Old
French has only the sense "youth."

(5) *"Eunuch."* εὐνοῦχος Matt 19,12[92] (Pal. Syriac סריסין); but the
εὐνοῦχος of Ethiopia (Act 8,27) is a royal official. Pesh. מהימנא "trust-
worthy" with the old sense. Bib. Hebr. סָרִיס mostly of court officials;
Potiphar the סָרִיס of Pharaoh (LXX εὐνοῦχος) has a wife (Gen 39,1.7).
At Sefire (KAI 224.5) "one of my officers or brothers or eunuchs,"

חד פקדי או חד אחי או חד סרסי

At Esther 2,14 of a castrate, "the king's eunuch (LXX εὐνοῦχος)
guarding the concubines," סְרִיס הַמֶּלֶךְ שֹׁמֵר הַפִּילַגְשִׁים.[93] In Rabbinic
only "impotent": Mishna *Yeb.* VIII.4 distinguishes סריס אדם "one

---

pp. 459-466 of J. Delobel (ed.), Logia... (Mémorial Joseph Coppens), Bib. Eph.
Theol. Lov. LIX; Leuven: University, 1982; New Documents 1979, 20-24.

88   Charles Williams, He Came Down from Heaven; London: Faber, 1950; 63: "The
     taunt flung at that Christ, at the moment of his most spectacular impotency, was:
     'He saved others; himself he cannot save.' It was a definition as precise as any in
     the works of the medieval schoolmen.... It was an exact definition of the kingdom
     of heaven in operation, and of the great discovery of substitution which was then
     made by earth."

89   Hence a denominative verb: Bab. Talm. *Sotah* 11a "Whoever makes building
     his business will get poor," כל העוסק בבנין מתמסכן "; at II Kor 8,9 "though
     rich he became poor (ἐπτώχευσεν)," the Peshitto אתמסכן.

90   CAD x.II.275; Kaufman 74, who finds himself "unable to isolate or compre-
     hend the linguistic forces which caused this specific value term to become the
     most widespread and long-lived of the Akkadian loanwords."

91   J. Corominas & J. A. Pascual, Diccionario crítico etimológico castellano e
     hispánico; Madrid: Gredos, vol. iv (1981) 62-63.

92   εὐνή + ἔχω "keeping the bedchamber" Herodotus 3.130 (Persian); Latin
     eunuchus.

93   So at Isa 56,3 a סָרִיס is one incapable of having children (reason unspecified),
     "I am a dry tree." At Ahiqar 61-68 the סריס is a slave and surely emasculated.

emasculated by man" and סריס חמה "one emasculated by the sun."[94]
From Akkadian *ša rēši* "head man" (Kaufman 100); later the harem-
keeper monopolized the name.

(6) *"Merchant."* ἔμπορος Matt 13,45, Pesh תגרא. Discussion at
III.66. Same equivalence in the *Hymn of the Pearl* and Palmyrene.
From Akkadian *tamkaru* (Kaufman 107), it from Sumerian DAM-
GAR. Quran 24.37 *tijāratun* تِجَٰرَة "merchandise."

(7) *"Adversary."* ἀντίδικος Matt 5,25 "Make friends quickly with
your adversary," Pesh בעל דינך; Luk 18,3 the widow: "Vindicate me
against my adversary," Pesh בעל דיני.[95] From Akkadian *bel dīni*
(Kaufman 43) "master of judgement".[96] *Avoth* IV.22: "[God] is the
judge, the witness, the adversary":

הוא הדין הוא העד הוא בעל דין

Jer. Talm. *Ned.* 41c31 "the legal adversary of a certain one was
rich,"[97]

חד בר נש היה בעל דיניה עתיר

These legal systems (Babylonian?) have no prosecuting attorney, the
aggrieved party goes to court. With God as adversary see Aššur and
Šamaš in an Akkadian text.[98] At Luk 18,3 the unjust judge is wearied

---

94   These are precisely the first two categories of Matt 19,12. The third, "those
      who made themselves eunuchs for the sake of the kingdom," was understood
      by "enervate Origen" in "too literal and immature a sense," ἁπλούστερον καὶ
      νεανικώτερον (Eusebius *H.E.* 6.8.2).

95   Both places the Palestinian Syriac transcribes the Greek, אנטידיקוס with vari-
      ations; at *Gen. Rabbah* 82.8 God is the אנטידיקוס of Israel's enemies. With the
      story of the widow see *Pesiqta de Rav Kahana* 15.9:
           There was a woman who 'honored' (i.e. bribed, שכיבדה) a judge with a
           silver lamp. Then her adversary (אנטידיקוס) went and 'honored' him with a
           golden foal. The next day she went and found the previous judgement in her
           favor reversed. She said, "My lord, let the previous judgement in my favor
           shine before you like a lamp." He said, "What can I do? The foal has
           overturned the lamp."
      But the Akkadian is a more likely antecedent. The Rabbinic tale seems a
      reversal of the Gospel parable (III.262)! —Jesus' little parable (Matt 5,25) can
      hardly be allegorized, for is the "adversary" God or Satan? At I Pet 5,8 the
      Devil is the ἀντίδικος (Pesh בעלדבבכון!), and so Rabbinically (Sperber Legal
      Terms 45 citing "AgBer 23.3, 47") "the good inclination which has no adver-
      sary":

                                    יצר טוב שאין לו אנטידיקוס

96   CAD iii.155.
97   And so in the Qumran *Book of the Giants* (J. T. Milik, The Books of Enoch:
      Aramaic Fragments of Qumran Cave 4; Oxford: Clarendon 1976, 307-8,
      citing from 4QEn Giants^c) one calls "my accusers," בעלי דיני, powerful.
98   CAD iii.155b.
99   CAD iii.156a.

into overruling the adversary; in Neo-Babylonian[99] a chief judge is superior to the adversary.

(8) *"Tax-collector."* τελώνης, Pesh מכסא. Both literal and ironical (I.248). Biblical Hebrew מֶכֶס "tax"; noun of agent from Akkadian *mākisu*. Full discussion at III.102.

(9) *Less certain classes.* *"Partner"*: κοινωνοί Matt 23,30, Pesh שותפי. Rabbinic שותף "business partner," Jer. Talm. *Sanh.* 19b1

שותף ליסטיס כליסטיס

"the partner of a bandit (λῃστής) is as a bandit." Akkadian *šutappu* (or *šutāpu*), Kaufman 105. Palmyrene שתף "take as partner" (PAT 1614.9).[100] —*"Enemy."* ἐχθρός, Pesh. (e.g. Matt 10,36) בעלדבבוהי. Rabbinic בעל דבב (*Cant. Rabbah* VII.10); Kaufman 42 from Akkadian *bēl dabābi*, origin uncertain. But old Hebrew for "enemy" is still living, Mishna *Sanh.* III.5 "a friend and an enemy (האוהב והשונא)" are disqualified as witness or judge. —*"Colleague."* Matt 18,29 σύνδουλος "fellow-slave," Pesh. כנתה. So reversed Ezra 4,7 כְּנָוֹתָו where the LXX συνδούλοις. כנות frequent in Egyptian Aramaic. Akkadian *kinattu* both "colleague" and "menial" Kaufman 64. Jer. Talm. *Git.* 48a36[101] "slaves who fled to their colleagues":

עבדיה עקרין לכנותהון

—*"Neighbor."* Luk 14,12 γείτονάς σου, Pesh. שבביך. Bab. Talm. *BB* 29a "the neighbors know well day and night" what is going on in the next house:

שיבבי מידע ידיעי ביממא ובליליא

Kaufman 101 from conjectural Akkadian *šе bābi* "neighbor" (idiom unexplained). —*"Farmer."* γεωργοῖς Matt 21,33, Pesh. פלחא (Arabic *fellaḥeen*). But at James 5,7 for γεωργός Pesh. has אכרא; Bib. Hebr. אִכָּר Amos 5,16 (LXX γεωργός); Mishna *Arakh.* VI.3 אכר. Kaufman 58 from Akkadian *ikkaru* "farmer."

23.2.2 Akkadian elements of urban design

(1) *"Temple."* An alleged saying Mark 14,58 "I shall destroy this temple (ναόν) made with hands," Pesh היכלא.[102] Aramaic היכלא in

---

100 At I Kor 10,20 "partners with demons," κοινωνοὺς τῶν δαιμονίων, the Pesh שותפא לשאדא is pure Akkadian (III.229).
101 As cited or emended by Sokoloff 264 where the standard text has לבנותהון.
102 At Matt 26,61 the Pal. Syr. for ναόν transliterates נוסה. At II.43,223 we suggested from Bernal that να(ϝ)ός was cognate with Bib. Heb. נָוֶה "abode." ναός also was borrowed into Nabataean. In a text from Rawwafah of Arabia (J. T. Milik, "Inscriptions grecques et nabatéennes de Rawwafah," Bulletin of

Megillath Taanith 11.[103] I Reg 21,1 "the palace of Ahab," הֵיכַל אַחְאָב;
the Temple as the palace of Yahweh Isa 6,1. A very early loan from
Akkadian (Kaufman 27) *ekallu* "palace", it from Sumerian É.GAL
"big house." Ugaritic *bhth* and *hklh* run parallel "his house, his palace";[104] the house is Baal's. The West-Semitic development "palace →
temple" is already anticipated in Akkadian where É.GAL is used for
the temple of Šamaš (CAD iv.55a). Ahiqar 17 בבב היכלא "in the gate
of the palace" of Esarhaddon. Palmyrene (PAT 1347) "who dedicated
the temple of Bel," דיחנך היכלא די בל.

(2) *"Rooftop."* Greeks used δῶμα for "rooftop": Matt 10,27 "proclaim on the rooftops," κηρύξατε ἐπὶ τῶν δωμάτων, Pesh אכרזו על אגרא;[105]
Mark 13,15 "on the rooftop," ἐπὶ τοῦ δώματος, Pesh דבאגרא.[106] *Ruth
Rabbah* 3.2 אינר פלטין "the roof of the palace (παλάτιον)". Kaufman
57 takes it from Akkadian *igāru* "wall"; Palestinian builders named
their style from a different Akkadian original.

(3) *"Bridechamber."* Mark 2,19 "sons of the bridechamber," οἱ υἱοὶ
τοῦ νυμφῶνος, Pesh בנוהי דגנונא; Bab. Talm. *B.B.* 14b בני גננא ("sons
of the canopy" בני החפה *Sukkah* 25b). *Gen. Apocryphon* 20.6[107] "No
virgins or brides who enter a bridal chamber are more beautiful than
[Sarah]":

וכל בתולן וכלאן די יעלן לגנון לא ישפרן מנהא

---

the Institute of Archaeology [London] 10 (1971) 54-57) "this is the temple that
the federation (?) of the Thamudeans built":

דנה נוסה די עבדת שרכת תמודן

But it is unlikely that this Hellenism underlies "Temple" in the sayings.

103 Fitzmyer-Harrington 186.

104 KTU 1.4.V.36-37; translated ANET³ 133b 98-99.

105 Bib. Aram. כָּרוֹזָא Dan 3,4 'herald' would seem formed on κῆρυξ (so LXX and
      Theod. here), so that the root כרז would be denominative, Dan 5,29 וְהַכְרִזוּ
      "proclaim," Theod. ἐκήρυξεν. But there may be conflation with an Iranian
      word.

106 Matt 17,15 "Pity my son for he is moonstruck (σεληνιάζεται)"; Pesh
      דאית לה בר אגרא "for he has a [demon] son of the roof." Both languages are
      convinced that sleeping out in the open under the moon causes epilepsy or
      'lunacy.' Cf σεληνιασμός (LSJ). Paulus *Digest* 21.1.43.6 *si furiosum aut
      lunaticum sit [mancipium]* "if a slave is mad or moon-struck." Bab. Talm. *Pes.*
      111b demons dwell on roofs, "the name of the demons on roofs is 'sparks'":

שידי דבי אגרי רישפי

      Locals in the Dominican Republic in the 1930's carried an umbrella if they had
      to walk out at night under a full moon.

107 Ed J. A. Fitzmyer, The Genesis Apocryphon of Qumran Cave I; 2 ed.; Biblica
      et Orientalia 18a: Rome: Bib. Inst. Press, 1971; 63. Reprinted in Fitzmyer-
      Harrington p. 113. Similarly in the Fragment Targum of Ex 12,2, cited by
      Sokoloff 133.

Kaufman 51 from Akkadian *ganūnu* "living quarters, bedroom." Babylonian architecture adapted for Palestinian local custom.

(4) *"Table."* Domestic: "the rich man's table (τραπέζης)" (Luk 16,21, cf 22,30), Pesh פתורה. "Banker's table" Luke 19,23 ἐπὶ τράπεζαν, Pesh על פתורא.[108] Rabbinic פתורה in both senses.[109] Hatra פתרא "altar" (KAI 253). Connected to Akkadian *paššuru* "table" (Kaufman 81) in spite of abnormal phonetics. The banker's table a Babylonian novelty.

(5) *"Furnace."*[110] Matt 6,30 "into the furnace," εἰς κλίβανον, Pesh בתנורא. Bib. Hebr. תַּנּוּר "portable oven." Some connection (Kaufman 108) with Akkadian *tinūru* "oven." In both Akkadian and Aramaic of the Tell Fekherye inscription[111] in a curse of scarcity; cf Lev 26,26 "Ten women shall bake your bread in one oven (בְּתַנּוּר אֶחָד)": LXX ἐν κλιβάνῳ ἑνί. The Aramaic has ומאה נשים לאפן בתנור לחם "And may a hundred women bake bread in an oven..." where the Akkadian has *tinūra*.[112]

(6) *"Street"* and *"alley."* Pesh. שוק for both ἀγορά "market" (Mark 7,4; Matt 11,6) and πλατεῖα "broad street" (Luk 10,10, Matt 6,5). πλατεῖα went into Semitic פלטיא.[113] Proverb at Matt 20,3 "standing idle in the market," ἑστῶτας ἐν τῇ ἀγορᾷ ἀργούς, Pesh דקימין בשוקא ובטילין. Bab. Talm. *Pes.* 55a "Go and see how many idle there are in the market":

פוק חזי כמה בטלני איכא בשוקא

In late Bib. Hebr. שׁוּק as Aramaism: Cant 3,2 (cf Prov 7,8; Koh 12,4-5) "in the streets and the squares," בַּשְּׁוָקִים וּבָרְחֹבוֹת, LXX ἐν ταῖς ἀγοραῖς καὶ ἐν ταῖς πλατείαις. Easement in a deed, Cowley 5.14 "in the street

---

108 At Matt 25,27 "You should have given my money to the bankers," τοῖς τραπεζίταις Pesh has just "to the table," על פתורא. For τραπεζίτης in Latin and Rabbinic see I.75; τράπεζα as a loanword at *Gen. Rabbah* 64.10 טרפיזין plural.
109 Jerus. Targum Gen 23,16 as cited by Jastrow 1250b.
110 κάμινος "furnace" (Matt 13,42), Pesh אתונא, may represent Akkadian *atūnu* (Kaufman 110), cited by Sokoloff 79 from Targum Neofiti on Ex 19,18 נהינם דמתילה באתונה "Gehenna which is compared to a furnace."
111 E. Lipiński, Studies in Aramaic Inscriptions and Onomastics; Orientalia Lovaniensia Analecta 57; Leuven: Peeters, 1994 chapter 2.
112 Arabic تَنّور *tannūr* Quran 11.40 has a different sense.
113 πλατεῖα entered Rabbinic through a Targum on Gen 19,2 (Krauss 457) which for LXX πλατείᾳ has פלטיא. Bab. Talm. *Shabb.* 6a המוציא מחנות לפלטיא "one who carries [an item] from shop to street." Palmyrene פלטיא (PAT 0041.7) is "corridor inside a tomb." *Thr. Rabbah* on I.1 "full of people" optimistically reckons that Jerusalem had 24 פלטיות, each of 24 entries (מבאות), each of 24 roads (שווקים), each of 24 streets (שקקים), each of 24 courts (חצרות), each of 24 houses (בתים)—or 191,102,976 houses in all. πλατεῖα became Latin *platea*, whence French and English *place*.

between us" (בשוקא זי בינין)." Palmyrene "market" in an elegant calque, רב שוק = ἀγορανομήσαντα PAT 0278, "market-overseer"; so *Num. Rabbah* 20.18 בעל השוק.[114] *Gen. Rabbah* 91.6 שוק של זונות "market of the harlots."

From Akkadian *šūqu* (Kaufman 94). Hence Arabic *sūq*: Quran 25.8 "What ails this messenger [the Prophet!] that he eats food and walks in the markets (*'aswāq* فى آلٱسۡوَاق)?" Cf. Jesus as "glutton," Matt 11,19; Luk 13,26 "You taught in our streets (πλατείαις, בשוקין)"! Hence in the picturesque settings celebrated by Orientalism: "[A Tunis] c'est le souk des selliers qui commence" (Gide 1896).[115] "There is a large 'Suk,' or market-place in the usual form, a long narrow lane darkened by a covering of palm leaves, with little shops let into the walls of the houses on both sides" (Burton 1855, of Medinah).[116]

Contrasted to the broad *sūq* is the narrow alley: Luk 14,21 "into the streets and alleys of the city," εἰς τὰς πλατείας καὶ ῥύμας τῆς πόλεως, Pesh לשוקא ולבריתא דמדינתא. Same contrast (Kaufman 44) in a text of Sennacherib,[117] *ribâtišu ušandilma bi-re-e-ti u sūqāni ušperdi* "I widened its (Nineveh's) squares and let light into its alleys and streets." Bab. Talm. *BB* 40b "in streets and alleys," בשוקא ובבריתא. Qumran on the New Jerusalem: ברית שוק "a portico of a street."[118] The narrow 'alleys' of Mediterranean cities even today recall the centuries when only camels delivered goods (III.320). Broad streets and squares were an innovation, already at Elephantine, first from Babylon, then Hellenistic. Bab. Talm. *Shabb.* 33b credits Romans with building streets (שווקים)—but only to put harlots (זונות) in them, with bridges for collecting tax (מכס); see I.248.

23.2.3 Other Akkadian loanwords

(1) *"Gratis, freely."* Matt 10,8 "Freely have you received, freely give," δωρεὰν ἐλάβετε, δωρεὰν δότε; Pesh מגן נסבתון מגן הבו. A verb in Ugaritic *mgn* (KTU 1.4.I.21) with מָגֵּן Gen 14,20 "has delivered."

---

114 The Athenian ἀγορανόμος was taken over into the Latin of Plautus as *agoranomus*.
115 Cited in Trésor de la langue française s.v.
116 Cited from OED.
117 CAD ii.252a.
118 5Q New Jerusalem (5QJN ar [5Q15]) frag. 1 col. 1 line 1, Fitzmyer-Harrington 54.
119 "This foreign word...occurs in early Akkadian in the sense of 'gift,' but only as a Hurrianism, and in late Akkadian in the meaning 'gratis' as an Aramaism. The Western forms were probably also borrowed directly from Hurrian."

Palmyrene (PAT 0282) "who brought up the caravan *gratis*, from his own purse":

ἀνακομίσα[ντα τὴν] συνοδίαν προῖκα ἐξ ἰδίων

די אסק שירתא מגן מן כיסה

Bab. Talm. *BQ* 85a (III.222) "a physician without pay" אסיא דמגן is a pure Akkadian phrase. *Lev. Rabbah* 34.16 "Does anybody work for nothing?" אית בר נש דלעי מגן. Kaufman 67 notes Akkadian *magannu* "gift," thence adverbially "as a gift":[119] "my house is worth one talent of silver, *u ana ma-gannu naši* but he has taken it for nothing."[120] The original may be Vedic *magham* "gift" with Indo-European cousins, e.g. Latin *magnus*.

(2) *"Cock."* Mark 14,30 "before the cock crows," πρὶν ἤ...ἀλέκτορα φωνῆσαι, Pesh. קדם דנקרא תרנגלא. Jer. Talm. *Sukkah* 55c19 etc. "the cock crowed," קרא תרנגלא. Kaufman 108 from Akkadian *tarlugallu*, it from Sumerian DAR.LUGAL. The earlier Greek form of the name is ἀλεκτρύων, Theognis 864 ἀλεκτρυόνων φθόγγος ἐγειρομένων "the sound of awakened cocks"; Levin takes it from the Akkadian by a "complicated metathesis." It is unclear whether the Homeric men (both in the genitive) Ἀλέκτορος *Odyssey* 4.10 and Ἀλεκτρυόνος *Iliad* 17.602 are "Cock" or "Protector"; or whether the man's name Linear B *A-re-ku-tu-ru-wo* (DMG² 58) is the same.

(3) *"Demon."* δαιμόνιον is beneficent in Plato, later malevolent (Josephus *BJ* 7.185); but Jesus' usage surely rests on some Aramaic word. The Old Syriac in the sayings of Jesus has Akkadian שאדא throughout; the Peshitto sometimes Iranian דיוא. At Matt 12,24 in a saying of Pharisees the versions make a distinction: "This fellow (οὗτος) only casts out demons (δαιμόνια, שאדא) by Beelzebul prince of the demons (ἄρχοντι τῶν δαιμονίων, רשא דדיוא)." While the Akkadian has a better claim as the original, the Iranian deserves a note here.

δῖος "divine," Latin *deus*, & Buddhist Pali *devānaṃ* (*Dhammapada* 30) are honorific like Sanskrit *deva*; but Iranian cognates like Syriac דיוא are all pejorative. So Zarathushtra (*Yasna* 32.1) of the *daēvā*; Xerxes[121] at Persepolis overthrew worship of the *daivā*. The flying letter in the *Hymn of the Pearl* 50 is sealed to keep it from "savage demons," דיוא מרירא, Greek δαίμονας. דיוא in the Peshitto then suggests Sasanid influence.

---

120 CAD x.I.32 which considers it a "loanword from Indo-European by way of Hurrian."

121 Kent 151, lines 35-41.

Syriac שאדא is Hebr. שֵׁדִים "demons" Deut 32,17, where LXX δαιμονίοις.[122] In a Pseudo-Daniel from Qumran[123] the Israelites "[sacri]ficed their children to the demons of error":

[וֹהוו זב]חין לבניהון לשידי טעותא

Bab Talm. *Pes.* 110a on "Asmodaios king of the *šedim*," אשמדאי מלכא דשידי makes him parallel to Beelzebul "prince of the demons".[124] *Šed* beside דיוא in Syriac incantations.[125] Loan from Akkadian *šedu* (Kaufman 101), "a spirit representing the vital force" of a man or temple, propitious or malevolent.[126] The "unclean spirit" that leaves a man and then returns "to my house from which I came" (Matt 12,43-45) is surely a *daimonion*; see "the evil (portended) by an evil *š[edu]* that flits about restlessly in the house of a man."[127]

(4) *"Purple."* Dives (Luk 16,19) wore "purple and byssus," πορφύραν καὶ βύσσον, Pesh reversed בוצא וארגונא; so Esther 8,15 בּוּץ וְאַרְגָּמָן, LXX βύσσινον πορφυροῦν.[128] Hebr. אַרְגָּמָן once in Aramaic form with *waw* II Chron 2,6 אַרְגְּוָן; Dan 5,7 אַרְגְּוָנָא; Palmyrene ארגונא Tariff 137. Ugaritic *argmn* is either "tribute" (so Akkadian *argamannu* at Boghaz-Köy)[129] or "purple." Old loan from Akkadian (Kaufman 35). ἀργεμώνη "purple poppy" (Dioscorides, II.335) may reflect it. πορφύρα in turn to Latin *purpura* and Rabbinic: "beds (κοῖται) of byssus and beds of purple":[130]

קימטאות של בוץ קיטיות של פורפירן

(5) *"(Gold) ring."* A clear mistranslation is Matt 7,6 "Give not the holy (τὸ ἅγιον, Pesh קודשא) to dogs, and cast not your pearls before swine." The Pesh by luck points to the intended "earring": cf. Prov 11,22 "a gold ring in the nose of a pig," נֶזֶם זָהָב בְּאַף חֲזִיר, which Jesus

---

122 שֵׁדִים also at Ps 106,37, describing the apostasy of Deut 32,17 as human sacrifice; conjectured at Amos 2,1 (less plausibly at Ps 91,6) "That they burned the bones of the king of Edom to a *demon*" where MT לַשִׂיד "to lime."

123 Fitzmyer-Harrington 6 = 4QpsDan arᵃ⁻ᶜ, c-2.

124 Ἀσμοδαῖος Tobit 3,8; he is Avestan *Aešma Daēva* "Demon of Wrath."

125 "I speak the secret (רזה) of this house against all that is in it; against *šedu* (שידא), against *devas* (דיוא)...against all messengers of idolatry (אזגנדא דפתכרותא)." The last phrase is pure Iranian: see on "messenger" (III.89) and *patikara* (III.96). See J. Naveh & S. Shaked, Amulets and Magic Bowls: Aramaic Incantations of Late Antiquity; Jerusalem: Magnes & Leiden: Brill, 1985; Bowl 1.4-5, p. 124.

126 CAD xv.256-8.

127 CAD xv.258b.

128 Similarly in Aramaic, *Genesis Apocryphon* 20.31 "many garments of byssus and purple (בוץ וארגואן)," Fitzmyer-Harrington 116.

129 CAD i.II.253.

130 Krauss 528a citing "Yelammedenu as quoted by Aruch completum."

doubles. Akkadian *qudāšu* "earring";[131] Gen 24,22 Onqelos has קדשא דדהבא for Hebrew נֶזֶם זָהָב "gold ring." The Qumran *Job Targum* ends with each of Job's friends giving him a gold ring, קדש חד די דהב.[132]

(6) *"Pay."* μισθός frequent, Pesh אגרא. Literal: Luk 10,7 "The laborer is worthy of his pay;" mostly symbolic, Matt 5,12 "Your pay is great in the heavens." Rabbinic: "a doctor's fee," אגר אסיא —a wholly Akkadian phrase;[133] "a hired man's pay," אגרא דאגירא;[134] "the reward of the righteous," אגרהון דצדיקיה.[135] R. Simon b. Shetah would rather hear 'Blessed be the God of the Jews' "than all the profit of this world," מאגר כל הדין עלמא (Jer. Talm. *BM* 8c31). Kaufman 33 finds the Aram. root אגר simply cognate with Akkadian *agāru* "to hire." But the noun seems derived: Old Assyrian *ig-ri rābiṣi* "hire of the police-man"; *ig-ri šiprē* "hire of the messengers."[136] *'ajr(un)* أَجْر is common in the Quran, always symbolic: Quran 12.57 "And the reward of the Hereafter is better," وَلَأَجْرُ ٱلْآخِرَةِ خَيْرٌ; 3.57 "He will pay them their wages," فَيُوَفِّيهِمْ أُجُورَهُمْ.

(7) *"Throne."* θρόνος, Pesh mostly כורסיא, but varies at Matt 19,28 "When the Son of Man shall sit on the throne of his glory (ἐπὶ θρόνου δόξης αὐτοῦ, Pesh תרונוס דשובחה), you also will sit on twelve thrones (θρόνους, כורסון)."[137] Akkadian *kussû* seems a very early loan to Ugaritic *ksu*.[138] The curse "overthrow the throne of one's kingship" (I.276-277) runs from Ugaritic through Byblos to the NT: Dan 5,20 "he was deposed from the throne of his kingship":

הָנְחַת מִן־כָּרְסֵא מַלְכוּתֵהּ

For the Aramaic form in *r*, כרסא KAI 216.7 (Bar-Rekab, 8th cent BC). The divine claim "Heaven is my throne" runs from Isa 66,1 כִּסְאִי (III.244) to Quran 2.255 "His throne (*kursiyyuhu*) includes heaven and earth":

وَسِعَ كُرْسِيُّهُ ٱلسَّمَٰوَٰتِ وَٱلْأَرْضَ

(8) *"To save."* Forms of σῴζομαι "be saved" mostly in the Pesh. from the root חיא "live"; but Luk 13,23 οἱ σῳζόμενοι in the Pal. Syr.

---

131 Kaufman 86; the CAD xiii.293 has "woman's ring" but not specifically "ear-ring"; this word has no demonstrable connection, either by original or folk etymology, with the root קדשׁ "sanctify."

132 Fitzmyer-Harrington 46 = 11QtgJob 38:11.

133 Sokoloff 34-35 citing the Fragment Targum on Ex 21,19.

134 Targum Neofiti on Lev 19,13.

135 Targum Neofiti on Num 24,23.

136 CAD i.45.

137 θρόνος went into Rabbinic also, תרונוס.

138 Kaufman 28 leaves it open whether the West-Semitic word is a loan from Akkadian or cognate; but its form is alien to West-Semitic root structure.

comes out משתוזבין from שוזב. Jennings[139] quoting Burkitt thinks that Palestinian Aramaic had no special term for "safety" and asks:

> May we not believe that this is the genuine Aramaic usage, and that the Greek Gospels have in this instance introduced a distinction [between "life" and "safety"] which was not made by Christ and His Aramaic-speaking disciples?

At Mark 5,23 "be saved" and "live" are synonyms, ἵνα σωθῇ καὶ ζήσῃ. But the root שוזב is well attested in Sokoloff 546. Kaufman 105 derives it from Akkadian *šūzubu* "to save," uncertain whether a "shaphel" of a simpler root. At Neh 3,4 a father מְשֵׁיזַבְאֵל has an old name-type newly formed in Akkadian Aramaic. At Dan 3,28 שֵׁיזִב in the LXX ("3,95") is ἔσωσε; so translating σῴζω at Palmyra (PAT 0197, AD 132) "saving from great danger," διασώσαντα...ἐκ...μεγάλου κινδύνου = שוזבה מן קדנס רב. Ahiqar 46 "I am that Ahiqar who formerly saved you from an undeserved death":

אנה הו אחיקר זי קדמן שזבך מן קטל זכי

(9) *Possible loans.* —"*Yoke.*" Matt 11,29-30 ὁ...ζυγός μου, Pesh נירא; נירי Targumic. But Kaufman 77 thinks Akkadian *nīru* simply cognate with Aramaic. —"*Divorce.*" Mark 10,4 βιβλίον ἀποστασίου cites Deut 24,1 LXX where Heb. סֵפֶר כְּרִיתֻת, Onqelos גט פיתורין "a bill of divorce." גט means "the document" *par excellence*, i.e. of divorce, in Mishna *Gittin.* From Murabbaʿat we have an actual "writ of divorce," גט שבמן (prob. AD 111).[140] גט is Akkadian *gittu* "(one-column) document." —"*Silver coin*". δραχμαί Luk 15,8-9 comes out in the Pesh זוזין.[141] If not an elegance of Luke, this reflects frequent זוז since Elephantine; Kaufman 114 from Akkadian *zūzu* "half-shekel"—a weight, not a coin.[142] In the Hellenistic-Roman period only in revolts did locals coin in silver, so the *zūz* named foreign silver, esp. the denarius. —"*Cross.*" We saw at III.109 that σταυρός must represent West-Semitic צליבא rather than (with the Pesh.) Edessene זקיפא from Akkadian *zaqīpu.*

---

139 W. Jennings & U. Gantillon, Lexicon to the Syriac New Testament; Oxford: Clarendon, 1926; p. 6.
140 Fitzmyer-Harrington 158.
141 "Drachma" is conflated with "daric" in West Semitic (II.296,335).
142 CAD xxi.170.

23.3 Iranian in the Aramaic of the sayings

We discussed Iranian influence on Judaism at III.100-101. The best guide for Iranian loanwords in Aramaic is Telegdi.[143] Early attestation of Iranian languages is limited; if I controlled the *Shahnameh* of Firdausi (AD 941-1020), the data would be improved. I cite: the Old Persian cuneiform texts of the Achaemenids, edited by Kent; parts of the Avesta and esp. its *Yasnas*, edited by Insler, some likely original verse of Zarathushtra; and the trilingual of Sapor at Naqš-i-Rustam in Greek, Parthian (the Arsacid dialect) and Pehlevi (Sasanid), ab. AD 265.[144] Some Iranian loanwords in both Greek and West-Semitic are noted at I.342, II.296; there are longer treatments in Chapter 20 of "satrap" (III.86), "legate" (III.89), "sword" (III.99), "magus" (III.91) and "image" (πάταχρον etc., III.96). Here are a few more.

—"*Danakē.*" δανάκη "coin put on the eyes of the dead"; Callimachus frag. 278;[145] Bab. Talm. *B. M.* 60b דנקא "small coin"; Persian *dāng*.[146] —"*Kapithē.*" καπίθη "dry measure" Xenophon *Anab.* 1.5.6; καπέτιες or καπέζιες plural Polyaenus 4.3.32. Pehlevi *kapīč*.[147] Bab. Talm. *Pes.* 48b top קפיזא. —"*Parasang.*" παρασάγγης "measure of distance" (time of march?) Herodotus 2.6.3. Middle Persian *frasang*.[148] Bab. Talm. *B.Q.* 82b פרסה with folk-etymology to פרס "Persia." — "*Dastikirt.*" δαστικίρτης "domain, property" Sapor *Res Gestae* 70 for Parthian *dstkrt*; Old Persian *dastakarta* "handiwork" (same word?).[149] Bab. Talm. *Erub.* 59a דאיסקרתא "village."[150] —"*Argapetes.*" In a Palmyrene bilingual (*PAT 0286*, AD 262), Septimius Worodes has three titles, respectively transliterated from Greek, Latin and Iranian:

קרטסטוס אפטרפא דקנרא וארגבטא

τὸν κράτιστον ἐπίτροπον Σεβαστοῦ δουκηνάριον ἀργαπέτην

---

143 S. Telegdi, "Essai sur la phonétique des emprunts iraniens en araméen talmudique: Glossaire," Journal Asiatique 226 (1935) 224-256.
144 For editions of the Res Gestae see III.73. For the Greco-Parthian bilingual of Vologases III of Parthia (AD 151) on a votive statue of Heracles/Verethragna see III.70. Scattered Iranian Arsacid texts represent Parthian, in large part expressed in Aramaic ideograms. The Aramaic script of a Greek bilingual from Armazi of Georgia must represent Parthian (Gignoux 44); KAI 276 treats it as aberrant Aramaic.
145 Ed. Pfeiffer i.262.
146 Telegdi 239 no. 51; Frisk iii.68.
147 Telegdi 254 no. 124.
148 Frisk iii.167.
149 Kent 190.
150 Telegdi 239 no. 52.

(Greek) "most eminent procurator of Augustus, *ducenarius, argapetes.*" Bab. Talm. *Zeb.* 96b ארקפטא; Parthian *hrkpty* "chef des impôts."[151] —*"(Gold) necklace,"* μανιάκης.[152] Plutarch *Cimon* 9.3: in the Persian wars Greeks took as booty "golden circlets and necklaces and torques," ψέλια χρυσᾶ καὶ μανιάκας καὶ στρεπτούς. Part of a bride's dowry is a golden περιτραχήλιον μανιάκην.[153] Certainly Persian,[154] with other words of the same ending, καυνάκης (Aristoph. *Vespae* 1137)[155] and ἀκινάκης (Xenophon *Anab.* 1.2.27) "cloak...dagger" (suitable for a spy-novel...).[156] At Gen 41,42 Aquila and Symmachus[157] have μανιάκην for רְבִד הַזָּהָב "gold chain" where Onqelos (from such a version) מניכא דדהבא; so Dan 5,7 (K) הַמְוֹנְכָא דִי־דַהֲבָא where LXX μανιάκην χρυσοῦ; *Deut. Rabbah* 4.2 מוניק של זהב.

23.3.1 Abstract Iranian loanwords in the sayings.

Greek supplied abstract words to concrete Semitic, but was anticipated by Iranian. -γούνη is a suffix in women's names: Ῥοδογούνη "Rose-Color";[158] *Hymn of the Pearl* 97 "and my toga, brilliant with colors," גוון ולטמי נציח גונא; "color" Bab. Talm. *Erub.* 53b. Parthian *gwnk* Sapor *Res Gestae* 37 "sort, kind."[159]

(1) *"Limb."* μέλος: Matt 5,29 "It is better that one of your limbs (μελῶν, Pesh. הדמך) be lost than that your whole body (σῶμα) be thrown into Gehenna."[160] Dan 2,5 הַדָּמִין תִּתְעַבְדוּן "You shall be cut up into members"; a Rabbinic verb הִדֵּם "dismember." Avestan *handāman,*[161] "NW Pehlevi" *handām,*[162] both "member." Paul's idea of persons as "members" of a larger "body" is Hellenistic: I Kor 12,12 "As the body (σῶμα)...has many members (μέλη, הדמא)". It appears in later Semitic, *Odes of Solomon* 3.2 "[The Lord's] members are with him," והדמוהי לותה אנון.

---

151 Gignoux 52.
152 See my treatment in "LXX and Targum" 203-204.
153 *P.Oxy.* 1273.7 (vol. x.207); the weight is given in "common gold on the standard of Oxyrhynchus."
154 Frisk iii.149.
155 Also Rabbinic, Targum Jonathan Jud 4,18 בגוונכא; Latin *gaunaca* (OLD).
156 Frisk at iii.149 cites Armenian *maneak* "Halsband" and at iii.24 Sogdian *kyn'k* "dagger."
157 Field i.59.
158 Ctesias FGH 688 frag. 13.24.
159 Gignoux 51; see Telegdi 236 no. 39. O. Szemerényi, "Iranica VI (Nos. 71-75)," Studia Iranica 9 (1980) 23-68, has an elaborate study of Iranian *gauna-* etc.
160 Cf. Kol 3,5 "Put to death your earthly members (μέλη, הדמא)."
161 Bartholomae 1772.

(2) *"Weapon."* ὅπλον uncompounded at Joh 18,3, Pesh. זינא. Luk 11,22 "seizes his panoply (πανοπλίαν, Pesh. זינה)." Cowley 31.8 זניהום "their weapons." Qumran Job Targum לנקשת זין "in the clash of arms."[163] Bab. Talm. *Sanh.* 104a זין אוכל זין "weapon eating up weapon."[164] Sapor *Res Gestae* 58, Deran is "chief of the armory," Parthian *zynpty*, Pehlevi *zynpt*, ζηνιπιτ. Avestan *Hymn to Mithra* 96,[165] Mithra wields the "strongest of weapons," *amavastəməm zaēnąm.*

(3) *"Time, season."* καιρός, Pesh. זבנא, marks not elapsed time (χρόνος) but a *kind of time*: favorable, II Kor 6,2 εὐπρόσδεκτος; unfavorable, II Tim 3,1 καιροὶ χαλεποί. Mark 1,15 is hopeful, "The time is fulfilled (πεπλήρωται ὁ καιρός, Pesh שלם לה זבנא, Vg *impletum est tempus*)."[166] Mark 13,33 demands watchfulness, "You do not know when the time is," πότε ὁ καιρός, Pesh. אמתי הו זבנא, Vg *quando tempus sit.*[167]

זבנא with *b* is Syriac and Palmyrene; elsewhere זמנא with *m*. In the Palmyrene Tariff for both Greek words: at I.4 בזבניא קדמיא = [ἐν τοῖς] πάλαι χρόνοις "in former times"; at I.10 בזבן זבן = κατὰ καιρόν "from time to time." At Esther 9,27, Purim is to be observed "at the [original] times," כִּזְמַנָּם; at Dan 2,16, Daniel asks the king "to set him a time," דִּי זְמָן יִנְתֶּן־לֵהּ (LXX χρόνος). Bab. Talm. *Hag.* 4b, "Does anyone die before his time?" איכא אזיל בלא זימנה. Koh 3,1 has two words for "time," "For everything there is a season, and a time for every matter under the heavens"

לַכֹּל זְמָן וְעֵת לְכָל־חֵפֶץ תַּחַת הַשָּׁמָיִם

The LXX reverses expectation, τοῖς πᾶσιν χρόνος, καὶ καιρὸς τῷ παντὶ πράγματι. This cyclic pessimism gives way in the NT Peshitto to time seen as a critical novelty, whether hopeful or dangerous.

Most take זְמָן from Iranian, comparing Pehlevi *zamān*, Persian *zāmān*.[168] Perhaps in Parthian *zmn*;[169] I cannot determine if it names the Zoroastrian heresy of *Zurvan* "Time." Kaufman 92 thinks the

---

162 Telegdi 241 no. 59.
163 11QtgJob 33.6, Fitzmyer-Harrington 40.
164 This picks up the international theme "sword against sword," III.25.
165 Ed. Ilya Gershevitch, Cambridge: University, 1959 p. 121; see Telegdi 242 no. 66.
166 More hopeful than not are Luk 12,42 "to give their ration in due time (ἐν καιρῷ)"; Luk 18,30 "manyfold in this time."
167 More dangerous than not are Luk 21,8 where false prophets say, "The time is at hand"; Luk 12,56 "Why can you not interpret the present time?"
168 Telegdi 242 no. 68.
169 Gignoux 68.

Aramaic is rather from Akkadian *simānu* "set time." But the initial consonants are problematic. The double coloration of N.T. καιρός[170] reflects Latin influence. In classical Greek καιρός is by itself positive, only an adjective makes it negative. But in Polybius often καιρός is by itself "a dangerous time": 18.11.8 τὸν παρόντα καιρὸν ἐκφυγεῖν "to avoid the difficult current situation."[171] Dubuisson saw that Latin *tempus* brought about the shift in Polybius, continuing to later Greek: Cicero (*Cael.* 13) says Catiline "helped his friends in the time of their troubles," *seruire temporibus suorum*; again (*Cat.* 1.22) he urges Catiline "to yield in face of the dangers of the State," *ut temporibus reipublicae cedas*. As in the N.T. καιρός is a critical time with possibilities for good or ill, compare Valerius Flaccus 1.306 *tempus adest; age, rumpe moras* "the time is at hand, put off delay."[172]

(4) *Other possible abstract terms. —"Ration."* Luke 12,42 σιτο-μέτριον might rest on Iranian פַּת־בַּג Dan 1,5 with Sanskrit *pratibhāga* "daily gift," concretely ποτίβαζις Athenaeus 11.503F "Persian bread"; rations were handed out in the Persian court (Xenophon *Anab.* 1.9.25-26). *—"Response."* Matt 12,36 "They shall give account (λόγον, Pesh. פתגמה) of it." Parthian *ptgm* "message";[173] Esther 1,20 פִּתְגָם הַמֶּלֶךְ "the king's edict"; Koh 8,11 פִּתְגָם מַעֲשֵׂה הָרָעָה "sentence against an evil deed": at Elephantine גסת פתגם "reprimand (?)" (Driver 4.3, 7.9). Also Targumic. But cf *Avoth* III.1 "You are to give account and reckoning (דין וחשבון)." *—"Kind, sort."* Mark 9,29 "This kind (γένος, Pesh. גנסא) comes out only by prayer"; Matt 13,47 "of every kind [of fish] (παντὸς γένους, גנסא)."[174] At I Kor 12,10 "kinds of tongues," γένη γλωσσῶν Pesh. has the Iranian cognate זניא דלשנא; cf. Dan 3,5 "all kinds of music," זְנֵי זְמָרָא, LXX παντὸς γένους μουσικῶν. Old Persian *vispazana-* (Kent 208) "with men of all kinds," Driver 7.3 "craftsmen of all kinds" אמנן וספזן. It is doubtful whether either the Greek or Iranian cognate underlies γένος in the Aramaic.

---

170 Conversely καιρός goes into Rabbinic, *Qoh. Rabbah* on 11,3 "when the student's time comes" to teach, אם הגיע קירסו שלתלמיד. But this cannot underly N.T. καιρός.

171 Dubuisson 177-178.

172 The OLD at *tempus* includes "a favorable or convenient time," but not specifically "a dangerous time," though it cites several passages with that coloration.

173 Gignoux 61; Telegdi 253 no. 119.

174 Same equivalence to the Greek loanword at Palm. Tariff I.13 "of every kind" כלמא גנס = παντὸς γένους.

23.3.2 Iranian cultural terms in the sayings

Many are treated elsewhere in these volumes.

(1) *"Demon."* While δαιμόνιον probably rests on Akkadian *šedu* via Aramaic שאדא (III.229), Iranian *deva* via Aramaic דיוא is barely possible.

(2) *"Legate."* For πρεσβεία "embassy" Luk 14,32; 19.12-14; Pesh. איזגדא "ambassadors." Discussion at III.89-91 of the Iranian original. Conversely πρεσβευτής went into Rabbinic פרוזבוטיס which however cannot underly it.[175] Legates in the ancient world have a far-reaching symbolism.[176]

(3) *"Sword."* Pesh sees μάχαιρα as Iranian at Matt 26,52 "Put your sword (μάχαιραν, ספסרא) back in its place"; 26,55 "Have you come as against a bandit (λῃστήν, Pal. Syr. לסטיא) with swords (μαχαιρῶν, בספסרא) and staves to take me?." At III.99-100 we note its source in Parthian *spsyr*, and its use in Aramaic and Greek σαμψηρά (Josephus *AJ* 20.32).[177] When Paul (Rom 13,4) writes "he bears not the sword (μάχαιραν, Pesh ספסרא) in vain," he anticipates the later *ius gladii*,[178] in language which Syriac hears as Iranian.

(4) *"Pearl."* Matt 13,45 (cf. 7,6), the trader finds a pearl (μαργαρίτην, Pesh מרגניתא, Pal. Syr. מרגלי). The "pearl" is Eastern, Middle Persian *marvarit*, Quran 55.58 مَرْجَان *marjān*. Discussion at III.62-63.

(5) *"Conscription."* Matt 5,41 "Whoever conscripts you one mile...," with denom. verb ἀγγαρεύσει, Pal. Syr. צאד לך אנגריא "exercises conscription on you." אנגריא in Aramaic was a Greek term for a

---

175 Levy iv.106 citing *Yelammedenu* on Deut. praef. from the *Aruch*: "[Speakers of] seventy languages stood at the entrance to Pharaoh's palace (פלטין), so that, if there should come legates (פרוזבטין) of a king, they would speak with him in his language."

176 Margaret M. Mitchell, "New Testament Envoys in the Context of Greco-Roman Diplomatic and Epistolary Conventions: The Example of Timothy and Titus," JBL 111 (1992) 641-662; Anthony Bash, Ambassadors for Christ: An Exploration of Ambassadorial Language in the New Testament; WUNT 2 Reihe no. 92; Tübingen: Mohr, 1997. Elsewhere ("Inversion of Social Roles in Paul's Letters," NovT 33 [1991] 303-325, pp. 316-317) I treat the transformation of the role of ambassador in Paul.

177 μάχαιρα went into early Latin: Ennius 519 Skutsch *succincti corda machaeris* "girt with swords over their hearts." But μάχαιρα hardly underlies Gen 49,5 מְכֵרֹתֵיהֶם "their swords?," although *Gen. Rabbah* 99.7 says "This is Greek, in which swords are called מכירין."

178 An early attestation of *ius gladii* at Heliopolis/Baalbek in ILS 9200 (=IGLS 2794 with photo): the veteran of the Jewish War C. Velius Rufus has been *proc(uratori) prouinciae Raetiae ius gladi* "procurator of the province of Rhaetia with *ius gladii*."

Roman practice (II.52). Greek ἀγγαρεία rests on ἄγγαρος "Persian messenger"; but the Roman meaning may rest on an unrecorded Persian or Akkadian original.

(6) *"Paradise."* Luk 23,43 "Today you will be with me in Paradise." See Chapter 21 for Avestan and Old Persian originals; Quran 18.107 "the gardens of Paradise," جَنَّتُ ٱلْفِرْدَوْسِ. Under the Achaemenids the παράδεισοι were the perquisites of the Great King and satraps, so Jesus, while suffering the penalty inflicted on rebel satraps, claims their legitimacy (III.108,140).

(7) *"Mystery."* Mark 4,11 "To you is given the mystery (μυστήριον) of the kingdom of God," Pesh ארזא.[179] Dan 2,19 "the mystery was revealed," רָזָא גֱּלִי, Theod. τὸ μυστήριον ἀπεκαλύφθη; *Ahiqar* 175 "in a hiding place of mysteries," בסתר ארזא.[180] Qumran רזי אל "secrets of El" in the *Rule* (1QS 3.23), *War Scroll* (1QM 3.9 etc.) is one of the rare non-Semitic words in the Scrolls.[181] A "Messianic" text[182] of a new-born child "He will know the secrets of mankind; his wisdom will go forth to all peoples, he will know the secrets of all living things":

ידע רזי אנשא וחוכמתה לכול עממיא תלך וידע רזי כול חייא

Odes of Solomon 8.10 "Keep my mystery, you who are kept by it":

טרו ארזי הנון דמתנטרין בה

Avoth VI.2 Torah "gives [the student] sovereignty and dominion and the searching out of judgement; and [these reciprocally] reveal to him secrets of the Torah":

ונותנת לו מלכות וממשלה וחקור דין ומגלין לו רזי תורה

The word is Iranian: Pehlevi *rāz*, and prob. Avestan *razah-* "Einsamkeit, Abgelegenheit".[183] Conversely μυστήριον went into Rabbinic, *Gen. Rabbah* 68.12 "who revealed the secret of the Holy One":

שגלו מיסטירין של הקדוש

Cicero *de orat.* 1.206 *illa dicendi mysteria* "those secrets of oratory."

---

179 Matt 13,11 and Luk 8,10 agree against the best MSS of Mark 4,11 in adding γνῶναι "to know." But most MSS of Mark add γνῶναι also. If this is taken as assimilation to Matthew or Luke, the Synoptic relations are puzzling; but if Matthew and Luke knew an edited form of Mark which already contained γνῶναι, all is clear. See my "An Early Revision of the Gospel of Mark," JBL 78 (1959) 215-227, p. 221.

180 At Hatra (KAI 252) the ארזא which has been built could be either a "cedar" structure or a "mystery" one.

181 Another Iranian word in the Scrolls is נחשיר "slaughter," 1QM 1.9 etc. See Gen 25,27 Onqelos נחשירכן "hunter"; Hatra 112.3 Vattioni נחשרפט "huntmaster" just as Parthian *nhšyrpty* Sapor *R.G.* 59.

182 4QMess ar i.8, Fitzmyer-Harrington 98.

183 Telegdi 254 no. 125, Ellenbogen 153, Bartholomae 1514.

(8) *"Lamp."* λύχνος, Pesh שרגא: Luk 15,8 a woman "lights a lamp"; 12,35 "let your lamps be lit";[184] Matt 6,22 (= Luk 11,34) "the eye is the lamp of the body," followed by a discussion of the "evil eye".[185] Matt 5,15 with a Latin loanword *modius* (III.255) "They do not light (Aramaic passive) a lamp and put it under a peck-measure," οὐδὲ καίουσιν λύχνον καὶ τιθέασιν αὐτὸ ὑπὸ τὸν μόδιον, where the Old Syriac recognizes the Latinism:

ולא אנש מנהר שרגא וסאם לה תחית מודיא

A lamp may be covered on the Sabbath (Mishna *Shab.* XVI.7), not to put it out, but "they may put a basin on a lamp (נר) so as not to set fire to a rafter." The same equivalence λύχνος ~ שרגא in the proverb "lamp at midday" (I.321): Diogenes (Diogenes Laertius 6.41) "lit a lamp at midday," searching for an honest man, λύχνον μεθ' ἡμέραν ἅψας; Bab. Talm. *Hull.* 60b "What is the use of a lamp at midday?" מאי רבותיה דשרגא בטיהרא.

Bib. Heb. knows domestic lamps, Prov 31,18 "Her lamp (נֵרָהּ, LXX λύχνος) does not go out at night." שרגא is Persian *čirāγ*;[186] perhaps Persians brought an improved model. Symbolic uses: *Odes of Solomon* 25.7 "A lamp you set for me," שרגא סמת לי. At Rev 21,23 New Jerusalem can dispense with sun and moon, seen as lamps, for "its lamp is the Lamb," ὁ λύχνος αὐτῆς τὸ ἀρνίον, Philox. ושרגא...אמרא. Hence of a man, Joh 5,35 John Baptist was the "burning and shining lamp," ὁ λύχνος ὁ καιόμενος καὶ φαίνων, Pesh שרגא...דדלק ומנהר. The Aramaic of these two passages is echoed in Arabic. Quran 71.16 Allah has created the seven heavens (for the seven luminaries)"and made the moon a light in them, and the sun a lamp":

وَجَعَلَ ٱلْقَمَرَ فِيهِنَّ نُورًا وَجَعَلَ ٱلشَّمْسَ سِرَاجًا

The Prophet besides being a "bringer of good news" (Quran 33.45-46 cf Isa 52,7 מְבַשֵּׂר) is a "lamp that gives light": وَسِرَاجًا مُّنِيرًا. مُبَشِّرًا

---

184 An alternative to Matthew's parable of the ten virgins, where the enigmatic oil-fed "torches" (II.173) have become unambiguous lamps.

185 Here the Gospels come down square on the predominant Greek theory that vision was caused by rays proceeding *from* the eye (and therefore that darkness must be an actual impenetrable substance). Matt 6,22 = Luk 11,34 contrast the "evil eye" (ὀφθαλμὸς πονηρός) with the "simple eye" (ἁπλοῦς) as *Avoth* II.9 עין טובה...עין רעה. See Sirach 14,10 (Heb עין רע) ὀφθαλμὸς πονηρός. The "evil eye" of these passages is envious or grudging, but not magically malignant as in Latin, Grattius 406 *oculi...uenena maligni*. See Thomas Rakoczy, *Böser Blick, Macht des Auges und Neid der Götter: Eine Untersuchung zur Kraft des Blickes in der griechischen Literatur*: Classica Monacensia 13. Tübingen: Narr, 1996.

186 Telegdi 255 no. 129.

(9) *"Treasure."* γάζα; Act 8,27 for the eunuch of Candace, γάζης Pesh גזה (II.296). Bilingual compound Mark 12,43 γαζοφυλάκιον "treasury," Pesh בית גזא. Esther 3,9 "the treasures of the king," גִּנְזֵי הַמֶּלֶךְ, LXX γαζοφυλάκιον. Ezra 5,17 "in the king's treasury," בְּבֵית גִּנְזַיָּא דִּי־מַלְכָּא. Polybius 11.39(34).12 γάζης of a king of India; but it was naturalized early (Theophrastus *Hist. Plant.* 8.11.5). In form assimilated to Gaza the city, Γάζα. Always exotic in Latin, Vergil *Aen.* 1.119 *Troia gaza.*

Attested as Persian *ganj* and Parthian *gnz*.[187] Ezra 1,18 הַגִּזְבָּר "treasurer" (also Bib. Aram.); *Hymn of the Pearl* 79 גזברא, ταμειούχους. In the Parthian of Sapor *Res Gestae* 66 one Mihrkhwast is treasurer, *gnzbr*, γανζοφύλακος. It becomes the ultimate 'treasure' awaiting the blessed. Bab. Talm. *Hag.* 12b "the treasures of life, of peace, of blessing":

גנזי חיים וגנזי שלום וגנזי ברכה

Hymn of the Pearl 4 "from the wealth of our treasury," ומן עותרא דבית גזן = ἀπὸ δὲ πλούτου τῶν θησαυρῶν. Quran 28.76 "so much treasure مِنَ ٱلْكُنُوزِ (*kunūzi* pl.) that its stores would have been a burden for a troop of mighty men"; thus Jer. Talm. *Ned.* 41c40-43 all the camels of Arabia "could not carry the keys to my treasure-houses (אפותיקי, i.e. ἀποθῆκαι)", III.243. Quran 18.82 "under the wall was a treasure (كَنْزٌ, *kanzun*)," in the context of the familiar Haggadic theme where seeming unjust acts turn out for the best when all is known (III.331). The Mandaean sacred corpus is the *Ginza.*

In the sayings "treasure" is θησαυρός, Pesh סימתא from סום "set";[188] a loanword in Rabbinic, Jer. Talm. *Sanh.* 27d70 תסברין של פרעה "the treasures of Pharaoh."[189] It entered Aramaic in the Targum of II Chron 12,9 תסברי for LXX θησαυρούς (Heb. אֹצָרוֹת). It translates גזא in the *Hymn of the Pearl* 4, so Esther 4,7 Vg *thesaurus* for גִּנְזֵי and Ezra 7,20 Vg *de thesauro et de fisco regis* for

מִן בֵּית גִּנְזֵי מַלְכָּא

Perhaps then "treasure in heaven," θησαυρὸς ἐν οὐρανοῖς (Matt 19,21),

---

187 Telegdi 237 no. 42; Gignoux 51.
188 It is confusing that Rabbinic has three words with identical spelling סימא for "sign" (σῆμα, σημαία); "silver" (back-formation from ἄσημον "uncoined"?); and "treasure."
189 Like *gaza*, *thesaurus* is exotic in Latin. Plautus *Trin.* 100 *thesaurum effodiebam* "I was digging up a treasure." In Dido's dream her slain husband (Vergil *Aen.* 1.358-359) *ueteres tellure recludit / thesauros* "reveals old treasures in the earth," which she took to Carthage; Nero (Suetonius *Nero* 31.4) believed her *thesauros antiquissimae gazae* could still be found. That would be Aramaic תיסברין די גנזא עתיקא*!!! From the Latin, French *trésor* and English *treasure.*

Pesh סימתא בשמיא, rests on Iranian גנזא. Winston[190] traces the subsequent history of the *gaza*, which in later Zoroastrian texts seems to mean a "treasury" in the hereafter; it is unclear whether any threads lead from them to the definition of the "treasury of merit" by Pope Clement VI, AD 1343.

23.4 Greek loanwords in the Aramaic of the sayings

Even before Alexander, the Near East was being Hellenized.[191] Ab. 400 BC a Greek-Phoenician stele (*KAI* 53) at Athens records the names of Artemidoros son of Heliodoros, עבדתנת בן עבדשמש = Ἀρτεμίδωρος Ἡλιοδώρου. Before Alexander a king of Sidon had the Greek name Στράτων (Athenaeus 531A). On May 12, 257 BC Toubias the wealthy Jew of Transjordan wrote Greek letters to Apollonios the minister of Ptolemy II.[192] Under Antiochus IV Epiphanes (175-164 BC) the High Priest Ἰησοῦς (*Yešua*) changed his name to Ἰάσων (the hero Jason), and his brother Ὀνίας to Μενέλαος (Josephus *AJ* 12.239); the same Jason set up a gymnasium in Jerusalem (II Makk 4,9). Almost the first recorded Rabbi is Antigonos (אנטיגנוס) of Socho (*Avoth* I.3).

Between Alexander and Islam, thousands of Greek loanwords (some masking Latin ones, 23.5) entered Aramaic dialects; and above all Rabbinic, which often anticipates Israeli Hebrew in sounding like a modern European language. But it is not always easy to tell whether under a Greek word in the sayings of Jesus lies the same word borrowed into Aramaic. The strongest criteria are:

(1) The loanword appears in a Syriac version of the passage.
(2) It is well attested in Rabbinic (or elsewhere in Aramaic).[193]

---

190 D. Winston, "The Iranian Component in the Bible, Apocrypha and Qumran: A Review of the Evidence," History of Religions 5 (1965/5) 183-216, p. 194.

191 The literature on the Hellenization of Judaea is endless. For Phoenicia, see Josette Elayi, Pénétration grecque en Phénicie sous l'empire perse; Travaux et mémoires; études anciennes 2; Nancy: Presses universitaires, 1988; Fergus Millar, "The Phoenician Cities: A Case-Study of Hellenisation," Proceedings of the Cambridge Philological Society 29 (1983) 54-71; John D. Grainger, Hellenistic Phoenicia; Oxford: Clarendon, 1991.

192 *CPJ* i.4-5. Toubias is sending Aeneas the eunuch with four slave boys 7-10 years old (two circumcised, two not) and a menagerie of wild animals for the King. He is surely a younger relative of that Tobiah the Ammonite who gave Nehemiah so much trouble (Neh 2,19 etc.).

193 See Samuel Krauss, Griechische und lateinische Lehwörter im Talmud, Midrasch und Targum; mit Bemerkungen von Immanuel Löw; Teil II; Berlin 1899; repr. Hildesheim: Olms, 1964; Daniel Sperber, A Dictionary of Greek and Latin Legal Terms in Rabbinic Literature; Jerusalem: Bar-Ilan University, 1984.

(3) The Targum uses it following the LXX.

(4) It names an element of Greek culture imported into Palestine.

(5) There is no obvious Aramaic alternative.

(6) The word shows its mobility by also moving into Latin.

But there is a grey area; here we treat the clearest cases.

(1) *"Crowd."* Mark 8,2 "I have compassion on the crowd (τὸν ὄχλον, Pal. Syr. אכלוסיא)." Act 21,34 Pesh. אכלוס for ὄχλος. In Targumic "army": Bab. Talm. *BM* 108a a "corvée" for digging wells; Jer. Talm. *Dem.* 24a32 "I saw crowds around you," והמית אוכלוסין עלך. Hellenized Palestine developed a new class of village unemployed for which a new name was needed.

(2) *"Steward."* Jesus praises both the "faithful steward" (Luk 12,42) ὁ πιστὸς οἰκονόμος and the "steward of injustice" (16,8, Semitic idiom) οἰκονόμον τῆς ἀδικίας. A semantic parallel in the Pesh. רביתא (i.e. רב ביתא) "master of the house." But the Greek went into Semitic: Jer. Talm. *B.M.* 11d16, a cow may be leased from "a well-keeper (הבייר) or a guard (סנתר)[194] or a steward (האיקונומוס)." Latin *oeconomia* (Quintilian 1.8.9) "arrangement."

(3) *"Stranger."* Matt 25,44 "When did we see you hungry or thirsty or a stranger (ξένον, Pesh. אכסניא) or naked or sick (ἀσθενῆ, III.247) or in prison (ἐν φυλακῇ, III.243)?" ξένος entered Aramaic in the anomalous form אכסניא; see III.15 for full discussion. Latin *xenium* "present given by host to guest." The confluence of loans points to an Aramaic original of Matt 25.

(4) *"Inn."* Luk 10,34, the Samaritan takes the victim to an inn, πανδοχεῖον, Pesh. לפותקא, Pal. Syr. better פונדקיא, Arabic NT[195] فُنْدُق *funduq*—Syrian dialect for classical خَان *khān*. Hence to Italian *fóndaco* (Boccaccio), with the article in *alfóndega* (11th century). The "bandits"(λῃσταί) are just right in this setting. Inns were felt alien, Mishna *AZ* II.1 "inns of idolaters," פונדקאות של עובדי גלולים.[196] Jesus' parable either varies a well-known theme, or generates a parody: *Gen. Rabbah* 92.6 an innkeeper (פונדקי) gets his guests out at night on a pretext; bandits (לסטיא) fall on them and share the spoil with him.

(5) *"Gate."* Matt 7,13 "the narrow gate (πύλης)"; 16,18 "the gates of Hades," πύλαι ᾅδου;[197] Luk 16,20 "Lazarus lay at his gate

---

194 Back-formation from συντηρέω "to guard."

195 American Bible Society, 1899.

196 A man may sleep with two women in an inn (בפונדקי, Mishna *Qidd.* IV.12) so long as his wife is with him (as one of the two or a third?).

197 Matthew echoes Isa 38,10 LXX πύλαις ᾅδου which in turn simply continues *Iliad* 5.646 πύλας Ἀΐδαο, a beautiful archaic parallel to the Hebrew (I.123-124). Frequent in the later LXX: Sap Sol 16,13; III Makk 5,51; Ps Sol 16,2.

(πυλῶνα)." Pesh. תרעא which might seem to underly. But Aramaic פילי is common (Sokoloff 431) and פילין (for πυλών or πύλην) occasional. It entered Rabbinic through a Targum at Gen 19,1, with בפילי דסדום for τὴν πύλην Σοδόμων "the gate of Sodom." Often symbolic: David asked the Holy One, "Master of the ages, tell me which gate is opened to the hereafter":[198]

רבון העלמים הודיעני איזה פילון מפורש לעתיד לבא

At *Lev. Rabbah* 18.1 (II.264) Greco-Roman ranks enter the city of the hereafter by "the one gate," בפילון אחד. Latin *Pylae* "mountain-pass."

(6) *"Storehouse" and "barn."* Luk 12,14 "[crows] with neither storehouse nor barn (ταμεῖον οὐδὲ ἀποθήκη)"; Old Latin (Bezae) *neque promptuarium neque apotheca.* Josephus *AJ* 9.274, Hezekiah built ἀποθήκας δὲ καὶ ταμιεῖα. ἀποθήκη in the saying of John Baptist "He will gather his wheat into his barn," Matt 3,12. Latin *apotheca* common since Cicero. Levin takes the Romance for "shop" (Spanish *bodega*, Italian *bottega*) from ἀποθήκη via Arabic. Both nouns טמיון and אפותיקי are frequent in Rabbinic, once together. Jer. Talm. *Ned.* 41c40-43:

A case involves a rich adversary (בעלדיניא, III.224). Rab summons him. "With such a one as this [plaintiff], should I come to court? All the camels of Arabia could not carry the keys to my treasure houses (אפותיקי)."[199] Rab curses him. "Forthwith a decree (קלווסיס = κέλευσις) came from the government that all he owned should fall to the treasury (טמיון)." But Rab by prayer secures his life.

(7) *"Prison."* Matt 25,44 "When did we see you in prison (ἐν φυλακῇ, Pal. Syr. בפילקי)?" Plautus *Capt.* 751 *abductus...in phylacam* "carried to jail." Rabbinic פילקי common.[200] A bandit (III.260) belongs there. Joh 18,40 calls Barabbas a λῃστής, and Luk 23,19 has him in prison, ἐν τῇ φυλακῇ. Josephus *AJ* 20.215 describing an amnesty "The prison was cleaned out of captives, and the countryside was filled with bandits," ἡ μὲν φυλακὴ τῶν δεσμωτῶν ἐκαθάρθη, ἡ χώρα δὲ λῃστῶν ἐπληρώθη. *Lev. Rabbah* 30.6 "After some days that bandit was captured and put in prison":

בתר יומין אצתיד ההוא ליסטא ואתחבש בפיליקי

(8) *"Chair."* Matt 23,2 "the chair of Moses," Μωϋσέως καθέδρας, Pesh. כורסיא דמושה, Vg *cathedram Mosi.* καθέδρα can be "academic chair": Nikagoras, a descendant of Plutarch, was the "sophist in the

---

198 *Pesiqta de Rab Kahana* 27.2.
199 Sokoloff 69 treats אפותיקי here as from ὑποθῆκαι "title deeds," and likely the two Greek words were confused, but "treasure houses" makes better sense.
200 Sperber Legal Terms 143-144.

chair," ἐπὶ τῆς καθέδρας σοφιστής[201]—the "throne of sophists at Athens," τὸν Ἀθήνησι τῶν σοφιστῶν θρόνον.[202] καθέδρα is the bishop's teaching chair. Juvenal 7.203 *paenituit multos uanae sterilisque cathedrae* "Many have regretted an empty and useless professorship." Mishna *Keth.* V.5 "If the wife brought four maids, she may sit in the chair [all day long]":

ארבעא יושבת בקתדרא

The chief synagogue at Alexandria had seventy golden cathedras, קתידראות של זהב (Jer. Talm. *Sukkah* 55a75 = Bab. Talm. *Sukkah* 51 b). Matthew's exact phrase in Rabbinic: Solomon's throne (I Reg 10,19) is "like the seat of Moses," קתדרא דמשה.[203] Chairs in ancient synagogues may actually be the "seat of Moses."[204]

(9) *"Footstool."* Matt 5,34-35 "Do not swear at all: not by heaven, for it is the throne (θρόνος) of God; nor by earth, for it is the footstool (ὑποπόδιον) of his feet."[205] Jesus quotes Isa 66,1 LXX "Heaven is my throne (θρόνος) and earth the footstool (ὑποπόδιον) of my feet." He may follow a Targumic tradition with איפופודין for "footstool."

Beit Hillel and Beit Shammai debated which was made first, heaven or earth.[206] Beit Hillel said Earth, citing Gen 2,4 "In the day that the Lord God made earth and heaven"; and Isa 48,13 "My hand laid the foundation of the earth, and my right hand spread out the heavens": "It is like a king who built a palace (פלטין, i.e. παλάτιον); after he has laid the foundation he builds the upper stories." Beit Shammai (which we now know was right!) naturally quoted Gen 1,1, and then Isa 66,1, "It is like a king who made a throne; after it, he made his footstool":

למלך שעשה כסא משעשאו עשה איפופודין שלו

---

201 SIG³ 845, ab. AD 250.

202 Philostratus *Vit. Soph.* 2.27 (618).

203 *Pesiqta de Rab Kahana* 1.7.

204 Cecil Roth, "The 'Chair of Moses' and its Survivals," PEQ 81 (1949) 100-111 (including a synagogue from China!); Benedict T. Viviano, "Social World and Community Leadership: The Case of Matthew 23.1-12, 34," JSNT 39 (1990) 3-21; *idem*, review of H.-J. Becker, Auf der Kathedra des Mose...Arbeiten zur neutestamentlichen Theologie und Zeitgeschichte 4; Berlin: Institut Kirche und Judentum, 1990 [not seen by me] in CBQ 54 (1992) 141, with further literature.

205 Elsewhere (III.231) θρόνος appears in the Peshitto as תרונוס, but it is unlikely that this is the underlying Aramaic when כרסיא was available.

206 Bab. Talm. *Hagigah* 12a; Jer. Talm. *Hagigah* 77c68—77d2; *Gen. Rabbah* 1.14; *Lev. Rabbah* 36.1. Here I mostly follow the Jerusalem Talmud. The Sages (in the Bab. Talm.) held a mediating position, that heaven and earth were created at the same time.

(10) *"Belt" and "sandal."* Mark 6,8-9 "No copper in your belt (ζώνην) but wearing sandals (σανδάλια, Old Syr. סדלא),[207] and not taking two tunics (χιτῶνας, Pesh כותינין)." Vg *neque in* zona *aes sed calciatos* sandaliis *et ne induerentur duabus* tunicis. The words for "tunic" go back to antiquity (I.204-209). Rabbinic זוני and סנדל common, together at Mishna *Kelim* XXVI.3-4. *Num. Rabbah* 4.20 "girt with a belt around his loins," חגור מתנין בזינו. Matt 3,4 of John Baptist "with a leather belt around his loins," ζώνην δερματίνην περὶ τὴν ὀσφὺν αὐτοῦ, Pal. Syriac: וזונא דמשיך אסיר בחרצין.[208] Latin *zona* common; *sandalium* rare (Terence *Eu.* 1028) except for the "sandalmakers' street," *Vicus sandaliarius*. Greek dress brought its names to Palestine.

(11) *The Prodigal Son.* While its narrative style is Greek (III.217), it has four Greek words which went into Syriac and Rabbinic.[209] The underlying story was expressed in vocabulary familiar to an Aramaic speaker.

(11.1) *"Robe."* Luk 15,22 "the best robe (στολήν, Pesh. אסטלא, Vg *stolam*)."[210] Cur. Syr. tr. ἱματίου Matt 14,36 as אסטלא. It entered Rabbinic through the Targum: Gen 45,22 Onq. has אסטלין for LXX στολή. Latin *stola* a man's or woman's long garment. Luxury dress in Rabbinic. A debtor should not wear a robe (איצטלא) worth a hundred minas (Bab. Talm. *Shabb.* 128a); Mishna *Gitt.* VII.5: "In Sidon a man said to his wife, 'This is your *geṭ* on condition you give me back my robe (איצטליתי)'."

(11.2) *"Estate."* Luk 15,12 "Give me my share of the estate (οὐσίας, Pal. Syr. אוסיא)." *Gen. Rabbah* 49.2 "Parable of a king who gave an estate to his friend," משל למלך שנתן אוסיא לאוהבו; *Num. Rabbah* 23.11 "[A king] used to give to his servants in marriage handmaidens from another estate (אוסיא)."

(11.3) *"Profligacy."* Luk 15,13 "There he dissipated his estate living riotously (ἀσώτως)." The noun at Eph 5,18 "wine wherein is excess (ἀσωτία)," where Pesh. has a Syriac abstract אסוטותא, used at Luk

---

207 The Pesh. for "sandals" has טלרא, which must be Latin *talaria* "winged sandals"!

208 משיך is Akkadian *mašku* "hide," Targumic משך (Num 31,20 Onq.); thence a loan to Old Persian *maškāuvā* loc. pl. fem. "on [inflated] skins" (Darius *Beh.* I.86, Kent 203); and Greek μέσκος (Hesychius citing Nicander).

209 Also the "carob pods" (Luk 15,16 κερατίων) appear in the Sin. Syr. as קרטא; but this is mere transcription since it seems to appear nowhere else in Semitic in this sense.

210 See Mark 12,38 (par.) "the scribes who wish to walk about in robes (στολαῖς, Pesh. באסטלא)"; but the Sin. Syr. has באסטוא, evidently reading στοαῖς "to walk about in stoas."

21,34 for κραιπάλη "drunkenness."[211] Latin adopted the Greek for the exact situation of the parable! Gellius 10.17.3 *sumptum plurimum asotiamque adulescentis* "the excess spending and extravagance of a youth"; Plautus *Merc.* Argument 2 "A merchant father sends out his dissolute son to make purchases,"

Mercator mercatum asotum filium extrudit pater.

(11.4) *"Symphony."* Luk 15,25 "music (συμφωνίας, Sin. Syr. צפוניא, Vg *symphoniam*)." Already in Aramaic at Dan 3,5 (II.329), סוּמְפֹּנְיָה, LXX συμφωνίας, Vg *symphoniae*. It should represent a particular instrument in a Seleucid orchestra, unclear which. Mishna *Kelim* XI.6 "a *symphonia* or flute of cast metal," סומפוניא וחליל של מתכת. Latin *symphonia*.

(12) *"Key."* Luk 11,52 "the key of knowledge," τὴν κλεῖδα τῆς γνώσεως, Pesh. קלידא דידעתא. Matt 16,19 "the keys (κλεῖδας) of the kingdom of heaven," Pesh. קלידא but Pal. Syr. מפתחיא. Greek keys had some special feature. Bab. Talm. *Gitt.* 56a "R. Hisba would hand all his keys (אקלידי) to his servant except that of wood." The Holy One has three keys (II.169). Quran 39.63 "the keys (*maqālīdu*) of heaven and earth": مَقَالِيدُ ٱلسَّمَٰوَٰتِ وَٱلْأَرْضِ.

(13) *"Scabbard."* Joh 18,11 "Put your sword back in its scabbard (θήκην, Old Latin *tecam*)." θήκη as "scabbard" at Josephus *AJ* 7.284. Mishna *Kelim* XVI.8 "the sheath of a sword or knife or dagger (Latin *pugio*)," תיק הסייף והסכין והפגיון.[212] Latin *theca* mostly in other senses.

(14) *"Necessity."* Matt 18,7 "It is necessary (ἀνάγκη, Pesh אננקא) that scandals come." Also in Rabbinic as "distress" (Luk 21,23), *Cant. Rabbah* pref. "A man does not recount his distress except in the hour of his relief":

לית בר נש מתני אננקי די זיה בשעת רווחיה

As "necessity," *Gen. Rabbah* 12.13 "When a man of flesh and blood stretches a tent, necessarily in the course of time it becomes loose":

בשר ודם מותח אהל אננקי ידי שהות הוא רפה

As divinity, Aeschylus *PV* 105 "The strength of Anangke is irresistible":[213]

---

211 The adjective ἄσωτος is marginal in Rabbinic: Krauss 86 finds אסיט at *Gen. Rabbah* 17.2 etc.

212 Cicero *Phil.* 2.30 *Brutus...cruentem pugionem tenens* "Brutus, holding the bloody dagger..." [with which he had killed Caesar]. Semitic שַׂכִּין "knife" Prov 23,2 went into συκίνη (Hesychius).

213 Cf. Simonides (Page PMG 282, Simonides 542.29, from Plato *Protag.* 339A-346D) "Even the gods do not fight against Anangke," Ἀνάγκᾳ/δ᾽ οὐδὲ θεοὶ μάχονται.

τὸ τῆς Ἀνάγκης ἔστ᾽ ἀδήριτον σθένος

"Necessity" is a Greek concept lacking from Palestine.

(15) *"Mask, [sculptured] face."* With "hypocrites" (III.211): Luk 12,56 "Hypocrites (נסבי באפא), you can discern the face (πρόσωπον, Pesh פרצופא) of earth and sky"; Matt 6,16-17 "[The hypocrites] disfigure their faces (πρόσωπα, Pesh פרצופיהון)...but you are to wash your face (πρόσωπον, Pesh אפיך)."[214] We saw how נסב באפא "a respecter of persons" is one with a false face—an actor's mask or a "beam in his eye." πρόσωπον had the sense "mask" lacking from Semitic: Aristotle *Poetics* 5.2 (1449a36) "the comic mask is ugly," τὸ γελοῖον πρόσωπον αἰσχρόν. Hence Bab. Talm. *AZ* 12a "faces [in fountains] which spurt out water in cities":

פרצופות המקלחין מים לכרכין

Jer. Talm. *AZ* 42c68 "There were all kinds of carved faces in Jerusalem except those of human beings":

כל פרצופות היו בירושלם חוץ משל אדם

(16) *"Yoke."* Luk 14,19 "five yoke of oxen," ζεύγη βοῶν, Pesh זוגין תורא.[215] The Pesh is identical with *ζεύγη ταύρων.[216] ζεῦγος or ζυγόν went into Aramaic to express a novel Greek understanding of "yoked pair, married couple."[217] Xenophon *Oec.* 7.18 τὸ ζεῦγος...ὃ καλεῖται θῆλυ καὶ ἄρρεν, "the yoke called female and male." At Heb 13,4 the Pesh for γάμος has זווגא. In Palestinian mostly "spouse" feminine; thus at Gen 7,9 for "male and female" (זָכָר וּנְקֵבָה) Neofiti has דכר וזוגה.[218] But Quran 2.230 زوج zawjun is "husband" and so in modern Arabic.

(17) *"Sick."* Matt 10,8 "Heal the sick (ἀσθενοῦντας)"; 25,44 "When did we see you sick (ἀσθενῆ)?"; Mark 14,38 "but the flesh is weak (ἀσθενής)." Mishna *Yoma* III.5 "If the High Priest was old or sick":

אם היה כהן גדול זקן או איסטניס

A euphemism of Greek doctors, "without strength," which caught on.

(18) *Key concepts of Judaism.* Before the challenge of Jesus' movement, Palestinian Judaism borrowed names for its principal terms from Greek.

---

214 פרצופא may have entered Aramaic through a Targum to Psalms 34,17 and 17,15 transcribing πρόσωπον (Krauss 495).

215 The Pesh. has Akkadian ניר for "yoke" in other contexts (III.232)

216 Mishna *Peah* II.6 the five "Pairs" of Rabbis down to Hillel and Shammai are the זוגות.

217 In the animal sense, at II Reg 5,17 for צֶמֶד Targum Jonathan transcribed LXX ζεύγους as זוג. Hence a Rabbinic verb זוג "marry" and זווג "marriage."

218 Cited by Sokoloff 173.

(18.1) *"Law."* "The Law and the Prophets" (ὁ νόμος καὶ οἱ προφῆται) Matt 7,12 in the Pesh. is נמוסא ונביא; but at 22,40 אוריתא ונביא with the Aramaic equivalent of תורה. In the Palmyrene Tariff (I.6) נמוסא corresponds to νόμῳ; a marriage contract from Murabbaʿat[219] envisages birth "legitimately," כנמסא. Rabbinic נימוס can refer to foreign laws, *Gen. Rabbah* 48.14 "When you enter a city, behave according to its customs":

עלת לקרתה הלך בנימוסה

Or to the law of Israel in the mouth of foreigners: at Jer. Talm. *Berakh.* 9a29 a proconsul says "Leave him alone; he is studying the law of his creator":

ארפוניה בנימוסא דברייה הוא עסיק

If Jesus ever delivered the Sermon on the Mount in Greek, he had only νόμος for "Law," which might have affected his Aramaic in reverse.

(18.2) *"Covenant."* Matt 26,28 "blood of the new covenant (διαθήκης)," Syriac דיתקא. Classically διαθήκη is mostly "last will and testament," though see Aristophanes *Aves* 439 "unless they make an agreement with me":

ἢν μὴ διάθωνταί γ᾽ οἵδε διαθήκην ἐμοί

Rabbinic דייתיקי is *only* "will, testament": Bab. Talm. *BB* 135b "A [new] will cancels an [old] will," דייתיקי מבטלת דייתיקי. Jer 31,31 בְּרִית חֲדָשָׁה (LXX 38,31 διαθήκην καινήν) originally meant "new covenant," Vg correctly *foedus nouum*. But Jews came to see God's covenants as unilateral acts like the will of a testator, and the old sense of διαθήκη prevailed. Jesus' words at the Last Supper are a kind of will, for which דייתיקי would be appropriate; also the Vg there as at Heb 8,8 has *nouum testamentum*.

(18.3) *"Sanhedrin."* In the sayings, συνέδρια refers to local bodies, Matt 10,17 = Mark 13,9, where Pesh. has the correct Jewish בית דינא. But for the Jerusalem body, סנהדרין was universal (II.107), though the Syriac translator no longer knows it; likely it was used also for the local bodies. The Hebrew spelling shows that the Greek internal *h* was pronounced, and the ending reduced to *-in*.

(19) *"Daughter-in-law."* Matt 10,35 "to divide a daughter-in-law (νύμφην, Pesh. כלתה) from her mother-in-law." Greek νύμφη in this sense first in the LXX for כַּלָּה (Gen 11,31).[220] It entered Rabbinic as "bride," Targum Cant 4,8 נינפי from LXX νύμφη.[221] *Ex. Rabbah* 36.1

---

219 Fitzmyer-Harrington 42.11.
220 Hebrew כַּלָּה also means "bride," designating the same young woman at an earlier stage.
221 Krauss 361.

"In Greek they call a כלה *nymphē* (נינפי)." Greek marriage customs also entered Rabbinic in זוג "marriage" (III.247).

(20) στρατιώτης "soldier" Matt 8,9, Pesh. אסטרטיוטא. Saying of the "centurion" of Capernaum, surely speaking Aramaic; *Ex. Rabbah* 15.22 "A king of flesh and blood enlists stout and strong soldiers (סטרטיוטין)."[222] Novel Hellenistic/Roman military discipline warranted a foreign name.

(21) *A certain meal.* ἄριστον is "breakfast" Luk 14,12, "dinner" Matt 22,4, uncertain Luk 11,38. "Breakfast" in Homer, ἄριστον ἄμ' ἠοῖ "at dawn" Od. 16.2. Jer. Talm. *Berakh.* 7b46 "If you are invited to dinner (אריסטון) and the sixth hour has come." The heavenly banquet as at Matt 22, *Lev. Rabbah* 13.3 "The Holy One will prepare dinner for his righteous servants":

אריסטון עתיד הקדוש...לעשות לעבדיו הצדיקין

A parody of the Gospel banquet parable Matt 22 at Jer. Talm. *Hag.* 77d51ff:

Bar Maʿyan the publican (מוכס) never did a meritorious deed; except once he made a dinner for his counsellors (βουλευταί),

אלא חד זמן עבד אריסטון לבולוטייא

But they did not come to eat it. He said, "Let the poor (מיסכייניא) eat so it will not go to waste."

So at Luk 14,21 the servants invite the poor (πτωχούς, Pesh למסכנא).

(22) *"Platter, tablet."* Luk 11,39 "wash...the platter (πίνακος, Old Syr פינקא)." Matt 14,8 "the head of John on a platter (πίνακι, Pesh. בפינקי)." Classical πίναξ "plank" was anything flat, e.g. a "writing tablet," *Iliad* 6.169 (I.49). Luk 1,63 Zachariah calls for a πινακίδιον, Pesh. פנקיתא. Jer. Talm. *Shabb.* 6b23 פינקא דאורזא "a dish of rice (ὄρυζα)"; *Avoth* III.17 (I.75) הפנקס פתוח "the ledger is open." Jer. Talm. *Rosh hash.* 57a58 "There are three account books (פינקסיות) [before the Holy One]: one for the fully righteous, one for the fully wicked, one for those in between." *Odes of Solomon* 23.21 "[God's] letter became a big *pinax*,"

הוה דין אגרתא פנקיתא רבתא

(23) *Marginal Greek loanwords.* In previous sections we noted Greek words entering Rabbinic, but in the sayings resting on something other than themselves: ἀντίδικος, δραχμή, ἔμπορος, καιρός, μυστήριον, ναός, πορφύρα, τραπεζίτης. Here are some other doubtful cases.

(1') ἄρχων (Luk 12,58, Pesh ארכונא) "archon" may rest on the loanword. ארכונא entered the Targum. Annual archon used for dat-

222 Also of the heavenly hosts *Num. Rabbah* 7.3; *Ex. Rabbah* 15.22.

ing.[223] Jer. Talm. *Berakh.* 5c54 "the governor was judging a robber
(ληστής)":

והוא ארכונא קאים דאין חד ליסטיס

(2') δανειστής (Luk 7,41, Pal. Syr. דניסטיס) "creditor"; דניסטיס *Ex.
Rabbah* 29.9; God as creditor, *ibid.* 31.1. Latin *danista* only in Plautus.

(3') δῶρον "gift" prob. rests on קורבן, not Rabb. דורון.

(4') εἰκών (Mark 12,16) "image" may rest on איקוניא (III.217).

(5') εὐγενής (Luk 19,12) "nobleman" could rest on Rabbinic: *Qoh.
Rabbah* praef. Solomon is אבגינוס בן אבגינוס "a noble son of a noble."

(6') ἔχιδνα "viper" orig. in a saying of John, Matt 3,7, Pesh אכדנא.
Rabbinic has only חכינא; the Baptist surely used a native word.

(7') ζημιόω (Matt 16,28, cf Phil 3,7 ζημίαν) "lose" can hardly rest
on זימיא "fine," *Lev. Rabbah* 33.6; Latin *zamia* Plautus *Aul.* 197.

(8') ζιζάνια (Matt 13,40, Pesh זיזנא) "tares" here first in Greek
(Sumerian ZIZAN "grain"[?]) and nowhere else in Semitic; mere transcription.

(9') κάλαμος (Matt 11,7) "reed" went to Rabbinic only as קולמוס
"pen."

(10') κοίτη (Luk 11,7) "bed"; Rabb. קיטא is luxury only (III.230).

(11') κόφινος (Matt 16,9-10, Pesh קופינין, Vg *cophinous*) "basket";
not Rabbinic; usage of Roman Jews, Juvenal 3.14 "Jews whose only
furniture is a basket and a bale of hay (to keep food warm on Sabbath?)," *Iudaeis quorum cophinus faenumque supellex*; Pesh transliterates the Greek.[224]

(12') κράσπεδον (Matt 23,5) "fringe" went from Num 15,38 LXX
to Targumic כרוספדין but nowhere else in Rabbinic.

(13') μωρός "foolish" in Matt, vocative μωρέ 5,22. Both at *Pesiqta
de Rav Kahana* 14.5 מורה...מורה. But μωρέ could also represent *Hebrew* מֹרֶה "rebellious" Deut 21,18-20 in a pun.

(14') πέλαγος "sea": Matt 18,6 "in the depth of the sea," ἐν τῷ
πελάγει τῆς θαλάσσης, Old Latin (Bezae) *in pelago maris*. Elsewhere
high style: Ap. Rhod. 2.608 πέλαγός τε θαλάσσης. *Lev. Rabbah* 12.1
"boat tossed on the high sea":

כחדא אלפא דמטרפת בפילגוס דימא

(15') πήγανον Luke 11,42 "rue," Pesh פגנא; הפיגם an *untithed* wild
herb at Mishna *Sheviith* IX.1.

---

223 So at Bab. Talm. *BB* 164b ארכן; Palmyrene Tariff i. 2, ארכוניא = ἀρχόντων;
ארכון to date the building of the Dura synagogue (Carl H. Kraeling, The
Synagogue: The Excavations at Dura-Europos VIII Part I; New York: Ktav,
1979; p. 263). Latin *archon* of the office at Athens, Velleius 1.2.2.

224 In the same text, the other word for "basket" (σπυρίς, Pesh אספרידין, Vg
sporta) likewise has no Rabbinic base.

(16') πόλεμος (Luk 14,31) "war"; פולמוס in Roman context, Mishna *Sotah* IX.14 "the war of Vespasian (בפולמוס של אספסיינוס)...of Titus (טיטוס)."

(17') σημεῖον when "sign" (III.257) may rest on סימא.

(18') στατήρ (Matt 17,27, Pesh אסתרא) "stater" prob. on Rabbinic אסטירא (II.299,335; III.63).

(19') ὑπηρέτης (Matt 5,25, Pal. Syr. הבריטא) "guard," cf. rare Rabbinic אפיריטוס (Krauss 108): III.113.

23.5 Latinisms in the Aramaic of the sayings

The first recorded contact between Jews and Romans is the embassy sent by Judas Maccabaeus to Rome (I Makk 8, 161 BC) and the following treaty, which agrees well with contemporary Roman treaties (in Greek) on stone (I.266).[225] We have from literary sources *senatus consulta* on Jewish affairs: I Makk 15,16-21 (140-139 BC); Josephus *AJ* 13.260-264 (132 BC); 14.145-148 (earlier?). Pompey took Jerusalem in 63 BC; Syria was under Roman governors since M. Aemilius Scaurus (65-62 BC, SVMB i.244). Augustus divided the realm of Herod the Great after his death in 4 BC (SVMB i.333), an event envisaged at Luk 19,12-14. Judaea was under governors (originally *praefecti*) since Coponius (AD 6-9). Rome governed the east in Greek, and the names of Roman institutions went into Greek in two ways: (1) as simple transcription of the Latin; (2) as Greek equivalents, often created by the chancery in Rome. Aramaic words for Roman things simply transcribe the Greek, whether it itself is transcription or equivalent; they show no new knowledge of Latin.[226]

---

225 W. Virgin, "Judah Maccabee's Embassy to Rome and the Jewish-Roman treaty," PEQ 101 (1969) 15-20; D. Timpe, "Der römische Vertrag mit den Juden von 161 v. Chr.," Chiron 4 (1974) 133ff.

226 The fullest listing of Latin loanwords in Greek is Herbert Hofmann, Die lateinischen Wörter im Griechischen bis 600 n. Chr.; Inaugural-Dissertation, Univ. Erlangen-Nürnberg, after 1989; I was unable to find a copy in the States. The fullest study of Latinisms in New Testament Greek is Corrado Marucci, "Influssi latini sul greco del nuovo testamento," Filologia Neotestamentaria 6 (1993) 3-30. BAGD records N.T. Latinisms in secular Greek. For Latinisms in Rabbinic see Krauss; in Semitic generally, Maria Gabriella Angeli Bertinelli, "I Semiti e Roma: Appunti da una lettura di fonti semitiche," pp. 145-181 of Serta historica antiqua; Pubbl. dell'Ist. di storia ant. & scienze ausiliare dell'Univ. degli studi di Genova XV; Roma: Bretschneider, 1986.

Three texts of Luke from the "Q" tradition have Latinate idioms lacking from Matthew.[227] If (as we assume) the sayings rest on Aramaic, the Latinisms are either work of the original translator deleted by Matthew; or editorial work of Luke on a less Latinate original.— Luk 7,4 (Galilaeans speaking) "He is worthy that you should do this for him," ἄξιός ἐστιν ᾧ παρέξῃ τοῦτο, a unique Greek version of a Latin "relative clause of characteristic." The Vulgate is pedestrian, *dignus est ut hoc illi praestes*; classically it would have been **dignus est cui hoc praestes*, thus Plautus *As.* 80 *me dignum quoi* [for later *cui*] *concrederet habuit* "he held me worthy for him to trust."[228] —Luk 14,18-19 ἐρωτῶ σε ἔχε με παρῃτημένον, Vg correctly *rogo te, habe me excusatum* "I beg you, have me excused"; so Martial 2.79.2 *excusatum habeas me rogo.*[229] —Luk 12,58 δὸς ἐργασίαν ἀπηλλάχθαι ἀπ' αὐτοῦ "work hard to be reconciled with him," Vg correctly *da operam liberari ab illo.*[230] Already in a papyrus of the 2nd century BC (*P. Oxy.* 742.11) δὸς ἐργασίαν and in a *senatus consultum* of 81 BC,[231] δίδωσίν τε ἐργασίαν. The Latin in Terence *Hec.* 553 *dare operam id scire* "to take pains to know it."[232]

---

227 I note one of several Latinisms in Mark's narrative. Mark 15,15 "wishing *to satisfy* (τὸ ἱκανὸν ποιῆσαι) the crowd," where the Vg correctly *satisfacere*. The idiom already in Greek at Polybius 32.3.13 ἐὰν τὸ ἱκανὸν ποιῇ συγκλήτῳ "if he should satisfy the Senate, which would be exactly **si senatui satisfaciat*. It was not until the Middle Ages that "satisfaction" became a technical term of theology for the Atonement: thus Anselm *Cur Deus Homo* i.20 *secundum mensuram peccati oportet satisfactionem esse* "satisfaction must be according to the measure of sin." So Cranmer in the Canon of 1549 *a full, perfect, and sufficient sacrifyce, oblacion, and satysfaccyon, for the sinnes of the whole worlde*. When Eliot has the Magi say of the Nativity *it was (you may say) satisfactory*, behind the colloquial understatement we can hear an echo of the rigid Latin theology.

228 Similarly Ovid *Met.* 10.681-682, Venus complains that Hippomenes failed to show gratitude for her help in winning Atalanta, *Dignane, cui grates ageret... fui?* "Was I not worthy for him to give me thanks?"; Vergil *Aen.* 7.653-4, of Lausus the noble son of the arrogant Mezentius, *dignus...cui pater haut Mezentius esset* "worthy of not having Mezentius as father."

229 More distant is *P. Oxy.* 2.292.5 (ab. AD 25) παρακαλῶ σε...ἔχειν αὐτὸν συνεσταμένον "I urge you to treat him as one recommended."

230 But the Vulgate misinterprets the second half "to be freed from his lawsuits." There is another Latinism in Matthew's version, κοδράντην = *quadrantem* Matt 5,26 (III.254); perhaps both stood together in an original version, with Luke deleting the transcribed word and Matthew the idiom.

231 Sherk no. 18.11, p. 109.

232 And above all in the text of the emergency decree of the Senate, which Caesar (*de bello ciuili* 1.5.3) quotes, *dent operam consules, praetores...ne quid res publica detrimenti caperet* "Let the consuls, praetors...take care that the state receive no harm."

23.5.1 Latin transliterated in the sayings

(1) *"Sudarium."* Luk 19,20 a mina "in a napkin (ἐν σουδαρίῳ, Vg *sudario*)"; Pesh incorrectly בסדינא (Bib. Hebr. סדין = σινδών, I.209). But for Lazarus' shroud (σουδαρίῳ) Joh 11,44 (cf 20,7) Pesh as it should has בסודרא. Bab. Talm. *Keth.* 67b "he wrapped *zuz* in his napkin" for the poor, היה צייר זוזי בסודריה. Latin *sudarium* "sweat-cloth"; a blushing woman "hides her face with a napkin," *faciem sudario abscondit*, Petronius 67.13.[233]

(2) *"Assarion."* Matt 10,29 two sparrows go for an ἀσσαρίου, Vg *duo passeres asse*, Pesh באסר.[234] Greek ἀσσάριον here first appears with a Latin suffix as if *assarium*. The *as* was once 1/10 *denarius* (whence the name) but later 1/16; a fee for exchange (*collybus*) was an *as* per *denarius* or 6 2/3 %.[235] Aramaic אסר and Greek *as* in the Palmyrene Tariff. In the Mishna the איסר is 1/24 דינר (Danby 797). That the *as* is near worthless echoes Latin verse, where Catullus (5.3) proposes to Lesbia that they should so reckon old men's gossip, *omnes unius aestimemus assis*.

(3) *"Sextarius."* Mark 7,4 as vessels ξεστῶν, Pesh קסטא. From Latin *sextarius* (but not Vg here) by metathesis; equivalents in Diocletian's Edict. Mostly a measure: Arrian *Epict.* 1.9.34 a coward is "a corpse and a pint of blood," πτῶμα...καὶ ξέστης αἱματίου. "Measures of wine," *Lev. Rabbah* 12.1 קסטין דחמרא; "vessels of kings," קיסטות דמלכים Mishna *Kelim* XV.1. Measures at Palmyra are pure Roman (Tariff 69), "Pure salt is charged one *assarion* per *modius* of 16 *sextarii*":

[מל]ח טב [יתג]בא אסרא חד למדיא די קסטין עשר ו[ש]ת

At Quran 17.35 a weight, "and weigh with a right balance":

بِٱلْقِسْطَاسِ

---

233 The napkin as means of life and death. At Act 19,12 healing is brought by σουδάρια (Pesh סודרא) ἢ σιμικίνθια, Vg *sudaria uel semicintia* "sweat-cloths and aprons"; the latter is a unique loan from *semicinctium* Petronius 94.6. A *sudarium* can bring death by suffocation (Valerius Maximus 9.12.7), and so at Mishna *Sanh.* VII.2 of execution by strangling.

234 At Luk 12,6 five sparrows go for two assaria, so that Matthew shows slight inflation. The Maximum-Price Edict of Diocletian (4.37, AD 301) illustrates the devaluation of the denarius, no longer silver: 10 *passeres* go for 16 denarii, where in Luke they would go for 4 assaria = 1/4 denarius (above), so that the denarius is 1/64 its Gospel value. More inflationary data at III.256 below. Mishna *Hull.* XII.5 says that mother bird and her young (Deut 22,6) must not both be taken from the nest to cleanse the leper; and adds that this is a "light commandment of the value of an *issar*," מצוה קלה שהיא כאיסר; if that is the price of the mother bird, it shows 100% inflation from Matthew.

235 OGIS 484.13, Pergamum, 2nd century CE, καθ' ἕκαστον δηνάριον εἰσέπρασσον ἀσσάριον ἕν.

(4) *"Quadrans."* Matt 5,26 "the last farthing," τὸν ἔσχατον κοδράντην, Vg *quadrantem*. The parallel Luk 12,59 has an even smaller coin, the λεπτόν; two for a quadrans at Mark 12,42, the widow's "mite," λεπτὰ δύο, ὅ ἐστιν κοδράντης (Vg *quadrans*, Pal. Syr. קודרנטיס). Plutarch *Cic.* 29.5 makes the smallest copper coin the κουαδράντην; Rabbinic קדריונטס;[236] at Lepcis in neo-Punic[237] דנריא...וכנדרם "de-narii...quadrantes." Livy 3.18.11 "plebeians threw quadrantes [all they could afford!] into the consul's house" for a grander funeral, *in consulis domum plebes quadrantes...iactasse.* In Latin verse as minimum coin.[238] Petronius 43 of a self-made man, *ab asse creuit et paratus fuit quadrantem de stercore mordicus tollere* "He began with a penny and was ready to pick a farthing out of a dung-hill with his teeth."

(5) *"Legion."* "More than twelve legions of angels" Matt 26,53, λεγιῶνας ἀγγέλων, Pesh לגיונין דמלאכא. So the demoniac of Gadara in Galilaean Aramaic, Mark 5,9 "my name is Legion," λεγιὼν ὄνομά μου, Pesh לגיון שמן "our name." *Legio* early in Greek λεγεών (Diodorus 26.5);[239] other renderings occasional, στρατόπεδον[240] and τάγμα.[241] The demoniac has a psyche coopted by the legions of Varus in 4 BC. For לגיונא in Palmyrene see III.65. *Gen. Rabbah* 12.16 "parable of a legion first to proclaim a king [i.e. emperor]":

משל ללגיונא שהמליך את המלך תחלה

Exod. Rabbah 15.13 has a combination of Latinisms not in any Latin text easily discoverable, "Parable of a *dux* to whom his *legions* have thrown the *purple*":[242]

משל לדוכוס שדרכו הלגיונות פורפירא

---

236 Jer. Talm. *Qidd.* 58d33, where the denarius (דינר) is 24 assaria (איסר) and the issar is 4 quadrantes.

237 G. Levi della Vida & M. G. Amadasi Guzzo, Iscrizioni puniche della Tripolitania (1927-1939); Monografie di Archeologia Libica XXII; Roma: Bretschneider, 1987; p. 42, no. 17.2.

238 Horace *Sat.* 2.3.93-94; Martial 5.32; Juvenal 7.8; Phaedrus the fabulist 4.21.23.

239 Plutarch *Rom.* 13 attributes a legion to Romulus. His spelling λεγεών is preferable because Latin short i was heard by Greeks as *e*.

240 Polybius calls legions στρατόπεδα because that is his general term for an army; then Luk 21,20 "When you see Jerusalem surrounded by armies (ὑπὸ στρατοπέδων)" need not have the specific sense "legion."

241 Dionysius Hal. 20.1.4 calls a legion τάγμα numbered πρῶτον etc. So Josephus *AJ* 15.72 of queen Alexandra προσφυγεῖν τοῖς σημείοις τοῦ Ῥωμαϊκοῦ τάγματος "to flee to the standards of the Roman legion." This usage may apear at *Odes of Solomon* 35.4

אנא שלא הוית בתגמה דמריא

which Charlesworth translates "But I was tranquil in the Lord's legion."

242 But in Palestinian Aramaic (Levy ii.475, Sokoloff 281) לגיונא can be used for a single soldier or "legionary"—a peculiar parallel to the Gadarene.

Romans called foreign military units legions: Livy 24.49.4 *Cartha-giniensibus legionibus*. The Gospels use *legion* of supernatural beings, unclean spirits and angels; each host is structured like a Roman army. In Rabbinic only the heavenly host: *Lev. Rabbah* 16.9 "The Holy One, blessed be He, calls to his legions": קורא הקדוש...ללגיונות שלו.

(6) *"Mile."* Matt 5,41 "And whoever conscripts you one mile, go with him two." Discussion at II.52-53. In *mille passuum* the word is a number; the back-formation μίλιον is a distance or even a milestone. In a Phrygian inscription[243] a villager describes the requisitioning of oxen (and carts?) laid on them: "We provide service for those coming from Synnada from the fifth mile (ἀπὸ πεμπτοῦ μειλίου)...and also from Meiros as far as Kamaxos four milestones (τέσσαρες μειλιάρια) are laid on us."

(7) *"Peck-measure."* Matt 5,15 "They do not light a lamp and put it under *the* peck-measure (ὑπὸ τοῦ μοδίου, Old Syriac תחית מודיא, Vg *sub modio.*)"[244] The *modius* was a dry measure of 16 *sextarii*; a μόδιος of grain Polybius 21.42.9. Concretely as the container, Josephus *AJ* 9.85 μόδιον Ἰταλικόν; wooden, ὁ μόδιος ξύλον ἐστὶ Arrian *Epict.* 1.17.9; tipped with iron, *modium praeferratum* Cato *de agr.* 11.3. Cicero *de amic.* 67 "many pecks of salt (*multos modios salis*) must be eaten" before two become friends. Bab. Talm. *Erub.* 83a מודיא דקונרס "a peck of artichokes (κινάρα)."

A Latin motif has precious metal in a peck-measure;[245] Plautus *Mil.* 1064 *plus mi auri mille est modiorum Philippi* "I have more than a thousand pecks of gold Philips." Livy (23.12.1) says that the gold rings (*anulos aureos*) from the Roman dead at Cannae poured out by Hannibal at Carthage amounted (according to some authors) to ·3½ pecks (*dimidium supra tris modios*), although in his opinion they filled only a single *modius*. So *Esther Rabbah* 2.3 extravagantly imagines the gift to a Rabbi of a "peck of (gold?) denarii," unattested **modius denariorum*, חד מודיא דדינרין.

(8) *"Denarius."* The silver coin of 10 *as*, δηνάριον, Pesh. דינר, *denarius. denarius* is masculine (Cicero *Verr.* 2.3.220), but went into Greek as neuter. *Periplous Maris Rubri* 8 a collective, "a small amount

---

243 SEG 16 (1959) 754 = W. H. C. Frend, "A Third-Century Inscription relating to *Angareia* in Phrygia," JRS 46 (1956) 46-56.

244 We saw (III.239) that the lamp is Iranian; the verb-forms are Aramaic passives. This house has just one peck-measure and one lamp (Mark 4,21).

245 Otto 225. Add *modium argenti* Juvenal 3.220 "a peck of silver"; Trimalchio's wife Fortunata "measures her sestertii by the peck," *nummos modio metitur* (Petronius 37.4).

of coinage of gold and silver," δηνάριον οὐ πολὺ χρυσοῦν τε καὶ ἀργυροῦν. דינרא pan-Aramaic.[246] Our Semitic sources assume "gold dinars," perhaps the aureus = 25 denarii. In a Palmyrene bilingual (PAT 0294) of AD 193 χρυσᾶ παλαιὰ δηνάρ[ια] = דינרין די דהב עתיקין "gold denars of old [weight]"; *Avoth* VI.9 דינרי זהב; the *dīnār* (دِينَار) at Quran 3.75 is thought gold. At Matt 20,2 a day's wage, ἐκ δηναρίου τὴν ἡμέραν, Pesh מן דינרא ביומא; so Bab. Talm. *BB* 86b היום בדינר. In Diocletian's *Edict* at 7.1 a farm laborer gets 25 denarii per diem plus food (*operario rustico p[asto diu]rni*) and more skilled workers 50; near enough the inflation of 1:64 for sparrows.[247]

(9) *Other possibilities.* —"*Grabatus.*" Mark 2,11 "Arise, take up your bed (κράβαττον)." The Greek is S. Italian vernacular, cf. Arrian *Epict.* 1.24.14 our possessions and body are no more ours than "the cot in the inn (III.270)," τὸν κράββατον ἐν τῷ πανδοκείῳ which we use for a night. Literary in Latin, Catullus 10.22 "the broken leg of an old cot," *fractum...ueteris pedem grabati.* Uncertain if Rabbinic: Bab. Talm. *Qidd.* 70a (cf. *Moed Qatan* 10b) אקרפיטא is something to sit on. Word of popular usage and uncertain origin.[248] —"*Census.*" Matt 22,19 "money of the census," τὸ νόμισμα τοῦ κήνσου, Pesh דינרא דכסף רשא "head-tax", but Pal. Syr. דינרא דקניסון. This can have the classical sense "assessment"; elsewhere κῆνσος is popularly "the coin of the head-tax" itself. Here the Pesh may be the Aramaic original & the Palestinian a late transliteration. Uncertain whether Rabbinic קנס "fine, compensation" (Mishna *Keth.* III.1)[249] is a Greco-Latin loanword, for the corresponding root קנס may be original Semitic.

The Latin originals become concrete in Greek and thence Aramaic. The numbers in *denarius, sextarius, quadrans* and *mille* are lost. *Sextarius* and *modius* from measures become vessels, the μίλιον from a measure becomes a milestone; *census* from a tax becomes the coin that pays it. *Sudarium* loses its connection with sweat, *legio* names celestial or infernal militias. But literary themes associated with coin-

---

246 From the Babatha archive, Fitzmyer-Harrington 62.12; in the Palmyrene tariff; in Punic and at Hatra (KAI 257.4).

247 For the price of sparrows see note 234 above. A third figure for the inflation comes from Mark 6,37, where 200 denarii is barely adequate to feed 5,000 persons; then a denarius fed about 25. By Diocletian's time a modius of grain (*Edict* 1.1) costs 100 denarii, and undoubtedly more on real markets. If a modius fed 50 persons, to feed one person cost 2 denarii, again a 1:50 inflation.

248 For more such vulgar vocabulary, all (as it happens) attested in Paul, see Excursus J below.

249 Also Nabataean, CIS 2.98.8.

age carry over: *as* denotes an insignificant amount, *quadrans* an even smaller amount carefully held on to; the *modius* is the container of extravagant wealth in gold and silver.

23.5.2 Greek equivalents for Latin in the sayings

Some Greek words exist only to translate Latin: ἀνθύπατος Polybius 28.5.6 for *pro consule* with Pesh אנתופטוס. Others went into Rabbinic and name things existing in Latin, but with only marginal coloration from the Latin; φυλακή "prison" with Rabbinic פילקי and Vg *carcer*, reflecting no special features of a Roman prison (III.243). As in 23.4, the Greek of the sayings rests phonetically on itself as loanword in the reconstructed Aramaic; but now both are colored to some degree by the Latin equivalent.

(1) *"Ensign."* Mostly σημεῖον just means "sign" and may rest on the Hellenism סימא (III.251). But elsewhere it may stand for *signum*; Matt 24,30 "the ensign (σημεῖον, Vg *signum*) of the Son of Man in the sky." At Josephus *AJ* 15.72 (III.254) σημείοις are legionary standards; Augustus *R.G.* 29 recovered military standards, *signa militaria* = σημέας. In AD 37 L. Vitellius avoided carrying images (εἰκόνας) attached to standards (σημαίαις) through Jerusalem (*AJ* 18.121); in AD 26 Pilatus deliberately had brought in "the medallions of Caesar attached to the standards," προτομὰς Καίσαρος αἳ ταῖς σημαίαις προσῆσαν (*AJ* 18.55, cf *BJ* 2.169). The desecration is recorded as reversed by *Megillat Taanith* 9 "On the third of Kislev the standards were removed from the Outer Court":[250]

בתלתא בכסלב אתנטילו סימואתא מן דרתא

Hence Targumic: Jer 6,1 "Raise a standard," שְׂאוּ מַשְׂאֵת, LXX ἄρατε σημεῖον, Vg *leuate vexillum*; Targ. Jonathan following the LXX זקפו סימותהון.

Rabbinic also has the Latin loanword סגנון. *Ex. Rabbah* 45.3 "Parable of a king who had a *legion* that rebelled against him. What did the commander of his troops do? He took the king's *standard* and fled":

משל למלך שהיה לו לגיון אחד ומרד עליו מה עשה שר צבאו נטל
סגנוס של מלך וברח

---

250 Ed. Fitzmyer-Harrington 187. Eusebius *Dem. Ev.* 8.2.123 quotes Philo (inaccurately?) as saying that Pilatus "set up the imperial [standards] by night in the Temple"; anyway *Megillath Taanith* supports this version. Discussion by Carl H. Kraeling, "The Episode of the Roman Standards in Jerusalem," HTR 35 (1942) 263-289.

A papyrus of ab. AD 335 records how Athanasius treated the Meletian bishops: his partisans locked them up at Nikopolis "until the *praepositus* came into the storage-room of the military standards," μέχρις τοῦ τ[ὸν] πραιπόσιτον προερθιν [i.e. προελθεῖν] ἐν τοῖς σίγνοις.[251] Hence σίγνον went into Coptic to mean "prison" and further into Arabic: Quran 12.100 "[Allah] took me out of the prison,"

أَخْرَجَنِي مِنَ ٱلسِّجْنِ

(2) *"Governor."* Matt 10,18 "You will be brought before governors and kings," ἐπὶ ἡγεμόνας καὶ βασιλεῖς, Pesh וקדם הגמונא ומלכא, Vg *et ad praesides et reges.*[252] ἡγεμών and *praeses* both are general terms.[253] Pilatus is ἡγεμών (Matt 27,2), and so Felix (Act 23,24). At Act 26,30 "the king and the governor arose," the king is Agrippa II and the governor Festus. At I Peter 2,13-14 "Be subject to the king, to governors," the "king" is the Emperor.[254] In Nabataean הגמונא is the Roman governor of a province; at Rawwafa "Antistius Adventus the governor (הגמונא)" sets up a dedication to Marcus Aurelius and Lucius Verus.[255] In the Palmyrene Tariff 74 the היגמונה may be Gaius Licinius Mucianus, *legatus Augusti pro praetore* of Syria in AD 68-69 (cf PAT 0278). Vague in Rabbinic: *Ex. Rabbah* 31.17 Esau (Rome) is compared to ἡγεμόνες, *duces* and eparchs who plunder cities:

היגמונים ודכסים ואפרכין

(3) *"Steward."* Matt 20,8 "The owner of the vineyard says to his steward (ἐπιτρόπῳ, Vg *uineae procuratori*)." ἐπιτροπος has four senses in the N.T., each attested in Aramaic as אפיטרופוס or the like.

(3.1) *"Steward" of a private estate* as at Matt 20,8. de Ste. Croix 140 holds that he is normally a slave. Classical since Herodotus. Jer. Talm. *B.M.* 10c29-30, "A Jew who appointed a Gentile as steward...a Gentile who appointed a Jew as steward":

ישראל שמינה גוי אפיטרופא...וגוי שמינה ישראל אפיטרופא

Agrippa I (*AJ* 18.194) made Thaumastos *"epitropos* of his estate," τῆς οὐσίας ἐπίτροπον; he may appear at Bab. Talm. *Sukk.* 27a with wives in Tiberias and Sepphoris as *"epitropos* of king Agrippa":

אפיטרופוס של אנריפס המלך

251 H. Idris Bell, Jews and Christians in Egypt: The Jewish Troubles in Alexandria and the Athanasian Controversy...; London: British Museum, 1914; no. 1914 line 18.
252 Plutarch *Comp. Thes. et Rom.* 4 βασιλεῖς...καὶ ἡγεμόνας.
253 Macer (*Digest* 1.18.1) *Praesidis nomen generale est...proconsulis appellatio specialis est,* "The word *praeses* is general...the name *proconsul* is specific."
254 Strabo 17.3.25 restricts ἡγεμών to governors of imperial provinces, but this distinction is not elsewhere observed.
255 J. T. Milik, "Inscriptions grecques et nabatéennes de Rawwafah," Bulletin of the Institute of Archaeology (London) 10 (1971) 54-58.

(3.2) *"Steward" of a realm.* Luke 8,3 "Chouza (Χουζᾶ) steward (ἐπιτρόπου, Old Syriac אפטרופא, Vg *procuratoris*) of Herod [Antipas]." In view of the Nabataean name כוזא (CIS 2.227), Chouza may be named for the Edomite god Κωζέ (Josephus *AJ* 15.253), a fellow-Edomite with the Herods and perhaps a relative.[256] The Nabataean king ruled Petra by a relative with the rank ἐπίτροπον whom he called "brother" (Strabo 16.4.21).[257] Seleucid usage: Lysias *"epitropos* of the king [Antiochus IV] and a relative and over his affairs (ἐπὶ τῶν πραγμάτων)," II Makk 11,1, also acts as general. Josephus (*BJ* 1.199, *AJ* 14.143) says that Caesar made Antipater ἐπίτροπος of all Judaea; Hellenistic or Roman usage?

(3.3) *"Guardian" of an orphan.* Gal 4,1-2 "The heir...is under guardians (ἐπιτρόπους)," Pesh אפטרופא. Classical since Herodotus. Mishna *Git.* V.4 "A guardian who was appointed for orphans by their father":[258]

אפטרופוס שמינהו אבי יתומים

The Babatha archive from the Dead Sea speaks of the "guardian of [Babatha's] orphan son Jesus son of Jesus,"[259] ἐπίτροπον Ἰησοῦ Ἰησοῦτος υἱοῦ αὐτῆς ὀρφανοῦ and so in Aramaic אפטרפא דיתמא "guardian of the orphan."[260]

(3.4) *Roman "procurator."* A *procurator* was an equestrian finance official; from Claudius on it was the title of the governor of Judaea. Previously he was *praefectus* = ἔπαρχος as Pilate's inscription from Caesaraea shows.[261] Here Seleucid and Roman usages flow together. At Palmyra (*PAT* 0286, AD 262) Septimius Worod is ἐπίτροπον

---

256 Discussion Hoehner 303. Chouza has been interpreted as Antipas' "finance minister" (Hoehner 120) and as manager of his estate (Fitzmyer on Luk 8,3, The Anchor Bible, 1981, i.698). Either way he could have been present at the execution of John Baptist and sent the story by his wife Joanna to Jesus' entourage. Was she there when Jesus called Antipas "jackal" (Luk 13,32) to convey the word back to her husband? – Does Josephus mean the Edomite god Qos (בַּרְקוֹס Ezra 2,53, DDD² 674-677)?

257 The Nabataean inscriptions show "brother of the king" (RES 675) and "brother of the queen" (CIS 2.351), probably for persons with the rank of *epitropos*.

258 Cited by Sperber Legal Terms 56-57 with numerous similar texts.

259 Naphtali Lewis et alii, The Documents from the Bar Kokhba Period in the Cave of the Letters: Greek Papyri; Judaean Desert Studies [2]; Jerusalem: Israel Exploration Society etc.; 1989; no. 15.4, p. 59. The double form of the genitive "of Jesus" is peculiar.

260 Y. Yadin, "Expedition D—The Cave of the Letters," IEJ 12 (1962) 247. The full publication of these important texts is being long delayed.

261 Josephus varies his usage and at *BJ* 2.169 calls Pilatus ἐπίτροπος; Tacitus *Ann.* 15.44 *per procuratorem Pontium Pilatum* shows the same inaccuracy.

Σεβαστοῦ = אפטרפא; a claim to legitimacy rather than a record of it? Jerusalem Targums[262] make Joseph Potiphar's אפיטרופוס. *Mekilta*[263] has an ascending series of seven offices in vague context with אפוטרופוס the lowest. *Procurator* also was "steward" of an estate small or large; hence, when an equestrian title, it was natural for the Roman chancery to adopt ἐπίτροπος as its translation.

(4) *"Bandit."*. Matt 26,55 "Have you come out as against a bandit (ἐπὶ λῃστήν, Vg *ad latronem*)?," Pal. Syr. (& Pesh of Luk 22,52) לסטיא. Luk 10,30 "A man fell among bandits (λῃσταῖς)," Pesh לסטיא, Vg *in latrones*. Matt 27,38 "Then there were crucified with him two bandits (λῃσταί, Pesh לסטיא, Vg *latrones*)."[264] The λῃσταί throughout Josephus seem more an (ill-defined) party than individuals. The partner of a bandit is considered a bandit (III.225). Bab. Talm. *BQ* 57b distinguishes an armed bandit (לסטיס מזויין) from an unarmed (לסטיס שאין מזויין).[265] In a Jewish district most bandits will be Israelites (Bab. Talm. *Bezah* 15a). Such belong in prison, φυλακή (III.243) and are subject to crucifixion (III.109). The Roman claim of universal peace gave disturbers special outlaw status; hence λῃστής went into Aramaic to express the new category of *latro*.

The social ambiguity of banditry led severe moralists to see it in established institutions. Mark 11,17 quoting Jer 7,11 LXX makes the Temple a "cave of bandits," σπήλαιον λῃστῶν, Vg *speluncam latronum*, Pesh מערתא דלסטיא (III.218). Augustine asks (*De Civ. Dei* 4.4), *remota iustitia quid sunt regna nisi magna latrocinia?* "without justice, what are kingdoms but big banditries?" In those fictional documents the "Acts of the Alexandrian Martyrs," Appian[266] calls the Emperor (Commodus?)

---

262 Krauss p. 104; see Sperber Legal Terms 56-59.

263 Lauterbach ii.150.

264 There is a large literature on Palestinian banditry and political unrest: Richard A. Horsley with John S. Hanson, Bandits, Prophets and Messiahs: Popular Movements in the Time of Jesus; San Francisco: Harper & Row, 1988; John Dominic Crossan, The Historical Jesus: The Life of a Mediterranean Jewish Peasant; San Francisco: Harper, 1991; pp. 168-206.

265 Jer. Talm. *Keth*. 26d44 prefers invaders and bandits to regular forces! It treats Mishna *Keth*. II.9 "If a city was overcome by a besieging troop, all women in it of priestly stock become ineligible [for marriage with a priest on the presumption they have been raped]," and distinguishes. The rule applies when the siege was on the part of the [local] government [where soldiers are at leisure]; "But in the case of a siege by another government, they are to be considered in the category of bandits [where both parties must operate quickly and have no leisure to rape indiscriminately]":

אבל כרקום של מלכות אחרת כליסטים הן

266 CPJ ii.159b iv.8.

a "bandit chief," λῄσταρχος. Ezekias of Galilee whom Herod the Great captured was a "chief bandit," ἀρχιλῃστής (Josephus *BJ* 1.204);[267] hence ארכיליסטיס *Deut. Rabbah* 4.5.

(5) *"Trumpet."* Matt 24,31 "He will send out his angels with a great trumpet (σάλπιγγος, Pesh שיפורא, Vg *tuba*)." σάλπιγξ went into Rabbinic סלפנגס for Gentile armies with connotations of *tuba*: II.262.

(6) *"Soldier's pay."* In the mouth of John Baptist, Luk 3,14 "be content with your wages (ὀψωνίοις, Pesh אפסוניתכון, Vg *stipendiis uestris*)." Rom 6,23 "the pay (ὀψώνια) of sin is death." See II.110, III.94. ὀψώνιον "victuals" translated *stipendium*, the soldier's pay (Polybius 6.39.12). Antiochus IV (I Makk 3,28) opens his *gazophylakion* "and gave his troops their pay for a year," ἔδωκεν ὀψώνια ταῖς δυνάμεσιν εἰς ἐνιαυτόν.[268] The Greek went into Latin *obsonium* in a less specialized sense: Pliny the Younger *Ep.* 10.118 *athletae... obsonium petunt pro eo agone* "the athletes are asking their upkeep for that game." In the Roman sense, Mishna *Sanh.* II.4 "the king must not multiply for himself silver and gold" (Deut. 17,17) "except to pay [his soldiers'] wages": אלא כדי ליתן אפסניא. *Mekilta* Ex 15,3-4[269] the "king of flesh and blood" must pay אפסניא.

23.6 *A lingua franca*

Akkadian and Iranian were donor languages, not recipients. As the Babylonian and Old Persian texts of Darius' Behistun inscription went into Aramaic of Elephantine, so those languages contributed vocabulary to Aramaic; later the two Iranian texts of Sapor's *Res Gestae* went into Greek. But little vocabulary and no texts went from Greek or Aramaic into them. Thus Greek, Aramaic (with other West-Semitic languages) and Latin play special roles in the interplay of East Mediterranean cultures.

23.6.1 Roles of the member languages
The role of Greek. Greek is the sole intermediary between Aramaic and Latin (apart from rare Punic loans in Latin). Latin words went into Aramaic in Greek form only, whether transcription or translation. In

---

267 Ezekias the bandit was the father of Judas the Galilaean (*AJ* 17.271); Act 5,37 surely refers to Judas, but at the wrong date.
268 It was unheard-of in the first century CE that it should be a denarius a day, Tacitus *Ann.* 1.26 *ut denarius diurnum stipendium foret*. For the soldier, unlike the day laborer, had his food provided.
269 Lauterbach ii.34.

the Hellenistic-Roman age, Aramaic as substrate hardly contributed to pagan Greek (or Latin) other than "sabbath." Earlier, when Greek and Phoenician were trading equals, West-Semitic words of various origin found parallels in Greek, and many further to Latin. Thus of old Greek words with Semitic parallels and appearing in the sayings of Jesus, these appear in Latin also (including the Gospel Vulgate): *byssus* "fine linen," *cadus* "jar," *camelus* "camel," *cuminum* "cummin," *lampas* "torch," *mina* "weight," *saccus* "sack," *taurus* "bull," *tunica* "tunic" (deformed from χιτών), *uinum* "wine" (but the old Semitic was replaced in Peshitto and Aramaic by חמרא). Along with the names of spices and jewels, and a few other words, they form the oldest stratum of what we may call a *lingua franca*—the commonality of Greek, Aramaic and Latin.

The role of Aramaic. It became the business language of successive empires, and anticipated Arabic moving into Canaanite. It may have been the intermediary in the takeover of Akkadian words in Ugarit and Phoenicia. It was surely the language in which unorthodox Jewish or Christian groups influenced Islam—so that the symbolism of the Akkadian "throne" is continuous from Ugarit to Mecca. As the language of the Jewish Exile in Babylon, it brought Akkadian for social classes and urban features—with their reality—to Palestine. Many Greek loanwords entered Aramaic[270] from the use of the Septuagint by the oral tradition which became the written Targums; hence the LXX in Jesus' quotations need not all be the work of the Evangelists.

The parables of Jesus were enough known in Aramaic to get *polemical reversal or parody*. At Matt 13,45-46 it is good luck for the trader who "went and sold all he had" to buy a pearl; bad luck for the Gentile (Bab. Talm. *Shabb.* 119a, III.63). The reliable innkeeper of the Samaritan parable for one wounded by bandits (Luk 10,30) is replaced by the rascally innkeeper of *Gen. Rabbah* 92.6 in cahoots with bandits (III.242). The householder who gives a banquet (Matt 22,4) for the poor (Luk 14,21) is replaced by the publican (Jer. Talm. *Hag.* 77d51) who does no other meritorious deed (III.249). At Luk 18,2-8 the unjust judge is swayed by the insistence of the widow to be vindicated from her adversary; at *Pesiqta de Rab Kahana* 15.9 a woman and her adversary both bribe the judge, and he is swayed by the bigger bribe of her adversary (III.224). At Matt 7,5 = Luk 6,42 the one with a "beam" in his eye unfairly criticizes the one with the "mote"; at Bab.

---

270 See further my "The Septuagint as a Source of the Greek Loan-Words in the Targum," Biblica 70 (1989) 194-216.

Talm. *Arakh.* 16b (III.329) the saying becomes a pretext to avoid *legitimate* reproof.—Often the Rabbinical parables are treated as pre-existing materials adapted by Jesus. But this is upside down. For (a) Jesus is above all the teacher remembered as a maker of parables; (b) the Rabbinical materials are much later; (c) their consistently negative theme suggests polemic; (d) they may lose the original reference, as in "the mote and the beam" to the actor-hypocrite's wooden mask.

The role of Latin. At first it was the borrower from Greek. Legendary Thebes is described in six Greek loans at Plautus *Amph.* 1011-1012:

> nam omnis *plateas* perreptaui, *gymnasia* et *myropolia*,
>
> apud *emporium* atque in *macello*, in *palaestra* atque in foro.

"For I walked through all the streets, gymnasia and perfumeries, at the market and the meat market, at the wrestling-floor and the forum." Three appear in the N.T. and four in Semitic: πλατεῖα with פלטיא; ἐμπόριον Joh 2,16 with Rabb. אמפורין; μάκελλον I Kor 10,25 (Pesh מקלין); PAT 1406 גמנסירכס with γυμνασίαρχος "gymnasium-supervisor."[271] Later, Latin becomes an equally generous donor to Greek, both in transcription and translation. Of Greek words we discussed above (23.4), Latin borrowed many first declension feminines—*apotheca, asotia, cathedra, stola, symphonia, theca, zona*—all of which also went into Aramaic. Hellenistic culture spread to Palestine and Italy during the same centuries; social conditions were enough alike that many of the same items were taken up by both peoples, with their names.

Here are a dozen more words from the Greek N.T. in their Latin form which were borrowed in the Latin and Syriac versions, and are also documented in Rabbinic and pagan Latin: *aloe* Joh 19,39 "aloes"; *barbarus* Acts 28,2 "barbarian"; *charta* II Joh 2,12 "paper"; *cithara* I Kor 14,7 "zither"; *gubernator* Act 27,11 "pilot"; *hydropicus* Luk 14,2 "dropsical"; *idiotes* Act 4,13 "private person"; *philosophus* Act 17,18 "philosopher"; *spongia* Matt 27,48 "sponge"; *stadium* I Kor 9,24 "stadium"; *stomachus* I Tim 5,23 "stomach"; *theatrum* Act 19,29 "theatre."

23.6.2 Trilingual texts

Where the three languages are on a par, *trilingual texts* appear. Cleon the salt-official dedicates a bronze altar at Sardinia in 200-150 BC (KAI 66) in Latin, Greek and Punic; the Punic notes that it weighs "100

---

271 [Plato] *Eryx.* 399A; *gymnasiarchus* Cicero *Verr.* 2.4.92.

pounds," לטרם מאת, the S. Italian word behind λίτρα. Nicodemus (Joh 19,39) brings a hundred pounds of ointment, λίτρας ἑκατόν, Pesh מאא ליטרין, Vg *libras centum*. At Palmyra (PAT 1413, AD 174)[272] L. Antonius Callistratus, a tax-collector, gets an honorific inscription in Latin, Greek and Palmyrene from Galen his agent (*actor* = πραγμα-τευτής = פרגמטתא). Cf Luk 19,13 πραγματεύσασθε "go into business"; Bab. Talm. *Bab. Mes.* 42a "keep a third [of your capital] in land, a third in goods (פרגמטיא), a third in cash."

The New Testament, itself to become a trilingual text, has in it the text billed (Joh 19,20) as in "Hebrew, Latin and Greek," Ἑβραϊστί, Ῥωμαϊστί, Ἑλληνιστί where presumably John as elsewhere by "Hebrew" meant Aramaic. (The Vulgate and Peshitto change the order, *hebraice graece et latine*.) The Peshitto of John correctly has ישוע נצרי "Jesus the Nazarene," for the town Nazareth is known in Hebrew from the Caesarea list[273] of priestly courses as נצרת. In a Crucifixion by El Greco (1605-1610) at Cleveland the *titulus* is a neat board against agitated clouds. The Greek painter, working in Toledo, follows the Vulgate change of order; he correctly puts the Greek in capitals (with ligatures); and so the Latin, with IVDEOR[um] abbreviated. The Hebrew is corrupt; he is copying an unknown translator at several removes. In a near-contemporary work, the Crucifixion by Rubens, the figures are in motion, even the *titulus* is wind-blown. Rubens' Greek is in MS style with capitals and small letters, breathings and accents; the Latin is correct. The Hebrew is again corrupt, now with vowel-points in what pass for the letters. The Greek mannerist conveys the feeling of an ancient trilingual in capitals, while the Flemish realist reproduces printed books of his own age.

23.6.3 The emergence of a lingua franca

When discourse in Greek, Aramaic or Latin aimed at users of one of the other languages, the speaker restricted syntax, topics and vocabulary for maximum ease of translation. While this accommodation seldom reached mutual intelligibility, it simplified learning another tongue. Thus arose a common vocabulary shared by all three tongues. The original *lingua franca* was the trading language of the central Mediterranean during the Renaissance, a fusion of Italian and Provençal with Arabic, like other pidgins comprehensible to each party, but in a

---

272 Trilingual epitaphs for the local Hairanes (PAT 2801, AD 52); and the Roman Lucius Spedius Chrysanthus, another publican, מכסא (PAT 0591, AD 58).

273 Jack Finegan, The Archeology of the New Testament...; Princeton: University, 1969; p. 29 with photo.

limited semantic realm. (*"Lingua franca"* itself seems a calque on Arabic *lisān al-faranğ* "tongue of the French [i.e. foreigner].") Molière parodies it in *Le Bourgeois Gentilhomme* IV.viii on the mufti's lips:

Se ti sabir, / Ti respondir; / Se non sabir, / Tazir, tazir.

Mi star mufti, / Ti qui star, ti? / Non intendir? / Tazir, tazir.

"If you know, answer; if you don't know, be quiet, be quiet. I am the mufti, who are you? You don't understand? Be quiet, be quiet."

What is known about the *lingua franca* is gathered in two works by Cifoletti.[274] In both he substantially reproduces our primary source, an anonymous little dictionary of 1830 for travelers and traders.[275] The first attestations (in the 1989 work) are from 1528 and 1612. The language appears to be today extinct. In the 19th century it got a more French coloration, and the old pronouns *mi* and *ti* become *moi* and *toi*. Throughout the verb is used only in the infinitive; words are adopted from various Romance languages, ideally where they overlap with Arabic. Thus Louis Léon César Faidherbe of "L'Alliance française pour la propagation de la langue française dans les colonies et les pays étrangers" in a study of 1884 attests among others the phrases: *Moi meskine, toi donnar sordi. Lui tenir drahem bezzef. Quand moi gagner drahem, moi achetir moukère.* "I am poor, give me sous! He has much (*beaucoup*) money. When I get money I will buy a wife." Two words are shared by French and Arabic, *meskine* (III.223) and *drahem* (II.335).

From this marginal and poorly attested original, in modern usage the phrase *lingua franca* becomes an existing language used for specific purposes beyond the range of its native speakers. French was long the lingua franca of diplomacy, and English names military ranks after it: *général, colonel, capitain, lieutenant.* English is the lingua franca of business: the French say *software* while the Académie vainly boosts *logiciel.* Rosén finds Roman Palestine "one of the few areas of inter-section (*Überschneidungsflächen*) of these two linguae francae [Greek and Imperial Aramaic]."[276] Fitzmyer[277] sees Aramaic in the Near East "serving as the *lingua franca* during the latter part of the Neo-Assyrian

---

274 Guido Cifoletti, Il Vocabolario della Lingua Franca; Padova: Clesp, 1980; La Lingua Franca Mediterranea; Quaderni Patavini di linguistica; monografie 5; Unipress, 1989. My xeroxes of these works (both short) lack page-numbers.

275 Dictionnaire de la Langue Franque ou Petit Mauresque; Marseille: Feissat & Demonchy, 1830.

276 Haiim B. Rosén, "Die Sprachsituation in römischen Palästina," pp. 489-513 of his East and West: Selected Writings in Linguistics; I. General and Indo-European Linguistics; München, W. Fink 1982: p.489. Strictly speaking, *lingua franca*, being Italian, should not have this Latin plural.

277 P. 29 of Fitzmyer (note 7 above).

Empire and during the Persian period"; and so for Greek (pp. 32, 35) in the Hellenistic and Roman periods.

Here I use "lingua franca" to denote the commonality of two or more languages in the same area, ever more assimilated without creating a full pidgin or creole (a trading pidgin become the language of a whole people). The Near Eastern lingua franca is nearly all nouns (with a few "denominative" verbs from nouns): the mutual intercourse of peoples keeps expanding the universe of things that require discourse—sabbaths, inns, legions.

Recognition of this lingua franca puts an enlarged burden on lexicography, whether of the New Testament or an ancient language generally. If the sayings of Jesus in our Gospels are truly a translation, their meaning is not exhausted by prior usage of the *translator's* vocabulary. If the underlying Aramaic is filled with loanwords from other languages, we need to look at them also. You would think at least that the N.T. lexica, when they come to a word transliterated from Latin, would cite Latin texts; they do not. καιρός is an egregious example: it surely rests on Aramaic זְמָן, which rests on Iranian; and its occasional meaning "dangerous time" rests on the influence of Latin *tempus* upon Polybius.

23.6.4 The New Testament as primary witness to the lingua franca.

The New Testament thus is really a trilingual text; and the Versions, in particular Syriac and Latin, not merely illustrate the coloration of its vocabulary, but again and again restore to its original form the actual situation. The Peshitto of Jesus' sayings, though not his original Aramaic, is one step closer than the Greek.

The versions of the N.T. come nearest mutual intelligibility in dealing with Roman administration. Matt 27,26-28: "Then he released Barabbas to them, and *scourged* Jesus and turned him over to be crucified. Then the *soldiers* of the *governor* took Jesus into the *praetorium* and collected the whole *cohort* against him. And they stripped him and put on him a scarlet *cloak*."

τότε ἀπέλυσεν αὐτοῖς τὸν Βαραββᾶν, τὸν δὲ Ἰησοῦν φραγελλώσας παρέδωκεν ἵνα σταυρωθῇ. τότε οἱ στρατιῶται τοῦ ἡγεμόνος παρα-λαβόντες τὸν Ἰησοῦν εἰς τὸ πραιτώριον συνήγαγον ἐπ᾽ αὐτὸν ὅλην τὴν σπεῖραν. καὶ ἐκδύσαντες αὐτὸν χλαμύδα κοκκίνην περιέθηκαν αὐτῷ.

Tunc dimisit illis Barabban, Iesum autem *flagellatum* tradidit eis ut crucifigeretur. Tunc *milites praesidis* suscipientes Iesum in *praetorio* congregauerunt ad eum uniuersam *cohortem*. Et exuentes eum, *clamydem* coccineam circumdederunt ei.

הידין שרא להון לבר אבא ונגד בפרגלא לישוע ואשלמה דנזדקף .הידין
אסטרטיוטא דהגמונא דברוהי לישוע לפרטורין וכנשו עלוהי לכלה אספיר.
ואשלחוהי ואלבשוהי כלמיס דזחוריתא.

All six Pesh. nouns are Greek loanwords for Roman institutions
available in Rabbinic. The Vulgate in each case has the Latin original.
For the *whip* see III.106; *soldiers* III.249; *governor* III.258; *cohort*
III.116. Rabbinic borrows *chlamys*.[278] Both in Jerusalem (Mark 15,16)
and Caesarea (Act 23,35) the *praetorium* or headquarters of the provincial governor took over a Herodian palace. At Mishna *Sanh.* II.3 the
"king" has a פלטורין as if the Latin had always existed in Israel
(II.110). The Roman soldier Scribonius Demetrius in Eboracum (York)
put up a Greek dedication (IG 14.2548) "to the gods of the governor's
praetorium," θεοῖς τοῖς τοῦ ἡγεμονικοῦ πραιτωρίου.[279] —The Latin of
Matt 27 restores the original language of the event. And the Peshitto
also restores a possible original of the text; for it can pass as reconstruction of an Aramaic eyewitness account.

Just like the older shared vocabulary of Hebrew and Greek, the
lingua franca of the Roman period generates *international phrases*,
where Greco-Latin and West Semitic say the same thing in the same
way. Here are some of the phrases we have found. With one word
Latin: "a string (*linea*) of pearls" (III.62); "to conscript a mile (*mille*)"
(II.52-53 etc.); "theatres and circuses (*circi*)" (III.211). With one or
both words a Greek equivalent for Latin: "bandits (*latrones*) at the
inn," "...in prison" (III.242-243); "chiliarch (*tribunus militum*) and
cohort (*cohors*)" (III.93,116). Three words all of which fall under the
lingua franca: in Latin, *thesauros antiquissimae gazae* (III.240); in
West Semitic, *dux...legio...purpura* (III.254).

Likewise phrases of Greek words: "storehouse and barn" (III.243);
"adversary and advocate" (III.330); "purple and byssus" (III.230);
"belt and sandals" (III.245); with a Semitic name, "*kathedra* of Moses" (III.243). Here is one further: *pedagogue and school. Cant. Rabbah*
II.5.2 explains why after the Exodus God delayed putting on Israel the
burden of the Law. "It was like a king's son who got up from his
illness. His pedagogue (פדגוגו) said to the king, 'Let your son go to
school (לאיסכולי)'. But the king said he should first spend three months
getting his strength back." παιδαγωγός since Herodotus 8.75.1 is a
slave who takes a boy to instruction. σχολή, originally "leisure" (Ar-

---

278 *Yelammedenu* on Gen. xxv, 23.25 as cited by Levy 341 "Esau [i.e. Rome]
wears the *chlamys*," עשו מלובש כלמוס.

279 Scribonius adds a second dedication specifically to "Ocean and Tethys,"
Ὠκεανῷ καὶ Τηθύϊ; he hopes to get safely across the English Channel.

istotle *Pol.* 1334a21 οὐ σχολὴ δούλοις "slaves have no leisure") becomes concrete as "school" (*ibid.* 1313b3). Both went into Latin as *paedagogus* (Plautus) and *schola* (Quintilian). They come together in later Latin. A Roman boy speaks:[280] "I went ahead...with the pedagogue following me directly through the portico that led to the school," *processi...sequente me paedagogo recte per porticum quae ducebat ad scholam.* Augustine[281] *sine paedagogis posse pueros pergere in scholam* "boys can get to school without pedagogues." Act 19,19 σχολῇ where Pesh באסכולא and Vg *in schola*. Later the "pedagogue" becomes a tutor, and all the literatures use it metaphorically (I.330-331).

The borrowed language naming new cultural elements paradoxically confers *invulnerability* upon texts containing it. A weaker society is vulnerable when it tries to hold on to old traditions in old language against the attraction and repression of an occupying power. That happened to the Keltic enclaves in Scotland and Ireland. But where the weaker society adopts the foreign culture in its foreign language, and then proceeds to express its native thought in those borrowed terms, the occupying regime has no power over it. Thus Jesus' thought is expressed precisely through examples derived from one of the foreign cultures, and named in its language. Since the objects named by the lingua franca have become a common Mediterranean (and modern) heritage, the message they convey is self-explanatory. And since the situation of Galilee was that of poor people on the land under a double layer of control, native and foreign, the message is self-explanatory wherever the narrative situation repeats itself, as in Latin America today.

Scholars have studied the Versions mostly as a witness to an earlier state of the Greek text. Since the Old Latin and Old Syriac may go back to the second century of our era, from which we have few papyri of the N.T., this is a valuable use of them. Here we rather use them as a witness to an earlier *cultural and linguistic state of the New Testament materials.* To the historian, the Latin and Syriac Versions are of no less value than their Greek original in assessing the original meaning of the text. For they represent a restoration of the historical setting by well-informed scholars with a vast fund of concrete knowledge and linguistic understanding now lost to us.

The Pentecost story is often taken as an interpretation of glossolalia —unintelligible ecstatic speech. Luke is presumed to have in mind the

---

280 *Corpus glossariorum latinorum* III.380.47-54.
281 *de gestis Pelagi* 1.3, PL 44.321.

spread of the Gospel to many of the peoples he lists (Act 2,9-11). We may extend his interpretation: Jews speaking Parthian recognized the loans from their language in the texts; Jews speaking Edessene Aramaic, Greek, the Latin of Rome were to acquire full versions of the texts in their own languages. The new Church is surprised and delighted that the barriers of Babel have been overthrown. The limitations on the language of Jesus, screening off what was not directly transferable to Greek and Latin, were the condition of its universality.

Excursus J: Vernacular words in Paul

What I have called the Near Eastern lingua franca under the Roman Empire has a very large vocabulary—nearly all Latin and Greek words passing through Greek into Aramaic. There is no way I can do full justice to it even in this thick volume. But of especial interest are people's words of fluctuating form, uncertain origin, and surprising success. We have briefly discussed two such which appear to come from the Greek vernacular of southern Italy: in their Latin form *grabattus* (III.256) "cot-bed," frequent in the Gospels and Act 5,15; 9,33 (to make up for Luke's omission of it in his Gospel); and *libra* "pound" (Joh 12,3; 19,39; III.264). Here are three more with special features, all (as it happens) attested or nearly so in Paul, even though his usage is less vernacular than that of Epictetus as transcribed by Arrian (thus Arrian 1.24.14 τὸν κράββαατον ἐν τῷ πανδοκείῳ "the bunk in the inn," III.256). Inevitably they have hangers-on worthy also of note.

(1) *The cloak.* At II Tim 4,13 Paul asks for the cloak (τὸν φαιλόνην, Vg *paenulam*) which he left behind at Troas, and the books, especially the parchments (τὰς μεμβράνας, Vg *membranas*). (An old puzzle at fundamentalist seminaries: is Paul's inerrancy compromised if in fact he left the cloak at Thessalonike?) Here first μεμβράνα appears in Greek; it is originally Latin *membrana*, Pliny 13.70 *Varro membranas Pergami tradit repertas* "Varro records that parchments were discovered at Pergamum," which gave them their modern name, *pergamenorum nomen ad hanc usque diem* "the name of 'parchments' came down to our own day," Jerome *Epist.* 7.2. φαιλόνης is a more popular variant of φαινόλης (both appear in the papyri): first attested in the Sicilian comic poet Rhinthon (3rd century BC) attested by Pollux 7.61 ἔχοισα καινὰν φαινόλαν "a woman with a new cloak." Epictetus (Arrian *Epict.* 4.8.34) says that the false Cynic takes up a threadbare cloak (τρίβωνα) in imitation of Socrates, and quarrels with a man wearing a better one, ἐν φαινόλη.

By contrast Latin *paenula* is fully literary: Plautus *Most.* 991 *libertas paenulast tergo tuo* "liberty is a cloak for your back"; Cicero *pro Milone*

29 *cum...hic de raeda reiecta paenula desiluisset* "when [Milo] threw off his cloak and jumped out of the carriage." (*Raeda* itself is Gallic along with *carrus*, Caesar *Bell. Gall.* 1.51 *Germani...aciem suam raedis et carris circumdederunt* "the Germans surrounded their line with carriages and wagons" to prevent retreat; it went into the NT [but not Semitic] as a Latin loanword, Rev 18,13 ἵππων καὶ ῥεδῶν "horses and chariots," Vg *equorum et redarum*.) Undoubtedly *paenula* appeared in a lost section of the *Edict. Diocl.* 19.63-64 (ed. Giacchero) where the Greek has φαινουλα, παινουλα. The more vulgar Greek form went into Rabbinic, mostly in false spelling: Jer. Talm. *Hagigah* 76d7-10 a certain Rabbi "released vows while wearing a *paenula*," התיר בפלניס (printed text בפלנים) for lack of a Talith (טלית). Most likely the word was south Italian like *grabattus* and *litra*, perhaps first entering Latin, then Greek, then Rabbinic.

(2) The (meat-) market.

Paul at I Kor 10,25 says "Eat whatever is sold 'at market'," πᾶν τὸ ἐν μακέλλῳ πωλούμενον ἐσθίετε, Vg *omne quod in macello uenit manducate*, and so Pesh במקלון. Cadbury[1] illustrates an actual fragmentary inscription from Corinth including MACELLV[M]. We saw (III.263) the *macellum* in Plautus' Thebes; at Plautus *Aul.* 373-4 you can get fish there, and also lamb (*agninam*), beef (*uitulinam*) and pork (*porcinam*)—all at high prices. The TDNT describes the Roman *macellum* in general, partly from the excavated one in Pompeii:[2] "a rectangular court of pillars with a fountain in the middle and over it, supported by the pillars, a dome-shaped roof (Tholus); the booths on the sides; before them porticos." Dessau[3] has gathered together building-inscriptions of *macella* from around the Empire which illustrate those features. They were so far as possible elegant and permanent stone buildings. So of a μάκελλος...πολυτελής (*SIG*[3] 783.45) "expensive *macellum*." Dio Cassius 16.19.1 notes Nero's dedication of a food-market, defined more generally as τὴν ἀγορὰν τῶν ὄψων, τὸ μάκελλον ὠνομασμένον. A life of Aesop[4] speaks of the "market of sacrificed pigs," τὸν μάκελλον τῶν τεθυμένων χοιριδίων; here μάκελλον comes closest to suggesting "butcher's shop" and nothing else.

Rabbinic takes the word from Greek, always in the sense of "meat-market." *Gen Rabbah* 86.2 is a parable of "a cow that they brought to the *makellon*":

---

1   Henry J. Cadbury, "The Macellum of Corinth," JBL 53 (1934) 134-141.
2   J. Schneider at TDNT iv.370-372.
3   *ILS* 5578-5592.
4   *Vita Aesopi* "G" 51, ed. Perry p. 52.

לפרה שהיו מושכין אותה למקולין

they drag her calf in front of her to get her to follow. There is a partial parallel to Paul's ruling in Bab. Talm. *Hullin* 95a (Rabbi): "[In the case of] *macella* and slaughterers of Israel, meat found in possession of a Gentile is permitted":

מקולין וטבחי ישראל בשר הנמצא ביד גוי מותר

That is, in the presumed case where the meat-market employs Jewish kosher butchers, even if the clerk is non-Jewish the meat may be bought.

The early history of the word and its origin are uncertain. The temple of Asklepios at Epidaurus, according to a Doric inscription of the 4th century BC,[5] contained a μάκελλον (neuter) which boasted an architect's plan (παραδείχματος), had "rings and pins," and required iron; the editors call it a "lattice" or "screen" (*Gitter*), LSJ an "enclosure." Nothing suggests that it is a market. Could the source be Hebrew מִכְלָה Hab 3,17 "sheepfold"? Compare Ps 78,70 "And [Yahweh] took [David] from among the sheepfolds"

וַיִּקָּחֵהוּ מִמִּכְלְאֹת צֹאן

But neither at Epidaurus nor elsewhere is there any indication that the Greco-Latin institution or its name were borrowed from Semitic; and when Rabbinic and Syriac took over the Greek name for the thing, they saw no connection with the native word מִכְלָה.

(3) *The blow.*

Matt 26,67 (cf. Mark 14,65) "Then they spat in his face (πρόσωπον) and struck him (ἐκολάφισαν)," Vg *colaphis eum ceciderunt*. We saw the takeover in Aramaic פרצופא of the word for "face" (III.247). The verb κολαφίζω appears first in the NT, but existed in the vernacular in a weaker sense. Thus in a letter of the second century CE (*Select Papyri* i.121.22-24),[6] Sempronius writes perhaps from Alexandria to his brother Maximus in upper Egypt, "If any of our brothers contradicts [our mother], you must cuff them," εἰ δέ τεις τῶν ἀδελφῶν ἀντιλέγει αὐτῇ, σὺ ὀφείλεις αὐτοὺς κολαφίζειν. It is formed from a noun κόλαφος only attested in lexica, but surely colloquial in Greek since it is regular in Latin: Plautus, *Per.* 846 *colapho me icit* "He hit me a blow"; Terence *Ad.* 199 *plus quingentos colaphos infregit mihi* "He hit me more than five hundred blows." From the bottom of society the Latin word rose to the top in French *coup*, Spanish *golpe*, Italian *colpo*! At I Kor 4,11 κολαφιζόμεθα, Vg *colaphis caedimur*, it is used of the ill-

---

5   SGDI pp. 140ff, no. 3325, esp. lines 296-301.
6   A. S. Hunt & C. C. Edgar, Select Papyri i pp. 318-321 (LCL 1952) = Revue Egyptien 1919 p. 204 = Sammelbuch iii.6263.

treatment of the apostles. At II Kor 12,7 for ἵνα με κολαφίζη "so that ['the thorn in the flesh'] might buffet me" the Vg creates a verb *ut me colaphizet*. Paul, who emphasizes in general his participation in the suffering of Jesus, here is in agreement with the actual language of the Passion narrative. At I Pet 2,20 it is used of slaves, ἁμαρτάνοντες καὶ κολαφιζόμενοι "if you are beaten when you make a mistake,..." Vg *si peccantes et colophizati*; the context suggests that all believers likewise participate in the suffering of Christ.

The Palestinian Syriac of Matt 26,67 in agreement with the Vulgate from the Greek verb restores a noun as loanword:

ומחו יתה קולפסין

"and struck him blows." As the noun was vulgar in Greek and Latin, it went also into popular Aramaic, from which the Palestinian has it. For there is a remarkable parallel in Rabbinic, e.g. תרי קולפי בלעת (Bab. Talm. *Berakh.* 56a) "you get two blows."

Chapter 24: From Particularity to Universalism

This final chapter is an historical summary of these volumes which rearranges the material from new points of view. It avoids introduction of new citations except where they force themselves upon us. It drops Hebrew and Greek fonts; where international words are essential, they appear in transcription. It is intended as an overview of the work as a whole, available to any educated reader of English, and short enough to provide a bird's-eye view of the argument. It could have stood at the beginning, if the author had known then what he believes he does now.

We presuppose the emergence of a new genus, and several species, of free societies at the fringe of the absolutist ancient Near Eastern empires. Vol. I outlined the social enterprises of the new societies through a common link, their shared vocabulary; Vol. II chronicled sacred institutions where Italy as much as Hellas echoes the Near East; Vol. III records the social and individual changes under Near Eastern imperialism and its Western successors—Macedon, Carthage, Rome. Here we review that history from perspectives in part already introduced.

(1) We include the *complementarity* of Israel and Hellas worked out in Chapter 22, without compromising the new beginning which they jointly represent.

(2) At each stage of the historical development, we note the *guarantee* for its continuance represented in the symbolism of the High God and his equivalents, which especially came to undergird Volume II. And we ask, How far can that guarantee be translated into terms generally acceptable today?

(3) So far as Israel and Hellas run parallel, the evidence for all these themes is their shared invention of the *book*, both as record of their historical novelty and its main product. —Not so much the book in the sense of a physical object, the fourth-century codices of Latin Vergil and the Greek Bible, or the ninth-century codices of the Hebrew Bible; but the book as a living tradition, whose text, pronunciation and meaning are handed down from one generation to another. (Hellas

provides a second body of evidence, its art and architecture, which both illustrate its books and are illustrated by them.)

(4) After the novelty represented by Israel and Hellas is fully developed, we chronicle a fundamental change in both from *particularity* to *universalism* (or perhaps better *cosmopolitanism*), correlated with a basic *shift* from autonomy to incorporation into new empires. Each society moves from saying "We are different from all the others" to saying "We have something of infinite value which should be made available to all the others."

(5) This universalism has an opposite side with two features. The reality that the walled city-state was not eternal but transitory brings the *fragility* of the natural created order also into new awareness. Above all, there emerges a new *individualism* replacing family solidarity and requiring a victory over death.

(6) When warring empires are replaced by Rome, and the Church begins to represent a new worldwide community, to some degree in a *second shift* the old particularity is restored. The walls of the city-state are replaced by the frontier armies of the Roman Empire; and a new set of outsiders is recognized. The lost solidarity of the genetic family is replaced by the universal brotherhood of the Church. Still, the new individualism with its demand for a life beyond death, once generated, is never lost; likewise the expectation of an end to the natural order remains—although with a more hopeful coloration. But the full story and documentation of this second shift lies beyond the limits of these volumes.

Underlying everything is the concept of *emergence*. Here my thought rests on several readings of Bernard Lonergan's *Insight*. Emergence is the link which unites cosmic expansion, biological evolution, and historical development. It says that galactic and stellar formation cannot be fully explained from particle physics, though depending on it and presupposing it, but represents a higher level of organization; that chemistry cannot be fully explained from physics, nor living organisms from inorganic, nor animals from plants, nor human beings from (other) animals. The present work carries the logic a step further. It maintains that, while the new free societies presuppose the ancient Near Eastern empires and rest on them, they cannot be fully understood from the inner life of those empires, but represent a higher level of organization.

A level far from predetermined: the new thing being born had (as always) an even broader range of potentialities than previous ones. The very differences among Israel, Hellas, and Rome too show this. In the Greek sculpture of the youth or *kouros* (III.164) we see a permanently valid image of the new humanity, which could have been (we may imagine) very different, but, once it came into being, imposes itself thereafter on our imaginations. The pressure for emergence reflects the undetermined character of the novelties—which however, once realized, constitute the necessary framework for any further emergences in the following two millennia up to the present. Still, some or all the characteristics of the new Mediterranean world already in principle were available in the Near Eastern empires of Egypt, Mesopotamia, Anatolia; but blocked, stunted, enslaved. It goes without saying that the novelties of Israel and Hellas were all along possible, since at the right time they became actual. Can we say that they existed potentially in the ancient Near East?

That question suggests a search for antecedents of the new free societies in the empires—a search which I do not here carry out, in my ignorance of cuneiform and hieroglyphic. It would be worthwhile for somebody with other skills to ask: How far does the simple phonetic script of the alphabet rest on previous scripts? Do the decrees of Assyrian kings embody a true idea of justice going beyond their ruling interests? Does the infantry of Near Eastern empires ever express itself (as in the new societies) through the demand or reality of political power? Do any Near Eastern texts represent an internal critique of ruling monarchs or entrenched priesthoods? Can we properly speak of a Near Eastern humanism?

Cosmic emergence is slow, taking billions of years, because each stage represents the appearance of events with low probability. Historical emergence operates much faster, because to an ever-increasing degree it springs from conscious human planning. Any doctrine of emergence presupposes that it never stops, but is ongoing. That raises the question for us: has the novelty of the Hebrew and Greek societies been, in part or in whole, superseded by subsequent emergences; or does it still hold the field? The point of view here adopted is that the insights of Hebrew and Greek texts, far from being rendered obsolete by the progress of technology or anything else, remain rather a standard for us to rise up to, than an accomplishment on which we can build new structures. They were such a big step that assimilation takes a long time.

The one novelty *of the same kind* as their innovations that I can see is the musical notation permitting the conception and record of large-scale compositions. Of course we know a lot of new things—cosmic history, planetary evolution, calculus, quantum mechanics, molecular biology. Even more remarkable: we behave the same old way and understand our behavior the same old way. Harold Bloom credits Shakespeare with the "invention of the human," characters capable of change; but a greater step was the emergence, both in literature and real life, of creatures possessing character in the first place. Surely a new emergence is in the cards: but to identify it with the Internet or anything else would not merely usurp the role of prophet, but affirm that it was already in our midst. Each emergence remains as a substructure for what follows. Far from being replaced, it achieves its true meaning by the revelation of what can be built on it—and on its successors. A true novel emergence is literally unimaginable; for if we could imagine it, it would already be upon us. Opinions differ whether nonviolent direct action (III.201) is a step beyond the New Testament or simply a contemporary application of it. Still, the prospect of the new emergence should not trouble Christian theologians who see the New Testament as not to be superseded; for it itself contains the promise, "And greater works than these shall he do" (Joh 14,12).

In the sections of this chapter we survey in sequence the phases that Israel and Hellas jointly passed through, striving to do justice both to their shared novelty and their differences. In each section we cite a few texts which define the phase most exactly.

In (24.1) we discuss the *physical environment* of Israel and Hellas so far as shared: hills and valleys, the defensible citadel; farming with the staples of wheat and barley, raising the noble fruits of fig and olive, grazing of sheep and goats; the technology of iron and lime; ambivalence about the forest cover of the land with its predators; the *rain* (with other "elements") from the High God which makes all possible; the interpenetrating sea and a first cosmology.

In (24.2) we survey the *external human environment*: the complementary relation of both peoples to the Ancient Near Eastern empires and to the maritime palace societies; seafaring and land-trade; warfare and the treaty; the foreign woman and exotic imports; the ethnic paradigm naming foreign peoples, and their interchange between societies.

In (24.3) we lay out the *internal organization* of the new societies, with rings of agriculture and grazing around the central citadel: kingship and its successors the magistrates, council of elders, and assembly of the people; larger structures in which they are included; the sacrificial cult of the bull and the seer; the central role of ecstasy from the fruit of the vine; the myth of dragon combat (with the tuna-fishery).

In (24.4) we summarize the *primary discoveries* of the two societies: the objective depiction of heroic *honor and shame*; the critique of sacral institutions; the discovery of *humanism*, along with family solidarity. Above all the idea of *justice* and the possibility of its historic realization, attributed to the High God but announced by people's spokesmen with sacral immunity, initially as validating land-tenure, and carried by land trade. The record of all this in the invention of the *book*; the inturning of the new societies on themselves in *particularity*, "We have a unique treasure."

In (24.5) we chronicle the *loss of independence to new empires*: the destruction of the city *wall*; the function of imperial *sanctions* and *legitimation*; discovery of world citizenship or membership in the entire human race as outsiders pass from presumed enemy to potential friend; the ladder of debt; the saving role of the rebel victim. The concept of war as spiritualized. Increased awareness of the world's likely end. As a result the societies pass from particularity to *universalism*: "We are custodians of a treasure for all"—in particular, of the old texts. The appearance of a near-universal Church and Empire as a *second historical shift*.

In (24.6) we look at a new *individualism* facing the enigma of death. As historical continuance of the state, the family, even the natural order becomes problematical, all hope is laid on the *continuance of the individual beyond death*. We survey each principal type of symbolism and ask: How far does this rely on previous hopes? How far is it demonstrable in the sense of previous novelties?

24.1 The physical environment

All the features we discuss here are shared by much of the Mediterranean: the Levant, Anatolia, the Balkans, Italy, Spain. Only the Mediterranean itself plays a different role in Greek and Hebrew symbolism. Thus the reason why the new step was taken in Palestine and Greece rather than elsewhere is more due to the human environment than the physical, which imposes necessary but far from sufficient conditions.

24.1.1 The geographical setting

The earth. Semitic and Germanic share a name for the land, Arabic ʾarḍa (accusative) and German *Erde* (II.68), modified by regular rules in Hebrew ʾoreṣ and English *earth*. Levin compares Akkadian *ina er-ce-tim* with English *in earth*. The agreement seems an old one, perhaps denoting the earth as female deity, preceding Greek, where only scholars know a noun *eras* (Strabo 16.4.27). But poets know a derivative *eraze*, i.e. **eras-de*, which appears in particular with the element *snow* (Russian *sneg*, Hebrew verb *taʾšleḡ*), perhaps then as a Northern word: Job 37,6 "For he says to the *snow*, Fall to the *earth*"; *Iliad* 12.156 "[the missiles] fell like *snow*flakes to *earth*."

Mountains. In contrast to the alluvial valleys of Mesopotamia and Egypt, Mediterranean lands are marked by hills and mountains. Hebrew *hɔr* and Greek *orʲos* "mountain" are surely related (II.65); they appear as quasi-determinatives in names of mountains, e.g. Lebanon (Jud 3,3; Strabo 16.2.15).[1] The mountain is the property of the High God, Sinai of Yahweh (Num 10,33) and Kithairon of Zeus (Pausanias 9.2.4). In the Near East the mountains *are* gods (II.9, Lebanon and Carmel). Each people knows a mountain to the north, not strictly speaking part of its territory, where the gods assemble and death is overcome, mounts Kasios and Olympus (III.48). The Aramaeans (though unaware of Hebrew monotheism) correctly observed "their gods are gods of the hills but not of the valleys" (I Reg 20,28; II.8, 242). No invader will follow the locals up into their mountain fastnesses: *montani semper liberi.* Especially as snow-capped and forested, the mountain provides permanent streams during the long dry summer: Amos 5,24, "But let justice roll down like waters, and righteousness as an ever-flowing stream" (II.35); Yahweh "makes springs break out in the valleys; they run between the hills" (Ps 104,10) as at Afqa of Lebanon (III.134). The flow of water is described in detail by Plato *Laws* 761A (II.72). The role of the mountain backdrop in maintaining independent life is expressed by assigning the mountain to the High God or gods who watch over the people.

The defensible citadel. Again in contrast to flat and arid Egypt and Mesopotamia where the only water-supply comes from the river, the new societies build a city around a fortified citadel with a natural spring inside the city-wall (I.24). It is surrounded with a magic circle (II.218-224). Somewhere nearby is the "navel of the land" (II.4), perhaps thought of as united by an umbilical cord to heaven: Ezek 38,12; Aeschylus *Eum.* 166 (Delphi); Cicero *Verr.* 2.4.106 (Enna of Sicily). The Siloam inscription (KAI 189, ab. 700 BC) tells how the two parties of diggers in the Jerusalem tunnel met. Limestone karst is "the hydrogeological basis of civilization" (Dora P. Crouch). The citadel may be called a "high place," Heb. *Rɔmɔh* (Neh 11,33); perhaps *Roma* (not the true Latin name of the city!, II.245) was so named by

---

1   This was seen by A. Cuny, "Les mots du fonds préhellénique en grec, latin et sémitique occidental," Revue des Etudes Anciennes 12 (1910) 154-164, p. 161. Other parallels for "land" are less certain: Hebrew *gey'* "valley" and Greek *gaia* "earth" (I.58), though appearing in contrast with the words for "mountain." If Greek *aia* "earth" came in the plural it would be a good phonetic parallel to Hebrew *'iyyey* "coastlands" (III.54). Words apparently meaning "mountain glen" run parallel (II.72): Greek *napē* and Hebrew *nɔpaî*.

Phoenicians in residence (I.24). As the High God has his own proper house on a mountain (*Iliad* 8.442-3, Exod 15,17; II.92), a grateful people sets up a temple to him (or one of his associates) on their citadel (I.159-160). He can be identified with it as a *feste Burg*. Beside it is the palace of the king, a Priam or Solomon or Tarquin. As the spiritual center of the people's continuity, the god is naturally established at the site which is the physical center of their continuity.

24.1.2 Farming and grazing

Wheat and barley. In the rain-watered fields around the citadel are grown the two long-domesticated grains (II.9-11, 90). There is a possible link in a subordinate name of the grain: Latin *far* "spelt," Greek *pyros* and Hebrew *bɔr* "grain" generically. Besides the physical conditions for their flourishing, the texts add a social one: disguised Odysseus compares Penelope (*Odyssey* 19.111-112) to a king(!) whose judgements ensure the growth of wheat and barley; Job (31,40) wagers his crops on his own justice, and so with the Davidic king (Ps 72,16). In further ways the crops are compared to humanity. The death of soldiers in an infantry battle (*Iliad* 11.67-69) is compared to the falling of wheat and barley at the hands of mowers; Eliphaz tells Job (5,26) that "you shall come to your grave in ripe old age, as a shock of grain [to the threshing floor] in its season." In those texts there is no thought of human beings living as individuals beyond the grave: the Homeric hero looks forward to permanent renown through poetic remembrance (I.11); Job's vindication (Job 42,13) comes from restoration of his family as before. But in the New Testament the death and life of the seed signifies the death and life of the individual (I.81): Joh 12,24 "if it dies, it bears much fruit"; I Kor 15,36 "That which you sow is not quickened unless it dies."

The noble trees. Jotham (Jud 9,7-15, II.11) thinks of three "noble trees" fit to rule over the others: fig, olive and vine. We treat the vine below (III.296) and add the pomegranate here. Each of the trees symbiotically joins the human family. The fig in both lands stands for a woman's sexual maturity (II.12). Its lengthy maturation makes a fully grown fig tree a living witness of peace: when swords have been beaten into plowshares, every man may sit unafraid under his vine and figtree (Micah 4,4 etc.); Athenians carrying sacred things from Eleusis to the city rested under the sacred fig, given by Demeter (Pausanias 1.37.2). Gautama became the Buddha sitting under the royal fig; Adam and Eve achieved enlightenment near a figtree (perhaps parodistically *under* it), for they straightway made aprons of its leaves, Gen 3,3-6; Jesus so saw Nathanael (Joh 1,48); Augustine was converted lying under a figtree (*Conf.* 8.28), III.320. For it is *the* fruit tree *par excellence*. The bride of Cant 4,13 is a "paradise of pomegranates," and Hades wed Persephone by making her eat the pomegranate seeds (*Hom. Hymn* 2.412-413). The marriage bed of Odysseus and Penelope is built into a living olive tree (*Odyssey* 23.190); children are olive shoots (Ps 128,3). Israel *is* an olive tree (Jer 11,16; Hos 14,6); Athens is identified with the olive planted by Athena (Herodotus 8.55), which sent up a fresh shoot the day after Xerxes burned it (I.60-61).

All the trees are old in the Mediterranean and their names have at best distant connections. The words for "fig" are closest: Heb. *paggɔh*, Greek *sykon* with dialect *tykon*, Latin *ficus*.[2] In contrast, the close relation among words for the "vine" and "wine" suggests a later entry into the languages. Americans and North-Europeans must make an effort to realize how intrinsic these fruits are to Mediterranean life; Deissmann called Paul's world the world of the olive-tree (I.60).

Legumes. It took centuries of experiment and failure to discover the necessities of agriculture in fields not fertilized by a rising Nile or Euphrates: fallow-periods, mulch and manure, rotation with legumes. The humble bean made its way across the Mediterranean: Hebrew *powl* "beans," Greek *pyanios poltos* and Latin *puls fabata* "pease porridge" (II.15). The Sabbatical year "so that the poor of your people may eat" (Exod 23,11, II.25) perhaps originally was for the land to recover; Greeks understood fallow time and manuring (II.14).

Sheep and goats. The two animals were early domesticated and usually grazed in mixed herds (II.15-18); the adult names are distinct except for the doubtful comparison of Greek *oïs* with Egyptian *ʿwt* "sheep and goats, flocks."[3] But names for "lambs" and "kids" can plausibly be compared. While bovines are of course known, and the bull is the noblest animal for sacrifice (III.295), the grazers are much better suited to the hilly and infertile Mediterranean. The docile and unenterprising lamb is everywhere known as the natural prey of the wolf; and even in the shepherd's family it plays an ambivalent role, a favorite of father and children, but in the end to be slaughtered. In the landscape the herds of goats play a clearly destructive role. After the native forest and second growth have been cut down for temples and ships, the goats graze the former forest floor, nibbling off each shoot before it can grow above the animal's height. On the mountain of

---

2   Heb. *ḥelēb* at Num 18,12 "fat" of the olive distantly suggests Greek *elai(w)a* and Latin *olīua*; Hebrew *rimmown* and Greek *rhoē* "pomegranate" could be brought together (II.12).

3   Bomhard & Kerns 521.

Lebanon today the writ of no government has force, and the Bedouin goatherds roam freely, their flocks annually cropping off the new growth of the cedar; only in the precincts of Maronite chapels and a few far-sighted villages is it protected (III.135).

24.1.3 Technology: iron and lime

Metallurgy of iron. As long as copper was the only metal available, and the process of its alloying with scarce tin to make bronze remained a trade secret, there was no possibility of arming whole populations, or giving them metal tools to cut down brush, plow the fields, and dig cisterns (I.25-26). Iron ore, once identified, was common: Canaan is a land whose "stones are iron" (Deut 8,9) and the Caucasus is the "mother of iron" (Aeschylus *PV* 301, II.227). Just possibly Latin *ferrum* reflects Hebrew *barzɛl*. Iron was thought regenerated in the mines of Elba (Strabo 5.2.6), and so perhaps Job 28,1 "There is a spring of silver" (II.224-5). The Philistines at first tried to keep the monopoly of iron farm tools "lest the Hebrews make themselves sword or spear" (I Sam 13,19-20); Porsenna in the vassal treaty he imposed on the Roman people forbade it "to use iron except in agriculture" (Pliny 34.139, I.171). The high temperatures required for smelting iron were at first seen as magical, "tempering" iron is called *pharmassōn* (*Odyssey* 9.391-3). But rapidly the secret got out and the new Polis found its whole citizenry under iron arms—if necessary by beating them out of plowshares and pruning hooks (Joel 4,10; Vergil *Aeneid* 7.635-636; I.172). Only so could it defend itself against another such city, and war became a regular occurrence. So the Delphic oracle was vindicated, and "iron was discovered to the hurt of man" (Herodotus 1.68.4), "created to shorten man's days" (Mishna *Middoth* III.4). But only so, it seems, could the assembly of citizen-soldiers achieve their own share of political power (III.293).

Plastered cisterns. In neither Palestine nor Greece was any territory distant from permanent streams truly habitable unless it could store water over the long dry summer for human beings, animals and crops. Cisterns could be dug with the new iron tools; the technology of lime was necessary to make them watertight. The Hebrew Bible understands whitewashing, and Theophrastus (*de lap.* 64-69, I.26) describes the burning of iimestone to lime in Phoenicia for cement; the precise use of lime in cisterns is attested at Mishna *Avoth* II.8, where a retentive student is a "plastered cistern that does not lose a drop" (II.324).

24.1.4 The wild and its animals

The forest. From the beginning, written record shows progresive defor-estation in Mediterranean lands. Already in the time of classical Israel, Palestine was not heavily forested, to judge by the reverence paid to certain individual trees like the terebinths of Mamre (Gen 13,18). Shepherds and farmers had been going over it for many centuries, and in well-populated areas the only trees or groves remaining were those with sacral protection. In Greece, the Mycenaeans did less damage to the countryside, but their successors more; Plato (*Critias* 111C) knew large buildings in Attica with roofs of wood cut from mountains "which can only produce nourishment for bees today" (III.133-134). Short-sighted Eratosthenes (Strabo 14.6.5) saw the forests of Cyprus (even though reduced by smelting the local copper) mainly as an impediment to farming. Ecologists today correlate "ruined cities and ruined land" (III.144).

Most tree-names like themselves were local; but shipbuilding timber might be international, for cypress (Latin *cupressus*, Vegetius 3.34) is used to build a galley as Hebrew *gopεr* the Ark (Gen 6,14; I.329). Only special sites such as the cedar forest of Lebanon attracted the admira-tion alike of Hebrews and of Greeks such as Theophrastus (*Hist. Plant.* 5.8.1, III.123). Persian kings and satraps (III.124) planted forests afresh and walled in the ancient ones they found as "enclosures," Greek *paradeisoi*—Lebanon was already one such in the time of Theophrastus. No doubt it was in large part for hunting-preserves, but coming as they did from desolate Iran, it seems they were also touched by the reality of the forest, as Nebuchadrezzar built the "hanging gardens" (Berossos, III.124) for his homesick Median wife.

Gilgamesh/Gilgamos (I.16), who gets such a fine press as a proto-humanist today, seemingly (III.129) went and cut cedars in the West, against the opposition of their guardian Humbaba, because they were there. While Lebanon naturally attracted the attention of kings build-ing palaces or temples, far more devastating was the Hellenistic and Roman push for naval fleets (III.145). Israel, in spite of perplexing texts which show Yahweh as logger (Isa 10,33-34, II.268), sees the Assyrian successors of Gilgamesh as impious. The axe is the token of the woodsman-God as of magistrates who represent him (II.269). For it was Yahweh who planted the cedars of Lebanon (Ps 104,16, III.125) as originally he planted the garden of Eden (Gen 2,8). The trees belong to the High God, the "cedars of El" (Ps 80,11); at Troy a special oak was the property of Zeus (*Iliad* 5.693).

A few texts (II.268, III.146) record a dawning realization that the life of a city is bound up with its forest, as in Germanic mythology the whole human race is bound up with the health of the world-tree. The Egypt of Pharaoh (Ezek 31) is compared to a world-cedar. At *Iliad* 13.389-391 (= 16.483-485) the death of a hero on the battlefield is compared with the cutting down of a mountain tree for ship-timber. Vergil (*Aen.* 2.626-631), enlarging the Homeric passage, compares the fall of Troy to the logging of a mountain-ash.

Lion and bear. The other side of the forest, and the wild generally, is the shelter it gives to the great enemies of the shepherd and his flock, the lion and bear (II.4). (The wolf can live anywhere and is more nearly taken for granted in the texts [II.16].) A lion or bear is equally probable (I Sam 17,34; Amos 5,19; Thr 3,10); in Greek art they appear together (*Odyssey* 11.611). The names of the lion in Mediterranean languages are related (I.340, III.320). Although Herodotus (7.126, I.197) confidently affirms the presence of lions in Thrace in his own day, it seems that no first-hand knowledge of them underlies the Homeric tradition: T. J. Dunbabin points out that the Homeric lion "is never heard to roar," although its roar would be very suitable in comparison with roaring heroes.[4] Contrast Amos 3,8 "The lion has roared (*šɔ'aḡ*), who will not fear?; Lord Yahweh has spoken, who will not prophesy?" The king like the High God may appear as a lion or (in Israel) a bear (II.3); the shamanistic seer has a deep connection with the bear (II.177-185). Odysseus has a she-bear among his ancestors (II.182) and Elisha calls out she-bears against his tormentors (II Reg 2,24). Nowhere does the terrible demonic force of the god or his human agents come out more clearly than in these comparisons.

24.1.5 Rain from the High God

Both Deut 11,10-12 and Herodotus 2.13.3 (I.22-23) contrast irrigated Egypt with their own land watered by the rain of the High God. The rain was unreliable, and urged on by various forms of rain-making (II.169). We found two parallel names for the rain: words meaning "water" (Greek *hydōr*, Heb. *mɔṭɔr*, II.71); and meaning a "blessed rain" (*brochē*, *bɔrɔkɔh*, II.73). The "water" of rain is said specifically to be of the High God, Sach 10,1 & Plato *Laws* 761A (II.72). Of all the geographical features we discuss, rain is the most absolutely necessary for an autonomous society independent of any authority opening and shutting a river's sluice-gates. Here and there a brook will spread out into a "soft meadow" full of lilies with their several Mediterranean names (I.331; III.44-46): Persephone (*Hom. Hymn* 2.427) and Europa

---

4   T. J. Dunbabin, The Greeks and their Eastern Neighbors (London 1957) p. 46, cited by Hainsworth in the Cambridge Iliad on 10.485 (iii.200).

(Moschus 2.32) were abducted while picking lilies in such a meadow, and the Shulamite (Cant 2,1) is a "lily of the valleys"; Jesus (Matt 6,28) sees the lilies as evidence of God's universal care. Somehow two sets of river-names spread across the Mediterranean: Hebrew Jordan (*Yarden*) and Homeric *Iardanos* (I.35; II.89, 207) with "Scythian" *dan* "river"; Hebrew Arnon, Greek Orontes, Etruscan Arnus, Hurrian *arinni* "well, spring" (III.323). The High God is the name given by the two societies for the agency that guarantees the rain. He may be thought of in physical terms as urinating through the rain (Aristophanes *Clouds* 373); or as the artisan who perforates the sky (Mal 3,10; Herodotus 4.158.3; II.71, 170). Once in Greek and regularly in Latin the "rainbow" (Gen 9,13; Ezek 1,28; II.146-9) is described as the bow of warfare.

24.1.6 The sea and cosmology

All the symbolism of irresistible power that we associate with the Ocean, the ancients invested in the Mediterranean (which can get very rough at times, as Odysseus, Paul and Aeneas can testify); Mark (4,35-41; 6,45-52) transfers it down yet further to the Sea of Galilee! Israel, effectively landlocked, knows storms at sea mostly by rumor (Jonah; Ps 107,23-30). Here complementarity separates them from Hellenes. But both see the plane of land and sea as circular: Yahweh inscribes a circle on the face of the Deep (Prov 8,27; Job 26,10; I.112-115) as Earth is wheel-shaped (Herodotus 4.36.2, I.110). The sky overhead is bronze (*Iliad* 5.504 etc.; Deut 28,23; I.106-7; later iron), and held up by pillars (*Odyssey* 1.52-54; Ps 75,4 and frequently; I.114). Where Hephaestus hammers out sky and earth on Achilles' shield (*Iliad* 18, I.108) he parallels the action of God in Genesis 1. Human beings "live around the Sea like ants or frogs around a marsh" (Plato, *Phaedo* 110C); Yahweh "sits on the circle of the earth, and its inhabitants are as grasshoppers" (Isa 40,22; I.88,110). Later the heavens become an imperial star-spangled cope (III.57-59).

Our difference from the ancients lies in a more developed science; we may translate their "High God" as the mysterious synchronization of planetary conditions with the evolution of a species ready to take advantage of it. Thus the confluence of elements that came together to make independent societies possible is named by them as the work of a High God: the Mediterranean hilly terrain blocking movements of imperial armies; the defensible citadel with its providential limestone strata channeling water to a spring; the wheat and barley that must die to be quickened; the sacred fig and olive; the inherited domestication of sheep and goats; the forest planted in the beginning by the god; the emblematic violence of lion and bear; the indispensable and unpredictable rain. It is not easy for the historian of planetary evolution to explain how all came together at the right time to make the first free societies possible; the High God is *their* name for it.

24.2 *The external human environment*

The presence of other human societies determined both the time and place where free societies emerged. We saw (III.158-160) the *differences* between Israel and Hellas, especially with relation to the ancient Near Eastern empires: the new pattern arose in Israel just *inside* the realm of the empires, in Hellas just *outside*. Here as in the previous section (24.1) we mostly return to features which the two societies exhibit in common—except again in their relation to the sea and seafaring (24.2.2). Those features do not yet define the special novelty represented by Israel and Hellas, but are shared by a broader circle of states. Still, they are best attested in Hebrew and Greek; and each cultural item jointly borrowed acquires in its new setting a halo of symbolic meaning unattested in the empires or elsewhere in their fringe of lands. Exotic products from far-off places are felt suitable as images of the High God, distant and inscrutable. Both war and its resolution, the treaty, are carried out in his name. The special roles of women mediate a unique relationship to the unseen world.

24.2.1 The ancient Near Eastern empires

From the empires, the peoples at their periphery received the novelties of city-life, commerce and organized warfare, with all their features of central administration, technology, a formalized cult, and writing. But the city lived under absolutist regimes, relied on irrigation by rivers rather than rainfall (except in Anatolia), and kept writing as a difficult scribal monopoly. The imperial reality both fostered the new free states, and in the end swept over them—but not until they had rendered their innovation independent of its civic birthplace. The texts and arts of both Israel and Hellas witness their close relations to the empires: some vocabulary items which they share show a cross-section of cultural influence.

(1) *Assyria and Babylonia* (II.292-293). Some Greeks by the fourth century BC knew the actual beginning of *Enuma Eliš*, and both peoples the figure of Gilgamesh (I.16-17). From Mesopotamia Hebrew and Greeks received the linen garment of the tunic (Heb. *kuttonεï*, Greek *chitōn*, Latin *tunica*, I.204-209), both outer and inner, more for leisure

than work. It came to be seen as a second skin standing for the private matters of birth, sexuality, mourning and death. The stratum of Hebrew recorded in the book of Proverbs got from Akkadian a name of gold (*ḥɔruwṣ*) universally adopted in Hellas (*chrysos*, I.307-8), along with its measure of a kilo or so, the mina (Heb. *mɔnɛh*, Greek *mnā*, Latin *mina*). As a special feature of Babylonian building both societies noted the brick (Hebrew *lɔbenɔh*, Greek *plinthos*, I.83-85). A spectacular example is the Ishtar gate, now in the Pergamon Museum, Berlin. Greeks for their temples borrowed the feature and name of the precinct (*temenos*, Akkadian *temennu*), which Hebrews also used as the first word of a city name (*Timnaī*); it is taken over further in Latin *templum*, a "space for augury" before it became a building (II.221-3).

(2) *Egypt* (II.294-6) The Hebrew Bible, with all its knowledge of Egypt, says nothing of the pyramids or Sphinx; Jeremiah (43,13) does mention the obelisks (*maṣṣɔbowī*, Jerome "statues") and temples of Heliopolis; possibly the mythical phoenix-bird appears (III.317); the hippopotamus and crocodile, which so struck Herodotus, show up as the Behemoth and Leviathan of Job. In contrast both peoples note and adopt the cosmetics used in Egypt to enhance the living and the dead (I.241, III.41). Egyptians discovered and exported to Lydia (the inventor of coinage) the touchstone for assessing the purity of gold (Hebrew *boḥan*, Greek *basaníos*, I.305-307). Two precious materials, ivory and ebony, were always thought of as Egyptian, though imported from farther south (I.89, 197, 337; II.295; III.325).

Egypt was the land of the ancient Near East the most accessible to both Hebrews and Greeks. As a result they are most aware of their differences from it rather than from the other empires. (1) Both noted their own rain-watered fields as over against its irrigation. (2) Romans especially noted the merits of the phonetic alphabet over against awkward hieroglyphics, a system both defective and redundant. (3) Both were struck by the obsession of the Egyptians with the preservation of the dead. (4) The Greek naked *kouros* is an Egyptian pharaoh striding into life (III.164).

(3) *Anatolia* (II.297-8). The Hittite empire was known to Israel and Hellas only by remote tradition (II.85-86), for the "Hittites" of the Hebrew Bible, though carrying the old name, are hardly closer related to the kingdom than the Lydians and Lycians. From the Anatolian world both peoples remembered an old name for the helmet (Hebrew *qobaʿ*, Greek *kymbachos*, I.165), and a designation of oppressive rulers (Philistine *sarney* and Greek *tyrannoi*, I.65). Almost certainly from the same land came the name of the torch as a designation of lightning (*lappiyd*, *lampas*, II.67, 172) and the woman's tambourine (below).

The culture of the empires was less well known to Hebrews and Greeks at first hand than at one remove through the palace societies of the Mediterranean coasts: Ugarit and the Phoenician cities, the cities of Cyprus and Cretan Cnossos, Mycenae and Pylos. While the alphabetic scripts of Ugarit and later Phoenicia are well understood, they were preceded by syllabic scripts—pseudo-hieroglyphic at Byblos and Linear A of Crete for unknown languages, syllabic Cypriote and Linear B for Greek—which present many problems. Relations among all these peoples are best understood through the remains of their arts and industries, and through such shipwrecks as those of Cape Gelidonya[5] with its cargo of "ox-hide" copper ingots and of Ulu Burun.[6]

24.2.2 Seafaring

Although certain concepts were carried mainly by overland trade (in particular the full notion of justice), diffusion of imperial civilization and interchange of novelties happened more readily by sea. Inland sites like Jerusalem, Boeotian Thebes and the Etruscan cities had connections with nearby seaports: much to Nehemiah's displeasure, in the fifth century BC resident Tyrians sold marine fish in Jerusalem on the Sabbath with their indispensable iodine (Neh 13,16; I.129). That does not reduce the dangers of the sea, as in Odysseus' shipwreck; "it is a fearful thing to die among the waves" says Hesiod (*Opera* 687); "they went up to heaven, they went down to the depths" (Ps 107,26). Not to mention pirates: one who got safely to land like Damon of Ascalon would set up a stele (I.213, II.332), or a votive anchor like Sostratus at Graviscae (II.211) and nameless dedicants at Byblos (III.317). The later flood-legends as of Noah and Deucalion surely rest in part on the great tsunami of (perhaps) 1628 BC (I.104); folk-memory may have retained some relic of the great cataract when the level of the Black Sea was raised 350 feet about 5600 BC (II.327).

Since Greek *gaulos* with different accents can mean both a table "vessel" and a ship (I.146), Heb. *gullɔh* "bowl" surely also meant "round (Phoenician) ship." The earliest anchors, Greek *eunai*, may be just Semitic "stones" (I.19). Archilochus (I.144) testifies that sailors were accustomed to sample the wine-cargo held in big pottery amphoras (Heb. *kad̄*, Greek *kados*, Latin *cadus*). That may account for some

---

5   George F. Bass et alii, Cape Gelidonya: A Bronze Age Shipwreck; Transactions of the Anerican Philosophical Society n.s. 57.8 (1967); Philadelphia.

6   George F. Bass, "A Bronze Age Shipwreck at Ulu Burun (Kas): 1984 Campaign," AJA 90 (1986) 269-305 etc. Two Phoenician wine-ships were recently found off Tyre by Robert Ballard (NYT June 24, 1999).

of the shipwrecks.... Both by sea and land prudent buyers insisted on *"full"* containers with a world-wide adjective (II.320). Another fleet went out after the enormous annual run of tuna (Hebrew *tanniyn*, Greek *thynnos*, I.128-130), today reduced to a small fraction of what it was even in the 1500s. The catch was assimilated to the aboriginal battle of the god against the great sea-monster (I.127).

24.2.3 Caravans and traders

As the wine-trade at sea has the common vocabulary of the carrier and container, so on land the ass (Heb. *ʾɔ̄town*, Latin *asinus*) with its twin pannier sacks (*śaq*, Greek *sakkos*, Latin *saccus*; II.51). The crafty Gibeonites put "wornout sacks on their asses" (Jos 9,4); the parvenu Trimalchio serves olives in an *asellus...Corinthius cum bisaccio* "an ass of Corinthian silver with twin pannier sacks" (Petronius 31.9). The caravans are an extension of the upland farmer bringing his produce in to the city market. The wool-trade brought the international name *sēs* of the clothes-moth between lands (I.73). By land or sea, the merchant-banker is the most familiar representative of a neighboring culture. The down-payment he asks for his goods is a Phoenician term (Heb. *ʿerɔb-own*, Greek *arrhabōn*, I.74-78; II.326). He is the custodian of the touch-stone (I.298-308). And since that test is the primary metaphor for human excellence in the proverb-books of Solomon and Theognis, he must be the carrier of the equally international proverbs—embodying an international practical wisdom, with a marked upper-class bias.

24.2.4 Warfare

Trade and warfare are the two occupations whereby men of neighboring peoples learn to know each other. —In war, as enemies, allies, merce-naries. In the Bronze Age when only affluent heroes could afford weapons and armor, the panoplies got so heavy (I.164) that the com-batants must be carried to and from the fight in chariots; and the horse with its old international name (II.304) acquired an honorific character (II.6) which it never lost even when iron weapons brought in the clash of infantry lines. It was the light weapons whose names were carried back and forth between languages as the weapons changed sides: lances (Heb. *rɔmḥey*, Greek *longchai*, Latin *lanceae*, I.174); arrows (*ḥiṣṣey*, *oistoi*, *sagittae*, II.140). With ambivalence of life and death, the bow is assimilated to the lyre: David, Odysseus and Apollo are equally skilled at handling each (II.153). The military tent (Greek *skēnē*, I.177) was probably named after an unattested Phoenician word, adapted as Rabbinic *šəkiynɔh* "'tabernacling' Presence of God" (II.330) which continues in Syriac Christian verse and Quranic *sakīnah*.

Hebrews and Romans professed that victories were won by the military *numen* of the state, sent out to battle from a box or building—the Ark of the Covenant, the Temple of Janus (II, Chapter 16). A prominent part of sacral theory was the effort to win over the opposing deity by *evocatio* (II.242-7). Ceremonially, the fighting was ended by the "triumphal" return of one claiming to be victor; legally, by a treaty, which, as an international document, achieved a nearly fixed format throughout the Near East and Mediterranean world (I, Chapter 8). The earliest attestations are the vassal treaties of the Hittite Great King. In Israel his role is taken by Yahweh, and the formularies of the covenant follow the vassal-treaty given by a benevolent deity to his people. When it is laid by a superior on an inferior, it always has the provision "to have the same enemies and friends" as the giver (I.263-4, III.10). The cosmic elements—Earth and Sky, sea and winds and rivers—appear as witnesses in the Hittite treaties (I.267-272) and in literary adaptations: "Listen, heavens, and hear, earth" (Isa 1,2); Prometheus' complaint about the injustice done him by a fellow-god (Aeschylus *Prom. V.* 88-92). The anthology of curses which the weaker party must lay on himself (I.272-283) is current throughout the Mediterranean.

24.2.5 Foreign women and imports

Hebrews and Greeks both had a taste for the exotic, above all in the foreign woman and the enticing items she brought in her trousseau. She came on three levels (I.229-232). Topmost is the foreign queen or princess. The lowest level is the harlot, who (we boldly proposed) is known in Hebrew as a Greek "woman": with certain Greek for "Pelasgian woman," *gynē Pelasgis* we compared probable Hebrew "Philistine harlot," *zonɔh Pəlištiyī* (I.226). It was the middle level of the concubine (I.65-70, 231-2; II.91) who became the international figure with her (seemingly Indo-European) name, Hebrew *piylɛḡɛš*, Greek *pallakis*, Latin *paelex*. For a prince to take his father's concubine is the most radical claim to the throne; so with Amyntor (*Iliad* 9.452) as with Reuben, Abner, Absalom, Adonijah. It is her qualifications that are closest scrutinized (I.232): Cant 4,7 "There is no flaw (*muwm*) in you"; a girl in Hesiod *Theog.* 259 is "without flaw," *a¦mōm¡os*.

Probably it was the foreign woman who first brought in the cosmetics (I.241) taken for granted by the matrons of Alexandria: Praxinoa sends her husband (*pappa*) off to the store for soap (*nitron*) and rouge (*phykos*), Theocritus 15.16. Perhaps both were originally Egyptian, but Greek "rouge" usurped the proper name of "mascara." Israel as harlot washes with soap (*nɛīɛr*, Jer 2,22) and sets off her eyes with mascara (*puwk̄*, Jer 4,30) like Jezebel (II Reg 9,30); in Propertius 2.18C.31-32 *caeruleo...fuco* is "steel-blue eye-shadow."

It was surely also the concubine or harlot who brought in the diaphanous tunic worn only to be taken off (Herodotus 1.8.3, Cant 5,3; I.207-208). Her exotic scents, each with its proper international name, are imagined as growing on Lebanon (Cant 4,13-14; I.71, 91-98); she sings (Prov 7,17) "I have perfumed my bed with myrrh, aloes and cinnamon." The spices are earlier attested at the epithalamium of a foreign princess. In Sappho's wedding-song for Hector and Andromache "myrrh, cassia and libanos were mixed"; of the groom marrying a Tyrian princess (Ps 45,9) "myrrh, aloes and cassia are on all your garments." The true home of cassia and cinnamon was the land we have learned to call Viet Nam (I.72, II.331).

In cult the women had a monopoly on two seeming contrasted opposites: ecstatic dancing with the Anatolian tambourine (Hebrew *tuppiym*, Greek *tympana*, I.152-5; II.166); and abandoned mourning (I.244) as for Tammuz/Adonis. But Aristophanes (*Lys.* 387-389) combines *tympanismos* and *Adoniasmos* as if features of a single ceremony. Jephthah's daughter comes out with her tambourine and is mourned annually by the daughters of Israel (Jud 11,34-40); Ezek 8,14 found women sitting in the Temple and wailing for Tammuz. Both peoples in their art represent the female tambourinist (my "Images and their Names..." Figs. 14-15).

Perhaps also jewels with their international names were early known on the fingers of fancy women, as Cynthia's beryl in Rome (Propertius 4.7.9, I.333). But in our texts they first appear in myths of a better world (I.87-90): jasper and emerald in the myth of Plato's *Phaedo* (110D) and in Ezekiel's myth (28,13) of the garden of Eden (which adds sapphire). And they are even more worn by men: the Jewish High Priest (Ex 28,20), Maecenas in Augustus' imagination.[7] The griffin (*gryps*) or cherub (*kəruwb̄*), its form learned from some Near Eastern artwork (I.85-87),[8] has its own place in the art and literature of both lands. It watches over gold in Eden and Scythia (Herodotus 4.13) and forms a throne for kings and gods.

24.2.6 The ethnic paradigm

As Israel and Hellas agree in such relations to the surrounding human world, they also agree in the grammatical form of names by which they

---

7 Macrobius *Sat.* 2.4.12; I.89.
8 A Jewish sarcophagus from the Catacomb Torlonia in Rome has a griffin taking the place of the indigenous cherub; Brown "Images and their Names" Plate 3.

designate foreigners (II.305-315). A *masculine singular* names the eponymous founder of a people or the people itself: thus Sidon as man and city, Ascalon, Ionian (Greek *Iaōn*, Heb. *Yɔwɔn*), Arab (Heb. *ʿărab̄*, Greek *Araps*), Cilician (Heb. *Ḥeylek*, Greek *Kilix*). A *masculine collective or plural* for groups of soldiers, colonists, slaves, traders: Aramaeans (Heb. *ʾĂrammiy*, Greek *Eremboi*), Pelasgians (*Pelasgoi*) and Philistines (*Pɔliŝtiy*), Achaeans (*Achaioi*) and "Hivites" (*Ḥiwwiy*). A *feminine singular* for a foreign woman or land: Sidonian (Heb. **Ṣedǝniyyɔh*, Greek *Sīdoniē*). The forms are extended for common nouns and in some special features of men's language (II.317-319). Anatolian peoples with Libyans are known as mercenaries to both Israel and Hellas (I.29-31). Prehistoric migrations brought foreign peoples to Hellas, Cadmeans (I.37) and Danaans (I.227); and to Canaan—Dorians, Cretans, Pelasgians, Achaeans ("Hivites," I.32 etc.) and Gergithes (II.193-8).

Omne ignotum pro magnifico (Tacitus *Agricola* 30.4). Since the God or gods are far from humankind and not often seen, rare imports from distant or unknown lands partake of the nature of divinity. Spices or aromatics unknown in Mediterranean lands are most suitable for the divine cult. Especially jewels witness a better land associated with the divine.

When two peoples are at war with each other, the underlying reality (II.242) is a combat between their respective tutelary divinities. In such a matter of life and death, more clearly than elsewhere the grounding of a people in the nature of things is expressed. At the end of a war, the format of the treaty is paralleled by the ongoing relationship or "covenant" (I.254) between a people and its eternal principle.

In the special roles of women, rejoicing and mourning, even though transmitted to us by male informants, we catch a glimpse of the feminine relationship (otherwise hidden from us) to the unseen world. Those polar opposites of emotion define an essential aspect of what it means to be human. In the predominantly masculine world that emotional level is only achieved through the outside assistance of the noblest tree, the vine (below)—and (in Hellas but not Israel) for the victor in the games.

24.3 Internal organization

We progressively narrow down the realm where the birth of freedom took place. The suitable physical environment (24.1) extends over much of the Mediterranean; the external human environment (24.2) reduces it further to states in touch with the ancient Near Eastern empires by sea or land. Here we discuss the internal social enterprises actually developed by peoples who built a city around a defensible citadel. None of the structures quite reach the essential novelty represented by Israel and Hellas (and later Rome) which accounts for the preservation of their literature. They are in principle (to the best of our knowledge) shared by other contemporary societies: Phoenicians, Aramaeans of Damascus, the Anatolian states, Etruscans, Italic peoples. But Hebrew and Greek (with Latin) texts are by far our best evidence for them—both domestically and in the other states as well. Each appears to be a necessary condition for the joint novelty of Israel and Hellas: human nature as it is, and as it might be, recorded in a people's phonetic alphabet. Even more than features of the external human environment (24.2) are they colored by the new emergence of which they become an essential part.

24.3.1 Social structure of the city-state

While history or legend records a *king with divine attributes* in the origins of the city-state or Polis, his powers were from the beginning limited by the necessary conditions for its survival—which in the end either entirely replaced him by a body of magistrates, or reduced him to a vestigial ceremonial status. Originally (II.90-92) he is seen by his justice as maintaining the fertility of the land, so that it bears wheat and barley; as a consequence he is the father of heroes. His palace adjoins the temple of the High God on the citadel; and, like that God, he leads his people in war.

When improved metallurgy showed iron to be abundant, the old heroic combat of bronze-clad heroes one on one was replaced by a people's army. Its role of succoring the state in wartime could not be denied it in peace, where its muster (now without arms) became a citizens' assembly (I.26, 235-6; II.5, 97). A beautiful text (Dio Cassius 37.28, 63 BC; III.315) shows the interchangeability of the assembly and militia in Rome: all who bore arms must attend the *comitia* in the Campus Martius; but an armed guard must hold the Janiculum, and if it broke up, the assembly was dissolved—to restore the militia. Since the assembly is the opposite face of the state under arms, there was no question of women entering it.

As the officers of the militia approached old age, class differences among them were intensified, and the aristocratic formed themselves into a council of elders or Senate (II.97-109). By election up from the Senate or devolution from the monarchy there appeared a small group of magistrates advising or replacing the king. Thus the continued existence of the state imposed on it the threefold structure of magistrates, council and assembly.

The mysterious unity of the Mediterranean world is illustrated where the magistrates are a college of two (II.101): two annually elected suffetes in Carthage and consuls in Rome, two lifelong hereditary kings in Sparta, the two complementary kings of Judah and Israel (often warring). The council of elders often "sits at the gate" and has a (sub-)committee of thirty (II.106) at Carthage and Sparta. The people's army has a ceremonial military force of three hundred in Israel, Sparta, Thebes, Rome and Carthage (II.84). As political body it acquires spokesmen with sacral immunity (II.107): Israelite prophets, statesmen like Solon and the reforming Spartan kings, the tribunes of the plebs at Rome.

Subordinate classes in the city still have a quasi-civic structure in their own right: women, youth, even slaves with their Saturnalia (I.234, 246); the Roman plebeians (II.42, 108); resident aliens (II.26-27, III.11-12). In the fully developed city-state the woman has only the choice of housewife and harlot: the two roles are made the objects of an allegorical choice for young men (Xenophon, Prov. 7,5-10; I.233).

The city-state acquires law-codes. Civil codes: the great inscribed code of Cretan Gortyn (II.278) runs parallel to Num 36,6, where heiresses must marry sons of their father's brother to keep property in the family (I.238-9). Criminal codes: Plato's proposed legislation in *Laws* 9 (also set in Crete!) has many of the same provisions as the Covenant Code of Exodus 21 in the same order (II.278-9), including permission to kill a thief at night (but not daytime), shared also by the Roman XII Tables (I.4).

24.3.2 Larger structures

Cities or tribes joined themselves into groups of twelve, to which we gave the Greek name "amphictyony" (II.203-8, cf. 239, 271): so in Israel, Ionia, around Delphi, Etruria; perhaps also in the Latin league at Lavinium (II.205). Since the group in each case has a cult-center, the obvious explanation is that each member of the league administered it for a month per year. Hebrews did not recognize any larger grouping than that of *lineage*: the tribes physically or conventionally descended from the twelve sons of Jacob/Israel (III.168-172). Greeks put *language* first: a Greek state recognized as part of *to Hellenikon* any people speaking Greek, and welcomed trade-partners in Anatolia or Libya who started to learn it (any such kinship of course did not block, but rather encouraged, warfare). Hebrews and Romans recognized an extended generation or *saeculum* of all those alive at a founding event, and computed the longevity of states on that basis, "unto the tenth generation" (Deut 23,3-4; II.228-234); this concept seems unknown in Hellas.

The new energy of the city-state increased its wealth and population, and led to extension by conquest at home or colonization overseas. Phoenician trade resulted in one colony, Carthage, which for centuries outshone the homeland states; but its early history is nearly unrecorded. Many Greek city-states founded overseas colonies, but again almost lacking history except for inscriptions from Cyrene. Thus the pattern of colonization (unearthed by Weinfeld, II.215) is best recorded in the legends of the Israelite conquest and the *Aeneid*. Weinfeld sees two phases: an initial phase of trade attributed to a single patriarch (Abraham and Aeneas); a second phase of true colonization inaugurated by a priestly oracle.

24.3.3 Sacrifice and the seer

The sacral life of the state is divided between an inherited sacrificial priestly cult taken for granted, and the charismatic activity of individual seers with some relation to boreal shamanism.

It is unclear how far the *sacrificial priestly cult* (I, Chapter 6) extended around the Mediterranean. Israel and Hellas (with Rome too) share special features: the primary act is the slaughter of a large animal which bloodies an altar; the inedible portions are offered to the High God or another as their smoke goes up to heaven (I.186), the meat provides a banquet for the participants. The shared vocabulary is very extensive (I.190-204). The ideal victim is a bull (Hebrew *šowr*, Greek *tauros*) with its horns, perhaps gilt (Hebrew *qεrεn*, Latin *cornu*), sacrificed (Hebrew *-zbaḥ*, Greek *sphag-*) on an altar (*bɔmɔh*, *bōmos*). The bull-sacrifice may be accompanied by the libation of wine with *its* common name (I.152). The herd of cattle further has a common name, Hebrew *bɔqɔr* and Latin *pecorіa* (II.18-19); in an old Semitic and Indo-European theme it is the natural object of theft, Heb. *gɔnebaī*, Greek *klepos* (II.322-3).

The charismatic *seer* combines seemingly disparate elements. The seer is of ambiguous sexuality, likely handicapped, hysteric (II.157-163). In the Mediterranean of uncertain rainfall, one of his tasks is rainmaking (II.171). Salmoneus of Elis claimed to be Zeus and threw lighted torches (*lampades*) at the sky, imitating lightning (Apollodorus 1.9.7); Rabbi Simeon b. Gamaliel juggled lighted torches at the Feast of Booths when rain was prayed for (Bab. Talm. *Sukkah* 53a, II.176), where the torches might as well have been *lappidiym*. (The names of "lightning bolts" are very old, Hebrew *bɔrɔqіiym*, Greek *phlogіes*, II.64.) Hebrew and Greek seers have close connections with the *bear*, hibernating and risen. The witch of En-Dor (I Sam 28,7, II.190) like Circe controls access to a seer still powerful in death; her practice seems Sibylline and could have been transmitted to Palestine by the Trojan *Gergithes* with their relation to the Hebrew *Girgashites* (II.193).

24.3.4 The fruit of the vine and ecstasy

Viticulture again has a strong international vocabulary, in particular the name of wine (Hebrew *yayin*, Greek *(w)oinos*, Latin *uīnum*; I.137). The great enemy of the vine is the boar (Ps 80,14; *Iliad* 9.539; I.135). (Note also the fox, Cant 2,15 "Catch us the foxes that spoil the vines"; Varro *de re rust.* 1.8.5 in Asia the vine lies on the ground, *quae saepe uulpibus et hominibus fit communis*, "which often is shared between foxes and men.") Yahweh brought a vine out of Egypt and planted it (Ps 80,9); "Oineus king of Calydon was the first to receive from Dionysus the plant of the vine" (Apollodorus 1.8.1). Since cistern water is barely drinkable, normal practice was to *mix* water with wine, and the verb was taken over from Indo-European (likely Greek) into West-Semitic (I.142-3). The wine-hall (Hebrew *liškɔh* and *niškɔh*, Greek *leschē*; I. 141-2) appears in both societies. As wine "makes glad the heart of gods and men" (I.139), in both societies it is the original element opening awareness of a transcendent world.

24.3.5 Dragon-combat

Of all mythical themes, that of combat with a primeval dragon is most deeply rooted in both societies. Before the High God could go about the work of creation, it seems, he had to overcome the sea-dragon of chaos (Ps. 74,14-16). At the Pillars of the world or beyond them (I.124-128) his combat is assimilated to the tuna-fishery; in the eastern Mediterranean at the foot of Mount Kasios he fights the monster with his toothed sickle (Heb. *ḥerɛb*, Greek *harpē*; I.80). Perhaps the great tsunami from the explosion of Thera is mythologized as the sea-monster; only after it has been taken care of is the regular order of the environment possible.

In each of these internal social structures or enterprises the High God (or his associates) plays a key role. He validates the status of the king before new conditions disperse the king's authority to magistrates, senate and people's assembly. He is the object of the official sacrificial cult and the validator of the charismatic seer who (among other things) conspires with him to bring the rain. Himself (or in Hellas through his agent Dionysus) he bestows the gift of the vine whose fruit makes glad the hearts of men and gods as well. Above all through his struggle with the oceanic and monstrous forces of disorder he makes possible the emergence of a stable environment friendly to human beings.

In the ascription of all these structures to the High God, ancient peoples explain, legitimate and guarantee the existence of their own societies. Modern anthropology is only partly able to account for the appearance of such structures. When did there come into being a divine kingship both able to hold a society together and to permit its own replacement by dispersal of power? How does the ritual slaughter of a bull act to validate the society? What is the relation of the sacrificial cult to the charismatic seer and rainmaker? By what genetic and historical processes does intoxication by wine come to stand for a higher level of existence? (For many non-Mediterranean peoples like American Indians lack genetic resistance to alcoholism....) How was the development of civilization synchronous with the softening of the glacial and tectonic catastrophes? About all we can do is to chronicle those parallel environmental and social developments, and observe how each in its way is essential to the birth of the Polis, and underlies the mysterious emergence of freedom and a sense of justice.

24.4 Freedom and particularity

None of the structures we have summarized so far was peculiar to the new societies of Israel and Hellas. All were shared to some degree by a number of other Mediterranean societies, even though the evidence often rests on Hebrew, Greek or Latin texts. On them as foundation a new level of society came into existence in Israel and Hellas, and later at Rome. And our records of earlier structures are lit up by the emergent novelties they held in potentiality.

We begin with the climax of old Mediterranean self-awareness (24.4.1) in *heroic honor and shame*, where the novelty in Israel and Hellas lies less in the facts themselves, than in the objectivity with which our texts present them—plus at times an implied rebuke proceeding from a new understanding. That rebuke becomes explicit (24.4.2) in the *critique of sacrifice and priesthood*. The new understanding (24.4.3) is the emergence of *humanism*: a celebration of weakness and grandeur in a setting of family solidarity arising from a realistic facing of death. Over against the faults of heroes and the sacrificial cult stands the central discovery (24.4.4) of the *justice of the High God* as revealed by feminine memory-figures to shepherd-prophets. From the beginning there was a realization that the new insights needed to be made permanent (24.4.5) in a *book* available to all through precious alphabetic script. The impact of these steps was so overwhelming that, as long as the autonomous city-state continued, the new culture is infused (24.4.6) with a common *particularity*: "We are different from the others."

24.4.1 Heroic honor and shame

Such historical or legendary works as the ancient Near East produced celebrate the deeds of kings, at peace or in their capacity as generals; the king appears in a uniformly good light because he has commissioned the works. In Israel and Hellas there appear literary works, at first more oral than written, proceeding from elsewhere than the court, and displaying the motives and actions of the leaders, historic or legendary, for better or worse—a David or Achilles—in categories which we may summarize as honor and shame. Their motives—"help friends, harm enemies" (III.8-10)—are precisely those which achieved international status through the vassal treaty. The father of Glaucus (*Iliad* 6.209, III.19) told him "not to shame the generation of his fathers"; Prov 28,7 "A companion of gluttons shames his father." It is the duty of vassals to have the same friends and enemies as their liege lords (I.263).

Archilochus, a near-contemporary of the Homeric poets, says "I know how to love my friend and hate my enemy"; Odysseus tells Nausicaa that a man and woman happily married "bring many pains to their ill-wishers, and joy to their well-wishers" (III.8). More subtly the author of II Sam 19,6-7 has Joab criticize David for mourning his rebel son Absalom: "You have shamed the face of all your servants...by loving those who hate you and hating those who love you" (III.3). It is left up to the hearer to determine whether David is doing better or worse by breaking convention. The tragedy of the Iliad is Achilles' exaggerated sense of being "unrewarded" (*atīmos, Iliad* 1.171) while the other Achaeans are given booty and women. Greek history in Thucydides, and tragedy throughout, build on the epic insight.

Hebrew for "love" at II Sam 19 is the root *'ohab*; a near-parallel occurs in the rare Homeric verb (later common) *agapaō, Odyssey* 16.17 "As a father loves his son." Perhaps the word (exceptionally, for a verb) moved between cultures precisely in the context of the vassal-treaty (III.18). Later in Hellas but more definitely than in Israel the doctrine arises that retaliation or "doing injustice in return" is excluded (Plato *Crito* 49B, III.30). A prerequisite for this realism and critique of the motives of leaders is the sharing of power between the leaders and the infantry under arms that made up the city's fighting force.

24.4.2 Critique of sacral institutions

Hebrews and Greeks inherited a common sacrificial cult from an unknown source—perhaps one of themselves, perhaps elsewhere in the

Minoan area. Quite early, thinkers and poets looked at the cult with their new realism of human motivations and rejected it—as much in puzzlement as in abhorrence (I.188-190). Empedocles (himself a charismatic seer who offered to teach rainmaking and raising of the dead, II.155) celebrates the chaste cult of Cyprian Aphrodite in the Golden Age: "But no altar was wet with the unmixed blood of bulls." (For, he felt, in view of the "transmigration of the soul" to animals, sacrifice of such was equivalent to murder, I.217.) This is not competition between religious professionals, since Greek sacrifice is laicized, but critique of popular cult by the *only* professional religious class. So the prophets, "He who slaughters a bull is a man-slayer" (Isa 66,3), though it is not clear what if anything the critics would put in the place of sacrifice. Lucian spoke for freethinkers when he made the gods into flies around the sacrifice (*de sacr.* 9, II.330), parodying a theme from Gilgamesh (I.186; 219-221).

24.4.3 Humanism and family solidarity

The clear look of the new societies generated a description of humanity which still today stands ahead of us and not behind us. Israel understood the potential *dominion* of humanity (I.55), Ps 8,7 "Thou hast put all things under his feet"; Gen 1,28 "And have dominion," Vg *dominamini*. The Chorus in Sophocles' *Antigone* 332-375 celebrates control over birds, beasts and fish; Ovid *Met.* 1.77 defines humanity as a being which could have dominion (*dominari*) over the others— Jerome remembered this. The other side of this is a new *realism* about old age and death (I.56-57, II.37, 325). Human beings are creatures of a day, like grass rising in the morning, faded by evening (Ps 90,5-6); a generation of leaves (*Iliad* 6.146); creatures of a day, the dream of a shadow (Pindar *Pyth.* 8.95-96). Each people somehow inherited the image of the dark underworld with its immovable gates (I.123-4) and chaotic torrents (I.57, II.187). Still over against this recognition of necessity stands the naked human being (I.58-60), at once vulnerable and defiant.

Paradoxically, while moderns look to Hellas for a notion of immortality, and to late Israel for resurrection, the historical societies are marked by their *freedom* from the Egyptian obsession with death. Their this-worldliness is in fact temporary and unique, for it is lost again after imperial conquest. What made their efflorescence of humanism possible was a *confidence in the future*, symbolized by the state with its walled citadel. The Homeric hero goes on fighting in the presumption that he will have "eternal fame" through the words of a sacred bard in an ongoing society more or less like his own. (I.10-11).

Later in both Israel and Hellas men are glad to fight and die for the state out of a sense of *family solidarity*: provided the state remains, what they fail to accomplish, their sons or grandsons may. A son's duty is to maintain his father's honor: a man's life rests in his sons, the greatest misfortune is to die childless. When Horace (*Carm.* 3.2.13) says "It is sweet and proper to die for one's country," *dulce et decorum est pro patria mori*, he is expressing a genuine truth for the ancient world. Still, war both vindicates solidarity and undermines it.

We have not previously described family solidarity. Nothing is more important for a man than having sons. If a man's wife cannot bear them he has recourse to her handmaids: thus Abraham (Gen 16,1-16) and Jacob (Gen 30,1-13); so Menelaus when Helen has only a girl (*Odyssey* 4.11-14, see II.284). Obedient sons are needed (III.9) to punish (family) enemies and honor friends (Sophocles *Antigone* 643-4). Above all to bury their father, as with Abraham (Gen 25,8-9) and Isaac (Gen 35,29). Croesus tells Cyrus (Herodotus 1.87.4), "In peace, sons bury their fathers; in war, fathers bury their sons." Joseph's great-grandchildren are born on his knees (Gen 50,23) and so Job 42,16. "The sons of sons are the glory of the aged" (Prov 17,6). In Aristotle's analysis of the mutual love of relatives, "parents love their children *as themselves*, for being from the parents by separation they are as it were *other selves*," *Eth. Nic.* 8.12.3 = 1161b26-27. Lev 19,34 (cf 19,18) "You shall love the stranger *as yourself*, for you were strangers." Both peoples presuppose love of self (III.3), and love of others as proceeding from self. *Eth. Nic.* 1.8.16 = 1099b3-6 "one cannot be truly happy who is...solitary and childless; even less if one's children are wicked...or were virtuous and have died." The tradition which made Absalom without sons (contrast II Sam 14,27) has him say, "I have no son to keep my name in remembrance" (II Sam 18,18, cf II.133). That is what sons are for.

24.4.4 The God of justice

Besides their insight into the actuality of human motivations, the new societies also achieved a new insight into what human motivations *should* be. You might think this a later phenomenon. But opinions can differ whether Hesiod's *Works and Days*, with its exposition of the justice of Zeus, is later or earlier than the *Iliad*; and whether Amos with the early strata of the Pentateuch are later or earlier than the analysis of David's character in the "Court Chronicle" (II Sam 9-20) as we have it. In any case the discovery of justice is a *different* (though related) insight, appearing in a different stratum of the people and communicated back and forth between Israel and Hellas very likely by land.

In the ancient Near East such a king as Ammisaduga of Babylon (II.47) proclaims his just acts—whether or not they were truly such. The new understanding of the High God as guarantor of justice arose (it seems likely) in a crisis of land-tenure. (Levin pushes that understanding yet further back in the recognition during patriarchal Israel of rightful ownership of cattle.) The geographical factor which marked Israel and Hellas above all was the land-tenure made possible by the rain from the High God; in its crisis, with the confusion of boundaries and the buying-up of large estates (II.23), the new guarantee was the maintenance or restoration of original holdings. (The process came later in Rome with the buildup of *latifundia* in the early Empire, III.321.) Farmers who doubled as upland shepherds in annual "transhumance" (II.2) "*see*" a new state of affairs (Amos 1,1); they are shown it by feminine memory-figures (II.36-37), the Muses (Hesiod *Theogony* 22-23) or spirits of God (Isa 11,2). And what they are shown is the concrete image of Justice, enthroned with the High God (II.45). Those uplanders communicate with others of their kind through overland transport, an extension of the ass with its sacks by which they carry their produce to the city-market (II.47).

The original definition of justice, as of the American republic, has what might seem strong built-in limitations. The supreme virtue of both is their *dynamism*, by which the definition is progressively enlarged. It was self-evident to the signers of the Declaration of Independence that "all Men are created equal." Initially that was not seen as applying to Negro slaves or women; but by an inexorable logic of history both came to be included. In neither Israel or Hellas was justice initially seen as going beyond Cicero's definition, "a state of mind granting each his own," *animi affectio suum cuique tribuens* (*de fin.* 5.25, and see its expansion by Ulpian of Tyre, II.29). At first one's "own" was above all *land*; and so land-owners (all or nearly all men, so that *his own* is a correct translation!) were the main or only beneficiaries of the new concept. But a development culminating in the new Church came to see that the landless, aliens, women, and slaves had in principle intrinsic rights of equal value which equally could be called their own, and which in the end justice could not deny them.

We saw the agreement (II.34) between Hesiod *Opera* 279 that Zeus "gave justice to men [rather than animals]" and Ps 98,2 Yahweh "has revealed his justice in the eyes of the nations"; and hence Rom 1,17 "the justice (*dikaiosynē*) of God is revealed in [the good news]." But we should add that while the N. T. Vulgate, followed by Catholic versions, translates the Greek as *iustitia*, Protestant versions have *righteousness* (since the KJV) and *Gerechtigkeit* (since Luther). For Paul has a special understanding of what it means for a human being to be just and how that state is reached, "we are justified by faith" (Rom 5,1).

The realistic description of the hero motivated by honor and shame, as soon as it came into being, had natural protection in the circle of the civic militia, among whom it was recited. The fact that the phonetic alphabet was available there kept the historical or legendary tale alive. The shepherd's proclamation of divine justice was more vulnerable, for it had its natural adversaries in the big landowners who exercised disproportionate power in the state. The shepherd-poet with the word of justice therefore required an extra element of legitimation; and found it in a status of *sacral immunity* (II.40-42, 107). In Israel the word of justice is carried by "prophets" who have fallen heir to a charismatic status in the society; in Hellas by poets who can claim a special connection with their patroness the Muse; in Rome by the tribunes of the *plebs* with a "sacrosanctity" supposedly from an old vote of the people, perhaps even before that a lost sacral status. The audience addressed by those spokesmen had enough overlap with the citizen-soldiers who heard the heroic legends that eventually the two sets of texts were grouped together: Hesiod joined Homer in an epic tradition; the Latter Prophets (Amos and his followers) joined the Former (or historians, from Joshua to Kings) in the category of commentators on the five books of Law.

24.4.5 The invention of the book

Horace (*Carm.* 4.9.25-28) imagines that "strong men lived before Agamemnon" but unknown "because they lacked a sacred bard" (I.10-11). Actually heroic honor would have been something different without Achilles' expectation of "imperishable fame" (*Iliad* 9.413); for though the phrase is old Indo-European, any earlier heroes to whom it might have been applied are in fact unknown. Hebrew shifts the application to its God, "The grass withers, the flower fades, but the word of our God abides for ever" (Isa 40,8). It was the simplicity of the alphabet (along with the excellence of the texts themselves) which ensured that the texts would remain when the independent societies that generated them were overthrown: a Roman historian contrasts complex hieroglyphs with the "fixed and simple series of characters" which "expresses whatever the human mind can conceive" (Ammianus 17.4.10, I.28, though he overestimates the ideographic character of Egyptian writing). In Crete about 500 BC one Spensithios in an archaic inscription is commissioned in a new role and an old, "to write and to remember" (I.51-52); earlier in Israel (II Reg 18,18) the scribe and the remembrancer are already different persons.

The new art moved from Canaan westward, for the names of the alphabet letters are Semitic (but neither Hebrew nor Phoenician, I.42), as is the name of the "tablet" (*deltos*, I.52). We discussed (I.40-43) how Greeks adapted and improved it. In Israel only a simple document could be read by one who had not previously seen it (I.49), like the baneful letter from David to Joab carried by Uriah (II Sam 11,15), echoed in the letter carried by Bellerophon (*Iliad* 6.168-9). In Israel, any more complex work needed a double tradition, both written (as *aide-mémoire* of the unpredictable materials coming up), and oral (to supply the vowels), as Levin has shown (I.47-50, II.325). Both in Israel and Hellas, the habit of the messenger, poet or historian reading his document out loud was so fixed that silent "reading" was a rare curiosity (Augustine, *Conf.* 6.3).

What initially sets Israel and Hellas apart from all their neighbors is that, when they lost political independence, they retained scribal groups whose job was to preserve their people's books. The book was produced under particularity but preserved under universalism. Literacy was widespread enough among both peoples so that such groups survived war and exile. The intrinsic interest of the books was great enough to give the scribes lifetime motivation—and to persuade their sons or students to carry the tradition on. In Egypt and the cuneiform world the scripts were so cumbersome that their knowledge was lost when the courts, temples and businesses that employed the scribes fell away. The texts (it appears) were not seen as valuable enough to generate groups committed to preserve them. (But perhaps the Achaemenid Persians held in their hands or their heads the actual texts of our Avesta.) Elsewhere in the world of alphabetic scripts—Ugarit, Phoenicia, Damascus, Anatolia—, literacy (though more easily acquired) must have been still the monopoly of a royal, priestly, mercantile class.

The different size and character of the two canons of texts (III.180) reflects a complementarity both of language and of script. Greek epics could be longer because the metrical hexameter was easier to memorize than the mixed style of Hebrew narrative books. But the bardic tradition was always liable to forgetfulness and improvisation. Long works surely came into being first when their writing-down was already possible or actual. As time went on, the written text became more and more necessary as a corrective to oral changes or mistakes. But (in different ways in the two lands) the written text had always to be supplemented by the oral. So, down to some time in the Latin Middle Ages, the "book" was a double tradition of written text and oral performance. Its custodians were a scribal community so self-contained as to survive the fall of the independent societies which had given it birth.

24.4.6 Particularity

During the age of their political autonomy, Hebrews and Greeks were so overwhelmed by the power of what they had produced, seeing themselves in the mirror of their own books, as to contrast themselves with the rest of the world. Thales (Diogenes Laertius 1.33, III.16) thanks Tychē that he was born "a human being and not a beast, a man and not a woman, a Hellene and not a barbarian." The synagogue service to this day begins with thanks to the God who has not made the worshipper a *goy*, a slave, a woman; it may follow Aristotle (*Pol.* 1.1.5) who recognizes the same three classes of inferiors, barbarians and women and slaves (I.234-5). (In Paul's universalism [Gal 3,28], precisely the same three groups are *affirmed*.) The Greek contrasts himself with the barbarian who speaks the wrong language, the Hebrew with the *goy* of different lineage who engages in the wrong cult (III.168-172).

The separateness of the new societies was concretely marked by the *city wall*, surrounding a citadel with a spring of water. Ovid (*Met.* 1.97, III.12) imagines a Golden Age "when steep moats did not yet surround cities"; Vergil more realistically (*Geor.* 2.155-7) celebrates the walls of Italian hill-towns. In an age of "fire and sword" (I.159-161) the smoke of an inadequately defended city "rises up to the heavens" (Jos 8,20; *Iliad* 21.522-3); and the city wall was indispensable to protect the law which it enclosed. Heraclitus says "the people must fight for its law as for its wall." If the wall goes, all goes (Thr 2,8-9). Only Sparta (of all places!) points to the future, "A city is not unfortified which is crowned with men and not with bricks" (Plutarch *Lyc.* 19.4; II.329); already the new departure which she represents is fully realized in the character of her men, and in that alone.

Each of the novelties we have chronicled here could only have first come into being in an autonomous state guarded by a city wall: the fighter and hero motivated by honor and shame (24.4.1); the advanced thinker in a society where the old sacrificial cult persists (24.4.2); the humanistic poet contemplating the attitudes of his fellows towards death (24.4.3); the shepherd-prophet seeing land-tenure as guaranteed by a God of justice (24.4.4); the poet, writer or scribe inventing the book to record new thoughts (24.4.5). The prophetic word is the agency by which latent justice and the other novelties break through into history. The new free society proclaims a better order of things striving to emerge into the time-sequence, whose primary evidence is that proclamation. The participants in each of those revolutions knew that they were bringing something novel into the world, and had no choice but to contrast themselves with outsiders; hence their particularity, "We are different from the others" (24.4.6). But the wall was destined to be pulled down; and the books, once completed and turned over to scribes or grammarians, no longer needed its protection. The "fence around the Torah" (*Avoth* I.1, I.161) changed character.

Most of the novelties in the fully developed city-state here noted can be seen as humanistic. But the old preeminence of the High God comes out more strongly than ever in the affirmation of his work as sustainer and promoter of justice. Here (for the last time!) we can rationalize his role as the personified justification of land-tenure—the prerogative of the only full members of the society, the landed citizen militia. When their central status disappears in the breakdown of the city and its walls, provisionally this semi-final role of the High God disappears. But when Paul renews the affirmation of a God revealing justice, it is no longer on behalf of those who have unjustly lost what once they had, but of those who deserve to be given what they never had— women, slaves, foreigners. Even this can be seen as a legitimate historical development from what preceded. But the replacement of family solidarity by the individual hopeful of a victory over death permits no such easy rationalizing.

24.5 Empire and universalism

The autonomy of the city-state was ended in a series of conquests by imperial powers. The northern kingdom of Israel was taken by Assyria, and Jerusalem itself by the Babylonians; under the Achaemenid Persians a partial return was permitted and control relaxed. Many of the Greek states in Asia Minor fell under Persian control, and the Greek mainland itself twice repelled Persian invaders. The new power of Macedon took over the Greek mainland, Asia Minor, Syria, Egypt, and much of Persia; control continued under the Successors of Alexander until Rome swept all away (III.74). About 587 BC Nebuchadrezzar broke down the walls of Jerusalem (II Reg 25,10; I.161); in 404 BC the Long Walls of Athens between the city and Piraeus were torn down "to the music of flutegirls" (Xenophon *Hell.* 2.2.23), perhaps by the returning exiles themselves.

Besides an end of political independence, the new imperial control imposed *sanctions* (24.5.1) on the subject states. The symbolic themes of *self-legitimation* set up by the Persian regime (24.5.2) were boldly adopted by subject peoples on their own behalf. But the loss of the city-wall raised the possibility that the natural order itself might be torn down (24.5.3). The new imperial control in both lands was providentially delayed until the primary treasures enshrined in the walled cita-

del had been transformed into a shape adapted for survival in exile.
And so particularity is transformed into a cosmopolitan *universalism*
(24.5.4): "we are different from the others" becomes "we have a
mandate to carry our novelty to all." All these changes are partially
reversed in the universal Church and Empire (24.5.5)—but within a
new context.

24.5.1 The imperial sanctions

Imperial control consisted in sanctions applied to the goods and above
all to the bodies of its subjects. The Persian *taxation* attested in late
Biblical Hebrew (III.102) was carefully noted by the Athenians and
adopted for control of their own maritime empire. By the Roman
period the whole world was arranged in a universal ladder of debt
(I.249-250; III.33). Rabbinic and Greco-Roman documents illustrate
the *requisitioning* (II.52-53) of ships and draught animals taken over
from Persia by the Hellenistic kingdoms and eventually Rome; the
same international name of *angaria* was applied to the *conscription* of
individuals for varying periods of service, with two notable instances
in the Gospels. Recalcitrant individuals are singled out for public
notice by *tattooing* (perhaps also branding); and punished by savage
forms of *flogging,* where Aramaic inherited both an Iranian and a
Latino-Greek name for the sanction (III.104-106)—no doubt the victims carefully distinguished their treatment by the two empires.

The ultimate sanction from the Persian period to the Roman was
execution by *crucifixion* (III.106-110) with the triple motives of vengeance, deterrence and public humiliation. Hebrew Midrash and Roman
law agree in the doctrine that "bandits" are to be strung up on the
scene of their depredations. The execution of a solitary symbolic figure
with a woman companion proclaims the fate of a *rebel victim*
(III.72-82): Prometheus in Aeschylus' play and the Servant of Yahweh
(Isa 53) each is a representative figure pegged up and attacked by birds
or beasts (as in all-too-historical crucifixions, I.247-8, 280-282); Jesus
is so treated by the Romans, apt pupils of the Persians and Alexander's
Successors. But in a historical reversal the rebel victim is seen as
ultimately victor and the savior of his people.

24.5.2 Imperial legitimation

As the fate of the rebel victim is reversed in poetry and doctrine, the
symbols of imperial legitimation are boldly plundered by resistance
movements for their own banner. The Persian monarch calls himself
"king of kings" (III.83-86), in part realistically as limitation of his

power, for he left numerous kinglets in their place—along with satraps more powerful than most previous kings. Aeschylus (*Sup.* 524) calls Zeus "lord of lords"; so (Deut 10,17) Yahweh is "God of gods and Lord of lords," where the Mishna goes one step further and makes him "King of the kings of kings." Alexander's title of *cosmocratōr* "world ruler" is taken over by Rabbinic (III.88-89) for various parties. The Iranian "ambassador" (rare Greek *askandēs*, III.89-91) is supernaturalized in the Syriac *Hymn of the Pearl* and in Mandaean; Paul (II Kor 5,20) speaking for himself says "We act as ambassadors on behalf of Christ" where in the Syriac translation the same Iranian word appears. What the ambassador rescues is the supernatural *pearl* known under the same name *margarita* in all languages (III.61-64). All armies and militias are reorganized in the now standard pattern of bodies of a hundred and a thousand (III.92-95). The royal and satrapal hunting-parks known to Xenophon and the Hebrew Bible as the king's *paradise* (III chap. 21) are seen as the utmost symbol of felicity, and claimed for the rebel victim executed as pretender to the status of the Great King.[9] The languages of four empires—Babylonian, Iranian, Greek and Roman—are put to work in Jesus' sayings (Chapter 23), defining a novel alternative to empire.

24.5.3 The end of the world

A corollary of confidence in the future within the autonomous city-state is the general reliance on the preservation of the natural order. We saw the making of Achilles' shield by Hephaestus (*Iliad* 18, I.108) as a demythologized creation-narrative parallel to Genesis. Early on, temporary breakdown of social order is regularly expressed in the symbolism of cosmic disruption. Both peoples envisage the likelihood of cosmic destruction by flood (I.104) or earthquake (I.123). Israel, always more vulnerable to disruption, both external and internal, is more aware of cosmic collapse. Both peoples find the sky held up by pillars, but in Israel they are much more liable to fall (I.114-115). In Amos, the predicted invasion of Israel is seen as eclipse and flood (Amos 5,8; 8,9; 9,6). The fear is intensified with permanent breakdown of old social order. Greek philosophy of the *ekpyrōsis* or destruction of the earth by fire magnified the threat.[10] Vergil (*Georg.*

---

9 Also the attributes of the Great King (III.95-100)—his image, diadem, gate, sword, the obeisance due him—to some degree are taken over in the symbolism of the subject peoples.

10 Zeno (Tatian, *Oratio ad Graecos* 3.3); but he strangely sees the entire course of history identically repeated after as before.

1.468, III.332) imagines an eclipse become "eternal night" at the murder of Caesar, and the younger Pliny sees the event in the eruption of Vesuvius. The epics see the fall of a tree as the fall of a hero or a city (III.211), and obscurely sense the connection between deforestation and fall of society; although official thought (III.197) short-sightedly regards timber-cutting like the tuna-fishery (I.130) as victories over chaos.

Two developments are seen by moderns as key to the "decline of the ancient world"—an eventuality mostly beyond our scope here. Environmentalists like J. Donald Hughes ("Pan's Travail") see it as an ongoing destruction of resources—most clearly documented for the two societies as deforestation. Marxists like de Ste. Croix see it as the equally short-sighted destruction by an urban elite of the peasant populations needed both for agriculture and the legions. How far did the ancients see what was going on? A genuine outsider in the late first century, John of Patmos, on that lovely island saw both the earth and its peoples as progressively destroyed by the folly and crime of its rulers. In Rome during the same decades rhetoric overcomes even class interest in a parallel revelation of underlying realities. Tacitus entered so far into the mind of the barbarian enemy Calgacus as to ascribe him the deathless formulation of Roman policy, *ubi solitudinem faciunt, pacem appellant* (*Agricola* 30.6)—which works equally well when applied to the farmer-soldiers on the land and the land itself.

24.5.4 The new universalism

In both Israel and Hellas, precisely the themes seen earlier as marking the people's particularity are reversed as features of a universal mission. Whereas (24.4.6 above, I.234-5) Aristotle and the synagogue agree in seeing barbarian, slave and woman as inferiors, Paul (Gal 3,28) affirms "In Christ there is neither Jew nor Hellene, slave or free, male or female." Eratosthenes (Strabo 1.4.9, III.17) realistically notes that "many Hellenes are bad and many barbarians civilized." (But all along by anticipation in both societies to fear God is to love the stranger, III.12-14; for the stranger might be a valuable trading partner or an old friend in disguise.)

In later texts of the Hebrew Bible, the *goyim*, once rejected, are seen in pilgrimage to Jerusalem, where (Isa 2,2) "the mountain of the house of Yahweh" is established "and all the *goyim* shall flow to it" (III.17); "all the ends of the earth shall remember and return to Yahweh" (Ps 22,28). That centripetal vision is theory, symbolically realized at the Christian Pentecost. A centrifugal reverse really happened: in the Hellenistic period, as Jewish artisans spread across the Mediterranean, the

Hebrew Bible in its Greek translation was made available to Gentile "God-fearers," surely for the most part not circumcised. At Antioch of Pisidia in the synagogue Paul speaks to "Men of Israel and God-fearers" (Act 13,16; III.173-174). (But the very success of Paul's mission within a few centuries closed shut the door so opened to Gentiles). In Hellas, precisely the education (*paideia*) seen by men like Isocrates (III.169) as the special property of Greeks is spread throughout the world of Alexander and of Rome; the Greek names of the *pedagogue* and *school* are taken over as a common phrase into Latin and Rabbinic (I.330-331; III.267-268).

Above all, the fact of Roman citizenship, steadily approaching total universalism (and effective meaninglessness) under Caracalla (AD 212),[11] is paralleled by a philosophical universalism (I.161-162). Epictetus the former slave defines man as a "citizen of the world" (Arrian 2.10.3); Cicero (*Leg.* 1.61) defines the mind exactly so, *ciuis totius mundi*. The former military panoply becomes spiritualized (I.168-9); the military tent (*skēnē*) is transformed into the *Shekhīnah* or Presence of Yahweh (I.179-180; II.330). For when the city-wall crumbles, the division between insiders and outsiders, friends and enemies, also is shaken, and the conditions are in place to envisage humanity as a universal "brotherhood." Jesus in effect sees all human beings as brothers and sisters (*adelphoi*), Mark 3,35; Matt 25,40 (III.179). In fact the word means "of the same womb" (*delphys*), originally applied to full brothers in the king's harem; but it has been conjectured that the entire human race is descended from one African Lucy.

To the extent that the new situation is seen positively, there is a reversal of the focus in which the societies see themselves. They retain, more strongly than ever, the conviction of their own excellence over against other peoples—including, at a late date, each other! But the breakdown of the wall came to be seen as a breakdown of the barriers between themselves and other peoples. It corresponded with a modification of their excellences into a form available for export. The new imperial situation opened the possibility of making their achievement open to others. (a) In part the novelty takes a *common* form in the availability of the *book*: in its original Greek for Hellas, in the Greek Bible of the Septuagint for Israel. The Hellenization of the Near East by the successors of Alexander, along with the Hellenization of Rome by a literary culture and a diplomatic chancery, provided a reading (or

---

11 Dio Cassius 77.9; Ulpian in the *Digest* 1.5.17, *In orbe Romano qui sunt ex constitutione imperatoris Antonini ciues Romani facti sunt*; a fragmentary papyrus (*Pap. Giessen* 40), see OCD[3] 383 "constitution, Antonine."

rather a *hearing*) public for the Septuagint. (b) Thus the novelty shared in the growing *complementarity* of the two societies: Hellas exported a language and a culture, with religious themes but more so secular; Israel supported a revised cult and a set of convictions. From particularity they moved to universalism; not quite completely in either case.

24.5.5 Partial reversal in the universal Church

The new imperialism with all its consequences leads to a second shift whereby the old solidarity and particularity are partially recreated in the new universal family of the Church under an empire with full citizenship (involving more duties than benefits ...). For the universalism of both Israel and Hellas by themselves was incomplete. What we must now call Jewish cult could not dispense with circumcision, and pagan semi-converts were relegated to the second category of *theosebeis*, God-fearers. The Greek language could not displace Latin in the West. The new Christian church with its entrance rite of baptism (non-threatening except for the danger of persecution), and the complete translatability of its book, eliminated both blockages.

But the new insights which emerged with the first imperialism and the breaking-down of the wall could not be eliminated. (1) Although the old solidarity of the "blood" family is replaced by the universal family of the Church, a newly discovered individualism cannot thereafter be denied; and the Church (less clearly so the synagogue) retains and deepens the doctrine of resurrection (popularly modified as immortality). (2) The new awareness of the fragility of the natural order likewise persists; and over against the universality of the City of God, the affirmation of an end of the world remains—but with a new promise of restoration. (3) Some degree of the old particularity remains even under the new universalism. Whenever the Church comes up against a novel external paganism, it reverts to the old particularity, emphasizing its unique benefits and initially ignoring whatever the outside society might bring to it. —Thus in general the second shift from the individual under Empire to the universal Church restores the unifying structures previously lost—but with a difference.

So far the themes under universalism are secular: the High God hardly appears, and no transcendent guarantee is in effect. That is because we postpone until the next section the final result of universalism, seen predominantly as negative: a new *individualism* with special demands on the cosmos. The former role of the High God as vindicator and guardian of his people is transformed into an oversight of each individual.

24.6 *The individual and the enigma of death*

Up until nearly the beginning of our era, in Hellas and especially Israel, family solidarity held together (24.4.3). That solidarity presupposes the continuation of history. If the suffering and death of the rebel victim results ultimately in the redemption of his people, that retroactively is seen as his vindication. But developments undercut that solidarity. The reality of death, always from the beginning an enigma, is intensified in three ways. (1) Initially in both societies the threat of individual death was blunted by reliance on the continuity of the family and of the people. This reliance was already reduced when the people lost political independence; it was intolerably reduced in Israel by the actual destruction of Jerusalem, first in anticipation and then in actuality. (2) The Israelite understanding of the High God as both sustainer of the people and maker of the created order raised the possibility that the created order might end when the people and its city also could be destroyed. (3) The new individualism created a new set of hopes independent of a man's future fame, his descendants, his clan and tribe, his people; it became more and more difficult to find a way of vindicating those hopes in the face of personal death.

This new universalism puts a further demand on the guarantees traditionally associated with the High God, which unlike all the previous guarantees is not easily rationalized into environmental or social conditions. Several schemes of symbolism raised the possibility that death might be overcome.

24.6.1 Recompense of benefits as of injuries

Early, the conviction of the justice of the High God led to the affirmation that those who did injuries would have injury done to them: certainly through the punishment of their sons or descendants for their wrongdoings; very likely in their own lives; as the concept was spiritualized, in the conviction that the act of wrongdoing in itself degraded the human image as much as obvious external retribution or more so. But then (III.30-32) the converse was affirmed: that an act of rightdoing brought its inevitable recompense—perhaps not in a man's external circumstances or in those of his descendants, but internally in his own character, and somehow also in a realm where the recompense of benefit would be visible to all. Meditation on the justice of the High God, which previously could be counted on in recompensing ill for ill visibly in history, either in the current or a succeeding generation, inevitably led to the extension of recompensing good for good. The

new individualism in an imperial society full of injustice led necessarily
to the affirmation of a realm in which the divine justice operated as
surely in the realm of rewards as that of punishments, or *more so*. And
that meant a realm in which somehow death was overcome.

24.6.2 The Beatitude

The old form of the Beatitude (III.35-39) leads to the same conclusion.
In the old days, the blessedness of the man who does so-and-so, if not
clearly visible in his own vindication during his lifetime, could be satis-
factorily postponed to his descendants. With the new individualism, in
a society where the self-determination of peoples had been replaced by
imperial control, that route is foreclosed. It became necessary to affirm
somehow a realm where the death of the individual was overcome or
compensated for, in which the justice of the High God was mathemati-
cally exact. The future acquires a new grammar (III.42-44).

24.6.3 Better lands

In both Israel and Hellas systems of symbolism arose to make concrete
that realm of vindication. In Hellas the symbolism appears most clearly
in the Islands of the Blessed (III.49-51), originally for military heroes,
later in Plato ethicised for all (women hardly yet figure). In Israel we
saw (III.59-61) hints of a blessed better life, Ps 16,10 "For thou dost
not give up my life to Sheol." Later the mode by which the dead are
raised is more and more specified. The vision of the valley of dry bones
in Ezekiel (37,1-14) originally was meant in the old way for the
restoration of "the whole house of Israel." But its concrete symbolism
"I will open your graves" was taken literally and individualistically
when the hope of restoration of the people as a whole became more
and more distant; precisely this passage is quoted in the Talmud to
prove the existence of a "key of the raising of the dead" (II.169).
Already the transition to individuals has been made at Dan 12,2 "And
many of those who sleep in the dust of the earth shall awake."

24.6.4 Immortality and resurrection

Roughly speaking we may see the two affirmations as complementary
and parallel: Plato on the immortality of the soul, Judaism on the
resurrection of the body. It marks the preponderance of the Greco-
Latin strain in the West that in Christian funerals, whether evangelical
or liberal or Catholic, immortality wins out, though inconsistent with
any Biblical understanding of the psychosomatic makeup of the human
being. The Rabbinic doctrine of the "raising of the dead," *təḥiyyat*

ham-mēṯiym, is downplayed in Judaism, perhaps so as not to seem too like Christianity (III.178). Even the massive historical fact of the Holocaust or *Šo'ɔh*, which drove some Jewish theologians into a paradoxical atheism, turned world Judaism towards the old political state, "Never again!," rather than to a reaffirmation of the Resurrection.

The unmeasured energy of the new Christian church arose in the first place from the conviction that Jesus had been raised from the dead; and that in union with him the believer likewise was raised from the dead, after physical death and burial indeed, but also in an anticipatory way in the midst of life. We may take the doctrine as the central place where Israel and Hellas in their full complementarity merged. The doctrine of the resurrection, wherever believed and affirmed, becomes the final guarantee of the goodness and justice of God. In contrast to previous guarantees, there is no easy way fully to rationalize it in society or psychology.

As long as the human race continues, the doctrine of the resurrection can be explained more or less in rationalistic historical terms. We may say that Jesus is one who fully, like others in part, turned over everything important about himself—above all his words and actions—into the keeping of his followers. In that sense we may say that he did indeed overcome death. And to the extent that his followers do the same, preferring the well-being of their children, students, associates, followers, to their own, they too live on in succeeding generations. In a sense that understanding represents a reversal of the individualism of the late Hellenistic and early Roman worlds. The old solidarity of family is extended to a community which serves as one big extended family, in principle the whole human race: "Behold my mother and brothers and sisters."

But two obstinate facts undercut that simple rationalization of the resurrection in the time-arrow of the historical process. (1) The new individualism, once grasped, cannot thereafter be denied. Precisely as men and women are liberated onto a new level of existence, each becomes precious in theirself, and death continues necessarily to be seen as the last enemy. (2) Further, the tenure of human beings on this earth is finite. Some day the sun (it seems) will melt off the planets before it collapses into a cinder. If humanity before then has succeeded in implanting itself around newer suns, the whole history of its birth here will be denied. Something is already lost when each species becomes extinct: the mammoths whose corpses still litter Arctic wastes, the passenger pigeon, the dodo, perhaps in some near future the tiger or elephant in the wild.... And in the end the whole transmission of the "torch of life" (II.174) from one to another will become as if it had never been.

So the vindication of the justice of God in the end demands the affirmation of a transcendent realm where death is definitively overcome. The historical rationalization of the early Christian experience of the resurrection is (I propose) true and necessary so far as it goes, but not sufficient. Up until this point the affirmations of the High God or gods in Israel and Hellas can be explained as symbolism of processes within the historical timeline. Here no longer. Now everybody must stake out their own claim. The parallel development and final merger of Israel and Hellas lead to a point where the human race must take a leap into the dark. One may say: the fact that many human beings (most in some ages) take that leap vindicates the affirmation. But many today simply see death as the end, whether for themselves as individuals or for the human race as a whole. Bleak and comfortless as this prospect ultimately must be, it does not always necessarily lead to despair. Perhaps in some future it will, and the affirmation of the realm beyond death will become necessary for the continuation of the race. Certainly the first witnesses to what they reported as the raising of Jesus from the dead saw a breakthrough of the divine reality into history. The High God and the realm beyond death are equivalent formulations of the same hope. So we end with the sobering reflection that the successive guarantees testified to in the rise of free humanity, which initially we can rationalize within the historical process, by the logic of their own sequence lead to the affirmation of a guarantee which cannot be so rationalized. Still, believers historically have not as a rule been much interested in rationalization of their stance. The affirmations that God is good and that death has been overcome have their own internal structure, which, far from deprecating the struggle for a better present, intensifies and validates it; and which in the past has warranted many books in its own right, and will in the future warrant many more.

Appendix 3: Additions and Corrections to Vols. I-III

(I.23) *Irrigation in Mesopotamia and Egypt.* Here and elsewhere, over against the Mediterranean rain-watered fields I compare dependence on the Tigris-Euphrates and Nile. Hughes (Pan's Travail 35,40) contrasts the two river systems. "The need for irrigation canals in Mesopotamia produced a salinization of the soil through water-evaporation; and (the canals rising above ground level through sediment) there was no way of flushing it out." But in Egypt "the Nile flood leached salt from the soil." Thus Egypt remained and remains fertile, whereas Iraq is much desertified. But this difference does not affect the larger contrast between political centralization in the two river-valleys, over against the autonomy of the Mediterranean farmer with rain-watered soil—until deforestation and erosion washed it out to sea.

(I.27) *Citizen militia and voting assembly.* They are the same body meeting under different circumstances (I.235-6; II.5, 97). Fergus Millar (The Crowd in Rome in the Late Republic; Ann Arbor: Univ. of Michigan, 1998; p. 198) cites Dio 37.28, describing a *comitia centuriata* (ταῖς κατὰ τοὺς λόχους ἀθροιζομέναις ἐκκλησίαις) in the Campus Martius, 63 BC. Dio observes "all who bore arms were obliged to attend the assemblies," πάντες οἱ τὰ ὅπλα ἔχοντες ἀνάγκην εἶχον ἐς αὐτὰς συνιέναι— and of course *vice versa*, since they had identical composition! In ancient times (he says), with many enemies near the city, not all voted at once; but an armed guard at all times held the Janiculum across the river with a raised standard (σημεῖον). If the standard was lowered the assembly was dissolved; in effect, it reverted to its normal status as standing militia. In the third century CE Dio adds "And even today this is done for form's sake," καὶ ἔτι καὶ νῦν ὁσίας ἕνεκα ποιεῖται.

(I.33) *Dor of Palestine.* A fragment of the Athenian Tribute Lists (ed. B. D. Meritt et alii, Cambridge; Harvard: vol. I [1939] pp. 154, 204, 483) lists a Δῶρος as giving tribute in 454 BC, and the editors think this is Dor of Palestine.

(I.33) *Atargatis the goddess.* We saw her at Ascalon; Lucian *de dea Syria* 14 calls her Derceto (Δερκετώ) as alternative transliteration, Strabo 16.4.27 identifies them. An Ἀταργατεῖον (II Makk 12,26) stood at Qarnayim E of the Sea of Galilee. At Hatra, KAI 248.7 "Baal-Shamin and Atargatis," בעלשמן ואתרעת. A Palmyrene bilingual (PAT 0273 cf 0197) among good gods lists עתרעתה = ['Ατα]ργάτει. Above all at Bambyke/Hierapolis, Βαμβύκη (Strabo 16.1.27); its coins show עתרעתה (Head 777); among five idolatrous temples (Bab. Talm. *Avoda Zara* 11b, בתי עבודה זרה) the Rabbis listed "Atargatis at Mabbug," תרעתא שבמבג. Most assume her name was originally double, ʿAshtoreth-ʿAnat, עשתרת ענת*. See DDD² 114-116.

(I.38) *Creation of the Greek alphabet*. Barry B. Powell ("Homer and Writing," A New Companion 3-32) has summarized and revised his previous book Homer and the Origin of the Greek Alphabet (1991). In the languages and scripts here studied I presuppose de Saussure's doctrine (Powell p. 48) that "the spoken language is primary and writing is essentially a means of representing speech in another medium"; but this seems not the case for Chinese script, and only partially for hieroglyphic and cuneiform. Powell (p. 10) writes as if the only vowels hidden by West-Semitic script were a, i and u; but each of the 7 Masoretic vowels is transcribed on a different pattern in early loanwords to Greek. Powell's absolute distinction between the "West-Semitic syllabary" and the "Greek alphabet" is only relative. For each script leaves out enough that the oral reader must by intuition grasp the intended speech from the written signs: Greek script adds vowels but (like the Semitic) omits the indispensable accents, and (even more regularly than the Semitic) word-dividers. Easy Hebrew letters could be read without an accompanying oral version; Homeric epic, even if read from a scroll, was always familiar to the reciter. I do not know what data prompted Powell to write (p. 11):

> The oblique narrative descriptions in familiar English versions of the Hebrew Bible, when compared with Homeric descriptions, or the tragedians', reflect the inability [!] of West Semitic writing to come close to natural language.

(I.65) *Pelasgians and Philistines* (see also I.170). The doctrine of this work—not absolute, but in the author's mind the most probable one—is that the Biblical Philistines brought up from "Caphtor" (Amos 9,7) carry the name of the Aegean Pelasgians; that Hebrew for "helmet," "tyrants," and "concubine" is from their language, along with the names of Achish (II.298) and Goliath; and that their neighbors, Greeks and Hebrews, gave them a bad name for a matriarchy betraying their menfolks (I.226). Robert Drews ("Canaanites and Philistines," JSOT 81 [1998] 39-61) does not touch the linguistics, but agrees from excavations at Ashdod, Ashkelon, Ekron and elsewhere that "there was a significant immigration to the southern Levantine coast from the Aegean—and more directly from Cyprus—in the twelfth century BCE." But (in line with his rejection of any "Sea-People" theory, II.212) he dissociates the name "Philistine" or "Palestine" from the Aegean invaders, and takes it to be an old Canaanite designation, although his documentation is scrappy. That leaves the Aegeans without a name and passes by their foreign vocabulary. I regret that this uncertain debate has been pressed into service on both sides to support present-day claims of both Jews and Palestinians to their common land—as if the demands of political justice, self-preservation and social harmony were so weak as to require validation from conjectural prehistory.

(I.72) *The phoenix.* Herodotus 2.73 describes the fabulous bird, and Hesiod frag. 304 M-W makes its lifespan 9x4x3x9 = 972 times that of a human being. Job 29,18 surely refers to it, "Then shall I die in my nest, and prolong my days like the *ḥol* (כַּחוֹל)": for *Gen. Rabbah* 19.5 calls the *ḥol* a bird, and says it lives a thousand years and then is reborn. Job 29,18 LXX has "Like the trunk of a *phoenix* (στέλεχος φοίνικος) I shall live a long time": here exceptionally we find a redactor at work, where the original version meant *phoenix* as the mythical bird, and a reviser reinterpreted it as a palm tree.

(I.88) *Goethe's further sources.* When Mephisto says of the grasshopper

      Und gleich im Gras ihr altes Liedchen singt

he echoes Vergil *Georg.* 2.378 on frogs

      et ueterem in limo ranae cecinere querelam

(I.138) *Wine for Kittiyim.* In the best-preserved of the Arad Inscriptions (ed. Yohanan Aharoni; Jerusalem: Israel Exploration Society, 1981; no. 1) Eliashib is instructed to "give wine to the Kitttiyim," נתן לכתים יין along with flour for bread. These appear to be Cypriote mercenaries in a Judaean army.

(I.146) *Cults and harbor duties in the sea-trade.* With the anchor-stone dedicated by Sostratos at Italian Graviscae (II.211) we may compare the stone anchors in the Temple of Obelisks at Byblos and the Temple of Baal at Ugarit, as well as at Kition of Cyprus. Aaron Jed Brody ("Each Man Cried Out to his God": The Specialized Religion of Canaanite and Phoenician Seafarers; Harvard Semitic Monographs 58; Atlanta: Scholars, 1998, 42-52) illustrates them and interprets them as votives for a safe sail, perhaps after a storm; we may conjecture that the very anchor which held fast is dedicated.

In a sensational find from Elephantine, Ada Yardeni ("Maritime Trade and Royal Accountancy in an Erased Customs Account from 475 B.C.E. on the Ahiqar Scroll from Elephantine," BASOR 293 [1994] 67-

78) has found 40 columns of an erased Aramaic customs text on both recto and verso of the fragments of the Ahiqar scroll from Elephantine. The full text was published in Porten-Yardeni TAD III no. C3.7. Some ships are Ionian (יוני) and others carry Sidonian wine (צידנים). It is unclear whether the actual harbor-duties were assessed so far upstream at Elephantine, or whether the scroll was erased and taken up there to be reused for the literary text Ahiqar. The Phoenician ships carried among other goods cedar (עק ארז) and iron (פרזל). Much of the vocabulary remains unclear (with Persian or Egyptian elements?) and further study will throw totally new light on sea-trade under the Achaemenids.

(I.164) *Goliath as personal name*. It appears in a remarkable monumental tomb with Greek and Hebrew inscriptions at Jericho (Rachel Hachlili, "The Goliath Family in Jericho: Funerary Inscriptions from a First Century A.D. Jewish Monumental Tomb"; BASOR 235 [1979] 31-73; commentary in New Documents 6 [1980/1981] 162-4). Among the three generations of the family represented, several inscriptions in the second generation have the name of Goliath, some bilingual, e.g.:

Σελαμσίους μητρὸς Ἰωέζρου Γολιάθου

שלמשיון אמה זי יהועזר גלית

"Of Shelomsion [the matriarch] mother of Yeho‘ezer Goliath." Several bodies are noted as tall, one (another Yeho‘ezer) as "Very tall (femurs 53 cm long); est. stature: 1.885 m." It is rare sardonic humor that these tall Jews were at adolescence given the nickname of the Philistine giant!

Another loculus has the inscription "Ossuary of Theodotus, *libertus* of Queen Agrippina," Θεοδότου ἀπελευθέρου βασιλίσσης Ἀγριππείνης. The editors agree in making this Agrippina the Younger, wife of Claudius AD 50-54; and conjecture how Theodotus was enslaved, presumably taken to Rome, and freed. There was a synagogue of a Theodotus son of Vettenus in Jerusalem (Θ[ε]όδοτος Οὐεττηνοῦ Gabba no. 23 with photo) and a synagogue of Libertines ("*liberti?*" συναγωγῆς ... Λιβερτίνων Act 6,9; but the addition "and men of Cyrene and Alexandria and Cilicia" suggests that "Libyans" was intended, whether or not we should emend to *Λιβυστίνων). Other Hellenizing Jews had the name Theodotus (Josephus *AJ* 14.248) and I am not prepared to make any connections.

(I.175) *Gyges, Kimmerioi, Lygdamis*. E. Lipiński ("Gyges et Lygdamis d'après les sources neo-assyriennes et hebraïques," pp. 159-165 of XXXIV Rencontre Assyriologique Internationale [1987]; Ankara, 1998) makes partly speculative but attractive combinations. Herodotus 1.15 describes the invasion of Lydia by the Kimmerioi (Κιμμέριοι) under Ardys the successor of Gyges. Lipiński identifies Lygdamis (Λύγδαμις) ruler of the Kimmerioi (Callimachus *Hymn* 3.252-3) who captured Sardes (Strabo 1.3.21) with Tugdamme king of the Umman-Manda (M. Streck, Assurbanipal und die letzten Assyrischen Könige...; II Teil; Leipzig: Hinrichs, 1916; p. 281); for the alternation l/t is plausible in Lydian. (Assurbanipal also knows Guggu king of the Luddi [Streck 21, see I.175] and the Gimirraa [23].) Lipiński then in turn identifies Tugdamme with Biblical Togarmah (תֹּגַרְמָה) assuming a graphic error d → r. For Togarmah is the son of Gomer (גֹּמֶר, Gen 10,3), surely the eponym of the Kimmerioi; and at Ezek 38,6 Gog, Gomer and Togarmah all appear together.

(I.194) *Paul's companion Barnabas.* Βαρναβᾶς is said (Act 4,36) to have been so named by the Apostles, inexplicably translated "son of consolation," υἱὸς παρακλήσεως; for it must be a pagan name (in contrast to his original Levitical name of Joseph!) "son of Nebo," Isa 46,1 נְבוֹ, Sfire (KAI 222 A8) נבא.

(I.242) *"Sacred" prostitution.* Mary Beard & John Henderson ("With this Body I thee Worship: Sacred Prostitution in Antiquity," Gender and History 9 [1997] 480-503) attribute the sacrality to 19th century stereotypes, but miss the point: the protection that the temple setting gave to foreign merchants with presupposed sexual needs.

(I.244) *Valley of the Adonis in Lebanon.* But the pages describing at second hand the "wild, romantic, wooded gorge of the Adonis" by Frazer (The Golden Bough, 3rd ed.; London: Macmillan, 1955, IV.i.28-29 = Adonis Attis Osiris i.28-29) are greatly touched up from the geographical reality.

(I.331) *Opium, musk, haoma.* Here besides cannabis are three more products of special status. *Opium* is ὄπιον Dioscorides 2.152. *P. Oxy.* 1088.6, 65 has recipes for opium as styptic and soporific(!). Jer. Talm. *AZ* 40d11 אופיון warns against it. Pliny 20.199 *non ui soporifera modo, uerum, si copiosior [sucus] hauriatur, etiam, mortifera per somnos* "its effect is not just to bring sleep, but also, if poppy-juice is drunk more copiously, to bring death through sleep."

Musk. The only ancient animal fragrance, from the musk deer of eastern Asia (S. Levin, "The Perfumed Goddess," Bucknell Review 24 [1978] 49-59), μόσχος Aetius 1.131. Jerome on Jeremiah 23,21-22 (Corp. Christ. 74.223.17) of heretics *frequentes adeant balneos, musco fraglent* "they attend crowded baths and are fragrant with musk." Persian *mušk* with Sanskrit *muškah* "testicle" (Monier-Williams 824) referring to the deer's musk-sack; it is a "little mouse," Hesychius μύσχον "genitals." Bab. Talm. *Berach.* 43a gives מושק or מושך a special blessing as an animal product.

Haoma. This is the Avestan form of Sanskrit *soma*, almost certainly the juice of a hallucinogenic mushroom, *Amanita muscaria* (R. G.

Wasson & D. H. H. Ingalls, "The Soma of the Rig Veda: What Was
It?," JAOS 91 [1971] 169-191). It appears unwittingly in illustrated
books of European fairy-tales; the mushroom which made Alice bigger
and smaller must somehow reflect it. The Old Persian *Sakā haumavargā*
of Darius (Kent 137, 211) are "haoma-preparing Scythians"; hence at
Herodotus 7.64.2 for Σκύθας 'Αμυργίους we should read one of the
variants Αὐμυργίους or Εὐμυργίους. At Elephantine a Jew belongs to
the "[military] detachment of Haumadata," לדגל הומדת (Cowley 8.2;
9.2). This can only be Iranian "gift of *haoma*." It is less certain that
Haman's father הַמְּדָתָא (Esther 3,1) holds the same name, but see
DDD² 384, which also suggests other plants as the original psych-
edelic. I cannot see that the name is clearly attested in the Elamite
tablets (M. Mayrhofer, Onomastica Persepolitana...; SB, Öster. Akad.
der Wiss., phil.-hist. Klasse 286, Wien 1973).

(I.334) *More Egyptian gods.*—The cat-goddess *Bastet*: her name in
the city Ezek 30,17 פִּי־בֶסֶת, Herodotus 2.137 Βούβαστις; DDD² 164-
6. —*Neith* in the name of Joseph's wife Asenath, Gen 41,45 אָסְנָת; Νηϊθ
Plato *Tim.* 21E (III.169); DDD² 616-8. —*Bes*: Βησᾶς Athenaeus
11.497D; *Besae dei...oraculum* Ammianus 19.12.3; Ezra 2,49 בֵּסָי;
DDD² 173.

(I.338) *The camel and the wheel.* Greek κάμηλος is well-known
since Herodotus and Aeschylus. Richard W. Bulliet (The Camel and
the Wheel; Cambridge: Harvard, 1975) proposed that ox-carts were
largely replaced by camels throughout the Near East and north Africa
some centuries before Islam; and that the typical narrow winding
streets of Arab cities even today show them to have been built up when
only camels were needed for deliveries. The contrast between broad
streets or squares and alleys in Akkadian, Greek (πλατεῖα/ῥύμη) and
Rabbinic (בריתא/שוק), see III.227, would suggest on the contrary that
all along both types of delivery were used. David F. Graf ("Camels,
Roads and Wheels in Late Antiquity," Electrum [Kraków] I [1997] 43-
49) proposes (p. 49) that

> Oxen remained invaluable and indispensable for hauling loads of great
> size and weight short distances. Camels have by far the greater range and
> capability especially in traversing desert terrain.

(I.340) *Names of the lion.* See E. Lipiński, "'Lion' and 'Lioness' in
Northwest Semitic," pp. 213-220 of Michael [M. Heltzer FS], eds. Y.
Avishur & R. Deutsch; Tel Aviv-Jaffa, Archaeological Center, 1999.

(II.13) *Sitting under the figtree.* To the citations listed for this to be
a site of enlightenment and peace, add Augustine *Confes.* 8.28 where
at the climactic moment of his conversion *ego sub quadam fici arbore*

straui me "I lay down under a certain fig tree." Likely he is seeing himself as undoing Adam's fault; at Gen 3,3-6 the two trees of life and knowledge seem combined, and the man and woman immediately find figleaves to cover themselves. The theme is attached specifically to the fig tree because it is the *principal* old pan-Mediterranean fruit-tree.

(II.23) *Large estates.* The Hebrew prophetic denunication of large estates (Micah 2,2; Isa 5,8) is paralleled less in Greece than in Rome, where unlimited funds made acquisition rampant. Pliny 18.35 in support of his doctrine "sow less, plow better" (*minus serere et melius arare*) comments *latifundia perdidere Italiam, iam uero et prouincias; sex domini semissem Africae possidebant, cum interfecit eos Nero princeps*; "big estates have ruined Italy [in what way?], and provinces also; six masters held half of Africa when Nero as *princeps* killed them." Seneca moralizing against wealth (*Epist.* 89.20) says that it is not enough "until you have surrounded seas with your estates," *latifundiis uestris maria cinxistis*. For theories about the nature of the *latifundia* and their "ruin" see OCD³ 816-7.

(II.39) *Vohu Mana.* The Avestan deity (DDD² 891-2) appears in Cappadocia, where the Magians in the temple of Anaitis and Omanos (Strabo 15.3.15 ἐν τοῖς τῆς Ἀναΐτιδος καὶ τοῦ Ὠμάνου ἱεροῖς) carry in procession a wooden image (*xoanon*) of the latter; at Strabo 11.8.4 the unidentified god Anadatos (Ἀναδάτου genit.) is added. So the first of the eunuchs of "Ahasuerus" (Xerxes) at Esther 1,10 is מְהוּמָן which will go well for Vohu Mana ("Best Purpose") with the regular equivalence of m and u. In contrast to Semitic, men carry the names of Iranian deities with no predicate, as of Ahuramazda himself in Cilicia and Palmyra; Armenians and Parsees to this day call their daughters Anahid. Diodorus 1.94.2 records "Good Spirit" in a passage worth quoting in full:

They say that among the Arians, Zathraustes claims that the Good Spirit (παρά ... Ἀριανοῖς Ζαθραύστην ... τὸν ἀγαθὸν δαίμονα) gave him laws; that among the Getae, who call themselves immortal, Zalmoxis (παρά ... Γέταις τοῖς ἀπαθανατίζουσι ... Ζάλμοξιν II.171.178) said the same of their common god Hestia; and so among the Jews Moyses of their god called Iao (παρὰ δὲ τοῖς Ἰουδαίοις Μωυσῆν τὸν Ἰαὼ ἐπικαλούμενον θεόν).

(II.47) *Prophecy in Israel and Assyria.* We have what moderns call "prophecies" from Assyria (but anciently not under such a name): Simo Parpola, Assyrian Prophecies; State Archives of Assyria IX; Helsinki: University, 1997. The editor correctly describes most of them as "Oracles of Encouragement" to Esarhaddon etc.: "Your enemies will roll before your feet like ripe apples. I am the Great Lady; I am Ištar of Arbela, who cast your enemies before your feet" (p. 4, cf ANET³

449 etc.). Their role is rather that of the 400 "prophets" of Ahab (I Reg 22,6). The great originality of Israel is that prophecy acquires the strength and backing to stand against the king.

(II.52) *Conscription*. See the excellent pages of de Ste. Croix (14-16) on *angareia*.

(II.86) *Telephos of Mysia*. Though associated with the *Kēteioi* (Hittites?), he has an extensive Greek legend. He is a son of Heracles, exposed on Mt Parthenius of Arcadia, and there suckled by a doe (Apollodorus 2.7.4). He goes to Mysia and becomes heir of king Teuthras (Apollodorus 3.9). He was wounded by Achilles' spear and healed by its rust, and led the Greeks to Troy (Apollodorus *Epit.* 3.17-20). The whole cycle appears in the lesser frieze on the altar of Zeus at Pergamon, now in Berlin.

(II.100) *Roman Democracy*. As over against interpretations of the Roman Republic which see it as controlled by aristocratic cliques for their own ends, Fergus Millar (The Crowd in Rome in the Late Republic; Ann Arbor: Univ. of Michigan, 1998) sees the "open-air meetings (*contiones*) of the *populus Romanus* as central to Roman politics" (p. 1); and finds (p. 11):

> it is difficult to see why the Roman Republic should not deserve serious consideration, not just as one type of ancient city-state, but as one of a relatively small group of historical examples of political systems that might deserve the label "democracy."

(II.119) *Names of Syrian kings*. Here, parallel to Greek versions of Punic notables, we gather names of Syrian kings attested in Greek, and (for different persons) in Palmyrene bilinguals.

Abgar. Ἄβγαρος Dio 40.20.2, dynastic name of kings of Edessa; *Acbarus* Tacitus *Ann.* 12.14.1 called *Arabum rex* must be an error for the same. Palmyrene bilingual PAT 0306 אבגר = Ἀβγάρου.

Iamblichus. Ἰάμβλιχος king of Emesa, Strabo 16.2.10 (Dio 50.13.7, Josephus *AJ* 14.129, Cicero *fam.* 15.1.3 *Iamblicho phylarcho Arabum*); same name borne by the philosopher of Chalcis and a Greek novelist. Palmyrene bilingual PAT 0472 ימלכו = Ἰάμλιχος. Perhaps hypocoristic "The God N shall make him rule," cf I Chron 4,34 יַמְלִיךְ.

Sampsigeramus. Σαμψιγέραμος dynastic name of kings of Emesa. S. I at Strabo 16.2.10, Diodorus 40.1b; Cicero *Att.* 2.14 uses *Sampsigeramus* as a nickname for Pompey. S. II was one of five kings convened by Herod Agrippa I in AD 43 at Tiberias (Josephus *AJ* 19.338); his name at Heliopolis/Baalbek (IGLS 6.2760) REGI MAGNO C. IVLIO SOHAEMO REGIS MAGNI SAMSIGERAMI F(ilius) ... PATRONO COLONIAE "To the great king Gaius Julius Sohaemus, son

of the great king Samsigeramus...patron of the colony (Heliopolis)";
tombs of their descendants at Emesa, IGLS 5.2212-2217. Palmyrene
bilingual (AD 75, PAT 1375) שמשגרם = Σαμσιγεράμου.

Sohaemus. Σόαιμος name of numerous dynasts: of Emesa, Josephus
BJ 2.501 (and see previous entry); of Petra, *BJ* 1.574; of Ituraea,
Tacitus *Ann.* 12.23 (*Sohaemus*); of Sophene *Ann.* 13.7. PAT 2761
שהימו. An Arabic diminutive *suhaym* "little dagger" like Ὀδαίναθος =
אדינת (PAT 0291, 0558) "little ear," *'uḏaynatun.* Again the underlying
Semitic throughout these dynasties is Arabic.

(II.123) *The seven-day week. Sambathaion* as personal name in
Egypt shows that knowledge of the Sabbath recurring every seven days
was widespread. It is unclear when and where the names of the seven
Babylonian "planets" (including Sun and Moon) were attached to the
seven. Martial 12.60.1 knows that his birthday was a Tuesday, *Martis
alumne dies*; otherwise the Latin day-names are attested poorly and
late. The church Father Filastrius (ab. AD 370), *de Haeresibus* 103, PL
12.1257B, includes a heresy that regards the seven as so named from
the beginning of the world: *nomina dierum: Solis, Lunae, Martis,
Mercurii, Iouis, Veneris, Saturni.* Dio Cassius 37.18.1 (writing after
AD 229) says that the custom of naming days from the seven planets
was begun by the Egyptians, universal (ἐπὶ πάντας ἀνθρώπους) in his
time, but of recent introduction.

(II.145) *Resheph.* See E. Lipiński, "Rᵉšafim: From Gods to Birds of
Prey," pp. 255-259 of A. Lange et al. (eds.), Mythos im Alten Testament
und seiner Umwelt [Hans-Peter Müller FS]; Berlin; de Gruyter, 1999.

(II.158) *Scythian impotence.* Hippocrates (*Airs* 22) goes on to explain that it arises from wearing trousers and constant riding on
horseback.

(II.207) *River-name "Arnus."* Besides the widespread river-name
"Jordan," another seems part of Luvian toponymy. The river *Arnus* of
Etruria (Livy 22.2.2) bears a name seemingly going back to Hurrian
arinni "well, spring" (Friedrich 319). Pausanias 8.8.2 attests a spring
Ἄρνη near Mantinea of Arcadia. It also names cities beside rivers. And
their founders, the legendary king *Arno* of Silius 5.7. Orneai (Ὀρνεαί
Iliad 2.571, Strabo 8.6.24) near Argos was named for its river. The old
name of Lycian Xanthos was probably Hittite *Arinna* (RLA i.150);Ἄρνα
Stephanus 123; in the Xanthos trilingual the Lycian *Arñna* (dat.) = Aramaic בורן; perhaps this is also the name of the river Xanthos. Compare
the river Orontes (Ὀρόντης Strabo 16.2.7) and man's name Ὀρόντας
(Xenophon*Anab.* 2.4.8); and the river Arnonאַרְנוֹן Num 21,13 (Moabite
ארנן KAI 181.26). (But Arauna the Jebusite [II Sam 24,16 Q הָאֲרַוְנָה, I
Chron 21,15 אָרְנָן] fits better Hurrian *iuri* "king," Friedrich 322.)

(II.233) *Symbolism of the U.S. dollar bill*. Add the single eye on the detached top of the pyramid with the single eye of the High God (Ps 33,18; Hesiod *Opera* 267), discussed I.272; II.34-35.

(II.233) *The Greek dining-room*. *Avoth* IV.16 "This age is like a *prozdor* before the age to come" continues "prepare yourself in the *prozdor* so that you may enter the *triclinon*":

התקן עצמך בפרוזדור כדי שתכנס לטרקלין

The dining-room with three couches (or couch with room for three recliners?) is barely recorded before the Hellenistic world; Antiochus IV Epiphanes had a banquet with a thousand τρίκλινα (Polybius 30.26.3). Then the ἀρχιτρίκλινος of Joh 2,9 (Vg *architriclinus*) could rest on Aramaic; so in Latin Petronius 22.6 *tricliniarches*. The synagogue at Stobi, Macedonia (CIJ 694, Williams 34) had a τρίκλεινον, perhaps with some symbolic usages.

(II.235) *Date of the Triumphal Entry*. Placing it at Tabernacles is no novelty; that dating was already seen by T. W. Manson, "The Cleansing of the Temple," Bulletin of the John Rylands Library 33 (1950/1) 271-282, and has been sporadically revived since.

(II.243 note 21) *Footprints of departing deities*. Outside the temple at ʿAin Dara in Syria meter-long bare footprints (evidently of the deity) are carved into limestone slabs entering the temple (Biblical Archaeology Review 26.3 [May/June 2000] 26-27).

(II.280) *Epic narrative*. Sarah Morris ("Homer and the Near East," A New Companion 599-623) summarizes narrative materials more fully treated by West (EFH), omitting common vocabulary and formulas, but with abundant bibliography. She is helpful on Homeric knowledge of various Mediterranean societies.

(II.289). *The tower*. Here is a wandering word of exceptional mobility with unique history. Troy had at least one great tower, πύργος, *Iliad* 6.386 πύργον ... μέγαν Ἰλίου. This is surely a loan from Germanic, Gothic *baurgs*, modern German *Burg*; Latin *burgus* (CIL 8.2494, Africa) "tower for watchmen, *speculatorium*" is probably an independent loan from the same Germanic; see further Hesychius φύρχος: τεῖχος "wall." The related Germanic word *Berg* "mountain," probably by a different route, underlies ἡ Πέργαμος the actual citadel of Troy as well as πέργαμα Aeschylus *PV* 956 "citadel"; see further Πέργαμον of Mysia (Xenophon *Anab*. 7.8.8), Πέργη of Pamphylia (Polybius 5.72.9, Act 13,13). Behind both sets of words lies an Indo-European source, Hittite *parku* "high," Sanskrit *bṛhant*. Rabbinic בורגין "tower, station for travelers" (Mishna *Maas*. III.7 plural בורגנין) with its *b* would seem to be from soldiers' Latin rather than old Greek πύργος; but βοῦργος also is attested late (LSJSup 71b). Hence to Arabic plural *burūj*, Quran 4.78 فى بروج "in towers," elsewhere "signs of the Zodiac." So it is appropriate that the great frieze of Eumenes II at *Pergamum*, the Gigantomachy, was transferred to the great *Burg* of Berlin.

(II.295) *Alchemy.* From Eg. *Km.t* "Egypt" perhaps came χυμεία or χημεία "alchemy" (as Egyptian specialty?), Zosimus Alchimista in Syncellus 24.13 (CSHB 30); the form is affected by χύμα "fluid." In English, the Arabic article *al-* distinguishes exotic *alchemy* from proper *chemistry*.

(II.295) *Ebony and ivory.* Latin rather than Greek has the Egyptian form of the names for both, *ebenus* and *ebur*. They appear together in the Vulgate of Ezek 27,15 (I.197), in Sidonius *Carm.* 27.53 *ebur... ebenusque et aurum*; and in a letter of Augustus to Maecenas (I.89) calling him *ebenum Medulliae, ebur ex Etruria*. An inscription from the vizier Rh-my-rʿ of Thutmose III at Thebes, 15th century BC (K. Sethe, Urkunden der 18. Dynaste, Bd 4, 2nd ed., Berlin: Akademie, 1927 [repr. 1961], no. 332, p. 1149) shows workmen making furniture. The text was transcribed for me by Gary Rendsburg, Gerald Kadish and Saul Levin: ʾirt ʾipdw "making furniture," *m 3bw* "out of ivory," *hbny* "ebony," and various woods.

This is the sole instance I have found where an Egyptian phrase reappears in Greek or Latin. Herodotus' account of embalming (2.86, III.41) has three Egyptian loanwords for "nitre, gum, *sindon*"; but I do not easily find an Egyptian mortuary text with those three, if indeed such exist.

(II.299) *The Akkadian goddess Nanaea.* She appears as Ναναία at II Makk 1,13 in Elymais (I Makk 6,1-4); at Palmyra with Resheph as gods, PAT 2766 ולנני ולרשף אלהיא; at Hatra (KAI 238) גלף נני גדיה "Gadaya [cf the god Gad Isa 65,11] carved [the statue of] Nanaya"; DDD[2] 612-4.

(II.301) *Mediterranean plant-names.* To this list add henna (κύπρος = כֹּפֶר, I.92), aloes (ἀλόη = אֲהָלוֹת, I.96), and perhaps crocus (κρόκος =? כַּרְכֹּם, I.93). Levin (SIE 401) notes the phonetic discrepancies between words for "sixty," ἑξήκοντα and *sexāgintā*; he surmises that the phonology of groups that habitually counted (mostly shepherds?) "diverged somewhat from the prevailing habits of the rest of the community." Two thoughts. First, is the divergence for the "sixty" words in particular the result of linguistic interference from sexagesimal Babylonia? Second, did herbalists or country folk generally also have different phonetic habits from the cities? If so, that reduces the evidence for a substrate "Mediterranean" language or languages naming plants and other local products.

(II.307) *Pumathon and Pygmalion.* For the perplexing relationship between these two, see Lipiński *Dieux et Déesses* 302-306.

(II.313) *Feminine city-names.* Αἴλα Strabo 16.2.30 "Aila" on the gulf is אֵילַת II Reg 14,22, אֵיל'ת I Reg 9,26; hence prob. a Phoenician fem. sing "Palm"—for אֵילִם Ex 15,27—16,1 has 70 palms (תְּמָרִים).

(II.325) *Hebrew consonantal inventory.* The language certainly also had Arabic *ghayn.* "Gomorra," עֲמֹרָה Gen 14,2 is Γομορρας in the LXX; the judge Othniel Jud 1,13 עָתְנִיאֵל is Γοθονιηλ; the queen Athaliah II Reg 11,13 עֲתַלְיָה is Γοθολια.

(II.335) *Rabbis as known in Greek and Latin.* Josephus *AJ* 15.3 speaks of "Pollio the Pharisee and his disciples Samaias," Πολλίων ὁ Φαρισαῖος καὶ Σαμαίας ὁ τούτου μαθητής. These are probably intended as Shemaiah and Abtalion (שמעיה ואבטליון) *Avoth* I.10, who however were colleagues, not master and student. Jerome on Isa. 8,11 (Corp. Christ. 73.116.43-48):

> ...Sammai et Hellel, ex quibus orti sunt Scribae et Pharisaei, quorum suscepit scholam Akibas, quem magistrum Aquilae proselyti autumant et post eum Meir, cui successit Ioannan filius Zachaei, et post eum Eliezer, et per ordinem Telphon, et rursum Ioseph Galilaeus, et usque ad captiuitatem Hierusalem Iosue.

> ...Sammai and Hellel, from whom arose the scribes and Pharisees, whose school Akibas took over, whom men call the teacher of Aquila the proselyte, and after him Meir, to whom there succeeded Ioannan son of Zachaeus, and after him Eliezer, and in order Telphon, and again Ioseph the Galilaean, and until the loss of Jerusalem Iosue.

The sequence seems hopelessly confused. Here anyway we have in Latin guise Hillel and Shammai (הלל ושמאי *Avoth* I.12, ca 25 BC); ʿAqiba (עקיבא III.14, ca 50-134 CE); Aquila perhaps identified with the translator Onqelos; Meir (מאיר IV.10, ca 110-175 CE); Yohanan b. Zakkai (יוחנן בן זכי II.8, ca. 1-80 CE); Eliezer b. Hyrcanus (אליעזר בן הורקנוס II.8, ca 40-117 CE); Tarphon (טרפון II.15, ca 46-117 CE); Jose the Galilaean (Jose the priest of *Avoth* II.8,? יוסי הכהן); and Joshua b. Hananiah (יהושע בן חנניה, II.8, ca 50-135 CE). Three of these *Avoth* II.8 considers disciples of Johanan b. Zakkai: Eliezer, Joshua, and Jose the priest.

Since the Maccabees (II Makk 3,11) Jews were called Ὑρκανός; had a group been exiled among the Ὑρκάνιοι (Herodotus 7.62.2) SE of the Caspian? Old Persian *Varkāna* Darius *Beh.* II.92 (Kent 122) is "Wolf-land," see Sanskrit *vŕka-* "wolf."

(II.337) *The citadel.* See E. Lipiński, "Origins and avatars of *birtu*, 'stronghold'," *Archív Orientální* 67 (1999) 609-617.

(III.33) *Giving and receiving*. Act 20,35 "it is more blessed to give than to receive," μακάριόν ἐστιν μᾶλλον διδόναι ἢ λαμβάνειν, while in the spirit of Jesus, seems to show that Thuc. 2.97.4 had become proverbial: he says of the Thracians that the custom (νόμον) was "to receive rather than to give," λαμβάνειν μᾶλλον ἢ διδόναι. Luke may assume that hearers will remember this and note its opposite with Jesus.

(III.62) *Losing a pearl*. Othello (V.ii) speaks of one who "threw a pearl away / Richer than all his tribe." Who? The Folio has "Like the base Iudean," the Quartos "the base Indian." H. H. Furness (A New Variorum Edition of Shakespeare; VI, Othello; Philadelphia: Lippincott, 1886; 327-331) has numerous comments. Those who read "Judaean" mostly assume him to be Herod the Great in the murder of his wife Mariamme (Josephus *AJ* 15.231). (Furness proposes Judas Iscariot!) But *Judaéan* is unmetrical, and the reference is both strained and inappropriate for Othello. *Indian* seems preferable as a proverb or pseudo-reference; Shakespeare may not clearly distinguish "Indians" of India and North America.

(III.85) *Septimius Wahballath Athenodorus*. The son of Zenobia, "king of kings," is in Palmyrene (PAT 0317) ספטימיוס והבלת אתנדר[וס]. A Greek papyrus (U. Wilcken, Zeitschr. für Numismatik 15 [1887] 330-333) shows him as Σεπτιμίου Οὐαβαλλάθου Ἀθηνοδώρου; Alexandrian coins (PIR[1] iii.215-216) prefix Ἰ(ούλιος) Α(ὐρήλιος) "Julius Aurelius." His Greek name "Gift of Athena" translates his Semitic name "Gift of the goddess Allath," Arabic in view of *wahaba* "he gave"; Herodotus 1.131 knows that Arabs call "the heavenly goddess Alilat," τὴν δὲ Οὐρανίην Ἀλιλάτ. But Aramaic אלהתא (Cowley 14.5), the same word, is just "goddess," not a proper name.

(III.95) *Speculator*. Originally "scout, spy" (Livy 22.33.1); later "executioner," with ten in a legion (one per cohort, ILS 2375, 2382). As in Mark 15,24 they claim the clothing of those executed, *Digest* 38.20.6 *ultro sibi uindicent*. In the semi-fictional *Acta Appiani* (CPJ ii.159a col. II.12 = Musurillo Pagan Martyrs no. 11 p. 65) an Emperor calls for the σπεκουλάτωρ in effect "off with his head!" Sperber Legal Terms 133-5 citing *Midrash Gadol* on Lev 10,2, "Forthwith he ordered the executioner (לספקלטור) and he cut off his head."

(III.103) *Satraps*. Here besides Bigwai and Sanballat are further satraps known in Greek, and on Aramaic coinage. Mazaios satrap of Cilicia 361-333 BC: Μαζαῖος Arrian *Anab.* 3.8.6. His coins (Head 731):

מזדי די על עברנהרא וחלך

"Mazday who is over the Land Beyond the River [Euphrates, i.e. Syria from the viewpoint of Persia] and Cilicia"; hypocoristic from Old Persian *Mazdah* "Wise one." Pharnabazos satrap of Cilicia, 397-374 BC, Φαρνάβαζος Thucydides 8.80.2, פרנבזו חלך Head 730. Tiribazos playing many roles in the time of Xenophon, e.g. *Anab.* 4.4.4 Τιρίβαζος; תריבזו Head 730.

(III.135) *Original habit of the cedar.* I owe to the newsletter of Peter Ian Kuniholm (Aegean Dendrochronology Project) the photo of a 60' cedar (measured by human figures) from the Turkish Taurus. Lateral branching is not at expense of height, and the tree preserves more of the presumed original tall habit.

(III.161) *Babylonian astronomy.* Pliny 2.39 cites the Babylonian astronomer *Cidenas* on the distance of Mercury from the Sun; Strabo 16.1.6 puts Κιδήνα (genit.) among "Chaldaean astronomers." O. Neugebauer (Astronomical Cuneiform Texts; 3 vols.; Princeton: Inst. for Advanced Study; 1955; i.22-23) published two British Museum tablets with *te-ir-si-tu₄ šá ¹Ki-din* "tablet of Kidenas"; he is probably of the 3rd century BC.

(III.166) *American-Danish scholarship.* Here I briefly note my awareness of a school of thought which comes to see much or all of the Hebrew Bible as late enough to have been influenced *by* Herodotus. Sara Mandell and David Noel Freedman (The Relationship between Herodotus' *History* and Primary History; Atlanta: Scholars, 1993; p. ix) presuppose as a fact that Ezra "rearranged the text of Primary History so as to form a Pentateuch and a four book sequel, the Former Prophets" and that Herodotus with his nine books knew at one or more removes of this work. John van Seters (In Search of History: Historiography in the Ancient World and the Origins of Biblical History; New Haven: Yale, 1983; p. 53) originally suggested that Greek historiography was influenced by Eastern; but later ("The Primeval Histories of Greece and Israel Compared," ZAW 100 [1988] 1-22, p. 22) he sees the clue to the problem of form in Genesis as "the Greek national antiquarian tradition, in its early historiography." Niels Peter Lemche (The Canaanites and Their Land: The Tradition of the Canaanites; JSOT Sup. Series 110; Sheffield, 1991; p. 169) writes:

> It may even be argued that instead of considering Old Testament history writing a unique feature of ancient Oriental society...it would be preferable to turn to the Greek historians and consider the older among them to be also the forefathers of the Jewish history writers of the post-exilic period.

—I would just say that an age which produced the romantic Esther and Judith, along with Ezra-Nehemiah in its confused chronology, is not a plausible candidate to have produced the subtle history of David's reign out of fading legend or patriotic speculation.

(III.173) *Hellenistic synagogues.* Louis H. Feldman (Studies in Hellenistic Judaism, Arbeiten zur Geschichte des antiken Judentums and des Urchristentums 30; Leiden: Brill, 1956; p. 578) lists 66 known from inscriptions and papyri.

(III.205) *Abdalonymus king of Sidon.* Phoenician was still current under Alexander. Abdalonymus was made king by Alexander, Justin 11.10.8: a bilingual from Kos (Charis Kantzia & M. Sznycer, Arkhaiologikon Deltion 35 [1980, pub. 1986] A. 1-30)

ʼΑβδαλωνύμου [Σιδ]ῶνος βασιλέως = עבדאלנם מלך צדנם.

(III.212) *The mote and the beam.* Jesus' saying became proverbial and is reflected in the Talmud—secondarily, for its origin in the actor's mask is lost. Jesus says (Matt 7,5, cf Luk 6,42) "'Let me take the speck (κάρφος, Pesh גלא, Pal. Syr. קיסמא) out of your eye,' and lo! there is a log (δοκός, Pesh קריתא, Pal. Syr. שדיתא) in your own eye." Bab. Talm. *Arakh.* 16b (R. Tarphon) "I wonder whether there is any in this generation (בדור הזה) who accepts reproof; for if one says to somebody, 'Take out the speck from between your eyes,' טול קיסם מבין עיניך he answers, 'Take out the log from between *your* eyes," טול קירה מבין עיניך." The Rabbinic for "speck" agrees with the Palestinian Syriac of Jesus' saying, its word for "log" with the Peshitto. As always, Rabbinic usage inverts or parodies Jesus' saying: it claims that the saying became proverbial as a pretext to avoid *legitimate* reproof.

(III.222) *The physician.* Hector Avalos (Illness and Health Care in the Ancient Near East: the Role of the Temple in Greece, Mesopotamia, and Israel; Harvard Semitic Monographs 54; Atlanta: Scholars, 1995) finds two connections between Semites and Greeks. Corresponding to the bronze serpent (Num 21,8) which cured snake-bites (i.e. Nehushtan, נְחֻשְׁתָּן II Reg 18,4), a dozen or so bronze serpents have been found at Palestinian sites (Avalos 339), and also at the Asclepieion of Pergamum (p. 62); military doctors still wear the bronze insignia of two serpents on the caduceus. The *dog* is associated with the Mesopotamian healer-goddess Gula (p. 203) and Asclepius (p. 60). Burkert (Orient. Rev., English ed., 76) illustrates a Babylonian bronze figurine of Gula and her dog, found in the sanctuary of Hera at Samos! Burkert further derives ʼΑσκληπιός and his title Asgelatas (Ασγελατα [genit.] SIG³ 977.8, 27) from Akkadian *azugallatu* "great physician" (p. 78). Numerous Hellenistic statues (LIMC) show bearded Asclepius standing with a serpent entwined on his staff; Pausanias 2.27.2 describes his statue at Epidaurus, seated, with serpent and also dog. The healing power of the serpent is homoeopathic in Numbers but unexplained in

Greece. The symbolism of serpent on staff is an exceptionally clear case of Greek borrowing from the Orient.

(III.224) *Adversary and advocate.* Both in Greece and the near East, the typical court procedure, whether criminal or civil, is one in which the defendant is attacked by the opponent or plaintiff himself acting as prosecution, and calls in advocates for his defence. Rabbinic expresses the situation in Greek loanwords. Mishna *Avoth* IV.11 (R. Eleazer b. Jacob):

קונה לו פרקליט אחד   העושה מצוה אחת

קונה לו קטגור אחד   העושה עברה אחת

"He who does one precept gains for himself one advocate; and he who does one transgression gains for himself one accuser." The Greek originals are παράκλητος (since Demosthenes 19.1), literally "one called in" like Latin *aduocatus*, and κατήγορος, common in Greek law. Semitic treats them both as athematic, whence by back-formation from the Hebrew κατήγωρ Rev 12,10 MS "A." Jesus is made to speak of the advocate or "paraclete" (παράκλητος Joh 14,26) where Pesh פרקלטא, Vg *paracletus*, explained as the Holy Spirit. (But at I Joh 2,1 the παράκλητος becomes Christ.) The "accuser of our brothers (Rev 12,10), the κατήγωρ, is defined at 12,9 as the Dragon, the Devil, Satan. At Act 23,35 κατήγοροί σου the Pesh has קטגריך. Elsewhere the Talmud has a different contrast: Bab. Talm. *Rosh hash.* 26a "A prosecutor cannot serve as defender":

אין קטיגור נעשה סניגור

Behind the latter lies συνήγορος. At Aeschines *ag. Ctesiphon* 199 the *synegoroi* are advocates for the *prosecutor*: he wishes there were a law making it "forbidden for either the accuser to call in advocates," or for the defendant, μὴ ἐξεῖναι μήτε τῷ κατηγόρῳ συνηγόρους παρασχέσθαι...

(III.236) *Latin influence on N.T. Greek.* Here are two more words whose N.T. meaning shows Latin interference.—ἑτοιμάζω "buy." Luk 23,56 (cf 24,1) the women ἡτοίμασαν ἀρώματα καὶ μύρα, Vg *parauerunt aromata et unguenta*. Did they already have spices and unguents and just needed to "get them ready"? More likely they had to go out and "buy" them. Thus Hermas *Sim.* 1.1 of those living in this world, "You are buying (ἑτοιμάζετε) houses and fields." BDF 5 derive this meaning from Latin *comparare* which moved from "prepare" to "purchase": Apuleius *Met.* 9.31 where a gardener buys the hero-ass for 50 coins, *me denique ipsum... hortulanus comparat quinquaginta nummis*. Likewise with the simple *paro* as with Luk 23,56 Vg, Cicero *Att.* 12.19.1 *cogito interdum trans Tiberim hortos aliquos parare* "I sometimes think of buying some gardens across the Tiber."—τόπος "chance, opportunity," frequent in the N.T. and Hellenistic Greek. Act 25,16 πρίν...τόπον τε ἀπολογίας λάβοι "until he get a chance to make a defence," Vg *priusquam...locumque defendendi accipiat*. Dubuisson 209 shows that this unclassical usage is due to Latin *locus*, with many illustrations.

(III.240) *Theodicy*. Quran 18.82 echoes the lost Jewish original of the story of Elijah and his companion R. Joshua b. Levi, while turning this Joshua into Moses (Louis Ginzberg, The Legends of the Jews, IV.223-226 [with the late sources at VI.334-335]; Philadelphia: Jewish Pub. Soc. of America, 5714/1954). Elijah prays that the good man's cow should die from his knowledge that his wife's death had been ordained in heaven; that the miser's wall should be rebuilt lest he find a treasure hidden under it. Probably גנז "treasure" stood in the original.

(III.241) *Greek names in Judaea*. About 150 BC Jonathan the Maccabee sent to Rome Noumenios the son of Antiochos and Antipater son of Jason (I Makk 12,16); Josephus (*AJ* 14.146) adds a third envoy, Alexander son of Dorotheos. Their fathers were born at least 60 years earlier; and already their grandfathers were so Hellenized by 210 BC as to give their sons those pure Greek names.

(III.243) *Barabbas*. He is a doublet or *Doppelgänger* of Jesus (like Thomas, whom the late *Acts of Thomas* make a twin of Jesus). A few MSS at Matt 27,16-17 have Pilatus make the contrast "Jesus Barabbas" with "Jesus called the Christ," Ἰησοῦν [τὸν] Βαραββᾶν ἢ Ἰησοῦν τὸν λεγόμενον Χριστόν. Origen (BAGD 133a), *In Matt. Comm. Ser.* 121 (ed. Klostermann 1933, 255-7) found the same reading. The name suggests "Son of the Father," although Jerome (*Comm. in Matt.* 27,16; Aland Synopsis *ad loc.*) reports that his "Hebrew Gospel" read *filius magistri eorum*, i.e. probably בר רבן*. Barabbas is a bandit, λῃστής (Joh 18,40), and Jesus complains of being treated like one (Matt 26,55 etc.).

(III.244) *The sexton in the synagogue*. One of the rare words that went from the Aramaic or Hebrew of the synagogue into Greek and Latin is חזן, "sexton, caretaker." The sumptuous synagogue of Alexandria with its 71 golden *kathedrae* (Bab. Talm. *Sukkah* 51b, see III.244) had a wooden βῆμα (בימה לעץ) where the חזן הכנסת stood with a *sudarium* (סודרין) in his hand; when the time for Amen came, he waved the napkin, for the building was too large for the reader to be heard. From Apamea of Syria we have the inscription (IGLS 4.1321, Seleucid era 703 = AD 391):

Ἐπὶ Νεμια αζζανα καὶ τοῦ διάκονος ἐψηφώθη ἡ πρόσθεσις [τοῦ] ναοῦ. "Under Nehemiah the *hazan* and deacon the porch of the sanctuary was paved in mosaic." Epiphanius (*Panarion* 30.11, GCS 25.346.16,

PG 41.424B) tells how one Joseph *apostolos* in Cilicia ab. AD 390 deposed a number of ἀρχισυναγώγων καὶ ἱερέων καὶ πρεσβυτέρων καὶ ἀζανιτῶν, whom he describes as διακόνων ἢ ὑπηρετῶν (full translation in Williams 82 with cross-references). Both texts show further an infusion of Church terminology into Diaspora usage.

(III.308) *The dark night of the cosmos*. Latin writers agree in forecasting universal destruction—from Stoic sources? Lucretius 5.91-109, referring to a threefold division of the universe, *maria ac terras caelumque* (I.267; II.56,241), affirms *una dies dabit exitio* "one day shall reduce [all three] to destruction"; perhaps Memmius will shortly see it (*forsitan...in paruo tempore cernes*), but perhaps a Providence (!) will avert it, *quod procul a nobis flectet fortuna gubernans*. Ovid (*Met.* 1.256-8) has Jupiter prefer Deucalion's flood to destruction by fire:

> esse quoque in fatis reminiscitur, adfore tempus
>
> quo mare, quo tellus correptaque regia caeli
>
> ardeat et mundi moles obsessa laboret.

"He remembered that it was in the Fates, that a time would come when sea, land, the palace of the sky would catch fire and burn, and the fabric of the universe should fall under siege." Especially is the destruction seen as a *nightfall*. At Caesar's death (Vergil *Georg.* 1.468) the sun hid itself,

> impiaque aeternam timuerunt saecula noctem

"and impious times feared eternal night." Later the night became proverbial. Pliny the younger (*Ep.* 6.20) at the eruption of Vesuvius says that many "interpreted [the event] as *that* eternal and last night for the world," *aeternamque illam et nouissimam noctem mundo interpretabantur*. Once Rabbinic approaches this usage: R. Simeon b. Yohai (Jer. Talm. *Taanith* 64a26) quotes Isa 21,12 "Morning comes, and also the night" and interprets, "Morning for the righteous, and night for the wicked," בוקר לצדיקים ולילה לרשעים. I suspect that a large-scale comparison of classical usage with Jewish-Christian apocalyptic is possible.

Some final notes:

(I.11) *Continuity of the book*. Herodotus in his introduction says that he writes so that the deeds of Hellenes and Barbarians should not lack fame (*kleos*), just as in Homer; and prefaces this by saying "lest things done by man should become faded through time (*chronos*)." Here Time as the enemy of preservation is explicitly perceived.

(I.227) *Matrilocal succession*. Why does not Hamlet become king on his father's death? Evidently the succession passes through Gertrude, as with Helen, Jocasta, Penelope, Saul's daughter, the Philistine women. Claudius is presumed to know this, and to have had hopes of marrying Gertrude, otherwise he would not have risked killing his brother.

(II.84) *Ceremonial forces of 300 men*. Unaccountably from this list I omitted the Sacred Band of 300 at Thebes (I.240)! It was supposed to consist of pairs of lovers; did the others have some comparable special status?

(II.113) *Imperium maius*. The phrase does occur at Tacitus *Ann.* 2.43, where however *maius* remains a true comparative. Germanicus is given by the Senate "an *imperium* greater than those who had gotten it by lot [in senatorial provinces] or the will of the Princeps [in imperial provinces]." I am unclear how far this corresponds to the deduced extra power of Augustus; or whether the phrase was ever used in Latin, as in English, with *maius* absolute rather than comparative.

(III.75) *Rule from sunrise to sunset*. Azitawadd of Karatepe (KAI 26A.1.4) with less justification claimed such for himself.

(III.115) *High Priesthood as hereditary*. Ananos son of Ananias (latter High Priest AD 47-59) is a totally distinct person from Ananos son of Ananos, where the father, the (honorary) High Priest of the Gospels was in office AD 6-15 (SVMB ii.230); the son, after four brothers himself High Priest in AD 62, in his brief tenure had James brother of Jesus stoned (Josephus *AJ* 20.197).

(III.115) *Gischala*. This home town of the rebel John is Gush-Halab of Galilee (Mishna *Arakh.* IX.6). Jerome (*de Viris Illustr.* 5) says that when it was captured by the Romans, the future apostle Paul and his parents emigrated to Tarsus. This capture seems unattested; Titus occupied the city much later without siege in AD 67 (*BJ* 4.112).

Appendix 4: Mishna texts from the Kaufmann codex

The primary written texts we deal with in these volumes all represent a series of phonemes—a language as it was actually spoken. The only exceptions are symbols for numerals and a few abbreviations: even so a Roman, reading Augustus' *Res Gestae* 22 out loud, would pronounce *XV uirorum* as *quindecim uirorum* and *collega M. Agrippa* (ablative) as *collega Marco Agrippa*. In contrast, cuneiform, hieroglyphic and Linear B have numerous ideograms (and Old Persian a few), which as we have them may look like the things denoted (or once did); it is often uncertain whether those texts were ever read out loud and, if so, whether or how the ideograms were pronounced.

The numerous phonetic comparisons in these volumes demand that the reader should be given such traditional information as has come down to us how the texts were pronounced. Sometimes we supplement the tradition: Hellenistic Greek inscriptions, where we are reasonably sure of the pronunciation, are given Byzantine accents and breathings; not so dialect inscriptions. We optimistically assume that readers can supply Latin long vowels. In West-Semitic texts to some degree we fall short of the tradition. (1) In Biblical Hebrew (except for pausal accents which change the vowels) we omit the accents available in printed editions; as also the supralineal lines on consonants (which normally convey no new phonetic information, and as such are omitted even from printed editions, but available in the facsimile of the Leningrad Codex). (2) In rare references to the Targums we omit the special set of vowels, since few presses have the fonts, and readers who can use the Targums will have the full edition of A. Sperber at hand. (3) Also we omit the vowels and consonantal dots in the Peshitto New Testament, available in the 1950 edition of the British and Foreign Bible Society. (The MSS of the Old Syriac Gospels and of the "Palestinian Syriac" lectionary are unvocalized.)

For some West-Semitic texts the vocalization is attested very sparsely or not at all. Ugaritic (like Arabic) had just the three vowels a, i and u, marked only on the glottal stop ("'aleph"). We have the Greek transcription of a fixed Punic dedication (in less usual order) "To the

Lord Baal-Hamon and to the Mistress Tinith 'face of Baal'" (KAI 102, Constantine, where פען marks the vowel *a*):

לאדן לבעל חמן ורבתן תנת פען בעל

in the form (KAI 175):

λαδουν λυ βαλαμουν ου λυ ρυβαοων θινιθ φανε βαλ

Here ρυβαοων (if that is indeed the text on the stone) is thought an error for ρυβαθουν. Plautus in the *Poenulus* 930-939 transcribes a Punic text with translation, where *Yth alonim ualonuth* represents *deos deasque*; אלנם "gods" is known since Byblos (KAI 10.10) and "goddess" singular in neo-Punic from Sardinia (KAI 172.3) להרבת לאלת "to the Mistress the goddess." Just these two citations suggest a substantial inventory and fluctuation of vowels in Phoenician as in Hebrew.

The MSS of the two Talmuds and Midrash are unvocalized. All the more important then is the fact that a complete vocalized text of the Mishna exists in the Kaufmann MS, now in Budapest, date uncertain; and a partially vocalized one in Parma. These MSS provide the *only* authenticated extension of Biblical vocalization to Rabbinic materials, with numerous surprises. Many modern editions of the Mishna print what contemporary scholars consider a correct vocalization. But the Kaufmann MS is the place we should start from! I have not seen the original publication by Georg Beer (Haag: M. Nijhoff, 1929), but the rare reprint (Veröffentlichungen der Alexander Kohut-Gedächtnis-stiftung; Faksimile-Ausgabe des Mischnacodex Kaufmann A 50...; 2 vols.; Jerusalem, [5]728 [=1967/8]). The backwardness of Rabbinic (as compared with classical) studies is marked by the fact that no modern critical text of the Mishna exists, even for the numerous MSS containing the consonants only, much less for the two with vocalization.

From the beginning Prof. Levin has urged me to provide from the Kaufmann MS the vowels of the Mishnaic texts here quoted. It is of special value for the numerous transcriptions from Greek and Latin in the Mishna. Here at last in Levin's camera-ready copy are the principal texts of the Mishna cited in these volumes. The Kaufmann MS lacks accents but does add the supralinear lines, which we are able to include. Regretfully I omit the individual transcriptions of Greek words also cited in these volumes from the Mishna. Still, readers have in their hands the *first* printed transcription (to the best of my knowledge) of any part of the Kaufmann vocalization.

The Kaufmann MS is not a very careful one. Nearly every page shows omitted words or phrases entered by one or more second hands. There is a plain error at *Avoth* III.14 where two phrases are collapsed into one: "Masorah is a fence for the Torah; tithes are a fence for wealth" becomes "Tithes are a fence for the Torah." The vowels are often surprising: Latin *castra* becomes *qǝṣɔrɔh*; πίναξ becomes *happiynqaś*. The vowels themselves are thought to be by a second hand, and their authority is uncertain. A comparison with the Parma MS would be highly constructive. But we should hesitate to correct the only tradition of the vowels we have from any doctrine of what they ought to have been!

It might have been better to print these texts at their places in this study. However they would have lacked the supralineal lines, here faithfully transcribed by Levin, along with their position often joining two fricatived consonants. They will serve as a tiny forerunner of the much-desired critical edition of the Mishna. Perhaps some reader would like to begin with *Avoth*, the tractate of most general interest. The sequence of tractates and the numbering of paragraphs here follows standard usage, where the Kaufmann MS is eccentric. The facing translations are mostly due to Levin also; only major variations from the standard text printed in Vols. I-III above are here noted.

1   ברכות II.2   יְקַבֵּל עָלָיו מַלְכוּת שָׁמַיִם תְּחִילָה וְאַחַר כָּךְ
יְקַבֵּל עָלָיו עוֹל מִצְווֹת

2   שביעית X.4   זֶה הוּא גּוּפוֹ שֶׁל פְּרוֹזְבּוֹל

3   ביכורים III.3   וְהַשּׁוֹר הוֹלֵךְ עִימָּהֶן וּקְרָנָיו מְצוּפּוֹת זָהָב וַעֲטָרָה
שֶׁלַּזַּיִת בְּרֹאשׁוֹ וְהֶחָלִיל מַכֶּה לִפְנֵיהֶם ...
הַפַּחוֹת וְהַסְּגָנִים וְהַגִּיזְבָּרִים יוֹצְאִין לִקְרָאתָם

4   יומא III.4   פֵּרְסוּ סָדִין שֶׁלַּבּוּץ בֵּינוּ לְבֵין הָעַם

5   יומא III.5   אִם הָיָה כֹהֵן גָּדוֹל זָקֵן אוֹ אַסְתְּנַס

6   סוכה V.4   הַחֲסִידִים וְאַנְשֵׁי הַמַּעֲשֶׂה הָיוּ מְרַקְּדִים לִפְנֵיהֶם בַּאֲבוּקוֹת

7   מגילה I.8   וּתְפִילִים וּמְזוּזוֹת אֵינָן נִכְתָּבוֹת אֶלָּא אַשּׁוּרִית

8   יבמות VIII.4   סְרִיס אָדָם ... סְרִיס חַמָּה

9   כתבות V.5   אַרְבַּע יוֹשֶׁבֶת בְּקַתֶּדְיָרָה   (אַרְבַּע added in margin)

10 שוטה I.7   בַּמִּידָה שֶׁאָדָם מוֹדֵד בָּהּ מוֹדְדִין לוֹ

11 שוטה II.5   אָמֵן שֶׁלֹּא סָטִיתִי ... אָמֵן שֶׁלֹּא נִטְמֵיתִי

12 שוטה VII.6   בַּמִּקְדָּשׁ אוֹמְ' אֶת הַשֵּׁם כִּכְתוּבוֹ וּבַמְּדִינָה בְּכִנּוּיוֹ

13 גיטים V.4   אַפִּיטְרוֹפוֹס שֶׁמִּינָהוּ אֲבִי יְתוֹמִים

14 גיטים VII.5   הֲרֵי זֶה גִיטֵיךְ עַל מְנַת שֶׁתִּתְּנִי לִי אִיסְטְלִיתִי   (' before דֶּ
in גיטך is a later insert)

15 קידושין IV.12   בִּזְמַן שֶׁאִשְׁתּוֹ עִמּוֹ יָשֵׁן עִמָּהֶם בַּפּוּנְדְּקִי
מִפְּנֵי שֶׁאִשְׁתּוֹ מְשַׁמַּרְתּוּ

1 *Berakhoth* II.2: A man will take upon himself the kingdom of heaven at first, and afterwards take upon himself the yoke of the commandments. (I.283; III.212) [Other MSS "*the yoke of* the kingdom of heaven"].

2 *Sheviith* X.4: This is the essence of a *prozbol*. (I.250)

3 *Bikkurim* III.3: And the bull (cf ταῦρος) goes with them, and its horns (Latin *cornu*) overlaid with gold and a wreath of olive-leaves on its head, and the flute plays before them. ...The governors and the prefects and the treasurers (Parthian *gnzbr*) go out to meet them. (I.198; III.104,240,295)

4 *Yoma* III.4: They spread a sheet (σινδών) of fine linen (βύσσος) between [the High Priest] and the people. (I.209)

5 *Yoma* III.5: If a High Priest was old or infirm (ἀσθενής).... (III.247)

6 *Sukkah* V.4: The *Hasidim* (I Makk 7,13 Ἀσιδαῖοι) and men of good works [wonder-workers?] used to dance before them [the assembly] with torches. (II.175) [Other MSS add *burning in their hands.*]

7 *Megillah* I.8 And *tephillim* and *mezuzoth* are written only in Assyrian. (I.324)

8 *Yevamoth* VIII.4: ...a eunuch made by man...a eunuch made by the sun.... (III.223)

9 *Kethuvoth* V.5: [If the wife brought] four [bondwomen,] she sits in a chair (καθέδρα). (III.244)

10 *Sotah* I.7: With the measure by which a man measures, they measure to him. (III.4)

11 *Sotah* II.5: "Amen (ἀμήν) that I have not gone astray... Amen that I have not been defiled." (III.216)

12 *Sotah* VII.6: In the Temple they pronounce the Name according to its writing, but in the country by its substitute. (II.246)

13 *Gittin* V.4: A guardian (ἐπίτροπος) whom the father of orpans appointed [must be sworn]. (III.259)

14 *Gittin* VII.5: "See, this is your bill of divorce on condition you give me back my robe (στολίς)." (III.245)

15 *Qiddushin* IV.12: While [a man's] wife is with him, he goes to sleep with [two other women] at the inn (πανδοχεῖον), because his wife is watching him. (III.242)

16 בבא קמא VII.1   אֵין הַגּוֹנֵב אַחַר הַגַּנָּב מְשַׁלֵּם תַּשְׁלוּמֵי כֶפֶל

17 בבא קמא X.1   אֵין פּוֹרְטִין לֹא מִתֵּבָה הַמּוֹכְסִים וְלֹא מִכִּיס שֶׁלַּגַּנָּבַּיִים

18 בבא מציעא VI.3   שָׂכַר אֶת הַחֲמוֹר וְהִבְרִיקָה אוֹ שֶׁנִּישֵׂאת אַינְגַּרְיָיא

19 בבא בתרא III.1   שְׂדֵה הַבַּעַל

20 סנהדרין I.6   סַנְהֶדְרִין גְּדוֹלָה הָיְתָה שֶׁל שִׁבְעִין וְאֶחָד

21 סנהדרין II.1   וְהוּא מֵסֵב הַסַּפְסֵל

II.3   מֵת לוֹ מֵת אֵינוּ יוֹצֵא מִפֶּתַח פָּלְטוֹרִין שֶׁלּוֹ

II.4   וְכֶסֶף וְזָהָב לֹא יַרְבֶּה לוֹ אֶלָּא כְדֵי שֶׁיִּתֵּן אָפְסַנְיָיא

22 סנהדרין III.2   נֶאֱמָן עָלַי אַבָּא

23 סנהדרין VI.4   כָּל הַנִּיסְקָלִים נִיתְלִים

24 סנהדרין VII.5   הַמְגַדֵּף אֵינוּ חַיָּיב עַד שֶׁיְּפָרֵשׁ אֶת הַשֵּׁם

25 סנהדרין VII.6   וְהַזּוֹרֵק אֶבֶן בַּמַּרְקוּלִיס זוֹ הִיא עֲבוֹדָתוֹ

26 סנהדרין VII.7   וּבַעַל אוֹב זֶה הַפִּיתוֹם וְהַמְדַבֵּר מִשֶּׁחְיוֹ

27 אבות I.1   וַעֲשׂוּ סְיָיג לַתּוֹרָה

28 אבות I.13   נְגַד שְׁמָא אָבַד שְׁמָא

29 אבות II.1   עַיִן רוֹאָה וְאוֹזֶן שׁוֹמַעַת וְכָל מַעֲשֶׂיךָ בְּסֵפֶר נִכְתָּבִים:

30 אבות II.4[5]   אַל תַּאֲמִין בְּעַצְמְךָ עַד יוֹם מוֹתָךְ

16 *Baba Qamma* VII.1: He who steals from a thief does not incur a [double] money penalty (Exod 22,3). (I.323)

17 *Baba Qamma* X.1: They do not take change from the table (θῖβις) of the tax-collectors nor from the wallet of the tax-gatherers. (III.103)

18 *Baba Metziah* VI.3: [If a man] hired an ass and she was blinded or was taken [for] *angareia* (ἀγγαρεῖα) [he is not liable]. (II.52) [This word for "ass" is masculine in Biblical Hebrew.]

19 *Baba Bathra* III.1: a field of Baal [i.e. rain-watered]. (II.75)

20 *Sanhedrin* I.6: A great Sanhedrin (συνέδριον) was made up of seventy-one. (II.107, cf. III.62)

21 *Sanhedrin* II.1: [At a funeral meal the High Priest] sits on a bench (Latin *subsellium*, συψέλιον). II.3: If any of his kin dies he does not go forth from the door of his residence (*praetorium*, πραιτώριον; but with an echo of *palatium*, παλάτιον). II.4: He does not multiply silver or gold for himself (Deut 17,17) except to pay [his soldiers'] wages (*obsonia*, ὀψώνια). (II.110; III.261)

22 *Sanhedrin* III.2: "My father (ἀββᾶ) is acceptable to me." (II.317, III.211)

23 *Sanhedrin* VI.4: All that have been stoned are hanged. (II.246)

24 *Sanhedrin* VII.5: The blasphemer (Lev 24,10) is not culpable until he explicitly pronounces the Name. (II.246)

25 *Sanhedrin* VII.6: And he who throws a stone at the *Marqulis* (*Mercurius*) [is to be stoned], because this is how it is worshipped. (II.134)

26 *Sanhedrin* VII.7: And a necromancer (Lev 20,27, Vg *pythonicus*) is the *pithom* (πύθων), and the one who speaks from his armpits. (II.190)

27 *Avoth* I.1: "And make a fence around the Torah" (I.161)

28 *Avoth* I.13: (Hillel) "A name made great is a name lost" (III.206) [Meaning unclear.]

29 *Avoth* II.1: (Rabbi) "...a seeing eye and a hearing ear, and all your deeds written in a book." (II.316)

30 *Avoth* II.5: (Hillel) "Do not trust yourself until the day of your death." (II.336)

31 אבות II.6[7] עַל דְּאַטִיפְתְּ אַטִיפוּךְ בְּסוֹף מַטִיפַיִיךְ יְטוּפוּן:

32 אבות II.8 אֱלִיעֶזֶר בֶּן הוֹרְקָנוֹס בּוֹר סוּד שֶׁאֵינוּ מְאַבֵּד טִיפָּה

33 אבות II.9 ... עַיִן טוֹבָה ... עַיִן רָעָה

34 אבות II.12 יְהִי מְמוֹן חֲבֵירָךְ חָבִיב עָלֶיךָ כְּשֶׁלָּךְ

35 אבות III.1 דַּע ... לִפְנֵי מִי אַתָּה עָתִיד לִיתֵּן דִּין וְחֶשְׁבּוֹן לִפְנֵי
מֶלֶךְ מַלְכֵי הַמְּלָכִים הַקָּבָּ"ה:

36 אבות III.2 הֱוֵי מִתְפַּלֵּל בִּשְׁלָמָהּ שֶׁלַּמַּלְכוּת שֶׁאִילוּלֵי מוֹרָאָהּ אִישׁ
אֶת רֵעֵהוּ חַיִּים בָּלָעְנוּ:

37 אבות III.2 אֲבָל שְׁנַיִם שֶׁיּוֹשְׁבִים וַעֲסוּקִים בְּדִבְרֵי תוֹרָה שְׁכִינָה בֵּינֵיהֶם

38 אבות III.5 כָּל מְקַבֵּל עָלָיו תּוֹרָה מַעֲבִירִים מִמֶּנּוּ עוֹל מַלְכוּת
וְעוֹל דֶּרֶךְ הָאָרֶץ:

39 אבות III.7 תֶּן לוֹ מִשֶּׁלּוּ שֶׁאַתְּ וְשֶׁלָּךְ שֶׁלּוֹ

40 אבות III.14 מַעֲשָׂרוֹת סְיָיג לַתּוֹרָה

41 אבות III.17 הַכֹּל נָתוּן בַּעֲרָבִים וּמְצוּדָה פְרוּשָׂה אַל כָּל הַחַיִּים
הֶחָנוּת פְּתוּחָה וְהַחֶנְוָנִי מַקִּיף הַפִּינְקַס פְּתוּחָה וְהַיָּד
כּוֹתֶבֶת וְהַגַּבָּאִים מְחַזִּירִים תָּמִיד בְּכָל יוֹם וְנִפְרָעִין
מן in margin הָאָדָם לְדַעְתּוֹ: וְשֶׁלֹּא לְדַעְתּוֹ וְהַדִּין דִּין אֱמֶת הַכֹּל
מְתוּקָּן לִסְעוּדָה:

42 אבות IV.11 הָעוֹשֶׂה מִצְוָה אַחַת קָנָה לוֹ פְרַקְלִיט אֶחָד הָעוֹבֵר
עֲבֵירָה אַחַת קָנָה לוֹ קַטֵיגוֹר אֶחָד

31 *Avoth* II.7: (Hillel) "Because you drowned [somebody], they drowned you; in the end those who have drowned you will drown." (III.29)

32 *Avoth* II.8: (Johanan b. Zakkai) "Eliezer b. Hyrcanus is a plastered cistern that does not lose a drop." (II.324; III.282)

33 *Avoth* II.9: ...a good eye...an evil eye. (III.239)

34 *Avoth* II.12: (R. Jose) "Let the property (μαμωνᾶς) of your associate be as dear to you as your own." (III.210)

35 *Avoth* III.1: (R.ʿAqabya) "Know...before whom you will give account and reckoning: before the King of the kings of kings, the Holy One, blessed is he." (II.297; III.86,236).

36 *Avoth* III.2: (R. Hananiah the Prefect) "Pray for the peace of the Government, since but for fear of it we would have swallowed each other up alive." (III.104,115)

37 *Avoth* III.2: (R. Hananiah b. Tardion) "But [when] two sit together and are occupied in words of Torah, the *Shekhinah* [rests] between them." (I.179)

38 *Avoth* III.5: (R. Nehunya) "Every one who takes upon himself the Torah, they shall take from him the yoke of the government and the yoke of life in the world." (I.283) [Other MSS add *the yoke of* the Torah."]

39 *Avoth* III.7: (R. Eleazar) " Give him out of what is his, for you and what you have are his (I Chron 29,14)." (III.217)

40 *Avoth* III.14: (ʿAqiba) "Tradition [מעשרות of the text is an error for מסורת] is a fence to the Torah." (I.162; III.197)

41 *Avoth* III.17: (ʿAqiba) "All is given on pledge [text בערבים seems an error for בערבון of other MSS, cf ἀρραβών], and the net is spread over all the living; the shop is open and the shopkeeper extends credit; the account-book (πίναξ) is open and the hand writes; [and every one who would borrow, let him come and borrow] (*Kaufmann MS omits this phrase*); and the collectors go around continually every day and exact payment from a man with his knowledge or without his knowledge; and the judgement is a true judgement. All is ready for a banquet." (I.75; III.33,179,249)

42 *Avoth* IV.11: (R. Eliezer) "He who does one commandment has gotten for himself one advocate (παράκλητος); and he who does one transgression has gotten for himself one accuser (κατήγορος)." (III.330)

43 אבות IV.16 הָעוֹלָם הַזֶּה דּוֹמֶה לִפְרוֹזְדּוֹד לִפְנֵי הָעוֹלָם הַבָּא הַתְקֵן עַצְמָךְ לִפְרוֹזְדּוֹר שֶׁתִּיכָּנֵס לִי טְרִיקְלִין

44 אבות IV.22 הַיְּלוּדִים לָמוּת וְהַמֵּתִים לִחְיוֹת

45 אבות IV.22 הוּא הַדַּיָּין הוּא עֵד הוּא בַּעַל דִּין

46 אבות V.5 וְלֹא נִרְאָה זְבוּב בְּבֵית [המטבחים added in margin]

47 ערכין II.3 לֹא הָיָה מַכֶּה בָּאַבּוּב נְחוֹשֶׁת אֶלָּא בָּאַבּוּב שֶׁלְקָנֶה מִפְּנֵי שֶׁקּוֹלוֹ עָרֵב

48 ערכין III.2 בְּפַרְדְּסוֹת סְבַסְטַא

49 ערכין IX.6 קְצָרָה שֶׁהַיְשָׁנָה שֶׁלְצִיפֶּרִין

50 מידות III.4 שֶׁהַבַּרְזֶל נִבְרָא לְקַצֵּר יָמָיו שֶׁלְאָדָם

51 מידות III.8 וְגֶפֶן שֶׁלְזָהָב הָיְתָה עוֹמֶדֶת עַל פִּיתְחוֹ שֶׁלַהֵיכָל וּמוּדְלָה עַל גַּבֵּי כְלוֹנְסוֹת

52 כלים XI.6 וְסוּמְפּוֹנִייָא וְחָלִיל שֶׁלַמַּתֶּכֶת

53 כלים XVI.8 תִּיק הַסַּיִיף וְהַסְכִּין וְהַפִּגְיוֹן

54 ידים III.5 כִּתְבֵי הַקּוֹדֶשׁ מְטַמְּאִין אֶת־הַיָּדַיִם .... אָמַ׳ ר׳ עֲקִיבָה .... שֶׁכָּל הַכְּתוּבִים קוֹדֶשׁ וְשִׁיר הַשִּׁירִים קוֹדֶשׁ קָדָשִׁים

43 *Avoth* IV.16: (R. 'Aqiba) "This age is like a *prozdod* before the age to come; get yourself ready in the *prozdor* so that you may enter the banquet-hall (τρίκλινον)." (II.233; III.204,324) [Other MSS attribute the saying to R. Jacob. Levin suggests that the first transcription *prozdod* of the puzzling Greek word is correct, and points to an original πρόσοδος.]

44 *Avoth* IV.22: (R. Eleazar ha-Kappar) "Those born are such in order to die, and those who die are in order to live." (I.311)

45 *Avoth* IV.22: "[God] is the judge, the witness, the plaintiff." (III.224)

46 *Avoth* V.5: And no fly was seen in the slaughterhouse. (I.219)

47 *Arakhin* II.3: He would not play with a flute (cf Latin *ambubaia* "flute-girl") of bronze but with a flute of reed, because its sound was sweeter. (II.329)

48 *Arakhin* III.2: ...in the gardens (παράδεισοι) of Sebaste. (III.137)

49 *Arakhin* IX.6: ...the old camp (Latin *castra*) of Sepphoris. (III.204) [The initial letter of the second word was cancelled by the punctator.]

50 *Middoth* III.4: "For iron was created to shorten man's days." (I.172; III.282)

51 *Middoth* III.8: And a golden vine stood by the door of the Temple and was trained over the tops of the columns (Latin *columnas*). (I.158)

52 *Kelim* XI.6: And a 'symphony' (συμφωνία) or flute of cast metal. (III.246)

53 *Kelim* XVI.8: The sheath (θήκη) of a sword or knife (συκίνη) or dagger (Latin *pugio*). (III.246)

54 *Yadayim* III.5: The holy Writings render the hands unclean. ... R. 'Aqiba said, "...All the Writings are holy, but the Song of Songs is the Holy of Holies." (III.181)

Cumulative Indexes to Vols. I-III

Do not be intimidated by their size! It is as easy to look something up in a long index as in a short one—with more hope of finding it. Principles best grasped by use dictated what to include and where to put it. In general I followed the rule: When in doubt, include. I have eliminated quite a few errors from the Indexes to Vols. I & II—and doubtless introduced new ones.

Index 1, "Words Discussed," treats the text as an etymological dictionary: in principle exhaustive for Greek and Semitic parallels in common nouns before Alexander; selective otherwise. In 1.1 it was impractical to specify West-Semitic dialects or list variants. For several languages the transcriptions, from diverse sources, are inconsistent. For the type of connection discussed in each case, and my judgement on it, consult the text.

Index 2, "Texts Cited," tells users with some completeness whether a given text is here treated. Note especially Index 2.2.7 "Rabbis cited"; no work known to me systematically collects their sayings by maker.

Index 3, "Objects described," would be an index to the plates in a fully illustrated edition.

Index 4, "Modern scholars," in place of a general bibliography tells users *where* the author is cited. Editors of reference works and collective volumes are normally omitted. Entries for authors very frequently cited are abbreviated but analyzed.

Index 5, "Proper names," contains much information not in the text: distinctions between persons of the same name, their (often conventional) dates. Entries with more than about five citations are analyzed. Some entries, in particular "High God," cry out for separate treatment.

Index 6, "Topics," contains all left over. See in particular the collective entries "Grammar," "Phrases, international," and "Proverbs."

Index 1: Words Discussed

Words with phonetic equivalents in other languages. See the whole Semitic-Greek equivalent phrases at III.197,336.

1.1 West-Semitic

1.1.1 West-Semitic common nouns (with verbs and adjectives)

אבא	father II.317; III.211,341	איקונומוס	steward III.242
אבגינוס	noble III.250	איקוניא	likeness III.90,217,250
אבוב	flute II.329; III.345	אכסניא	stranger III.15,242
אַבְנֵי	stones I.19; III.288	אִכָּר	farmer III.225
אגרא	rooftop III.226	אָלָה	curse I.258; II.277
אגרא	pay III.231	אֵלָה	some tree I.342; II.314
אִגֶּרֶת	letter I.342; II.172	אלהי	"my God" III.208
אָדוֹן	lord I.41,154	אלנם	gods III.336
אָדָם	man II.78	אלף	Aleph I.42
אֲדָמָה	earth II.78	אלפבטרין	alphabet-song I.46
אֲדַרְכֹּנִים	darics/drachmas II.296, 335	אלת	goddess II.314; III.327, 336
אַהֲבָה	love I.21; II.311; III.17,298	אֵם	mother II.317
אֲהָלִים	aloes I.71,92,96; III.325	אָמֵן	Amen III.215-6,339
אוכלוס	crowd III.242	אמפורין	market III.66,263
אונגליון	Gospel II.114	אנגריא	conscription II.52; III.237,306,341
אוסיא	estate III.245	אנטידיקוס	adversary III.224
אופיון	opium III.319	אֲנִיָּה	mourning I.21; II.312; III.29
אורזא	rice III.249	אֲנִיָּה	ship II.50
אָזְנַיִם	ears I.196; II.279,316	אננקי	necessity III.246
אֲחַשְׁדַּרְפְּנִים	satraps I.342; II.297; III.87	אנתופטוס	proconsul III.257
		אסוטותא	profligacy III.245
אֵטוּן	linen I.41	אסטוא	stoa III.245
אטונס	tuna I.133	אסטיר	stater II.299,335; III.251
איזגדא	legate III.90-91,230, 237,307	אסטלא	robe III.143,245,339
		אסטר[טומא]	army III.15
אִיֵּי	coastlands III.54,279	אסטרטיוטא	soldier II.264;III.249,267
איסטניס	weak III.247	אסיא	physician III.222,229-31
איסכולי	school III.267	אספיר	cohort III.113-116,267
איספקלטור	executioner III.95,327	אסר	as (Roman coin) III.253
איפופודין	footstool III.218,244		

אַפַּדְנוֹ	(Persian) palace III.126
אפוטרופוס	steward II.100; III.233, 258,339
אפותיקי	storehouse III.243
אפיריטוס	guard III.251
אפנרתמא	corrector III.85
אפסניא	wages II.110; III.94, 261,341
אֶפְעֶה	serpent I.340; III.302
אפרכין	eparchs II.264
אקלידא	key II.169; III.246
אקנא	enamel I.88; II.326
אקרפיטא	bed III.256
אַרְגְּמָן	purple II.96,335; III.230
ארגנפטא	Persian title III.233
אֲרוֹן	ark, chest II.292
אריסטון	some meal III.249
ארכון	archon III.114,249
ארכיליסטיס	chief bandit III.261
אֶרֶץ	earth I.20; II.68,304; III.278
ארר	to curse I.258
אָתוֹן	she-ass I.19; II.51,301; III.289
אתליטא	athlete III.142
אתפתח	"be opened!" III.208
באין	palm branch II.265
בָּאַשׁ	to stink II.321; III.19
בולא	senate II.100
בּוּץ	byssus I.209; II.293,331; III.230,339
בוקינוס	trumpet II.262
בורנין	towers III.324
בורלא	beryl I.333; II.293; III.143
בּוֹשׁ	be ashamed II.321; III.3,19
בַּחוּן	tower I.131
בֹּחַן	touchstone I.19,303-7; II.280,295; III.287
בימה	bema III.218,331
בִּירָה	citadel II.337
בַּיִת	house I.42; II.93,318
בֵּיתְאֵל	house of God I.337

בְּלוֹ	tax III.102
בלוט	senator II.107; III.249
בָּמָה	altar I.188-190,201-4; II.30,223,299,303; III.295
בָּנָה	to build II.318
בסלקא	basilica II.327
בֹּסֶר	unripe grapes I.155-6; II.302
בעל דבב	enemy III.225
בעל דין	adversary III.224
בָּצְרָה	stronghold II.219
בָּקָר	herd I.194; II.16-18,309; III.295
בָּר	grain II.10,302,320; III.280
בַּרְזֶל	iron II.227; III.25,282
בריתא	alley III.227,320
בְּרָכָה	blessing I.24; II.73,322; III.284
בְּרֵכָה	pool I.24; II.73,322
בָּרָק	lightning I.18,330; II.63,319; III.295
בָּרֶקֶת	emerald I.18,87,122,332; II.293; III.54
ברתא	juniper III.131
בֹּשֶׂם	balsam I.92,96; II.291
גְּדִי	kid II.16
גָּדֵר	wall I.119
גונא	color III.234
גונכא	cloak III.234
גּוֹרָל	pebble, lot II.22
גושכיא	"Ears" (office) III.78
גִּזְבָּר	treasurer III.240
גזירפטי	chiliarch III.93
גט	divorce paper III.232
גַּיְא	valley I.58; II.65,302; III.279
גיורא	sojourner II.291; III.14, 206
גַּלְגַּל	circle II.205-6
גֻּלְגֹּלֶת	skull II.221
גֻּלָּה	bowl I.19,40,109,146-8; II.291; III.288

חֹתָם signet I.75

טַבּוּר navel I.330; II.4
טָבַח to slaughter I.199-201
טוֹגִי toga III.63,234
טוּר mountain I.191; II.8,330
טטרגנון square I.339
טליתא girl III.208
טלרי sandals III.245
טמיון storehouse III.243
טריקלין triclinium III.324,345
טרני rulers I.65
טרפסיטיס banker I.75

יַיִן wine I.41,137-41; II.304,320; III.296,317
יְרָא to fear II.321
יָשְׁפֵּא jasper I.40-2,87-90; II.293

כַּבִּיר great I.36-7; II.311-2
כַּד amphora I.19,40,143-5; II.302,311,320; III.288
כַּרְכֹּד some jewel III.143
כּוֹבַע helmet I.20,65,136, 165-6; II.297
כּוחל mascara II.332
כֵּיפָא rock III.210
כִּירִי "Lord!" II.117
כִּכָּר talent I.307; II.172
כֶּלֶב dog II.17
כְּלוּב bird-cage I.341; II.291
כלונסות columns I.158; III.345
כלירכא chiliarch III.94,113
כלמוס cloak III.267
כַּמּוֹן cummin I.335; II.301
כִּנּוֹר lyre I.155; II.330
כְּנָת colleague III.225
כָּסֵא throne I.276; III.231
כְּסוּת covering II.289
כֶּסֶף silver II.226
כֹּפֶר henna I.92-3,149; III.325
כְּרוּב cherub, griffin I.18,85-7; II.91,303,309; III.291
כָּרוֹזָא herald III.226

כרוספדין fringe III.250
כרז proclaim III.91,226
כרך fortified city III.65
כַּרְכֹּם crocus I.92-3, 150;III.325
כַּרְפַּס cotton I.339; II.293
כִּשְׂבָּה ewe-lamb II.16-17
כְּתֹנֶת tunic I.59,188-90,204-9; II.292,309; III.57,286
כֶּתֶר Persian headdress II.296

לָבִיא lion I.340
לָבָן white II.8, 291
לְבֵנָה brick I.16,76,83-5,332; II.293,314,329; III.287, 304
לְבֹנָה frankincense I.40,70-2, 92-5,150,188-90,210-3; II.291,314
לגיונא legion III.65,116,254, 257
לולרי harness-makers I.179
לוניא string III.62
לֹט some aromatic I.332
לטרם pounds III.264
ליסטיס bandit III.62,103,109, 218,225,237,242-3, 260-1
לַיִשׁ lion I.42,340; II.92,291
למד Lamedh I.44
לַפִּיד torch, lightning I.21; II.67,90,172,298,309; III.287,295
לקנה dish I.343
לקק to lick I.282
לִשְׁכָּה wine-hall I.18,43,141-2; II.96,300,311; III.296

מֶגֶד greatness II.303
מַגָּן *gratis* III.228
מגשיא magus I.342; II.296; III.92
מַדְבְּחָא altar I.202
מוֹדְיָא peck III.239, 253-5
מוכסא tax collector III.102,225, 249

סְפַּסְרָא	sword III.99-100,237
סַרְבָּלֵיהוֹן	trousers II.296
סָרִיס	eunuch III.223,339
סָרְנֵי	rulers I.65; II.213,298; III.87,287
סַתְּתָרִי	staters II.299,335
עֶבְרָה	arrogance I.107,294
עָנַב	have intercourse III.18
עֵנֶל	calf II.16,311
עַד־מְאֹד	very much II.291
עוּנְגְלִיוֹן	Euangelion II.115
עוֹף	birds I.281; II.277,304, 309
עֲזַבְתָּנִי	"you forsook me" III.208
עֲטַלֵּף	bat? II.301
עַיִט	eagle II.216,309
עַיִן	eye I.196; II.279,316
עֶלְיוֹן	most high I.35
עַקְרָב	scorpions I.146,336; II.301
עֹרֵב	raven I.313; II.12,311
עֶרֶב	evening I.57-8; II.303
עֵרָבוֹן	pledge I.18-19,74-8; II.291,309; III.289,343
עֲשֵׂה	"do!" II.319
עַתִּיק	old I.119; II.172,311, 327: III.240
פַּגָּה	fig II.12,302; III.281
פִּגְיוֹן	dagger III.246,345
פִּגָנָא	peganon (herb) III.250
פּוּחַ	to blow II.335, III.20
פּוּךְ	mascara I.241-2; II.302; III.291
פּוֹל	beans I.19; II.13,302, 309; III.281
פּוּלְמוֹס	war III.251
פּוֹמְבִּי	procession II.253
פּוּנְדּוּק	inn III.242,339
פּוֹרְפִירָא	purple III.230,254
פִּידָגוֹג	pedagogue I.330; III.267
פִּילְגּוֹס	deep sea III.250
פִּילֶגֶשׁ	concubine I.19,65-70; II.281,298; III.290

פִּילוֹן	gate II.264; III.243
פִּילְקוֹס	axe II.269
פִּילְקִי	prison III.243,260
פִּיתוֹם	necromancer II.190; III.341
פַּךְ	oil-flask I.342; II.15,299
פְּלַגּוֹת	divisions? II.5
פְּלַטְיָא	public square III.227,263
פְּלַטִין	palace III.237,341
פֶּלֶךְ	spindle II.269
פִּלְפֵּל	pepper I.151,335; II.293
פְּלוּנִיס	cloak III.271
פְּלַתְרִין	praetorium II.110; III.267,341
פִּנָּה	corner I.343
פִּנְקָס	tablet I.75; III.33,249,343
פַּסָּא	pebble, lot III.52
פֶּסַח	Passover II.291; III.208
פְּסִיפָס	mosaic cube III.53
פְּסַנְתֵּרִין	psaltery II.96,329
פְּרַגְלָא	whip III.106,267
פְּרַגְמַטְיָא	wares III.62,264
פַּרְדֵּס	paradise I.21,95-6,140; II.12,296,311; III.123-143, 238,283,307,343
פְּרֵה	"bear fruit!" I.43; II.318
פְּרוֹזְבּוּטִיס	legate III.89-91,237
פְּרוֹזְבּוּל	cancellation I.250; II.25; III.339
פְּרוֹזְדּוֹר	forecourt II.233; III.345
פַּרְזֶל	iron II.227; III.318
פַּרְסָה	parasang? III.233
פַּרְצוּף	face, statue III.247
פְּרַקְלִיט	defender III.330,343
פַּת־בַּג	ration III.236
פִּתְגָּם	response III.236
*פַּתָּה	"open!" II.172
פְּתוֹרָא	table III.227
פֶּתֶךְ	image III.96-7,230
פֶּתֶן	serpent II.190,302,309
*פתניה	Lady(?) II.298
צְדָקָה	justice II.33,299

שכינה	Presence I.20,179-80; II.150,291,311,330; III.142,289,343	תְּהוֹם	Deep II.324; III.123
שֵׁכָר	strong drink I.154	תּוֹר	bull I.18,190-5; II.304, 311-2,330
שֶׁלֶג	snow I.330; II.68,96,319; III.278	תיטרא	theater III.211
שלם	to be safe II.195	תיק	sheath III.246,345
שֶׁמֶשׁ	sun II.7,60,223	תִּירוֹשׁ	new wine I.154-8; II.302
שֶׁנְהַבִּים	ivory I.197,337; II.295	תֻּכִּיִּים	peacocks? I.44
שפטם	suffetes II.102,125	תלגא	snow II.8
שַׂק	sack I.19,41; II.50,302, 311,320; III.289	תָּלָה	hang I.307; II.246,321
שֶׁקֶל	sheqel I.307; II.292,310	תַּלְמִיד	student III.221
שִׁקְמָה	sycomore I.342	תִּמְנַת	precinct? I.21; II.93,96, 221,293,303; III.287
שרגא	lamp III.239	תַּנּוּר	oven III.227
שְׂרֵשׁוּ	flogging III.106	תַּנִּין	great fish I.19,128-33; II.301; III.289
שֵׁשׁ	six II.316,320	תסבר	treasure III.240
ששמן	sesame I.335; II.301	תֹּף	tambourine I.152-5; II.166,172,298; III.291
תְּאוֹמִים	twins I.146; II.328	תְּקַל	shekel I.50,307; II.292
תֵּבָה	ark I.35; II.168,295; III.341	תרונוס	throne III.231,244
תגמא	army III.254	תרנגול	cock III.229
תגרא	merchant III.65-66,224	תרסו	"take heart" II.282; III.208

1.1.2 West-Semitic proper nouns

אבגר	Abgar, dynasts III.322	אלגשיא	Vologaisia III.65
אֲגַג	Agag I.37; III.57	אלהיתס	Alasiotes II.145
אנדר	Gadeira I.119	אליעזר	R. Eleazar III.326
אנרגנת	Agrigentum II.125	אֱלִישָׁה	Elisha (Cyprus?) I.178; II.145
אנריפס	Agrippa III.258	אלכסנדוס	Alexander the Great III.88
אדינת	Odainathos III.85,323	אלפקי	Lepcis II.100
אדנבעל	Hannibal II.102,124,138	אָמוֹן	Amon of Thebes I.329
אהורמזד	Ahuramazda II.40	אמן	Ammon god of Libya I.329
אהורמיז	Ahriman II.40	אנטיגנוס	R. Antigonos III.241
אזתוד	Azitawad, king II.324	אס(י)	Isis I.333
אחיקר	Ahiqar I.309	אָסְנַת	Asenath III.320
אחרם	Ahiram I.334	אספסנא	of Spasinos III.67
אֲחַשְׁוֵרוֹשׁ	Xerxes III.84	אספסיינוס	Vespasian III.251
אֵילָת	Elath III.326	אֱסַר־חַדֹּן	Esarhaddon I.309
אינצים	Isle of Hawks II.109	אסרשמר	Osir-Shamar I.333
איתנם	Isle of Tuna II.301		
אָכִישׁ	Achish of Ekron I.164; II.298		

	III.292,327
חִירָם	Hiram I.334
חָם	Ham (Egypt) II.296
חֹמֶלכֹת	Himilco II.121
חנא	Hanno I.41; II.102,124
חנבעל	Hanobal II.127
חַנָּה	Hannah I.336
חנוב	Chnub, Eg. god I.338; II.337
חנינא	R. Hanina III.115
חסידים	Hasidim III.339
חפי	Apis I.334
חָפְרַע	Hophra, Pharaoh II.286
חֲצַרְמָוֶת	Hadhramaut I.210
חרתת	Aretas II.117
חִתִּי	Hittite I.31; II.86,314
טוּבִיָּה	Tobias I.40
טיטוס	Titus III.251
טרפון	R. Tarphon III.326
טַרְפְּלָיֵא	men of Tripolis I.34
יב	Elephantine I.338
יהושע	R. Joshua III.326
יוחנן	Yohanan II.120
יוחנן בן זכי	R. Yohanan b. Zakkai III.326
יוֹכֶבֶד	Iochebed m. of Moses I.68; II.167
יָוָן	Ionia I.18,42,82; II.307, 315; III.169,292,318
יוסי	R. Jose III.326
יוֹסֵף	Joseph II.336
יַמְלִיךְ	Iamblichus III.322
יָפוֹ	Joppa I.82
יֶפֶת	Japheth I.42,82-3; II.308
יַרְדֵּן	Jordan I.34,42; II.89, 207; III.285
כאפא	Cephas III.210
כבבה	Cybebe I.328
כותר	Kothar I.245,332
כישריא	Caere of Etr. II.210
כלדאי	Chaldaeans III.63
כספי	Caspian? II.227
כָּרִי	Carian I.29-30; II.307
כרך	Caria I.29
כרך	Charax III.65
כַּרְמֶל	Carmel II.9
כְּרֵתִי	Cretan I.32,69,231; II.308
כַּשְׂדָיֵא	Chaldaeans I.97; II.326
כתי	Kition II.307; III.317
לְבָנוֹן	Lebanon I.95,101,210, 245; II.8; III.125
לֹד	Lydda I.30
לוּבִים	Libyans I.29,165; II.308
לוּד	Lydia I.29-30,42,165; II.310
לֵוִי	Levi I.38; II.167,310
לַפִּידוֹת	Lappidoth II.63,174
לפש	Lapethos II.108
מאיר	R. Meir III.326
מבג	Bambyce III.316
מַגֹן	Mago II.129
מִדְיָנִי	Midianite II.310
מְהוּמָן	"Vohu Mana" III.321
מהרבעל	Merbalos I.42,330
מונבז	Monobazus III.82
מזדי	Mazaeus satrap III.327
מישן	Mesene III.64-71
מלקרת	Melqarth I.120; II.109, 183
מֹף	Memphis I.329
מפש	Mopsus I.33
מקדנון	Macedonian III.88
מרקוליס	Mercury cairn II.134; III.341
מֶשֶׁךְ	Meshech I.174-5
מֹשֶׁה	Moses III.243,321
מַתָּן	Mattan I.330; II.307
נְבוֹ	Nebo III.319
נבני	Nabonidus II.286
נִינְוֵה	Nineveh I.329
נירון	Nero III.215
נְכוֹ	Necho Pharaoh II.286

תִּבְרִיָּא	Tiberius, Etr. II.210	תַּמּוּז	Tammuz I.244-5,332
תֹּגַרְמָה	Togarmah III.319	תִּפְסַח	Thapsacus I.329
תַּדְמֹר	Tadmor I.19; III.66	תִּרְחָנָה	Tirhana Calebite II.209
תִּדְעָל	Tid'al king II.86	תִּרִיבַזּ	Tiribazus satrap III.328
תְחוֹת	Thoth Eg. god I.334	תַּרְמִילָא	Lycia I.29; III.172
תַּחְפַּנְחֵס	Daphnae of Egypt I.100, 333; II.49	תַּרְשִׁישׁ	Tarshish I.7,115
תִּירָס	Tiras s. of Japheth II.212	תִּשְׁבִּי	"Tishbite" I.35; II.324

1.2 Greek

1.2.1 Common nouns (and verbs)

ἀββᾶ	father II.317; III.211, 341
ἀβέλιος	sun (Cretan) II.60
ἀγάλοχον	fragrant wood I.96
ἀγάπη	love I.21; II.311; III.17,298
ἀγγαρεία	conscription II.52; III.102,237,341
ἄγγαρος	Persian messenger I.342; II.172; III.102,238
ἄγγελος	messenger I.342; III.102
ἄγε	"lead!" II.319
ἀγορανόμος	market supervisor III.228
ἀγρός	field II.140,311
ἀδελφεός	brother I.225
ἀζανίτης	synagogue sexton III.331
ἀζαραπατεῖς	chiliarchs III.93
ἀθλητής	athlete III.142
αἶα	land III.54,279
αἰετός	eagle II.216,271,309, 334
ἀλεκτρύων	cock III.229
ἀλόη	aloes I.71,96; III.325
ἄλφα	alpha I.42-3
ἀλφαβητάριον	alphabet-song I.46
ἀμήν	amen III.215-6,339
ἀμνός	lamb II.16,311
ἄμπελος	grapevine I.136-7,156; II.96,302
ἀμύμων	flawless I.232

ἀνάγκη	necessity III.246
(ϝ)άναξ	king I.200; II.96,299, 309
ἀνεμώνη	anemone I.246
ἀνεψιός	nephew II.212
ἀνθύπατος	proconsul III.257
ἀνίη	grief I.21; II.312; III.9,29
ἀντίδικος	adversary III.224
ἀξίνη	axe II.269
ἄπιος	pear II.300
ἀποθήκη	storehouse III.243
ἀρά	curse I.258; II.277
ἀργαπέτης	Persian title III.233
ἀργεμώνη	purple flower II.335; III.230
ἄργυρος	silver I.301; II.226
ἄριστον	some meal III.249
ἅρπη	sickle I.21,78-83; II.303,312;III.296
ἀρραβών	pledge I.18-19,74-8; II.291,309,326; III.289, 343
ἀρσενικόν	arsenic II.296
ἀρχιληστής	chief bandit III.261
ἄρχων	archon III.249
ἀσθενής	weak, sickly III.247,339
ἀσσάριον	as (Roman coin) III.253
ἀστάνδης	Persian courier III.89, 307
ἀσφόδελος	asphodel III.46
ἀσωτία	profligacy III.245

ἀττέλεβος | locust II.302

βάϊα | palm branches II.256, 265
βαίτυλος | betyl I.337
βάλσαμον | balsam I.96; II.289,291
βάρβαρος | barbarian III.171
βᾶρις | citadel II.337; III.326
βάσανος | touchstone I.19,305-7; II.280,295,309,321; III.287
βασιλική | basilica II.327
βάτραχος | frog I.336; II.60,301
βῆμα | bema III.218
βήρυλλος | beryl I.333; II.293; III.291
βῆτα | beta I.42
βιός | bow II.135
βόρατον | juniper III.131
βότρυς | grapes I.155-6; II.302
βουκάνη | horn II.262
βουλευτής | senator II.107; III.249
βουλή | senate II.100
βοῦργος | tower III.324
βράθυ | juniper III.131
βροχή | rain I.24; II.73,322; III.284
βύβλος | papyrus I.329
βύρσα | hide II.219
βύσσος | byssus I.209; II.293, 331; III.41,230,339
βωμός | altar I.188-90,201-4; II.30,223,299,303; III.295

γάζα | treasure I.40; II.296; III.240
γαῖα | earth I.58; II.65,302; III.279
γαυλός | wine-vessel I.19, 40, 109,146-8; II.50,291
γαῦλος | Phoen. freighter I.19, 146-8,179; II.291; III.288
γέεννα | gehenna III.210
γένος | type, kind III.236
γέφυρα | bridge I.35

γῆ | earth I.58
γιώρας | sojourner II.291; III.14
γλύφειν | to carve II.299; III.173
γλωσσόκομον | purse III.62
-γόνε | begetting II.54,319
-γούνη | -color III.234
γρύψ | griffin I.18,85-7; II.91,303,309; III.291
γυμνασίαρχος | gymnasiarch I.121; III.263
γυνή | woman I.226; I.299, 311; III.290
γύψ | vulture I.85,281; II.277,304,309

δάκτυλος | date-palm I.19; II.291, 327
δανάκη | Persian coin III.233
δανειστής | creditor III.250
δαρεικός | daric II.296,335
δαστικίρτης | village III.233
δέλτα | Delta I.44
δέλτος | tablet I.18,40,46,52-3; II.45,291,311; III.303
δέμειν | to build II.318
δῆμος | people II.100
δηνάριον | denarius III.253-6
διάβολος | devil I.13
διάδημα | diadem III.82,97
διαθήκη | covenant, will III.248
διάταγμα | decree III.218
δίδυμοι | twins II.328
δίκη | justice II.299
δῖος | divine III.229
δόγμα | decree II.100
δουκηνάριος | ducenarius III.233
δράκων | dragon I.13
δραχμή | drachma I.301; II.296, 335; III.232,265
δωρεά | gift III.89
δῶρον | gift III.250

ἔβενος | ebony I.42,197,338; II.295
ἕδος | seat II.92; III.129
εἰκών | image III.96,217,250
ἐλαί(ϝ)α | olive III.281

ἐλάτη	fir tree I.342; II.314	θύννος	tuna I.19,128-133; II.301; III.289
ἐλωι	"my God" III.208		
ἐμπόριον	market III.66,224	θύρσος	thyrsus I.154-8; II.265, 302
ἕξ	six II.316,320		
ἐξατράπης	satrap III.87		
ἑξήκοντα	sixty III.325	ἴασπις	jasper I.40,42,87-90, 301; II.293; III.291
ἐπανορθωτής	corrector III.86		
ἔπαρχος	eparch II.264	ἰδιώτης	private person III.142
ἐπικάρ	headlong I.195	ἰμπεράτωρ	commander (Latin) II.260
ἐπίτροπος	steward II.100; III.233, 258-260,339		
		ἰξός	mistletoe II.300
ἑπτά	seven II.316,320	(ϝ)ίον	violet II.300
ἔραζε	earthward I.20; II.68, 304; III.278	ἰός	arrow, poison (two words) II.141-2
ἐρέβινθος	vetch II.300	ἵππος	horse II.6-7,304
ἔρεβος	darkness I.57; II.303	ἶρις	rainbow II.147
ἐρών	ark II.292		
εὐαγγέλιον	good news II.114	κάγκαμον	some spice II.326
εὐγενής	noble III.250	κάδος	jar I.19,40,143-5; II.173,302,311,320; III.288
εὐναί	anchor-stones I.19; III.288		
		καθέδρα	chair III.243,339
ἔφφαθα	"be opened!" III.208	καιρός	right time III.236
ἔχιδνα	serpent III.250	κάλαμος	reed, pen I.54,330; III.250
ἔχις	serpent II.302		
		κάμηλος	camel I.210,338; II.291, 311; III.320
ζαφθανι	"you have forsaken me" III.208		
		κάμιλος	cable I.338
ζεῦγος	yoke, couple III.247	κάννα	reed I.94; II.301
ζημία	fine III.250	κάνναβις	cannabis I.331
ζιζάνια	tares III.250	καπίθη	Persian measure III.233
ζίκαια	just things II.299	κάρδαμον	cardamum I.335
ζμύρνη	myrrh I.95-6	κάρπασος	cotton I.339; II.293
ζώνη	belt III.245	κασᾶν	blanket II.289
ἡγεμών	governor III.258,266	κασία	cassia I.18,42,70-72; II.293,311; III.41
ἥλιος	sun II.7,60,223		
ἡλί	"my God" III.208	κάστρα	camp (Latin) III.204
		κατήγορος	accuser III.330,343
θαρσεῖτε	"take heart!" II.282; III.208	καυνάκης	cloak III.234
		κέδρος	cedar I.329; II.300
θέατρον	theater III.211	κεντυρίων	centurion III.93-95
θήκη	sheath III.246,345	κέρας	horn I.195-9; II.316
θησαυρός	treasure II.226; III.240	κεφαλή	head II.336
θῖβις	chest, ark I.35; II.168, 295; III.341	κῆβος	monkey I.44; II.295
		κῆνσος	census III.256
θρίαμβος	triumph II.252,300	κήρ	(angel of) death III.61
θρόνος	throne III.231,244	κῆρυξ	herald III.91,226

μάκελλον	meat-market III.263, 271	νέτωπον	almond-oil I.331
μάλθα	mortar I.41	νῆρος	six hundred II.335
μάμμη	mother II.317	νίτρον	nitre I.241; II.96,295; III.290
μαμωνᾶ	wealth III.210,343	νίφα	snow I.330; II.68,319
μανιάκης	necklace III.234	νόμος	law III.248
μάννα	"manna," granule I.210	νύμφη	girl III.248
μάραγδος	emerald I.332; II.293		
μαραναθα	"Lord, come!" II.117	ξαδράπης	satrap III.87
μαργαρίτης	pearl II.293; III.62-4, 237,307	ξένος	stranger III.15,206,242
		ξέστης	sextarius III.253
μάρρον	hoe I.145		
μάχαιρα	sword I.342; III.237	ὀθόνη	fine linen I.41
μέγαρον	cave I.244; II.289,303	οἰκονόμος	steward III.242
μέγεθος	stature II.303	(ϝ)οῖκος	house II.93,318
μέθυ ἡδύ	sweet mead I.139	(ϝ)οῖνος	wine I.41,137-41;
μέλαν	ink I.54,330		II.304,309,320-1;
μέν	particle III.155		III.296
μέσκος	skin, hide III.245	ὄϊς	sheep III.281
μίλιον	mile II.53; III.255	ὀϊστοί	arrows I.20; II.70,140-
μίνθη	mint II.300		1,302,311; III.289
μίσγειν	to mix I.142-3; II.299, 321	ὀνία	grief (dial.) III.29
		ὄνος	ass II.50,301
μνᾶ	mina I.43, 307-8; II.292; III.287	ὄπιον	opium III.319
		ὀπυίειν	to marry II.214,278
μόδιος	peck-measure III.239, 255	ὁράω	to see II.321
		ὄροβος	vetch II.300
μόλυβδος	lead (metal) II.300	ὄρος	mountain I.342; II.65,
μόσχος	musk III.319		302; III.279
μύρον	ointment I.96	ὄρυζα	rice III.249
μύρρα	myrrh I.40,70-2,95-6, 210-3; II.291	οὐάτοιν	two ears I.196; II.279, 316
μῶμος	flaw I.194,232; II.302; III.28,290	οὐρανός	heaven II.72
		οὖρος	aurochs I.192-3
μωρός	fool III.216,250	οὐσία	estate III.245
		ὄφις	serpent I.340; II.302
νάβλας	lute I.155; II.291	ὄχλος	crowd III.117,242
να(ϝ)ός	temple II.43,223,303; III.225	ὀψώνιον	wages II.110; III.94, 261,341
νάπη	glade I.342; II.72,302; III.279	παιδαγωγός	pedagogue I.54,330; III.267,309
νάρδος	nard I.92,148-151; II.293	παλάτιον	palace III.237,341
νάρναξ	chest II.96	παλλακίς	concubine I.19,65-70,
ναῦς	ship II.50		231-2; II.281,298;
νάφθα	naphtha I.279; II.277		III.290
νέκταρ	nectar I.91; II.326	πανδοχεῖον	inn III.242,256,339

σκηνή	tent I.20,179-180; II.150,291,311; III.289, 309	ταλιθά	girl III.208
		ταμεῖον	treasury III.243
σκορπίος	scorpion I.146,336; II.301	ταῦρος	bull I.18,146,152,188-195; II.304,309,311, 321,330; III.295,339
σμάραγδος	emerald I.87,122,332; II.293; III.291	ταῶς	peacock I.44
σμύρνη	myrrh I.95-6; III.41	τεῖχος	wall II.296
σουδάριον	handkerchief III.253	τελώνιον	customs-house III.95, 103,225
σοῦσον	lily I.331; II.296; III.46	τέμενος	precinct I.21; II.93,96, 222-4,293,303; III.287
σοφία	wisdom II.299		
σπάθη	broadsword II.271	τέρμινθος	terebinth II.334
σπεῖρα	cohort III.95,113,266	τέρμων	boundary II.24
σπεκουλάτωρ	executioner III.95,327	τετράγωνος	square I.339
σπόγγος	sponge II.300	τευθίς	cuttlefish II.336
σπορδακᾶς	frog (modern Gk) I.336	τλῆ	to endure I.307; II.321
σπυρίς	basket III.250	τόγα	toga III.64,234
στατήρ	stater II.299,335; III.173,251	τόξον	bow II.141
		τράπεζα	table III.227
στίμμι	mascara I.241-2	τραπεζίτης	banker I.75; III.227
στοά	stoa III.245	τρίβουνος	tribune III.93
στολή	robe III.143,245,339	τρίκλινον	triclinium III.324,345
στράτευμα	army III.15	τῦκον	fig (dial.) II.12,302; III.281
στρατιώτης	soldier II.264; III.249, 266		
σύγκλητος	senate II.85	τύμπανον	tambourine I.152-5; II.166,172,289,298; III.291
συκάμινος	sycomore I.342		
συκίνη	knife III.246,345		
συκόμορος	sycomore I.342	τύραννος	tyrant I.65; II.213,298; III.287
σῦκον	fig II.12,302; III.281		
συμφωνία	"symphony" II.329; III.246,345	ὑάκινθος	hyacinth II.300
		ὑάκινθος	jacinth III.62
συμψέλιον	bench II.110; III.341	ὕβρις	arrogance I.107,294
συνέδριον	council II.107; III.114, 248,339	ὕδωρ	water I.22,330; II.70, 319; III.284
συνήγορος	defender III.67,330	ὑπατικός	consul II.117
συνοδία	caravan III.66-67,229	ὑπηρέτης	assistant III.95,113,251
συντηρέω	to oversee III.242	ὑποθήκη	contract III.243
σφάζειν	to slaughter I.188-90, 199-201; II.291,321; III.295	ὑποπόδιον	footstool III.218.244
		φαινόλης	cloak III.64,270
σφενδόνη	sling II.300	φακός	bean I.342; II.15,298
σχολή	leisure, school III.267, 309	φάλαγξ	phalanx II.5
		φέρε	"bear!" I.43; II.317-8
σῶσσος	sixty II.335	φητιάλιος	fetial priest II.241
		φλόξ	lightning I.330; II.64, 319; III.295
τάγμα	army III.254		

1.2.2   Greek proper nouns

Ἀσιδαῖοι Hasidim III.339
Ἀσκάλων Ascalon II.307
Ἀσκληπιός Asclepius III.329
Ἀσμοδαῖος Asmodaeus demon III.230
Ἀσπαθίνης Aspathines II.6; III.99
Ἄσπενδος Aspendos II.324
Ἀσσυρία Assyria I.42-3; II.313
Ἀσσωρός Assoros, Bab. god I.17
Ἀστάρτη Astarte I.213; II.314, 332
Ἀτάβυρις Atabyris, mt of Rhodes I.330; II.4
Ἀτάργατις Atargatis goddess III.316
Αὐμύργιοι Aumurgioi, *haoma*-people III.319
Ἄφακα Aphaka spring I.245; II.333
Ἀφροδίτη Aphrodite I.213
Ἀχαιοί Achaeans I.32; II.30,85, 141,282,310-5; III.292

Βαβυλών Babylon I.83,334
Βαιτοκαίκη Baitokaike I.331
Βαλμαρκώδης Balmarcodes god II.329
Βαμβύκη Bambyce (Hierapolis) III.316
Βαραββᾶς Barabbas III.331
Βαργιώρας Bargioras III.15
Βαρθολομαῖος Bartholomew III.207
Βάρκας Barcas (Hamilcar) II.63, 123,174
Βαρναβᾶς Barnabas III.319
Βεελζεβούλ Beelzebul I.219-221; III.210
Βεελσάμην Beelsamen II.88
Βελλεροφῶν Bellerophon I.49
Βῆλος Bel god I.195; II.341
Βησᾶς Bes, Eg. god III.320
Βοανηργές Boanerges II.63; III.210
Βόστρα Bostra II.219
Βότρυς Botrys of Phoen. I.156
Βούβαστις Boubastis of Egypt III.320
Βοῦττα Buddha II.13
Βράθυ Brathy, mt III.131

Βραύρων Brauron II.181
Βύβλος Byblos I.93, 329; II.290
Βύρσα Bursa of Carthage II.219

Γάββαθα Gabbatha III.170
Γάδειρα Gades I.119,129
Γάζα Gaza I.40
Γάμαλιήλ Gamaliel II.176
Γαμφάνη Gamphane of Cyprus I.335
Γεργῖθες Gergithians I.31; II.193-8,308; III.296
Γέσκων Gisgo II.126,307
Γεφυραῖοι Gephyraeans I.35
Γίλγαμος Gilgamesh I.16; II.324
Γολγοθά Golgotha II.221; III.170
Γολιαθος Goliath as PN III.318
Γύγης Gyges I.175; III.318
Γωβρύης Gobryas III.99

Δαμασκός Damascus II.334
Δανάη Danaë I.227
Δαναοί Danaans I.227; II.208
Δάφναι Daphnae of Egypt I.333; II.49
Δάχης? Daches, Bab. god I.17
Δειδώ Dido I.336; II.312,337
Δερκετώ Derketo goddess III.315
Δίδυμον Didymon, mt II.328
Δοῦρα Doura of Pal. I.33; II.308; III.315
Δουσάρης Dusares, Arab god I.333; III.94
Δωδώνη Dodona I.7
Δῶρος Dorian II.308,315; III.168

Ἔδεσσα Edessa III.101
Εἴρωμος Hiram I.334
Ἐλιεύς Elieus (Zeus) I.35
Ἐρεμβοί Aramaeans? I.18,80; II.310; III.292
Ερεσχιγαλ Ereschigal, Bab. goddess I.328
Ἔσμουνος Eshmun, Phoen. god I.35

Λιβύη Libya I.29,165; II.308
Λύγδαμις Lygdamis III.318
Λύδδα Lydda I.30
Λυδός Lydian I.29,42,165; II.308-312

Μάγων Mago II.126
Μαζαῖος Mazaeus satrap III.327
Μαρνᾶς Marnas god of Gaza II.71,117
Ματιηνοί Matieni II.310
Ματτήν Matten I.330; II.307
Μελικέρτης Melicertes II.184
Μέλκαρθος Melqarth I.120; II.183
Μέμφις Memphis I.329
Μέρβαλος Merbalos I.42,330
Μεσήνη Mesene III.65-71
Μεσσίας Messiah I.60
Μέσχοι Moschi I.174-5
Μηριόνης Meriones II.86
Μίδης Midas I.175; II.330
Μίλητος Miletus II.85
Μίναια Minaia of Arabia I.210
Μιριδάτης Mithradates III.69
Μισώρ Misor, Phoen. god II.33
Μονόβαζος Monobazus III.82
Μόξος Mopsus I.33
Μόσχοι Moschi I.174-5
Μότυλος Muwattalis? II.85
Μοῦσα Muse II.39
Μόψος Mopsus I.34; II.196
Μόψου Ἑστία "Hearth of Mopsus" I.33
Μυρτίλος Myrtilos (Homeric) II.86
Μυτιλήνη Mytilene II.85
Μωΰμίν Bab. god? I.17
Μωυσής Moses III.243,321

Ναζαρέθ Nazareth III.264
Ναναία Nanaea goddess III.325
Νεκῶς Necho Pharaoh II.286
Νέφθυς Nephthys Eg. god II.8
Νηΐθ Neith Eg. goddess III.169,320
Νιβαρός Nibaros, mt II.8
Νίνος Nineveh I.329; III.101

Νιφάτης Niphates, mt II.8

Ξίσουθρος Xisouthros (Gilgamesh) I.16

Ὀβόδας Obodas of Nabataea I.43
Ὀδαίναθος Odaenathus of Palmyra III.85,323
Οἰνεύς Oineus I.137
Οἰνωτρίη Oenotria I.138
Ὀλογαισία Vologaisia III.66
Ὀλόγασος Vologasus III.69
Ὀρόντης Orontes river III.323
Ὀρνεαί Orneai III.323
Ὄσιρις Osiris I.333
Οὐαβαλλάθος Vaballathus III.327
Οὐαρδάνης Vardanes I.339
Οὐορώδης Vorodes I.339

Πάκορος Pacorus III.69
Παλαιστίνη Palestine I.170-1; II.310
Πάλμυρα Palmyra I.19
Πάνδαρος Pandarus I.33; II.138
Παπίας Papias II.317
Πάτουμος Patoumos I.329
Πάχυνος Pachynos of Sicily I.131
Πελασγός Pelasgian I.65,170-1, 226; II.308-315; III.290-2
Πελαστικέ title of Zeus I.170-1
Πέργαμον Pergamum III.324
Πέργη Perge III.324
Πέρσης Persian I.40,165
Πήγασος Pegasus II.6
Πιοδασσης Priyadarsi (Ašoka) II.13
Πολλίων R. Pollio III.326
Πότνια Lady II.298,314
Πρίαμος Priam II.85-6
Πυγμαλίων Pygmalion II.307; III.326
Πυθώ Pytho (Delphi) II.190
Πύθων Python, serpent II.190, 302,309
Πυμάθων Pumathon of Cyprus II.307; III.326

1.3 Latin

Note further lists of Latin words at III.262, 263.

admodum	extremely II.291	castra	camp III.204,337,345
ager	field II.311	cathedra	chair III.244
agnus	lamb II.16,311	census	worth III.256
agoranomus	market-supervisor III.228	centurio	officer of a hundred III.92
albus	white II.8	cerebrum	brain I.195
aloe	aloes I.71,96	ceruus	stag I.195
amarus	bitter I.314; II.291	charta	paper I.330
ambubaia	woman flautist II.329	chlamys	cloak III.266
angaria	conscription II.52; III.102,237	cinnamomum	cinnamon I.71,94
anguis	serpent II.302	circulus	circle II.206
antiquus	old I.119; II.172,311; III.240,267	circus	arena III.211,267
		citrus	some tree II.300
apotheca	storehouse III.243	clauis	key III.143,246
architriclinus	banquet-chief III.324	clepo	to steal II.19,321-3
archon	Greek magistrate III.250	cohors	cohort of 600 III.93, 116,266
arcus	bow II.141		
argentum	silver I.301; II.226	colaphus	blow III.272
arra(bo)	pledge I.74-8	columna	column I.158; III.345
as	small coin III.254	cophinus	basket III.250
ascia	axe II.269	cornu	horn I.195-9; III.295, 339
asinus	ass I.19; II.51,301; III.289	coruus	raven I.57,313; II.12, 311
asotia	profligacy III.245	costus	Indian spice I.149-150
athleta	athlete III.142,261	crocus	crocus scent, dye I.71, 93; III.52
aurum	gold II.226		
		cumba	skiff I.167
baetylus	betyl I.337	cupressus	cypress I.329; II.302; III.283
beryllus	beryl I.89,333; III.291		
brasilium	some wood II.228	custodia	guard III.117
bucina	cow's horn II.262	cymbium	flat bowl I.167
burgus	tower III.324	cyminum	cummin I.335
buxus	box-tree II.300		
		danista	creditor III.250
cadus	wine-cask I.19,143-5; II.302,311,320; III.288	decem	ten II.327
		denarius	coin III.255
calamus	reed, pen I.330-1	deus	god III.229
camelus	camel I.338; II.311	diabolus	devil I.13
camisia	shirt I.322	diadema	diadem III.97
canna	reed I.94	digitus	finger II.327
carpasus	cotton, sail I.339	dolium	bucket I.145; II.72,176, 291
casia	cassia I.70-2,89		

nardus	nard I.148-151	quadrans	small coin III.252-4
nepos	nephew II.212		
nix	snow II.68,319	rosa	rose I.339
nomen	name II.96	rumpia	broadsword I.174
obsonium	wages II.110; III.261, 341	sabbata	sabbath II.292
		saccus	sack I.19; II.50,302, 311,320; III.289
oeconomia	arrangement III.242		
oliua	olive III.281	sagitta	arrow I.20; II.70,140, 151-2,302,311; III.289
onus	burden III.29		
opium	opium III.319	sandalium	sandal III.245
		sapphirus	sapphire I.87
paedagogus	tutor I.330-1; III.268	satrapa	satrap III.87,126
paelex	concubine I.19,65-70; II.298	schola	school III.268
		semicinctium	apron III.253
paenula	cloak III.270	septem	seven II.316,320
palatium	palace II.110; III.237, 341	sex	six II.316,320
		sexaginta	sixty III.325
pampinus	grapevine I.136-7; II.96,302	sextarius	measure III.253
		signum	ensign III.257
pande	"open!" II.172	simula	flour I.343
pappa	father II.317	smaragdus	emerald I.89
paradisus	paradise III.126-151	smyrna	myrrh I.95-6
pauo	peacock I.44	sol	sun II.60
pecus	herd I.194; II.18,309, 321,323; III.295	speculator	executioner III.95
		stigma	brand, tattoo III.104-6
pelagus	deep sea III.250	stola	robe III.245
phylaca	prison III.243	subsellium	bench II.110; III.341
pirus	pear-tree II.300	sudarium	handkerchief III.253, 331
platea	public square III.227, 263		
		sufes	suffete II.102
plenus	full II.143,320	symphonia	music III.246
plumbum	lead (metal) II.300	synhodos	assembly III.67
pompa	procession II.253		
praepositus	officer III.258	talaria	winged sandals III.245
praetorium	praetorium II.110; III.266,341	tarpezita	banker I.75
		taurus	bull I.146,152,190-5; II.304,311
primus	first II.86		
pudet	be ashamed II.321; III.20	taxus	yew II.141
		teloneum	customs house III.103
pugio	dagger III.246,345	templum	precinct I.21; II.96, 223,293; III.287
puls	beans I.19; II.15,302, 309; III.281		
		tenebrae	shadows II.58
purpura	purple III.230,267	terminus	marker II.24
putet	to stink II.321; III.20	theatrum	theater III.211
python	necromancer II.190; III.341	theca	scabbard III.246
		thesaurus	treasure III.240,267

Mago	Punic PN II.129
Marnas	god of Gaza II.71,117
Meir	rabbi III.326
Mercurius	Mercury II.109,134
Neptunus	Neptune II.9
Odenathus	Odainath III.86
Oenotri	Oenotrians I.138
Pacorus	Sasanid III.71
Parthi	Parthians III.77
Populonia	Etruscan city II.199
Roma	Rome I.24; II.103,209, 245; III.279
Sabaei	Sabaeans I.338
Sammai	rabbi III.326
Sampsigeramus	dynasts III.322
Sarra	Tyre I.329
Sohaemus	dynasts III.322
Spaosines	Iranian PN III.68
Tanais	Don r. II.207
Tarchon	Etruscan II.208
Tarquinii	Etr. city II.208
Telphon	rabbi III.326
Thamuz	Syrian Adonis I.244
Utica	city of Africa I.119, II.327
Vardanes	Persian PN I.339
Vascones	Basques I.177
Winlanda	"Vineland" I.138
Zachaeus	rabbi III.326

1.4 Other Languages

Akkadian

argamannu	purple II.335; III.230
ašpû	jasper I.88
asû	physician III.222
atūnu	furnace III.227
azugullatu	great physician III.329
bamâtu	open country? I.201
barbaru	wolf III.171
barraqtu	emerald I.333; II.293
bēl dabābi	enemy III.225
bēl dīni	adversary III.224
bēl paḫâti	governor III.103
biltu	tax III.102
biretu	alley III.228
birtu	castle II.337
bûṣu	byssus I.209
ekallu	palace III.226
embūbu	flute II.329
ganūnu	bedroom III.227
giṭṭu	document III.232
gullatu	bowl I.146-8
ḫabaṣillatu	reed III.46
ḫaṣṣinnu	axe II.269
ḫurāṣu	gold I.84,197,301; II.292
igāru	wall III.226
igru	pay III.231
ikkaru	farmer III.225
ilku	tax III.102
ina er-se-tim	on earth II.68; III.278
kilubi	bird cage I.341; II.291
kinattu	colleague III.225
kitu	linen, tunic I.205; II.292; III.286
kuribu	guardian? I.85; II.304
kurkanu	some aromatic I.93
kussû	throne III.231
labbu	lion I.340
ladanu	ledanon I.331
laḫannu	dish I.343
libittu	brick I.84; II.293

Labnanu	Lebanon I.210		'arḍa	earth I.20; II.68,304,
Laḫ(a)mu	I.17			325
Luddi	Lydians I.175; III.319		ʿaqabatu	ascent II.47
Lukka	Lycians III.172		ʿatīq	old II.327
			balamīda	young tuna I.133
Mita	Midas I.175		burr(un)	grain II.10
Mi-il-qar-tu	Melqarth I.120		burūj	towers III.325
Muski	Moschoi I.174-5		darāhima	drachmas II.335
			dīnār	denarius III.256
Nabu-naid	Nabonidus II.96		ḍarra	oppress II.325
			ḍabaha	slaughter I.199; II.331
Ṣapuna	Saphon I.100		fellaḫin	peasants III.225
			firdaws	paradise III.147,238
Tabal	Tibareni I.174-5		funduq	inn III.242
Tiawat	Ocean I.17; II.324		ǧarb(un)	West I.58; II.303
Tugdamme	king III.319		ǧrāb	raven II.12
			'injīlu	Gospel II.114
Yamani	Ionian II.96		jabal(un)	mountain II.336
			jamal(un)	camel I.338
			jaral(un)	stones II.22
	Anatolian		kaʿb(un)	die III.53
ϝαναϰτει	king (Phrygian) II.96		kalb(un)	dog II.17
kssadrapa	satrap (Lycian) III.87		kanz(un)	treasure III.240
λάβρυς	axe (Lydian) II.269		kursiy	II.334; III.231
χssaθrapazate	act as satrap		laban(un)	milk II.8
	(Lycian) II.297; III.87		layt(un)	lion I.42,340
			maguš	magician II.296
Arñna	river III.323		malik(un)	king II.96
Artimuλ	Artemis (Lydian) I.336		maqlīd	key II.169; III.246
Εστϝεδιιυς	Aspendus II.324		marjān	pearl III.62,237
Μᾶ	mother-goddess II.317		miskīn	poor III.223
Ματαρκυβιλε	mother Cybele		mizāj	mixed II.300
	(Phrygian) II.336		qāḍī	judge I.97
Μιδαι...ϝαναϰτει	Midas king		qalam(un)	pen I.330
	(Phrygian) I.175		qamīṣ(un)	shirt I.322
Οἰνόανδα	Oenoanda city I.138		qarn(un)	horn I.195-6
Παναμύης	Panamyes (Carian) II.85		qaṣr(un)	fortress III.204
Śfardak	Sardes (Lydian) I.336		qirṭās(un)	paper I.330
Tešub	weather-god II.324		qisṭās	weight III.253
Trm̃mile	Lycians (Lycian) I.31;		quṭ(u)n	cotton I.205
	III.172		sakīnah	messenger II.330;
Valveś	Alyattes (Lydian) I.164;			III.142,289
	II.298		sārabīla	trousers II.296
			sijn(un)	prison III.258
	Arabic		simsim(un)	sesame I.336
'ajr(un)	pay III.231		sirāj	lamp III.239
'al-kuḥul	alcohol II.333		suhaym	little dagger III.323

bᶜj   palm II.265

bhn   some stone I.305-7; II.295

bi3   some metal II.227

db3.t   basket I.35; II.295

dt   olive II.294

gjf   monkey I.44; II.295

hbny   ebony I.338; II.295; III.325

hms.t   crocodile II.294

hrr.t   flower I.331; III.46

htm   signet I.75

hšdrpn   satrap III.87

ir.t   eye II.147

k3   aspect of soul III.61

k3k3   castor I.331

kmj.t   gum III.41

m3ᶜ hrw   "justified of voice" III.39

mᶜr   fortunate III.39

mśdm.t   mascara I.241

ntr   nitre I.241; II.96,295; III.41

p3 shnt   double crown II.294

rw   lion I.340

s3b   jackal II.294

šmšm.t   sesame I.336

šndwt   linen II.295; III.41

śśmt   horse II.6

'Imn   Amoun of Thebes I.329

Dhw.tj   Theuth I.334

Hp   Apis I.334

Hr   Horus I.334

Km.t   Black Land II.295; III.325

Mn-nfr   Memphis I.329

Nb.t-h.t   Nephthys II.8

P3-nhsj   Penhase "the Negro" I.181-2; II.295

Pr-jtm-tkw   Pithom I.329

Pth   Ptah I.334

Stš   Seth II.326

Ś.t   Isis I.333

Tbn   Daphnae I.333

Wś-ir   Osiris I.333

English

aex   ax (OE) II.269

arwe   arrow (OE) II.141

beaver   II.181

bere   barley (OE) II.10

bolca   gangway (OE) II.5

bras   brass (OE) II.227

brasil   red dye (ME) II.227

brown   II.181

clan   II.214

dēofol   devil (OE) I.13

dike,ditch   II.296

draca   dragon (OE) I.13

eare   ears (OE) II.316

egan   eye (OE) I.196; II.316

eorðan   earth (OE) II.68,304; III.278

feoh   herd (OE) II.18

flint   I.83

gable   II.336

guest   III.11

heorot   hart (OE) I.195

host   III.11

lēod   people (OE) I.38

place   III.227

pshent   Eg. crown II.295

queen, quean   I.226

snow   III.278

steer   I.191

suk   III.228

sunnan hweoʒul   sun's wheel I.272; II.60

swetter...med   sweeter...mead (OE) I.139

treasure   III.240

ūr   wild ox (OE) I.192-3

water   II.71,96,319; III.284

whelp   II.17

Ethiopic

---   II.16

bərät   some metal (Amharic) II.227

br(r)   silver (Cushitic) II.227

wayn   wine (Geez) II.304

Suppiluliuma	king II.86
Tarhund	weather-god II.209
Telipinus	king I.31; II.86
Tudhaliyas	king II.86
Wilusa	Ilion? II.85

Hurrian
arinni	well, spring III.285,323
iuri	king III.323

Indo-European
Βραύρων	"Bear Town"? II.181
θρίαμβος	triple beat? II.252
Ὄλυμπος	white mountain? II.9
paelex	concubine II.281; III.290

Iranian
'st'nk	messenger (Sogdian) III.89,237
apadāna	palace (Old Persian) III.126
asa	horse (OP) II.6
aspa	horse (Median) II.6
byrt'	castle (Parthian) II.337
čirāγ	lamp (Persian) III.239
daiva	demon (OP) III.229,237
dāng	coin (Persian) III.233
dastakarta	handiwork (OP) III.233
didā	wall (OP) II.296
dydymy	diadem (Pehlevi) III.97
farna-	glory (OP) II.297
frasang	parasang (mid. Pers.) III.233
ganǰ	treasure (Pers.) II.296; III.240
gauša	ear (OP) III.78
gnzbr	treasurer III.240,339
gwnk	sort, kind (Parth) III.234
handām	limb, member (Pehl) III.234
hrkpty	title (Parth) III.234
hštrp	satrap (Parth) III.87
hzrwpt	chiliarch (Parth) III.92
kapič	dry measure (Pehl) III.233
kyn'k	dagger (Sogd.) III.234

maguš	Magian II.296; III.91
μανιάκης	circlet III.234
marvarit	pearl (Mid Pers) III.62, 237
maškāuvā	on hides (OP) III.245
mgwpt	chief magus (Pehl) III.92
mušk	musk III.319
nḥšyrpty	huntmaster (Parth) III.238
paradayadama	enclosure? (OP) II.296; III.128
patikara	image (OP) III.96
pirosen	some acclamation III.84
ptgm	message (Parth) III.236
rāz	secret (Pehl) III.238
saansaan, σεγανσαα	king of kings III.71,84
šalvar	trousers (mod Pers) II.296
spsyrdr	sword-bearer (Parth) III.99,237
taχs	arrow (mod Pers) II.141
*urda	rose I.339
vispazana	men of all kinds (OP) III.236
xšaçapāvā	satrap (OP) II.296; III.87
xšāyaθiya	king (OP) III.83
zamān	time (Pehl) III.235
zarniq	arsenic (mod Pers) II.296
zynpty	armorer (Parth) III.235

'ršk	Arsakes III.70
'wrḥ'y	Urha/Edessa III.101
Aršāma	PN (OP) II.297
Aspacana	PN (Median) II.6; III.99
Auramazda	High God (OP) II.40
Çušāyā	Susa (OP) I.331; II.296
Gaubaruva	Gobryas III.99
H'rn	Carrhae III.101
Haumavargā	haoma-people (OP) III.320
Karka	Caria (OP) I.31
Mtrdt	Mithradates (Parth) III.70

Pali

damasaccena	damask II.334
deva	god III.229
haṃšâ	swans II.165
samaṇa	ascetic II.154
veḷuriya	beryl I.333
Aṃtiyoge	Antiochus II.13
Taṃbapaṃṇī	Taprobane II.13

Russian

gosti	guest (OCS) III.11
снег	snow I.330; II.68,96, 319
чар	tsar I.263
тоуръ	bull (Old Ch Slav) I.190-5
кесар	Caesar I.263

Sanskrit

açvaḥ	horse II.6,304
aghil	aromatic wood (Prakrit) I.96
ahiḥ	serpent II.302
barbara	non-Aryan III.171
bṛhant	high III.324
bhrāj	flash I.330; II.64
çiraḥ	head I.195
çṛṅgam	horn I.195
dānu	river II.208
deva	god III.229
dyaùs pítaḥ	Sky Father II.55
ibha	elephant I.338
iṣu	arrow II.141
jyā	bow-string II.135
kalama	pen I.331
kardama	some spice I.335
karpasa	cotton I.339; II.293
kurkuma	turmeric I.93
kuṣṭa	costus I.149-150
magham	gift III.229
marakata	emerald I.18,332; II.293
melā	ink I.331
muškaḥ	testicle III.319
naladah	nard I.148-151; II.293
nṛ	man II.158
paçú	herd II.18

paraśuh	axe II.269
pippali	pepper I.335
pratibāgha	ration III.236
rajas	darkness I.58
ságarbhya	maternal brother I.225
sahásra	thousand III.92
soma	a psychedelic III.319
śramaṇa	ascetic II.154
śrávo...ákṣitam	undying fame I.11; II.39
stṛbhis	stars I.339
sūrya, suvar	sun II.60
súras cakrám	wheel of the sun I.272
svādór...mádhvaḥ	sweet mead I.139
tu(m)pati	hurt II.298
vīṣám	poison II.142
vṛkaḥ	wolf II.17; III.326

Buddha	Enlightened One II.13
Chandragupta	king II.13
Dānavaḥ	demon II.208
Priyadarsi	Asoka II.13
Vṛtrahan	Slayer of Vrtra III.71

Scandinavian

aesir	gods (Old Norse) II.213
hreinn	reindeer (ON) I.195
lo	lynx (Swedish) II.17
sunnu-hvél	sun's wheel (ON) I.272
þiorr	steer (ON) I.192-3
vatten	water (Swedish) II.71

"Scythian"

*dan	river I.227; II.208; III.285
Ἐνάρεες	unmanly II.158
οἰόρπατα	ruling men I.224; II.158
Τάξακις	man's name II.141
Τόξαρις	" " II.141

Siberian

šaman	shaman (Tungus) II.154
tüngür	drum II.166,298

Spanish

alcalde	judge I.97
bodega	shop III.243
golpe	blow III.272

Index 2: Texts Cited

2.1 Biblical

2.1.1 Hebrew Bible

13,9 III.164
14,2-9 I.100
15,1 II.37
15,3 II.93
15,8 I.104
15,11 II.66,105,319
15,17 II.92; III.280
15,20 I.154; II.159
15,21 II.236
15,27 III.326
16,15 I.210
16,25 II.292
16,28 III.208
16,31 I.210
17,5-6 II.284
17,8-13 II.241
17,14 I.44; III.156
18,21 III.92
19,4 II.165
19,16 II.64,79
20,3 I.262
20,4 I.267
20,5 I.310; II.34
20,18 II.67
20,25 II.220
21,10 II.289
21,15-29 II.279; III.24,27,162,294
21,37–22,3 I.4,202,323; II.16,18,
    279,323; III.341
22,21 II.281
22,26 I.207
23,10-11 II.14,25; III.281
23,22 I.263; III.10,17
24,4-8 I.200,260; II.206; III.156
24,10 I.84,106,332; II.314
24,12 I.44
24,16 II.316
25,8 I.179
25,39 II.172
28,4 III.57
28,9-11 II.299
28,17-20 I.87,332; III.54,291
28,40 I.166
28,42-43 II.110
30,13 II.335
30,23-24 I.94-5
30,34-37 I.150,213,331

31,17 II.316
31,18 II.327; III.156
32,4 I.194
32,19 I.259; II.259
32,24 I.307
32,29 II.322
33,19 I.231
34,29 I.199; II.331
35,21 II.334
38,28 I.44
38,42-43 I.205
39,10-13 I.87
39,27 I.204-5; II.110
41,42 III.156

Leviticus
1.9 I.184
2.2 II.314
2,11 II.110
3,2 I.203
3,9-16 I.184-5; II.330
4,10 I.199
4,15 II.99
5,6 II.16
5,15 II.297
6,2-8 I.213
7,8 I.214
7,15 I.185
7,24 II.322
7,30-34 I.184
8,13-15 I.189
9,4 I.194
9.18 I.189
11,19 II.301
11,22 II.301
11,37 I.81
16,3-4 I.189
16,30 II.246
18,21 II.29
19,18 III.2,300
19,21 II.29
19,28 II.163,180
19,34 I.310; III.300
19,36 II.46
20,3 II.29
20,20 I.336; II.312
20,27 III.341

12,14 II.271
12,27 I.203
13,1 I.261
13,10 I.266
15,1-6 I.250; II.25
15,12 II.312
16,6 I.58
17,1 I.194
17,16-20 II.83,110; III.261,341
18,10-11 II.191
19,21 II.279; III.27
20,5-8 I.236; II.83
20,10-12 I.160
20,19-20 II.83
21,3 I.216
21,18-20 II.106; III.250
21,22 II.247; III.108
22,5 II.159
22,21 II.322
23,3-4 II.230; III.294
23,15 II.237
24,1 III.232
25,5-10 I.238
25,11 III.20
26,5 I.18; II.310
27,2 I.26
27,5 II.220
28,12 I.249; II.74,169
28,18 I.278
28,23-33 I.5,107,280; III.110,285
28,40 I.60
28,48 I.283
28,49 II.48
28,51 I.157
28,53-57 I.280
29,3 I.196; II.316
29,10-22 I.256-8; II.31,318
30,15 I.55
30,19 I.269
31,10-11 I.261
31,16 I.259
32,5 III.212
32,6 II.91
32,11-12 II.165
32,14 I.135
32,17 III.230
32,23-24 II.144

32,38 I.215
32,39 II.58
32,42 II.142
33,13 II.303
33,17 I.152,198; II.92
33,20-22; II.42,92
34,6 II.169

Josua
2,10 II.188
2,15 I.243
4,19 II.205
4,22 II.207
5,2-3 I.80; II.319
5,6 II.229
6 II.218,237
6,15 II.316
6,17 II.239
6,22-25 I.243
6,26 II.220
7,14 I.235
7,25 II.240
7,26 II.132
8,18 II.137,241
8,20 I.159; III.304
8,29 II.132
9,3-9 I.201; II.30-31,51; III.289
9,21 II.31
10,1 II.43
10,3 II.86
10,11 II.69
10,12-14 II.59, 221; III.180
11,8 I.42
11,19 II.30,282
12,4 II.314
13–19 II.22
13,3 I.334
13,4 I.245
15,59 II.314
17,11 I.33
18,3 II.283
18,16 III.210
19,28 II.307
19,45 I.330; II.63; III.210
19,46 I.182
19,50 II.221
21,27 II.314

21,42 II.222
22,10-13 I.181,201
23,14 II.333
24,1 II.205
24,26 II.133
24,29 II.228
24,30 II.221
24,32 II.216

Judices
1,8 I.159
1,12 I.228
1,13 III.326
1,19 I.171
1,27 I.33
1,33 II.314
1,35 II.222
2,7-10 II.221,228-9
3,2 II.229
3,3 I.32; II.65,313; III.279
3,31 I.44; II.137,314
4,3 I.171
4,4-10 II.63,123,159,174
4,21 II.242
5,3 II.37
5,6 II.137
5,8 I.173
5,11 II.42
5,15 II.5
5,21 II.80,236
5,26 II.242
5,31 III.17
6,4 I.40
6,25-6 I.189; III.160
6,33 I.37; II.175
6,38 I.343
7,6 II.84
7,16 I.144; II.90,173
7,25 I.281; II.185
8,5 II.175
8,18-21 II.266
8,30 II.91
9,4 I.257
9,7-15 I.60,136-140; II.11,55; III.280
9,37 I.330; II.4
9,45 I.273
9,48 I.26

11,34-40 I.154,244,255; III.291
12,6 III.170
12,34 II.251
13,2 I.227
13,3-20 I.137; II.91,166,246
14,9 II.183
14,11-20 I.226,229,313; II.307
15,1 I.228; II.167
15,4-5 II.177
15,11 III.4,28
15,16 II.260
16,1 I.226
16,3 I.123
16,5 I.65
16,8 III.87
16,19 I.226
16,23 II.71
16,30 I.123
17,5 II.93
18,5 II.217
18,16 II.216
18,31 II.93
19,29 I.231,274
20,16 I.56
20,27-28 I.181
20,40 I.159
20,43 II.60
21,5 I.257
21,21 I.246
21,25 III.160

I Samuel
1,2 I.336
1,3 I.181
1.11-19 II.167
2.1-10 I.114,199; II.35,80,151; III.16
2,13-14 I.182,214
2,20 I.81
2,21-22 II.167
2,23 I.182
2,30 III.10
3,2 I.182
4,4-8 II.91,237
4,11 I.182
4,21-22 II.237,243
5,1-5 II.243

5,6 II.282
6,7-12 I.216; II.284
6,19 II.237
7,5 II.94
7,10 II.67,80,236; III.16
7,12 II.133
8,5 III.160
9,12 I.201
9,22 I.142
10,1 I.342
10,3 I.140
10,5 I.155
10,6 II.40,163,189
10,9-13 II.163
10,21 II.73
11,7 I.231,274
12,17 II,73,90,170
13,4 III.19
13,19-20 I.25-26,171; II.269; III.282
13,22 II.50
14,3 I.181
14,24 II.284
14,32 II.163
14,50 I.67
15,1 II.95
15,12 II.133
15,22 I.217
15,33 II.266
16,11 II.20,36
16,13 II.189
16,16 II.153
16,18 II.94
16,23 II.20
16,26-28 II.89
17,4 II.189
17,5-7 I.164; II.137,297
17,8 I,226; II.310,315
17,21 I.22
17,33 II.94
17,34-37 II.3,36,182; III.284
17,38 I.165-7
17,39 II.97
17,44 I.280
18,6-7 I.155; II.251,260
18,10 II.20,163
18,17-25 I.228
19,6 III.215

19,9 II.20
19,12 II.333
19,18-24 I.59; II.41,163,189
20,20-23 II.140
20,30 III.19
21,11 II.260
21,12 I.164
22,7 III.92
22,18-20 I.181
25,2 II.16
25,41 II.31
25,43 I.67
26,12 II.282
26,19 I.186
27,8 I.35
27,12 III.19
28,7-13 II.190; III.295
28,17 II.89
29,5 II.260
31,10 I.213; II.314,332

II Samuel
1,14 II.89
1,19-27 I.240-4; II.313; III.180
3,2-7 I.67; II.74,91
3,29 I.278
3,30 I.49
3,35 I.256; II.284
4,4 II.160
5,3 II.5
5,8 I.24
5,11 I.334; III.131
5,13-16 I.67; II.91
5,18 II.188
6,2 II.237
6,5 I.155
6,7 II.237
6,9 II.321
6,12-23 I.60,155,199-200; II.251,
 258-61
7,2 II.251
7,6-9 I.180
7,14 II.87,91,152
7,23 III.171
8,3 I.273
8,18 I.32,231,304; II.308
10,5-6 III.19-20

14,31 II.91
15,18 II.334
16,34 II.220
17,1 I.35; II.73,170
17,6 II.183
17,12 I.144
17,17-22 II.186
18,1 II.70
18,12 II.165,183
18,21-26 II.9,160
18,27 I.122
18,28 I.174; II.163
18,34 I.144
18,41-44 II.73,171
18,46 II.165,183
19,8-13 II.80,183
19,19 II.183
20,23-28 II.8,242; III.279
20,36 II.4
21,1 III.226
21,8 I.7,230
21,19 I.282
21,24 I.280
22,6 III.322
22,11 I.199
22,16 III.198
22,19-23 II.105
22,38 I.282; II.73,322

II Reges
1,2-16 I.219; II.183; III.210
1,8 II.183
2,8-14 II.38,183,189
2,23-24 II.4,183; III.284
3,22 I.313
4,9 II.41
6,5 I.26
6,30-31 I.272; III.216
9,21 II.94
9,24 II.140
9,30 I.241; II.210; III.291
9,31 I.7
9,36 I.282
11,4 I.30
11,13 III.326
11,18-19 II.307
11,24 II.334

12,10 II.292
12,14 II.289
13,14-19 II.135,138
14,14 I.76
14,22 III.326
16,15 II.313
17,21 II.89
17,26 II.4
18,4 III.329
18,13 I.341; II.286
18,18 I.52; III.302
18,24 III.103
18,25 II.282
18,26 I.7; II.314; III.170,205
18,31 II.13
18,34-35 II.242
19,16 II.316
19,23 I.101; III.130
19,32 II.138
19,37 I.309
20,8-11 II.59
20,20 I.24
22,8 I.50
22,14 II.159
22,19 II.54
23,5-13 I.213; II.7
23,29 III.72
23,31 II.74
25,1 II.296; III.128
25,5 I.97
25,9 III.145
25,10 I.161; III.305

Isaiah
1,2 I.270; III.290
1,11 I.217
1,13 I.213
1,18 I.312
1,26 II.246
2,2-4 I.26,172-3; III.17,308
2,12-13 II.268
3,23 I.209
5,1-7 I.137; II.61,70,319
5,8 I.250; II.23; III.321
5,12 I.155
5,22 I.143
6,1-5 II.161,175; III.226

14,6-7 I.60; II.75,79; III.281

Joel
1,10-12 II.11
2,3 III.138
2,16 II.99
2,24 II.320
4,9 II.239
4,10 I.26,172-3; III.282
4,20 II.230

Amos
1 III.38
1,1 II.36; III.301
1,15 II.242
2,1 I.26; III.230
2,6-7 II.27-29
2,15 II.153
3,5 I.342
3,8 II.92; III.284
4,6-13 II.56,73,170
5,8 III.307
5,10-15 II.27,106
5,16 III.225
5,19 II.4,182; III.284
5,24 II.35; III.279
5,25 I.217; II.332
5,26 III.96
6,4 II.328
6,6 I.60
7,10 II.40
7,14-15 I.342; II.36; III.222
8,1 I.342
8,6 II.27
8,9 III.307
9,6 III.307
9,7 II.282; III.159,316

Obadiah
20 I.336

Jonah
1,3 I.112,182
4,6 I.331

Micha
1,3 I.203

2,2 I.250; II.23,27; III.321
3,5 I.160
3,9 II.46
4,3 I.26,173
4,4 II.13,19; III.280
4,12 II.44
6,2 I.269
6,15 I.60
7,3 II.27
7,6 II.34
7,19 II.281

Nahum
2,5 II.174
2,8 I.153
3,8 I.329; II.94
3,9 I.29
3,17 II.302
3,18 II.3

Habakkuk
1,4 II.46
3,4-15 I.196; II.8,70,94,136,144-5,
    316
3,17 III.272

Zephaniah
1,5 III.96
1,14-15 III.178
2,5 I.32,69; II.308

Haggai
1,10 II.74
2,14 II.221
2,19 II.11

Sacharia
2,14 I.180
3,10 II.13
6,10 I.304
7,2 I.337
8,12 II.74
9,3 I.147,301
9,9-10 II.53,150
9,11 I.200
9,14 II.70
10,1 II.72; III.284

72,10 I.338
72,16 II.10,90; III.280
74,5 I.26
74,8 I.161
74,13-17 I.103,126,133; II.89; III.296
75,4 I.114; III.285
75,9 I.143
76,4 II.144
78,45 I.336
78,65 I.122
78,70 III.272
80,2 I.86; II.3,94
80,9-14 I.135-7; III.125,283,296
82,1 II.105; III.48
85,11-12 II.43-45
87 I.162
88,7-13 II.187-9
89,2 II.37
89,7-8 II.66,105
89,9-11 I.103,126
89,16 II.262
89,26-27 II.87,152
89,36-38 I.268
89,45 I.276
90,5-10 I.57; II.187; III.299
91,4 III.198
91,5-6 II.144; III.230
95,3 I.10,55; II.54,74,88; III.163
95,10 II.229
95,11 III.215
96,1-11 I.271; II.36; III.45,163
97,2 II.45
97,4 II.62
97,11 III.61
98,2 II.34; III.301
98,8 I.272
102,27 III.58,166
103,6 II.33
103,17-18 III.50
104 III.135
104,2 II.159; III.58
104,7 II.64,79
104,10 III.134,279
104,15 I.139
104,16 III.125,283
104,26 I.103
104,29-30 II.78,186

105,23 II.296
106,19-20 I.194,202
106,37 III.230
107,18 I.123
107,23-32 I.102; II.99; III
109,29 II.322; III.21
110,3 I.111
115,3 II.283
116,8-9 III.50,61
118,19-25 II.251,256-7,263
121,4 I.121
124,7 II.45
125,1 II.230
127,3-5 II.152
128,3 I.60; III.281
132,8 II.236,251
136,2-3 III.83
139,9 I.112; III.51
139,17-18 I.315; III.165
139,21-22 I.263; III.10
140,4 II.301
141,10 II.44
143,10-11 III.61
144,4 II.187
144,6 II.64,145,319
145,14 III.109
146,9 III.13
147,4 I.315; III.165
147,16 II.68
148,7 I.103,133
148,8 II.59

Job
1,21 I.58
2,13 II.316
3,9 I.111
3,10 II.311
4,11 I.340
5,26 II.10; III.280
6,4 II.140-1
7,12 I.132-3
9,6 I.114,126
9,7 II.221
9,8 I.203
9,13 I.126
10,16 II.3
10,21 II.325

9,27 III.235
10,2 III.181

Daniel
1,5 III.236
2,4 I.97; III.205
2,5 II.326; III.234
2,16 III.235
2,19 III.238
2,26 I.97
2,32-33 I.302
2,35-45 III.74,83
2,47 III.83
3,2 III.104
3,3 II.297; III.87
3,4 III.226
3,5 II.96,299,329; III.236,246
3,27 II.296
3,28 III.232
4,34 II.88
5,7 III.230,234
5,20 III.231
5,23 III.209
5,25-26 I.50,307
5,29 III.226
7,13 III.213
9,3 II.51
11,45 III.126
12,2 III.177,312
12,3 I.108

Ezra
1,8 III.104
1,18 III.240
2,22 I.331
2,49 III.320
2,69 I.308
3,7 III.123
4,6 III.84
4,7 III.225
4,8 I.342
4,9 I.34
4,13 III.102
5,14 III.103
5,17 II.296; III.240
6,2 II.337
6,9 I.191

6,11 III.110
7,12 II.297; III.84
7,20 III.240
7,24 III.102
7,26 III.106
8,36 III.87
10,15 II.123

Nehemiah
1,1 I.331
2,8 I.96; II.296; III.122,135
2,10 I.40; III.103
2,16 III.104
2,19 II.310; III.241
3,4 III.232
3,30 I.141
4,7 I.173; II.311
4,16-18 I.161
5,3 I.76
5,13 I.272
6,14 II.159
7,70 II.335
8,8 I.54; III.221
9,13 II.46
10,30 I.256
11,33 I.24; III.279
11,35 I.30
12,23 III.180
12,31-43 II.219
13,11 III.114
13,16 I.129; III.288
13,23-24 II.313-5

I Chronica
1,7 I.339
2,16 I.67
2,48 II,209
4,18 II.312
4,34 III.322
5,35-36 II.120
7,14 I.43; II.312
7,40 III.85
9,35-39 II.30
9,40 II.160
12,9 I.174
15,15 II.282
17,21 III.171

18,5 II.334
21,15 II.221; III.323
21,16-29 I.203; II.144,310
25,8 III.221
27,1-15 II.206
29,7 II.335
29,14 III.217,343

II Chronica
2,3 II.318
2,6 III.230
2,13 I.304
2,15 II.50

3,9 II.310
6,41 II.236
11,21 I.67
12,3 II.308
12,9 III.240
13,20-21 II.91
15,13-15 I.262
16,14 I.211
19,11 II.104
29,14 III
31,5 II.157
32,21 III.217

2.1.2 Septuagint
(Selective for canonical works)

Dan 3,46 I.279
Deut 32,43 II.105
Gen 1,26 III.217
    2,8 III.125
    41,42 Aq Sym III.234
Isa 8,21 III.96
    37,38 III.96
    66,1 III.244
Jer 7,11 III.218,260
Job 4,11 Aq I.340
    29,18 III.317
Jos 10,12-13 III.180
    21,42 II.222
Jud 16,8 III.87
Judith 15,12 I.158
    16,20 I.154
I Makk 1,22 III.59
    3,3 I.167
    3,28 III.261
    3,55 III.93,113
    5,13 I.40
    6,1-4 III.325
    6,49-53 II.25
    7,13 III.339
    8 III.251
    8,25-27 I.258, 266
    10,30 II.52
    11,34 I.30
    12,16 II.123; III
    13,37 II.265

13,51 II.265
15,16-21 III.251
II Makk 1,13 III.325
    1,36 I.279
    3,11 III.326
    4,9 III.241
    4,12 I.246
    6,7-21 I.157,186
    8,23 III.116
    10,7 I.157; II.265
    11,1 III.259
    12,26 III.315
    12,43-5 III.177
    13,4 III.86
    14,4 II.265
    14,5 II.107
III Makk 4,6 I.89
    5,51 I.124; III.242
Prov 9,18c I.296
Ps 22,17c III.82
Ps of Solomon 14,3 III.139; 16,2
    I.124; III.242
I Reg 8,53a III.180
II Reg 1,2 Aq Sym I.219
    25,1 III.128
Sap Sol 5,17-20 I.168-9; II.93
    8,7 I.237
    11,16 III.29
    13,14 I.241; II.258
    15,9 I.304

2.1.3 Targums (various)

2.1.4 Vulgate

2.1.5 Apocrypha

Baruch (Syriac) 29 I.126
Enoch (Eth.) 9 III.86
    32 III.139
    60 I.126
    65 II.226

IV Esdras (Latin) 6.52 I.126
    8.52 III.139
Jubilees III.181
Test. XII Patr. III.181
Test. Levi 18.10 III.139
Tobit (Aram) III.181

2.1.6 New Testament
See also texts listed at III.263.

Matt
2,1 III.92
2,11 I.95, 212; III.98
3,2 III.213
3,4 III.245
3,7 III.250
3,9 I.83
3,10 II.271; III.112
3,12 II.44; III.243
4,9 III.98
4,10 I.262
5,3-12 III.36,42,231
5,14 I.24
5,15 III.239,255
5,21-48 I.252
5,22 III.208,250
5,25 III.224,251
5,26 III.252-4
5,29 III.234
5,33-37 I.270; III.216,218,244
5,38 III.27
5,39-40 I.207; II.53; III.81
5,41 II.52; III.237,255
5,43-47 II.56,80; III.2,22,214
6,2-16 III.211
6,5 III.227
6,9-10 II.29
6,11 III.207
6,12 I.250; III.31,209
6,16-17 III.247
6,18 III.215
6,19 I.74; II.19
6,22 III.239
6,24 III.210,214
6,25-33 III.46,227,285

6,34 I.295
7,1-2 III.4,31
7,5 III.212,262,329
7,6 III.208,230
7,7-8 III.33
7,12 III.248
7,13 II.263; III.242
7,15 II.17
7,21 III.213
7,25 II.73-74
8,5 III.94
8,9 III.249
8,11 III.75
8,12 III.207,213
8.19 I.264
8,20 III.78,219
9,9 III.103
9,17 I.140
10,3 III.103
10,8 III.228,247
10,16 II.17
10,17 III.248
10,18 III.258
10,24 III.221
10,25 I.220, 318; III.210
10,27 III.226
10,29 III.253
10,30 I.316
10,34 III.100
10,35 II.34; III.248
10,36 III.225
10,37-38 I.265; III.109
11,6 III.227
11,7 III.250
11,17 III.208

11,19 III.213-4,228
11,21-23 III.207
11,25 III.209
11,29-30 I.283; III.232
12,24 I.219; III.229
12,26-28 III.214
12,32 II.233; III.34
12,36 III.236
12,43-45 III.210,230
13,11 III.238
13,31-33 III.214
13,38 III.207,213
13,40 III.250
13,42 III.227
13,45-46 III,62,66,224,237,262
13,47 III.236
13,55 III.222
14,8 III.249
14,27 III.208
14,36 III.245
16,9-10 III.250
16,13-23 III.210
16,17 III.207
16,18 I.124; III.209,242
16,19 II.169; III.246
16,24 III.109
16,28 III.250
17,15 III.226
17,17 III.212
17,27 I.304; III.63,251
18,1 III.213
18,6 I.275; III.250
18,7 III.246
18,21-22 III.27
18,29 III.225
19,12 III.223
19,21 III.240
19,23 III.215
19,24 I.338
19,28 II.263; III.231
20,2 III.256
20,3 III.227
20,8 III.258
21,8-9 II.256-7
21,17 II.256
21,19 II.114
21,31 I.248; II.333; III.214

21,32 II.46
21,33 III.225
22,4 III.249,262
22,5 III.66
22,19 III.256
22,40 III.248
23,2 III.243
23,5 III.206,250
23,7-8 III.207
23,13-22 I.270; III.36,216
23,15 III.14,206,207,210
23,23 I.335
23,26 III.207
23,27 III.211
23,30 III.225
24,2 III.215-6
24,19-31 II.234, 262, 271
24,28 I.281
24,30 III.257
24,31 III.261
24,40-41 III.214
25,1-12 II.173
25,27 I.75; III.227
25,35 III.13
25,40 III.309
25,43 III.11
25,44 III.15,242-3,247
26,2 III.208
26,24 I.312
26,28 III.248
26,52-55 III.25,99,237,254,260,331
26,57 III.117
26,58 III.114
26,61 III.225
26,65 II.247
26,67 II.53; III.292
27,2 III,258
27,6 III.207
27,16-17 III.331
27,26-29 II.118; III.118,266
27,32 II.53
27,33 II.221
27,35 II.53
27,38 III.260
27,43 III.81
27,46 III.208
27,51 III.59

14,12 III.225,249
14,15 III.213
14,18-19 III.247,252
14,21 III.228,249,262
14,26 I.265
14,27 III.109
14,31 III.251
14,32 III.90,237
15,2-10 III.214,217,232,239
15,11-32 III.214,245
15.25 II.329
16,8 III.34,207,242
16,9-11 I.180; III.210
16,13 III.210
16,15 III.215
16,19 III.230
16,20 III.242
16,21 III.227
17,4 III.27
17,20 III.213
17,24-30 II.64, 80
17,34-35 III.214
17,37 I.281; II.271
18,3 III.224,262
18,9-14 III.214
18,24 II.19
18,30 III.235
19,2 III.103
19,12-14 III.90,237,250-1,264
19,20 III.253
19,23 I.75; III.227
20,34-35 II.233; III.34,207
20,36 III.207
21,8 III.235
21,20 III.254
21,23 III.246
21,24 III.207
21,34 III.246
22,4 III.114
22,19 I.218
22,25 II.115
22,28 III.140
22,30 II.263; III.227
22,37 III.81
22,52 III.99,114,260
23,19 III.243
23,28 I.244

23,31 III.222
23,42-43 III.108,140,218,238
23,47 III.95
23,56 III.330
24,2 II.185
24,31 III
24,42 II.184
24,52 III.98

John
1,14 I.180
1,41 III.209
1,42 I.60
1,48 II.13; III.280
2,9 III.324
2,15 III.106
2,16 III.66,263
2,19 III.34
3,1 III.114
3,14 III.110
4,2 II.183
4,25 I.60
4,42 II.116
4,46-53 III.94
5,2 III.170
5,35 III.239
6,15 II.114
6,31 I.210
7,1-13 II.176, 256-7; III.113
7,32-46 III.114
7,37-38 II.176, 256
8,28 III.110
9,31 III.174
10,9 II.264
10,12 II.17
10,22 II.256
11,16 I.146
11,44 III.253
11,48 III.109
11,54 III.67,207
12,3 I.95, 151; III.270
12,13 II.256-7,265
12,24 II.11; III.280
12,29 II.65
12,32-34 III.110
12,38 III.81
13,1-16 II.31; III.216,221

2.1.7 N.T. Apocrypha

2.2 West Semitic

2.2.1 Palmyrene inscriptions (most bilingual with Greek)

PAT 0041 tomb described III.227
0050 physician III.222
0197 Atargatis III.65,232,316
0259 Tariff
    Intro. II.100; III.103,235-6,
      248-250
    47 II.333
    69 III.253
    74 III.258
    103 III.215
    137 III.230
0273 Atargatis III.316
0278 market-overseer III.228
0282 Shallamallath III.229
0286 Worodes I.339; III.233,259
0290 Hairanes II.85,219
0291 Odainath II.117; III.323
0292 Odainath III.85
0294 Thaimassa III.67,256
0298 basilica II.327
0305 Hadrian II.116; III.15
0306 Abgar III.322
0317 Zenobia III.85,327
0320 *apkallu* II.39

0345 Baraq II.63,123,174
0420 Hormazd II.40
0472 Iamblichus III.322
0558 Odainath III.323
0591 Chrysanthus trilingual III.264
1347 temple of Bel III.226
1373 Asclepiades II.107; III.66-67
1374 Yarhai III.70
1375 Sampsigeramus III.323
1397 Maximus III.65,94
1406 gymnasiarch I.121; III.263
1409 Yarhai III.66
1412 Vologaisia III.66
1413 Callistratus trilingual III.264
1575 Hormazd II.40
1614 partners III.225
1719 sculpture II.299
1918 spring II.333
2065 bull tessera I.195
2761 Suhaimu III.323
2766 Nanaea III.325
2769 consular governor II.100
2801 Hairanes III.264
2817 cave II.333
— Vologaisia III.65

2.2.2 Other West-Semitic Inscriptions

Abydos, graffiti (KAI 49) I.152;
    II.123
Afis, Zakar (KAI 202) II.88,281
Aleppo, Bar-Hadad (KAI 201) I.120
Arad, ostraca III.317
Asshur, ostracon (KAI 233) I.341
Athens, ʿAbdtinit (KAI 53) III.241
    Noumenios (KAI 55) II.123

Bambyke, coins III.316
Beth-Alpha, Zodiac mosaic I.146
Byblos, Abibaal (KAI 5) I.7
    Ahiram (KAI 1) I.276,334; III.104
    Batnoam (KAI 11) II.314

Hasdrubal (KAI 3) I.330
    tax I.88; II.326
    Yehawmilk (KAI 10) III.336
    Yehimilk (KAI 4) II.33,88,105

Caesarea, priestly courses III.264
Capernaum, synagogue II.120
Cappadocia, Mithraic (KAI 265)
    III.92
Carthage, Agrigentum (CIS 1.5510)
    II.102,124-7
    Eshmun (CIS 1.4834-6) I.160,332
    funerary (KAI 90) I.121
    genealogy (KAI 78) III.156

2.2.3 Elephantine (TAD numbers in [square brackets])

1.14 III.244
6.4 II.100
12.13 III.246
12.16 III.254
17.2 III.246
19.5 III.317
23.4 III.222
28.6 I.330
30.9 I.321
48.14 III.248
49.2 III.245
58 III.209
64.10 III.227
68.12 III.238
73.4 II.169
74.14 III.205
77.3 III.142
82.8 III.224
86.2 III.271
91.6 III.228
92.6 III.242,262
99.7 III.237
Exodus Rabbah 5.14 III.89
15.13 III.254
15.22 III.249
29.9 III.250
30.16 III.218
30.24 III.62
31.17 III.258
36.1 III.248
42.3 III.90
45.3 III.257
46.4 II.85
Lev Rabbah 12.1 III.250,253
13.3 III.249
16.9 III.255
18.1 II.264, 332; III.243
18.3 III.89
22.4 III.208
29.4 II.262
30.2 II.265
30.6 III.243
32.1 III.106
33.36 III.250
34.3 III.15,206
34.16 III.229
36.1 III.244

Num Rabbah 4.8 I.75
4.20 III.245
7.3 III.85,249
19.26 III.95
20.18 III.228
23.11 III.245
Deut Rabbah 1.16 III.204
4.2 III.234
4.5 III.261
7.6 II.169
Ruth Rabbah 3,2 III.226
3,13 I.46
Shir Rabbah praef. III.246
on 1,8 II.269
1,10 III.62
1,14 I.322
2,5 III.267
7,10 III.225
Qoh Rabbah praef. III.250
on 7,4 I.322
7,9 I.322
9,11 I.341
11,3 III.236
12,7 III.94
Eka Rabbah 1,1 III.227
1.7 I.322
Esther Rabbah 1,12 III.89,109
2,3 III.255

Mishna
(many texts printed III.338-345)
Arakhin II.3 p. II.329
III.2 p. III.137
IV.1 p. II.134
VI.3 p. III.225
IX.6 p. III.204,333
Avoda Zara II.1 p. III.242
IV.1 p. II.134
Avoth I.1 p. I.161; III.142,305
I.3 p. III.241
I.13 p. III.206
II.1 p. II.316
II.5 p. II.336
II.7 p. III.29
II.8 p. II.324; III.282
II.9 p. III.239
II.12 p. III.210

2.2.7 Sayings of named Rabbis

"Rabbi" (Judah the prince) eye & ear
    II.316; III.341
Samuel b. Nahman Holy One honors
    Aramaic III.205

Shammai two Torahs III.197
Simeon b. Yohai rejects Romans I.248
    night for the wicked III.332
Yehuda praises Romans I.248

2.2.8 Syriac

Ahiqar 54 I.318
Baruch 29.4 I.126
Ephrem Syrus
    Paradise II.330; III.141-3
    Pearl III.63
Hymn of the Pearl I.333; II.334;
    III.64-66,83,91,98,143,229,
    240
Melito (pseudo-) I.245,332
Odes of Solomon 3.2 III.234
    8.10 III.238

17.6 III.15
23.21 III.249
25.7 III.239
28.5 III.99
35.4 III.254
Peshitto (selected) Gen 2,8 III.125
    Matt 12,24 III.229
    Matt 26,52 III.100
    Matt 27,26-28 III.267
    Joh 19,6 III.110

2.2.9 Mandaean III.91

2.3 Greek

2.3.1 Literary Greek

Abydenus frag. 2a (FGH 685) II.325
    frag. 3 I.16
Achilles Astron. *Eisagoge* 4 I.108
Achilles Tatius 1.1.2 I.213
    2.2 I.135,157; II.328
    3.6 I.102
Acta Alexandrinorum III.260,327
Acta Cononis 4 I.212
Acta Thomae III.63
Aelianus *de natura anim.*
    2.39 II.309
    5.17 I.219
    6.51 I.16
    7.1 III.129
    11.8 I.219
    11.15 II.316
    12.21 I.16
    15.3 I.132
    frag. 22 II.45
Aeschines
    Embassy 2.79 III.105
        2.111-116 I.256,265-6,278;
        II.205-6,240

Ctesiphon 3.110 II.240
    3.125 II.95-100
    3.132 III.75
    3.199 III.330
Aeschrio II.147
Aeschylus
    Agamemnon 28 II.173
        114 II.334
        239 I.93; II.181
        383 I.201
        404 I.174
        437-444 I.300
        763-770 II.44
        827-8 I.282
        1115 II.187
        1291 I.123
        1440 II.30
        1450 II.285
        1478 I.283; II.319
        1593 I.280
        1624 III.80
    Choephori 66 III.24
        200 III.14

Hist. Anim. 490a34 I.57
    502a19 I.44
    521b21-25 I.132
    547b15 I.343
    552b16 II.337
    557b3 I.74
    571a8-23 I.131
    600b3 II.179
    602a25 I.129
    607b31 I.130
    614a10 I.341
    630a18 I.191
Magna Moralia 1196a36 II.264
    1208b10 III.28
Meteor. 324a10 I.19
Poetica 5.2 III.247
    11.4 III.14
    13.5 III.166
    16 III.14
Politica 1.1.5-9 = 1252b5-1253a3
    I.234-5; III.16,91,304
    1.4.5 = 1259a12 I.77
    1.5.6 = 1260a10 I.234
    2.1.10 = 1261b33 I.319
    2.3.10 = 1265b36 II.100
    2.6.2-3 = 1269a34 II.30
    2.8.1-3 = 1272b27 II.100,102
    3.5.10 = 1280a36 II.210
    3.5.14 = 1281a1 I.235
    3.10.2 = 1285b36 II.95
    3.11.9 = 1287b30 III.78
    4.10.10 = 1297b16 I.235
    5.5.5 = 1305b33 II.5
    5.6.1 = 1306b30 I.246
    5.9.2 = 1313b3 III.268
    6.5.4 = 1321b31 III.135
    6.5.4 = 1321b39 I.52
    7.4.4 = 1326a23 II.5
    7.11.4 = 1331b15 III.135
    7.13.4 = 1333a35 I.160
    7.13.17 = 1334a21 III.268
[*Prob.*] 966b28 II.296
Rhet. 1371b10 III.28
    1373b5 III.197
frag. 144 Rose I.66
frag. 610 Rose II.211
Ith. Pol. II.182

apud Diog. L. I.325
Arrianus
    Anab. 1.11.6 I.152,199
    2.3.3 II.219
    2.5.2-4 I.324
    2.26.1 I.40
    3.8.6 III.327
    4.10-12 III.98
    6.22.5 I.151
    6.26.3 I.340
    6.28 II.252
    6.29.4 III.126
    7.14.10 III.94
    7.20.2 I.151
    7.22 III.97
    Epict. 1.3.1-3 III.176
    1.9.34 III.253
    1.11.12-13 III.176
    1.17.9 III.255
    1.22.4 III.176
    1.24.14 III.256,270
    1.25.21 I.207; II.309
    2.10.3 I.162; III.309
    3.7 III.86
    3.22.54 III.22
    3.24.34 I.168
    3.24.85 II.258
    4.1.79 II.52
    4.1.86 I.162
    4.1.91 III.67
    4.8.34 III.170
    Parthica III.99
    frag. 95 (FGH 156) II.194
Asclepiades II.68
Athenaeus 1.4C I.131
    3.94B I.332
    3.116C I.129
    4.158C II.182
    4.167D II.307
    5.195 I.72
    5.201-202 I.72,91,198,210
    5.208B I.118
    6.253C I.122
    6.256-257 II.194
    7.297E I.133
    7.301F I.132
    7.302C I.129

[17.]15 II.25
18.154 II.205
19.1 III.330
19.254 II.45,48
21.33 I.167
21.150 III.16
23.53 I.69
23.68 I.214
23.72 III.24
24.113 I.4
24.140 II.279; III.27
24.149 II.25
[25.]11 II.45
34.6 I.304
35.11 I.249
35.32 II.309
42.7 II.51
[59.]49 I.233
[59.]74 II.109
[59.]122 I.69, 233
Didache 1.3 III.2
10.6 II.117
Dinon frag. 27 (FGH 690) I.66
Dio Cassius 16.19.1 III.271
36.52.3 III.98
37.18.1 III.323
37.28 III.293,315
37.40.2 II.260
40.14.3 III.77
40.20.2 III.322
42.38.2 III.183
47.10.4 III.105
48.24-26 III.101
49.15.5 II.41
49.22.6 III.101
50.4.5 II.241
50.13.7 III.322
51.7.4 II.209
52.42.3 II.41
53.12 II.112
53.16.7 II.111
53.17.4 II.112
53.27.2 I.117
53.32.5-6 II.112-113
54.1.3 II.112
65.7.1 III.15
68.28.4 III.65

68.29 III.69
69.2.1 I.99
71.3.3 II.95
77.9 III.309
78.6a III.15
Dio Chrysostomus 2.75 III.86
10.19 II.51
33.47 I.120
53.1 III.182
Diocletianus *see* Latin inscr.
Diodorus 1.1.2 III.197
1.25.6 I.16
1.47.4 III.85
1.65.6 I.215
1.91.4 I.81
1.94.2 III.321
1.97.2 II.72,176
2.10.2 III.124
2.13.2 I.27
2.47.3 II.206
2.49.3 I.151
3.3.3-5 I.28
3.4.1 I.28
4.18.5 I.127
4.31.5 II.207
5.12.13 II.224
5.13.4 II.211; III.144
5.14 I.176
5.20 I.119; II.211
5.66.3 I.83
5.81.7 II.86
12.13.2 I.51,260
12.17.4 II.279; III.27
13.43.5 II.125
13.80 II.125-127
13.85.5 II.125
14.54.5 II.126
14.80.2 III.125
14.93.4 II.211
15.15.2 II.126
16.41 I.34; II.107; III.125
17.66 II.335
18.39.1 III.126
18.48 III.93
19.58 III.135,145
19.79.4 II.307
19.98 I.96

9.413 I.10; III,302
9.447-457 I.66; II.281; III.290
9.[458-461] I.66-68
9.497-500 I.186
9.539-540 I.135; III.296
9.566-567 I.258

10.5-7 II.59
10.154 II.62
10.220 II.334
10.292-294 I.216
10.429 II.310
10.437 I.312
10.485-486 II.15

11.17-43 I.163; II.147
11.67-69 II.10; III.280
11.86 II.31
11.201 II.55
11.269-272 II.283
11.395 III.20
11.492 II.208
11.512-518 III.222
11.559 II.51
11.624-641 I.94,142
11.792 II.283

12.25-26 II.61,70
12.156 II.68; III.278
12.208 II.302
12.278-287 II.68-69
12.451 II.18

13.21-31 II.8,94
13.302 II.64
13.356-357 I.228
13.389-391 II.268; III.146,284
13.429-430 II.214
13.685 I.82; II.307
13.796 II.65
13.830 III.46

14.171 I.96
14.200-207 II.324; III.50
14.231 I.121
14.301-306 III.50
14.321 I.69

14.325 II.199
14.348 I.93
14.351 II.74
14.444 I.232

15.36-38 I.267
15.128-129 II.316
15.187-193 I.225,267; II.56
15.275 I.340
15.463-464 I.277
15.469 II.149
15.478-482 I.163
15.498 II.22
15.532 III.10
15.535-538 I.166; II.298
15.694-695 III.165

16.131-139 I.164
16.152 II.6
16.233 I.170
16.235 I.70
16.297-298 II.64
16.385-388 II.27,46,73,95,170
16.392 I.195
16.483-485 II.268; III.146,284
16.542 II.95

17.200 II.282
17.336 III.19
17.424-425 I.106
17.447 II.283
17.547-549 II.147
17.602 III.229

18 III.57,285
18.23-25 II.284
18.29 I.40
18.239-242 II.59
18.271 I.281
18.318-320 I.340
18.397 II.160
18.399 I.109
18.417-420 I.87
18.468-471 I.87; II.335
18.480 I.118
18.483 I.267; III.58
18.487-489 II.177

4.613 I.109
4.746 I.139

5.1-2 I.111
5.55 III.55
5.62 I.237
5.68-71 I.141; III.55
5.121-4 I.112
5.184-186 I.267
5.216-218 III.56
5.239 I.342
5.273-275 I.111; II.177
5.306 III.38
5.333-335 II.184

6.10 II.22
6.42-46 II.92; III.48
6.57 II.317
6.120-121 III.13
6.184-185 III.8
6.188-189 II.283
6.207-208 III.10,13
6.221 I.59
6.244-245 I.224
6.292 III.46
6.309 I.139

7.71 II.321
7.80 II.314
7.100 I.201
7.112-117 II.11; III.55
7.127 III.56
7.197-198 I.238

8.63-64 II.160
8.312 I.312
8.390-391 I.194; II.205
8.488 II.36
8.543 III.10
8.546 II.26
8.570-571 I.295
8.575-576 III.13

9.81 I.332
9.97 I.332
9.105-111 I.136-137; II.11,90
9.175-176 III.13

9.208 I.139
9.215 II.33
9.222-223 I.147
9.240 II.185
9.244 II.15
9.270-271 II.26; III.10
9.284 III.50
9.296 II.19
9.379ff II.241
9.391-393 I.171; III.282

10.80 II.316
10.238 II.190
10.276 II.190
10.333 III.100
10.492-495 II.158,189
10.513-514 II.187
10.532 I.199

11 III.40
11.155-158 II.187
11.206-208 II.186
11.236 II.171
11.261 II.168
11.263 II.314
11.301 III.54
11.315-316 I.84
11.489-491 I.57
11.521 I.31; II.86
11.571 I.123

12.61 II.165-168
12.81 I.58
12.92 II.320
12.397 II.316

13.181-187 I.194, 201
13.201-202 III.13

14.54 II.284
14.80 II.317
14.202-203 I.69
14.211-212 I.228
14.249 II.316
14.257 I.329
14.288ff I.69
14.457-458 II.70

Ignatius *ad Eph.* 20.2 I.16
   ad Polyc. 1.3 III.142
     6.2 I.169
Irenaeus *con. Haer.* 5.5.1 III.125
Isaeus 8.19 I.243
   8.23 I.76
Isocrates 3.24 II.126
   4.49-50 III.169
   9.12-19 II.195; III.157
   12.259 II.25
   15.235 II.39
Johannes Chrysostomus I.78; [II.318]
Johannes Lydus II.220
Josephus
   Ant. Jud. 1.71 I.84
     1.129 I.97
     3.134 II.292
     3.144 II.172
     3.153 I.209
     3.161 I.208; III.57
     3.225 I.184
     4.73 III.207
     7.101 I.273
     7.347 III.137
     8.186 III.137
     9.85 III.255
     9.274 III.243
     12.15 III.205
     12.138 II.107
     12.141 III.135
     12.145-146 III.116
     12.233 III.137
     12.239 III.241
     13.52 II.52
     13.260-264 III.251
     13.395 II.145
     14.36-37 I.158
     14.54 I.81
     14.129 III.322
     14.143 III.259
     14.145-8 III.251,331
     14.167 II.107
     14.190 II.101
     14.248 III.318
     14.330 III.101
     15.3 III.326
     15.72 III.254-7

15.231 III.327
15.253 III.259
15.268 III.211
15.269 III.142
15.373 III.94
15.395 I.158
15.403 II.337
15.417 III.115
16.163-164 II.292
16.220 I.43
17.215 III.113,117
17.271 III.261
17.289 III.222
17.300 III.90
18.21 III.257
18.52 III.101
18.55 III.257
18.114 III.90,94
18.121 III.257
18.194 III.258
19.338 III.322
20.11 II.101,107
20.20 II.107
20.22-34 III.68,82,96,99
20.65 III.98
20.71 I.339
20.131 III.104,115,117
20.197 III.333
20.215 III.243
Bellum Judaicum 1.3 III.206
   1.97 I.247; III.107
   1.138 I.96
   1.159 II.308
   1.199 III.259
   1.204 III.261
   1.269 III.101
   1.422 III.211
   1.574 III.323
   1.656 III.114
   2.11 III.113
   2.169 III.257-9
   2.243 III.115
   2.331-6 II.107
   2.365 III.197
   2.427 I.250
   2.501 III.323
   2.521 III.14

3.71.6 II.121
5.45.10 I.94
5.66.1 I.33
5.70.6 I.330
5.72.9 III.324
6.11.12 II.101
6.15.8 II.253
6.23 I.163
6.24.5 III.93
6.31.10 I.339
6.39.12 III.261
6.51.2 II.100
7.9 I.254-270
10.18.1 II.84
10.27.12 I.84
10.32.11 I.31
11.23.1 III.116
11.39(34).12 III.240
12.5.6 I.246
13.3.7 II.241
15.12.2 II.262
16.12.3 II.74
18.11.8 III.236
20.6.12 II.240
21.42.9 III.255
30.20.8 I.323
30.26 I.72; III.324
31.12.11-12 II.102
32.2.5 III.182
32.3.13 III.252
34.7 I.129
34.11.8 II.53
36.4.6 II.84
apud Plinium III.109
Polycarpus *ad Phil.* 2.3 III.31
Porphyrius *Antr. Nymph.* 18 II.184
de Abst. 2.20 I.188
2.26 I.184
4.7 II.265
Vita Pyth. 14-15 II.179
29 II.164
apud Euseb. I.334
Posidonius I.168; III.144
Proclus *in Tim.* 3.176 II.76
Procopius *Hist.* 4.10.17ff II.197
8.2.24 I.176
8.22.23-25 I.101

Proverbia Byz. I.332-333
Ptolemaeus 3.3 II.109,213
5.17.7 II.219
Ptolemaeus Heph. I.44

Quintus Smyrnaeus 6.218 I.79

Rhinthon III.270

Saporus *Res Gestae* see 2.6 Iranian
Sappho frag. 1 (PLF) I.112,399; III.29
2 I.212
44 I.70; III.291
140 I.41,204,208,245
Scylax 111 I.119
112 I.148,178
Scymnus 162 I.132
Semonides frag. 36 I.328
Sextus Emp. *adv. Math.* 1.287 II.44; III.31
Simonides frag. 37 PMG I.236
542.29 III.246
543 II.168
Solon frag. 4.14 IEG II.45,48
4a II.42
6.3-4 II.44
28 II.48
36.1-7 II.23
36.8-15 II.28
Sophocles
Aias 243-244 II.163
944 I.283
1228 II.30
Antigone 100-104 I.111
332-375 I.55; III.299
643-644 III.9,300
847 II.130
944-950 II.75
966-976 I.182
1163 II.96
1222 I.209
Electra 1223 III.14
Oedipus Col. 425-426 I.277
448 II.334
700-701 I.61
952 I.257; II.277
1225-1226 I.311

14.1.27 I.33; II.196
14.1.38 III.78
14.2.7 I.79
14.2.12 I.330
14.2.28 I.30
14.4.3 I.33; II.196
14.5.9 I.324
14.5.10 II.195
14.5.16-19 I.33; II.196
14.6.3 II.108
14.6.5 III.133,283
15.1.14 II.13
15.1.20 I.209
15.1.29 II.8
15.1.34 II.293
15.1.58 I.139
15.3.15 III.321
16.1.6 III.328
16.1.11 III.127
16.1.15 I.279
16.1.16 III.328
16.1.27 III.316
16.2.5 I.99
16.2.7 III.323
16.2.9 I.134
16.2.10 III.322
16.2.15 II.65; III.279
16.2.16 I.94
16.2.18 I.156,329
16.2.19 III.126
16.2.20 III.77
16.2.22 I.36
16.2.23 I.123; II.312
16.2.28 I.182
16.2.30 III.326
16.2.33 I.100
16.2.39 I.309
16.3.4 III.71
16.4.17 I.241
16.4.19-25 I.72,333; III.259
16.4.27 III.278,315
17.1.27 II.294
17.1.28 III.164
17.1.33 III.124
17.1.46 I.70
17.1.48 I.338
17.1.50 II.130

17.2.4 I.342
17.3.14 I.160
17.3.16 I.131
17.3.25 II.112; III.258
apud Josephum I.158
Suda 1.509 I.147
3.39 I.99
4.319 III.99--- II.180,225,333,335

Tatianus, *Orat.* 3.3 III.307
16 I.169
Thallus frag. 2 (FGH 276) I.126
Theocritus 1.12 II.318
2.28-29 I.274
2.73 I.209
4.43 II.56
5.58-59 I.147
10.54-55 I.335; II.15
12.36-37 I.306
15 I.245
15.16 I.241; II.317; III.290
15.93 II.315
15.149 I.41
Epigr. 1.5 I.203
Theodoretus I.78; III.96
Theodoridas I.129
Theognis 25-26 II.70
31-32 I.292
43 I.293
69-72 I.292
112 I.292
141-142 I.295
145-148 I.308
151-152 I.294
159-160 I.295
179 I.292
233-234 I.293
268 I.292
284 I.293
425-426 I.311
449-452 I.305
499-500 I.303
573 I.293
621 I.293
697-698 I.293
743-753 I.292-293
824 I.257

2.3.2 Greek Inscriptions

2.3.3 Greek Papyri

2.4 *Latin*

2.4.1 Literary Latin

Augustus
  Comment. II.232
  Epist. I.89; II.295; III.62,
    291,325
  Res Gestae 4 II.112.253
    7 II.112
    10 II.113
    13 II.112, 138
    19 II.65
    22 II.231; III.335
    25 I.262
    26 I.338
    29 III.257
    34 II.112, 332
    35 II.113--- I.40
  apud Suet. I.89
Ausonius 1.2 III.3
  7.23.15 II.109
Auienus *Ora Maritima* 520 II.228

Baebius 955 III.26
Baeda 2.2 III.204
Basingstoke III.190

Caesar
  Bell. Ciu. 1.5.3 III.252
  Bell. Gall. 1.51 III.271
    3.1 II.8
    6.25 II.207
    6.28 I.193
Calpurnius Flacc.
  Decl. 49 II.322; III.19
Capito apud Macrob. I.215
Carmen Saliare III.86
Cato
  de agr. 11.3 III.255
    37.2 II.14
  frag. I.331
Catullus 3.12 II.325
  5.3 III.253
  7 I.315
  10.22 III.256
  13.8 II.320
  36.1 I.330
  63 I.80, 328
  72.4 I.251
  80.2 I.313

  85 III.17
  108.4-6 I.281
  109.6 I.251
Celsus 1 pr. 9 II.300
Censorinus 2.5 II.232
  4.13 II.220
  17 II.229-231
Cicero
  Acad. 2.1 I.53
  ad Att. 2.14 III.322
    7.11.2 II.321
    12.19.1 III.330
    13.23 I.250
    14.17a.2 III.85
  ad Fam. 7.12.2 I.276
    13.4-7 II.249
    15.1.3 III.322
  Aratus 320-331 I.145
  Brutus 169 II.248
  de Amicit. III.255
  de Div. 1.40 I.106
    2.42 II.66
    2.50 II.219
    2.110-12 II.111
    2.146 I.325
  de Domo 38 II.110
    66 I.250, 259
  de Finibus 4.56 I.318
    5.25 II.29; III.30,301
  de Lege Agr. 2.94 II.27
  de Legibus 1.61 I.162; III.309
  de Nat. Deorum 2.93 I.40
    3.68 II.19
    3.84 II.63
  de Off. 1.35 I.160
    1.37 I.53; III.11
    1.77 I.58; III.64
    2.25 III.105
  de Oratore 1.206 III.238
    1.249 p. 27
    2.262 I.317; III.30
    3.43 II.248
    3.213 III.197
  de Republica 1.65 II.143
    2.14 II.106
    2.40-41 II.97, 101
    2.58 II.42

40.42.8 II.110
42.40.3 I.259
49 *per.* II.106
67 *per.* II.266
Lucanus 3.217 I.123
   3.228 I.30
   7.197 II.65
   7.317 II.143; III.23
   10.434-5 I.100
   Schol. 2.137 II.249
Lucretius 1.90 I.217
   1.250-251 II.76
   2.75-79 II.173
   2.618-620 I.154
   2.991-1000 I.311; II.78
   3.18-22 III.49
   3.750-751 I.196
   3.1034 II.123
   5.91-109 III.332
   5.727 I.97
   5.1286-1294 I.172
   6.526 II.148

Macer (*Digest* 1.18.1) III.258
Macrobius *Sat.* 1.4.19 I.4
   1.6.7 II.271
   1.6.9 II.259
   1.9.17-18 II.239
   1.23.17 I.273
   2.4.12 I.89; III.62,291
   3.4.9 I.37
   3.5.5 I.216
   3.9.1-5 II.243
   3.10.3-7 I.215
   5.19.13 II.219
Maecenas apud Isid. I.89
Mago II.7, 328
Manilius 4.16 I.311
Martialis 1.43.8 I.145
   2.79.2 III.252
   4.19.12 I.209
   5.8.1 II.116
   5.32 III.254
   9.37.6 I.240
   10.51 I.198
   10.72.8 II.116
   12.60.1 III.323

13.10.1 I.343
Mela 3.46 I.119

Nepos *Hamilcar* 1 II.121
   Hannibal 1.1 II.63,121
   7.4 II.103
Nicolaus Hussovianus II.331
Nouella 98.359 III.211

Orosius 5.3.7 II.261
   6.20.2 II.252
Ouidius *Amores* 3.11A.6 I.199
   Ars Amat. 1.59-60 I.314
   1.475-6 I.314
   3.239 I.240
   3.327 I.155
   ex Ponto 2.1.20 II.253
   2.5.37-38 I.313
   3.18.15-16 I.314
   4.10.5 I.320
   Fasti 1.186 I.145
   1.267-281 II.238
   1.699 I.173
   2.171 I.208
   3.59 II.87
   4.681-682 II.177
   4.898 I.152
   6.577 II.210
   Heroides 8.46 III.85
   9.116 I.279
   16.251-2 I.313
   21.1-2 I.48
   Metamorphoses 1.74-77 I.55; III.299
   1.91-92 I.53
   1.97 III.12,304
   1.99 I.172
   1.111-112 I.4, 140
   1.144 III.11
   1.237 II.185
   1.256-8 III.332
   1.335 II.262
   1.414 I.83
   2.80 I.198
   2.496-507 II.181
   3.136-137 II.336
   3.194 I.196

40 II.221
59.1 I.302
Tabulae XII I.4; III.11,30
Tacitus *Agricola* 12.6 III.62
    30.4 I.10; III.292
    30.6 III.308
    Annales 1.3 II.112
    1.8 I.261; II.263
    1.12 II.112
    1.26 III.261
    2.24 I.116
    2.27 III.92
    2.43 III.333
    2.58 III.101
    6.31 III.101
    6.43 III.97
    11.10 I.339
    11.11 II.231
    12.14 III.322
    12.23 III.323
    12.41 II.112
    12.47 I.283
    12.63 I.131
    13.7 III.323
    14.13-15 III.214
    15.1 III.82
    15.13 III.77
    15.44 I.208; II.316; III.259
    Germania 17.2 I.116
    34 I.117
    40.2-3 II.304
    Historiae 1.4 II.248
    1.72 III.20
    2.78 II.9
    2.81 I.262
    3.72 II.270
    4.58 II.254
    5.5 I.158
    5.6 I.81; II.68; III.135
    5.12 II.324; III.14
    5.13 II.243; III.114
Terentius
    Adelph. 199 III.272
    958 III.25
    Eu. 709 II.56
    1028 III.245
    Heaut. 452-3 III.87

603 I.76
Hec. 553 III.252
Phormio 506-7 I.323
Tertullianus
    ad. Nat. 2.8.5 I.333
    adv. Marc. 4.25.4 II.190
    4.26.12 I.220
    adv. Prax. 19.4 II.190
    Apol. 11-13 III.146
    33.4 II.258
    50.3 II.264
    de Anima 55.5 III.143
    de Pr. Haer. 7.9 I.161; II.85; III.152
[Thomas à Kempis]
    de imit. Christi 1.19.2 I.295
[Thomas de Celano] *Dies irae* III.179
Thomas Aquinas III.191
Tibullus 1.1.67 II.187
    1.1.75 I.251
    1.3.80 I.145
    1.7.26 I.23
    1.10.1-2 I.251
    2.5.23 II.230
    2.5.67 II.197
    2.5.117-118 II.264
    3.6.63-64 I.149

Ulpianus (*Digest* 1.1.10) II.29; III.301
    (*Digest* 1.5.17) III.309
    (*Digest* 49.18.4) II.52

Valerius Flaccus 1.306 III.236
Valerius Maximus 2.7.12 III.108
    2.8.1 II.260
    6.9.2 I.283
    9.12.7 III.253
Valerius Soranus II.249
Varro *de Lingua Lat.* 5.3 III.11
    5.86 II.241
    5.100 I.338
    5.143 II.219
    5.165 II.238
    6.14 II.262
    6.68 II.252
    6.88 II.103
    7.6-8 II.223

2.4.2 Latin Inscriptions

2.5 Treaties

Citations (all in Vol. I, Chapter 8) of provisions from treaties and the like as numbered at I.284-286.

2.6 Other Languages

For texts in languages not listed here, see under their vocabulary in Index 1.4.

Index 3: Objects Described

Index 4: Modern Scholars

Index 5: Proper Names

For kings, emperors etc. with long reigns, "r(uled)." marks regnal years, not birth and death.

264; III.215
Claudius Lysias (NT) III.116,169
Clearchus of Heracleia (366-353 BC) II.258
Clement VI Pope (1342-1352) III.241
Cleomenes I of Sparta (520-490 BC) I.199
Cleomenes III (235-222 BC) I.249
Cleopatra w. of Phineus I.182
Cleopatra VII (69-30 BC) I.68,333; II.241,251,294; III.85
Clio Muse II.39
Clitophon hero of novel I.102
Clusium of Etruria II.270
Cluvia whore of Capua (210 BC) I.243
Clytemnestra I.208,283; II.287
Cnossus I.87,206; II.269; III.288
Colchis on Black Sea I.176,240
Cold War III.76
Colline Gate, battle (82 BC) II.250
Columbus III.119
Comana of Cappadocia I.70
Commodus (AD 180-192) III.28
Constantinople III.190
Constantinus I (AD 306-337) II.269; III.89
Constantius II (AD 337-361) III.84
Coponius gov. of Judaea (AD 6-9) III.251
Corcyra I.101,263; III.7
Corinth I.212,242; II.245; III.107
Cornelia m. of Gracchi I.249
Cornelius Cinna, L. (consul 87 BC) I.276
Cornelius Scipio Aemilianus Africanus, P. (185-129 BC) II.123; III.74
Cornelius Scipio Africanus, P. (236-183 BC) II.123,259
Cornelius Sulla Felix, L. (138-79 BC) I.276; II.232,249
Cornificia d. of Marcus (AD 150-215) III.15
Corsica I.176; III.132
Corycian Cave in Cilicia I.80,124
Court Chronicle III.43
Covenant Code II.278

Crassus *see* Licinius
Crete: name I.32; II.308-315; III.292; all liars? I.30-32; II.315; III.171; in story of Odysseus I.69; David's mercenaries I.231; its unfree peoples II.30; naked athletics I.59; constitution II.100; Dictyaean cave II.179.
Croesus of Lydia (560-546 BC): rich from alluvial gold II.226, dedicates it at Delphi I.305; commissions prophecies I.48; punished for sin of ancestor II.34; "count no man happy" II.336; "in war fathers bury sons" III.300.
Crusaders III.190
Cumae, battle (474 BC) I.124; II.210
Cumae, city II.191-2
Cupid II.151
Cushites II.282
Cutilia of Italy II.4
Cybebe goddess I.16,328
Cybele goddess I.154,328; II.336
Cyclopes: Brontes & Steropes II.174; meaning of their name? II.19. Unsocialized, unaware of justice II.33; III.13; pre-agricultural I.137; II.11, 90; but pastoral I.147, II.15.
Odysseus invokes Zeus Xenios II.26; trapped by rock II.185; blinds Polyphemus I.171, II.241.
Cydonians of Crete I.32
Cynic theme in Gospels? III.60,245
Cynthia of Propertius I.252,333; II.186; III.291
Cyprus: named from henna? I.92; its copper II.145; syllabary II.325; deforestation III.133,283; temple of Aphrodite at Paphos II.223, the "Cyprian queen" I.188; honors Tiberius I.286.
Cypselus tyrant of Corinth (657-627 BC) I.118
Cyrene I.285; II.25,217; III.295
Cyrus the Great (r. 557-530 BC): conquers Astyages II.89; takes Babylon III.72; his Akkadian decree

III.95; called shepherd of Yahweh II.3, Messiah I.60; advice to sons III.9; tomb at Pasargadae III.126.

Cyrus the younger (d. 401 BC) I.225; III.107,121,124

Cyzicus of Propontis I.131

Dagon Philistine god I.123; II.71, 243

Damarchus werewolf II.185

Damascus I.28,243; II.334

Danaans I.227; III.292

Danaë I.227; II.75,168

Danaids I.72,145,227; II.72,176

Danaoi I.6,227; II.208; III.38

Danaos I.181,227; III.172

Danapris r. II.207

Danastius r. (Dniester) II.207

Daniel I.50

Danites I.6,227; II.217

Danuvius II.207

Daphnae in Egypt (Tahpanhes) I.100, 333; II.49

Dardanus II.194

Dardas r. of Syria III.121

Dar es-Salaam of Tanzania II.195

Darius I the Great (r. 522-486 BC): "from courier to king" III.89; name & titles in 4 languages III.82; "Great King" II.88; "King of kings" II.297; creates satraps II.296, III.86; his gold "darics" II.335.

Crucifies 3,000 in Babylon III.107; law-codes in Egypt III.27; builds stone-heap II.130; letter to Greeks III.84; at Behistun III.97; his spirit consulted II.191.

Darius II Ochus (424-404 BC) III.121

Darius III (336-330 BC) III.72

Darius prince I.66

Dascyleium of Phrygia III.127

David: as shepherd II.36; kills a bear but ursine II.3,182; charms animals like Orpheus? II.20-21; as man of war II.94; rejects bronze armor I.167; II.97; kills Goliath II.89 and thousands II.260; like

Alexander, pours out water I.340.

Has spirit of Yahweh II.20,36; son of Yahweh II.21; handles bow & lyre as Apollo II.153; as poet I.244; III.180. His wives & concubines I.67,228; II.31,91; impotent in old age I.67; II.90; affair with Bathsheba, letter to Joab I.3, 49; II.37; III.167.

Complex relations with Saul & Jonathan I.240,244; II.163; III.18, 180,215; his Cretan mercenaries I.69; enters Jerusalem as victor and exposed I.59,155; II.251,259-261.

Wood from Lebanon for his palace III.131; Joab condemns his mourning for Absalom I.3; II.284, 322; III.3,18,298; Davidic kingship I.60; II.20,89,95,218.

Day, Dorothy III.201

Deborah II.63,159,174.

Decalogue *see* Ten Commandments

Declar. of Indep. (U.S.) III.301

Dedan (uncertain place) II.328

Deianeira w. of Heracles I.66,188.

Delilah I.170,226.

Delos I.36,203.

Delphi (*see also* Apollo): its serpent II.190; navel of the earth II.4; rapacity of Delphians at sacrifice I.186,214,323. Its amphictyony II.205; III.294; oath I.256; vengeance required I.265-6 in sacred war II.239-240.

Its Sibyl Herophile II.191; the Pythia counts sand & waves I.315, but may get a dumb spirit II.163. Oracles: iron brings woe I.172; III.282; Croesus punished for 5th ancestor II.34; Therans to colonize Libya, rain withheld II.25, 73,170. Moral maxims III.163.

Demeter: doesn't drink wine I.142; Persephone abducted II.4; III.45; gives Triptolemus grain II.11; her fruits come from rain II.76; gives Athens figtree II.12; III.280; seen

Egypt: scholarship I.6; relations to Israel, Hellas **III.287**; loanwords II.294-6; places I.329; gods I.333-4; gift of the Nile I.22; II.4,13, 34,169; III.279,315; imperial past III.72; and the future life III.39-41,299; Solon & Jeremiah there II.48.

Einstein III.53

Ekron in Philistia I.219,247; II.298

El, god I.195; II.89,133; III.125

Elagabalus god, emperor (AD 218-222) II.336

Elaious on Hellespont II.223

Elba II.200,224; III.144,282

Electra III.14

Elephantine I.7,338; III.72,170,221, 317

Eleusis II.11-12,76; III.37-8,280

Eli priest II.167,237

Eliezer b. Hyrcanus rabbi III.326, 343

Elijah: hairy; has magic mantle; fasts for 40 days, fed by ravens, lives in caves **II.183**; runs tirelessly II.165; withholds & restores rain II.73--for he holds its key II.170.

Taunts priests "Is Baal sleeping?" I.122; "Why do you limp?" II.160; his opponent Melqarth? II.183. Raises widow's son II.186 —for he has key of raising dead II.170. Gives Elisha double measure of spirit II.38,189; himself raised as Jesus? II.183; legend of Elijah & R. Joshua III.331.

Elim II.54,66,91,105

Elisha prophet: ursine character & allies II.4,182; III.284; has king as enemy I.272; II.216; "holy man of God" II.41; magical arrow II.138; double measure of Elijah's spirit II.38, 189; Elijah's mantle II.183.

Elisha (Cyprus) I.178; II.145

Elizabeth I III.191

Elohim I.85

Elymas magus III.92

'Elyon III.48

Elysian fields I.112; III.51,60,147

Emesa of Syria III.322

Emmaus III.14

Empedocles of Acragas (492-432 BC) I.217; II.155; III.299

Enarees of Scythia II.158

En-Dor, witch of I.243; II.190-3; III.295

Enkidu II.316

Enna of Sicily see Henna

Enoch, translated III.138

Enosin, isl. II.109

Enuma Elish I.17,64,127; III.286

Eos I.71,112; III.51

Ephesus I.308; III.124

Ephialtes giant I.84

Ephrem of Nisibis (AD 306-373) II.330; III.141,220

Epicasta m. of Oedipus II.168

Epictetus III.176,270

Epidaurus II.31; III.272,329

Epimenides seer II.179

Epyaxa q. of Cilicia (401 BC) I.225

Eremboi I.18,79; II.310; III.292

Ereschigal Bab. deity I.328

Ereuthalion giant II.89

Erichthonius Attic hero I.340

Eridanus r. (several) II.207

Erinyes I.283; III.24

Eros II.151

Erytheia isl. I.125

Erythrae of Ionia II.192

Esarhaddon (see Treaty **17**) (680-669 BC): "true shepherd" II.3; realm from sunrise to sunset III.75; his agent Ahiqar I.309; logging on Lebanon III.130; his palace III.226; court prophets III.321; inscription at Lycus r. I.209; Vassal curses I.5,107; treaty with Baal of Tyre I.101,255; II.150.

Esau II.15-16,183

Eshmun I.7,35-6,159

Eshmun'amas (suffete 406 BC) II.102, 124

Eshmunazar of Sidon (early 5th c. BC) I.45; II.120

II.296); gifts to Jesus I.95,212;
III.98,252; in Talmud II.40; desig-
nate Parthian king III.98; crucified
III.108; at Cappadocia III.321.
Magnesia I.118
Mago agric. author I.134; II.7,328
Mago br. of Hannibal (d. 203 BC)
II.121,129
Mago founder of dynasty II.102
Mago general (383 BC) II.126
Mago general (296 BC) III.107
Maia II.55
Maimonides III.178
Mallus in Cilicia I.33; II.196
Mammon III.210,214
Manaen fr. of Antipas III.94
Mandaeans III.91,240
Manes II.187
Mani prophet (AD 216-276) III.69
Manoah II.166
Manto d. of Tiresias II.166,196
Mantua II.207-8
Mantiklos I.45; III.84
Marathon III.87
Marathus I.93
Marcius Coriolanus, Cn. (490 BC)
II.105
Marcus Aurelius (AD 161-180) II.95,
262; III.88,258
Mardonius (d. 479 BC) I.178; III.108
Marduk I.127
Marius, C. (157-87 BC) II.232,267
Marnas god of Gaza II.71,117; III.88
Marpessus in Troad II.191-193
Mars I.47; II.7,87
Marsyas r. of Phrygia III.121
Marx III.80,200
Marxism I.222; II.21; III.308
Mary I.177; III.111
Maryland (U.S.) III.120
Masoretes: supplement oral recitation
I.12,48; their Qeri primary text
I.50; III.185; annotate codex, not
scroll III.188; Heb. vowels com-
plex III.185,316; mark varying
pron. of consonants II.325; poetic
pointing I.290; special pointing

I.179,203.
Massilia I.134; II.211
Mati-ilu (ab. 750 BC) II.149
Matienoi II.310
Matten Phoen. PN I.330; II.307
Matthew III.36,103,156
Mausollus of Caria (377-353 BC)
III.87
Mazaios satrap (r. 385-328 BC)
III.327
Mecca III.262
Medea I.240
Media II.6,174,297; III.74,87
Medinah III.228
Mediterranean seer II.157
Mediterranean words II.12,300-3
Medusa I.79
Megara I.240
Meges Achaean I.166
Megiddo III.72
Mehuman eunuch of Xerxes III.321
Meidias (time of Demosthenes) III.16
Meir rabbi III.326
Melanippus (two) II.6
Melchizedek II.43
Meles k. of Lydia I.70
Melikertes II.184
Melos isl. III.7
Melqarth (*see* Heracles) Baal of Tyre
I.7,160; "king of the city"? I.120;
king of Tyre I.86; III.48; carries
axe at Aleppo III.164.
    His cult with Heracles pan-
Mediterranean **I.119-122**; dedica-
tion from Cyprus I.167; Baal of
Carmel? II.9; Heracles of Forum
Boarium? I.220-221; ursine like
Melikertes **II.183-4**; III.131; men's
names in -Melqarth II.122-123.
Memnon II.75
Memory II.37-39
Memphis I.329; II.176
Menahem Essene (50 BC) III.94
Menelaus: nurtured by Zeus II.87; like
a lion II.92; m. Helen & becomes
k. of Sparta I.227; has son by slave

284,308; II.86

Noah: the Ark II.168; its wood II.302; Noah & Deucalion **I.82-83**; 40 days' rain II.146; story rests on tsunami of Thera? I.104; II.327; III.288. Echos in Greek **II.168-169**; invents sacrifice I.186; his covenant I.267; maltreated by son I.82.

"Nostratic" II.323

Noumenius PN II.123

Numa Pompilius 2nd k. of Rome I.69; II.24,238

Numidia II.197

Nymphs II.179

Nysian plain III.45

Obodas Nabataean I.43,333

Ocean I.109-111,123-5; II.177,188; III.49,62

Oceanids III.44

Oceanus god III.78

Octavian *see* Augustus

October equus II.7

Odainathus *see* Septimius

Odysseus (Ulysses; *see also* Calypso, Penelope): Zeus-born II.87; ursine ancestry II.182; feigns madness II.334; and Helen's suitors I.230; at Troy I.206; II.22.

Blinds Cyclops II.241; in the underworld I.57; II.171,186-189; with Calypso III.56; tests each strange people III.13; shipwrecked in Scheria I.101; III.285; with Nausicaa I.59; III.8,298; hears bard II.36; invents birth from Cretan concubine I.69.

In disguise at Ithaca I.141; II.31,65; III.13; with Penelope I.60; II.10; III.280; his arrows poisoned? II.141; checks his bow as if a lyre II.140,153; III.289; twelve axes of his kingship II.271.

His last voyage II.117; Andocides his descendant III.157.

Oedipus: his flocks III.49; his hot tem-

per III.166; trapped by devious Apollo I.68; marrying his mother & supplanting his father a single package I.227-228; condemns Tiresias III.92.

Compared with Moses: male forebear a seer; mother involved in incest; exposed in ark; grave unknown **II.167-169**.

The riddle in folklore II.332; its hidden meanings & the devious Sphinx I.228; Oed. self-cursed I.255,278; or an innocent victim? I.218.

Oenotria (Italy) I.138

Oeta, mt. of Thessaly I.120

Og of Bashan II.188

Ogenos II.188; III.58

Ogygia III.55

Ogygos I.37; II.188; III.56

Oineus of Calydon I.135-7; III.296

Oinoanda I.138

Olbe of Cilicia II.195

Olbos "Blessedness" II.44

Olenus Etr. seer of Cales II.220

Ologasos *see* Vologases

Olympia I.219; III.59

Olympian gods: twelve in all II.206; as pantheon I.54; II.54; two levels of assembly II.99; seat at Olympus II.92; Hestia their homebody II.93; receive sacrifice I.183; make four metal ages I.301.

Olympias m. of Alexander III.88

Olympus: giants make it ladder to sky I.84; sky its bronze floor I.106; golden home of the gods II.92 and their assembly II.105; compared with Kasios III.279; generic name "snowy"?; Zeus thunders from its snow II.65,68; III.49; but once seen as immutable & snowless III.48.

Omanos Iranian deity III.321

Omphale princess I.279; II.207,269

On (Heliopolis of Egypt) II.9,48

Onan I.81

Index 6: Topics

Quotation marks as on "aloes" indicate that the entry both is discussed as a topic and translates an item of the common vocabulary. Where the original is less obvious it is added in rough transliteration, especially when the English represents two or more originals.

abduction III.45,51
abecedaria I.39
absolutism *see* Ancient Near East (Index 5)
academy & church I.1,161; III.154, 200
accountability, civic III.79
"accuser" (*katēgoros*) III.330,343
actors III.212
adamant I.78
adoption of king II.87-91
"adversary" (two words) III.224,330
"advocate" (*paraklētos*) III.330,343
afterlife, beatific III.40
"agent" (*pragmateutēs*) III.264
agronomy III.167
aide-mémoire I.11,47-48; III.185,303
alchemy III.325
alien, resident II.29
alienation of land II.23
allegory of vice & virtue I.233; III.294
allegory of weapons I.162
"alley" III.227
"almond-oil" I.331
"aloes" I.71,96
"alpha" I.42
"alphabet-song" I.46,193
"altar": name and discussion I.201-204; II.303; function in sacrifice I.188-190; III.295; Great Altar I.201,220; II.30,209.
alter ego III.3,300
"ambassador" III.67,89-91,237,307
ambiguous oaths I.269

"Amen I say" III.215
amphictyony: of twelve peoples I.22; II.271; III.168,294; discussed II.203-208; Delphic oath and curse I.256,265; in a sacred war II.239; they sacrifice twelve bulls I.194.
"amphora" (*cadus*) I.19,40,143-5; II.302,311, 320; III.288
anagnorisis III.14
"anchor-stones" I.19; II.211; III.288, 317
androgyny II.158
"anemone" I.246
angel II.144
aniconic worship III.164
animal foster-mothers II.182
"anointed" I.60,95,149; II.326
antecedents in Near East III.276
anthropomorphism III.164
anxiety I.295
apocope of herms II.131
arcanum II.248
archaic implements I.275; II.63,219-222,241
archery I.33; II.55,**135-153**
architecture I.7
archives I.250
argapetēs III.233
"arise!" III.208
aristocracy I.292
"ark" (*larnax*) II.96,168
"ark" (*thibis*) II.168,295; III.341
Ark of Covenant (*aron*) *see* Index 5
armor, putting on I.164

foreigners & slaves III.11-12
forest I.130; III.127,133,283
forgiveness III.31
formulas, oral I.13
fortress, God as I.160
founding of cities II.202,216
four ages I.302; III.74
four rivers III.55,120
four species of tree III.134
four virtues I.237; II.332
foursquare man, city I.236-7,339;
    II.332
fowler II.44
foxes I.156; II.176-7; III.222,296
fragility of natural order III.310
"frankincense": use, source I.210-
    213; mystique of its source I.72;
    name, falls together with Lebanon
    I.72,95; II.291,314; in sacrifice,
    I.188-190; in embalming III.41; in
    ideal realm III.45.
free society, conditions for I.22-28;
    II.49; III.158
"freighter" (Phoen., gaulos) I.19, 146-
    8; II.291; III.288
friend & enemy II.333; III.8-22
friend to friends I.263
"frogs" I.336; II.60,301; III.55,221
fruit trees II.11-13
fulguric names II.174
"full" II.143,320; III.289
"furnace" (klibanos) III.227
furrow, magic II.218

"galbanum" I.150; II.293,311
gall & wormwood I.314
game, ritual II.260
garden I.140-1; II.311; III.55,136-
    7,345
garments, iridescent I.59; III.143
    over & under I.206-7
"gate" II.105,263-4,327; III.242
gate of Great King III.98
    of heaven II.327
gates of sea I.115
gates of underworld I.123-4; II.327;
    III.242

genealogy III.156-7,172
genealogy of justice, injustice II.43-
    45
generation, long II.229-233; III.294
generation, "this" III.212
genres, literary I.63
gentleness of divinity III.31
geographical conditions I.22-25;
    III.278-280
geography, mythical III.44
geopolitical world I.14-17,328-9
giants 89,188-9
"gift" (qorban) III.207
"girl" III.208
give to giver III.1-5,32
giving & receiving III.33,228,327
glaciation III.123,132
glossolalia II.41,163; III.268
goats II.15-18; III.135,145,281
"god" (Etruscan) II.213
goddess at window II.210
goddess naming city II.313
gods I.55; II.55,282
"gold": gold-economy I.299-308; as
    Akkadian II.292; III.287; suffixes
    II.309; in Lydia II.226; as tested
    II.280; gold bricks I.84; gilt horns
    I.197-8; gold leaf I.198; golden
    eagle III.114; golden vine I.158;
    III.345; by the peck III.255; with
    moth I.73-4; and wisdom II.226;
    III.36,165.
"gold ring" III.208,230
goldsmith-bankers I.299-308; II.50,
    226,280; III.289
good and bad I.55-56,297; II.325
goring ox II.279
"governor" (hegemòn) III.258,267
governors, Persian III.103,339
grace III.1-8
grain III.4
grammar
    abstract & concrete III.15,17,256
    accents I.12,146,204,290,301;
        II.55,174,275,318
    acrostics I.46
    active & stative forms II.73,322;

III.282

test gold I.18,306; II.19,280, 321; III.289

theatres & circuses III.211

thunder out thunder III.16

torches in jars II.173

treasures of ancient wealth III.240

wine in drinking-hall I.142

Summary: III.267-8

Reconstructions:

mix wine in golden bowl I.148

bills of lading II.320

physical environment III.278-286

"physician" I.75; III.221,329

physiology, Medit. II.38,186

pilgrimage of nations III.17,75,308

pillar for orientation II.161

pillar of Hermes II.130-4

pillars of heaven I.21,113-123; III.307

piracy: Cilician I.30; Lycian III.172; Tyrsenian I.137,171; II.213; Damon of Ascalon saved I.213; II.332; anchor-stones dedicated II.211; III.288,317.

plague as arrow II.143

plains & uplands I.8; II.14

plant-names II.300

"platter" (*pinax*) III.249

plebeians II.41-2,108,113

"pledge" (*arrabon*): word & thing from Phoenicia **I.74-78**; II.291; III.289; inscription from Gaul II.326; Aqiba's parable I.75; III.343.

poetry as revealed II.37; of commerce I.71,210-1; of justice II.32-42; Semitic III.219

poison (& witchcraft) I.171; II.141

polemarch II.109

political animal I.51,235

politics II.83

pollution, sacral II.281

polygamy III.258

polytheism I.55

pomegranate II.12; III.138,281

pomerium II.262,267

"pool" I.24; II.73

"poor" III.223

"porridge" I.19; II.15

ports of trade I.25,302

"pound" III.264

praetor II.201

praetorium II.110; III.117,267,341

prayer II.281; in Aramaic? II.205

"precinct" (*temenos*) I.21; II.93,96, 200,221-4,293; III.287

prefects III.104,117,339

prescription & description III.1-9, 25

"presence" I.177-180

preservation of texts I.10

priesthood, hereditary III.160

princeps II.112

princess, foreign I.230

principalities & powers II.266

prison (*phylakē*) III.114,243; (*sijnun*) III.258

prisoners of war II.30

"private person" III.142

procession with bull I.198; III.104, 339

proclamations, royal II.1,47,275,280

proconsular authority II.112

proconsuls II.82

procreation, role of male II.167

procurator II.110; III.145,259

profanation of Name II.29

"profligacy" III.245

prohibition implies practice I.213; II.330

prohibition of metallurgy I.25,171

proletarians II.97

prophetism I.27; II.41,48,163; III.321

proscriptions III.105

prose and verse I.63-64

"proselyte" III.14,197,206

prosopography, Punic II.119

prostitution: ritual in Anatolia I.70; at Babylon, Byblos, Rome, Pompeii I.242; in temple of Aphrodite at Corinth I.212,242; serving needs of merchants I.242; III.319; taxed I.248; a potentially disloyal enclave I.243; II.333; imperialism prostitutes women III.111; 'publicans

and harlots' (*q.v.*) I.248.
prostration III.97
prototype of Greek alphabet I.38
proverb and fable I.156,320,325
proverb-book I.290-299
proverbs (most international)
  a wolf by the ears I.323
  all who take the sword III.25, 100
  as many as stars, sand I.314-6
  as you sow, so reap I.317; III.30
  better foot slip than tongue I.318
  better not born I.311; II.335
  bitten by a serpent I.322
  bitter as gall I.314
  black as a raven I.57,313
  blood thicker than water I.206
  blood will have blood I.5; II.279;
    III.24,184
  born but to die I.311; III.345
  bread on the waters I.321
  constant dropping I.320
  count none happy II.336; III.341
  cross my heart I.255
  dice of Zeus fall well III.53
  drink from your own well I.296
  early to bed I.298
  earth to earth I.311; II.77-79
  eat, drink & be merry I.324
  eye for an eye III.27
  foxes have holes III.78
  frog to drink water II.60
  hand washes hand III.28
  hard as stone I.314
  he that cannot beat the ass I.319
  if I be hanged I.317
  iron sharpens iron III.25
  kick against goads III.80
  king of the beasts I.340; birds
    II.334
  kingdom of the blind I.321; II.336
  lamp at midday I.321
  liar not believed I.325
  like master, like man I.318
  man proposes I.295
  many hands, light work I.319
  measure for measure III.4,30
  mills of the gods II.44; III.31

money is man I.299
of battle the end is peace I.160
of ill debtors men take oats I.323
ox to the slaughter I.201,218
physician, heal yourself III.222
place doesn't honor man I.319
place sheweth the man I.319
pride goeth before a fall I.294
raven's palm II.12
rich folk have plenty of friends
  I.293
sawing cummin-seed I.335
scorpion under every stone I.336
sour grapes I.156
standing idle in market III.227
steal from a thief I.323; III.341
sticks and stones I.255
student not above teacher III.221
sufficient unto the day I.154, 295
sweet as honey I.313
the ox fell, men sharpen I.322
thief knows thief III.28
too many cooks I.319
wash an Ethiop white I.320
white as snow I.312
who spits against heaven I.322
wine is the master's I.316; II.336
you can't take it with you I.324
Summaries I.290-308; II.226, 280,
  336; III.289
Delphic maxims III.163
provinces II.81,112
prozbol I.250; II.25; III.339
prudence I.326
prytanis II.213
psyche of the dead II.185-6
publicans and harlots I.248-9; II.333;
  III.214
"purple" I.88; (*argaman*) II.335;
  III.63,230; (*porphyra*) III.230,254
"purse" (*glōssokomon*) III.62
pyramids I.11; II.294; III.287

"*quadrans*" III.254
quasi-civic structures III.294
quiver II.151